HORACE

Oklahoma Series in Classical Culture

Oklahoma Series in Classical Culture

Series Editor
Susan Ford Wiltshire, *Vanderbilt University*

Advisory Board

Alfred S. Bradford, *University of Oklahoma*
Ward W. Briggs, Jr., *University of South Carolina*
Susan Guettel Cole, *State University of New York, Buffalo*
Carolyn J. Dewald, *University of Southern California*
Thomas M. Faulkner, *The College of Wooster*
Elaine Fantham, *Princeton University*
Nancy Felson-Rubin, *University of Georgia*
Arther Ferrill, *University of Washington*
Helene P. Foley, *Barnard College*
Ronald J. Leprohon, *University of Toronto*
Thomas R. Martin, *College of the Holy Cross*
A. Geoffrey Woodhead, *Corpus Christi College, Cambridge/
    Ohio State University*

HORACE

Epodes and Odes
A New Annotated Latin Edition

by Daniel H. Garrison

University of Oklahoma Press : Norman

By Daniel H. Garrison

Mild Frenzy: A Reading of the Hellenistic Love Epigram (Wiesbaden, 1978)
The Language of Virgil (New York, 1984)
The Student's Catullus (Norman, 1989)

Library of Congress Cataloging-in-Publication Data

Horace.
  [Carmina]
  Odes and Epodes / Horace ; a new annotated Latin edition by Daniel H. Garrison.
    p.   cm. — (Oklahoma series in classical culture ; v. 10)
  Latin text; commentary in English.
  Includes bibliographical references.
  ISBN 0-8061-2374-5
  I. Garrison, Daniel H. II. Horace. Epodi. 1991. III. Title. IV. Series
PA6393.C2 1991
874'.01—dc20   91-3224
                                                               CIP

Horace: Epodes and Odes, A New Annotated Latin Edition is Volume 10 of the Oklahoma Series in Classical Culture.

The paper in this book meets the guidelines for permanence and durability of the Committee on Production Guidelines for Book Longevity of the Council on Library Resources, Inc.

Maps 1-4 courtesy of The Cleveland Museum of Art.

Excerpt from *Alexandria* by Edward Morgan Forster, copyright © 1961 by Edward Morgan Forster. Used by permission of Doubleday, a division of Bantam Doubleday Dell Publishing Group, Inc.

3   4   5   6   7   8   9   10   11

CONTENTS

MAPS

PREFACE

This edition began four years ago as a revision of the 1934 Bennett and Rolfe commentary, from which generations of scholars (my own included) first read our Horace. It soon became clear that something more than a revision was necessary if students of this fine poet were to have a clear view of his achievement. So many of the basic assumptions with which we read poetry have changed since the beginning of the twentieth century (when the school editions still in use at this writing first appeared), that it has been necessary to write a new book. What has emerged preserves the scope and some of the actual language of the 1934 Bennett and Rolfe, but makes different assumptions about the poet and the business of reading him—about which more later.

Though in respect to the *dis manibus* of Bennett and Rolfe I cannot present this edition as a revision of their work, it still owes much to their example, as it attempts to anticipate the problems of today's reader as comprehensively as they did. At the same time, the 1896 commentary of E. C. Wickham, the 1903 C. L. Smith, the 1910 Shorey and Laing, the 1930 Kiessling and Heinze, the 1970-78 Nisbet and Hubbard, and the 1980 Quinn have each made important contributions. Besides these commentaries, I have regularly consulted Fraenkel, Commager, Williams (on *Odes* 3), and Putnam (on *Odes* 4), and as many articles on individual poems as time permitted. David Armstrong's *Horace* and the typescript of Gregson Davis' *Polyhymnia* also contributed to my work in its later stages. My own students over the past twenty-two years have made no small contribution, and my colleagues Francis Dunn and Diane Rayor suggested dozens of improvements as the commentary grew. In addition, William S. Anderson, Gregson Davis, and the anonymous readers of the University of Oklahoma Press each contributed several pages of suggestions. Barbara Siegemund-Broka edited the final draft for the Press with meticulous care and good humor. I owe particular thanks to David Armstrong, who with his students at the University of Texas spent a considerable amount of the fall of 1990 helping me improve what now goes to press. My own conception of each poem has necessarily colored the notes, but the chief task has been to select what should be included of everything I have learned. In that respect this book, though eclectic, is new and its faults are my own.

The method of this commentary is to provide aids to understanding Horace's Latin rather than to suggest a finished translation: in this I depart fundamentally from Bennett and others whose glosses imply that the end product of studying Horace should be a poetistic English version. Latin poetry, like other poetry, is by definition untranslatable in its essence. Though translation can clarify meaning at some basic level, it cannot go beyond that. Anyone reading a straight prose translation of Horace may well wonder why anyone bothers to read such stuff in any language, and why Horace bothered to write it in the first place. This commentary is written for students of Latin, not of translation. The genius of Horace is locked in his language: the order of his words, their flavor, their sound, and their rhythms, few of which are reproducible in English.

It is generally beyond the scope of these notes to make critical judgments, this being the privilege of each reader. It has not been easy to conceal my distaste in some cases or to restrain my enthusiasm in others, but I have endeavored to keep my personal preferences and prejudices out of the commentary. Most lovers of Horace will agree that his poetry is uneven, and may therefore sympathize with the plight of the neutral commentator. Critical neutrality does not, however, exclude rhetorical exegesis and the identification of poetic devices. Poetic, rhetorical, grammatical, and historical explanation are the main business of any commentary that proposes to serve the reader, whether first-time student or advanced scholar. But aesthetic doctrine, literary ideology, and critical opinion are another matter, best left to individual readers, classroom discussion, and written analysis.

In this respect I have kept to the traditional form of Horatian commentaries. I depart from tradition by restoring the original order of publication: instead of treating the misleadingly named *Epodes* as a regrettable appendage to the *Odes* (Bennett and Rolfe decline to comment on Epodes 8 and 12, Shorey and Laing refuse to print Epodes 8, 11, and 12 even in the decent obscurity of a learned tongue, while Quinn omits the *Epodes* entirely), this edition puts them first, as they were the first written and published. Likewise, the *Carmen Saeculare* is placed between *Odes* 1-3 and *Odes* 4, also reflecting the date of composition. For the Latin text, I have relied chiefly on the Wickham and Garrod Oxford Classical Text, with occasional departures where I felt there was a more readable alternative. As a general rule, for the sake of brevity I do not comment on textual controversies.

Latin scholars have long needed a commentary that emulates the helpfulness of the Bennett, Smith, and Shorey and Laing editions while avoiding their Victorian sense of decorum, Romantic preconceptions, and blindness to Hellenistic poetry's all-pervasive influence. With this edition, I hope to give readers of Horace a more authentic view of the poet and his work, combined with help in understanding the mechanics of his art.

DANIEL H. GARRISON

Northwestern University
January 1991

INTRODUCTION

Horace's Life

Quintus Horatius Flaccus was born December 8, 65 B.C., in Venusia, a small town on the Appian Way in the center of southern Italy. His father, a freed slave, had done well for himself as a minor financial official[1]—well enough, at least, to provide his son an expensive education at Rome and later at Athens, where the most wealthy young Romans received their higher education. Horace describes his father in his *Satires* as a devoted moral preceptor, but he makes no mention at all of his mother. Except for tributes to his father, Horace makes few credible references to his early childhood or to the dismally poor region of Italy where he spent it. Nor do his scant remarks about his first years in Rome give any hint of unusual formative experiences: he appears to have had hard teachers and a simple, conventional introduction to classical literature before going to Athens to complete his "liberal" education—the exposure to philosophy, science, and letters considered appropriate for a young man of good family about to enter a public career.

At Athens, he perhaps attended lectures at the Academy (*Epist.* 2.2.45), then headed by one Theomnestus. But the phrase *inter silvas Academi quaerere verum* may be only figurative, as Horace later proved more an Epicurean than a follower of Academic doctrines. This was in the mid-forties B.C., and when after the assassination of Julius Caesar the tyrannicide Brutus attended the lectures of Theomnestus (Plutarch *Brutus* 24), Horace was one of the Romans in Athens who took note of his presence and approved of his ideals. Along with Cicero's son Marcus, who was studying under the Peripatetic Cratippus, he joined the forces of Brutus and shared his defeat at Philippi in 42 B.C.—though he was not necessarily in charge of a legion, as he brags to Maecenas in *Sat.* 1.6.48. He eventually returned to Italy "with wings clipped" (*Epist.* 2.2.50, *decisis humilem pennis*) under the terms of a general amnesty, but his father was now dead, the farm confiscated, and the time had come for him to find a place for himself in the new order of things.

Horace says very little about this period of his life. Like any writer who places himself at the center of his own writings, he had in a sense to invent himself for his readers, and he chose to present a finished product rather than dwell on the process of self-creation. Suetonius reports in his brief *Vita Horati* that he obtained a civil service post (*scriptum quaestorium comparavit*). This would have been unavailable to someone without rank and a certain amount of independent wealth, and we must avoid the temptation to picture him slaving at some petty job and getting by on starvation wages, like Melville in his New York customs house or P. G. Wodehouse in his London bank, living on three pounds a week. Though Horace claims at one point that neediness forced him into his career as a poet (*Epist.* 2.2.51f., *paupertas impulit audax ut versus facerem*), it is unlikely that he ever earned his living by writing, or hoped to do so.

---

[1] In *Sat.* 1.6.86 Horace says his father was a *coactor*, a collector of goods for auction or collector of money at auctions; cf. Suetonius, *exactionum coactor*.

All that can be said with certainty of these years is that Horace made good connections with the powerful circle of young Octavian, who was two years his junior, and the Roman literary establishment. Virgil, whom he met in about 41 B.C., introduced him to the future emperor's wealthy friend Maecenas,[2] who was to become his patron. He also found time to write, as is testified by the publication in 35 B.C. (at the age of thirty) of his first book of *Satires*, or *Sermones*. These lightly satiric, humorous "talks" in dactylic hexameters are miscellaneous sketches ultimately derived from the Cynic-Stoic diatribe or "pastime" making fun of human foibles, particularly those committed in the quest of goals not worth achieving. A more immediate model for Horace's first writing was the *Satura* or "miscellany" developed by Q. Ennius (239-169 B.C.). These humorous pieces had no cutting edge of invective or attack, but they were so congenial to Horace that he called Ennius the *auctor* of his own art in the *Satires* (*Sat.* 1.10.66). C. Lucilius (180-101 B.C.), who fixed the meter of this emergent Roman genre and added the element of ridicule, is in turn credited as the *inventor* of Horace's *Satires* (*Sat.* 1.10.48). One feature of Roman satire that Horace found attractive was the centrality of the satirist himself as a dramatic character. The satirist personifies the point of view that he is promoting, taking on a character that is appropriate to his rhetorical style. In his *Sermones*, Horace adopted the persona of a detached, amused observer. It was a pose that served him well throughout his career.

Horace followed up this success five years later with a second book of *Satires*. Maecenas had presented him with the Sabine farm that provided the peace, privacy, and natural surroundings that his temperament required. Now in his mid-thirties, Horace had another type of poetry ready to show the world. In the same year as *Satires* 2, he published a collection of poems that came to be known as the *Epodes*, though Horace himself calls them *Iambi* because of their characteristic meters.[3] These too are something of a miscellany, and like the *Satires* they contain a thread of attack and ridicule. But they also introduce new themes, such as the political crisis that continued to threaten Rome and the love themes that would recur with the more serious political motifs in the *Odes*. An important difference from the *Satires* is that the *Epodes* are not a Roman genre: like their meters, they are consciously Greek, loosely modeled on the early Greek poet Archilochus, and they mark a critical turning point in Horace's career. Now he was to be a Hellenistic Roman poet, adapting Greek models to Roman life and taste. Catullus had shown a generation earlier that a wide range of Greek lyric meters could be employed successfully in Latin poetry, and that love and mockery, both with a personal flavor, were promising themes. With the *Epodes*, Horace began his career as a lyric poet.

The next seven years were the peak of his career as a lyricist, culminating with the publication in 23 B.C. of three books of *Odes*, or *Carmina*. They show Horace as the master of a poetic style chiefly inspired by Alcaeus of Mytilene (early sixth century B.C.) but influenced

---

[2] For more about Maecenas and other persons appearing in the *Epodes* and *Odes*, see appendix A.

[3] *Epod.* 14.7, *Odes* 1.16.3 and 24, *Epist.* 1.19.23. For the meaning of "epode," see appendix C.

by a range of Greek poets as early as Archilochus (early seventh century B.C.) and as late as Callimachus (early third century B.C.). Like Catullus, he espoused the virtues of brevity and wit set forth by Callimachus. Alcaeus' poems encouraged Horace's aspiration to write serious political lyrics as well as light poetry. Pindar, the all-time master of encomiastic poetry (sixth to fifth centuries B.C.), was the model for Horace's poems of praise. Though Horace's lyrics are eclectic in inspiration, they are thoroughly and self-consciously Roman in tone. Horace did not imitate his Greek models—he transformed them.

By the age of forty-two, Horace had demonstrably earned the title of *vates* to which he confidently laid claim. His *Satires* were readable and witty expositions of the best ethical values of his day, both Stoic and Epicurean. His lyrics, without diminishing his role as popular philosopher, showed his supremacy not only as a spokesman of the Augustan settlement of Rome's civil wars (the *Aeneid* remained unfinished at the time of Virgil's death four years later) but also as a fashioner of light verse that was never surpassed in Latin. He had molded Latin into a lyric medium comparable to Greek but with a character of its own.

Now something of a celebrity, he was offered the position of private secretary to the Princeps, which he declined. For all of his ambition, he remained protective of his freedom to dispose of his time as he liked, "a porker from the herd of Epicurus" (*Epist.* 1.4.16, *Epicuri de grege porcum*). He describes himself during these years as small of stature, prematurely gray, fond of the sun, easily annoyed but readily placated (*Epist.* 1.20.24-5, *corporis exigui, praecanum, solibus aptum, irasci celerem, tamen ut placabilis essem*). His advocacy of a simple diet did not prevent him from gaining weight; he admits to being fat and sleek (*Epist.* 1.4.15, *pinguem et nitidum*), and Suetonius preserves a letter from Augustus teasing him good-naturedly about his roundness. Though it appears from his own lyrics and the biography of Suetonius that Horace was no celibate, he never married and left no children.

His literary success having made him *de facto* Rome's dean of letters, he turned his attention to a series of personal and literary memoirs in hexameter verse, roughly equivalent to what a celebrated author today would provide in television interviews and campus lectures. His first book of *Epistles* appeared in 20 B.C. When Augustus decided to revive an ancient religious ceremony, the *Ludi Tarentini*, in 17 B.C., he commissioned Horace to write a Centennial Hymn to mark the occasion. As Virgil was two years dead, Horace was as near to being a national poet laureate as anyone could be, and he resumed his mantle of *vates* to write the solemn *Carmen Saeculare* for performance by a chorus of boys and girls on the night of June 3. Three other literary essays, now grouped as *Epistles* 2, came out between 20 B.C. and the end of the poet's life. The third and longest of these, the *Ars Poetica*, ranks with Aristotle's *Poetics* as one of the most important critical essays of the ancient world. It concentrates on epic and drama, but in a lively, easy-going, and humorous epistolary style.

Horace's last publication was a fourth book of *Odes*, published, according to the Suetonian life of Horace, at the request of Augustus. Many of these are laudatory odes for various important men of the Augustan regime, but some of the literary, philosophic, and erotic themes of the earlier odes also make their appearance.

Horace outlived his colleague Virgil by eleven years, his patron Maecenas by fifty-nine days. He died on November 27, 8 B.C., after naming Augustus his heir. He was buried near the tomb of Maecenas on Rome's Esquiline Hill.

On Reading Horace

More has been written about the lyric art of Horace than can be summarized in a few pages, and no simple formula can be offered as a key to his poetry. A few of the best guides to Horace are mentioned at the end of this introduction. What follows here are a few basic suggestions.

The reader's highest priority must be to stay as close to Horace's Latin text as possible. Translation can be a useful means of testing one's understanding of the language, and at its best it is a fine art, but it is not the final goal because ultimately poetry cannot be translated. Poetry is the sum of the sound, rhythm, word order, allusions, rhetoric, propositional content, and flavor of a poet's original language, and for this reason it is irreducible to a paraphrase in an alien tongue. To enjoy Horace's poems on their own terms, the reader must lay aside some already-learned reading habits. Instead of reading silently, read out loud or subvocalize, as the Romans did; instead of reading rapidly, read slowly enough to take in the sound of the words, and pause where meter or punctuation require a pause. Instead of reading once or twice, read many times. Instead of reading for content, read for familiarity, the ideal being total recall. Ancient readers often memorized poetry for pleasure and replayed it as they went about their business the way we listen to recorded music. Though memorization seems like pointless drudgery in a culture accustomed to throwaway language, it is still the best way to enjoy Greek and Roman poetry. For thousands of years, memorization has been a cornerstone of literary pleasure.

Rhythm is essential. It is a good idea to work out the meter of a poem even before determining what it says. Never read a poem as if it were prose, and always subvocalize as you read so as to keep the metrical values in place. Meter is the heartbeat of a poem; to understand how it works, consult appendix B at the back of this book.

Likewise, the sound of Horace's language is essential. Word music and euphony have always been important to the Italians, and words should keep the sound values they had in the Augustan age before the changes of the vulgate which are reflected in church Latin:

> *c* is always hard as in *cat*, never soft as in *city*.
> *g* is always hard as in *get*, never soft as in *gem*.
> *s* is always voiceless as in *sense*, never voiced as in *rise*.
> *t* is always mute as in *tell*, never fricative as in *nation*.
> *u* is always like the *-oo* in *boot* (if it is long) or in *foot* (if it is short), without the
>   *y* heard in *curious*.
> *v* is always a semi-vowel as in *window*, never a fricative as in *victor*.

In other respects, Augustan Latin sounds like modern Italian: double consonants, for example, should be sounded doubly, as in *pal-lida* and *non-ne*. When in Rome, do as the Romans do.

Just as we need to lay aside our learned habits of reading, we must also discard some romantic notions about poetry itself. The assumption that poetry is the frank outpouring of emotion, that it is sincere and spontaneous, and that a poet's declarations can be taken at face value as autobiographical—all of this ideological baggage must be discarded if we are to make authentic sense of Greek and Roman poetry. Like other writers and public men of his time, Horace adopted a *persona* (Latin for mask) that was tailored to his role and to the particular context in which he spoke. Truth in a discourse as public as poetry was considered less important than the effectiveness of the poem, and though as a rule Horace tells the truth, it is not always the whole truth. No other major poet in antiquity tells us more about himself and his life than Horace, but everything he says is calculated to fit the occasion. Horace's overall public image, something like the picture on the cover of this book, is mellow, good-humored, philosophic, detached, and rational. Such a persona is well suited to Horace's literary achievement, but once or twice he lets the mask slip just enough to reveal a more complicated person.[4] That too is calculated. We enjoy the personality Horace puts before us, we even feel affection for it, but we need not confuse it with historical fact.

While reading Horace, therefore, one walks a narrow line between the willing suspension of disbelief that all literature requires and the critical detachment (*nil admirari*) that Horace himself claimed is the key to happiness (*Epist.* 1.6.1). Much as every poet wishes to be read as if divinely inspired, all poets are human, fallible, and creatures of their time. When Horace flatters powerful Romans, repeats official propaganda, or says bloodthirsty things about foreign enemies, we gain nothing by hanging on his words as if they were holy writ.

Nor do we gain by supposing that every poem of Horace is as good as every other, that his taste was infallible, or that our taste will be the same as that of a Roman audience two millennia ago. Connoiseurship is the discrimination of quality, and every reader will come to like some odes of Horace more than others. The purpose of a commentary such as this is not to pronounce on the excellence of any particular poem, passage, or line, but to provide some information about the art of poetry as understood in Horace's tradition and then to leave it to the reader to make the necessary critical judgment. Reading Horace is traveling in time: as with all travel, one should not expect to love equally everything one sees or hears.

Horace became arguably the most successful writer of his generation, and remains one of the best-loved Latin poets of all time, in large part because he is a master stylist. His gift for memorable epigrammatic phrasing, his sense of humor, irony, and paradox, and his freshness of

---

[4] For example, in *Epist.* 1.20.25 where he admits to a short temper, or in *Sat.* 2.7, where he represents himself being twitted by his slave for gourmandizing and other vices.

language earned him a lasting place among the best sellers of classical literature.

The public for whom he wrote was small; before the printing press, relatively few copies of a poem, and even fewer of an entire *liber* or book-roll of poems, could be made, and the few in circulation were expensive. Partly because publication in the modern sense was not possible, Horace's public at first consisted chiefly of well-educated connoisseurs who would readily recognize quotations from Greek and Roman authors, poetic types and rhetorical figures, learned mythological allusions, and historical references. But within a century after his death at least two commentaries had been written, and by the time of Porphyrio (early third century A.D.) Horatian handbooks were a minor industry, so much had Horace's reading public expanded beyond the original audience. Commentaries proliferated not so much because Horace is obscure as because his art is sophisticated, learned, and often topical.

Horace and his readers enjoyed an artful style that was more complex and artificial than everyday speech. Highly wrought rhetorical structures such as chiasmus, interlocking word order, the tricolon crescendo, the priamel, the golden line, and other refinements were highly prized for their own sake. Natural language that imitated the usage and cadences of street life (as in Plautine comedy and Catullus' polymetric poems) was out; artifice, formality, and a lightly ornamental style were in. Horace did not attempt the sinewy economy found in the best modern prose, for example. Good Augustan poetry was well rounded out and so intricately constructed that it would not be read with unseemly haste. Pick a lyric at random and you will see that most of the nouns are paired with an adjective, and that most of these adjectives are not essential to the main meaning of the sentence but function mainly to fill out the diction and add color. Even where Horace is least formal or rhetorically elevated, adjectives abound. Look in any poem for examples of hyperbaton, that is, where words that would naturally stand together in simple prose are separated. In each of those cases of verbal hop-scotch, consider the word combinations that result and you will find the dramatic contrasts, humor, and sharp emphasis that made Horace famous.

These are more artifice than nature, more like an eighteenth-century formal garden than an untouched natural setting. Fine language is as much an end in itself as a means to an end. Much of the bulk of Horatian poetry consists of catalogs—lists of examples set out with wit and elegance to make the point of the ode memorable. Yet these lists, often organized in threes, seldom seem extraneous, as if they were effete decoration, literary dandyism, or filler. Horace is seldom flabby: his ideals, in fact, favored the short poem.

Horatian craftsmanship begins with metrical arrangement, but as a rule his choice of words or word order is not made for the sake of meter. On the scale of artistic priorities, meter does not rank high—though Horace always works within its limitations. The analysis of style and content does, though, consider how units of thought are placed in a metrical construction. Is a line heavily end-stopped, and do stanzas end with a period? Or are phrases enjambed between lines or stanzas, preventing us from stopping in expected places? The interplay of meaning and meter is an aspect of Horace's art.

Repetitions of a word or related words are also important. These signal a poet's theme as clearly as the actual predication of his sentences. Another index of meaning is word order. Horace follows the general tendency of Latin to push important words to the front of a construction. The first words of a poem are therefore a strong clue to the poet's intentions. Instead of the titles added to the Latin text in this edition, Horace's readers used the opening phrase to identify the poem. Fully aware of this convention, Horace chose his opening words with particular care.

Significant developments often occur near the midpoint of a Horatian ode. This is a favorite spot for emphatic language, and it is sometimes the place where a poem changes direction. Like any great performer, Horace likes to surprise his audience; the midpoint of an ode is one place to look for signals of the poet's intentions. Throughout any poem, an alert reader is always asking, "What is Horace up to *this* time?" A third key point is the closure. One classic Horatian ending is the peaceful diminuendo, where the rhetorical tone becomes noticeably quieter. Another is the ending that takes us back to a word or idea introduced in the first line or two. Horace's purpose is never to confuse the reader or to conceal his meaning; but an interesting poem is a complex, even playful structure, doing or saying a number of things simultaneously.

Though his artistry often results in complex verbal arrangements, Horace's vocabulary is relatively simple, reflecting in part the limitations of Latin itself, in part his own instinct for restraint. For example, superlatives in *-errimus* and *-issimus, -a -um,* used seventeen times in Catullus' 2,288 lines, appear only four times in Horace's 3,735 lyric lines, and only in the *Epodes.* For strong statements he prefers litotes and other periphrasis, such as *splendidior vitro* for the Bandusian spring (3.13.1).

The choice of *Sermones,* literally "talks," as Horace's first literary medium confirmed a tendency that remained a feature of his *Odes* and *Epistles.* All share a conversational quality that verges on the dramatic. Most of the *Odes* are addressed to a person, who is usually named. Some of these are real people, others are types; rhetorical questions and other verbal nudges remind us we are listening to part of a conversation, and exclamations add a note of spontaneity. There is sometimes a hint or two about the dramatic setting, particularly if the poem is symposiac or a love poem, but as a rule the details are left to our imagination.

Though intricate in structure and subtle in nuance, Horace's poems are clear and lively reading. But their meaning cannot be exhausted by translation or explanation. After all the analysis in the world, the wise reader goes back to Horace's own words and lets them speak for themselves.

Additional Reading

Commentaries

Charles E. Bennett and John C. Rolfe. *Horace Odes and Epodes.* New York: Allyn and Bacon. Rolfe's 1934 revision of Bennett's 1901 commentary. For generations the standard college commentary, though the latest reprints have been of the 1901 edition. Both are quite old-fashioned in their view of the Augustan period and Horace's poetry in general, but they are the most helpful with the Latin of all the commentaries listed here.

Adolf Kiessling. *Horaz: Oden und Epoden*. Rev. by Richard Heinze. Zürich: Weidmann 1984. The standard German commentary, this is a reprint of the 1930 edition with an updated bibliography.

R. G. M. Nisbet and Margaret Hubbard. *A Commentary on Horace: Odes Book I*. Oxford: Clarendon Press, 1970. The standard scholarly commentary, 488 pages on thirty-eight odes. Exhaustive, encyclopedic, and essential to the close study of any ode in Book 1, but sometimes unpersuasive in its literary judgments.

R. G. M. Nisbet and Margaret Hubbard. *A Commentary on Horace: Odes Book II*. Oxford: Clarendon Press, 1978. A continuation of the above volume, with the same great virtues and small vices.

Kenneth Quinn. *Horace: The Odes*. The only modern commentary in one volume, first published in 1980 by Macmillan/St. Martin's. Omits the *Epodes* and the *Carmen Saeculare*. Though spotty in their coverage and often indifferent to the mundane questions of the beginner, the notes add a valuable element of critical interpretation that is largely missing in the earlier commentaries.

Paul Shorey and Gordon J. Laing. *Horace: Odes and Epodes*. Univ. of Pittsburgh Press. A 1910 revision of Shorey's 1898 text, somewhat briefer than the Bennett and Rolfe, chiefly useful now for illuminating citations from other ancient authors. This text is also a standard in colleges, and is still in print at this writing.

Clement Lawrence Smith. *The Odes and Epodes of Horace*. 2d ed. Boston: Ginn and Co., 1903. The only edition in this century in English that provides text and notes to all 121 Horatian lyrics. Though long out of print, this is a sound commentary and is less biased than Bennett and Rolfe.

Gordon Williams. *The Third Book of Horace's Odes*. Oxford: Clarendon, 1969. Latin text, English translations, and brief running commentary. Of limited usefulness for details of language and technique, but provides excellent general analysis.

Critical Studies and Related Works

David Armstrong. *Horace*. New Haven, Conn.: Yale Univ. Press, 1989. An introduction to the works, life, and personality of Horace, ostensibly for the nonspecialist but with many valuable insights for specialists.

Steele Commager. *The Odes of Horace: A Critical Study*. New Haven, Conn.: Yale Univ. Press, 1962. Essential reading for several aspects of Horace's achievement.

Eduard Fraenkel. *Horace*. Oxford: Clarendon, 1957. Foundational to the modern study of Horace, the most important work published in this century.

Peter Green. *Alexander to Actium: The Historical Evolution of the Hellenistic Age*. Berkeley and Los

Angeles: Univ. of California Press, 1990. A refreshing and sometimes irreverent account of the culture from which the Romans took their cues.

Jasper Griffin. *Latin Poets and Roman Life*. Chapel Hill: Univ. of North Carolina Press, 1986. The cultural context as a component in poetry. Challenges the view that Latin poetry is purely literary convention.

G. Pasquali. *Orazio lirico*. Florence: Le Monnier, 1920/1964. The first critical study to pay attention to Horace's Hellenistic affinities, this is still one of the best in any language.

Michael C. J. Putnam. *Artifices of Eternity: Horace's Fourth Book of Odes*. Ithaca, N.Y.: Cornell Univ. Press, 1986. Latin text, English translation, and short critical essay on each of the fifteen odes.

Matthew S. Santirocco. *Unity and Design in Horace's Odes*. Chapel Hill: Univ. of North Carolina Press, 1986. Considers the *Odes* as components in the larger poetic design of a poetry book. *Odes* 1-3, he argues, approximate the unity of a single ode.

Hans Peter Syndikus. *Die Lyrik des Horaz*. 2 vols. Darmstadt: Wissenschaftliche Buchgesellschaft, 1973. The best poem-by-poem analysis in German.

L.P. Wilkinson. *Golden Latin Artistry*. Cambridge: Cambridge Univ. Press, 1963. Reprint. Norman: Univ. of Oklahoma Press, 1985. An essential guide to the poetic techniques of Horace and his contemporaries.

L. P. Wilkinson. *Horace and His Lyric Poetry*. 2d ed. Cambridge: Cambridge Univ. Press, 1951. The best short appraisal of Horace's life and lyrics.

Gordon Williams. *Tradition and Originality in Roman Poetry*. Oxford: Clarendon, 1968. With particular emphasis on the Augustan poets, this book describes characteristics of Roman poetry and the place of individual poets in the tradition.

Paul Zanker. *The Power of Images in the Age of Augustus*. Ann Arbor: Univ. of Michigan Press, 1988. How the Augustan principate created a system of visual imagery complementing the political agenda in the poetry of Virgil and Horace. Profusely illustrated.

HORACE

THE *EPODES*

1

A TRIBUTE TO MAECENAS

Ibis Liburnis inter alta navium,
    amice, propugnacula,
paratus omne Caesaris periculum
    subire, Maecenas, tuo.
Quid nos, quibus te vita si superstite   5
    iucunda, si contra, gravis?
Utrumne iussi persequemur otium
    non dulce ni tecum simul,
an hunc laborem, mente laturi decet
    qua ferre non mollis viros?   10
Feremus, et te vel per Alpium iuga
    inhospitalem et Caucasum
vel occidentis usque ad ultimum sinum
    forti sequemur pectore.
Roges, tuum labore quid iuvem meo,   15
    imbellis ac firmus parum?
Comes minore sum futurus in metu,
    qui maior absentis habet;
ut adsidens implumibus pullis avis
    serpentium allapsus timet   20
magis relictis, non ut adsit auxili
    latura plus praesentibus.
Libenter hoc et omne militabitur
    bellum in tuae spem gratiae,
non ut iuvencis illigata pluribus   25
    aratra nitantur mea,
pecusve Calabris ante sidus fervidum
    Lucana mutet pascuis,
neque ut superni villa candens Tusculi
    Circaea tangat moenia.   30
Satis superque me benignitas tua
    ditavit; haud paravero,
quod aut avarus ut Chremes terra premam,
    discinctus aut perdam nepos.

2
A BANKER'S REFLECTIONS ON COUNTRY LIFE

"Beatus ille qui procul negotiis,
    ut prisca gens mortalium,
paterna rura bobus exercet suis,
    solutus omni faenore,
neque excitatur classico miles truci,   5
    neque horret iratum mare,
forumque vitat et superba civium
    potentiorum limina.
Ergo aut adulta vitium propagine
    altas maritat populos,   10
aut in reducta valle mugientium
    prospectat errantis greges,
inutilisque falce ramos amputans
    feliciores inserit,
aut pressa puris mella condit amphoris,   15
    aut tondet infirmas ovis;
vel cum decorum mitibus pomis caput
    Autumnus agris extulit,
ut gaudet insitiva decerpens pira
    certantem et uvam purpurae,   20
qua muneretur te, Priape, et te, pater
    Silvane, tutor finium.
Libet iacere modo sub antiqua ilice,
    modo in tenaci gramine;
labuntur altis interim ripis aquae,   25
    queruntur in silvis aves,
fontesque lymphis obstrepunt manantibus,
    somnos quod invitet levis.
At cum tonantis annus hibernus Iovis
    imbres nivesque comparat,   30
aut trudit acris hinc et hinc multa cane
    apros in obstantis plagas,
aut amite levi rara tendit retia,
    turdis edacibus dolos,
pavidumque leporem et advenam laqueo gruem 35
    iucunda captat praemia.

Quis non malarum quas amor curas habet
  haec inter obliviscitur?
Quodsi pudica mulier in partem iuvet
  domum atque dulcis liberos, 40
Sabina qualis aut perusta solibus
  pernicis uxor Apuli,
sacrum vetustis exstruat lignis focum
  lassi sub adventum viri,
claudensque textis cratibus laetum pecus 45
  distenta siccet ubera,
et horna dulci vina promens dolio
  dapes inemptas apparet,
non me Lucrina iuverint conchylia
  magisve rhombus aut scari, 50
si quos Eoïs intonata fluctibus
  hiems ad hoc vertat mare,
non Afra avis descendat in ventrem meum,
  non attagen Ionicus
iucundior quam lecta de pinguissimis 55
  oliva ramis arborum
aut herba lapathi prata amantis et gravi
  malvae salubres corpori,
vel agna festis caesa Terminalibus
  vel haedus ereptus lupo. 60
Has inter epulas ut iuvat pastas oves
  videre properantis domum,
videre fessos vomerem inversum boves
  collo trahentis languido
positosque vernas, ditis examen domus, 65
  circum renidentis Lares."
Haec ubi locutus faenerator Alfius,
  iam iam futurus rusticus,
omnem redegit Idibus pecuniam,
  quaerit Kalendis ponere. 70

3

BLOCK THAT GARLIC!

Parentis olim si quis impia manu
  senile guttur fregerit,
edit cicutis alium nocentius.
  O dura messorum ilia!
Quid hoc veneni saevit in praecordiis?   5
  Num viperinus his cruor
incoctus herbis me fefellit? An malas
  Canidia tractavit dapes?
Ut Argonautas praeter omnis candidum
  Medea mirata est ducem,   10
ignota tauris illigaturum iuga
  perunxit hoc Iasonem;
hoc delibutis ulta donis paelicem
  serpente fugit alite.
Nec tantus umquam siderum insedit vapor   15
  siticulosae Apuliae
nec munus umeris efficacis Herculis
  inarsit aestuosius.
At si quid umquam tale concupiveris,
  iocose Maecenas, precor   20
manum puella savio opponat tuo,
  extrema et in sponda cubet.

4

HIGH ROLLER

Lupis et agnis quanta sortito obtigit,
  tecum mihi discordia est,
Hibericis peruste funibus latus
  et crura dura compede.
Licet superbus ambules pecunia,   5
  Fortuna non mutat genus.
Videsne, Sacram metiente te Viam
  cum bis trium ulnarum toga,
ut ora vertat huc et huc euntium
  liberrima indignatio?   10
"Sectus flagellis hic triumviralibus
  praeconis ad fastidium
arat Falerni mille fundi iugera
  et Appiam mannis terit
sedilibusque magnus in primis eques   15
  Othone contempto sedet.
Quid attinet tot ora navium gravi
  rostrata duci pondere
contra latrones atque servilem manum,
  hoc, hoc tribuno militum?"   20

5

CANIDIA'S INCANTATION

"At o deorum quidquid in caelo regit
  terras et humanum genus,
quid iste fert tumultus et quid omnium
  vultus in unum me truces?
Per liberos te, si vocata partubus   5
  Lucina veris adfuit,
per hoc inane purpurae decus precor,
  per improbaturum haec Iovem,
quid ut noverca me intueris aut uti
  petita ferro belua?"   10
Ut haec trementi questus ore constitit
  insignibus raptis puer,
impube corpus, quale posset impia
  mollire Thracum pectora,
Canidia, brevibus implicata viperis   15
  crinis et incomptum caput,
iubet sepulcris caprificos erutas,
  iubet cupressos funebris
et uncta turpis ova ranae sanguine
  plumamque nocturnae strigis   20
herbasque quas Iolcos atque Hiberia
  mittit venenorum ferax,
et ossa ab ore rapta ieiunae canis
  flammis aduri Colchicis.
At expedita Sagana, per totam domum   25
  spargens Avernalis aquas,
horret capillis ut marinus asperis
  echinus aut currens aper.
Abacta nulla Veia conscientia
  ligonibus duris humum   30
exhauriebat, ingemens laboribus,
  quo posset infossus puer
longo die bis terque mutatae dapis
  inemori spectaculo,
cum promineret ore, quantum exstant aqua   35
  suspensa mento corpora;

exsecta uti medulla et aridum iecur
  amoris esset poculum,
interminato cum semel fixae cibo
  intabuissent pupulae. 40
Non defuisse masculae libidinis
  Ariminensem Foliam
et otiosa credidit Neapolis
  et omne vicinum oppidum,
quae sidera excantata voce Thessala 45
  lunamque caelo deripit.
Hic irresectum saeva dente livido
  Canidia rodens pollicem
quid dixit aut quid tacuit? "O rebus meis
  non infideles arbitrae, 50
Nox et Diana, quae silentium regis,
  arcana cum fiunt sacra,
nunc, nunc adeste, nunc in hostilis domos
  iram atque numen vertite.
Formidulosis cum latent silvis ferae 55
  dulci sopore languidae,
senem, quod omnes rideant, adulterum
  latrent Suburanae canes,
nardo perunctum, quale non perfectius
  meae laborarint manus. 60
Quid accidit? Cur dira barbarae minus
  venena Medeae valent,
quibus superbam fugit ulta paelicem,
  magni Creontis filiam,
cum palla, tabo munus imbutum, novam 65
  incendio nuptam abstulit?
Atqui nec herba nec latens in asperis
  radix fefellit me locis.
Indormit unctis omnium cubilibus
  oblivione paelicum. 70
A! a! solutus ambulat veneficae
  scientioris carmine!
Non usitatis, Vare, potionibus,
  o multa fleturum caput,
ad me recurres, nec vocata mens tua 75
  Marsis redibit vocibus.

Maius parabo, maius infundam tibi
  fastidienti poculum,
priusque caelum sidet inferius mari,
  tellure porrecta super,   80
quam non amore sic meo flagres uti
  bitumen atris ignibus."
Sub haec puer iam non, ut ante, mollibus
  lenire verbis impias,
sed dubius unde rumperet silentium   85
  misit Thyesteas preces:
"Venena maga non fas nefasque, non valent
  convertere humanam vicem.
Diris agam vos; dira detestatio
  nulla expiatur victima.   90
Quin, ubi perire iussus exspiravero,
  nocturnus occurram Furor
petamque vultus umbra curvis unguibus,
  quae vis deorum est Manium,
et inquietis adsidens praecordiis   95
  pavore somnos auferam.
Vos turba vicatim hinc et hinc saxis petens
  contundet obscenas anus;
post insepulta membra different lupi
  et Esquilinae alites,   100
neque hoc parentes, heu mihi superstites,
  effugerit spectaculum."

6

TO AN ABUSIVE POET

Quis immerentis hospites vexas, canis
  ignavus adversum lupos?
Quin huc inanis, si potes, vertis minas,
  et me remorsurum petis?
Nam qualis aut Molossus aut fulvus Lacon,   5
  amica vis pastoribus,
agam per altas aure sublata nives,
  quaecumque praecedet fera;
tu cum timenda voce complesti nemus,
  proiectum odoraris cibum.   10
Cave, cave! Namque in malos asperrimus
  parata tollo cornua,
qualis Lycambae spretus infido gener
  aut acer hostis Bupalo.
An, si quis atro dente me petiverit,   15
  inultus ut flebo puer?

7

A THREATENED RENEWAL OF CIVIL WAR

Quo, quo scelesti ruitis? Aut cur dexteris
  aptantur enses conditi?
Parumne campis atque Neptuno super
  fusum est Latini sanguinis,
non ut superbas invidae Carthaginis   5
  Romanus arces ureret,
intactus aut Britannus ut descenderet
  Sacra catenatus Via,
sed ut, secundum vota Parthorum, sua
  urbs haec periret dextera?   10
Neque hic lupis mos nec fuit leonibus,
  umquam nisi in dispar feris.
Furorne caecus an rapit vis acrior
  an culpa? Responsum date!
Tacent, et albus ora pallor inficit   15
  mentesque perculsae stupent.
Sic est: acerba fata Romanos agunt
  scelusque fraternae necis,
ut immerentis fluxit in terram Remi
  sacer nepotibus cruor.   20

8

TO A SCORNFUL MATRON

Rogare longo putidam te saeculo
  vires quid enervet meas,
cum sit tibi dens ater et rugis vetus
  frontem senectus exaret,
hietque turpis inter aridas natis   5
  podex velut crudae bovis!
Sed incitat me pectus et mammae putres,
  equina quales ubera,
venterque mollis et femur tumentibus
  exile suris additum.   10
Esto beata, funus atque imagines
  ducant triumphales tuum,
nec sit marita, quae rotundioribus
  onusta bacis ambulet.
Quid quod libelli Stoici inter sericos   15
  iacere pulvillos amant?
Illiterati num minus nervi rigent,
  minusve languet fascinum?
Quod ut superbo provoces ab inguine,
  ore allaborandum est tibi.   20

9

AFTER ACTIUM

Quando repostum Caecubum ad festas dapes
    victore laetus Caesare
tecum sub alta—sic Iovi gratum—domo,
    beate Maecenas, bibam
sonante mixtum tibiis carmen lyra,   5
    hac Dorium, illis barbarum,
ut nuper, actus cum freto Neptunius
    dux fugit ustis navibus,
minatus urbi vincla, quae detraxerat
    servis amicus perfidis?   10
Romanus eheu—posteri negabitis—
    emancipatus feminae
fert vallum et arma miles et spadonibus
    servire rugosis potest,
interque signa turpe militaria   15
    sol adspicit conopium.
Ad hoc frementis verterunt bis mille equos
    Galli, canentes Caesarem,
hostiliumque navium portu latent
    puppes sinistrorsum citae.   20
Io triumphe, tu moraris aureos
    currus et intactas boves?
Io triumphe, nec Iugurthino parem
    bello reportasti ducem
neque Africanum, cui super Carthaginem   25
    virtus sepulcrum condidit.
Terra marique victus hostis Punico
    lugubre mutavit sagum.
Aut ille centum nobilem Cretam urbibus,
    ventis iturus non suis,   30
exercitatas aut petit Syrtis Noto,
    aut fertur incerto mari.
Capaciores adfer huc, puer, scyphos
    et Chia vina aut Lesbia,
vel quod fluentem nauseam coerceat   35
    metire nobis Caecubum.

Curam metumque Caesaris rerum iuvat
dulci Lyaeo solvere.

10

BAD LUCK TO MEVIUS!

Mala soluta navis exit alite,
    ferens olentem Mevium.
Ut horridis utrumque verberes latus,
    Auster, memento, fluctibus;
niger rudentis Eurus inverso mari   5
    fractosque remos differat;
insurgat Aquilo, quantus altis montibus
    frangit trementis ilices,
nec sidus atra nocte amicum appareat,
    qua tristis Orion cadit;   10
quietiore nec feratur aequore
    quam Graia victorum manus,
cum Pallas usto vertit iram ab Ilio
    in impiam Aiacis ratem.
O quantus instat navitis sudor tuis   15
    tibique pallor luteus
et illa non virilis heiulatio,
    preces et aversum ad Iovem,
Ionius udo cum remugiens sinus
    Noto carinam ruperit.   20
Opima quodsi praeda curvo litore
    porrecta mergos iuverit,
libidinosus immolabitur caper
    et agna Tempestatibus.

11

IN LOVE AGAIN

Petti, nihil me sicut antea iuvat
  scribere versiculos amore percussum gravi,
amore, qui me praeter omnis expetit
  mollibus in pueris aut in puellis urere.
Hic tertius December, ex quo destiti   5
  Inachia furere, silvis honorem decutit.
Heu me, per urbem, nam pudet tanti mali,
  fabula quanta fui! Conviviorum et paenitet,
in quis amantem languor et silentium
  arguit et latere petitus imo spiritus.   10
"Contrane lucrum nil valere candidum
  pauperis ingenium!" querebar applorans tibi,
simul calentis inverecundus deus
  fervidiore mero arcana promorat loco.
"Quodsi meis inaestuet praecordiis   15
  libera bilis, ut haec ingrata ventis dividat
fomenta vulnus nil malum levantia,
  desinet imparibus certare summotus pudor."
Ubi haec severus te palam laudaveram,
  iussus abire domum ferebar incerto pede   20
ad non amicos heu mihi postis et heu
  limina dura, quibus lumbos et infregi latus.
Nunc gloriantis quamlibet mulierculam
  vincere mollitia amor Lycisci me tenet;
unde expedire non amicorum queant   25
  libera consilia nec contumeliae graves,
sed alius ardor aut puellae candidae
  aut teretis pueri longam renodantis comam.

12
TO A REPULSIVE LADY

Quid tibi vis, mulier nigris dignissima barris?
  Munera quid mihi quidve tabellas
mittis, nec firmo iuveni neque naris obesae?
  Namque sagacius unus odoror,
polypus an gravis hirsutis cubet hircus in alis,   5
  quam canis acer ubi lateat sus.
Qui sudor vietis et quam malus undique membris
  crescit odor, cum pene soluto
indomitam properat rabiem sedare, neque illi
  iam manet umida creta colorque   10
stercore fucatus crocodili, iamque subando
  tenta cubilia tectaque rumpit.
Vel mea cum saevis agitat fastidia verbis:
  "Inachia langues minus ac me;
Inachiam ter nocte potes, mihi semper ad unum   15
  mollis opus. Pereat male, quae te
Lesbia quaerenti taurum monstravit inertem,
  cum mihi Cous adesset Amyntas,
cuius in indomito constantior inguine nervus
  quam nova collibus arbor inhaeret.   20
Muricibus Tyriis iteratae vellera lanae
  cui properabantur? Tibi nempe,
ne foret aequalis inter conviva, magis quem
  diligeret mulier sua quam te.
O ego non felix, quam tu fugis, ut pavet acris   25
  agna lupos capreaeque leones!"

13

STORMY WEATHER CALLS FOR DRINK

Horrida tempestas caelum contraxit et imbres
  nivesque deducunt Iovem; nunc mare, nunc siluae
Threïcio Aquilone sonant. Rapiamus, amici,
  occasionem de die, dumque virent genua
et decet, obducta solvatur fronte senectus.   5
  Tu vina Torquato move consule pressa meo.
Cetera mitte loqui: deus haec fortasse benigna
  reducet in sedem vice. Nunc et Achaemenio
perfundi nardo iuvat et fide Cyllenea
  levare diris pectora sollicitudinibus,   10
nobilis ut grandi cecinit Centaurus alumno:
  "Invicte, mortalis dea nate puer Thetide,
te manet Assaraci tellus, quam frigida parvi
  findunt Scamandri flumina lubricus et Simois,
unde tibi reditum certo subtemine Parcae   15
  rupere, nec mater domum caerula te revehet.
Illic omne malum vino cantuque levato,
  deformis aegrimoniae dulcibus alloquiis."

14

A TASK FORGOTTEN

Mollis inertia cur tantam diffuderit imis
    oblivionem sensibus,
pocula Lethaeos ut si ducentia somnos
    arente fauce traxerim,
candide Maecenas, occidis saepe rogando;   5
    deus, deus nam me vetat
inceptos, olim promissum carmen, iambos
    ad umbilicum adducere.
Non aliter Samio dicunt arsisse Bathyllo
    Anacreonta Teïum,   10
qui persaepe cava testudine flevit amorem
    non elaboratum ad pedem.
Ureris ipse miser: quodsi non pulchrior ignis
    accendit obsessam Ilion,
gaude sorte tua; me libertina, nec uno   15
    contenta, Phryne macerat.

15

THE LOVER BETRAYED

Nox erat et caelo fulgebat Luna sereno
        inter minora sidera,
cum tu, magnorum numen laesura deorum,
        in verba iurabas mea,
artius atque hedera procera adstringitur ilex   5
        lentis adhaerens bracchiis,
dum pecori lupus et nautis infestus Orion
        turbaret hibernum mare,
intonsosque agitaret Apollinis aura capillos,
        fore hunc amorem mutuum.   10
O dolitura mea multum virtute Neaera!
        Nam si quid in Flacco viri est,
non feret assiduas potiori te dare noctes,
        et quaeret iratus parem;
nec semel offensi cedet constantia formae,   15
        si certus intrarit dolor.
Et tu, quicumque es felicior atque meo nunc
        superbus incedis malo,
sis pecore et multa dives tellure licebit
        tibique Pactolus fluat,   20
nec te Pythagorae fallant arcana renati,
        formaque vincas Nirea,
heu, heu, translatos alio maerebis amores;
        ast ego vicissim risero.

16

AFTER PHILIPPI

Altera iam teritur bellis civilibus aetas,
  suis et ipsa Roma viribus ruit:
quam neque finitimi valuerunt perdere Marsi
  minacis aut Etrusca Porsenae manus,
aemula nec virtus Capuae nec Spartacus acer   5
  novisque rebus infidelis Allobrox,
nec fera caerulea domuit Germania pube
  parentibusque abominatus Hannibal,
impia perdemus devoti sanguinis aetas,
  ferisque rursus occupabitur solum.   10
Barbarus heu cineres insistet victor et urbem
  eques sonante verberabit ungula,
quaeque carent ventis et solibus ossa Quirini
  (nefas videre) dissipabit insolens.
Forte quid expediat communiter aut melior pars 15
  malis carere quaeritis laboribus.
Nulla sit hac potior sententia: Phocaeorum
  velut profugit exsecrata civitas
agros atque lares patrios, habitandaque fana
  apris reliquit et rapacibus lupis,   20
ire pedes quocumque ferent, quocumque per undas
  Notus vocabit aut protervus Africus.
Sic placet, an melius quis habet suadere? Secunda
  ratem occupare quid moramur alite?
Sed iuremus in haec: "Simul imis saxa renarint 25
  vadis levata, ne redire sit nefas;
neu conversa domum pigeat dare lintea, quando
  Padus Matina laverit cacumina,
in mare seu celsus procurrerit Appenninus,
  novaque monstra iunxerit libidine   30
mirus amor, iuvet ut tigris subsidere cervis,
  adulteretur et columba miluo,
credula nec ravos timeant armenta leones,
  ametque salsa levis hircus aequora."
Haec et quae poterunt reditus abscindere dulcis 35
  eamus omnis exsecrata civitas,

aut pars indocili melior grege; mollis et exspes
    inominata perprimat cubilia.
Vos quibus est virtus, muliebrem tollite luctum,
    Etrusca praeter et volate litora.   40
Nos manet Oceanus circumvagus: arva, beata
    petamus arva divites et insulas,
reddit ubi Cererem tellus inarata quotannis
    et imputata floret usque vinea,
germinat et numquam fallentis termes olivae,   45
    suamque pulla ficus ornat arborem,
mella cava manant ex ilice, montibus altis
    levis crepante lympha desilit pede.
Illic iniussae veniunt ad mulctra capellae,
    refertque tenta grex amicus ubera,   50
nec vespertinus circumgemit ursus ovile
    neque intumescit alta viperis humus;
pluraque felices mirabimur: ut neque largis
    aquosus Eurus arva radat imbribus,
pinguia nec siccis urantur semina glaebis,   55
    utrumque rege temperante caelitum.
Non huc Argoö contendit remige pinus,
    neque impudica Colchis intulit pedem;
non huc Sidonii torserunt cornua nautae,
    laboriosa nec cohors Ulixei.   60
Nulla nocent pecori contagia, nullius astri
    gregem aestuosa torret impotentia.
Iuppiter illa piae secrevit litora genti,
    ut inquinavit aere tempus aureum;
aere, dehinc ferro duravit saecula, quorum   65
    piis secunda vate me datur fuga.

17

MERCY, CANIDIA!

Iam iam efficaci do manus scientiae,
supplex et oro regna per Proserpinae,
per et Dianae non movenda numina,
per atque libros carminum valentium
refixa caelo devocare sidera,   5
Canidia, parce vocibus tandem sacris
citumque retro solve, solve turbinem.
Movit nepotem Telephus Nereïum,
in quem superbus ordinarat agmina
Mysorum et in quem tela acuta torserat.   10
Unxere matres Iliae addictum feris
alitibus atque canibus homicidam Hectorem,
postquam relictis moenibus rex procidit
heu pervicacis ad pedes Achillei.
Saetosa duris exuere pellibus   15
laboriosi remiges Ulixeï
volente Circa membra; tunc mens et sonus
relapsus atque notus in vultus honor.
Dedi satis superque poenarum tibi,
amata nautis multum et institoribus.   20
Fugit iuventas et verecundus color
reliquit ossa pelle amicta lurida,
tuis capillus albus est odoribus,
nullum ab labore me reclinat otium;
Urget diem nox et dies noctem, neque est   25
levare tenta spiritu praecordia.
Ergo negatum vincor ut credam miser,
Sabella pectus increpare carmina
caputque Marsa dissilire nenia.
Quid amplius vis? O mare et terra, ardeo   30
quantum neque atro delibutus Hercules
Nessi cruore, nec Sicana fervida
virens in Aetna flamma; tu, donec cinis
iniuriosis aridus ventis ferar,
cales venenis officina Colchicis.   35
Quae finis aut quod me manet stipendium?

Effare! Iussas cum fide poenas luam,
paratus expiare, seu poposceris
centum iuvencos, sive mendaci lyra
voles sonari: "Tu pudica, tu proba   40
perambulabis astra sidus aureum."
Infamis Helenae Castor offensus vicem
fraterque magni Castoris, victi prece,
adempta vati reddidere lumina:
et tu—potes nam—solve me dementia,   45
o nec paternis obsoleta sordibus
neque in sepulcris pauperum prudens anus
novendiales dissipare pulveres.
Tibi hospitale pectus et purae manus
tuusque venter Pactumeius, et tuo   50
cruore rubros obstetrix pannos lavit,
utcumque fortis exsilis puerpera.
"Quid obseratis auribus fundis preces?
Non saxa nudis surdiora navitis
Neptunus alto tundit hibernus salo.   55
Inultus ut tu riseris Cotyttia
vulgata, sacrum liberi Cupidinis,
et Esquilini pontifex venefici
impune ut urbem nomine impleris meo?
Quid proderit ditasse Paelignas anus   60
velociusve miscuisse toxicum?
Sed tardiora fata te votis manent:
ingrata misero vita ducenda est in hoc,
novis ut usque suppetas laboribus.
Optat quietem Pelopis infidi pater,   65
egens benignae Tantalus semper dapis,
optat Prometheus obligatus aliti,
optat supremo collocare Sisyphus
in monte saxum; sed vetant leges Iovis.
Voles modo altis desilire turribus,   70
modo ense pectus Norico recludere,
frustraque vincla gutturi in nectes tuo,
fastidiosa tristis aegrimonia.
Vectabor umeris tunc ego inimicis eques,
meaeque terra cedet insolentiae.   75
An quae movere cereas imagines,

ut ipse nosti curiosus, et polo
deripere lunam vocibus possim meis,
possim crematos excitare mortuos
desiderique temperare pocula, 80
plorem artis in te nil agentis exitus?"

[handwritten, top margin] 1st Asclepiadean ⏑ ⏑ —— ⏑ ⏑ — // — ⏑ ⏑ — ⏑ ×

THE *ODES*, BOOK 1

1

DEDICATION TO MAECENAS

Maecenas atavis edite regibus,
o et praesidium et dulce decus meum,
sunt quos curriculo pulverem Olympicum
collegisse iuvat metaque fervidis
evitata rotis palmaque nobilis   5
terrarum dominos evehit ad deos;
hunc, si mobilium turba Quiritium
certat tergeminis tollere honoribus,
illum, si proprio condidit horreo
quicquid de Libycis verritur areis.   10
Gaudentem patrios findere sarculo
agros Attalicis condicionibus
numquam dimoveas, ut trabe Cypria
Myrtoum pavidus nauta secet mare.
Luctantem Icariis fluctibus Africum *leisure*   15
mercator metuens otium et oppidi
laudat rura sui; mox reficit rates
quassas, indocilis pauperiem pati.
Est qui nec veteris pocula Massici
nec partem solido demere de die   20
spernit, nunc viridi membra sub arbuto
stratus, nunc ad aquae lene caput sacrae.
Multos castra iuvant et lituo tubae
permixtus sonitus bellaque matribus
detestata. Manet sub Iove frigido — *metonymy*   25
venator tenerae coniugis immemor,
seu visa est catulis cerva fidelibus,
seu rupit teretes Marsus aper plagas.
Me doctarum hederae praemia frontium
dis miscent superis, me gelidum nemus   30
Nympharumque leves cum Satyris chori
secernunt populo, si neque tibias
Euterpe cohibet nec Polyhymnia
Lesboum refugit tendere barbiton.
Quodsi me lyricis vatibus inseres,   35
sublimi feriam sidera vertice.

[handwritten annotation] poet

[handwritten annotation] Horace is reviving the Roman word for poet, moving away from the Greek "poetae"

Sapphic strophe — ᴗ — — — // ᴗᴗ — ᴗ — ×
— ᴗᴗ — ×

2

TO AUGUSTUS

Iam satis terris nivis atque dirae
grandinis misit pater et rubente
dextera sacras iaculatus arces
    terruit urbem,

terruit gentis, grave ne rediret   5
saeculum Pyrrhae nova monstra questae,
omne cum Proteus pecus egit altos
    visere montes,

piscium et summa genus haesit ulmo,
nota quae sedes fuerat columbis,   10
et superiecto pavidae natarunt
    aequore dammae.

Vidimus flavum Tiberim, retortis
litore Etrusco violenter undis,
ire deiectum monumenta regis   15
    templaque Vestae,

Iliae dum se nimium querenti
iactat ultorem, vagus et sinistra
labitur ripa, Iove non probante, ux-
    orius amnis.   20

Audiet civis acuisse ferrum,
quo graves Persae melius perirent,
audiet pugnas vitio parentum
    rara iuventus.

Quem vocet divum populus ruentis   25
imperi rebus? Prece qua fatigent
virgines sanctae minus audientem
    carmina Vestam?

Cui dabit partis scelus expiandi
Iuppiter? Tandem venias, precamur, 30
nube candentis umeros amictus,
    augur Apollo;

sive tu mavis, Erycina ridens,
quam Iocus circum volat et Cupido;
sive neglectum genus et nepotes 35
    respicis, auctor,

heu nimis longo satiate ludo,
quem iuvat clamor galeaeque leves
acer et Marsi peditis cruentum
    vultus in hostem; 40

sive mutata iuvenem figura
ales in terris imitaris almae
filius Maiae, patiens vocari
    Caesaris ultor:

serus in caelum redeas, diuque 45
laetus intersis populo Quirini,
neve te nostris vitiis iniquum
    ocior aura

tollat; hic magnos potius triumphos,
hic ames dici pater atque princeps, 50
neu sinas Medos equitare inultos,
    te duce, Caesar.

3 *2nd Asclepiadee*

TO VIRGIL SETTING OUT FOR GREECE

Sic te diva potens Cypri,
    sic fratres Helenae, lucida sidera,
ventorumque regat pater
    obstrictis aliis praeter Iapyga,

navis, quae tibi creditum   5
    debes Vergilium; finibus Atticis
reddas incolumem, precor,
    et serves animae dimidium meae.

Illi robur et aes triplex
    circa pectus erat, qui fragilem truci   10
commisit pelago ratem
    primus, nec timuit praecipitem Africum

decertantem Aquilonibus
    nec tristis Hyadas nec rabiem Noti,
quo non arbiter Hadriae   15
    maior, tollere seu ponere vult freta.

Quem mortis timuit gradum
    qui siccis oculis monstra natantia,
qui vidit mare turbidum et
    infamis scopulos, Acroceraunia?   20

Nequiquam deus abscidit
    prudens Oceano dissociabili
terras, si tamen impiae
    non tangenda rates transiliunt vada.

Audax omnia perpeti   25
    gens humana ruit per vetitum nefas.
Audax Iapeti genus
    ignem fraude mala gentibus intulit.

Post ignem aetheria domo
  subductum macies et nova febrium   30
terris incubuit cohors,
  semotique prius tarda necessitas

leti corripuit gradum.
  Expertus vacuum Daedalus aëra
pinnis non homini datis;   35
  perrupit Acheronta Herculeus labor.

Nil mortalibus ardui est;
  caelum ipsum petimus stultitia, neque
per nostrum patimur scelus
  iracunda Iovem ponere fulmina.   40

4

THE MEANING OF SPRING

Solvitur acris hiems grata vice veris et Favoni,
  trahuntque siccas machinae carinas,
ac neque iam stabulis gaudet pecus aut arator igni,
  nec prata canis albicant pruinis.

Iam Cytherea choros ducit Venus imminente luna,   5
  iunctaeque Nymphis Gratiae decentes
alterno terram quatiunt pede, dum gravis Cyclopum
  Vulcanus ardens visit officinas.

Nunc decet aut viridi nitidum caput impedire myrto
  aut flore, terrae quem ferunt solutae;   10
nunc et in umbrosis Fauno decet immolare lucis,
  seu poscat agna sive malit haedo.

Pallida Mors aequo pulsat pede pauperum tabernas
  regumque turris. O beate Sesti,
vitae summa brevis spem nos vetat incohare longam.   15
  Iam te premet nox fabulaeque Manes

et domus exilis Plutonia; quo simul mearis,
  nec regna vini sortiere talis,
nec tenerum Lycidan mirabere, quo calet iuventus
  nunc omnis et mox virgines tepebunt.   20

4th Asclepiadean

5

TO A FEMME FATALE

Quis multa gracilis te puer in rosa
perfusus liquidis urget odoribus
   grato, Pyrrha, sub antro?
    Cui flavam religas comam,

simplex munditiis? Heu quotiens fidem   5
mutatosque deos flebit et aspera
   nigris aequora ventis
    emirabitur insolens

qui nunc te fruitur credulus aurea,
qui semper vacuam, semper amabilem   10
   sperat, nescius aurae
    fallacis. Miseri, quibus

intemptata nites. Me tabula sacer
votiva paries indicat uvida
   suspendisse potenti   15
    vestimenta maris deo.

6

APOLOGIES TO A NATIONAL HERO

Scriberis Vario fortis et hostium
victor, Maeonii carminis alite,
quam rem cumque ferox navibus aut equis
    miles te duce gesserit.

Nos, Agrippa, neque haec dicere nec gravem   5
Pelidae stomachum cedere nescii
nec cursus duplicis per mare Ulixeï
    nec saevam Pelopis domum

conamur, tenues grandia, dum pudor
imbellisque lyrae Musa potens vetat   10
laudes egregii Caesaris et tuas
    culpa deterere ingeni.

Quis Martem tunica tectum adamantina
digne scripserit aut pulvere Troico
nigrum Merionen aut ope Palladis   15
    Tydiden superis parem?

Nos convivia, nos proelia virginum
sectis in iuvenes unguibus acrium
cantamus vacui, sive quid urimur,
    non praeter solitum leves.   20

7

IN PRAISE OF TIBUR

Laudabunt alii claram Rhodon aut Mytilenen
  aut Epheson bimarisve Corinthi
moenia vel Baccho Thebas vel Apolline Delphos
  insignis aut Thessala Tempe.

Sunt quibus unum opus est intactae Palladis urbem 5
  carmine perpetuo celebrare et
undique decerptam fronti praeponere olivam;
  plurimus in Iunonis honorem

aptum dicet equis Argos ditisque Mycenas:
  me nec tam patiens Lacedaemon 10
nec tam Larisae percussit campus opimae,
  quam domus Albuneae resonantis

et praeceps Anio ac Tiburni lucus et uda
  mobilibus pomaria rivis.
Albus ut obscuro deterget nubila caelo 15
  saepe Notus neque parturit imbris

perpetuos, sic tu sapiens finire memento
  tristitiam vitaeque labores
molli, Plance, mero, seu te fulgentia signis
  castra tenent seu densa tenebit 20

Tiburis umbra tui. Teucer Salamina patremque
  cum fugeret, tamen uda Lyaeo
tempora populea fertur vinxisse corona,
  sic tristis affatus amicos:

"Quo nos cumque feret melior fortuna parente, 25
  ibimus, o socii comitesque.
Nil desperandum Teucro duce et auspice Teucro;
  certus enim promisit Apollo

ambiguam tellure nova Salamina futuram.
  O fortes peioraque passi   30
mecum saepe viri, nunc vino pellite curas;
  cras ingens iterabimus aequor."

8

CORRUPTED BY LOVE

Lydia, dic per omnis
  hoc deos vere, Sybarin cur properes amando
perdere, cur apricum
  oderit campum, patiens pulveris atque solis,

cur neque militaris   5
  inter aequalis equitet, Gallica nec lupatis
temperet ora frenis.
  Cur timet flavum Tiberim tangere? Cur olivum

sanguine viperino
  cautius vitat neque iam livida gestat armis   10
bracchia, saepe disco,
  saepe trans finem iaculo nobilis expedito?

Quid latet, ut marinae
  filium dicunt Thetidis sub lacrimosa Troiae
funera, ne virilis   15
  cultus in caedem et Lycias proriperet catervas?

9

WINTER HEAT

Vides ut alta stet nive candidum
Soracte, nec iam sustineant onus
   silvae laborantes, geluque
    flumina constiterint acuto.

Dissolve frigus ligna super foco   5
  large reponens atque benignius
   deprome quadrimum Sabina,
    o Thaliarche, merum diota.

Permitte divis cetera, qui simul
stravere ventos aequore fervido   10
   deproeliantis, nec cupressi
    nec veteres agitantur orni.

Quid sit futurum cras fuge quaerere, et
quem Fors dierum cumque dabit lucro
   appone, nec dulcis amores   15
    sperne puer neque tu choreas,

donec virenti canities abest
morosa. Nunc et campus et areae
   lenesque sub noctem susurri
    composita repetantur hora,   20

nunc et latentis proditor intimo
gratus puellae risus ab angulo
   pignusque dereptum lacertis
    aut digito male pertinaci.

10

HYMN TO MERCURY

Mercuri, facunde nepos Atlantis,
qui feros cultus hominum recentum
voce formasti catus et decorae
    more palaestrae,

te canam, magni Iovis et deorum   5
nuntium curvaeque lyrae parentem,
callidum quicquid placuit iocoso
    condere furto.

Te, boves olim nisi redidisses
per dolum amotas, puerum minaci   10
voce dum terret, viduus pharetra
    risit Apollo.

Quin et Atridas duce te superbos
Ilio dives Priamus relicto
Thessalosque ignis et iniqua Troiae   15
    castra fefellit.

Tu pias laetis animas reponis
sedibus virgaque levem coerces
aurea turbam, superis deorum
    gratus et imis.   20

11

CARPE DIEM

Tu ne quaesieris—scire nefas—quem mihi, quem tibi
finem di dederint, Leuconoë, nec Babylonios
temptaris numeros. Ut melius quicquid erit pati,
seu pluris hiemes, seu tribuit Iuppiter ultimam,
quae nunc oppositis debilitat pumicibus mare   5
Tyrrhenum. Sapias, vina liques, et spatio brevi
spem longam reseces. Dum loquimur, fugerit invida
aetas: carpe diem, quam minimum credula postero.

12

IN PRAISE OF AUGUSTUS

Quem virum aut heroa lyra vel acri
tibia sumis celebrare, Clio?
Quem deum? Cuius recinet iocosa
    nomen imago

aut in umbrosis Heliconis oris   5
aut super Pindo gelidove in Haemo,
unde vocalem temere insecutae
    Orphea silvae,

arte materna rapidos morantem
fluminum lapsus celerisque ventos,   10
blandum et auritas fidibus canoris
    ducere quercus?

Quid prius dicam solitis parentis
laudibus, qui res hominum ac deorum,
qui mare ac terras variisque mundum   15
    temperat horis?

Unde nil maius generatur ipso,
nec viget quicquam simile aut secundum;
proximos illi tamen occupavit
    Pallas honores,   20

proeliis audax; neque te silebo,
Liber, et saevis inimica virgo
beluis, nec te, metuende certa
    Phoebe sagitta.

Dicam et Alciden puerosque Ledae,   25
hunc equis, illum superare pugnis
nobilem; quorum simul alba nautis
    stella refulsit,

defluit saxis agitatus umor,
concidunt venti fugiuntque nubes,   30
et minax, quod sic voluere, ponto
    unda recumbit.

Romulum post hos prius an quietum
Pompili regnum memorem an superbos
Tarquini fasces, dubito, an Catonis   35
    nobile letum.

Regulum et Scauros animaeque magnae
prodigum Paulum superante Poeno
gratus insigni referam camena
    Fabriciumque.   40

Hunc et incomptis Curium capillis
utilem bello tulit et Camillum
saeva paupertas et avitus apto
    cum lare fundus.

Crescit occulto velut arbor aevo   45
fama Marcelli; micat inter omnis
Iulium sidus, velut inter ignis
    luna minores.

Gentis humanae pater atque custos,
orte Saturno, tibi cura magni   50
Caesaris fatis data: tu secundo
    Caesare regnes.

Ille seu Parthos Latio imminentis
egerit iusto domitos triumpho,
sive subiectos Orientis orae   55
    Seras et Indos,

te minor laetum reget aequus orbem:
tu gravi curru quaties Olympum,
tu parum castis inimica mittes
    fulmina lucis.   60

13

JEALOUSY

Cum tu, Lydia, Telephi
   cervicem roseam, cerea Telephi
laudas bracchia, vae, meum
   fervens difficili bile tumet iecur.

Tum nec mens mihi nec color   5
   certa sede manent, umor et in genas
furtim labitur, arguens
   quam lentis penitus macerer ignibus.

Uror, seu tibi candidos
   turparunt umeros immodicae mero   10
rixae, sive puer furens
   impressit memorem dente labris notam.

Non, si me satis audias,
   speres perpetuum dulcia barbare
laedentem oscula quae Venus   15
   quinta parte sui nectaris imbuit.

Felices ter et amplius
   quos irrupta tenet copula nec malis
divulsus querimoniis
   suprema citius solvet amor die.   20

14

TO A BATTERED SHIP

O navis, referent in mare te novi
fluctus. O quid agis! Fortiter occupa
   portum. Nonne vides ut
      nudum remigio latus

et malus celeri saucius Africo   5
antemnaeque gemant, ac sine funibus
   vix durare carinae
      possint imperiosius

aequor? Non tibi sunt integra lintea,
non di quos iterum pressa voces malo.   10
   Quamvis Pontica pinus,
      silvae filia nobilis,

iactes et genus et nomen inutile,
nil pictis timidus navita puppibus
   fidit. Tu, nisi ventis   15
      debes ludibrium, cave.

Nuper sollicitum quae mihi taedium,
nunc desiderium curaque non levis,
   interfusa nitentis
      vites aequora Cycladas.   20

15

THE PROPHECY OF NEREUS

Pastor cum traheret per freta navibus
Idaeis Helenen perfidus hospitam,
ingrato celeris obruit otio
    ventos, ut caneret fera

Nereus fata: "Mala ducis avi domum   5
quam multo repetet Graecia milite,
coniurata tuas rumpere nuptias
    et regnum Priami vetus.

Heu, heu, quantus equis, quantus adest viris
sudor! Quanta moves funera Dardanae   10
genti! Iam galeam Pallas et aegida
    currusque et rabiem parat.

Nequiquam Veneris praesidio ferox
pectes caesariem grataque feminis
imbelli cithara carmina divides;   15
    nequiquam thalamo gravis

hastas et calami spicula Cnosii
vitabis strepitumque et celerem sequi
Aiacem: tamen (heu serus!) adulteros
    crines pulvere collines.   20

Non Laërtiaden, exitium tuae
gentis, non Pylium Nestora respicis?
Urgent impavidi te Salaminius
    Teucer, te Sthenelus sciens

pugnae, sive opus est imperitare equis,   25
non auriga piger. Merionen quoque
nosces. Ecce furit te reperire atrox
    Tydides melior patre,

quem tu, cervus uti vallis in altera
visum parte lupum graminis immemor,   30
sublimi fugies mollis anhelitu,
   non hoc pollicitus tuae.

Iracunda diem proferet Ilio
matronisque Phrygum classis Achilleï;
post certas hiemes uret Achaïcus   35
   ignis Iliacas domos."

16

RECANTATION

O matre pulchra filia pulchrior,
quem criminosis cumque voles modum
    pones iambis, sive flamma
        sive mari libet Hadriano.

Non Dindymene, non adytis quatit   5
mentem sacerdotum incola Pythius,
    non Liber aeque, non acuta
        sic geminant Corybantes aera,

tristes ut irae, quas neque Noricus
deterret ensis nec mare naufragum   10
    nec saevus ignis nec tremendo
        Iuppiter ipse ruens tumultu.

Fertur Prometheus, addere principi
limo coactus particulam undique
    desectam, et insani leonis   15
        vim stomacho apposuisse nostro.

Irae Thyesten exitio gravi
stravere et altis urbibus ultimae
    stetere causae cur perirent
        funditus, imprimeretque muris   20

hostile aratrum exercitus insolens.
Compesce mentem! Me quoque pectoris
    temptavit in dulci iuventa
        fervor et in celeres iambos

misit furentem; nunc ego mitibus   25
mutare quaero tristia, dum mihi
    fias recantatis amica
        opprobriis animumque reddas.

17

INVITATION TO A COUNTRY RETREAT

Velox amoenum saepe Lucretilem
mutat Lycaeo Faunus et igneam
   defendit aestatem capellis
     usque meis pluviosque ventos.

Impune tutum per nemus arbutos   5
quaerunt latentis et thyma deviae
   olentis uxores mariti,
     nec viridis metuunt colubras

nec Martialis haediliae lupos,
utcumque dulci, Tyndari, fistula   10
   valles et Usticae cubantis
     levia personuere saxa.

Di me tuentur, dis pietas mea
et Musa cordi est; hinc tibi copia
   manabit ad plenum benigno   15
     ruris honorum opulenta cornu.

Hic in reducta valle Caniculae
vitabis aestus, et fide Teïa
   dices laborantis in uno
     Penelopen vitreamque Circen;   20

hic innocentis pocula Lesbii
duces sub umbra, nec Semeleïus
   cum Marte confundet Thyoneus
     proelia, nec metues protervum

suspecta Cyrum, ne male dispari   25
incontinentis iniciat manus
   et scindat haerentem coronam
     crinibus immeritamque vestem.

18

IN PRAISE OF WINE

Nullam, Vare, sacra vite prius severis arborem
circa mite solum Tiburis et moenia Catili;
siccis omnia nam dura deus proposuit neque
mordaces aliter diffugiunt sollicitudines.
Quis post vina gravem militiam aut pauperiem crepat?   5
Quis non te potius, Bacche pater, teque decens Venus?
Ac ne quis modici transiliat munera Liberi,
Centaurea monet cum Lapithis rixa super mero
debellata, monet Sithoniis non levis Euhius,
cum fas atque nefas exiguo fine libidinum   10
discernunt avidi. Non ego te, candide Bassareu,
invitum quatiam nec variis obsita frondibus
sub divum rapiam. Saeva tene cum Berecyntio
cornu tympana, quae subsequitur caecus Amor sui
et tollens vacuam plus nimio Gloria verticem   15
arcanique Fides prodiga, perlucidior vitro.

19

LOVE'S FIRE

Mater saeva Cupidinum
　Thebanaeque iubet me Semelae puer
et lasciva Licentia
　finitis animum reddere amoribus.

Urit me Glycerae nitor,　　　　　　　　　　　　5
　splendentis Pario marmore purius;
urit grata protervitas
　et vultus nimium lubricus aspici.

In me tota ruens Venus
　Cyprum deseruit, nec patitur Scythas　　　　10
et versis animosum equis
　Parthum dicere, nec quae nihil attinent.

Hic vivum mihi caespitem, hic
　verbenas, pueri, ponite turaque
bimi cum patera meri:　　　　　　　　　　　15
　mactata veniet lenior hostia.

20

AN INVITATION TO MAECENAS

Vile potabis modicis Sabinum
cantharis, Graeca quod ego ipse testa
conditum levi, datus in theatro
    cum tibi plausus,

care Maecenas eques, ut paterni   5
fluminis ripae simul et iocosa
redderet laudes tibi Vaticani
    montis imago.

Caecubum et prelo domitam Caleno
tu bibes uvam: mea nec Falernae   10
temperant vites neque Formiani
    pocula colles.

21

A HYMN TO LATONA AND HER CHILDREN

Dianam tenerae dicite virgines,
intonsum, pueri, dicite Cynthium
    Latonamque supremo
      dilectam penitus Iovi.

Vos laetam fluviis et nemorum coma,   5
quaecumque aut gelido prominet Algido,
    nigris aut Erymanthi
      silvis aut viridis Cragi;

vos Tempe totidem tollite laudibus
natalemque, mares, Delon Apollonis,   10
    insignemque pharetra
      fraternaque umerum lyra.

Hic bellum lacrimosum, hic miseram famem
pestemque a populo et principe Caesare in
    Persas atque Britannos   15
      vestra motus aget prece.

$$- \cup / - - - / - / \cup \cup / - \cup / - x$$
$$- \cup \cup - x \quad 22$$

NOTHING CAN HURT A LOVER

A

Integer vitae scelerisque purus
non eget Mauris iaculis neque arcu
nec venenatis gravida sagittis,
    Fusce, pharetra,

sive per Syrtis iter aestuosas   5
sive facturus per inhospitalem
B Caucasum vel quae loca fabulosus
    lambit Hydaspes.

Namque me silva lupus in Sabina,
C dum meam canto Lalagen et ultra   10
terminum curis vagor expeditis,
    fugit inermem;

Portent
quale portentum neque militaris
C Daunias latis alit aesculetis
nec Iubae tellus generat, leonum   15
    arida nutrix.

Pone me pigris ubi nulla campis
Harsh places arbor aestiva recreatur aura,
B quod latus mundi nebulae malusque
    Iuppiter urget;   20

pone sub curru nimium propinqui
solis in terra domibus negata:
A dulce ridentem Lalagen amabo,
    dulce loquentem.

4th Asclepiadean

$$-\ -\ |\ -\ \cup\cup\ |\ -\ //\ -\ \cup\cup\ |\ -\ \cup\ |x$$
$$-\ -\ |\ -\ \cup\cup\ |\ -\ x$$
23 $-\ -\ |\ -\ \cup\cup\ |\ -\ \cup x$

TO A SKITTISH GIRL

Vitas inuleo me similis, Chloë,
quaerenti pavidam montibus aviis
    matrem non sine vano
       aurarum et siluae metu.

Nam seu mobilibus veris inhorruit   5
adventus foliis, seu virides rubum
    dimovere lacertae,
       et corde et genibus tremit.

Atqui non ego te tigris ut aspera
Gaetulusve leo frangere persequor: 10
    tandem desine matrem
       tempestiva sequi viro.

24

TO VIRGIL, ON THE DEATH OF QUINTILIUS

Quis desiderio sit pudor aut modus
tam cari capitis? Praecipe lugubris
cantus, Melpomene, cui liquidam pater
    vocem cum cithara dedit.

Ergo Quintilium perpetuus sopor   5
urget? Cui Pudor et Iustitiae soror,
incorrupta Fides, nudaque Veritas
    quando ullum inveniet parem?

Multis ille bonis flebilis occidit,
nulli flebilior quam tibi, Vergili.   10
Tu frustra pius heu non ita creditum
    poscis Quintilium deos.

Quid? Si Threïcio blandius Orpheo
auditam moderere arboribus fidem,
num vanae redeat sanguis imagini,   15
    quam virga semel horrida,

non lenis precibus fata recludere,
nigro compulerit Mercurius gregi?
Durum: sed levius fit patientia
    quicquid corrigere est nefas.   20

25

TO AN AGING HETAERA

Parcius iunctas quatiunt fenestras
iactibus crebris iuvenes protervi,
nec tibi somnos adimunt, amatque
    ianua limen,

quae prius multum facilis movebat   5
cardines. Audis minus et minus iam:
"Me tuo longas pereunte noctes
    Lydia, dormis?"

Invicem moechos anus arrogantis
flebis in solo levis angiportu,   10
Thracio bacchante magis sub inter-
    lunia vento,

cum tibi flagrans amor et libido,
quae solet matres furiare equorum,
saeviet circa iecur ulcerosum,   15
    non sine questu,

laeta quod pubes hedera virenti
gaudeat pulla magis atque myrto,
aridas frondes hiemis sodali
    dedicet Euro.   20

26

FOR LUCIUS LAMIA

Musis amicus tristitiam et metus
tradam protervis in mare Creticum
    portare ventis, quis sub Arcto
        rex gelidae metuatur orae,

quid Tiridaten terreat, unice   5
securus. O quae fontibus integris
    gaudes, apricos necte flores,
        necte meo Lamiae coronam,

Pipleï dulcis. Nil sine te mei
prosunt honores: hunc fidibus novis,   10
    hunc Lesbio sacrare plectro
        teque tuasque decet sorores.

27

WINE AND LOVE AT A SYMPOSIUM

Natis in usum laetitiae scyphis
pugnare Thracum est: tollite barbarum
   morem, verecundumque Bacchum
     sanguineis prohibete rixis.

Vino et lucernis Medus acinaces   5
immane quantum discrepat: impium
   lenite clamorem, sodales,
     et cubito remanete presso.

Vultis severi me quoque sumere
partem Falerni? Dicat Opuntiae   10
   frater Megillae, quo beatus
     vulnere, qua pereat sagitta.

Cessat voluntas? Non alia bibam
mercede. Quae te cumque domat Venus,
   non erubescendis adurit   15
     ignibus ingenuoque semper

amore peccas. Quicquid habes, age,
depone tutis auribus. A miser,
   quanta laborabas Charybdi,
     digne puer meliore flamma!   20

Quae saga, quis te solvere Thessalis
magus venenis, quis poterit deus?
   Vix illigatum te triformi
     Pegasus expediet Chimaera.

28

THE ARCHYTAS ODE

Te maris et terrae numeroque carentis harenae
   mensorem cohibent, Archyta,
pulveris exigui prope litus parva Matinum
   munera, nec quicquam tibi prodest

aërias temptasse domos animoque rotundum   5
   percurrisse polum morituro.
Occidit et Pelopis genitor, conviva deorum,
   Tithonusque remotus in auras

et Iovis arcanis Minos admissus, habentque
   Tartara Panthoïden iterum Orco   10
demissum, quamvis clipeo Troiana refixo
   tempora testatus nihil ultra

nervos atque cutem morti concesserat atrae,
   iudice te non sordidus auctor
naturae verique. Sed omnis una manet nox,   15
   et calcanda semel via leti.

Dant alios Furiae torvo spectacula Marti,
   exitio est avidum mare nautis;
mixta senum ac iuvenum densentur funera, nullum
   saeva caput Proserpina fugit.   20

Me quoque devexi rapidus comes Orionis
   Illyricis Notus obruit undis.
At tu, nauta, vagae ne parce malignus harenae
   ossibus et capiti inhumato

particulam dare: sic, quodcumque minabitur Eurus   25
   fluctibus Hesperiis, Venusinae
plectantur silvae te sospite, multaque merces,
   unde potest, tibi defluat aequo

ab Iove Neptunoque sacri custode Tarenti.
  Neglegis immeritis nocituram   30
postmodo te natis fraudem committere? Fors et
  debita iura vicesque superbae

te maneant ipsum: precibus non linquar inultis,
  teque piacula nulla resolvent.
Quamquam festinas, non est mora longa; licebit   35
  iniecto ter pulvere curras.

29

ICCIUS GOES TO WAR

Icci, beatis nunc Arabum invides
gazis et acrem militiam paras
   non ante devictis Sabaeae
      regibus, horribilique Medo

nectis catenas? Quae tibi virginum   5
sponso necato barbara serviet?
   Puer quis ex aula capillis
      ad cyathum statuetur unctis,

doctus sagittas tendere Sericas
arcu paterno? Quis neget arduis   10
   pronos relabi posse rivos
      montibus et Tiberim reverti,

cum tu coëmptos undique nobilis
libros Panaeti Socraticum et domum
   mutare loricis Hiberis,   15
      pollicitus meliora, tendis?

30

GLYCERA'S INVOCATION TO VENUS

O Venus, regina Cnidi Paphique,
sperne dilectam Cypron et vocantis
   ture te multo Glycerae decoram
      transfer in aedem.

Fervidus tecum puer et solutis   5
Gratiae zonis properentque nymphae
et parum comis sine te Iuventas
      Mercuriusque.

31

A POET'S PRAYER

Quid dedicatum poscit Apollinem
vates? Quid orat, de patera novum
    fundens liquorem? Non opimae
      Sardiniae segetes feracis,

non aestuosae grata Calabriae   5
armenta, non aurum aut ebur Indicum,
    non rura quae Liris quieta
      mordet aqua taciturnus amnis.

Premant Calena falce quibus dedit
Fortuna vitem, dives et aureis   10
    mercator exsiccet culillis
      vina Syra reparata merce,

dis carus ipsis, quippe ter et quater
anno revisens aequor Atlanticum
    impune. Me pascunt olivae,   15
      me cichorea levesque malvae.

Frui paratis et valido mihi,
Latoë, dones ac, precor, integra
    cum mente, nec turpem senectam
      degere nec cithara carentem.   20

32

INVOCATION TO THE LYRE

Poscimus, si quid vacui sub umbra
lusimus tecum quod et hunc in annum
vivat et pluris, age dic Latinum,
    barbite, carmen,

Lesbio primum modulate civi,   5
qui ferox bello tamen inter arma,
sive iactatam religarat udo
    litore navim,

Liberum et Musas Veneremque et illi
semper haerentem puerum canebat,   10
et Lycum nigris oculis nigroque
    crine decorum.

O decus Phoebi et dapibus supremi
grata testudo Iovis, o laborum
dulce lenimen, mihi cumque salve   15
    rite vocanti.

33   3rd Asclepiadean

TO A DESERTED LOVER

Albi, ne doleas plus nimio memor
immitis Glycerae neu miserabilis
decantes elegos, cur tibi iunior
    laesa praeniteat fide.

Insignem tenui fronte Lycorida   5
Cyri torret amor, Cyrus in asperam
declinat Pholoën; sed prius Apulis
    iungentur capreae lupis,

quam turpi Pholoë peccet adultero.
Sic visum Veneri, cui placet imparis   10
formas atque animos sub iuga aënea
    saevo mittere cum ioco.

Ipsum me melior cum peteret Venus,
  grata detinuit compede Myrtale
libertina, fretis acrior Hadriae   15
    curvantis Calabros sinus.

34

AN EPIPHANY

Parcus deorum cultor et infrequens
insanientis dum sapientiae
   consultus erro, nunc retrorsum
     vela dare atque iterare cursus

cogor relictos. Namque Diespiter,   5
igni corusco nubila dividens
   plerumque, per purum tonantis
     egit equos volucremque currum;

quo bruta tellus et vaga flumina
quo Styx et invisi horrida Taenari   10
   sedes Atlanteusque finis
     concutitur. Valet ima summis

mutare et insignem attenuat deus,
obscura promens; hinc apicem rapax
   Fortuna cum stridore acuto   15
     sustulit, hic posuisse gaudet.

35

A HYMN TO FORTUNE

O diva, gratum quae regis Antium,
praesens vel imo tollere de gradu
    mortale corpus vel superbos
        vertere funeribus triumphos,

te pauper ambit sollicita prece   5
ruris colonus, te dominam aequoris,
    quicumque Bithyna lacessit
        Carpathium pelagus carina;

te Dacus asper, te profugi Scythae
urbesque gentesque et Latium ferox   10
    regumque matres barbarorum et
        purpurei metuunt tyranni,

iniurioso ne pede proruas
stantem columnam, neu populus frequens
    ad arma cessantis, ad arma   15
        concitet imperiumque frangat.

Te semper anteit saeva Necessitas,
clavos trabalis et cuneos manu
    gestans aëna, nec severus
        uncus abest liquidumque plumbum.   20

Te Spes et albo rara Fides colit
velata panno, nec comitem abnegat,
    utcumque mutata potentis
        veste domos inimica linquis.

At vulgus infidum et meretrix retro   25
periura cedit, diffugiunt cadis
    cum faece siccatis amici,
        ferre iugum pariter dolosi.

Serves iturum Caesarem in ultimos
orbis Britannos et iuvenum recens   30
    examen, Eois timendum
        partibus Oceanoque rubro.

Eheu, cicatricum et sceleris pudet
fratrumque. Quid nos dura refugimus
    aetas? Quid intactum nefasti   35
        liquimus? Unde manum iuventus

metu deorum continuit? Quibus
pepercit aris? O utinam nova
    incude diffingas retusum in
        Massagetas Arabasque ferrum!   40

36

A JOYFUL RETURN

Et ture et fidibus iuvat
  placare et vituli sanguine debito
custodes Numidae deos,
  qui nunc Hesperia sospes ab ultima

caris multa sodalibus,   5
  nulli plura tamen dividit oscula
quam dulci Lamiae, memor
  actae non alio rege puertiae

mutataeque simul togae.
  Cressa ne careat pulchra dies nota,   10
neu promptae modus amphorae,
  neu morem in Salium sit requies pedum,

neu multi Damalis meri
  Bassum Threïcia vincat amystide,
neu desint epulis rosae   15
  neu vivax apium neu breve lilium.

Omnes in Damalin putris
  deponent oculos, nec Damalis novo
divelletur adultero,
  lascivis hederis ambitiosior.   20

37

THE FALL OF CLEOPATRA

Nunc est bibendum, nunc pede libero
pulsanda tellus, nunc Saliaribus
　　ornare pulvinar deorum
　　　　tempus erat dapibus, sodales.

Antehac nefas depromere Caecubum　　　　　5
cellis avitis, dum Capitolio
　　regina dementis ruinas,
　　　　funus et imperio parabat

contaminato cum grege turpium
morbo virorum, quidlibet impotens　　　　　10
　　sperare fortunaque dulci
　　　　ebria. Sed minuit furorem

vix una sospes navis ab ignibus,
mentemque lymphatam Mareotico
　　redegit in veros timores　　　　　15
　　　　Caesar, ab Italia volantem

remis adurgens, accipiter velut
mollis columbas aut leporem citus
　　venator in campis nivalis
　　　　Haemoniae, daret ut catenis　　　　　20

fatale monstrum. Quae generosius
perire quaerens nec muliebriter
　　expavit ensem nec latentis
　　　　classe cita reparavit oras;

ausa et iacentem visere regiam　　　　　25
vultu sereno, fortis et asperas
　　tractare serpentes, ut atrum
　　　　corpore combiberet venenum,

deliberata morte ferocior;
saevis Liburnis scilicet invidens   30
   privata deduci superbo
    non humilis mulier triumpho.

38 Sapphic

DOWN WITH ORIENTAL LUXURY

Persicos odi, puer, apparatus;
displicent nexae philyra coronae;
mitte sectari rosa quo locorum
    sera moretur.

Simplici myrto nihil allabores   5
sedulus curo: neque te ministrum
dedecet myrtus neque me sub arta
    vite bibentem.

THE *ODES,* BOOK 2

1

TO POLLIO WRITING OF THE CIVIL WARS

Motum ex Metello consule civicum
bellique causas et vitia et modos
   ludumque Fortunae gravisque
      principum amicitias et arma

nondum expiatis uncta cruoribus,   5
periculosae plenum opus aleae,
   tractas et incedis per ignes
      suppositos cineri doloso.

Paulum severae Musa tragoediae
desit theatris; mox, ubi publicas   10
   res ordinaris, grande munus
      Cecropio repetes cothurno,

insigne maestis praesidium reis
et consulenti, Pollio, curiae,
   cui laurus aeternos honores   15
      Delmatico peperit triumpho.

Iam nunc minaci murmure cornuum
perstringis auris, iam litui strepunt,
   iam fulgor armorum fugacis
      terret equos equitumque vultus.   20

Audire magnos iam videor duces,
non indecoro pulvere sordidos,
   et cuncta terrarum subacta
      praeter atrocem animum Catonis.

Iuno et deorum quisquis amicior   25
Afris inulta cesserat impotens
   tellure victorum nepotes
      rettulit inferias Iugurthae.

Quis non Latino sanguine pinguior
campus sepulcris impia proelia 30
   testatur auditumque Medis
      Hesperiae sonitum ruinae?

Qui gurges aut quae flumina lugubris
ignara belli? Quod mare Dauniae
   non decoloravere caedes? 35
      Quae caret ora cruore nostro?

Sed ne relictis, Musa procax, iocis
Ceae retractes munera neniae,
   mecum Dionaeo sub antro
      quaere modos leviore plectro. 40

2

THE USE AND ABUSE OF MONEY

Nullus argento color est avaris
abdito terris, inimice lamnae
Crispe Sallusti, nisi temperato
    splendeat usu.

Vivet extento Proculeius aevo,   5
notus in fratres animi paterni:
illum aget penna metuente solvi
    fama superstes.

Latius regnes avidum domando
spiritum, quam si Libyam remotis   10
Gadibus iungas et uterque Poenus
    serviat uni.

Crescit indulgens sibi dirus hydrops,
nec sitim pellit, nisi causa morbi
fugerit venis et aquosus albo   15
    corpore languor.

Redditum Cyri solio Phraäten
dissidens plebi numero beatorum
eximit Virtus populumque falsis
    dedocet uti   20

vocibus, regnum et diadema tutum
deferens uni propriamque laurum,
quisquis ingentis oculo irretorto
    spectat acervos.

3

TO DELLIUS: MEMENTO MORI

Aequam memento rebus in arduis
servare mentem, non secus in bonis
    ab insolenti temperatam
      laetitia, moriture Delli,

seu maestus omni tempore vixeris,   5
seu te in remoto gramine per dies
    festos reclinatum bearis
      interiore nota Falerni.

Quo pinus ingens albaque populus
umbram hospitalem consociare amant   10
    ramis? Quid obliquo laborat
      lympha fugax trepidare rivo?

Huc vina et unguenta et nimium brevis
flores amoenae ferre iube rosae,
    dum res et aetas et sororum   15
      fila trium patiuntur atra.

Cedes coëmptis saltibus et domo
villaque, flavus quam Tiberis lavit,
    cedes, et exstructis in altum
      divitiis potietur heres.   20

Divesne, prisco natus ab Inacho,
nil interest an pauper et infima
    de gente sub divo moreris;
      victima nil miserantis Orci.

Omnes eodem cogimur, omnium   25
versatur urna serius ocius
    sors exitura et nos in aeternum
      exsilium impositura cumbae.

4

LOVE FOR A SLAVE-GIRL

Ne sit ancillae tibi amor pudori,
Xanthia Phoceu. Prius insolentem
serva Briseis niveo colore
    movit Achillem;

movit Aiacem Telamone natum   5
forma captivae dominum Tecmessae;
arsit Atrides medio in triumpho
    virgine rapta,

barbarae postquam cecidere turmae
Thessalo victore et ademptus Hector   10
tradidit fessis leviora tolli
    Pergama Graïs.

Nescias an te generum beati
Phyllidis flavae decorent parentes:
regium certe genus et penatis   15
    maeret iniquos.

Crede non illam tibi de scelesta
plebe dilectam neque sic fidelem,
sic lucro aversam potuisse nasci
    matre pudenda.   20

Bracchia et vultum teretisque suras
integer laudo; fuge suspicari,
cuius octavum trepidavit aetas
    claudere lustrum.

5

NOT YET!

Nondum subacta ferre iugum valet
cervice, nondum munia comparis
    aequare nec tauri ruentis
      in venerem tolerare pondus.

Circa virentis est animus tuae   5
campos iuvencae, nunc fluviis gravem
    solantis aestum, nunc in udo
      ludere cum vitulis salicto

praegestientis. Tolle cupidinem
immitis uvae: iam tibi lividos   10
    distinguet Autumnus racemos
      purpureo varius colore.

Iam te sequetur (currit enim ferox
aetas, et illi quos tibi dempserit
    apponet annos), iam proterva   15
      fronte petet Lalage maritum,

dilecta quantum non Pholoë fugax,
non Chloris, albo sic umero nitens,
    ut pura nocturno renidet
      luna mari Cnidiusve Gyges,   20

quem si puellarum insereres choro,
mire sagacis falleret hospites
    discrimen obscurum solutis
      crinibus ambiguoque vultu.

6

IN PRAISE OF TARENTUM

Septimi, Gadis aditure mecum et
Cantabrum indoctum iuga ferre nostra et
barbaras Syrtis, ubi Maura semper
    aestuat unda,

Tibur Argeo positum colono   5
sit meae sedes utinam senectae,
sit modus lasso maris et viarum
    militiaeque.

Unde si Parcae prohibent iniquae,
dulce pellitis ovibus Galaesi   10
flumen et regnata petam Laconi
    rura Phalantho.

Ille terrarum mihi praeter omnis
angulus ridet, ubi non Hymetto
mella decedunt viridique certat   15
    baca Venafro;

ver ubi longum tepidasque praebet
Iuppiter brumas, et amicus Aulon
fertili Baccho minimum Falernis
    invidet uvis.   20

Ille te mecum locus et beatae
postulant arces; ibi tu calentem
debita sparges lacrima favillam
    vatis amici.

7

A HAPPY RETURN

O saepe mecum tempus in ultimum
deducte Bruto militiae duce,
   quis te redonavit Quiritem
     dis patriis Italoque caelo,

Pompei, meorum prime sodalium,   5
cum quo morantem saepe diem mero
   fregi, coronatus nitentis
     malobathro Syrio capillos?

Tecum Philippos et celerem fugam
sensi relicta non bene parmula,   10
   cum fracta virtus et minaces
     turpe solum tetigere mento.

Sed me per hostis Mercurius celer
denso paventem sustulit aëre;
   te rursus in bellum resorbens   15
     unda fretis tulit aestuosis.

Ergo obligatam redde Iovi dapem,
longaque fessum militia latus
   depone sub lauru mea nec
     parce cadis tibi destinatis.   20

Oblivioso levia Massico
ciboria exple, funde capacibus
   unguenta de conchis. Quis udo
     deproperare apio coronas

curatve myrto? Quem Venus arbitrum   25
dicet bibendi? Non ego sanius
   bacchabor Edonis; recepto
     dulce mihi furere est amico.

8

TO A HEARTBREAKER

Ulla si iuris tibi peierati
poena, Barine, nocuisset umquam,
dente si nigro fieres vel uno
    turpior ungui,

crederem. Sed tu simul obligasti   5
perfidum votis caput, enitescis
pulchrior multo iuvenumque prodis
    publica cura.

Expedit matris cineres opertos
fallere et toto taciturna noctis   10
signa cum caelo gelidaque divos
    morte carentis.

Ridet hoc, inquam, Venus ipsa; rident
simplices Nymphae ferus et Cupido,
semper ardentis acuens sagittas   15
    cote cruenta.

Adde quod pubes tibi crescit omnis,
servitus crescit nova, nec priores
impiae tectum dominae relinquunt,
    saepe minati.   20

Te suis matres metuunt iuvencis,
te senes parci miseraeque nuper
virgines nuptae, tua ne retardet
    aura maritos.

9

TO A MELANCHOLY FRIEND

Non semper imbres nubibus hispidos
manant in agros aut mare Caspium
    vexant inaequales procellae
      usque, nec Armeniis in oris,

amice Valgi, stat glacies iners   5
menses per omnis, aut Aquilonibus
    querqueta Gargani laborant
      et foliis viduantur orni:

tu semper urges flebilibus modis
Mysten ademptum, nec tibi Vespero   10
    surgente decedunt amores
      nec rapidum fugiente solem.

At non ter aevo functus amabilem
ploravit omnis Antilochum senex
    annos, nec impubem parentes   15
      Troïlon aut Phrygiae sorores

flevere semper. Desine mollium
tandem querellarum, et potius nova
    cantemus Augusti tropaea
      Caesaris, et rigidum Niphaten,   20

Medumque flumen gentibus additum
victis minores volvere vertices,
    intraque praescriptum Gelonos
      exiguis equitare campis.

10 *Sapphic*

THE GOLDEN MEAN

Rectius vives, Licini, neque altum
semper urgendo neque, dum procellas
cautus horrescis, nimium premendo
  litus iniquum.

Auream quisquis mediocritatem   5
diligit, tutus caret obsoleti
sordibus tecti, caret invidenda
  sobrius aula.

Saepius ventis agitatur ingens
pinus et celsae graviore casu   10
decidunt turres feriuntque summos
  fulgura montis.

Sperat infestis, metuit secundis
alteram sortem bene praeparatum
pectus. Informis hiemes reducit   15
  Iuppiter; idem

summovet. Non, si male nunc, et olim
sic erit: quondam cithara tacentem
suscitat Musam neque semper arcum
  tendit Apollo.   20

Rebus angustis animosus atque
fortis appare; sapienter idem
contrahes vento nimium secundo
  turgida vela.

11

A CALL TO PLEASURE

Quid bellicosus Cantaber et Scythes,
Hirpine Quincti, cogitet Hadria
   divisus obiecto, remittas
     quaerere, nec trepides in usum

poscentis aevi pauca. Fugit retro   5
levis iuventas et decor, arida
   pellente lascivos amores
     canitie facilemque somnum.

Non semper idem floribus est honor
vernis, neque uno luna rubens nitet   10
   vultu. Quid aeternis minorem
     consiliis animum fatigas?

Cur non sub alta vel platano vel hac
pinu iacentes sic temere et rosa
   canos odorati capillos,   15
     dum licet, Assyriaque nardo

potamus uncti? Dissipat Euhius
curas edacis. Quis puer ocius
   restinguet ardentis Falerni
     pocula praetereunte lympha?   20

Quis devium scortum eliciet domo
Lyden? Eburna dic, age, cum lyra
   maturet, in comptum Lacaenae
     more comas religata nodum.

12

IN PRAISE OF LICYMNIA

Nolis longa ferae bella Numantiae
nec durum Hannibalem nec Siculum mare
Poeno purpureum sanguine mollibus
    aptari citharae modis,

nec saevos Lapithas et nimium mero   5
Hylaeum domitosque Herculea manu
Telluris iuvenes, unde periculum
    fulgens contremuit domus

Saturni veteris; tuque pedestribus
dices historiis proelia Caesaris,   10
Maecenas, melius ductaque per vias
    regum colla minacium.

Me dulcis dominae Musa Licymniae
cantus, me voluit dicere lucidum
fulgentis oculos et bene mutuis   15
    fidum pectus amoribus;

quam nec ferre pedem dedecuit choris
nec certare ioco nec dare bracchia
ludentem nitidis virginibus sacro
    Dianae celebris die.   20

Num tu quae tenuit dives Achaemenes
aut pinguis Phrygiae Mygdonias opes
permutare velis crine Licymniae,
    plenas aut Arabum domos,

cum flagrantia detorquet ad oscula   25
cervicem, aut facili saevitia negat,
quae poscente magis gaudeat eripi,
    interdum rapere occupet?

13

A NARROW ESCAPE

Ille et nefasto te posuit die,
quicumque primum, et sacrilega manu
    produxit, arbos, in nepotum
        perniciem opprobriumque pagi.

Illum et parentis crediderim sui   5
fregisse cervicem et penetralia
    sparsisse nocturno cruore
        hospitis; ille venena Colcha

et quicquid usquam concipitur nefas
tractavit, agro qui statuit meo   10
    te, triste lignum, te caducum
        in domini caput immerentis.

Quid quisque vitet, numquam homini satis
cautum est in horas. Navita Bosphorum
    Poenus perhorrescit neque ultra   15
        caeca timet aliunde fata;

miles sagittas et celerem fugam
Parthi, catenas Parthus et Italum
    robur; sed improvisa leti
        vis rapuit rapietque gentis.   20

Quam paene furvae regna Proserpinae
et iudicantem vidimus Aeacum
    sedesque discriptas piorum et
        Aeoliis fidibus querentem

Sappho puellis de popularibus   25
et te sonantem plenius aureo,
    Alcaee, plectro dura navis,
        dura fugae mala, dura belli.

Utrumque sacro digna silentio
mirantur umbrae dicere; sed magis   30
    pugnas et exactos tyrannos
        densum umeris bibit aure vulgus.

Quid mirum, ubi illis carminibus stupens
demittit atras belua centiceps
    auris, et intorti capillis   35
        Eumenidum recreantur angues?

Quin et Prometheus et Pelopis parens
dulci laborem decipitur sono,
    nec curat Orion leones
        aut timidos agitare lyncas.   40

Alcaic

14

DEATH IS INEVITABLE

Eheu fugaces, Postume, Postume,
labuntur anni, nec pietas moram
  rugis et instanti senectae
    adferet indomitaeque morti;

non, si trecenis, quotquot eunt dies,   5
amice, places illacrimabilem
  Plutona tauris, qui ter amplum
    Geryonen Tityonque tristi

compescit unda—scilicet omnibus,
quicumque terrae munere vescimur,   10
  enaviganda, sive reges
    sive inopes erimus coloni.

Frustra cruento Marte carebimus
fractisque rauci fluctibus Hadriae,
  frustra per autumnos nocentem   15
    corporibus metuemus Austrum.

Visendus ater flumine languido
Cocytos errans et Danaï genus
  infame damnatusque longi
    Sisyphus Aeolides laboris.   20

Linquenda tellus et domus et placens
uxor, neque harum quas colis arborum
  te praeter invisas cupressos
    ulla brevem dominum sequetur.

Absumet heres Caecuba dignior   25
servata centum clavibus et mero
  tinguet pavimentum superbo
    pontificum potiore cenis.

15

THE INVASION OF LUXURY

Iam pauca aratro iugera regiae
moles relinquent, undique latius
   extenta visentur Lucrino
    stagna lacu, platanusque caelebs

evincet ulmos; tum violaria et   5
myrtus et omnis copia narium
   spargent olivetis odorem
    fertilibus domino priori.

Tum spissa ramis laurea fervidos
excludet ictus. Non ita Romuli   10
   praescriptum et intonsi Catonis
    auspiciis veterumque norma.

Privatus illis census erat brevis,
commune magnum; nulla decempedis
   metata privatis opacam   15
    porticus excipiebat Arcton,

nec fortuitum spernere caespitem
leges sinebant, oppida publico
   sumptu iubentes et deorum
    templa novo decorare saxo.   20

16

ODE ON TRANQUILLITY

Otium divos rogat in patenti
prensus Aegaeo, simul atra nubes
condidit lunam neque certa fulgent
  sidera nautis;

otium bello furiosa Thrace,   5
otium Medi pharetra decori,
Grosphe, non gemmis neque purpura ve-
  nale nec auro.

Non enim gazae neque consularis
summovet lictor miseros tumultus   10
mentis et curas laqueata circum
  tecta volantis.

Vivitur parvo bene, cui paternum
splendet in mensa tenui salinum
nec levis somnos timor aut cupido   15
  sordidus aufert.

Quid brevi fortes iaculamur aevo
multa? Quid terras alio calentis
sole mutamus? Patriae quis exsul
  se quoque fugit?   20

Scandit aeratas vitiosa navis
Cura nec turmas equitum relinquit,
ocior cervis et agente nimbos
  ocior Euro.

Laetus in praesens animus quod ultra est 25
oderit curare et amara lento
temperet risu. Nihil est ab omni
  parte beatum.

Abstulit clarum cita mors Achillem,
longa Tithonum minuit senectus;   30
et mihi forsan, tibi quod negarit,
    porriget hora.

Te greges centum Siculaeque circum
mugiunt vaccae, tibi tollit hinnitum
apta quadrigis equa, te bis Afro   35
    murice tinctae

vestiunt lanae; mihi parva rura et
spiritum Graiae tenuem Camenae
Parca non mendax dedit et malignum
    spernere vulgus.   40

17

CHEER UP, MAECENAS!

Cur me querelis exanimas tuis?
Nec dis amicum est nec mihi te prius
   obire, Maecenas, mearum
      grande decus columenque rerum.

A, te meae si partem animae rapit   5
maturior vis, quid moror altera,
   nec carus aeque nec superstes
      integer? Ille dies utramque

ducet ruinam. Non ego perfidum
dixi sacramentum: ibimus, ibimus,   10
   utcumque praecedes, supremum
      carpere iter comites parati.

Me nec Chimaerae spiritus igneae
nec, si resurgat, centimanus Gyas
   divellet umquam: sic potenti   15
      Iustitiae placitumque Parcis.

Seu Libra seu me Scorpios adspicit
formidulosus, pars violentior
   natalis horae, seu tyrannus
      Hesperiae Capricornus undae,   20

utrumque nostrum incredibili modo
consentit astrum. Te Iovis impio
   tutela Saturno refulgens
      eripuit volucrisque Fati

tardavit alas, cum populus frequens   25
laetum theatris ter crepuit sonum;
   me truncus illapsus cerebro
      sustulerat, nisi Faunus ictum

dextra levasset, Mercurialium
  custos virorum. Reddere victimas   30
    aedemque votivam memento;
      nos humilem feriemus agnam.

18

THE VANITY OF RICHES

Non ebur neque aureum
  mea renidet in domo lacunar,
non trabes Hymettiae
  premunt columnas ultima recisas
Africa, neque Attali   5
  ignotus heres regiam occupavi,
nec Laconicas mihi
  trahunt honestae purpuras clientae.
At fides et ingeni
  benigna vena est, pauperemque dives   10
me petit: nihil supra
  deos lacesso nec potentem amicum
largiora flagito,
  satis beatus unicis Sabinis.
Truditur dies die,   15
  novaeque pergunt interire lunae.
Tu secanda marmora
  locas sub ipsum funus et sepulcri
immemor struis domos,
  marisque Baïs obstrepentis urges   20
summovere litora,
  parum locuples continente ripa.
Quid quod usque proximos
  revellis agri terminos et ultra
limites clientium   25
  salis avarus? Pellitur paternos
in sinu ferens deos
  et uxor et vir sordidosque natos.
Nulla certior tamen

rapacis Orci fine destinata   30
aula divitem manet
    erum. Quid ultra tendis? Aequa tellus
pauperi recluditur
    regumque pueris, nec satelles Orci
callidum Prometheä   35
    revexit auro captus. Hic superbum
Tantalum atque Tantali
    genus coërcet, hic levare functum
pauperem laboribus
    vocatus atque non vocatus audit.   40

19

HYMN TO BACCHUS

Bacchum in remotis carmina rupibus
vidi docentem—credite posteri—
    Nymphasque discentis et auris
    capripedum Satyrorum acutas.

Euhoe, recenti mens trepidat metu,   5
plenoque Bacchi pectore turbidum
    laetatur. Euhoe, parce, Liber,
    parce, gravi metuende thyrso!

Fas pervicacis est mihi Thyiadas
vinique fontem lactis et uberes   10
    cantare rivos atque truncis
    lapsa cavis iterare mella;

fas et beatae coniugis additum
stellis honorem tectaque Penthei
    disiecta non leni ruina   15
    Thracis et exitium Lycurgi.

Tu flectis amnis, tu mare barbarum,
tu separatis uvidus in iugis

nodo coërces viperino
Bistonidum sine fraude crinis.   20

Tu, cum parentis regna per arduum
cohors Gigantum scanderet impia,
    Rhoetum retorsisti leonis
        unguibus horribilique mala;

quamquam choreïs aptior et iocis   25
ludoque dictus non sat idoneus
    pugnae ferebaris; sed idem
        pacis eras mediusque belli.

Te vidit insons Cerberus aureo
cornu decorum, leniter atterens   30
    caudam, et recedentis trilingui
        ore pedes tetigitque crura.

20

A PROPHECY OF IMMORTALITY

Non usitata nec tenui ferar
penna biformis per liquidum aethera
   vates, neque in terris morabor
    longius invidiaque maior

urbes relinquam. Non ego, pauperum   5
sanguis parentum, non ego, quem vocas,
   dilecte Maecenas, obibo
    nec Stygia cohibebor unda.

Iam iam residunt cruribus asperae
pelles, et album mutor in alitem   10
   superne, nascunturque leves
    per digitos umerosque plumae.

Iam Daedaleo notior Icaro
visam gementis litora Bosphori
   Syrtisque Gaetulas canorus   15
    ales Hyperboreosque campos.

Me Colchus et, qui dissimulat metum
Marsae cohortis, Dacus et ultimi
   noscent Geloni, me peritus
    discet Hiber Rhodanique potor.   20

Absint inani funere neniae
luctusque turpes et querimoniae;
   compesce clamorem ac sepulcri
    mitte supervacuos honores.

THE *ODES*, BOOK 3

1

SIMPLICITY

Odi profanum vulgus et arceo;
favete linguis. Carmina non prius
   audita Musarum sacerdos
     virginibus puerisque canto.

Regum timendorum in proprios greges,   5
reges in ipsos imperium est Iovis,
   clari Giganteo triumpho,
     cuncta supercilio moventis.

Est ut viro vir latius ordinet
arbusta sulcis, hic generosior   10
   descendat in Campum petitor,
     moribus hic meliorque fama

contendat, illi turba clientium
sit maior: aequa lege Necessitas
   sortitur insignis et imos,   15
     omne capax movet urna nomen.

Destrictus ensis cui super impia
cervice pendet, non Siculae dapes
   dulcem elaborabunt saporem,
     non avium citharaeque cantus   20

somnum reducent. Somnus agrestium
lenis virorum non humilis domos
   fastidit umbrosamque ripam,
     non Zephyris agitata Tempe.

Desiderantem quod satis est neque   25
tumultuosum sollicitat mare
   nec saevus Arcturi cadentis
     impetus aut orientis Haedi,

non verberatae grandine vineae
fundusque mendax, arbore nunc aquas   30
    culpante, nunc torrentia agros
        sidera, nunc hiemes iniquas.

Contracta pisces aequora sentiunt
iactis in altum molibus; huc frequens
    caementa demittit redemptor   35
        cum famulis dominusque terrae

fastidiosus. Sed Timor et Minae
scandunt eodem quo dominus, neque
    decedit aerata triremi et
        post equitem sedet atra Cura.   40

Quod si dolentem nec Phrygius lapis
nec purpurarum sidere clarior
    delenit usus nec Falerna
        vitis Achaemeniumque costum,

cur invidendis postibus et novo   45
sublime ritu moliar atrium?
    Cur valle permutem Sabina
        divitias operosiores?

2

VIRTUS

Angustam amice pauperiem pati
robustus acri militia puer
    condiscat et Parthos ferocis
        vexet eques metuendus hasta,

vitamque sub divo et trepidis agat   5
in rebus. Illum ex moenibus hosticis
    matrona bellantis tyranni
        prospiciens et adulta virgo

suspiret: "Eheu, ne rudis agminum
sponsus lacessat regius asperum   10
    tactu leonem, quem cruenta
        per medias rapit ira caedes."

Dulce et decorum est pro patria mori:
mors et fugacem persequitur virum,
    nec parcit imbellis iuventae   15
        poplitibus timidove tergo.

Virtus, repulsae nescia sordidae,
intaminatis fulget honoribus,
    nec sumit aut ponit securis
        arbitrio popularis aurae.   20

Virtus, recludens immeritis mori
caelum, negata temptat iter via,
    coetusque vulgaris et udam
        spernit humum fugiente penna.

Est et fideli tuta silentio   25
merces. Vetabo qui Cereris sacrum
    vulgarit arcanae sub isdem
        sit trabibus fragilemque mecum

solvat phaselon; saepe Diespiter
neglectus incesto addidit integrum,   30
   raro antecedentem scelestum
     deseruit pede Poena claudo.

3

JUSTICE AND CONSTANCY OF PURPOSE

Iustum et tenacem propositi virum
non civium ardor prava iubentium,
   non vultus instantis tyranni
     mente quatit solida neque Auster,

dux inquieti turbidus Hadriae,   5
nec fulminantis magna manus Iovis;
   si fractus illabatur orbis,
     impavidum ferient ruinae.

Hac arte Pollux et vagus Hercules
enisus arces attigit igneas,   10
   quos inter Augustus recumbens
     purpureo bibet ore nectar.

Hac te merentem, Bacche pater, tuae
vexere tigres, indocili iugum
   collo trahentes; hac Quirinus   15
     Martis equis Acheronta fugit,

gratum elocuta consiliantibus
Iunone divis: "Ilion, Ilion
   fatalis incestusque iudex
     et mulier peregrina vertit   20

in pulverem, ex quo destituit deos
mercede pacta Laomedon, mihi
   castaeque damnatum Minervae
     cum populo et duce fraudulento.

Iam nec Lacaenae splendet adulterae   25
famosus hospes nec Priami domus
    periura pugnaces Achivos
        Hectoreïs opibus refringit,

nostrisque ductum seditionibus
bellum resedit. Protinus et gravis   30
    iras et invisum nepotem,
        Troica quem peperit sacerdos,

Marti redonabo; illum ego lucidas
inire sedes, discere nectaris
    sucos et adscribi quietis   35
        ordinibus patiar deorum.

Dum longus inter saeviat Ilion
Romamque pontus, qualibet exsules
    in parte regnanto beati;
        dum Priami Paridisque busto   40

insultet armentum et catulos ferae
celent inultae, stet Capitolium
    fulgens triumphatisque possit
        Roma ferox dare iura Medis.

Horrenda late nomen in ultimas   45
extendat oras, qua medius liquor
    secernit Europen ab Afro,
        qua tumidus rigat arva Nilus.

Aurum irrepertum et sic melius situm,
cum terra celat, spernere fortior   50
    quam cogere humanos in usus
        omne sacrum rapiente dextra,

quicumque mundo terminus obstitit,
hunc tanget armis, visere gestiens
    qua parte debacchentur ignes,   55
        qua nebulae pluviiique rores.

Sed bellicosis fata Quiritibus
hac lege dico, ne nimium pii
   rebusque fidentes avitae
     tecta velint reparare Troiae.   60

Troiae renascens alite lugubri
fortuna tristi clade iterabitur,
   ducente victrices catervas
     coniuge me Iovis et sorore.

Ter si resurgat murus aëneus   65
auctore Phoebo, ter pereat meis
   excisus Argivis, ter uxor
     capta virum puerosque ploret."

Non hoc iocosae conveniet lyrae:
quo, Musa, tendis? Desine pervicax   70
   referre sermones deorum et
     magna modis tenuare parvis.

4

WISDOM AND ORDER

Descende caelo et dic age tibia
regina longum Calliope melos,
   seu voce nunc mavis acuta
     seu fidibus citharave Phoebi.

Auditis, an me ludit amabilis   5
insania? Audire et videor pios
   errare per lucos, amoenae
     quos et aquae subeunt et aurae.

Me fabulosae Vulture in Apulo
nutricis extra limina Pulliae   10
   ludo fatigatumque somno
     fronde nova puerum palumbes

texere, mirum quod foret omnibus,
quicumque celsae nidum Acherontiae
   saltusque Bantinos et arvum   15
      pingue tenent humilis Forenti,

ut tuto ab atris corpore viperis
dormirem et ursis, ut premerer sacra
   lauroque collataque myrto,
      non sine dis animosus infans.   20

Vester, Camenae, vester in arduos
tollor Sabinos, seu mihi frigidum
   Praeneste seu Tibur supinum
      seu liquidae placuere Baiae.

Vestris amicum fontibus et choris   25
non me Philippis versa acies retro,
   devota non extinxit arbor,
      nec Sicula Palinurus unda.

Utcumque mecum vos eritis, libens
insanientem navita Bosphorum   30
   temptabo et urentis harenas
      litoris Assyrii viator;

visam Britannos hospitibus feros
et laetum equino sanguine Concanum,
   visam pharetratos Gelonos   35
      et Scythicum inviolatus amnem.

Vos Caesarem altum, militia simul
fessas cohortes abdidit oppidis,
   finire quaerentem labores,
      Pierio recreatis antro.   40

Vos lene consilium et datis et dato
gaudetis, almae. Scimus, ut impios
   Titanas immanemque turbam
      fulmine sustulerit caduco,

qui terram inertem, qui mare temperat   45
ventosum et urbes regnaque tristia,
   divosque mortalisque turmas
     imperio regit unus aequo.

Magnum illa terrorem intulerat Iovi
fidens iuventus horrida bracchiis   50
   fratresque tendentes opaco
     Pelion imposuisse Olympo.

Sed quid Typhoeus et validus Mimas,
aut quid minaci Porphyrion statu,
   quid Rhoetus evolsisque truncis   55
     Enceladus iaculator audax

contra sonantem Palladis aegida
possent ruentes? Hinc avidus stetit
   Vulcanus, hinc matrona Iuno et
     numquam umeris positurus arcum,   60

qui rore puro Castaliae lavit
crinis solutos, qui Lyciae tenet
   dumeta natalemque silvam,
     Delius et Patareus Apollo.

Vis consili expers mole ruit sua: 65
vim temperatam di quoque provehunt
   in maius; idem odere viris
     omne nefas animo moventis.

Testis mearum centimanus Gyas
sententiarum, notus et integrae   70
   temptator Orion Dianae,
     virginea domitus sagitta.

Iniecta monstris Terra dolet suis
maeretque partus fulmine luridum
   missos ad Orcum; nec peredit   75
     impositam celer ignis Aetnen,

incontinentis nec Tityi iecur
reliquit ales, nequitiae additus
   custos; amatorem trecentae
      Pirithoum cohibent catenae.   80

5

MARTIAL COURAGE

Caelo tonantem credidimus Iovem
regnare; praesens divus habebitur
   Augustus adiectis Britannis
      imperio gravibusque Persis.

Milesne Crassi coniuge barbara   5
turpis maritus vixit et hostium
   (pro curia inversique mores!)
      consenuit socerorum in armis

sub rege Medo, Marsus et Apulus,
anciliorum et nominis et togae   10
   oblitus aeternaeque Vestae,
      incolumi Iove et urbe Roma?

Hoc caverat mens provida Reguli
dissentientis condicionibus
   foedis et exemplo trahentis   15
      perniciem veniens in aevum,

si non periret immiserabilis
captiva pubes. "Signa ego Punicis
   affixa delubris et arma
      militibus sine caede" dixit   20

"derepta vidi; vidi ego civium
retorta tergo bracchia libero
   portasque non clausas et arva
      Marte coli populata nostro.

Auro repensus scilicet acrior   25
miles redibit. Flagitio additis
   damnum: neque amissos colores
      lana refert medicata fuco,

nec vera virtus, cum semel excidit,
curat reponi deterioribus.   30
   Si pugnat extricata densis
      cerva plagis, erit ille fortis

qui perfidis se credidit hostibus,
et Marte Poenos proteret altero,
   qui lora restrictis lacertis   35
      sensit iners timuitque mortem.

Hic, unde vitam sumeret inscius,
pacem duello miscuit. O pudor!
   O magna Carthago, probrosis
      altior Italiae ruinis!"   40

Fertur pudicae coniugis osculum
parvosque natos ut capitis minor
   ab se removisse et virilem
      torvus humi posuisse vultum,

donec labantis consilio patres   45
firmaret auctor numquam alias dato,
   interque maerentis amicos
      egregius properaret exsul.

Atqui sciebat quae sibi barbarus
tortor pararet. Non aliter tamen   50
   dimovit obstantis propinquos
      et populum reditus morantem,

quam si clientum longa negotia
diiudicata lite relinqueret,
   tendens Venafranos in agros   55
      aut Lacedaemonium Tarentum.

6

RELIGION AND PURITY

Delicta maiorum immeritus lues,
Romane, donec templa refeceris
   aedisque labentis deorum et
    foeda nigro simulacra fumo.

Dis te minorem quod geris, imperas: 5
hinc omne principium; huc refer exitum.
   Di multa neglecti dederunt
    Hesperiae mala luctuosae.

Iam bis Monaeses et Pacori manus
inauspicatos contudit impetus   10
   nostros et adiecisse praedam
    torquibus exiguis renidet.

Paene occupatam seditionibus
delevit urbem Dacus et Aethiops,
   hic classe formidatus, ille   15
    missilibus melior sagittis.

Fecunda culpae saecula nuptias
primum inquinavere et genus et domos;
   hoc fonte derivata clades
    in patriam populumque fluxit.   20

Motus doceri gaudet Ionicos .
matura virgo et fingitur artibus
   iam nunc et incestos amores
    de tenero meditatur ungui.

Mox iuniores quaerit adulteros   25
inter mariti vina, neque eligit
   cui donet impermissa raptim
    gaudia luminibus remotis,

sed iussa coram non sine conscio
surgit marito, seu vocat institor   30
   seu navis Hispanae magister,
      dedecorum pretiosus emptor.

Non his iuventus orta parentibus
infecit aequor sanguine Punico
   Pyrrhumque et ingentem cecidit   35
      Antiochum Hannibalemque dirum;

sed rusticorum mascula militum
proles, Sabellis docta ligonibus
   versare glaebas et severae
      matris ad arbitrium recisos   40

portare fustis, sol ubi montium
mutaret umbras et iuga demeret
   bobus fatigatis, amicum
      tempus agens abeunte curru.

Damnosa quid non imminuit dies?   45
Aetas parentum, peior avis, tulit
   nos nequiores, mox daturos
      progeniem vitiosiorem.

7

BE FAITHFUL, ASTERIE!

Quid fles, Asterie, quem tibi candidi
primo restituent vere Favonii
   Thyna merce beatum,
     constantis iuvenem fide,

Gygen? Ille Notis actus ad Oricum   5
post insana Caprae sidera frigidas
   noctes non sine multis
     insomnis lacrimis agit.

Atqui sollicitae nuntius hospitae,
suspirare Chloen et miseram tuis   10
   dicens ignibus uri,
     temptat mille vafer modis.

Ut Proetum mulier perfida credulum
falsis impulerit criminibus nimis
   casto Bellerophontae   15
     maturare necem refert;

narrat paene datum Pelea Tartaro,
Magnessam Hippolyten dum fugit abstinens;
   et peccare docentis
     fallax historias monet.   20

Frustra: nam scopulis surdior Icari
voces audit adhuc integer. At tibi
   ne vicinus Enipeus
     plus iusto placeat cave;

quamvis non alius flectere equum sciens   25
aeque conspicitur gramine Martio,
   nec quisquam citus aeque
     Tusco denatat alveo.

Prima nocte domum claude neque in vias
sub cantu querulae despice tibiae,   30
    et te saepe vocanti
        duram difficilis mane.

8

ANNIVERSARY OF A CLOSE CALL

Martiis caelebs quid agam Kalendis,
quid velint flores et acerra turis
plena miraris positusque carbo in
    caespite vivo,

docte sermones utriusque linguae?   5
Voveram dulcis epulas et album
Libero caprum prope funeratus
    arboris ictu.

Hic dies anno redeunte festus
corticem adstrictum pice dimovebit   10
amphorae fumum bibere institutae
    consule Tullo.

Sume, Maecenas, cyathos amici
sospitis centum et vigiles lucernas
perfer in lucem; procul omnis esto   15
    clamor et ira.

Mitte civilis super urbe curas:
occidit Daci Cotisonis agmen,
Medus infestus sibi luctuosis
    dissidet armis,   20

servit Hispanae vetus hostis orae
Cantaber, sera domitus catena,
iam Scythae laxo meditantur arcu
    cedere campis.

Neglegens ne qua populus laboret,   25
parce privatus nimium cavere et
dona praesentis cape laetus horae ac
    linque severa.

9

RECONCILIATION

"Donec gratus eram tibi
    nec quisquam potior bracchia candidae
cervici iuvenis dabat,
    Persarum vigui rege beatior."

"Donec non alia magis   5
    arsisti neque erat Lydia post Chloën,
multi Lydia nominis
    Romana vigui clarior Ilia."

"Me nunc Thressa Chloë regit,
    dulcis docta modos et citharae sciens,   10
pro qua non metuam mori
    si parcent animae fata superstiti."

"Me torret face mutua
    Thurini Calaïs filius Ornyti,
pro quo bis patiar mori,   15
    si parcent puero fata superstiti."

"Quid si prisca redit Venus
    diductosque iugo cogit aëneo?
si flava excutitur Chloë
    reiectaeque patet ianua Lydiae?"   20

"Quamquam sidere pulchrior
    ille est, tu levior cortice et improbo
iracundior Hadria,
    tecum vivere amem, tecum obeam libens!"

10

A SERENADE TO LYCE

Extremum Tanaïn si biberes, Lyce,
saevo nupta viro, me tamen asperas
porrectum ante fores obicere incolis
    plorares Aquilonibus.

Audis, quo strepitu ianua, quo nemus   5
inter pulchra satum tecta remugiat
ventis, et positas ut glaciet nives
    puro numine Iuppiter?

Ingratam Veneri pone superbiam,
ne currente retro funis eat rota;   10
non te Penelopen difficilem procis
    Tyrrhenus genuit parens.

O quamvis neque te munera nec preces
nec tinctus viola pallor amantium
nec vir Pieria paelice saucius   15
    curvat, supplicibus tuis

parcas, nec rigida mollior aesculo
nec Mauris animum mitior anguibus.
Non hoc semper erit liminis aut aquae
    caelestis patiens latus.   20

11

THE CASE OF THE DANAIDS

Mercuri (nam te docilis magistro
movit Amphion lapides canendo),
tuque testudo resonare septem
    callida nervis,

nec loquax olim neque grata, nunc et   5
divitum mensis et amica templis,
dic modos, Lyde quibus obstinatas
    applicet auris,

quae velut latis equa trima campis
ludit exsultim metuitque tangi,   10
nuptiarum expers et adhuc protervo
    cruda marito.

Tu potes tigris comitesque silvas
ducere et rivos celeres morari;
cessit immanis tibi blandienti   15
    ianitor aulae

Cerberus, quamvis furiale centum
muniant angues caput eius atque
spiritus taeter saniesque manet
    ore trilingui.   20

Quin et Ixion Tityosque vultu
risit invito, stetit urna paulum
sicca, dum grato Danaï puellas
    carmine mulces.

Audiat Lyde scelus atque notas   25
virginum poenas et inane lymphae
dolium fundo pereuntis imo
    seraque fata,

quae manent culpas etiam sub Orco.
Impiae (nam quid potuere maius?)   30
impiae sponsos potuere duro
    perdere ferro.

Una de multis face nuptuali
digna periurum fuit in parentem
splendide mendax et in omne virgo   35
    nobilis aevum,

"Surge" quae dixit iuveni marito,
"surge, ne longus tibi somnus, unde
non times, detur; socerum et scelestas
    falle sorores,   40

quae, velut nanctae vitulos leaenae,
singulos eheu lacerant. Ego illis
mollior nec te feriam neque intra
    claustra tenebo.

Me pater saevis oneret catenis,   45
quod viro clemens misero peperci;
me vel extremos Numidarum in agros
    classe releget.

I, pedes quo te rapiunt et aurae,
dum favet Nox et Venus; i secundo   50
omine et nostri memorem sepulcro
    scalpe querelam."

12

NEOBULE'S SOLILOQUY

Miserarum est neque amori dare ludum neque dulci
mala vino lavere aut exanimari metuentis
   patruae verbera linguae.

Tibi qualum Cythereae puer ales, tibi telas
operosaeque Minervae studium aufert, Neobule,   5
   Liparaeï nitor Hebri,

simul unctos Tiberinis umeros lavit in undis,
eques ipso melior Bellerophonte, neque pugno
   neque segni pede victus,

catus idem per apertum fugientis agitato   10
grege cervos iaculari et celer arto latitantem
   fruticeto excipere aprum.

13

TO THE SPRING OF BANDUSIA

O fons Bandusiae, splendidior vitro,
dulci digne mero non sine floribus,
    cras donaberis haedo,
        cui frons turgida cornibus

primis et venerem et proelia destinat.   5
Frustra: nam gelidos inficiet tibi
    rubro sanguine rivos
        lascivi suboles gregis.

Te flagrantis atrox hora Caniculae
nescit tangere, tu frigus amabile   10
    fessis vomere tauris
        praebes et pecori vago.

Fies nobilium tu quoque fontium,
me dicente cavis impositam ilicem
    saxis, unde loquaces   15
        lymphae desiliunt tuae.

14

THE RETURN OF AUGUSTUS

Herculis ritu modo dictus, o plebs,
morte venalem petiisse laurum
Caesar Hispana repetit penatis
　　victor ab ora.

Unico gaudens mulier marito   5
prodeat iustis operata divis
et soror clari ducis et decorae
　　supplice vitta

virginum matres iuvenumque nuper
sospitum. Vos, o pueri et puellae   10
iam virum expertae, male ominatis
　　parcite verbis.

Hic dies vere mihi festus atras
eximet curas; ego nec tumultum
nec mori per vim metuam tenente   15
　　Caesare terras.

I pete unguentum, puer, et coronas
et cadum Marsi memorem duelli,
Spartacum si qua potuit vagantem
　　fallere testa.   20

Dic et argutae properet Neaerae
murreum nodo cohibere crinem;
si per invisum mora ianitorem
　　fiet, abito.

Lenit albescens animos capillus   25
litium et rixae cupidos protervae;
non ego hoc ferrem calidus iuventa
　　consule Planco.

15

LEAVE YOUTH TO THE YOUNG

Uxor pauperis Ibyci,
  tandem nequitiae fige modum tuae
famosisque laboribus;
  maturo propior desine funeri

inter ludere virgines   5
  et stellis nebulam spargere candidis.
Non, si quid Pholoën, satis
  et te, Chlori, decet: filia rectius

expugnat iuvenem domos,
  pulso Thyias uti concita tympano.   10
Illam cogit amor Nothi
  lascivae similem ludere capreae;

te lanae prope nobilem
  tonsae Luceriam, non citharae decent
nec flos purpureus rosae   15
  nec poti vetulam faece tenus cadi.

16

MONEY VS. HAPPINESS

Inclusam Danaën turris aëneä
robustaeque fores et vigilum canum
tristes excubiae munierant satis
    nocturnis ab adulteris,

si non Acrisium virginis abditae   5
custodem pavidum Iuppiter et Venus
risissent: fore enim tutum iter et patens
    converso in pretium deo.

Aurum per medios ire satellites
et perrumpere amat saxa, potentius   10
ictu fulmineo; concidit auguris
    Argivi domus, ob lucrum

demersa exitio; diffidit urbium
portas vir Macedo et subruit aemulos
reges muneribus; munera navium   15
    saevos illaqueant duces.

Crescentem sequitur cura pecuniam
maiorumque fames. Iure perhorrui
late conspicuum tollere verticem,
    Maecenas, equitum decus.   20

Quanto quisque sibi plura negaverit,
ab dis plura feret: nil cupientium
nudus castra peto et transfuga divitum
    partis linquere gestio,

contemptae dominus splendidior rei,   25
quam si quicquid arat impiger Apulus
occultare meis dicerer horreis,
    magnas inter opes inops.

Purae rivus aquae silvaque iugerum
paucorum et segetis certa fides meae   30
fulgentem imperio fertilis Africae
    fallit sorte beatior.

Quamquam nec Calabrae mella ferunt apes,
nec Laestrygonia Bacchus in amphora
languescit mihi, nec pinguia Gallicis   35
    crescunt vellera pascuis,

importuna tamen pauperies abest,
nec, si plura velim, tu dare deneges.
Contracto melius parva cupidine
    vectigalia porrigam,   40

quam si Mygdoniis regnum Alyattei
campis continuem. Multa petentibus
desunt multa: bene est, cui deus obtulit
    parca quod satis est manu.

17

PREPARE FOR A RAINY BIRTHDAY

Aeli vetusto nobilis ab Lamo—
quando et priores hinc Lamias ferunt
   denominatos et nepotum
     per memores genus omne fastus,

auctore ab illo ducis originem,   5
qui Formiarum moenia dicitur
   princeps et innantem Maricae
     litoribus tenuisse Lirim,

late tyrannus—cras foliis nemus
multis et alga litus inutili   10
   demissa tempestas ab Euro
     sternet, aquae nisi fallit augur

annosa cornix. Dum potes, aridum
compone lignum: cras Genium mero
   curabis et porco bimestri   15
     cum famulis operum solutis.

18

A PRAYER TO FAUNUS

Faune, Nympharum fugientum amator,
per meos finis et aprica rura
lenis incedas abeasque parvis
    aequus alumnis,

si tener pleno cadit haedus anno,   5
larga nec desunt Veneris sodali
vina craterae, vetus ara multo
    fumat odore.

Ludit herboso pecus omne campo,
cum tibi Nonae redeunt Decembres;   10
festus in pratis vacat otioso
    cum bove pagus;

inter audacis lupus errat agnos;
spargit agrestis tibi silva frondes;
gaudet invisam pepulisse fossor   15
    ter pede terram.

19

HARD DRINKING FOR MURENA

Quantum distet ab Inacho
    Codrus pro patria non timidus mori
narras et genus Aeaci
    et pugnata sacro bella sub Ilio;

quo Chium pretio cadum   5
    mercemur, quis aquam temperet ignibus,
quo praebente domum et quota
    Paelignis caream frigoribus, taces.

Da lunae propere novae,
    da noctis mediae, da, puer, auguris   10
Murenae: tribus aut novem
    miscentur cyathis pocula commodis.

Qui Musas amat imparis,
    ternos ter cyathos attonitus petet
vates; tris prohibet supra   15
    rixarum metuens tangere Gratia

nudis iuncta sororibus.
    Insanire iuvat: cur Berecyntiae
cessant flamina tibiae?
    Cur pendet tacita fistula cum lyra?   20

Parcentis ego dexteras
    odi: sparge rosas; audiat invidus
dementem strepitum Lycus
    et vicina seni non habilis Lyco.

Spissa te nitidum coma,   25
    puro te similem, Telephe, vespero
tempestiva petit Rhode;
    me lentus Glycerae torret amor meae.

20

THE RIVALS

Non vides quanto moveas periclo,
Pyrrhe, Gaetulae catulos leaenae?
Dura post paulo fugies inaudax
    proelia raptor,

cum per obstantis iuvenum catervas   5
ibit insignem repetens Nearchum:
grande certamen, tibi praeda cedat,
    maior an illa.

Interim, dum tu celeris sagittas
promis, haec dentes acuit timendos,   10
arbiter pugnae posuisse nudo
    sub pede palmam

fertur et leni recreare vento
sparsum odoratis umerum capillis,
qualis aut Nireus fuit aut aquosa   15
    raptus ab Ida.

21

HYMN TO A WINE JUG

O nata mecum consule Manlio,
seu tu querelas sive geris iocos
   seu rixam et insanos amores
     seu facilem, pia testa, somnum,

quocumque lectum nomine Massicum   5
servas, moveri digna bono die,
   descende Corvino iubente
     promere languidiora vina.

Non ille, quamquam Socraticis madet
sermonibus, te negleget horridus: 10
   narratur et prisci Catonis
     saepe mero caluisse virtus.

Tu lene tormentum ingenio admoves
plerumque duro; tu sapientium
   curas et arcanum iocoso   15
     consilium retegis Lyaeo;

tu spem reducis mentibus anxiis
viresque et addis cornua pauperi,
   post te neque iratos trementi
     regum apices neque militum arma.   20

Te Liber et si laeta aderit Venus
segnesque nodum solvere Gratiae
   vivaeque producent lucernae,
     dum rediens fugat astra Phoebus.

22

A DEDICATION TO DIANA

Montium custos nemorumque, Virgo,
quae laborantis utero puellas
ter vocata audis adimisque leto,
    diva triformis,

imminens villae tua pinus esto,   5
quam per exactos ego laetus annos
verris obliquum meditantis ictum
    sanguine donem.

23

ON SIMPLE OFFERINGS

Caelo supinas si tuleris manus
nascente luna, rustica Phidyle,
    si ture placaris et horna
        fruge Lares avidaque porca,

nec pestilentem sentiet Africum   5
fecunda vitis nec sterilem seges
    robiginem aut dulces alumni
        pomifero grave tempus anno.

Nam quae nivali pascitur Algido
devota quercus inter et ilices   10
    aut crescit Albanis in herbis
        victima, pontificum securis

cervice tinguet: te nihil attinet
temptare multa caede bidentium
    parvos coronantem marino   15
        rore deos fragilique myrto.

Immunis aram si tetigit manus,
  non sumptuosa blandior hostia,
    mollivit aversos Penatis
      farre pio et saliente mica.   20

24

ON CORRUPT GREED

Intactis opulentior
  thesauris Arabum et divitis Indiae
caementis licet occupes
    terrenum omne tuis et mare publicum,

si figit adamantinos   5
  summis verticibus dira Necessitas
clavos, non animum metu,
    non mortis laqueis expedies caput.

Campestres melius Scythae,
  quorum plaustra vagas rite trahunt domos,   10
vivunt et rigidi Getae,
    immetata quibus iugera liberas

fruges et Cererem ferunt,
  nec cultura placet longior annua,
defunctumque laboribus   15
    aequali recreat sorte vicarius.

Illic matre carentibus
  privignis mulier temperat innocens,
nec dotata regit virum
    coniunx nec nitido fidit adultero.   20

Dos est magna parentium
  virtus et metuens alterius viri
certo foedere castitas,
    et peccare nefas aut pretium est mori.

O quisquis volet impias   25
    caedes et rabiem tollere civicam,
si quaeret "Pater urbium"
    subscribi statuis, indomitam audeat

refrenare licentiam,
    clarus postgenitis: quatenus—heu nefas!—   30
virtutem incolumem odimus,
    sublatam ex oculis quaerimus invidi.

Quid tristes querimoniae,
    si non supplicio culpa reciditur;
quid leges sine moribus   35
    vanae proficiunt, si neque fervidis

pars inclusa caloribus
    mundi nec Boreae finitimum latus
durataeque solo nives
    mercatorem abigunt, horrida callidi   40

vincunt aequora navitae,
    magnum pauperies opprobrium iubet
quidvis et facere et pati,
    virtutisque viam deserit arduae?

Vel nos in Capitolium,   45
    quo clamor vocat et turba faventium,
vel nos in mare proximum
    gemmas et lapides aurum et inutile,

summi materiem mali,
    mittamus, scelerum si bene paenitet.   50
Eradenda cupidinis
    pravi sunt elementa et tenerae nimis

mentes asperioribus
    formandae studiis. Nescit equo rudis
haerere ingenuus puer   55
    venarique timet, ludere doctior,

seu Graeco iubeas trocho,
  seu malis vetita legibus alea,
cum periura patris fides
  consortem socium fallat et hospites   60

indignoque pecuniam
  heredi properet. Scilicet improbae
crescunt divitiae; tamen
  curtae nescio quid semper abest rei.

25

ODE TO BACCHUS

Quo me, Bacche, rapis tui
  plenum? Quae nemora aut quos agor in specus,
velox mente nova? Quibus
  antris egregii Caesaris audiar

aeternum meditans decus   5
  stellis inserere et consilio Iovis?
Dicam insigne, recens, adhuc
  indictum ore alio. Non secus in iugis

exsomnis stupet Euhias,
  Hebrum prospiciens et nive candidam   10
Thracen aut pede barbaro
  lustratam Rhodopen, ut mihi devio

ripas et vacuum nemus
  mirari libet. O Naïadum potens
Baccharumque valentium   15
  proceras manibus vertere fraxinos,

nil parvum aut humili modo,
  nil mortale loquar. Dulce periculum est,
o Lenaeë, sequi deum
  cingentem viridi tempora pampino.   20

26

A RETIRED LOVER'S FINAL PRAYER

Vixi puellis nuper idoneus
et militavi non sine gloria.
   nunc arma defunctumque bello
      barbiton hic paries habebit,

laevum marinae qui Veneris latus   5
custodit. Hic, hic ponite lucida
   funalia et vectes et arcus
      oppositis foribus minacis.

O quae beatam diva tenes Cyprum et
Memphin carentem Sithonia nive,   10
   regina, sublimi flagello
      tange Chloen semel arrogantem.

27

BON VOYAGE, GALATEA

Impios parrae recinentis omen
ducat et praegnans canis aut ab agro
   rava recurrens lupa Lanuvino
      fetaque vulpes;

rumpat et serpens iter institutum,   5
si per obliquum similis sagittae
   terruit mannos: ego cui timebo,
      providus auspex,

antequam stantis repetat paludes
imbrium divina avis imminentum,   10
   oscinem corvum prece suscitabo
      solis ab ortu.

Sis licet felix, ubicumque mavis,
et memor nostri, Galatea, vivas;
teque nec laevus vetet ire picus   15
    nec vaga cornix.

Sed vides quanto trepidet tumultu
pronus Orion? Ego quid sit ater
Hadriae novi sinus et quid albus
    peccet Iapyx.   20

Hostium uxores puerique caecos
sentiant motus orientis Austri et
aequoris nigri fremitum et trementis
    verbere ripas.

Sic et Europe niveum doloso   25
credidit tauro latus et scatentem
beluïs pontum mediasque fraudes
    palluit audax.

Nuper in pratis studiosa florum et
debitae Nymphis opifex coronae,   30
nocte sublustri nihil astra praeter
    vidit et undas.

Quae simul centum tetigit potentem
oppidis Creten, "Pater, o relictum
filiae nomen pietasque," dixit   35
    "victa furore!

Unde quo veni? Levis una mors est
virginum culpae. Vigilansne ploro
turpe commisum an vitiis carentem
    ludit imago   40

vana, quae porta fugiens eburna
somnium ducit? Meliusne fluctus
ire per longos fuit an recentis
    carpere flores?

Si quis infamem mihi nunc iuvencum   45
dedat iratae, lacerare ferro et
frangere enitar modo multum amati
    cornua monstri.

Impudens liqui patrios Penates,
impudens Orcum moror. O deorum   50
si quis haec audis, utinam inter errem
    nuda leones!

Antequam turpis macies decentis
occupet malas teneraeque sucus
defluat praedae, speciosa quaero   55
    pascere tigris.

'Vilis Europe,' pater urget absens,
'Quid mori cessas? Potes hac ab orno
pendulum zona bene te secuta
    laedere collum;   60

sive te rupes et acuta leto
saxa delectant, age, te procellae
crede veloci, nisi erile mavis
    carpere pensum

regius sanguis dominaeque tradi   65
barbarae paelex.' " Aderat querenti
perfidum ridens Venus et remisso
    filius arcu.

Mox ubi lusit satis, "Abstineto"
dixit "irarum calidaeque rixae,   70
cum tibi invisus laceranda reddet
    cornua taurus.

Uxor invicti Iovis esse nescis:
mitte singultus, bene ferre magnam
disce fortunam; tua sectus orbis   75
    nomina ducet."

28

A MUSICAL HOLIDAY

Festo quid potius die
  Neptuni faciam? Prome reconditum,
Lyde, strenua Caecubum
  munitaeque adhibe vim sapientiae.

Inclinare meridiem   5
  sentis ac, veluti stet volucris dies,
parcis deripere horreo
  cessantem Bibuli consulis amphoram.

Nos cantabimus invicem
  Neptunum et viridis Nereïdum comas;   10
tu curva recines lyra
  Latonam et celeris spicula Cynthiae;

summo carmine, quae Cnidon
  fulgentisque tenet Cycladas et Paphum
iunctis visit oloribus;   15
  dicetur merita Nox quoque nenia.

29

AN INVITATION TO MAECENAS

Tyrrhena regum progenies, tibi
non ante verso lene merum cado
    cum flore, Maecenas, rosarum et
      pressa tuis balanus capillis

iamdudum apud me est: eripe te morae,   5
nec semper udum Tibur et Aefulae
    declive contempleris arvum et
      Telegoni iuga parricidae.

Fastidiosam desere copiam et
molem propinquam nubibus arduis,   10
    omitte mirari beatae
      fumum et opes strepitumque Romae.

Plerumque gratae divitibus vices
mundaeque parvo sub lare pauperum
    cenae sine aulaeis et ostro   15
      sollicitam explicuere frontem.

Iam clarus occultum Andromedae pater
ostendit ignem, iam Procyon furit
    et stella vesani Leonis
      sole dies referente siccos;   20

iam pastor umbras cum grege languido
rivumque fessus quaerit et horridi
    dumeta Silvani, caretque
      ripa vagis taciturna ventis.

Tu civitatem quis deceat status   25
curas et urbi sollicitus times
    quid Seres et regnata Cyro
      Bactra parent Tanaïsque discors.

Prudens futuri temporis exitum
caliginosa nocte premit deus,   30
　　ridetque si mortalis ultra
　　　　fas trepidat. Quod adest memento

componere aequus; cetera fluminis
ritu feruntur, nunc medio alveo
　　cum pace delabentis Etruscum   35
　　　　in mare, nunc lapides adesos

stirpesque raptas et pecus et domos
volventis una non sine montium
　　clamore vicinaeque silvae,
　　　　cum fera diluvies quietos   40

irritat amnis. Ille potens sui
laetusque deget cui licet in diem
　　dixisse "Vixi: cras vel atra
　　　　nube polum pater occupato

vel sole puro; non tamen irritum   45
quodcumque retro est efficiet, neque
　　diffinget infectumque reddet
　　　　quod fugiens semel hora vexit."

Fortuna saevo laeta negotio et
ludum insolentem ludere pertinax   50
　　transmutat incertos honores,
　　　　nunc mihi, nunc alii benigna.

Laudo manentem; si celeris quatit
pinnas, resigno quae dedit et mea
　　virtute me involvo probamque   55
　　　　pauperiem sine dote quaero.

Non est meum, si mugiat Africis
malus procellis, ad miseras preces
　　decurrere et votis pacisci,
　　　　ne Cypriae Tyriaeque merces   60

addant avaro divitias mari:
tunc me biremis praesidio scaphae
tutum per Aegaeos tumultus
aura feret geminusque Pollux.

30

THE POET'S IMMORTALITY

Exegi monumentum aere perennius
regalique situ pyramidum altius,
quod non imber edax, non Aquilo impotens
possit diruere aut innumerabilis
annorum series et fuga temporum.   5
Non omnis moriar multaque pars mei
vitabit Libitinam; usque ego postera
crescam laude recens. Dum Capitolium
scandet cum tacita virgine pontifex,
dicar, qua violens obstrepit Aufidus   10
et qua pauper aquae Daunus agrestium
regnavit populorum, ex humili potens,
princeps Aeolium carmen ad Italos
deduxisse modos. Sume superbiam
quaesitam meritis et mihi Delphica   15
lauro cinge volens, Melpomene, comam.

THE *CARMEN SAECULARE*

Phoebe silvarumque potens Diana,
lucidum caeli decus, o colendi
semper et culti, date quae precamur
    tempore sacro,

quo Sibyllini monuere versus   5
virgines lectas puerosque castos
dis quibus septem placuere colles
    dicere carmen.

Alme Sol, curru nitido diem qui
promis et celas aliusque et idem   10
nasceris, possis nihil urbe Roma
    visere maius!

Rite maturos aperire partus
lenis, Ilithyia, tuere matres,
sive tu Lucina probas vocari   15
    seu Genitalis.

Diva, producas subolem patrumque
prosperes decreta super iugandis
feminis prolisque novae feraci
    lege marita,   20

certus undenos deciens per annos
orbis ut cantus referatque ludos
ter die claro totiensque grata
    nocte frequentis.

Vosque veraces cecinisse, Parcae,   25
quod semel dictum est, stabilisque rerum
terminus servet, bona iam peractis
    iungite fata.

Fertilis frugum pecorisque tellus
spicea donet Cererem corona;   30
nutriant fetus et aquae salubres
    et Iovis aurae.

Condito mitis placidusque telo
supplices audi pueros, Apollo;
siderum regina bicornis, audi,   35
    Luna, puellas.

Roma si vestrum est opus Iliaeque
litus Etruscum tenuere turmae,
iussa pars mutare Lares et urbem
    sospite cursu,   40

cui per ardentem sine fraude Troiam
castus Aeneas patriae superstes
liberum munivit iter, daturus
    plura relictis,

di, probos mores docili iuventae,   45
di, senectuti placidae quietem,
Romulae genti date remque prolemque
    et decus omne.

Quaeque vos bubus veneratur albis
clarus Anchisae Venerisque sanguis,   50
impetret, bellante prior, iacentem
    lenis in hostem.

Iam mari terraque manus potentis
Medus Albanasque timet securis,
iam Scythae responsa petunt superbi   55
    nuper et Indi.

Iam Fides et Pax et Honos Pudorque
priscus et neglecta redire Virtus
audet, apparetque beata pleno
    Copia cornu.   60

Augur et fulgente decorus arcu
Phoebus acceptusque novem Camenis,
qui salutari levat arte fessos
  corporis artus,

si Palatinas videt aequus aras,   65
remque Romanam Latiumque felix
alterum in lustrum meliusque semper
  prorogat aevum;

quaeque Aventinum tenet Algidumque,
quindecim Diana preces virorum   70
curat et votis puerorum amicas
  applicat auris.

Haec Iovem sentire deosque cunctos
spem bonam certamque domum reporto,
doctus et Phoebi chorus et Dianae   75
  dicere laudes.

THE *ODES,* BOOK 4

1

SPARE ME, VENUS!

Intermissa, Venus, diu
   rursus bella moves? Parce, precor, precor.
Non sum qualis eram bonae
   sub regno Cinarae. Desine, dulcium

mater saeva Cupidinum,   5
   circa lustra decem flectere mollibus
iam durum imperiis: abi,
   quo blandae iuvenum te revocant preces.

Tempestivius in domum
   Pauli, purpureis ales oloribus,   10
comissabere Maximi,
   si torrere iecur quaeris idoneum.

Namque et nobilis et decens
   et pro sollicitis non tacitus reis
et centum puer artium   15
   late signa feret militiae tuae;

et quandoque potentior
   largi muneribus riserit aemuli,
Albanos prope te lacus
   ponet marmoream sub trabe citrea.   20

Illic plurima naribus
   duces tura, lyraeque et Berecyntiae
delectabere tibiae
   mixtis carminibus non sine fistula;

illic bis pueri die   25
   numen cum teneris virginibus tuum
laudantes pede candido
   in morem Salium ter quatient humum.

Me nec femina nec puer
   iam nec spes animi credula mutui   30
nec certare iuvat mero
   nec vincire novis tempora floribus.

Sed cur heu, Ligurine, cur
   manat rara meas lacrima per genas?
Cur facunda parum decoro   35
   inter verba cadit lingua silentio?

Nocturnis ego somniis
   iam captum teneo, iam volucrem sequor
te per gramina Martii
   campi, te per aquas, dure, volubilis.   40

2

ON PRAISING AUGUSTUS

Pindarum quisquis studet aemulari,
Iulle, ceratis ope Daedalea
nititur pinnis vitreo daturus
    nomina ponto.

Monte decurrens velut amnis, imbres   5
quem super notas aluere ripas,
fervet immensusque ruit profundo
    Pindarus ore,

laurea donandus Apollinari,
seu per audacis nova dithyrambos   10
verba devolvit numerisque fertur
    lege solutis,

seu deos regesque canit, deorum
sanguinem, per quos cecidere iusta
morte Centauri, cecidit tremendae   15
    flamma Chimaerae,

sive quos Eleä domum reducit
palma caelestis pugilemve equumve
dicit et centum potiore signis
    munere donat,   20

flebili sponsae iuvenemve raptum
plorat et viris animumque moresque
aureos educit in astra nigroque
    invidet Orco.

Multa Dircaeum levat aura cycnum,   25
tendit, Antoni, quotiens in altos
nubium tractus. Ego apis Matinae
    more modoque

grata carpentis thyma per laborem
plurimum circa nemus uvidique   30
Tiburis ripas operosa parvus
    carmina fingo.

Concines maiore poeta plectro
Caesarem, quandoque trahet ferocis
per sacrum clivum merita decorus   35
    fronde Sygambros;

quo nihil maius meliusve terris
fata donavere bonique divi,
nec dabunt, quamvis redeant in aurum
    tempora priscum.   40

Concines laetosque dies et urbis
publicum ludum super impetrato
fortis Augusti reditu forumque
    litibus orbum.

Tum meae, si quid loquar audiendum,   45
vocis accedet bona pars, et "O sol
pulcher, o laudande!" canam, recepto
    Caesare felix.

Teque dum procedis, "io Triumphe!"
non semel dicemus, "io Triumphe!"   50
civitas omnis dabimusque divis
    tura benignis.

Te decem tauri totidemque vaccae,
me tener solvet vitulus, relicta
matre qui largis iuvenescit herbis   55
    in mea vota,

fronte curvatos imitatus ignis
tertium lunae referentis ortum,
qua notam duxit niveus videri,
    cetera fulvus.   60

3

MY DEBT TO THE MUSE

Quem tu, Melpomene, semel
  nascentem placido lumine videris,
illum non labor Isthmius
  clarabit pugilem, non equus impiger

curru ducet Achaïco   5
  victorem, neque res bellica Deliis
ornatum foliis ducem,
  quod regum tumidas contuderit minas,

ostendet Capitolio:
  sed quae Tibur aquae fertile praefluunt   10
et spissae nemorum comae
  fingent Aeolio carmine nobilem.

Romae, principis urbium,
  dignatur suboles inter amabilis
vatum ponere me choros,   15
  et iam dente minus mordeor invido.

O testudinis aureae
  dulcem quae strepitum, Pieri, temperas,
o mutis quoque piscibus
  donatura cycni, si libeat, sonum,   20

totum muneris hoc tui est,
  quod monstror digito praetereuntium
Romanae fidicen lyrae;
  quod spiro et placeo, si placeo, tuum est.

4
THE VICTORIES OF DRUSUS

Qualem ministrum fulminis alitem,
cui rex deorum regnum in avis vagas
   permisit, expertus fidelem
      Iuppiter in Ganymede flavo,

olim iuventas et patrius vigor   5
nido laborum propulit inscium,
   vernique iam nimbis remotis
      insolitos docuere nisus

venti paventem, mox in ovilia
demisit hostem vividus impetus,   10
   nunc in reluctantis dracones
      egit amor dapis atque pugnae;

qualemve laetis caprea pascuis
intenta fulvae matris ab ubere
   iam lacte depulsum leonem   15
      dente novo peritura vidit,

videre Raetis bella sub Alpibus
Drusum gerentem Vindelici (quibus
   mos unde deductus per omne
      tempus Amazonia securi   20

dextras obarmet, quaerere distuli,
nec scire fas est omnia), sed diu
   lateque victrices catervae
      consiliis iuvenis revictae

sensere quid mens rite, quid indoles   25
nutrita faustis sub penetralibus
   posset, quid Augusti paternus
      in pueros animus Nerones.

Fortes creantur fortibus et bonis;
est in iuvencis, est in equis patrum   30
   virtus, neque imbellem feroces
     progenerant aquilae columbam.

Doctrina sed vim promovet insitam,
rectique cultus pectora roborant;
   utcumque defecere mores,   35
     indecorant bene nata culpae.

Quid debeas, o Roma, Neronibus,
testis Metaurum flumen et Hasdrubal
   devictus et pulcher fugatis
     ille dies Latio tenebris,   40

qui primus alma risit adorea,
dirus per urbes Afer ut Italas
   ceu flamma per taedas vel Eurus
     per Siculas equitavit undas.

Post hoc secundis usque laboribus   45
Romana pubes crevit, et impio
   vastata Poenorum tumultu
     fana deos habuere rectos,

dixitque tandem perfidus Hannibal:
"Cervi luporum praeda rapacium,   50
   sectamur ultro quos opimus
     fallere et effugere est triumphus.

Gens, quae cremato fortis ab Ilio
iactata Tuscis aequoribus sacra
   natosque maturosque patres   55
     pertulit Ausonias ad urbes,

duris ut ilex tonsa bipennibus
nigrae feraci frondis in Algido,
   per damna, per caedes ab ipso
     ducit opes animumque ferro.   60

Non hydra secto corpore firmior
vinci dolentem crevit in Herculem,
    monstrumve submisere Colchi
        maius Echioniaeve Thebae.

Merses profundo, pulchrior evenit;   65
luctere, multa proruet integrum
    cum laude victorem geretque
        proelia coniugibus loquenda.

Carthagini iam non ego nuntios
mittam superbos; occidit, occidit   70
    spes omnis et fortuna nostri
        nominis Hasdrubale interempto."

Nil Claudiae non perficient manus,
quas et benigno numine Iuppiter
    defendit et curae sagaces   75
        expediunt per acuta belli.

5

COME HOME, AUGUSTUS

Divis orte bonis, optime Romulae
custos gentis, abes iam nimium diu;
maturum reditum pollicitus patrum
    sancto concilio redi.

Lucem redde tuae, dux bone, patriae;   5
instar veris enim vultus ubi tuus
adfulsit populo, gratior it dies
    et soles melius nitent.

Ut mater iuvenem, quem Notus invido
flatu Carpathii trans maris aequora   10
cunctantem spatio longius annuo
    dulci distinet a domo,

votis ominibusque et precibus vocat,
curvo nec faciem litore dimovet:
sic desideriis icta fidelibus   15
    quaerit patria Caesarem.

Tutus bos etenim rura perambulat,
nutrit rura Ceres almaque Faustitas,
pacatum volitant per mare navitae;
    culpari metuit fides,   20

nullis polluitur casta domus stupris,
mos et lex maculosum edomuit nefas,
laudantur simili prole puerperae,
    culpam poena premit comes.

Quis Parthum paveat, quis gelidum Scythen, 25
quis Germania quos horrida parturit
fetus, incolumi Caesare? Quis ferae
    bellum curet Hiberiae?

Condit quisque diem collibus in suis,
et vitem viduas ducit ad arbores;   30
hinc ad vina redit laetus et alteris
    te mensis adhibet deum;

te multa prece, te prosequitur mero
defuso pateris, et Laribus tuum
miscet numen, uti Graecia Castoris   35
et magni memor Herculis.

"Longas o utinam, dux bone, ferias
praestes Hesperiae!" dicimus integro
sicci mane die, dicimus uvidi,
    cum sol Oceano subest.   40

6

TO APOLLO AND HIS CHORUS

Dive, quem proles Niobaea magnae
vindicem linguae Tityosque raptor
sensit et Troiae prope victor altae
    Phthius Achilles,

ceteris maior, tibi miles impar,   5
filius quamvis Thetidis marinae
Dardanas turris quateret tremenda
    cuspide pugnax—

ille, mordaci velut icta ferro
pinus aut impulsa cupressus Euro,   10
procidit late posuitque collum in
    pulvere Teucro.

Ille non inclusus equo Minervae
sacra mentito male feriatos
Troas et laetam Priami choreis   15
    falleret aulam,

sed palam captis gravis, heu nefas! heu!
nescios fari pueros Achivis
ureret flammis, etiam latentem
    matris in alvo,   20

ni tuis flexus Venerisque gratae
vocibus divum pater adnuisset
rebus Aeneae potiore ductos
    alite muros.

Doctor argutae fidicen Thaliae,   25
Phoebe, qui Xantho lavis amne crinis,
Dauniae defende decus Camenae,
    levis Agyieu.

Spiritum Phoebus mihi, Phoebus artem
carminis nomenque dedit poetae.   30
Virginum primae puerique claris
    patribus orti,

Deliae tutela deae, fugacis
lyncas et cervos cohibentis arcu,
Lesbium servate pedem meique   35
    pollicis ictum,

rite Latonae puerum canentes,
rite crescentem face Noctilucam,
prosperam frugum celeremque pronos
    volvere mensis.   40

Nupta iam dices "Ego dis amicum,
saeculo festas referente luces,
reddidi carmen docilis modorum
    vatis Horati."

7

SPRING'S RETURN

Diffugere nives, redeunt iam gramina campis
    arboribusque comae;
mutat terra vices et decrescentia ripas
    flumina praetereunt;

Gratia cum Nymphis geminisque sororibus audet   5
    ducere nuda choros.
Immortalia ne speres, monet annus et almum
    quae rapit hora diem.

Frigora mitescunt zephyris, ver proterit aestas,
    interitura simul   10
pomifer autumnus fruges effuderit, et mox
    bruma recurrit iners.

Damna tamen celeres reparant caelestia lunae;
    nos ubi decidimus
quo pius Aeneas, quo Tullus dives et Ancus,   15
    pulvis et umbra sumus.

Quis scit an adiciant hodiernae crastina summae
    tempora di superi?
Cuncta manus avidas fugient heredis, amico
    quae dederis animo.   20

Cum semel occideris et de te splendida Minos
    fecerit arbitria,
non, Torquate, genus, non te facundia, non te
    restituet pietas;

infernis neque enim tenebris Diana pudicum   25
    liberat Hippolytum,
nec Lethaea valet Theseus abrumpere caro
    vincula Pirithoö.

8

A GIFT OF POETRY

Donarem pateras grataque commodus,
Censorine, meis aera sodalibus,
donarem tripodas, praemia fortium
Graiorum, neque tu pessima munerum
ferres, divite me scilicet artium,   5
quas aut Parrhasius protulit aut Scopas,
hic saxo, liquidis ille coloribus
sollers nunc hominem ponere, nunc deum.
Sed non haec mihi vis, non tibi talium
res est aut animus deliciarum egens.   10
Gaudes carminibus; carmina possumus
donare et pretium dicere muneri.
Non incisa notis marmora publicis,
per quae spiritus et vita redit bonis
post mortem ducibus, non celeres fugae   15
reiectaeque retrorsum Hannibalis minae,
non incendia Carthaginis impiae
eius, qui domita nomen ab Africa
lucratus rediit, clarius indicant
laudes quam Calabrae Pierides; neque   20
si chartae sileant quod bene feceris,
mercedem tuleris. Quid foret Iliae
Mavortisque puer, si taciturnitas
obstaret meritis invida Romuli?
Ereptum Stygiis fluctibus Aeacum   25
virtus et favor et lingua potentium
vatum divitibus consecrat insulis.
Dignum laude virum Musa vetat mori:
caelo Musa beat. Sic Iovis interest
optatis epulis impiger Hercules,   30
clarum Tyndaridae sidus ab infimis
quassas eripiunt aequoribus rates,
ornatus viridi tempora pampino
Liber vota bonos ducit ad exitus.

9

IN PRAISE OF LOLLIUS

Ne forte credas interitura quae
longe sonantem natus ad Aufidum
   non ante vulgatas per artis
     verba loquor socianda chordis,

non, si priores Maeonius tenet   5
sedes Homerus, Pindaricae latent
   Ceaeque et Alcaei minaces
     Stesichorive graves Camenae;

nec si quid olim lusit Anacreon
delevit aetas; spirat adhuc amor   10
   vivuntque commissi calores
     Aeoliae fidibus puellae.

Non sola comptos arsit adulteri
crinis et aurum vestibus illitum
   mirata regalisque cultus   15
     et comites Helene Lacaena,

primusve Teucer tela Cydonio
direxit arcu; non semel Ilios
   vexata; non pugnavit ingens
     Idomeneus Sthenelusve solus   20

dicenda Musis proelia; non ferox
Hector vel acer Deïphobus gravis
   excepit ictus pro pudicis
     coniugibus puerisque primus.

Vixere fortes ante Agamemnona   25
multi; sed omnes illacrimabiles
   urgentur ignotique longa
     nocte, carent quia vate sacro.

Paulum sepultae distat inertiae
celata virtus. Non ego te meis   30
   chartis inornatum silebo,
     totve tuos patiar labores

impune, Lolli, carpere lividas
obliviones. Est animus tibi
   rerumque prudens et secundis   35
     temporibus dubiisque rectus,

vindex avarae fraudis et abstinens
ducentis ad se cuncta pecuniae,
   consulque non unius anni,
     sed quotiens bonus atque fidus   40

iudex honestum praetulit utili,
reiecit alto dona nocentium
   vultu, per obstantis catervas
     explicuit sua victor arma.

Non possidentem multa vocaveris   45
recte beatum; rectius occupat
   nomen beati, qui deorum
     muneribus sapienter uti

duramve callet pauperiem pati
peiusque leto flagitium timet,   50
   non ille pro caris amicis
     aut patria timidus perire.

10

BEAUTY NEVER LASTS

O crudelis adhuc et Veneris muneribus potens,
insperata tuae cum veniet pluma superbiae
et quae nunc umeris involitant deciderint comae,
nunc et qui color est puniceae flore prior rosae
mutatus, Ligurine, in faciem verterit hispidam: 5
dices "Heu," quotiens te speculo videris alterum,
"quae mens est hodie, cur eadem non puero fuit,
vel cur his animis incolumes non redeunt genae?"

11

INVITATION TO PHYLLIS

Est mihi nonum superantis annum
plenus Albani cadus; est in horto,
Phylli, nectendis apium coronis;
    est hederae vis

multa, qua crinis religata fulges;   5
ridet argento domus; ara castis
vincta verbenis avet immolato
    spargier agno;

cuncta festinat manus, huc et illuc
cursitant mixtae pueris puellae;   10
sordidum flammae trepidant rotantes
    vertice fumum.

Ut tamen noris quibus advoceris
gaudiis, Idus tibi sunt agendae,
qui dies mensem Veneris marinae   15
    findit Aprilem,

iure sollemnis mihi sanctiorque
paene natali proprio, quod ex hac
luce Maecenas meus adfluentis
    ordinat annos.   20

Telephum, quem tu petis, occupavit
non tuae sortis iuvenem puella
dives et lasciva, tenetque grata
    compede vinctum.

Terret ambustus Phaëthon avaras   25
spes, et exemplum grave praebet ales
Pegasus terrenum equitem gravatus
    Bellerophontem,

semper ut te digna sequare et ultra
quam licet sperare nefas putando   30
disparem vites. Age iam, meorum
    finis amorum,

(non enim posthac alia calebo
femina) condisce modos, amanda
voce quos reddas; minuentur atrae   35
    carmine curae.

12

SPRINGTIME PLEASURES

Iam veris comites, quae mare temperant,
impellunt animae lintea Thraciae;
iam nec prata rigent nec fluvii strepunt
   hiberna nive turgidi.

Nidum ponit Ityn flebiliter gemens   5
infelix avis et Cecropiae domus
aeternum opprobrium, quod male barbaras
   regum est ulta libidines.

Dicunt in tenero gramine pinguium
custodes ovium carmina fistula   10
delectantque deum cui pecus et nigri
   colles Arcadiae placent.

Adduxere sitim tempora, Vergili;
sed pressum Calibus ducere Liberum
si gestis, iuvenum nobilium cliens,   15
   nardo vina merebere.

Nardi parvus onyx eliciet cadum,
qui nunc Sulpiciis accubat horreis,
spes donare novas largus amaraque
   curarum eluere efficax.   20

Ad quae si properas gaudia, cum tua
velox merce veni; non ego te meis
immunem meditor tinguere poculis,
   plena dives ut in domo.

Verum pone moras et studium lucri   25
nigrorumque memor, dum licet, ignium
misce stultitiam consiliis brevem;
   dulce est desipere in loco.

13

RETRIBUTION

Audivere, Lyce, di mea vota, di
audivere, Lyce: fis anus et tamen
   vis formosa videri
     ludisque et bibis impudens

et cantu tremulo pota Cupidinem   5
lentum sollicitas. Ille virentis et
   doctae psallere Chiae
     pulchris excubat in genis.

Importunus enim transvolat aridas
quercus, et refugit te, quia luridi   10
   dentes te, quia rugae
     turpant et capitis nives.

Nec Coae referunt iam tibi purpurae
nec cari lapides tempora quae semel
   notis condita fastis   15
     inclusit volucris dies.

Quo fugit venus, heu, quove color? decens
quo motus? Quid habes illius, illius,
   quae spirabat amores,
     quae me surpuerat mihi,   20

felix post Cinaram notaque et artium
gratarum facies? Sed Cinarae brevis
   annos fata dederunt,
     servatura diu parem

cornicis vetulae temporibus Lycen,   25
possent ut iuvenes visere fervidi
   multo non sine risu
     dilapsam in cineres facem.

14

ANOTHER VICTORY FOR AUGUSTUS

Quae cura patrum quaeve Quiritium
plenis honorum muneribus tuas,
    Auguste, virtutes in aevum
        per titulos memoresque fastus

aeternet, o, qua sol habitabilis   5
illustrat oras, maxime principum,
    quem legis expertes Latinae
        Vindelici didicere nuper,

quid Marte posses? Milite nam tuo
Drusus Genaunos, implacidum genus,   10
    Breunosque velocis et arces
        Alpibus impositas tremendis

deiecit acer plus vice simplici;
maior Neronum mox grave proelium
    commisit immanisque Raetos   15
        auspiciis pepulit secundis,

spectandus in certamine Martio
devota morti pectora liberae
    quantis fatigaret ruinis,
        indomitas prope qualis undas   20

exercet Auster Pleïadum choro
scindente nubes, impiger hostium
    vexare turmas et frementem
        mittere equum medios per ignes.

Sic tauriformis volvitur Aufidus,   25
qui regna Dauni praefluit Apuli,
    cum saevit horrendamque cultis
        diluviem meditatur agris,

ut barbarorum Claudius agmina
ferrata vasto diruit impetu   30
   primosque et extremos metendo
     stravit humum sine clade victor,

te copias, te consilium et tuos
praebente divos. Nam tibi quo die
   portus Alexandrea supplex   35
     et vacuam patefecit aulam,

Fortuna lustro prospera tertio
belli secundos reddidit exitus,
   laudemque et optatum peractis
     imperiis decus arrogavit.   40

Te Cantaber non ante domabilis
Medusque et Indus, te profugus Scythes
   miratur, o tutela praesens
     Italiae dominaeque Romae.

Te, fontium qui celat origines,   45
Nilusque et Hister, te rapidus Tigris,
   te beluosus qui remotis
     obstrepit Oceanus Britannis,

te non paventis funera Galliae,
duraeque tellus audit Hiberiae,   50
   te caede gaudentes Sygambri
     compositis venerantur armis.

15

AUGUSTUS, PEACEMAKER

Phoebus volentem proelia me loqui
victas et urbes increpuit lyra,
   ne parva Tyrrhenum per aequor
     vela darem. Tua, Caesar, aetas

fruges et agris rettulit uberes   5
et signa nostro restituit Iovi
  derepta Parthorum superbis
    postibus et vacuum duellis

Ianum Quirini clausit et ordinem
rectum evaganti frena licentiae   10
  iniecit emovitque culpas
    et veteres revocavit artis,

per quas Latinum nomen et Italae
crevere vires famaque et imperi
  porrecta maiestas ad ortus   15
    solis ab Hesperio cubili.

Custode rerum Caesare, non furor
civilis aut vis exiget otium,
  non ira, quae procudit enses
    et miseras inimicat urbes.   20

Non qui profundum Danuvium bibunt
edicta rumpent Iulia, non Getae,
  non Seres infidique Persae,
    non Tanaïn prope flumen orti.

Nosque et profestis lucibus et sacris   25
inter iocosi munera Liberi,
  cum prole matronisque nostris,
    rite deos prius apprecati,

virtute functos more patrum duces
Lydis remixto carmine tibiis   30
  Troiamque et Anchisen et almae
    progeniem Veneris canemus.

MAPS

1. The Classical World

BRITANNIA

GERMANS

GERMANIA

RAETIA

GALLIA

Lugdunum

ALPS

Rhodanum (Rhone)

ATLANTIC
OCEAN

CANTABRIA

HISPANIA
(HIBERIA)

Gades

MAURETANIA

Volubilis

GAETULIA

NUMIDIA

Carthage

Rome

ITALY

DALMATIA

GREECE

DACIANS

DACIA

HAEMUS MTS.

SCYTHIANS

Tanais

SEA
OF AZOV

BLACK SEA

PONTUS

COLCHIS

CAUCASUS

ARMENIA

ASIA MINOR

PHRYGIA

ASSYRIA

PARTHIA

PERSIA

CRETE

Paphos

CYPRUS

Antioch

Damascus

SYRIA

Tyre

Babylon

MEDITERRANEAN SEA

Syrtis

Cyrene

Alexandria

Naucratis

Memphis

EGYPT

Coptus

Thebes

LIBYA

AETHIOPIA

ARABIA

RED SEA

ARABIA FELIX

ETHIOPIANS

Meroë

2. Italy

ALPS

NORICUM

Po (Padus)

Padua

ILLYRICUM

Bologna

DALMATIA

Rimini
(Ariminum)

UMBRIA

Florentia
Metaurus
Ancona

ETRURIA
Arezzo
(Arretium)
Volterra

Siena

Macerata
(Apiro)

PICENUM

Perugia
(Perusia)

ELBA

Chiusi
(Clusium)

Orvieto
Volsinii

ADRIATIC SEA

CORSICA

Vulci
Falerii

Tarquinii

PAELIGNI

APENNINES

GARGANUS

Veii

MARSI

Cerveteri
(Caere)

LATIUM

Rome
Gabii

Ostia
Palestrina
(Praeneste)

LAKE
NEMI

SARDINIA

Capua

Herculaneum
Naples
Beneventum

APULIA

Cumae

Mt. Vesuvius
Salerno

Potenza
(Potentia)

Brundisium

Taranto
(Tarentum)

BAY
OF NAPLES

Pompeii
Paestum

Palinurus Pr.

LUCANIA

Thurii

TYRRHENIAN SEA

MAGNA

Lipara

Riace

Locri
Rhegium

GRAECIA

Mt. Eryx
Himera

Mt. Aetna

SICILY

Tunis
(Carthage)

Syracuse

SICULUM MARE

3. Greece

THRACE

MACEDONIA

Philippi

Abdera

Pella

Thessalonica

Vergina
(Aegae)

CHALCIDICE

Olynthus

Mt. Athos

LEMNOS

PIERIA

Mt. Olympus

EPIRUS

PINDUS MTS.

Peneus

Larisa

TEMPE

CORFU

Dodona

THESSALY

MAGNESIA

PAXOS ISLANDS

Iolcus

AEGEAN SEA

Actium

Artemisium

AETOLIA

Thermopylae

LOCRIS

EUBOEA

PHOCIS

Mt. Parnassus

Delphi

Orchomenus

OPUS

Chalcis

Eretria

BOEOTIA

Tanagra

Patras

GULF OF CORINTH

MT. HELICON

Thebes

Rhamnus

ACHAEA

Mycenae

MT. ERYMANTHUS

MT. CYLLENE

Corinth

Isthmia

Megara

ATTICA

Marathon

IONIAN ISLANDS

Elis

PELOPONNESE

Athens

Piraeus

ELIS

Olympia

ARCADIA

ARGOLIS

Argos

Epidaurus

AEGINA

CEOS

Tegea

DELOS

CYCLADES

Mt. Ithome

Messene

MYRTOAN SEA

PAROS

IONIAN SEA

Pylus

Sparta
(Lacedaemon)

LACONIA

Phylakopi

MELOS

Taenarum

CYTHERA

Anticythera

4. Asia Minor

BLACK SEA

THRACE

BITHYNIA

Izmit

Troy
(Ilium)

Scamander

MT. IDA

LESBOS

Mytilene

Pergamum

PHRYGIA

LYDIA

Myrina

Cyme

Phocaea

Hermus

CHIOS

Izmir
(Smyrna)

Sardis

Pactolus

Teos

Apamea

AEGEAN SEA

Ephesus

SAMOS

Magnesia

Priene

ICARIA

Laodicea

Miletus

Aphrodisias

ICARIAN SEA

CARIA

Halicarnassus

COS

Cnidus

LYCIA

RHODES

Patara

CARPATHIAN SEA

MEDITERRANEAN SEA

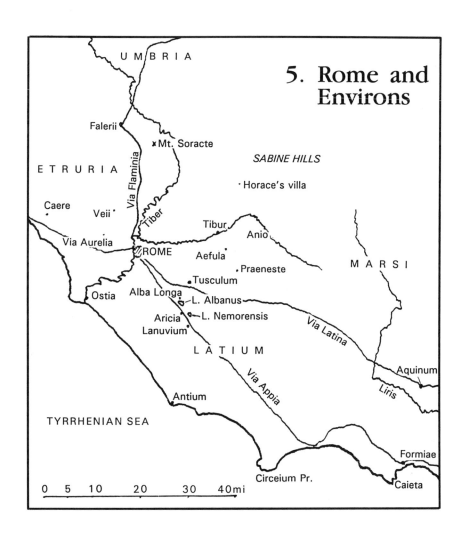

5. Rome and Environs

UMBRIA

Falerii

×Mt. Soracte

SABINE HILLS

Via Flaminia

ETRURIA

· Horace's villa

Caere

Veii

Tiber

Tibur

Anio

Via Aurelia

ROME

Aefula

·Praeneste

MARSI

·Tusculum

Ostia

Alba Longa

L. Albanus

Aricia

L. Nemorensis

Via Latina

Lanuvium

LATIUM

Via Appia

Aquinum

Antium

Liris

TYRRHENIAN SEA

Formiae

Circeium Pr.

Caieta

0 5 10   20   30   40mi

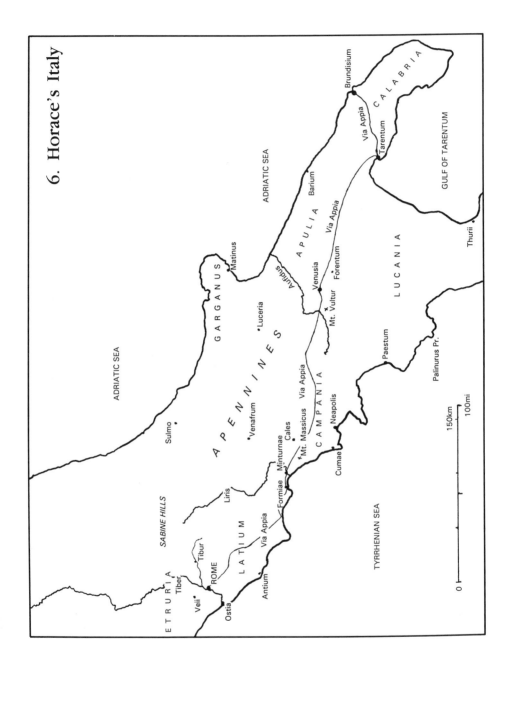

6. Horace's Italy

NOTES

ABBREVIATIONS

Aeschylus
  Ag.   Agamemnon
  Prom.   Prometheus Vinctus
A.P.   Anthologia Palatina
Caesar
  BCiv.   Bellum Civile
  BGall.   Bellum Gallicum
Cicero
  Amic.   De Amicitia
  De Div.   De Divinatione
  De Off.   De Officiis
  De Or.   De Oratore
  Fam.   Epistulae ad Familiares
  In Cat.   In Catilinam
  Luc.   Lucullus
  Orator   Orator ad M. Brutum
  Tusc.   Tusculanae Disputationes
CIL   Corpus Inscriptionum Latinarum
               (see References)
Dionysius Halicarnassensis
  Comp.Verb.   Περὶ ὁμοιοτήτων
Euripides
  Hipp.   Hippolytus
GP   A. S. F. Gow and Denys Page
               (see References)
Hesiod
  Theog.   Theogonia
  W&D   Works and Days
Homer
  Il.   Iliad
  Od.   Odyssey
Horace
  Ars P.   Ars Poetica
  Carm.Saec.   Carmen Saeculare
  Epist.   Epistulae
  Epod.   Epodes
  Sat.   Satires
LP   Edgar Lobel and Denys Page (see
               References)
LSJ   H. G. Liddell, R. Scott, and H.
               S. Jones (see References)
NH   R. G. M. Nisbet and Margaret
               Hubbard (see References)

OLD   Oxford Latin Dictionary (see
               References)
Ovid
  Am.   Amores
  Ars Am.   Ars Amatoria
  Her.   Heroides
  Met.   Metamorphoses
  Pont.   Epistulae Ex Ponto
  Rem. Am.   Remediae Amoris
Pindar
  Nem.   Nemean Odes
  Ol.   Olympian Odes
  Pyth.   Pythian Odes
Plato
  Phdr.   Phaedrus
Pliny (the Elder)
  Nat. Hist.   Naturalis Historia
Plutarch
  Ant.   Vitae Parallelae—Antonius
  Mor.   Moralia
  Symp.   Septem sapientium convivium
               (Moralia 146b-164d)
Shakespeare
  A&C   Antony and Cleopatra
  AYL   As You Like It
  Cor.   Coriolanus
  Ham.   Hamlet
  JC   Julius Caesar
  Macb.   Macbeth
  MM   Measure for Measure
  MND   A Midsummer Night's Dream
  R&J   Romeo and Juliet
  Timon   Timon of Athens
Suetonius
  Aug.   Divus Augustus
  Claud.   Divus Claudius
  Jul.   Divus Iulius
  Tib.   Tiberius
  Vesp.   Divus Vespasianus
Virgil
  Aen.   Aeneid
  Ecl.   Eclogues
  Georg.   Georgics

NOTES TO THE *EPODES*

1

A send-off poem to Maecenas (though not strictly speaking a *propempticon*), probably as he is about to leave for Brundisium in 31 B.C. prior to the battle of Actium. The poem has it that Maecenas is going into battle (1-2 *inter alta navium ... propugnacula*) and that Horace is eager to accompany his patron into this battle. In fact, Maecenas was at this time responsible for keeping order in Italy and would stay behind in Rome, and Horace, who admits he is no warrior (16 *imbellis ac firmus parum*), was a most unlikely companion in any such labor. The placement of this statement of loyalty as the first of the Epodes serves as a kind of dedication to Horace's benefactor. Meter: iambic strophe.

1-10 You are leaving to share the perils of Octavian in a sea battle: but what about me?

1. Ibis: the first word helps identify the occasion of the poem. **Liburnis:** sc. *navibus*; the Liburnians of Illyria made a fast galley, many of which were used in the battle of Actium. Cf. the *saevis Liburnis* in 1.37.30 sent to fetch Cleopatra back to Rome after the battle.

1-2. alta navium ... propugnacula: Antony's warships at Actium were equipped with high towers. Horace contrasts these heavy galleons with the fast "Liburnians" employed by Octavian's fleet under Agrippa. The inclusion of such details suggests this epode was written after reports of the battle had gotten back to Rome.

4. tuo: sc. *periculo*. Note the tendency to group the thoughts of this epode in quatrains: 1-4, 11-14, 15-18, 19-23, 31-34.

5. Quid nos: What about us? A "plural of modesty," for which see *OLD* 3 s.v. *nos*. **te superstite:** abl. absolute with si.

7. Utrumne: the interrogative suffix *-ne* is redundant and emphatic; English idiom requires the omission of both parts in translation.

9-10. laturi: ready to bear. The fut. participle may denote readiness, likelihood, or inevitability depending on context; cf. *latura* (22). **decet qua** = *qua decet*. **non mollis:** litotes for *fortes*.

11-22. I will bear the same hardships as you, wherever they are; unwarlike as I am, I will worry less than if you are far away.

12. inhospitalem et Caucasum: the mountainous region between the Black Sea and the Caspian, proverbially desolate country since Aeschylus' *Prometheus Bound*; cf. 1.22.6, *per inhospitalem Caucasum*.

13. occidentis ... sinum: some vague and savage western nook, probably for Horace in the wilds of Mauretania: cf. 2.6.3, *Maura ... unda*, 3.10.18, *Mauris ... anguibus*. For *sinus* as some remote but not necessarily cozy place, cf. Virgil *Georg.* 2.122 *India, extremi sinus orbis*.

15. tuum: sc. *laborem*.

16. imbellis, etc.: For Horace's inglorious military record, see 2.7.9ff. In *Sat.* 1.5.30 and 49 Horace described himself as *lippus*, having inflamed eyes; in *Epist.* 1.20.24 he would add that he is short, prematurely gray, and fond of sunbathing: *corporis exigui, praecanum, solibus aptum*. Here, *firmus parum* suggests weak health, but Horace's language is as playfully literary as it is autobiographic: cf. Homer *Il.* 2.201, ἀπτόλεμος καὶ ἄναλκις.

17. Comes: conditional, if I go along as your *comes*.

18. qui: anteced by *metu*. **maior:** adverbial. Anxiety grips people who are not there (**absentis**) more than those who are on the scene.

19. adsidens ... avis: bracketing word order; the participle takes the dat. **implumibus pullis,** her unfledged chicks. Still in his Homeric mode (line 16), Horace throws in this epic simile.

21. relictis: agrees with *pullis* (19).

21-22. a difficult adversative construction. **non ... latura:** though she is not likely to bring more assistance (**auxili ... plus**) even if she were there for them. **ut adsit** is a concessive subjunctive clause; **praesentibus** (lit. to them present) is an emphatic redundancy: and they were close by.

23-34. I will go through any war to win your gratitude; my needs are simple, and you have already given me all I need.

24. in tuae spem gratiae: Horace does not conceal his need for Maecenas' continued patronage, though he hastens to add in the next lines that his modest requirements are already being met.

26. aratra nitantur: poetic transference, perhaps with humorous intent. Instead of the usual pair of straining bullocks hitched to a plow, Horace imagines straining plows hitched to many bullocks.

27-28. Calabris ... Lucana: the herd, moving from Calabrian to cooler Lucanian pastures, receives the acc. *Lucana [pascua]* in exchange for the abl. *Calabris pascuis*. Only the wealthiest farmer would own grazing land in both Calabria and Lucania. For the construction, cf. 1.17.1f., *Lucretilem mutat Lycaeo*. **ante sidus fervidum:** before the hot season heralded by Canicula, the dog star Sirius.

29. superni ... Tusculi: Tusculum (see map 5), a dozen miles southeast of Rome, was a "lofty" place in more ways than one. The summer villas of Cicero, Lucullus, Hortensius, and other rich and famous Romans were located in this exalted hilltown, situated near Frascati. It is the dramatic setting of Cicero's *Tusculan Disputations*, and Horace would no doubt have been delighted to receive a villa here, notwithstanding his disclaimer.

30. Circaea moenia: legend had it that Tusculum was founded by Telegonus, Circe's son by Ulysses. **tangat:** the villas were just below the hilltop town, the closer to the walls the better.

31. ditavit: Horace refers to Maecenas' gift of the Sabine farm in 33 B.C. For more on this theme, cf. *Sat.* 2.6.1-5, *Odes* 3.16.33-44.

33. quod ... premam: rel. clause of purpose. **avarus ut Chremes:** a miser like the typical old man in comedy. Though no surviving comedy has a miser named Chremes, the name (perhaps suggested by χρήματα, money) is typical for the comic old man whose son fritters away the family

nest egg.

34. discinctus ... nepos: appositive with the subject of *perdam:* or waste it, [like] an ungirt spendthrift. This is another type from comedy and from Stoic diatribes against indecent wealth, which will sooner or later be squandered by a dissolute heir.

2

Praise of the simple country life became a standard theme of Augustan poetry, bordering on triteness. As Horace would later remark in *Epist.* 2.2.77, *Scriptorum chorus omnis amat nemus et fugit urbem.* It was also a standard topos of the Stoic *sermo*, which compared the futile hustle of city people with the wise serenity of rustics. See, for example, the fable of the town mouse and the country mouse in *Sat.* 2.6.79-117. In this epode, Horace plays ironically on the theme by putting the usual remarks in the mouth of a moneylender who has the desire but not the will to change careers. Similar ironic discourses can be found in the second Book of Horace's *Satires*, published the same year as the *Epodes*. Meter: iambic strophe.

1-8. "How happy the man who works his farm, free from war, seafaring, and city life!

1. Beatus ille: Some readers hear in this opening, and in the Epode as a whole, a parody of the grand conclusion of Virgil's *Georg.* 2 in praise of country life: *Fortunatis et ille*, etc. (493ff.).

2. prisca gens: the people of the Golden Age, prior to the evils of civilization.

4. faenore: debt, interest on debt, and the like.

5. miles: in apposition with *ille*; **classico truci:** the war trumpet is cruel because it calls him to battle. The list here of alternative occupations may be compared to similar lists at the beginning of *Sat.* 1.1 and *Odes* 1.1.

8. limina: Horace refers to the daily call of the needy *cliens* at the house of his *patronus* to see if he can be of service. Many talented but unpropertied Romans were forced to support themselves in this humiliating way.

9-22. "He goes about his rustic chores, and at harvest time pays his respects to the rustic gods.
9. Ergo: because he is free of the hassles of city life. **adulta:** abl. of association. Young vines were kept three years in a *seminarium* or nursery-garden before being transplanted.
10. maritat: a metaphor common among farmers for the trellising of grapevines on small trees; the poplar was the favorite tree for this purpose, providing light shade as well as support.
11. mugientium: used substantively of lowing cattle. Lucretius called sheep *lanigerae* (1.887); cf. Virgil *Georg.* 1.272, *balantum*.
14. feliciores inserit; fruit trees were maintained by constant grafting of fresh branches onto mature trees. Cf. *insitiva pira*, line 19. *Felix* is used here in its root sense of fruitful.
15. pressa mella: honey was squeezed out of the comb in a press; today it is done in a centrifuge.
16. infirmas ovis: gentle and unresisting, a standard poetic epithet for sheep: Cf. Ovid *Ibis* 44.
18. Autumnus: personified. For his association with fruit, cf. 4.7.11, *pomifer autumnus*, 3.23.8 *pomifero anno*.
19. ut: how. Exclamatory, as in line 61. **gaudet ... decerpens** is a Greek construction where Latin would normally use the infinitive *decerpere*: delights to pluck.
20. purpurae, dat. with *certantem*, is the expensive purple dye made from the murex, a genus of sea snail.
21. qua muneretur: rel. clause of purpose, with which to honor [by a gift]. **Priape:** originally from the Hellespont, this fertility demon was represented with an enormous phallus, which warded off evil influences and promoted fertility. His cult spread in Hellenistic times, and his figure carved from wood was a popular scarecrow and figure of fun in Roman gardens. Priapus is the speaker in *Sat.* 1.8.

22. Silvane: the old Italic god of uncultivated land and its boundaries, often associated with Pan and the satyrs. Cf. Virgil *Georg.* 2.494, *Panaque Silvanumque senem nymphasque sorores.*

23-36. "He enjoys loafing in the summer and hunting in the winter.
24. tenaci: thick and matted, clinging together. The details here and in the following four lines suggest the classic pastoral *locus amoenus* (see appendix C).
25. altis ... ripis: either brimming with water in spring or later in the summer, when the streams would be low relative to the banks.
26. queruntur: doves in particular have a mournful song, appropriate for romantic pastoral scenes; cf. Virgil *Ecl.* 1.58, *nec gemere aeria cessabit turtur ab ulmo*, and Ovid *Am.* 3.1.4, *dulce queruntur aves.*
28. quod invitet: relative clause of result with the antecedent *obstrepunt*, a sound to invite easy naps.
29. annus: with **hibernus**, season; cf. 3.23.8, *pomifero anno.*
33. amite lēvi: the smooth pole (*ames*) used to spread the wide-meshed nets (**rara retia**, as in Virgil *Aen.* 4.131). The initial iamb of this line is resolved into a dactyl.
35. pavidumque leporem: Horace imitates the trembling of the hare by substituting short syllables wherever the meter permits, yielding an anapest and a tribrach in place of two iambs. The Augustan poets placed a high premium on such metrical sound effects. **laqueo:** the fifth iamb is resolved into an anapest, as in 5.79 *inferius*, or the final syllables are slurred by synizesis.

37-60. "Instead of the cares of the lover, he has the pleasures of a happy husband, whose busy wife prepares the best of meals.
37. malarum quas amor curas habet: gen. with *obliviscitur*. **Curas** is appositive to **quas.** Prose would have it *malarum curarum quas amor habet.*

Horace contrasts the troublesome love affairs of city life with the manly sport of hunting and with the pleasure of life with a *pudica mulier* (39).

39. in partem iuvet: do her share in helping; *in partem* = *partim*. **iuvet** is subjunctive as the protasis of a future less vivid condition, together with *exstruat* (43), *siccet* (46), and *apparet* (48); the fut. perf. indic. *iuverint* (49) and the pres. subj. *descendat* (53) represent the apodosis: If a faithful wife should do her job, I won't need exotic gourmet foods.

41. Sabina qualis: such as a Sabine; word order reversed for emphasis. For more on the virtues of Sabine women, see 3.6.39ff. **solibus** is plural to emphasize repeated exposure. In this culture, a sunburn was less glamorous than indicative of hard field labor.

42. pernicis ... Apuli: fast-moving, hence hardworking. Cf. 3.16.26, *impiger Apulus*. This region, along the Adriatic coast from Garganus to the heel of the Italian boot, is now called Puglia (see map 6).

43. This chiastic line, arranged adjective a, adjective b, verb, noun b, noun a, is an iambic variant of the hexameter "golden line" (see appendix C).

45. textis cratibus: fences made of wicker work are still used in parts of Britain, Europe, and the Mediterranean.

47. horna: this year's; its sweetness is poetically transferred to the *dolium* in which it is stored.

49. Lucrina ... conchylia: the shallow *Lacus Lucrinus* on the north shore of the Bay of Naples produced fine oysters. Juvenal 4.140f.

50. rhombus ... scari: turbot and scarfish or parrot wrasse.

53. Afra avis: Numidian guinea fowl, the latest gourmet sensation from North Africa in Horace's time.

54. attagen Ionicus: an exotic species of grouse imported from Asia Minor.

57-58. herba lapathi prata amantis: interlocking word order; sorrel, recommended for constipation in *Sat.* 2.4.29. **malvae:** another laxative for sluggish bowels (**gravi ... corpori**), recommended again in 1.31.16. If one sticks to wholesome country fare, these medicinal herbs won't be necessary.

59. agna ... caesa Terminalibus: the rustic eats meat only on special occasions such as the Feb. 23 festival of the Boundaries (Ovid *Fasti* 2.655, *spargitur et caeso communis terminus agno*).

60. haedus ereptus lupo: another occasion for meat; the wolf was supposed to take only the tastiest kid (Plutarch *Symp.* 2.9). Cf. Martial 10.48.14, *haedus inhumano raptus ab ore lupi*.

61-70. "He enjoys seeing his flocks and oxen returning at day's end, and his household gathered around." So saying, the moneylender resolves to change careers, but within days he is back in his old business.

61. The fourth syllable, usually long, is resolved here into two shorts, as in *Odes* 2.18.34. **pastas:** pastured (*pasco*).

63-64. Cf. note on 35; here the opposite effect is achieved by the substitution of long syllables imitating the slow movement of the tired oxen. **vomerem inversum:** the plow was inverted on the yoke with the pole dragging behind so that it could be drawn home easily at the end of the day's work; cf. Virgil *Ecl.* 2.66, *aratra iugo referunt suspensa iuvenci*.

65. positos ... vernas, etc.: the wealth of the countryman was a swarm (*examen*) of home-born (not purchased) slaves arrayed (*positos*) around the hearth; this is old wealth, like the *paterna rura* of line 3.

66. renidentis Lares: the wooden household gods, polished with oil and wax, glow in the firelight.

67. locutus [est]: Horace's surprise. This idyllic praise of country life turns out to have been the effusion of a moneylender: *faenerator* ironically echoes line 5 *solutus omni faenore*. Alfius was a well known moneylender of Cicero's time (Columella 1.7.2), used as a type of his class. The technique of using a personage from the previous generation as a satirical type appears often in Horace's *Satires*.

69. redegit: called in his loans. The Ides, Kalends, and Nones were customary days for settling accounts.

70. quaerit Kalendis ponere: asyndeton and the shift to the present tense emphasize Horace's dry irony. The phrase is adversative: *but* he tries to [re]invest. So much for the reform of Alfius.

3

Maecenas has given Horace some food heavily laced with garlic. With comic hyperbole, Horace compares the garlic with various burning poisons of myth, and prays that if Maecenas ever repeats the joke no woman will have anything to do with him. Meter: iambic strophe.

1-8. Garlic is worse than hemlock. What kind of poison has afflicted me: viper's blood? a witch's brew?

1. Parentis: in the emphatic position, because the worst kind of evildoer is one who kills his own parent. For a similar formula, cf. 2.13.5, *parentis sui fregisse cervicem*. **olim:** some time in the past.

2. senile guttur: for extra horror, the epithet is transferred from the aged parent to the parent's neck. **fregerit** is future perfect.

3. edit: archaic subjunctive, colloquial for *edat*. **cicutis:** abl. of comparison. Hemlock, used to poison criminals in Athens, was used in the execution of Socrates.

4. messorum: for garlic in the diet of harvest hands, see Virgil *Ecl.* 2.11.

5. Quid … veneni: partitive gen. with the interrogative, the normal construction for a "what kind of …?" question. **praecordiis:** sc. *meis*. Horace's innards are protesting.

7. incoctus herbis: boiled into these vegetables; but *herba* is also used of herbs used for poisons and magical potions (*Epod.* 5.21). **me fefellit:** has

escaped my notice, a Grecism.

8. Canidia: the witch, probably more a type than a real person, made fun of in *Sat.* 1.8 and Epodes 5 and 17.

9-18. This is what Medea used to immunize Jason to fire-breathing bulls and to incinerate her rival; it is hotter than Apulia in summer and the cloak of Nessus that roasted Hercules.

9-10. Ut: when. The **candidum ducem** is Jason, who led the Argonauts in search of the Golden Fleece. On arriving in Colchis, he was aided by Medea, sorceress daughter of King Aeëtes, who fell in love with him at first sight (10, *Medea mirata est ducem*). When Aeëtes assigned him the impossible task of yoking fire-breathing bulls to plow a field, Medea rubbed him with a protective potion (12, *perunxit hoc Iasonem*).

11. tauris: an *apo koinou* construction, dat. with *ignota* and *illigaturum* (about to fasten on the bulls yokes unknown to the bulls). For more on this construction, see appendix C.

12-13. hoc … hoc: instrumental abl.: with this [garlic], repeated for emphasis. **delibutis … donis:** also instrumental: with gifts smeared with this [garlic] she got revenge on her rival (*ulta [est] paelicem*). When Jason decided to leave Medea and marry the princess of Corinth, Medea sent her as a wedding present a garment smeared with poison that burned her to death when she tried it on. She then killed her children by Jason and escaped on a chariot pulled by dragons (14, *serpente fugit alite*). See Euripides' *Medea*; the story was a favorite of the Roman stage.

15. siderum … vapor: summer's heat, connected with constellations (*sidera*) such as the dog star that were in the ascendant in July and August. For *vapor* = heat, cf. Lucretius 1.663, 2.150.

16. siticulosae Apuliae: dat. with *insedit*; Horace is joking about his native Apulia, as "thirsty" as it was hot; cf. General Sherman's remark that if he had houses in Hell and in Texas, he would live in the one in Hell.

17. **munus**: when Nessus the Centaur tried to rape Hercules' wife Deianira, Hercules shot him with a poisoned arrow; the dying Nessus gave Deianira a vial of his poisoned blood, telling her it was a love potion. Later when she applied it to a robe for him to wear, Hercules died in burning agony. See Sophocles' *Trachiniae*. Hercules is capable (*efficax*) because of his many labors.

19-22. **If you ever think of repeating this joke, may every girl give you the cold shoulder.**
19. **At**: used regularly at the beginning of imprecations as a gesture of emphatic speech; see Austin on *Aen.* 2.535, and Catullus 3.13, Horace *Sat.* 2.6.54. **concupiveris**: fut. perf., humorously emphatic, if you ever develop the craving, implies that the overdose of garlic was a practical joke—as does *iocose Maecenas* in the next line.
20. **puella**: i.e., any woman in whom you become interested. **savio tuo**, to your kiss, dat. with *opponat*. **opponat** and **cubet**: optative subjunctive with *precor*.
22. **extrema ... in sponda**: i.e., on the farthest couch from you she can find, referring to the couches on which diners reclined; but *sponda* is also bedroom furniture, as in Ovid *Am.* 3.14.26, *spondaque lasciva mobilitate tremat.*

4

In contrast to the mock invective of Epode 3, this lampoon is more in the spirit of *liberrima indignatio* (10) than good humor, attacking an obnoxious upstart who parades his new wealth. The type was common in the turbulent years of civil unrest before Actium; ancient commentators, misreading lines 1-2, sought to identify a personal enemy of Horace, but as usual Horace is attacking a type. For the topic, cf. Anacreon 43 Page. Meter: iambic strophe.

1-6. **You are my natural enemy, scarred with bonds and shackles. You flaunt your wealth, but** fortune doesn't change what you are.
1. **quanta sortito**, etc.: as great a *discordia* as exists by the law of nature.
3. **Hibericis ... funibus**: synecdoche for rope in general; Spain was a source of rope fiber. **peruste ... latus**: acc. of specification, lit. chafed as to your side. He has rope burns from being tied up; but there may also be an echo of Thallus' *inusta ... flagella* in Catullus 25.11.
4. **dura compede**: collective singular. Horace is not attacking this type simply because the man had been a slave (Horace's own father, after all, had also been a slave) but because he is now so *superbus* (5). The scars suggest he had been in constant trouble.
5. **ambules**: concessive subjunctive, with *licet*. **pecunia**: abl. with *superbus*.

7-10. **Don't you see the looks of disgust when you parade along the Via Sacra?**
7. **Sacram ... Viam**: the main promenade leading down into the Forum, where people went to see and be seen; this is where Horace meets the social climber in *Sat.* 1.9. **metiente**: walking the length of (with the sense of pompously measured steps).
8. **bis trium ulnarum toga**: a grotesquely wide toga, like a gangster's $3,000 suit, displaying nothing better than the wearer's vulgarity. The *ulna*, lit. forearm, is probably about half a meter.
9. **ora vertat**: turns their faces, i.e., makes them frown or flush (or perhaps turn away) with disgust. Cf. *Sat.* 2.8.35, *vertere pallor ... faciem.* Others interpret as "draws stares," as in *Epist.* 2.1.196, *vulgi converteret ora.*
10. **liberrima**: frank and unrestrained; characteristic of a free man. Cf. *libera bilis* in *Epod.* 11.16.

11-20. **People remark: "This much-flogged lout now carries on like a big shot. What good is it to have put down an army of desperadoes, when this one is a military tribune?"**
11. **Sectus**: cut by their lashes. **triumviralibus**:

the *triumviri capitales* inposed punishment on slaves, foreigners, and other riffraff.

12. praeconis ad fastidium: until even the crier had enough; the job of the *praeco* was to call out the crimes of the offender while the *tortor* applied the lash.

13. Falerni ... fundi: interlocked word order. Falernian farm land, on the border of Latium and Campania, was prized acreage, producing the famous Falernian wine.

14. Appiam [Viam]: the ancient superhighway south of Rome, Italy's premier roadway. Instead of the Maseratis and Lamborghinis of today's *autostrade*, Romans showed off their stylish Gallic ponies (**mannis**). Galatea's vehicle is powered by these in 3.27.7. **terit:** wears out by constant travel between Rome and his Falernian ranch.

15. magnus ... eques: i.e., he is now a big man of the equestrian order; *magnus*, though, is heavily sarcastic.

16. Othone contempto: abl. absolute. Lucius Roscius Otho, tribune in 67 B.C., passed a measure reserving the first fourteen rows in the theater for members of the equestrian order. He is scorned in this case because equestrians were supposed to be men of free birth, not ex-slaves.

17-18. ora navium ... rostrata = beaked warships. **gravi ... pondere:** abl. of description. **duci:** infin. subject of *attinet*: what does it accomplish that these ships were led?

19. latrones atque servilem manum: in a bid to defeat Octavian in the Sicilian War of 37-36 B.C., Sextus Pompey patched together a force of pirates and runaway slaves. Augustus claimed afterward to have rounded up and returned to their masters some 30,000 of the latter.

20. hoc, hoc tribuno: abl. abs. The emphatic repetition is especially common in the *Epodes*: cf. 5.53 *nunc, nunc*, 6.11 *Cave, cave!*, 7.1 *Quo, quo*, 14.6 *deus, deus*, 17.1 *Iam iam, 7 solve, solve.*

5

The iambic spirit of abuse continues in this dramatic dialogue between the witch Canidia and a boy she is about to kill to make a magic potion. But as this longish piece goes on it appears Horace is attempting something more than abuse, perhaps closer to the type of eldritch scene featured in the tragedies of Ennius (239-169 B.C.), which were still being performed in Horace's Rome. Canidia, aided by fellow hags Sagana, Veia, and Folia, has snatched a boy of good family off the street and is proceeding to bury him up to his face until he starves to death. Then they will use his marrow and liver to make a potion to draw a man named Varus (73) to Canidia's bed. The boy, rising to the occasion, pronounces a ringing curse on the witches. Romans of Horace's time were prone to superstition, and there were plenty of "witches" around to prey on their credulity. There is even a grave inscription (*CIL* 6.19747) purporting to record the death of a child at the hands of a witch. Porphyrio says that this Canidia, featured also in *Sat.* 1.8 and Epode 17 and mentioned in *Sat.* 2.1.48, 2.8.95, and *Epod.* 3.8, was a perfume maker at Naples named Gratidia. He adds the unlikely gossip that Horace had had an unhappy affair with her and was taking literary revenge. Meter: iambic strophe.

1-10: The Boy: "What is the meaning of this tumult and these fierce looks?"

1. At: the little drama opens abruptly with this outburst by the captive boy. No attempt is made to represent the speech of a child. He uses the hyperbaton and anaphora of high poetic, theatrical rhetoric. **o deorum quidquid:** exclamatory acc., by whatever (of) gods.

3. fert: i.e., what does it mean.

5-6. per liberos: seeing her age, the boy assumes Canidia has had children of her own in whose name he can appeal for mercy; but **partubus ... veris** insinuates that any such children were not her own but taken from others. See *Epod.* 17.50-52 and note. **Lucina** is the goddess of childbirth, usually associated with Juno or Diana.

7. hoc inane purpurae decus: suggests a gesture to the purple-bordered *toga praetexta*, which identifies him as the child of a good family.

9. ut noverca refers to the proverbial cruelty of the stepmother.

11-28. Meanwhile, Canidia and Sagana, heedless to the boy's protest, prepare their hideous ritual.

11. questus ... constitit: stood protesting.

12. insignibus raptis: his *insignia* would be the bordered toga indicating his rank and the *bulla* around his neck containing a good luck charm; as a *crepundia*, this locket would also show his identity. Their removal adds to the boy's pathos.

13. impube corpus: more pathos, in apposition to *puer*; he has been stripped naked.

14. Thracum: i.e., Thracian witches, or at any rate barbarians.

15-16. implicata ... crinis et ... caput: passive with middle force and inner acc.

17. caprificos: wild figs, chosen for this rite because they grow in the cracks of tombs and are thus associated with death.

19. turpis ... ranae: probably the venomous *rana rubeta*, an amphibious toad used in making drugs (Pliny *Nat. Hist.* 8.110).

20. strigis: a screech owl of evil omen, sometimes considered a kind of vampire; Tibullus 1.5.52 calls it the *strix violenta*. Pliny *Nat. Hist.* 11.232 was unable to identify it; Ovid *Fasti* 6.131-140 gives a gruesome account of its activities, which include snatching unguarded babies from their cradles. Cf. Shakespeare *2 Henry VI* 1.4.16ff.:

> Wizards know their times.
> Deep night, dark night, the silent of the night,
> The time of night when Troy was set on fire,
> The time when screech-owls cry and bandogs howl,
> And spirits walk, and ghosts break up their graves—
> That time best fits the work we have in hand.

21. Iolcos in Thessaly was famous for its witches; **Hiberia**, the territory of the Hiberes south of the Caucasus Mts. near Medea's Colchis, was also famous for witchcraft and poisons. Not to be confused with Spanish *Hiberia*.

23. ore .. ieiunae canis: a bone from the mouth of a starving dog will be magically imbued with the dog's craving and impart desire to anyone taking a drug made with it.

24. aduri is the object of *iubet* (17-18).

25. expedita: i.e., with her skirts hitched up to free her movements.

26. Avernalis aquas: Lake Avernus near Cumae in the Bay of Naples was regarded as an entrance to the underworld, giving its water special powers in black magic.

27-28. marinus ... echinus: the spiny black sea urchin common in Mediterranean waters.

29-46. Veia digs a hole in which to bury the boy until he starves; Folia too is there, who charms stars and moon out of the sky.

30. ligonibus duris: plural for singular. The mattock or *ligo* is a hoelike implement for trenching hard earth.

32. quo: antecedent is *humum*, relative clause of purpose.

33-34. longo die, etc.: he will die at the spectacle of a meal changed twice or thrice during the long day. *inemori* (pine away to death at) is a hapax legomenon, taking the dat. *spectaculo*. As with the magic of the bone snatched from the starving dog, this torture will imbue the boy's organs with longing that will pass into the potion made from them.

35. ore: abl. of respect.

36. suspensa mento: swimmers using a breaststroke would appear to be held up by the chin.

37. exsecta, aridum: both marrow and liver are to be cut out and dried. As the seat of passion, the *iecur* would be an especially good vehicle of the boy's longing. Victims of powerful longing (Gk. $\pi\acute{o}\theta o\varsigma$) are also said to be affected in their marrow: Catullus 64.93, *imis exarsit tota medullis* (of Ariadne's love for Theseus).

39. interminato: forbidden with threats, the same formation as in Eng. *interdicted.* **cibo** is dat. with both *fixae* and *intabuissent.*

40. intabuissent: same formation and meaning as *inemori* (34).

41. masculae libidinis: gen. of characteristic; witches are proverbially lustful and sexually aggressive.

42. Ariminensem: from Ariminum (mod. Rimini) in northeastern Umbria (see map 6).

43. otiosa ... Neapolis: idle, and therefore gossipy. For the proverbial idleness of Naples (originally named Parthenope), cf. Ovid *Met.* 15.711, *in otia natam Parthenopen.*

46. caelo deripit: for this power of witches, cf. Virgil *Ecl.* 8.69, *carmina vel caelo possunt deducere lunam*; cf. Propertius 1.1.19 calls it a *fallacia.*

47-82. Canidia's first attempt to bring in Varus fails.

47-48. irresectum ... pollicem: i.e., with the nail unpared for use in scratching and mauling her victims. For angry or frustrated nail-biting, cf. Propertius 2.4.3, *et saepe immeritos corrumpas dentibus unguis.* The tooth with which Canidia bites her thumbnail is necrotic, hence purple (*livido*).

50. arbitrae: overseers, with the dat. *rebus meis.*

53. hostilis domos: plural for singular, viz. the house of Varus, named on line 73.

57. senem ... adulterum: old lecher. As befits the character of a witch, Canidia's lust for Varus in no way alters her loathing. **quod omnes rideant:** rel. clause of purpose; the antecedent, *latrent,* follows.

58. Suburanae canes: the female dogs to be affected inhabit the Subura, a sleazy quarter of Rome between the Esquiline, Viminal, and Quirinal hills.

59. nardo perunctum, etc.: Canidia has substituted for Varus' usual scent a perfume containing a magic potion to make him come to her house.

61. Quid accidit? In baffled rage, Canidia asks herself what could have gone wrong. **minus ... valent:** fail.

62-66. Medeae, etc.: as dramatized in Euripides' *Medea,* the famous witch from Colchis got revenge on Jason when he planned to leave her and marry the daughter of Creon of Corinth. Medea sent a pretty gown dipped in poison (65 *tabo*) to her proud rival (63 *superbam paelicem*) as a wedding present; when it burned the young bride to death (65-6 *novam incendio nuptam abstulit*), Medea then killed her two sons by Jason and escaped in a chariot drawn by dragons. The *venena* that served Medea so splendidly have failed to do for Canidia—though her requirements are less caustic than erotic.

67-68. latens in asperis ... locis: the less accessible, the more potent. **fefellit me:** escaped my notice.

69. indormit unctis, etc.: apparently Canidia has smeared Varus' bed with her worthless unguent; he sleeps on it in oblivion not only of her but of all mistresses, *omnium ... paelicum,* adding insult to injury. (Others interpret *paelicum* as Canidia's rivals only, on the assumption she does not realize her failure until line 71; another possibility is that the rival witch mentioned in 71-72 got to Varus' bed first and smeared it with *her* unguent, which knocked him out.)

71-72. A! a!: Canidia imagines she has the answer: Varus has been freed by the incantation (**carmine**) of a cleverer sorceress or poison-maker (**veneficae**). **ambulat** here contrasts with *indormit* above.

73. Vare: apostrophe to the absent object of her lust, who is at last mentioned by name.

74. fleturum: in the same doomed sense as *morituri te salutant.* **caput,** referring by metonomy to a person, may express hatred (as here) or fondness, as in 1.24.2, *tam cari capitis.*

75-76. nec ... Marsis ... vocibus: i.e., not with merely Marsian incantations. The Marsi were

Italian rustics known for snake charming and magic cures (*Epod.* 17.29, Virgil *Aen.* 7.750) but not for anything of the power or sophistication that Canidia has in mind.

79. priusque caelum sidet: one of the common rhetorical topoi was the *adynaton*, the thing that will never happen. **inferius:** the fifth iamb is resolved into an anapest.

81. non ... flagres uti: i.e., the impossible will happen before you fail to burn with love. Emphatic litotes.

82. atris ignibus: an oxymoron for smoky flame.

83-102. The boy: "My spirit will torment you, the mob will stone you, wolves and birds will pick your bones, and my parents will enjoy the spectacle."

82. bitumen: tar or pitch used to kindle fires.

83. sub haec: thereupon.

84. lenire: historical infinitive with conative force, tried to soothe. Though it occurs in the *Satires* and *Epistles*, this is the only example of the construction in the *Odes* and *Epodes*.

85. unde: how, i.e., with what beginning words.

86. Thyesteas preces: like those of Thyestes cursing his brother Atreus after being tricked into eating the flesh of his murdered sons. This was a favorite scene in the violent and bombastic tragedies for which the Romans had a taste. Both Ennius and Seneca wrote a *Thyestes*; see Aeschylus *Ag.* 1590ff., Ennius frag. 309; Seneca's play survives intact.

87. Venena maga: magic potions; *maga non* is Haupt's conjecture for *magnum*, which is found in the transmitted texts.

88. convertere: by zeugma, to reverse *fas nefasque* and to repel *humanam vicem*. **vicem:** requital or revenge, especially evil for evil.

89. Diris: with curses; a *detestatio* is a ritual curse or execration.

91. Quin: furthermore. **perire iussus** implies that his death will be a summons for his spirit to begin tormenting the witches as a *Furor* (92).

93. umbra: as a ghost.

94. vis: a supernatural power (*OLD* 12). The *di Manes* are the spirits of the dead, especially potent to curse the wicked: Livy 3.58.11, *manesque Verginiae ... per tot domos ad petendas poenas vagati, nullo relicto sonte* [guilty person], *tandem quieverunt*.

97. vicatim: from neighborhood (*vicus*) to neighborhood or street to street.

98. obscenas anus: in apposition to *vos* above.

100. Esquilinae alites: the carrion birds of the Esquiline, a paupers' cemetery outside the city walls. Note the hiatus. Invective describing the gruesome dismemberment of an enemy's corpse is a topos with a history of its own, going back perhaps to Callimachus' *Ibis*. Cf. Catullus 108, Ovid *Ibis* 165-172.

101. parentes, heu, etc.: the thought of parents surviving their own children was especially pathetic; it is a persistent tragic motif of Virgil's *Aeneid*.

102. spectaculum: emphatically placed at the end of the poem, ironically echoes line 34, *inemori spectaculo*.

6

Horace tries on his Archilochian mantle. Archilochus, the Iambic poet who lived a generation or two after Homer, boasted, "I know one big thing: how to pay back somebody who does me wrong with fearful wrongs" (frag. 126 West). In this spirit Horace, who lacks Catullus' slashing élan, threatens an unknown bully, comparing himself to a spirited hound and his adversary to a cowardly cur. Meter: iambic strophe.

1-10. You cowardly cur, why don't you try your teeth on me? I am a hound that will run any beast to earth, while you bark loudly until someone throws you table scraps.

1. Quis ... vexas: i.e., who are you to harass. **hospites:** passersby, as often in epitaphs and other inscriptions.

2. ignavus: adversative, though you are cowardly

against real enemies.

3. huc: this way, i.e., toward me. For this per-haps fictive personal note, cf. *Epod.* 4.2, *tecum mihi discordia est.* **inanis:** futile. **si potes:** i.e., if you dare.

4. petis: attack, as often in Horace; cf. line 15, *petiverit.*

5. Molossus ... Lacon: two of the best hunting breeds; cf. Virgil *Georg.* 3.405, *veloces Spartae catulos acrem Molossum,* Shakespeare *MND* 4.1.118, "My hounds are bred out of the Spartan kind."

6. amica vis: a friendly force or pack; cf. Lucre-tius 6.1222, *fida canum vis,* Virgil *Aen.* 4.132, *odora canum vis.*

7. aure sublata: with ear pricked up. **per altas ... nives:** the picture of a hunter eager to chase game through snow but indifferent to *proiectum cibum* (10) owes something to Callimachus *A.P.* 12.102 (GP 1); see also Horace *Sat.* 1.2.105-6, *leporem venator ut alta / in nive sectetur, positum sic tangere nolit.*

9-10. tu is emphatic by position and adversative: but *you,* ... **cum comple**(vi)**sti ... odoraris:** the indicative *cum*-clause denotes the identity of the two situations: when you bark, [it is because] you will have scented food thrown out for you (or the possibility of such food). Horace may be hinting behind the metaphor that his enemy is a black-mailer raising a fuss in order to elicit hush money.

11-16. Beware! Like Archilochus and Hippo-nax, I have horns to gore scoundrels: do you think if attacked I will wail unavenged?

12. tollo cornua: Horace shifts his metaphor; cf. *Sat.* 1.4.34, *faenum habet in cornu; longe fuge!*

13. Lycambae ... gener: the story was that when Lycambes reneged on his promise to give his daughter in marriage to Archilochus, the poet avenged himself in verses so cutting that the old man hanged himself. **gener** would therefore mean the would-be son-in-law of Lycambes. **Lycambae ... infido** is dat.: just as the rejected (*spretus,* from

sperno) son-in-law was *to* the traitor Lycambes.

14. hostis Bupalo: more biographical gossip about early poets, this time Hipponax, who wrote iambic poetry sometime after 550 B.C. Pliny *Nat. Hist.* 36.5 reports that Bupalus was the son of an artist named Achermus, whose sculpture of an ugly man seemed to Hipponax to be a caricature of himself. His angry iambs, the story runs, drove both Bupalus and his brother to suicide. Like Lycambes (cf. Gk. λύκος = wolf), Bupalos (cf. Gk. βοῦς = bull, ox) carries on the poem's animal metaphor.

15. atro dente: metaphoric, with spiteful or malevolent words.

7

A harangue to his fellow Romans, perhaps on the breakdown of the Treaty of Misenum in the spring of 38 B.C. that led to the Sicilian War between Octavian and Sextus Pompey (see note to *Epod.* 4.19). The same themes are set forth at greater length in Epode 16. Meter: iambic strophe.

1-10. Why are you taking up arms? Has not enough blood been shed, not against foreign enemies, but in suicidal war?

1. Quo, quo scelesti ruitis? Instead of titles, Latin poems were known by their opening phrase. Even Virgil's *Aeneid* was sometimes referred to as the *Arma virumque cano,* and papal encyclicals in prose still employ the same convention. The first words of this poem reflect the care with which Horace has tried to communicate both the tone and the essence of his message. **ruitis** combines the sense of reckless haste and destruction, hasten to your ruin.

2. enses conditi: sheathed swords.

3. Parumne: too little, begins a rhetorical ques-tion that continues to the middle of the poem. **Neptuno** = the sea by synecdoche. **super:** delayed by anastrophe, governs both *campis* and *Neptuno.*

4. fusum est: impersonal (from *fundo*), has been

shed; governs the partitive gen. *Latini sanguinis.*

5. invidae Carthaginis, a hostile Carthage, refers to the Punic Wars, the last of which ended with the sack of the city in 146 B.C.

7. intactus ... Britannus: unlike Carthage, Britain had not succumbed to Roman attack.

8. Sacra catenatus Via refers to the ritual of the military triumph, in which captured chiefs were chained and paraded in front of the victor's chariot before being executed (it is this humiliation that Cleopatra avoids by suicide in 1.37.29-32). Cf. Shakespeare *JC* 1.1.34:

> What tributaries follow him to Rome
> To grace in captive bonds his chariot wheels?

9. secundum, etc.: adverbial, in accordance with the prayers of the Parthians, Rome's Iranian foes.

9-10. sua ... dextera: emphatic hyperbaton, made more so by its echo of line 1, *dexteris.*

11-16. Even wild beasts do not fight against their own kind. Is this insanity, destiny, or some ancient wrong? Their silence convicts them.

11. lupis ... leonibus, etc.: for the commonplace that man is the only animal that attacks its own kind, cf. Pliny *Nat. Hist.* 7.1.5, Seneca *Controv.* 2.9, Seneca *Ep. Mor.* 95.31, Juvenal 15.159.

12. umquam, etc.: never savage except against a dissimilar animal. The negative sense carries over from the preceding line. **in dispar** [animal]: i.e., against one of another species. **feris:** in apposition with *lupis* and *leonibus:* wild beasts though they are.

13. vis acrior: probably = fate; cf. 2.17.6 *maturior vis.* **culpa** is fault incurred, ancient guilt, miasma (as explained in lines 18-20).

14-15. Responsum date! Tacent: A histrionic effect. The poet turns from one imagined audience to another, drawing conclusions from the former's abashed silence and frightened pallor. Similar techniques are used in Tibullus and especially Propertius (1.8.27, 2.34.25).

16. perculsae stupent: are struck with dismay (*percello*), and stunned.

17-20. That is it: we are cursed by the fratricide of Romulus and Remus.

17. acerba fata echoes *vis acrior* (13). **agunt:** incite (to violence), harry, haunt (as in *Epod.* 5.89 *diris agam vos*).

18. scelus echoes line 1 *scelesti* and repeats the idea of *culpa* (14). Legends of an original act of violence creating a curse on posterity are common in the ancient Mediterranean: Adam's disobedience in the Garden of Eden, Cain's murder of Abel, and Atreus' crime against Thyestes are other well-known examples.

19. ut: ever since, as in 4.4.42.

20. sacer nepotibus cruor: in its bad sense, *sacer* applies to anything cursed because of an offense against divine law (*OLD* 2); here Remus' blood is a curse to his descendants, viz. the descendants of his brother Romulus.

8

Coarsely abusive sexual language is an early iambic tradition. It was brought into Latin poetry by Catullus, whose pungent wit Horace emulates in these lines. Satire against the growing class of wealthy Roman women who cultivated their minds instead of their wifely duties was a likely theme of the Stoic *sermo* by the time this epode was written. Juvenal was later to develop the topic in *Sat.* 6.434-456 as part of a long and vitriolic satire on women. For Horace's own jeremiad on unwifely wives, see 3.6.17-32.

Horace is also developing a theme that will recur in the *Odes* (e.g., 1.25, 4.13) of a woman who has rejected the poet's advances becoming old and ugly. Meter: iambic strophe.

1-10. You ask why I am low on energy, but you are the one who is truly decrepit.

1. Rogare: infinitive in indignant exclamation: to think that you would ask, etc. The acc. subject is **putidam te.**

3. dens ater: collective singular; cf. the *dente*

livido with which the witch Canidia gnaws her thumbnail in *Epod.* 5.47.

3-4. vetus ... senectus: old age, like *longo saeculo* in line 1. **exaret:** plows or inscribes. Like *sit* (3) and *hiet* (5), the subjunctive after *cum* is causal, explaining the poet's indignation: you have your nerve calling me feeble when you are such a wreck yourself.

5-6. hiet ... podex insinuates many years of anal intercourse. Cf. the εύρυπρώκτοι in Aristophanes *Clouds* 1084-99.

7. incitat me: ironic. Horace does not find the second triad of physical features (7-10) any more sexually exciting than the first (3-6).

9-10. femur ... suris additum: collective singulars. The unsightly combination of skinny thighs and fat ankles (*sura* is lit. the calf) is appropriately presented with interlocking word order.

11-20. I wish you the best, but does my lack of philosophic lore diminish my virility? If you want to interest *me,* you'll have to work harder!

11. Esto concessive fut. imperative, like the subjunctives *ducant* and *sit.* Be as wealthy as you like, etc.

11-12. imagines ... triumphales: death-masks of ancestors who had been honored with a triumph were displayed in the atrium of the house as status symbols and carried in funeral processions. Display of such *imagines* was permitted only to people of praetorian or consular rank.

13-14. marita: married woman. **rotundioribus ... bacis:** i.e., more perfect pearls. **ambulet** has a hint of insolence, as in *Epod.* 5.71.

15. Quid quod, etc.: what difference does it make that you have a few philosophical booklets among your silk cushions? **libelli** is contemptuously diminutive, insinuating that these are watered-down abridgements rather than serious philosophy. **sericos:** Chinese, hence silk.

17-18. Illiterati num, etc.: the position of *illiterati* indicates that it is predicative: you don't suppose, do you (*num*), that my muscles (or sexual

powers) are flabby because they are unlettered, or my penis unsoft (i.e., hard and ready for business)? Horace means that his lack of reading has nothing to do either way with his virility. For *minus = non,* cf. *Epod.* 5.61. Horace returns to the lady's scornful question *vires quid enervet meas,* which started the poem. **fascinum** is a phallic charm against the evil eye, hence an actual phallus. For the Stoic opposition of eros and philosophy, see Posidippus *A.P.* 5.134 (GP 1).

19. Quod: his *fascinum.* **superbo ... ab inguine:** his loins are proud or disdainful because he has been insulted. **provoces** is ironic because after challenging his ability to perform she must now do something special to challenge his *fascinum.*

20. The *ad-* prefix in **allaborandum** denotes additional work, i.e., fellatio; cf. 1.38.5. The *o*-sounds in the last couplet illustrate what Horace is talking about.

9

Addressed to Maecenas on the arrival, in September of 31 B.C., of news of the victory at Actium. Maecenas was at Rome at this time, and many believe neither he nor Horace was present at the battle. But the form is dramatic (cf. Epode 7), as if they had been at sea taking part in the victory, and one school of thought maintains Horace was present in person at the battle. In either case, this poem reads as a sequel to Epode 1. Meter: iambic strophe.

1-10. When, Maecenas, will you and I have a feast to celebrate Caesar's victory, like the one we had when Pompey was defeated?

1. repostum: syncopated from *repositum,* stored away, hence aged to perfection. **Caecubum:** sc. *vinum,* a choice wine from a marshy district in southern Latium; cf. 1.20.9. **dapes:** properly, a *daps* was a sacrificial meal. Cf. the *dapes* due on Cleopatra's defeat in 1.37.4 and 2.7.17 *obligatam Iovi dapem.*

3. sub alta ... domo refers to Maecenas' lofty

palace on the Esquiline; it had a tower that commanded a view of the city and the surrounding countryside. Cf. 3.29.10 and note. For the force of *sub*, within, cf. 1.5.3 *sub antro*.

5. sonante ... lyra: abl. abs.: while the lyre plays a song accompanied by flutes (*carmen* is the object of *sonante*).

6. hac ... illis: i.e., a *Dorium carmen* on the lyre and a Phrygian or *barbarum carmen* on the flutes. The Dorian style was military, the Phrygian appropriate to wild parties.

7. ut nuper: five years before, when Sextus Pompey was defeated at Naulochus and driven from the sea (**actus freto**) by Agrippa (36 B.C.). **Neptunius dux** refers sarcastically to Pompey's assumption of the title "son of Neptune" after his earliest naval successes.

10. servis: dependent upon both *detraxerat* and *amicus*; i.e., he had taken bonds from the slaves, and he was friendly to them. For such *apo koinou* constructions, see appendix C. For Pompey's use of slaves, see note on *Epod.* 4.19. Slave-owning Romans had no love for a Great Emancipator. **perfidis:** that is, from the point of view of a slave owner.

11-20. Roman soldiers have served a woman, bowed to eunuchs, and taken to canopied beds. No wonder the Galatians deserted to our side, and ships refused to enter battle against us.

11ff. The idea is that the victory at Actium partially redeems the shocking conduct of Antony's troops in submitting to the commands of a mere woman, Cleopatra.

11. Romanus ... emancipatus feminae: a Roman (soldier) handed over to a woman. *emancipo* = to place a person at someone's disposal, here with the dat. Cf. Shakespeare *A&C* 3.7.66, "so our leader's led, and we are women's men." Such an indignity will be hard for future ages to believe (*posteri negabitis*).

13. vallum: collective singular. *Valli* were stakes used in making a temporary barricade (*vallum*).

spadonibus ... rugosis: eunuchs were the usual attendants in oriental courts because they would not interfere with the harem and would have no outside family interests. Horace appeals to the Roman contempt of this class by calling them "wrinkled"; cf. 1.37.9 *contaminato cum grege turpium morbo virorum*.

14. servire ... potest: can bring himself to obey.

15-16. turpe ... conopium: a bed equipped with mosquito nets; Horace presents it as a "disgusting" symptom of oriental degeneracy.

17. Ad hoc: at this sight. **frementis verterunt,** etc.: two thousand Galatians (*Galli*), under the command of Amyntias and Deiotarus, had fought for a time in the army of Antony, but deserted (*verterunt equos*) to Octavian before the battle of Actium. The short second *e* of *verterunt* is short, reminiscent of the original quantity.

18. canentes Caesarem: i.e., chanting his name; cf. Virgil *Aen.* 7.698, *regem canebant*.

19. hostiliumque navium, etc.: the ships of Antony and Cleopatra hide in the harbor. No other account of the battle explains what *sinistrorsum citae*, "mustered to the left," refers to, but the general sense is that like the Galli, part of the fleet deserted before the battle started. The unusual expression *navium puppes* conveys the idea of turning their backs on the battle.

21-26. How can you wait to celebrate? No greater victor ever came back to Rome, not even from Carthage.

21. aureos ... boves: gilded chariots and bulls uncontaminated by the yoke or other earthly uses were part of the regular paraphernalia of the Roman triumph. The *triumphator* rode in a chariot decorated with gold and ivory to the temple of Jupiter on the Capitoline, where priests would sacrifice the *intactas boves* that had been led in the procession. They were actually bulls, in spite of the gender of *intactas*.

23-24. Iugurthino bello ... ducem: C. Marius' victory over Jugurtha in Numidia (106 B.C.) won him a military triumph and three successive consulships. At the time of this epode Sallust's *Iugurtha* had recently been published.

25. Africanum: understand *parem ducem* in apposition. This refers to the younger Publius Cornelius Scipio, given the title *Africanus* after his defeat of Hannibal at Zama in 202 B.C.

26. sepulcrum: a monument rather than a tomb.

27-38. Our enemy is on the run; so bring out bigger cups and better wines, and let us drown our cares.

28. Terra marique victus: an enthusiastic exaggeration. Though defeated at sea, Antony still had nineteen legions of infantry and some 22,000 cavalry at his disposal. These waited several days for his return before surrendering to Octavian. **Punico ... sagum:** has taken a mourning *sagum* (a common soldier's cloak) in exchange for his scarlet *paludamentum*, the mantle worn by commanding generals. Horace imagines Antony (the **hostis** here) taking the same prudent measures as Pompey after Pharsalus: *equum nactus detractis insignibus imperatoriis decumana porta se ex castris eiecit* (Caesar *BCiv.* 3.96.3).

29. centum ... urbibus: descriptive abl., the Homeric "hundred-citied Crete"; cf. 3.27.33, *centum potentem oppidis Creten*. **Cretam:** object of *petit* (31).

30. ventis iturus non suis: destined to go with winds not his own, i.e., not blowing in his favor, on the general principle that his star is waning and whatever he does will be fraught with disaster.

31. exercitatas ... Syrtis: the stormy shoals off mod. Libya; cf. 4.14.20f., *undas exercet Auster*.

32. incerto mari: because his destination is uncertain; transferred epithet.

33. puer: that is, slave, as often in sympotic contexts; cf. 2.11.18. **scyphos:** large beakers with two handles.

35. quod coerceat: relative clause of purpose, to restrain my *fluentem nauseam*; Horace speaks jokingly as if he were on one of Antony's fleeing

ships. Caecuban, like modern champagne, was supposed to prevent sea-sickness.

37. Curam ... rerum: concern for Octavian's fortunes. Though defeated at Actium, Antony and Cleopatra still had access to powerful resources. It was not until a year later that they were finally vanquished and Horace was able to burst out into the jubilant *nunc est bibendum* of *Odes* 1.37.

38. Lyaeo = *Baccho*, synecdoche for *vino*. **solvere:** set free. There is a pun on *Lyaeo*, the god who sets free. See notes on 1.7.22, 3.21.15.

10

This hostile send-off poem to Mevius uses the components of the traditional *propempticon* to wish him a disastrous instead of a prosperous voyage. Contrast the somber good wishes for Virgil in 1.3. An early Greek iambic fragment (Hipponax 115 West) is similarly conceived and may have provided the idea for this Epode. Meter: iambic strophe.

1-14. May all the winds blow up a storm when stinking Mevius sets sail.

1. Mala ... alite: circumstantial abl., under an evil omen, lit. wing (of a prophetic fowl). The first word of this poem indicates its theme. **soluta exit:** emphatic redundancy; it has been cast off (from its moorings) and leaves.

2. olentem Mevium: possibly the poetaster Mevius, mocked by Virgil in *Ecl.* 3.90, *qui Bavium non odit amet tua carmina, Mevi.* But all we learn about him here is that he is a stinker, *olentem* being widely understood here as metaphorical. Horace generally attacks types rather than individuals, and the name's particular reference may be unimportant.

3. Ut, with the force of *utinam,* governs the optative subjunctives *verberes, differat* (6), *insurgat* (7), *appareat* (9), and *feratur* (11). These imprecations for foul weather supplant the usual prayer for favorable winds in the *propempticon.*

5. niger ... Eurus: because it brings black storm

clouds; cf. 1.5.6 f., *aspera nigris aequora ventis*. In this part of his poem Horace invokes stormy south, east, and north winds (Auster, Eurus, Aquilo), saving the worst (Notus, from the south) for last (20). **inverso mari**: for the subjective language, cf. Virgil *Aen.* 1.43, *evertit aequora ventis*.

7-8. quantus ... frangit: as great as when it breaks.

10. qua: temporal, on which; the antecedent is *nocte*. The setting of Orion in early November was a season of storms.

13. usto ab Ilio: after the burning of Troy. This use of the participle is a common idiom in Horace.

14. impiam Aiacis ratem: transferred epithet, a kind of guilt by association (see appendix C, *hypallage*). Ajax the son of Oïleus raped Cassandra during the sack of Troy when she took refuge at the sanctuary of Athena. As punishment, Athena impaled him on a sharp rock during a storm on the trip home. See Virgil *Aen.* 1.39-45. The four lines describing this part of Horace's curse occupy the exact center of the poem.

15-24. What a panic will grip you, Mevius, when your ship breaks up! If the gulls eat your corpse, I will sacrifice a goat and a lamb to the Tempests.

15. O ... tuis: The second part of the poem is an apostrophe to Mevius.

16. luteus: mud-yellow, the kind of pallor that would appear on a dark Mediterranean complexion. The adjective also carries disreputable connotations.

17. illa ... heiulatio: that [well-known] whining of yours. Latin would normally use *ista* in this situation, but Horace is mocking Mevius' cowardice with liquid and nasal sounds.

19. Ionius ... sinus: the Ionian Sea, between the instep of the Italian boot and western Greece (see map 3). Note the distinction between Ĭŏnĭus and Īōnĭcus, the latter referring to the Greek-speaking Asia Minor coast. Mevius is sailing from Italy to Greece, like Virgil in 1.3.

21. Opima ... praeda: instead of the sacrifice for a friend's safe arrival usually promised in a *propempticon*, Horace prays that Mevius' corpse will be choice booty for the gulls.

23. libidinosus ... caper: the goat's sexual potency makes it a better sacrifice; for an expansion of this motif, see 3.13.4-5.

24. Tempestatibus: personified gods of the storm, as in Virgil *Aen.* 5.772-3, *Tempestatibus agnam caedere deinde iubet.*

11

Probably more literary than autobiographical, this conventional confession of the repeated buffets of love is one of the oldest and still most popular themes of erotic lyric (Sappho 130 LP, Alcman 59a Page, Anacreon 413 Page, etc.). It is combined here with a Hellenistic symposiac theme, in which a guest at a banquet tearfully reveals that he is in love. This comes down to us chiefly in the epigrams, e.g., Asclepiades *A.P.* 12.50 (GP 16). The idea that a man can as easily fall in love with a pubescent boy as with a woman is also traditional. In this poem Horace turns from the abusive iambic mood of the epodes that bracket it on either side and plays with the love themes to be developed in the Odes. Meter: third Archilochian.

1-4. I can no longer write poems, Pettius, because love has clobbered me again.

1. Petti: the otherwise unknown confidant is brought in to convey the feeling of a private conversation at a party. **nihil** = *non*: inner object of **iuvat**.

2. versiculos: ditties; the diminutive conveys mild disparagement. **percussum**: causal, because I am smitten. Anacreon (413 Page) likewise describes himself smitten by Eros as with an axe. The theme of love preventing poetic composition may be Archilochian (frags. 196/215 West).

4. mollibus in pueris: the tradition was pederastic (love for boys just before puberty) rather than pedophiliac (love for children) or homosexual (love for grown men). **puellis**: the conventional term for young unmarried women.

5-14. This is the third winter since I broke up with Inachia; what a state I was in when a wealthier rival edged me out!
5. tertius December, etc.: places the season of the scene depicted as well as the duration of time since he recovered from his passion for (the fictitious) Inachia. The usual metrical pause is missing here and in line 15.
6. Inachia: abl. of cause, as often with verbs like *furere* and *ardere* denoting love (but cf. *in puellis urere* above). **silvis honorem decutit**: with its winds; for *honor* = handsome growth or crop, cf. 1.17.16, 2.11.9.
8. fabula: cause for gossip, as in *Epist.* 1.13.9, *cognomen vertas in risum et fabula fias*. **Conviviorum**: the drinking parties or symposiums, with their spectacle of the lovelorn guest, were a common topic of Hellenistic epigrams. Such guests are represented as trying to conceal their condition.
9. quīs = *quibus*.
9-10. amantem ... arguit: accuses, convicts, proves me a lover.
10. spiritus: the lover's melancholy sigh.
11. -ne, normally attached to a personal pronoun, adds force to the exclamatory infin. **valere**: to think that a good-natured disposition (*candidum ingenium*) is worthless against wealth!—a traditional complaint of the lover edged out by a wealthier rival. For the wealthy rival theme, see *Epod.* 15.19-20, 4.1.18.
13-14. calentis: gen., governing **arcana** in the next line: my secrets, when I was warm with **fervidiore mero**, stronger wine. Note the hiatus after *mero*. **inverecundus deus**: Bacchus, because under his influence people feel no shame.

15-22. I angrily vowed to forget her, but after every party I staggered off to her doorstep and begged in vain to be let in.

15-18. Quodsi ... pudor: but if a free man's anger boils up (*inaestuet ... libera bilis*) so as to scatter to the winds all useless consolations, my pride (*pudor*) will stop competing with rivals I cannot match (*imparibus* refers to the rivals, their expensive gifts, and the unfair disadvantages he faces). **ut ... dividat**: result clause; the subject is *bilis*. **haec ingrata ... fomenta**: the unwelcome poultices are his friends' attempts to comfort him and his own vain hopes. For **nil** = *non*, cf. note on *nihil*, line 1.
19. haec severus ... laudaveram: sternly approved this plan.
20. incerto pede, etc.: he is drunk, and when told to go home he totters off instead to the woman's house, where he is unwelcome (*non amicos postis, limina dura*).
22. limina dura, etc.: It was the custom for the lover leaving the symposium to go off to his beloved's house and make a scene (see appendix C, *paraclausithyron*) outside the door, as represented in numerous Hellenistic love epigrams. Cf. 3.10.19-20 *non hoc semper erit liminis ... patiens latus*.

23-28. Now I am in love with Lyciscus, and no friendly counsel can untangle me—only another love for a boy or girl.
23-24. gloriantis Lycisci: objective gen. with **amor**. The new boyfriend boasts that he can outdo any girlie (scornful diminutive **mulierculam**) in *mollitia*; cf. line 4, *mollibus pueris*. The name is fictitious, like Inachia (6).
25. unde: i.e., from his new *amor*. Lyciscus is like Gyges in 2.5.21-24, playing on a Roman taste for boys who look like girls.
26. libera consilia: generous advice. *Liber* can be used to describe any self-respecting or magnanimous impulse typical of a free-born man; cf. *libera bilis* (16). The life described in such scenes is assumed to be that of the wealthy *jeunesse dorée*.
27-28. aut puellae ... aut ... pueri: repeats line 4, *mollibus in pueris aut in puellis*. The repetition in

ring structure gives an appropriate sense of closure.

28. longam renodantis comam: cf. Pyrrha in 1.5.4, *cui flavam religas comam?*, and Lyde's Spartan-style hairdo in 2.11.23f., *in comptum Lacaenae more comas religata nodum.* Here it is a boy's style, provocatively imitating a woman's.

12

A gigolo's lament, not for the squeamish or for the *virginibus puerisque* addressed in 3.1.4. Fraenkel condemned it as "repulsive," but the woman's character is conveyed through her words with subtle irony, and there is more high comedy than low obscenity. Composed in the same tradition as Epode 8, this poem of sexual invective differs in offering something of a narrative persona, a professional ladies' man or male prostitute complaining about an unsatisfied customer (in the first half) and reciting her complaint about him in the second half. Meter: Alcmanic strophe.

1-6. Why are you sending me all these gifts and letters, madam? I smell trouble.

1. nigris ... barris: dark elephants, probably from India. Only later does it become clear why she is worthy of these work animals, and how they might be employed.

3. firmo iuveni: dat. with *mihi*; he is not the tireless performer he used to be. **naris obesae:** gen. of description; thick, therefore insensitive. Horace is saying he is no fool. For the keen nose as a metaphor of mental acuity, cf. *Sat.* 1.4.8 (of Lucilius) *facetus, emunctae naris.*

4. sagacius: with *quam* (6). **odoror,** determine by smell, governs the indirect question that follows.

5. polypus: a tumor; cf. *Sat.* 1.3.40. The usual caesura is missing in this line. **hircus in alis:** cf. Rufus in Catullus 69 and 71 is similarly afflicted with goatish body odor.

7-12. What a sweat she works up in the heat of passion! Her makeup runs, and she breaks the bed.

7. Qui: exclamatory, with **sudor.** The adj. **vietis,** shrivelled or wrinkled, is pushed ahead of the copula *et* for emphasis.

8. pene soluto: i.e., after her male partner is exhausted.

9. rabiem sedare: to appease her own still-raging lust.

10. creta: a chalky clay used as a cosmetic; once *umida* with her perspiration, it begins to run. **color:** i.e., rouge, applied over the *creta* as a blush.

11. stercore fucatus crocodili: dyed with crocodile dung. This use is elsewhere unattested, though Pliny *Nat. Hist.* 28.108 refers to a fragrant substance *crocodilea* used as an eye salve and to clear the complexion.

11-12. subando ... rumpit: in the throes of her violent orgasm she wrecks the bed and its canopy. **tenta cubilia:** (pl. in sing. sense) the bed, made of a frame supporting stretched cords; *tentus* also has connotations of erotic tension (*OLD* b).

13-20. She complains: "You love Inachia less than me, but you serve her better; curses on Lesbia, who recruited *you* when I could have had Amyntas of Cos!

13. cum: temporal, with *agitat.* **agitat:** she arouses his disgust (*OLD* 6) at the same time as she criticizes it (*OLD* 10). The plural **fastidia** suggests he is often disgusted.

14. langues: with abl. **Inachia** (referring to some other woman), you are in love with; but the verb is ironic, because the point of the complaint is that his way with Inachia is anything but languid.

15. potes: the ellipsis omits the complementary infinitive, but it is easy enough to guess: you can "do" Inachia three times a night.

15-16. ad unum mollis opus: sc. *es,* too soft for a single "job." Her sexual vocabulary is crudely perfunctory. See appendix C, *ethos.*

17. Lesbia could be the slave-girl or procuress, perhaps from Lesbos, who suggested the liaison. Cf. the unnamed agent of Chloe in 3.7.9-20. But the association with Catullus' Lesbia, a promiscuous married woman, suggests she is another rich lady who goes in for midnight cowboys. **quaerenti:** sc. *mihi,* takes the object **taurum** (metaphoric for a prodigiously endowed sexual athlete).

18. mihi ... adesset: i.e., he was available. **Cous ... Amyntas,** another fictitious character, is the *taurus* who could have satisfied this lady's requirements. The name and the place both suggest pastoral poetry: Amyntas is Simichidas' Coan companion in Theocritus *Idyll* 7.2; cf. Virgil *Ecl.* 2.35, 3.66, 5.8, 10.37. The ironic pastoral note is repeated in the simile at the end of the poem: the world of this poem is anything but pastoral.

19. nervus: muscle, a significant euphemism for the business end of Amyntas.

20. nova ... arbor: a young tree, but no sapling. **collibus:** she may also be thinking of her own *mons veneris.*

21-26. "Why do you think I sent you those richly dyed woolens? How unlucky I am: you avoid me as the flock avoids wolves and lions!"

21. Muricibus Tyriis, etc.: some of the *munera* (2) with which the unnamed lady has been regaling the narrator, consisting of woolen fleeces (**vellera**) twice-dyed (**iteratae**) in expensive Tyrian dye extracted from the shellfish *murex.*

23. ne foret, etc.: i.e., so it would be clear to all that you had no peer. **aequalis inter:** among your contemporaries (suggesting that the woman is older). **conviva:** a guest (masc. nom. sing.)

24. mulier sua: probably another indication of her age; a younger or contemporary sexual partner outside of marriage was regularly called *puella,* as in Eng. *girlfriend.* Catullus referred to Lesbia as *mulier* only after the affair was broken off (70.1, 3; 87.1). **te:** sc. *diligo.*

26. agna lupos, etc.: the lady's metaphors give her away again, comparing herself to (male) predators and him to (female) prey. A *virago,* she has qualities usually attributed to the male of the species. Her words are adapted from Plato *Phdr.*

241d1: ὡς λύκοι ἄρνας ἀγαπῶσιν, ὡς παῖδα φιλοῦσιν ἐρασταί.

13

This best-loved of all the *Epodes,* praised by Fraenkel as "a perfect poem," adapts a sympotic theme found in Alcaeus (338 LP) that will reappear in another Horatian masterpiece (1.9, the Soracte Ode). The stormy weather outdoors and the worries of friends gathered indoors meet their match in wine and song. The poem ends with a paradigm from legend, where Chiron the Centaur teaches young Achilles how he will relieve future distress at Troy. Meter: second Archilochian.

1-5. Snow and wind are upon us; let us seize the occasion to celebrate youth while we have it.

1. caelum contraxit: the storm has narrowed the sky by lowering the clouds.

2. deducunt Iovem repeats the predication of the first line. For *Iovem = caelum,* see appendix C: synecdoche. **siluae** is trisyllabic, as in 1.23.4.

3. Threïcio: four syllables, separated from *Aquilone* by hiatus. Calling the north wind Thracian adds a Greek note. **Rapiamus:** an energetic note, as in 1.11.8 *carpe diem.*

4. dum ... virent genua: while our knees are springy. The knees are a measure of strength in general as early as Homer.

5. obducta ... fronte: from a clouded (i.e., troubled) brow. The weather metaphor latent in *obducta* (OLD 5c) picks up the theme of line 1, *caelum contraxit.* Note the antithetical juxtaposition of *obducta solvatur.*

6-11. Bring out the old wine, and let us forget our cares with a song such as the Centaur sang to Achilles.

6. Tu: one of the *amici* addressed in line 3. **Torquato ... consule ... meo:** in the consulship of "my" Torquatus because L. Manlius Torquatus was consul in 65 B.C.—the year of Horace's birth. Cf.

3.21.1 (to a wine jug), *O nata mecum consule Man-lio*. The personal note is typically Horatian. **move:** bring down from its place of storage under the rafters, as in 3.21.6-7

7. mitte: with *loqui*, stop (*OLD* 4b), as in 1.38.3 *mitte sectari*. In Horace, the imperative *mitte* always means stop, leave off. **haec:** i.e., these troubles, as suggested by the *tempestas* of line 1. **benigna ... vice:** with kindly compensation or exchange. The old Greek idea was that the gods alternately dispense good and bad fortune. Cf. 1.4.1 *grata vice* (of the change from winter to spring).

8. Achaemenio: Persian, by metonymy from the ruling dynasty.

9. fide Cyllenea gives the line a spondaic ending. The lyre is from Mt. Cyllene in Arcadia because its inventor Mercury/Hermes was born there.

10. diris ... sollicitudinibus: abl. of separation with *levare*, relieve. The troubles in the poems of Alcaeus were political. It is reasonable to infer behind the Alcaean mask of this poem a reference to the political unrest of Horace's own time.

11. grandi ... alumno: an oblique reference to Achilles, raised on the slopes of Mt. Pelion by Chiron the Centaur. For the arrangement of words in this line, see appendix C, golden line.

12-18. Chiron's song: "You are destined for Troy, whence it is fated you will not return. There you must find solace in wine and song."

12. mortalis dea: antithetical juxtaposition. Achilles inherited mortality from his father Peleus. Note the "golden" order of the last five words. **dea ... Thetide:** abl. of source depending on *nate*. Achilles' mother was the sea nymph Thetis.

13. Assaraci tellus: Troy, so-called after Ganymede's brother Assaracus, an early king and great-great-grandfather of Aeneas.

14. lubricus: slippery, treacherous.

15. subtemine: the weft or cross-threads on the loom of the Parcae or Fates. The use of this word recalls the refrain of the wedding song in Catullus 64 (lines 327, 333, etc.), where the Parcae predict

the bloody triumphs of Achilles: *currite ducentes subtegmina, currite, fusi*.

16. rupere (*ruperunt*): suggests the breaking of the thread of life, and Achilles' violent death. **mater ... caerula:** Thetis is sea-blue through her association with the sea.

17. levato: fut. imper., recalling *levare* (10). When Achilles' friends come to his shelter in *Il*. 9.186-89, they find him "delighting his heart with a lyre" even though he is angry at Agamemnon.

18. deformis aegrimoniae: for unlovely sorrow. Objective gen. depending on **alloquiis** (consolations), a rare word that recalls Catullus 38.5, *qua solatus es allocutione?*

14

An admission to his patron Maecenas that his current project, presumably the *Epodes*, has been delayed. The proffered excuse, a love affair, may or may not have been the actual reason, but through its thinly disguised *recusatio* the poem shows a significant shift from the polemical topics of iambic poetry to the love themes in lyric meters for which Anacreon of Teos (ca. 575-490 B.C.) was famous. Behind the conventional postures of poetry we may perceive a personal statement by the poet about the development of his art. Meter: first pythiambic.

1-8. You keep asking, Maecenas, why I am idle. It is a god who prevents me from finishing my iambic poems.

1. Mollis inertia: the opening words, as often, are thematic for the poem as a whole. Comparable to *otium* in Catullus 51, it represents the drugged state of the person in love (cf. *oblivionem* and *somnos*, lines 2-3). **diffuderit:** subjunctive in ind. question, depending on *rogando* (5).

3. Lethaeos ... somnos: object of *ducentia*, inducing Lethe-like sleep. *Lethaeos*, alluding to the river of forgetfulness in Hades, reinforces *oblivionem* in the previous line, the point being that

Horace has forgotten his iambic task. **ut si** is delayed (as such connectives often are in Horace) to give the line its symmetry: noun a, adjective b, *ut si*, adjective a, noun b.

4. arente fauce traxerim: i.e., thirstily guzzled. Perfect subjunctive after *ut si*.

5. candide: for the honorific epithet, cf. 1.18.11, *Sat.* 1.10.86, *Epist.* 1.4.1. **occidis:** sc. *me*; hyperbolic, you wear me out.

6. deus, deus: the god of love, as we learn in the second half of the poem. For emphatic repetition in the *Epodes*, see *Epod.* 4.20 n.

7. carmen: poetry. In apposition with *inceptos iambos*, this would have to mean a collection of poems, no doubt the *Epodes*, which would be published in 30 B.C.

8. ad umbilicum adducere: to finish off, complete, lit. bring to the rod. A completed book, its pages written left to right on a papyrus scroll, was attached to a rod at its right end and rolled up from right to left to make a *liber*. The ornamented knobs at the end of the rod (and hence the rod itself) were called *umbilici*.

9-16. Anacreon too was in love, and made his laments in lyric meters. You yourself are a lover. My tormenter is the unfaithful Phryne.

9. Samio ... Bathyllo: Anacreon of Teos spent some time on the island of Samos under the patronage of the tyrant Polycrates. His passion for Bathyllus is mentioned in several late sources. **arsisse:** as often, *ardeo* = be in love.

10. Anacreonta Teïum: the love poet (ca. 575-490 B.C.) from Greek Asia Minor just north of Samos. Placement of the name by itself on a single line gives it special emphasis, as if serving notice on the reader that Horace is contemplating a new poetic model. Described by D.A. Campbell as "perhaps the most meticulous craftsman of all the early lyric writers," his words are echoed by Horace in 1.23.1 and 1.27.1; see also 4.9.9.

11. cava testudine: i.e., on his lyre, according to legend first fashioned from a tortoise's shell.

12. non elaboratum ad pedem may refer to the fact that lyric meters are not as rigidly measured out in feet as are epic and iambic verses, or that Anacreon's meters were simple. Cf. his description of Pindar's meter in 4.2.11-12, *numeris ... lege solutis.*

13. Ureris and **miser**, like *arsisse* (9), belong to the standard vocabulary of love. **ignis** by metonymy = lover, the one who kindles your passions; it also refers to the fire that burned Troy in the war to win back Helen.

13-15. quodsi ... tua: the sense is, if Helen of Troy is no prettier than your lover, consider yourself lucky.

15. me: the sense is adversative: but *my* girlfriend is no exclusive lady. A **libertina** is a freed slave, of the class Horace recommends for love affairs in *Sat.* 1.2.47f. This one keeps a number of boyfriends on call (*nec uno contenta*). Cf. 1.33.13 ff., *me ... grata detinuit compede Myrtale libertina.*

16. Phryne is a stock name for courtesans. The original Phryne, a hetaera from Thespiae, was the model for Praxiteles' Cnidian Aphrodite; she offered to spend her vast earnings rebuilding the walls of Thebes after it was sacked by Alexander in 338 B.C. More about this celebrated beauty, who was said to be most beautiful "in the unseen parts," can be read in Athenaeus 13.590d-592f. **macerat:** torments (with jealousy), exhausts, softens (playing off *mollis* in line 1). Horace tends to treat his own love life—real or imagined—with self-mockery.

15

A lament for the infidelity of Neaera, suitably paired with Epode 14. Horace comforts himself that Neaera will be sorry when he finds himself another girlfriend, and taunts his rival that he too will be cast aside. Neaera appears again in 3.14.21; the name is probably meant to be understood as a hetaera's professional name, perhaps alluding to the central figure in Pseudo-Demosthenes' *In*

Neaeram. The motifs are common poetic topics, and the general tone of the poem suggests Latin love elegy, which was at this time emerging as a new Roman genre. Meter: first pythiambic.

1-10. One moonlit night you swore you would share my love forever.

1. Nox erat et: these words became the standard opening for the "quiet night" formula in Latin poetry (cf. Virgil *Aen.* 3.147, 4.522, 8.26; Ovid *Am.* 3.5.1, *Pont.* 3.3.5, *Fasti* 1.421, 2.792), but the topos is as old as Homer (*Il.* 2.1-2, 10.1-4, *Od.* 20.54-58). Horace's opening may owe something to a fragment sometimes ascribed to Sappho, frag. adesp. 976 Page. See also Asclepiades *A.P.* 5.167 and 189 (GP 14 and 42).

3. laesura: soon to outrage. The future participle suggests the inevitability, and perhaps even the intention, of treachery.

4. in verba iurabas suggests the technical term for the soldier's oath of allegiance, *iurare in verba.* **mea** makes it clear that the oath was prescribed by the lover himself to preclude artful evasions and leave no loopholes for Neaera.

5. artius atque: more closely than. **hedera:** for ivy as a metaphor of clinging devotion, Cf. 1.36.20.

6. lentis: supple, clinging. **adhaerens:** sc. *mihi.*

7-9. This three-part elaboration of the "forever" motif is a common rhetorical topos. The wolf will always be the herd's enemy, Orion will always bring on storms, the wind will always stir Apollo's traditionally long hair.

7. dum pecori lupus: sc. *infestus esset.* For the anacoluthon, see appendix C. **Orion:** the setting of Orion in early November was associated with the beginning of the stormy season.

8-9. turbaret, agitaret: the subjunctives show that the *dum-* clause was part of the actual oath, depending on *fore* (10).

10. mutuum: predicative, placed at the end for emphasis.

11-16. You'll regret your treachery, Neaera!

11. dolitura significantly echoes *laesura* (3). **virtute,** echoed by *viri* in the next line, emphasizes that Horace's manhood demands revenge. The abl. is causal, depending on *dolitura.*

12. Flacco: Horace's cognomen. Though this is one of just four places where Horace mentions himself by name, there is no reason to believe that this poem is necessarily more autobiographical than any other by Horace. Fraenkel suggests that the note of acrimony expressed here "may be intended to render the tone somewhat Archilochian."

13. assiduas ... noctes: night after night. **potiori:** to a more favored rival (with an undertone of machismo, as if the rival were more forceful or better entitled to her favors).

14. parem: a calculated insult, implying that Neaera has a peer (or peers). But in the context of *mutuum* (10), it also suggests that his new partner will be *his* equal in affection—a promise Neaera has failed to keep. For this second meaning, cf. 1.33.10 and Propertius 1.1.32.

15. offensi: emended from the manuscript *offensae,* this gen. masc. reading makes better sense: my constancy, once I am offended, will not yield to (your) beauty, if a known cause for resentment (*certus dolor*) has entered in. Compare the case of Barine in 2.8, who thrives on perfidy. There, the point of view is comic and more typically Horatian: here, it is elegiac.

17-24. (to his conceited rival) As for you, however rich and handsome you may be, you'll be cast aside as well and it will be my turn to laugh.

17-18. meo ... malo: abl. of cause with *superbus,* haughty at my misfortune.

18. incedis: implies a proud and stately walk, like Juno's in Virgil *Aen.* 1.46, Cynthia's in Propertius 2.2.6 and 1.2.1: *Quid iuvat ornato procedere, vita, capillo;* cf. also *Epod.* 4.5, *licet superbus ambules pecunia.*

19. sis: concessive subj., with *licebit.*

20. Pactolus: the river in Lydia whose golden

sands are supposed to have provided the wealth of Midas.

21. nec te ... fallant: litotes: and you understand (well enough to reproduce). **Pythagorae ... renati:** the philosopher Pythagoras included among his *arcana* the claim that in an earlier incarnation he was Nireus, "the handsomest man of all the Greeks who came beneath Ilion, except Achilles" (*Il.* 2.673).

24. ast: archaic for *at*, an affectation more suitable to Virgilian epic, which Horace abandoned in his later work. **risero:** the fut. perf. represents the rival's comeuppance as good as done.

16

Horace's disaffection with Rome's civil wars provides the theme for this declamatory poem. In language that mimics the formulas of Greek and Roman legislatures, Horace proposes that the "better part" (15 and 37 *melior pars*) leave Rome and colonize some utopian "wealthy isles" set aside by Jupiter to preserve the age of gold. This escapist fantasy is rhetorical rather than practical in intent, inspired in part by Virgil's fourth eclogue hailing the return of a golden age. This epode, much praised for its polish, reflects the tradition of Archilochus (early seventh century B.C.), who made political discontent a poetic theme. It comes from the period between Horace's return in defeat from Philippi in 41 B.C. and his acceptance into the circle of Maecenas and Octavian. The meter is second pythiambic.

1-14. Another age of civil wars is doing to Rome what no foreign enemy could do. Beasts and barbarians will occupy the city, and the bones of Quirinus will be scattered.

1. Altera ... aetas: a second generation, the first having begun in the time of Marius and Sulla ca. 88 B.C. **teritur:** is being worn away.

3. finitimi ... Marsi: leaders of the so-called Social War of 91-88 B.C., when Italian cities

unwillingly allied to Rome revolted and tried to make Cornifinium the capital of Italy.

4. minacis ... Porsenae: Lars Porsena was the Etruscan war lord who took up the cause of the banished king Tarquin when the Romans first declared themselves a republic but (according to this version) failed to take the city.

5. aemula ... virtus Capuae: Capua's rival valor. After Rome's disastrous defeat by Hannibal at Cannae in 216 B.C., Capua went over to Hannibal and tried to make herself capital of Italy, but was reduced to a Roman prefecture in 211. **Spartacus acer:** leader of the slave revolt in 73-71 B.C.; 6,000 of his followers were crucified along the Appian Way.

6. Allobrox: collective singular. The Allobroges, a southern Gallic tribe, are called unfaithful in revolution because after betraying the conspirator Catiline they themselves revolted against Rome. Cicero, *In Cat.* 3.4.8, Sallust *Cat.* 40.

7. caerulea ... pube: blue-eyed youth, abl. with *fera* or *domuit*. Horace refers here to the invasion of the Cimbri and the Teutones, defeated in 102-101 B.C. For the word order, cf. lines 33 and 55 and see appendix C, golden line.

8. Hannibal: his nearly catastrophic invasion of Italy in the Second Punic War (218-201 B.C.) made him hateful to Roman parents. For the construction, cf. 1.1.24-5, *bellaque matribus detestata*.

9. impia ... aetas recalls the opening line, *altera ... aetas*. **devoti sanguinis**, gen. of description, suggests the fratricide of Romulus and Remus, which curses the Romans as a kind of original sin. Cf. *Epod.* 7.18, *scelus fraternae necis*.

11. cineres insistet: will stand upon our ashes (i.e., those of our city).

12. sonante ... ungula: with thundering hoof. Horace unconsciously echoes Ezekiel 26:11: "With the hoofs of his horses he will trample all your streets."

13. ossa Quirini: postponed antecedent of *quae*. Romulus (Quirinus) was reportedly entombed behind the Rostra in the Forum. His bones, like those of any hero, were thought to have a protective power for the city.

15-24. The best proposal is to follow the example of the ancient Phocaeans and go somewhere else.
15. expediat: subjunctive in ind. question, depending on *quaeritis.* Horace imagines himself addressing an assembly of his fellow Romans deliberating how to deal with the crisis. **aut melior pars:** the monosyllabic line ending emphasizes that Horace's concern is not so much with the rank and file as with the elite; cf. 37, *aut pars ... melior.*
16. carere ... laboribus: to be free from our troubles; infin. of purpose, completing the sense of *expediat.*
17. sit: jussive subjunctive. A **sententia** is a resolution; Horace is imitating the formal language of the Senate. **Phocaeorum,** giving the line a spondaic ending, is emphatic. Herodotus 1.165 reports that the Phocaeans abandoned their city to Persian rule and sailed away to their colony in Corsica, vowing not to return until an iron bar that they threw into the sea should float to the surface.
18. exsecrata: transitive deponent, having cursed.
21. quocumque ... quocumque: emphatic repetition, stressing that the Romans will be more daring than the Phocaeans: they set out not for anywhere, but specifically for Corsica. Moreover, Herodotus adds that most of them went back on their oath and returned to their city.
23. Sic placet: more senatorial language: it is so resolved?
23-24. Secunda ... alite: circumstantial abl., with favorable omen (as indicated by bird flight). Cf. *Epod.* 10.1, *mala ... alite.*

25-34. But let us swear never to return. This section is a catalog of seven *adynata* or impossibilities, a poetic way of emphasizing the idea of

"never." It balances the list of seven failed enemies of Rome in lines 3-8.
25. saxa rena(ve)rint: a variant of the iron bar oath reported by Herodotus.
26. ne ... sit nefas: litotic: let it be lawful. See appendix C, litotes.
27. neu ... pigeat: litotes again. **conversa domum ... dare lintea:** turn around (by shifting the sail) and sail homeward.
28. The **Padus,** being a river in northern Italy, could never wash the **Matina ... cacumina,** heights far to the south in Apulia.
29. celsus ... Appenninus: the Apennine range—the mountainous spine of the Italian peninsula—is far from the sea on both sides.
31. iuvet ut: anastrophe of the conjunction: so that it is a pleasure for tigers **subsidere cervis,** to crouch beneath stags for mating (the more impossible because the predator is submitting to its prey).
32. miluo: here trisyllabic. Another case of a predator, the hawk, mating with its prey, the pigeon or dove.
33. The language echoes Virgil's *Ecl.* 4.22, *nec magnos metuunt armenta leones.* For the word order, cf. lines 7 and 55.
34. lēvis hircus: like *credula* in the previous line, the adjective is proleptic, because the normally shaggy goat will become sleek like a sea animal only after it has entered the water. See appendix C, prolepsis.

35-42. Let the best of us seek out the happy fields, wealthy islands.
36. exsecrata: having secured these resolutions (*haec,* lines 25-34)—and whatever else can prevent our return—by curses. The participle agrees with *omnis civitas*; it repeats *exsecrata* in line 18, but is used in a different sense.
37. indocili melior grege: as often, Horace clearly displays his antipopulist sentiment; cf. 3.1.1, *Odi profanum vulgus et arceo.* **mollis et exspes:** flabby and demoralized.

38. **inominata**: a *hapax legomenon*, = *male ominata*, ill-starred. **perprimat**: rest continuously (*per-*) upon.

39. **Vos**, etc.: adversative asyndeton. But as for you who have *virtus*, away with (*tollite*) womanish grief.

40. **Etrusca praeter et**: complex poetic anastrophe for *et praeter Etrusca*. By metonymy, Etruscan shores = Italy.

41. **Oceanus circumvagus**: the old Homeric flat-earth cosmology with an Ocean surrounding the lands was by Horace's time purely poetic, but geographers still believed that the habitable lands were surrounded by sea, and the mythic tone suits Horace's fanciful proposal. Appropriately, *circumvagus* is a Horatian coinage.

41-42. **arva, beata ... arva**: the repetition and the hendiadys (*arva divites et insulas* for fields *of* the wealthy isles) contribute to the rhapsodic spell Horace is trying to weave. Homer placed his Elysian Fields in the underworld (*Od.* 4.563ff.); Hesiod's Isles of the Blessed (*W&D* 170ff.) are by the streams of the Ocean, identified in later Roman thought with the Canaries or the Madeira Islands.

43-62. **The blessings of the new land.** This third and longest catalog is a well-known "Age of Gold" topos, featuring the spontaneous fruitfulness of nature and the innocence of man. It is essentially an expansion of Hesiod *W&D* 172-3, with details roughly comparable to those in Virgil's fourth eclogue, lines 18-45.

43. **Cererem**: grain, by metonymy.

44. **imputata**: unpruned. The root meaning of *puto* is to tidy up; cf. *amputans* in *Epod.* 2.13.

45. **numquam fallentis ... olivae**: the never failing (lit. deceiving) olive. Cf. 3.1.30, *fundus mendax*. **termes**: branch.

46. **suam ... arborem**: with emphasis on *suam*, because in real life the better varieties of fig were produced only by grafting to another tree. None of that will be necessary in the new land. **pulla ficus**:

the drab fig is a ripe one, having ripened from a bright green to a duller, darker color.

47. **mella ... manant**, etc.: the liquid *m, l, n* sounds contrast with the *c*'s of *cava ... ilice* to capture the effect of soft honey in the hard oak.

48. **levis crepante**, etc.: more sound effects, consisting of alternate *l* and *p* sounds (the *h* in *lympha* is weak) to suggest running and plashing water. **crepante ... pede**: giving water a splashing foot extends the metaphor of *desilit*; cf. Lucretius 5.272, *liquido pede detulit undas*.

49. **mulctra**: milking pails.

50. **tenta**: for *distenta*; cf. *Epod.* 2.46, *distenta ubera*.

51. **nec**: from here to the end of the catalog, the advantages of the *divites insulae* are expressed by a series of ten negatives, emphasizing the theme of escape. **vespertinus**: adverbial, at evening. The sequence of three spondees lends a sinister effect. **ovile**: the sheepfold.

52. **intumescit alta viperis**: swell high with vipers. The swelling of the vipers is transferred to the ground they infest.

53. **ut**: how, with *mirabimur*.

54. **aquosus Eurus**: the east wind is rainy because of the weather it brings. **radat**: erode.

55. Same word order as 33.

56. **utrumque rege temperante**: causal abl. absolute: because the king of the gods restrains both (rain and draught).

57. **pinus**: by metonymy, a ship **Argoö remige**, with oarage or oarsmen of the Argo. In the Hellenistic tradition, the exploits of legend are symptomatic of man's fallen state. For this example, cf. Virgil *Ecl.* 4.34f.

57-60. **contendit, impudica, torserunt, laboriosa** contrast the hasty, straining pushiness of the Bronze Age heroes with the happy ease of the *divites insulae*.

58. **Colchis**: the shameless Colchian is Medea.

59. **Sidonii ... nautae**: Phoenician sailors were the most daring in antiquity, the archetype of enterprise at sea. **torserunt cornua**: turned their

yardarms (so as to direct their ships), as in Virgil *Aen.* 3.549, 5.831f: *una ardua torquent cornua detorquentque.*

61-62. nullius astri ... aestuosa ... impotentia: no constellation's blazing fury, i.e., the hot weather that came with the rising of such summer constellations as the *canicula* or dog star. Cf. 1.17.17, *hic in reducta valle Caniculae vitabis aestus.*

63-66. Jupiter set those shores aside as a haven for the just; with me as prophet, there is a refuge.
64. ut inquinavit, etc.: when he debased the Golden Age with bronze. Horace leaves out the Silver Age mentioned by Hesiod. The ages grow harder and crueller as harder and baser metals are mixed in.
65-66. quorum ... secunda ... fuga: from which (worse ages) a happy escape is offered. Some readers detect a note of ironic despair here, as a purely poetic escape is not enough. **vate me:** abl. abs.; Horace revived the archaic notion of the poet-prophet as representing the high seriousness of his calling. For the use of *vates* instead of *poeta,* see note on 1.1.35.

17

Canidia, the more or less fictitious witch whom Horace mocked in *Sat.* 1.8 and Epode 5, is supplicated here with a mock apology. In reply, she lashes back with a savage refusal to have mercy. In this ironic palinode or recantation, Horace finds ways of repeating some of his past libels, while she in her fury repeats others. Meter: iambic trimeter.

1-7. By all the powers of magic I beg you, Canidia, undo your spells!
1. do manus: I yield. Defeated soldiers threw down their weapons and held out their hands to be bound. **scientiae** is ironic, as if Canidia's crude spells were based on anything more than ignorant superstition.

2. supplex et = *et supplex:* for this high-sounding displacement of the copula, cf. *per et* (3) and *per atque* (4). Throughout his address to Canidia (1-52) Horace subtly parodies the usages of elevated rhetoric. Cf. also **regna per** for *per regna.*
3. Dianae ... numina: the feminine powers of nature on earth, as Proserpina's are those of the underworld. Diana's usual name as the goddess invoked by witchcraft was Hecate: "Witchcraft celebrates pale Hecat's offerings" (Shakespeare *Macb.* 2.1.51). See note on *Odes* 3.22.4, where her epithet *triformis* reflects more universal powers (underworld, earth, sky).
5. devocare completes the sense of *valentium* in the preceding line: spells powerful [enough] to call down. **refixa ... devocare,** another poeticism, is ornamental redundancy. She is able to unhinge and call down stars.
6. Canidia: trisyllabic. **vocibus ... sacris,** dat. with *parce,* is a mocking euphemism for the gibberish she babbles as she whirls her *turbo.*
7. citum ... turbinem: the rhombus or *turbo* was a common piece of magical paraphernalia. Sometimes called a bull-roarer, it is "an oblong or diamond-shaped piece of wood or metal, to the point of which a cord is attached. When swung in a circle, the instrument emits a muttering roar which rises in pitch as the speed increases" (A.S.F. Gow on Theocritus 2.30). **retro solve,** probably magical jargon, suggests she should reverse the direction in which she is whirling her *turbo* and undo her evil spell.

8-18. Achilles took pity on his former enemy Telephus, and gave back to Priam the corpse of murderous Hector. Circe undid the magic that turned Ulysses' men to swine.
8. nepotem ... Nereïum parodies Hellenistic allusiveness by naming Achilles only as "the Nerean grandson," i.e., the grandson of Nereus. Telephus, king of the Mysians, wounded by Achilles during the siege of Troy, was told by the oracle of Apollo that his festering wound could be healed only by

the rust of Achilles' spear. His successful appeal to Achilles was dramatized in Euripides' *Telephus.* Achilles figures in the first two of Horace's persuasive exemplars because this part of the Epode loosely imitates the supplication to Achilles in Homer's *Iliad*, Book 9.

11. matres Iliae: the Trojan mothers; for the adj., cf. *Carm. Saec.* 37f., *Iliae turmae.* **addictum feris**: adversative, though he had been consigned to wild birds. Achilles was so angry when Hector killed his companion Patroclus that he at first refused to hand him over for a decent burial.

12. homicidam Hectorem translates Homer's formula ῞Εκτορος ἀνδροφόνοιο. In this metrically unusual line, the first foot is a spondee with the second syllable resolved, and the longum is resolved into two brevia in the third and fourth iambs.

13. rex: Hector's father Priam. The story of his supplication to Achilles in Book 24 is a moment of great pathos in the *Iliad*, as reflected by Horace's interjection *heu* in the next line.

15-17. Saetosa ... membra: the limbs of Ulysses' oarsmen were bristly because they had been turned into swine by the sorceress Circe. **exuere** (perf. indic.) takes the acc. of the thing laid bare and the abl. of the thing removed (*duris pellibus*). **laboriosi ... Ulixeï**, long-suffering Ulysses, corresponds to Homer's epithet πολύτλας 'Οδυσσεύς. **volente Circa** is abl. abs., like *Deo volente.* But Circe was willing because Odysseus threatened to kill her (*Od.* 10.321-345), an irony that would not be lost on Horace's readers. **sonus**: speech.

18. notus ... honor: the familiar grace of their human features.

19-26. I have suffered enough: my youth has fled, my body is an exhausted ruin.

19. For the caesura after the short syllable of the fourth iamb (after *superque*), cf. 38 and 60.

20. amata ... institoribus: like the traveling salesman of American humor, the *institor* or peddler was a notorious philanderer. Cf. 3.6.30.

21. verecundus color: the modest blush of youth.

22. pelle ... lurida: with a sallow hide. Canidia's persecution has left him skin and bones.

23. odoribus: perfumes laced with toxins that have made his hair white. For perfume as a vehicle for magical potions, cf. *Epod.* 5.59.

24. me reclinat: gives me respite.

25-26. neque est levare: a Greek idiom. It is not [possible] to restore my chest **tenta spiritu**, stretched with sighing or gasping.

27-35. I take back what I said about your spells. What more do you want? I burn in torment, and you will burn me to an ash.

27. negatum vincor ut credam: I am compelled to believe what I denied.

28-29. Sabella ... carmina, Marsa ... nenia: different kinds of magical incantations. For Sabellian or Sabine witches, cf. *Sat.* 1.9.30ff.; Canidia is scornful of Marsian folk magic in *Epod.* 5.76, though it was regarded as capable of splitting snakes if not heads: Lucilius 512, *Marsus colubras disrumpit cantu.* **nenia**, sometimes a dirge (2.20.21) or a gentle evening song (3.28.16), here a magical *carmen.*

31. quantum neque: litotes for *magis quam.* **delibutus**: smeared. The centaur Nessus, mortally wounded by Hercules for having tried to rape his wife Deianira, gave her a vial of his poisonous blood, telling her it was a love philter. Later put to use when Hercules takes a new mistress Iole, it causes Hercules to die in burning agony. The story is dramatized in Sophocles' *Women of Trachis.*

32-33. Sicana ... flamma: chiastic word order. The Sicilian flame thriving on burning Etna is its volcanic activity. Its first known eruption, in 475 B.C., was described by Pindar and Aeschylus. It is Europe's highest and most active volcano.

35. cales ... officina: i.e., you are as hot as a forge. Governs the preceding subj. *donec ... ferar*, indicating intention. **officina**, in apposition with *tu* (33), is an ironworking shop as in 1.4.8, *gravis*

Cyclopum Volcanus ardens visit officinas.

36-41. Tell me what I must do to set things right: I will even sing your praises.
36. stipendium: tax or tribute, like that levied on conquered states to pay the cost of their occupation.
37. fide: abl. of manner with adverbial force, faithfully. **poenas luam:** pay the penalty for defaming Canidia.
39. mendaci lyra leaves it unclear whether his poetic "lyre" was mendacious when he defamed her, or will be when he recants.
40-41. The midpoint of the poem is Horace's ironic recantation, consisting of two allusions to Catullus. For **pudica ... proba,** cf. Catullus' ironic praise of the *putida moecha* who refuses to return his tablets in poem 42, *Pudica et proba, redde codicillos!* (24). For the prophecy that Canidia will be transformed into a *sidus aureum,* cf. Catullus 66.60-64.

42-48. As Castor and Pollux revoked their curse on the poet Stesichorus, you can free me from maddening torment.
42. Infamis Helenae: gen. with *vicem,* lit. on account of disgraced Helen. **vicem** is an adverbial acc. depending on **offensus,** though he was offended.
43. frater: Pollux. Cf. Catullus 4.27, *gemelle Castor et gemelle Castoris.*
44. vati: the story is that after the Greek poet Stesichorus wrote about Helen's scandalous escapade with Paris, her half-divine brothers caused him to go blind; when he took back his libels in another poem, the Dioscuri (as they were also called) restored the poet's sight. Horace cites this as precedent for Canidia to revoke her curses on him.
46-48. By appearing to deny these rumors about Canidia, Horace gives them additional exposure, taking away with one hand what he appears to concede with the other. **paternis ... sordibus:** her

filth is in part inherited, according to the rumor here denied. **prudens ... dissipare:** skilled at scattering the **novendiales ...pulveres** of paupers who had no one to keep an eye on their ashes. Last rites were completed nine days after death; these would then be just buried.

49-52. Kind of heart and pure of hand, you are truly a mother.
49-50. tibi, tuus: sc. *est* or *sunt.* Pactumeius, otherwise unknown, is here acknowledged as the *bona fide* son of Canidia, the common belief being that witches were barren and only pretended by various frauds to have children of their own (cf. *Epod.* 5.5-6). Thus **tuo** is emphatic: the blood with which the midwife wets her towels is yours (not some chicken's).
52. fortis exsilis immediately undercuts the affirmation of Canidia's motherhood by having her leap up after childbirth in a suspiciously hearty condition (*fortis*).

53-59. Canidia replies: "How dare you plead for mercy after making fun of my sex orgies and filling the city with my name?
53. Quid ... fundis: why do you pour your prayers?
54. nudis ... navitis: unprotected, shipwrecked sailors.
55. Neptunus: by metonymy, the sea, as **salo** is the sea.
56. Inultus ut tu riseris, etc.: subjunctive in a repudiating question: to think that you would mock unpunished; so also *ut ... imple(ve)ris* (59).
56-57. Cotyttia vulgata: a so-called *ab urbe condita* construction, meaning the divulgence of the rites of Cotyto. Only women were admitted to the orgiastic rites of the Thracian goddess Cotyto, which men suspected were sexually licentious (*sacrum liberi Cupidinis*).
58. pontifex venefici: i.e., as if you were the high priest of Esquiline potion-making.

60-69. "Why do you think I have poisons? Yours will be a slow and painful death, and you will pray for relief as if you were Tantalus, Prometheus, or Sisyphus.

60. Quid proderit: what will it have profited me. **Paelignas anus:** crones from Paelignia, central Italian neighbors of the Marsi and like them adept in sorcery.

61. velocius ... toxicum: a faster, more potent poison.

62. tardiora ... votis: more lingering than you will pray for. **te ... manent:** are in store for you.

63. in hoc: for this purpose, as explained in the following *ut*-clause. The absence of a caesura in this line is very unusual.

64. suppetas: be available.

65. Pelopis ... pater: Tantalus, founder of the dynasty that would later produce Atreus, Agamemnon, and Orestes. In 1.28.7 he is *Pelopis genitor*, in 2.13.37 *Pelopis parens*. Pelops is *infidus* because he murdered the charioteer who helped him win the hand of Hippodameia. Cf. Catullus 64.346, *periuri Pelopis*.

65-68. Optat ... optat ... optat: mythic precedents for what Horace can expect to suffer, and their prayers for respite. Tantalus is suspended in a pool, always out of reach of needed food and drink; Prometheus is **obligatus aliti**, assigned to the vulture who eats at his liver; Sisyphus is assigned to a rock that always rolls out of control just as he is about to finish pushing it up a mountain.

70-75. "You will want to kill yourself, and I will ride in triumph on your shoulders.

71. ense ... Norico: Noricum, a territory roughly corresponding to mod. Austria (see map 2), produced a fine steel used in weaponry. Cf. 1.16.9, *Noricus ensis*.

73. fastidiosa tristis aegrimonia: depressed by tiresome grief. For bracketing word order in a three-word line, cf. lines 16, 48, 61.

74. eques: like a rider or equestrian; cf. the scene in Plautus' *Asinaria* 698ff., where the slave Libanus makes his master's son carry him around. Canidia likes to put on airs, as *insolentiae* in the next line admits. Iambs are resolved into tribrachs in the second and fourth feet of this line.

76-81. "With all my powers of magic, does it seem likely that my art will fail against you?"

76-81. An quae ... possim ... plorem: subjunctive in a repudiating question: would I, who am able to move wax figurines (of my voodoo victims), etc., complain about the outcome of my art?

77-78. polo deripere lunam: charm the moon down from the sky, as witches were supposed to do. Cf. Propertius 1.1.19, *vos, deductae quibus est fallacia lunae*. **vocibus ... meis:** with my words.

79. crematos excitare mortuos: i.e., raise the dead.

80. temperare: mix or blend love potions, **desideri ... pocula.** Epode 5 tells how Canidia prepares to brew such a potion out of the liver of a boy she has stolen.

81. agentis exitus: the poem (and the book) ends with Canidia's hissing speech.

1

The opening poem of *Odes* 1-3, published together in 23 B.C., is addressed to Horace's patron Maecenas, but except for the opening two lines it focuses on the poet himself. A long priamel lists other occupations and pleasures that put his own calling as poet into perspective. The poem ends with a prediction of his immortality. Meter: first Asclepiadean.

1-10. Some, Maecenas, like chariot racing at Olympia; this man loves politics, that one the grain market.

1. Maecenas: see appendix A. His name became a synonym for a patron of literature as early as the time of Martial, a century later. **atavis ... regibus:** royal stock, with **atavis** used substantively in the general sense of remote ancestors and **regibus** adjectivally, as in Virgil *Aen.* 1.273 *regina sacerdos*, a royal priestess. Maecenas traced his lineage back to the old Etruscan kings of Arretium (mod. Arezzo; see map 2), but preferred to remain a knight rather than be advanced to senatorial rank. Cf. 3.16.20, *Maecenas, equitum decus*.

2. o: hiatus occurs regularly after the interjections *o* and *a*. **praesidium,** bulwark, acknowledges the material and moral support of Maecenas; **dulce decus,** my cherished glory, honors the prestige of Maecenas' patronage.

3. sunt quos begins the priamel that focuses on *me*, line 29. For more about the priamel and other technical terms, see appendix C. **curriculo:** on the racing chariot, strictly speaking an instrumental abl. **pulverem Olympicum,** referring to the games held every four years, also suggests Greek games in general, like *labor Isthmius* (4.3.3). For particularizing adjectives, see appendix C, synecdoche, and note on *trabe Cypria* (line 13 below).

4. collegisse: subject (with *meta*) of *iuvat*; perfect tense, with present force. **meta ... evitata:** i.e., the act of clearing the turning point on the racecourse. For the participial idiom, cf. the common phrases *post urbem conditam* (after the founding of the city)

and *post reges exactos* (after the expulsion of the kings). The races regularly circled a long, low stone *spina* or "thorn," with a *meta* at each end consisting of a pier surmounted by three columns. Winning drivers had to round these ends at high speed (*fervidis rotis*). The excitement of such races is caught in a famous scene of the 1959 film *Ben Hur*.

5. palma: subject of *evehit*; the custom of placing a palm branch in the hands of the Olympic victor was adopted by the Romans in 293 B.C. **nobilis** = illustrious in the causative sense, because it makes its winner a celebrity.

6. terrarum dominos: ambiguously constructed to be read (a) in apposition with *quos,* the understood object of *evehit:* the victory exalts them as masters of the lands, and (b) in apposition with *deos.* Cf. the winning charioteers in 4.2.17, *quos Elea* [= *Olympica*] *domum reducit palma caelestis.* Roman interest in the Olympic games was keen. Germanicus and Tiberius, before he became emperor, competed in chariot races there. Nero tried to drive a ten-horse chariot and was awarded the victory even though he did not finish.

7. hunc: object of *iuvat,* line 4. **mobilium,** fickle, and **turba,** mob, express a typically Horatian distaste for popular politics. In *Epist.* 1.19.37 Horace characterizes the *plebs* as *ventosa,* fickle as the wind.

8. certat: strives. **tergeminis ... honoribus:** the triple honors are the offices of curule aedile, praetor, and consul.

9. illum: dependent (like *hunc* in line 7) upon *iuvat,* to be supplied in thought. **proprio ... horreo:** his own granary (as opposed to a state granary), with emphasis on *proprio.* **condidit:** has stored away. The type referred to here is a commodities trader, acquiring large supplies of grain and holding it until the market price is high.

10. quicquid: i.e., the entire harvest; he wants to corner the market. Cf. 3.16.26f., *si quicquid arat impiger Apulus occultare meis dicerer horreis.* **Libycis:** Africa was at this time one of the main sources of the Roman grain supply. Horace repeatedly alludes to the fertility of this district, e.g., 3.16.31 *fertilis Africae*; *Sat.* 2.3.87, *frumenti quantum metit Africa*, as much grain as Africa reaps. **verritur areis:** the threshing floor (*area*) was a circular paved space on which the grain was trampled out by cattle. It was then winnowed by being tossed in the wind with shovels until the chaff was blown away, and then swept up (*verritur*). The same process may be seen today in some parts of Greece and the orient.

11-18. The happy farmer cannot be tempted to go to sea, while the merchant fears the sea but soon repairs his ships because he cannot bear poverty.

11. Gaudentem seems at first to continue the *hunc ... illum* construction of the previous sentence, but turns out to be the object of *dimoveas* (13). **findere:** the clods are so hard that they have to be split and the field is so small that it is cultivated with a hoe (*sarculo*) rather than plowed; yet the man cannot be lured from his inherited plot of poor ground. The hard-working farmer, like the man who relaxes outdoors in 19-22, is seen more favorably than the grain speculator (9-10) or the *mercator* (15-18).

12. Attalicis condicionibus: the terms of an Attalus, like a king's ransom, would be a sum beyond the dreams of avarice. Attalus was the name of several kings of Pergamon in Asia Minor whose wealth, like that of Croesus, was legendary. In 133 B.C. Attalus III bequeathed his kingdom and his treasures to the Roman people.

13. dimoveas: pry loose, turn away. **ut ... secet:** to plow the sea instead of his field; depends on *dimoveas*, which functions as a verb of persuading. **trabe Cypria:** Cyprus (see map 1) was famous for shipbuilding; it was said that the island could furnish the material for building a ship from keel to masthead, with all its rigging and equipment. Horace follows the usual poetic practice of using a particularizing adjective; cf. 14 and 15 (*Myrtoum, Icariis*). This phrase combines metonymy with

synecdoche to make the description more vivid. For more about these terms and techniques, see appendix C.

14. Myrtoum: the Myrtoan sea, between the Peloponnesus and the Cyclades, was proverbially stormy. **pavidus nauta:** as a frightened sailor, in apposition with the subject of *secet*, the farmer described in line 11.

15. Luctantem: the wind, wrestling with the waves, is almost personified. **Icariis fluctibus:** another stormy body of water, in the Aegean Sea between Samos and Mykonos and connected by legend with the fall of Icarus. The construction is dat. with *luctantem*, a Grecism. **Africum:** the southwest wind, blowing up from Africa.

16. otium et oppidi rura sui: i.e., the peace and quiet of his home town and the surrounding countryside. Horace continues to build his case for the simple rustic life.

17. mox: i.e., soon after the storm that made him wish he was home. **rates quassas:** his damaged (lit. shattered) ships; poetic for *naves*.

18. pauperiem: poverty but not destitution, moderate circumstances as opposed to affluence. Horace is gently mocking the unwillingness of the *mercator* to take life as it comes. **pati:** completing the sense of *indocilis*, untaught to endure. This *mercator*, like the *faenerator Alfius* in Epode 2, is a compulsive hustler, representing a way of life that is anathema to Horace's values. For other anti-mercantile sentiments, cf. 1.31.11, 3.24.40.

19-28. Relaxation, war, and hunting attract others.

19-21. est qui ... spernit: One there is who does not scorn, perhaps Horace himself. The words are significantly placed at the midpoint of the ode. **Massici:** sc. *vini*. Synecdoche, like *Cypria* in line 13 and *Marsus* in 28. One of the famous Italian wines, made from grapes grown on Mons Massicus in northern Campania.

20. solido ... de die: *solidus dies* was the business day, extending from the early morning to the end of the ninth hour, i.e., to about 3:00 P.M.; to use a part of it for revelry was *de die potare* (Plautus *Asinaria* 825); cf. *Sat.* 2.8.3 *de medio potare die.* Here the time out is for loafing. **demere:** take away, subtract, object of *spernit.*

21. spernit: zeugma, taking both a noun object (*pocula*) and an infinitive object (*demere*). **membra:** object of *stratus*, stretching, here used with reflexive or middle force. **arbuto:** sometimes called strawberry tree because of the look of its berries, the arbutus was prized for its shade.

22. aquae ... sacrae: chiastic word order. The sacred spring has connotations of poetic inspiration going back to Hesiod *Theog.* 6, and appears regularly with that sense in Hellenistic poetry: Callimachus *Hymn to Apollo* 112, Alcaeus A.P. 7.55.5-6 (GP 12), Asclepiades A.P. 9.64.5 (GP 45). Cf. Lucretius 1.926-28.

23. lituo: for *litui sonitu*, probably abl. The *lituus*, used by cavalry, was a long straight horn, curved at the end; the *tuba*, an infantry trumpet, was straight throughout.

24. matribus: dat. of agent, a construction found even in prose with the perfect passive participle.

25. detestata: the deponent is here used passively like *modulate*, played, in 1.32.5 and *abominatus*, detested, in *Epod.* 16.8. **Manet:** stays out, spends the night. **Iove:** here equivalent (by metonymy) to *caelo.* Originally a sky and weather god, Jupiter is synonymous in poetry with both. The root *Iov-* (Indo-European *$d(i)ieu$-, Skt. *dyaúh*) originally meant sky, light. Latin *dies*, day, is the same word; cf. *Diespiter*, archaic and poetic for *Iuppiter.*

26. venator: the hunter. **tenerae:** young (as often).

27. catulis: hounds, fondly called pups. **cerva:** a deer.

28. teretes ... plagas: close-twisted nets. **Marsus:** synecdoche again; the form is a poetic variant of *Marsicus.* The Marsi inhabited a mountainous district of central Italy, about fifty miles east of Rome. **aper:** wild boar, prized by Roman gourmets and as a consequence much hunted.

29-36. As for me, poetry makes me like a god and distinguishes me from the mob if the muses give their aid. Rank me with the lyric poets, and my head will strike the stars.

29. Me: emphatically placed to introduce the climax of the ode, namely Horace's own aspiration. For this characteristic feature of Horatian style, cf. 1.5.13, 1.16.22, 1.31.15f., 2.12.13, 2.17.13, 4.1.29. **doctarum ... frontium:** poetry was conceived as a cerebral art; *doctus* was applied to one who had achieved distinction in philosophy, art, or letters. Catullus, for example, was often honored with this epithet after his death. **hederae:** nom., in apposition with *praemia.* Ivy was sacred to Bacchus, one of the patrons of poetry.

30. dis miscent: link me with the gods; cf. 5, *evehit ad deos*; for the case of *dis*, see note on 23, *lituo.* **gelidum nemus:** the cool grove is a type of the *locus amoenus*, far from the madding crowd and often linked in Horace's poetry to his creativity.

31. leves ... chori: light-footed bands of dancers or singers.

32. secernunt populo: set me apart from the common herd. For this Horatian attitude, cf. 3.1.1, *odi profanum vulgus.* **tibias:** two *tibiae* were regularly played together, fastened to a single mouthpiece. One was held in each hand.

33. Euterpe: the muse of music and lyric poetry, which was originally composed for singing to a musical instrument. Euterpe is represented in art with flutes in her hands. **cohibet:** withhold. **Polyhymnia**, another muse of poetry, particularly hymns to the gods. Here the muses are appropriate, but often their attributes are not sharply defined.

34. Lesboum ... barbiton: the lyre of the Lesbian poets Sappho and Alcaeus (ca. 600 B.C.). These were two of Horace's chief models in the composition of his lyric poems (as suggested by the names of his two favorite meters). **tendere:** to stretch or tighten the strings, hence to tune. The infinitive with *refugere*, refuse, is poetic; cf. *demere* (20). *barbiton* is Gk. acc.

35. lyricis vatibus inseres: i.e., if you rank me among the lyric poets of Greece, probably the nine Greek lyric poets of the Hellenistic canon. Horace sees his importance in literature as an introducer of the Greek lyric medium into Latin. This is made explicit in 3.30.13f., *princeps Aeolium carmen ad Italos deduxisse modos*. Originally meaning seer or prophet, *vates* was the earliest word for poet among the Romans. It gave place to the Greek *poeta*, ποιητής, but was revived by Virgil and Horace because of their interest in poetry as a medium of moral discourse and political exhortation. Cf. *Epod.* 16.66, *vate me*.

36. sublimi feriam sidera vertice: a proverbial phrase from the Greek, paraphrased in Ben Jonson's *Sejanus*, 5.1.8:

> And at each step I feel my advanced head
> Knock out a star in heaven.

Such hyperbolic affirmations of his immortality occur elsewhere in Horace: 2.20, 3.30.

2

Horace zealously adopted the role of court poet, seizing opportunities to sound every note of personal adulation, public urgency, and moral reform that his partisanship to Octavian suggested. The prominence in this book of odes that Horace gives this panegyric, hinting that the princeps is a god in human form, suggests the importance to Horace of his place near the center of power. The ode has been variously dated from 30 to 27 B.C.; it is often compared to Virgil's first Georgic, sometimes to Horace's disadvantage. Meter: Sapphic strophe.

1-12. Already Jove has sent enough dire portents; people fear a second flood will inundate the world.
1. terris: ind. object of *misit*. **nivis:** partitive gen. of *nix*, with *satis*. Snow is not unusual in central Italy in the winter months, though it rarely sticks; but an especially severe storm might seem a portent. **dirae:** i.e., portentous, to be taken with

both *nivis* and *grandinis* (hail).
2. pater: i.e., Jupiter, father of gods and men. **rubente:** glowing from the lightning he wields. Classical color terms are often imprecise: cf. Pindar's Δία τε φοινικοστερόπαν (Ol. 9.6).
3. sacras ... arces: the sacred hilltops, in particular the two summits of the Capitoline: the northern, or *Arx* proper, and the southern with the temple of Jupiter, Juno, and Minerva. **iaculatus:** here transitive, striking.
4-5. terruit ... terruit: such connection of clauses by anaphora is a favorite device of Horace. It also contributes to the dire mood Horace is setting in the first half of this poem.
5. gentis: mankind, all the races of the earth. **grave ne rediret:** the clause depends on the idea of fear involved in *terruit*. In poetry, words that ordinarily stand first are frequently postponed; so here *ne*; cf. *omne cum*, line 7, *piscium et* (9), *Prece qua* (26), *quam ... circum* (34), and see appendix C, anastrophe.
6. saeculum: age. **Pyrrhae:** wife of the classical Noah figure Deucalion. All mankind, except Deucalion and Pyrrha, had been destroyed by a flood. The flooding of the Tiber on January 16-17, 27 B.C. (see stanza four below) suggested fears of a second deluge. The length and detail of the Pyrrha digression, in which many readers see a note of humor, tends to undercut the seriousness with which the ode begins. **nova monstra:** acc. obj. of *questae*, strange portents, explained by the following clauses; *monstrum*, from *moneo*, means originally a warning or sign. The portents that preceded the death of Caesar were described in Plutarch's biography and Shakespeare's *JC* 1.3.3ff.
7. Proteus: the prophetic old man of the sea, visited by Menelaus in Homer *Od.* 4.384-570. **pecus:** Proteus' herd of seals.
8. visere: poetic infinitive of purpose.
9. summa ... ulmo: generalizing singular, the elm-tops. Dat. with *haesit*.
10. nota ... sedes ... columbis: the usual home for doves.

11. **superiecto:** lit. spread over the earth, i.e., overwhelming it. The emphasis of the clause rests on this word. Note also the interlocked order, a favorite arrangement in Horace.

12. **dammae:** lit. does, deer by metonymy.

13-24. We have seen the Tiber flood the Forum, calling itself Ilia's avenger. Our youth will hear of civil war instead of foreign conquest.

13. **flavum:** the regular epithet of the Tiber, made yellowish brown by alluvial mud.

14. **litore Etrusco:** The meaning of this is much disputed. Porphyrio and many modern editors refer to the belief that Tiber floods were the result of strong winds retarding its exit into the sea, and interpret *litore Etrusco* as the sea coast north of the Tiber. Others understand the Etruscan *litus* as the right or western bank of the Tiber. Just above the Island the river makes a sharp turn, so that the water seemed to be hurled back (*retortis*) from the bank opposite the city through the Velabrum to the Forum.

15. **deiectum:** to overthrow. Supine in *-um*, showing purpose. **monumenta regis:** a poetic plural. The so-called king's memorial was the *Regia* or official residence of the Pontifex Maximus at the southeastern end of the Forum. It was thought to date from the time of King Numa. Since the Forum was on low land, the Tiber sometimes rose high enough to flood the ground on which the Regia stood.

16. **templaque Vestae:** the round temple of Vesta near the Regia. For the plural, cf. *monumenta* in line 15.

17. **Iliae:** known also as Rhea Silvia, a Vestal Virgin and mother of Romulus and Remus. As punishment for breaking her vow of virginity, Ilia was killed by drowning in the Tiber; Horace has it that the river god made her his wife. Hence the flood is represented as intended to avenge her unjust execution and the assassination of her descendant, Julius Caesar. **dum se ... iactat:** boasting that he the *ultor*; the *dum*-clause explains the

preceding *ire deiectum.* **nimium:** vehemently, without the notion of excess.

18-19. **sinistra ... ripa:** over its eastern bank; abl. of the way by which. **vagus ... labitur:** gliding far and wide; *labitur* is part of the *dum*-clause, and *vagus* (lit. drifting) has adverbial force.

19. **ux-/orius amnis:** husbands who are overattentive to their wives are still called uxorious. The river god is too willing to gratify Ilia's vehemence. For hyphenation in *synapheia*, see appendix B on the Sapphic strophe and the definition in appendix C.

21. **audiet:** the subject is *iuventus*. **civis acuisse ferrum:** i.e., prepared for civil war. *Civis* is emphatic, fellow-citizens, or citizen ... against citizen. **acuisse:** whetted, related to *acer*.

22. **Persae:** The Persian empire had long since been destroyed by Alexander the Great, but to dramatize their eastern wars the Augustan poets apply the names *Persae* and *Medi* to the Parthians. The Romans first ran afoul of this loose confederation of tribes in 53 B.C., when Crassus was disastrously defeated at Carrhae. Though subsequently twice defeated in battle (39 and 38 B.C.), the Parthians remained hostile, but Horace patriotically exaggerates the threat they posed. **melius perirent:** had better perished; subjunctive of unfulfilled obligation.

23. **audiet:** for the repetition, see note on *terruit*, line 4. **pugnas:** battles too, besides mere preparations (*acuisse ferrum*). **vitio:** because of the sins, lit. fault; to be taken with *rara*, which here has the force of made fewer, diminished.

24. **rara iuventus:** the younger generation, thinned out by the civil wars started by their corrupted parents.

25-32. Whom shall the people call upon? What prayer should the Vestals make, and whom will Jupiter summon? Come at last, we pray, Apollo.

25. **ruentis:** falling, with the idea of rushing into ruin. Cf. *Epod.* 16.2, *suis ipsa Roma viribus ruit*.

26. **rebus:** the fortunes of the empire; dat. with

vocet, call upon (on behalf of). **Prece:** rarely used in the singular. **qua:** for the post-position, see on line 5. **fatigent:** importune with prayers for aid.

27. virgines sanctae: the Vestal Virgins. **minus** has the force of a negative. Vesta, offended by the assassination of Julius Caesar, her *pontifex maximus*, is deaf to their entreaties.

28. carmina: litanies; their prayer is in verse form.

29. partis: in the plural, duty or role.

30. Tandem: at last, since prayers have been in vain.

31. nube ... amictus: veiling your radiant shoulders in a cloud; a middle or reflexive construction. *Amicio* is lit. throw around (*am- + iacio*; for *am-* cf. *ambi-* in *ambit*, 1.35.5).

32. augur Apollo: the god of prophecy. According to Suetonius (*Aug.* 94.4), Augustus was thought to be the son of Apollo, and the god was credited with assisting him at the battle of Actium. Augustus did much to promote the worship of Apollo; in 28 B.C. he had a magnificent temple erected to him on the Palatine (referred to in 1.31). Horace plays often on the Augustus/Apollo theme. For the epithet *augur* as adjective, cf. *atavis regibus* (1.1.1).

33-44. Or will you help us, Venus, or you, Mars, or Mercury changed to the form of a youth, ready to be called Caesar's avenger?

33. sive tu = *vel tu, si*. **Erycina ridens:** the smiling lady of Eryx is Venus, so-called because of the temple dedicated to her on Mt. Eryx in Sicily (supposedly by Aeneas, *Aen.* 5.759, but more likely by Phoenicians to their goddess Astarte). She is invoked here as the ancestress of the Roman people, and especially of the Julian family.

34. quam ... circum: anastrophe, not uncommon with disyllabic prepositions. **Iocus:** Mirth personified.

35. genus et nepotes = *genus nepotum*, the race of your descendants.

36. auctor: Mars, founder of the Roman race.

37. heu: to be joined closely in thought with *nimis longo*. **satiate:** glutted, vocative by attraction to *auctor*, though logically in agreement with the subject of *respicis*. **ludo:** our game, as if civil war has become the Roman national sport.

38. iuvat: pleases. **clamor:** the battle cry (from *clamo*). **lēves:** polished; note the quantity.

39. acer ... vultus: the hostile glare. **Marsi** is Faber's correction for *Mauri*; the Moors were famous as cavalrymen, not infantrymen, while the Marsians were among the flower of the Roman infantry. For their location, see 1.1.28, note. The Marsian name makes them appropriate favorites of the war god Mars.

41. mutata ... figura: abl. absolute, changing your form to that of Mercury. **iuvenem ... imitaris:** i.e., take on the form of a young man, the usual image of Mercury, who may even now be present on earth in the form of young Octavian. Mercury is no doubt brought in here as patron of trade and commerce, peaceful activities that Augustus was endeavoring to promote. *Iuvenis* designates anyone of military age (17-45) and is thus appropriate to Octavian, who at this time was in his mid-thirties.

42-43. ales ... filius: in apposition with the subject of *imitaris*; Mercury is winged because of the wings on his cap (*petasus*) and ankle straps. **almae:** lit. fostering (>*alo*), hence benign or kindly.

43. Maiae: daughter of Atlas and mother of Mercury. **patiens vocari:** allowing yourself to be called, a Grecizing construction suggesting "the condescension of a superior being who consents to life on earth" (NH *ad loc.*). For the usage, cf. *Epist.* 1.16.30.

44. Caesaris ultor: the punishment of Caesar's assassins was an avowed object in the formation of the Second Triumvirate, and after the battle of Philippi Octavian erected a temple to Mars Ultor, of which a part is still standing.

45-52. Return to heaven at the end, and be involved with our state; have triumphs here, be

called our leader, and strike the Parthians, Cae-
sar.

45. serus: late, i.e., after you have done your
work on earth. Horace is covertly alluding to the
proposed deification of Augustus. Although the
subject was officially avoided as impolitic, it was a
pet subject of Virgil and Horace. See note on
3.2.21. **in caelum redeas:** these last two stanzas
are applicable both to the god and the man, but
the latter is gradually emphasized and fully brought
out at the end.

46. laetus intersis: willingly take an interest in as
our patron deity. **Quirini:** of Quirinus, the deified
Romulus.

47. vitiis: dat. with *iniquum*, which is here used
in the sense of hostile to, offended by. Cf. 1.10.15
iniqua Troiae castra.

48. ocior: lit. too speedy, untimely.

49. magnos triumphos: in August of 29 B.C.,
Octavian ordered three days of triumphs over the
Pannonians, Dalmatians, and Egyptians.

50. ames dici: the infinitive with *amo* is a poetic
construction frequent in Horace. **pater atque
princeps:** *pater* is here no more than a conven-
tional term of respect; the formal designation of
pater patriae was not conferred upon Augustus
until 2 B.C.; *princeps*, first citizen or chief, probably
suggested by *princeps senatus*, the head of the
Senate, was a title conferred upon Octavian in 28
B.C. It became the regular designation of the
emperor and is the root of our word "prince."

51. neu sinas: and do not permit. **Medos:** see
note on *Persae*, line 22. **equitare** refers to their
dreaded cavalry raids. **inultos:** unpunished by
punitive expeditions, which Horace fervently
advocates throughout the *Odes*. Augustus made
peace with them instead.

52. te duce: circumstantial abl. abs., a favorite
phrase with Horace: 1.6.4, 1.10.13, 3.14.16 *tenente
Caesare terras*, etc. **Caesar:** the family cognomen
was becoming the princeps' customary title, placed
here is the final position of emphasis.

3

A *propempticon* or send-off ode, to Virgil on setting
sail for Greece. Although Virgil's only known
voyage to Greece since his student days was in 19
B.C., it is likely there were others while Horace
was writing the *Odes*. It is not clear what the main
body of the poem, a digression on man's fatal
audacity, has to do with Virgil. It may be a half-
serious reflection on his undertaking of the *Aeneid.*
Meter: second Asclepiadean.

**1-8. To the ship: May the gods grant you fair
sailing, on condition you deliver Virgil safely.**

1-2. Sic ... sic, etc.: A common formula of
supplication or request in which a good wish is
offered in return for a desired favor. The thought
is, just as I wish you (the ship) happy sailing, so do
you deliver (*reddas*) my friend safely. Cf. Catullus
17.5-7, Virgil *Ecl.* 9.30, Horace *Epist.* 1.7.69f.: *sic
ignovisse putato me tibi, si cenas hodie mecum.* **diva
potens Cypri:** the goddess who rules over Cyprus.
Venus, as sprung from the sea, was regarded as a
patron goddess of sailing and was widely wor-
shipped on the island of Cyprus, where she had
many temples.

2. fratres Helenae: Castor and Pollux, famous as
the guardian divinities of seamen. **lucida sidera:**
sailors believed the constellation of the twin
brothers (Gemini) could calm a stormy sea; there
is also perhaps a reference to an electrical dis-
charge known as St. Elmo's fire. When seen
double on the yardarms of a vessel, these fires were
thought to represent the presence of Castor and
Pollux and were regarded as a favorable sign.

3. ventorum ... pater: Aeolus, traditionally the
master but not the father of the winds, as in Virgil
Aen. 1.52ff.

4. obstrictis: abl. abs. with *aliis*. A traditional
feature of the *propempticon* was a prayer for the
restraint of unfavorable winds. For the opposite of
such a wish, cf. *Epod.* 10.3-8. **Iäpyga:** Gk. acc.
Iapyx was the northwest wind, blowing across
Iapygia (mod. Calabria, the heel of the Italian

boot; see maps 2 and 6), which would be favorable for vessels sailing to Greece from the Italian port of Brundisium.

5-8. creditum debes ... reddas incolumem ... serves ... dimidium: Horace is playing with a banking conceit, in which Virgil is like money deposited or loaned and the ship is the bank.

6. debes Vergilium: the ship owes Virgil to his friends.

7. reddas: return him, as he has been entrusted or loaned (*creditum*, 5) to the ship. **incolumem:** safe and sound, without loss to the *caput* or capital.

8. animae dimidium meae: half of my soul; often compared to a phrase of Callimachus (ἥμισύ μευ ψυχῆς, A.P. 12.73.1, GP 4.1), this famous tribute to Virgil reflects current attitudes about friendship. Cf. 2.17.5 (to Maecenas) *te meae partem animae;* Cicero *Amic.* 25.92: *cum amicitiae vis sit in eo, ut unus quasi animus fiat ex pluribus.* There may also be a reference to the halved bronze coin (*dimidium assis*), usually representing the head of Janus, that was in common circulation at the time this poem was composed (see T.V. Buttrey, 1972).

9-20. Whoever first launched his boat on the cruel sea feared neither foul weather, sea monsters, nor rocky coasts.

9. robur et aes triplex: the idea is that the first seafarer had a heart well protected against fear by oak and triple bronze.

10. erat: Horace commonly uses a singular verb with two or more subjects. **fragilem truci:** antithetical juxtaposition, emphasizing the contrast between the frail bark and the angry sea.

11. pelago: like other poets, Horace uses many words for sea: *freta* (line 16), *vada* (24), etc. Although different in their exact meaning, they are often used interchangeably. Here, the choice of *pelago* initiates a running battle of mutes and liquids that goes on for three lines.

12. praecipitem: headlong, tempestuous, gusty.

13. decertantem: fighting it out; *de-* is intensive,

as in other Horatian compounds, *deproelior, debello.* **Aquilonibus:** with the north winds. The dat. with a verb of contending is a Grecism; cf. 1.1.15, *luctantem Icariis fluctibus Africum.*

14. tristis Hyadas: the Hyades are gloomy because rainy weather prevailed in October and November, when they rose and set. **rabiem Noti:** the rage of Notus, the south wind.

15. arbiter: more master or tyrant than settler of disputes. **Hadriae:** the Adriatic, between Italy and the Balkan peninsula.

16. maior: sc. *est.* **tollere seu ponere:** to raise or calm. With *tollere* understand *seu*, which is sometimes omitted; *ponere* is for *componere.* Cf. Virgil *Aen.* 1.135, *componere fluctus.* Poetic language often uses a simple verb in place of a compound. **freta:** see on *pelago*, line 11.

17. Quem mortis ... gradum: what step or form of death, personified as in Shakespeare MM 5.1.388:

... the swift celerity of his death,
which I did think with slower foot came on.

18. siccis oculis: i.e., without weeping in fear. **monstra:** sea monsters; for the original meaning of the word, see note on 1.2.6.

19. vidit: i.e., had the courage to gaze on.

20. Acroceraunia: lit. Thunderbolt Heights, a mountain ridge near the sea in Epirus known for its lightning storms. The cliffs where it meets the sea are *infamis*, ill-famed, because they were the scene of frequent shipwrecks. *Acroceraunia* is in apposition with *scopulos*, cliffs.

21-28. In vain did a prudent god separate land from sea; mankind audaciously breaks all rules.

21. Nequiquam: in vain; emphatically placed at the beginning of a stanza. **deus ... prudens:** God in his wisdom, a vaguely personified divine providence. **abscidit:** has severed in dividing land from sea.

22. dissociabili: estranging, incompatible with human life.

24. non tangenda: i.e., not meant to be touched;

hence the epithet *impiae* in line 23. **transiliunt:** dash across, lit. overleap, implying lawless audacity. **vada:** depths. See note on line 11.

25. omnia: everything, hence anything. Having detailed man's conquest of one element (water), the poet goes on to other transgressions, of fire (Prometheus), air (Daedalus), and earth (Hercules). **perpeti:** completes the sense of *audax*. Cf. 1.1.18, *indocilis pauperiem pati*.

26. per vetitum nefas: strong language about human perversity: men rush into wickedness even in the face of express prohibition.

27. Iapeti: the father of Prometheus, Iapetus was a son of Uranus and Gaea. **genus:** poetic language for *filius*.

28. ignem ... intulit: according to the familiar tradition, Prometheus stole fire from the gods, hiding it in a hollow reed and secretly giving it to mortals. **fraude mala:** by impious craft. Prometheus' trick is evil in the Hesiodic version of the myth, but heroic philanthropy in the more optimistic *Prometheus Bound* attributed to Aeschylus. **gentibus:** mankind; cf. *gentis*, 1.2.5.

29-40. The theft of fire brought a throng of troubles and hastened death; Daedalus took to the air, Hercules invaded the underworld; our folly is a constant cause of Jove's wrath.

29. Post ignem ... subductum: after the theft of fire. For the idiom, cf. 1.1.4 *meta evitata* and note. Prometheus' theft of fire was the immediate occasion of the results described in lines 30-33. **aetheria domo:** its home in heaven, lit. in the ether above the common air.

30. macies: emaciation, i.e., wasting disease.

31. incubuit: settled upon; cf. Virgil *Aen.* 1.89, *ponto nox incubat atra*. **cohors:** throng.

32-33. semotique prius ... leti: the doom of death, formerly slow and distant; *prius* is to be taken with both *tarda* and *semoti*. Hyperbaton puts a significant distance between the adjective *semoti* and its noun *leti*. See also appendix C on enjambment.

33. corripuit gradum: quickened its pace. See note on line 17 above.

34. Expertus: sc. *est*, essayed, tried. **Daedalus:** the legendary Athenian craftsman, said to have made wings and escaped by flight from Crete. Virgil tells the story himself in *Aen.* 6.14-33. **aëra:** Gk. acc., like *Iāpyga* (line 4 above).

35. non datis: litotes for *negatis*.

36. perrupit Acheronta: note the long *i*. One of Hercules' twelve labors was to bring Cerberus to the upper world. Acheron here denotes the lower world in general, not just the river. **Herculeus labor:** lit. the toil of Hercules, by ordinary poetic metonymy the toiling Hercules. Cf. 3.21.11 *Catonis virtus*, for the virtuous Cato. Like Daedalus, Hercules is a hero whose audacity got him into trouble.

37. Nil ... ardui est: lit. there is nothing (of) steep, no path is too steep. *ardui* is gen. with *nil*; a variant of *nil est arduum*.

40. iracunda: the epithet is transferred from *Iovem* to *fulmina*. **ponere:** in the sense of *deponere*, as it stands for *componere* in line 16 above.

4

A pretty description of the coming of spring gives way abruptly to thoughts about death. A fragment of a poem by Alcaeus (286 LP) indicates that Horace began with that model, but other Greek sources have played a part (see NH 1.58ff.). For other spring poems, cf. Catullus 46, Horace 4.7 and 12. The meter is the fourth Archilochian strophe. Note the tension between the rapid long lines and the slower short lines.

1-12. Winter is breaking up; spring with its delight is again at hand.

1. Solvitur has several applicable meanings: is being melted, is breaking up, is loosened (i.e., its grasp on the earth is loosened). Cf. *terrae ... solutae* in line 10. **grata vice:** welcome change. Cf. *Epod.* 13.8 *benigna vice* and 4.7.3 *mutat terra vices*. **veris:**

appositional gen. with *vice*. **Favoni:** the west wind or Zephyr, Favonius, was a regular accompaniment of spring.

2. trahunt: sc. *in mare*. **siccas ... carinas:** the dry hulls (lit. keels) of boats that have been hauled out of water for the winter. **machinae:** the winches and other gear used for launching.

3. neque iam: and no longer. **stabulis:** abl. with *gaudet*, in the pens where they have spent the winter. **igni:** the fire in his hearth.

4. prata: meadows. **canis albicant:** Latin poets often juxtapose words to emphasize contrast; here the poet links redundant words denoting whiteness.

5. Cytherea: Cytherean Venus, so-called from Cythera, an island off the southern coast of Laconia, near which Aphrodite rose from the sea. Usually *Cytherea*, "Lady of Cythera," is used alone. The Italian Venus, identified with Aphrodite, presided over gardens and fruits and hence over the springtime. **imminente luna:** while the moon stands overhead.

6. iunctae: i.e., linked (hand in hand) with. **Nymphis, Gratiae:** often mentioned as attendants and companions of the goddess, e.g., in 1.30.6. **decentes:** comely, traditionally nude but not provocatively so: 1.30.5f., *solutis Gratiae zonis*, 3.19.17 *Gratia nudis iuncta sororibus*.

7. alterno ... pede refers to their dance step. **quatiunt:** they tap or beat the earth as they dance. Note the metrical effect of the first four words of this line. **gravis:** with *officinas*, mighty. Horace's imaginary description, aided by the meter, contrasts the graceful dance of the nymphs and Graces with the heavy industry of Vulcan's workshop where the lightning bolts of summer storms are hammered out. **Cyclopum:** the Cyclopes were Vulcan's servants, employed in forging the thunderbolts of Jupiter. A fine passage in Virgil, *Aen.* 8.424ff., describes them at work. They are not the same as Polyphemus and his neighbors (*Aen.* 3.616ff.).

8. ardens: gleaming in the light from his forges,

as befits the god of fire. Also keen, eager, assiduous; Horace is laying the groundwork for the final couplet of his poem, esp. *calet* and *tepebunt*. **visit:** not Eng. "visits," but does the rounds of. **officinas:** workshops.

9. Nunc decet: now it is fitting. Cf. *decentes*, line 6, and *decet* again in 11. **nitidum:** glistening with perfumed oils, with which it was customary to anoint the hair on special occasions. **impedire:** to load or entwine with garlands; poetic for *cingere* or *vincire*. **myrto:** myrtle was sacred to Venus.

10. flore: used collectively of blossoms. **solutae:** freed from the bondage of winter frosts; cf. *solvitur* in line 1.

11. nunc et: intensive *et*, now too. **Fauno:** the god of shepherds and farmers. The root is *fau-*, the same as that of *faveo* and *Favonius* (line 1); hence originally "the propitious one." **immolare:** to sprinkle with meal (*mola*) before sacrificing, hence to sacrifice: the first hint of the death theme that will take over the ode in the next stanza. **lucis:** in Horace, *lucus* is used only of sacred groves, *nemus* of all others.

12. agna ... haedo: the ablatives with *immolare* are probably meant to lend an archaistic flavor; either abl. or acc. is used with verbs of sacrifice.

13-20. We all will die soon, and after death there will be no pleasures.

13. Pallida Mors ... pulsat pede: pale like his victims, Death is imagined knocking on doors (with his foot, as Romans customarily did); the alliterative *p*-sounds in this line imitate his knocking. **aequo:** impartial. **tabernas** are peasant huts.

14. regum: the rich and powerful, a frequent meaning of *rex* in Horace, e.g., *Sat.* I.7.1 (where it is ironic: "big shot"). **turris:** towered palaces. **beate Sesti:** the adjective has adversative and ironic force: fortunate as you are, Sestius. *beatus*, the participle of *beo*, originally meant blessed, hence favored, usually with wealth. This may be a reference to Sestius' election to the consulship in 23 B.C. For more about the person addressed, see appendix A.

15. vitae summa brevis: life's brief extent. **spem ... incohare longam:** enter on long-term hopes, i.e., for anything lasting.

16. Iam: with fut. *premet,* soon. The tone of the poem is set by repetitions of this word (lines 3, 5, 16, 20) and of *nunc* (9, 11); cf. also *mox* (20). **nox:** the night of death. **fabulae Manes:** the phantom shades; *fabulae,* in apposition with *manes,* means mere names or stories. "Life is eating us up. We shall be fables presently" (Emerson, *Representative Men,* chap. 4).

17. exilis: meager, bleak. **Plutonia:** for the adjective with gen. force, cf. *Herculeus labor,* 1.3.36. **quo simul mearis:** as soon as you get there; *simul* is for *simul ac,* as often.

18. regna vini: the lordship of the wine, i.e., the privilege of presiding at the festive board as symposiarch. **sortiere:** obtain by lot, in this case by the dice (abl. pl. *talis*). The highest throw (the *Venus,* as in 2.7.25) was when the numbers that appeared were all different.

19. tenerum: young and tender, as in 1.1.26, *tenerae coniugis.* **Lycidan:** Gk. acc.; he is probably fictitious and representative of a type, as often in Horace. **mirabere:** marvel at. The erotic world of the Greeks and Romans was bisexual; men particularly admired boys in early adolescence. **calet:** is hot with desire; cf. *tepebunt* below.

20. nunc ... et mox emphasizes the quick passage of time. The brevity of Lycidas' youth, like springtime, is another argument *spem non incohare longam.* **tepebunt:** will heat up with desire. As this Lycidas passes from adolescence to maturity, men will lose their interest and girls will begin to take notice. The last word of the poem takes us back to the warming trend with which the poem started.

5

The Pyrrha Ode, what the poet William Blake might have called a song of experience. Pyrrha, a courtesan whom not even Horace (if we believe him) could resist, is working on (or being worked on by) an innocent young victim. Both characters are classic types in Greek and Roman New Comedy, but could just as well have been drawn from life. Hyperbaton and enjambed lines come thick and fast here (see appendix C), fitting the complexity that will soon overwhelm the unnamed lover. The humor is high comedy, the ode an all-time favorite, the meter fourth Asclepiadean.

1-5. What youth is paying attention to you now, Pyrrha?

1. multa ... in rosa: we are asked to picture not a bed of roses, but an elaborately prepared grotto hung with flowers. **te:** the center of a chiastic arrangement of words, as Pyrrha is the center of this heavily intertwined scene.

2. perfusus ... odoribus: though men commonly used scents on such occasions as these, this teenage Lothario believes that more is better. **urget** suggests unreflective urgency.

3. grato ... antro: the Romans of Horace's time shared the Hellenistic taste for rustic grottoes. This one is probably artificial, not a natural cave. **Pyrrha:** the Greek name suggests reddish or auburn hair, and a fiery spirit (Gk. πῦρ = fire); Pyrrhus was the hot-headed, unscrupulous son of Achilles. **sub** = in, under the cover of, in the privacy of.

4. flavam ... comam: Romans preferred blondes, then as now a rarity in southern Italy. Cf. 2.4.14, *Phyllidis flavae,* 3.9.19, *flava Chloë.* **religas:** a certain provocative modesty seems to have come into fashion about this time, perhaps as a creative response to Augustus' concern for sexual morality. For hair suggestively tied up into a knot, cf. Lyde's coiffure in 2.11.23f., Neaera's in 3.14.22, Phyllis' in 4.11.5, and *Epod.* 11.28.

5. simplex munditiis: an oxymoron that says everything about this hair style and the woman who wears it: *munditia* is clean elegance, plural here to suggest that the effect is not as simple as it looks.

5-13. Alas! How little he knows.

5. quotiens: exclamatory, how often. **fidem:** his misplaced trust, her lack of good faith. Cf. 1.33.4, *laesa fide* and note.

6. mutatos ... deos: because when the affair was going well they were smiling on him. Now they are laughing at him. **flebit:** transitive: bemoan, lament. **aspera nigris aequora ventis:** interlocking word order.

7. nigris: transferred epithet; it is the storm clouds rather than the winds that bring them that are dark. We are to understand that the coming tantrums will extract ever more costly gifts. Pyrrha is no amateur.

8. emirabitur: *hapax legomenon,* invented as an intensified form of *mirabitur.* Her future theatrics will astonish him. **insolens:** adverbial: in surprise, because he is new to all this.

9. credulus aurea: the two epithets are a compendious expression, = *credens te auream esse*: she now seems to his credulity as golden as her hair.

10. vacuam: available, otherwise unoccupied.

11-12. aurae fallacis: the treacherous breeze, returning to the metaphor of lines 6f.

13. intemptata nites: shine untried; the latent metaphor is the dazzling sea, whose glittering surface can quickly become stormy.

13-16. As for me, I'm thankful to have escaped alive.

13. Me: subject of *suspendisse* (line 15), in an emphatic position; cf. *me* in 1.1.29. **tabula ... votiva:** abl. of means with *indicat.* **sacer ... paries:** one wall of a seaside shrine might contain votive tablets and offerings of thanks made by sailors who had escaped shipwreck alive. Literary Hellenistic epigrams sometimes imitated such inscriptions.

15. suspendisse: sailors sometimes hung up the garments in which they had been saved; Horace's, we are to believe, were still soaking wet after his "shipwreck."

16. maris: gen. with *potenti,* as in 1.3.1 *diva potens Cypri.* Debate has raged about whether *deo*

in the manuscripts should be emended to *deae* (i.e., Venus) because Neptune has nothing to do with love while Venus/Aphrodite was in many places venerated as a sea goddess and patroness of seamen. But *deus,* like Gk. θεός, may be masc. or fem. (Catullus 61.64 *quis huic deo [sc. Veneri] compararier ausit?*).

6

To Augustus' right-hand man Marcus Vipsanius Agrippa, a *recusatio* declining the privilege of writing his praises and suggesting that the epic and tragic talents of Varius (see appendix A) are more appropriate for the task. Horace argues that his talents lie on the lighter side, viz. the convivial themes of Hellenistic poetry. Behind this polite refusal, and subtly embedded in its words, some see a dislike of Agrippa. Virgil is said to have borne him no love, and Horace's patron Maecenas hated him as his chief rival for Augustus' favor. Meter: third Asclepiadean.

1-4. Varius, a bard of Homeric genius, will write of your victories on land and sea.

1. Scriberis: you will be written about. **Vario ... alite** is abl. of agent without the usual prep. *ab.* **fortis et ... victor:** predicate with *scriberis,* you will be represented as brave, etc.

2. Maeonii carminis: descriptive gen. with *alite.* Because Homer was by some accounts a native of Maeonia or Lydia, the adj. means Homeric. **alite,** bird, = poet or bard by the usual association of both with song. The usual image was of a swan, as in 2.20 and Ben Jonson's description of Shakespeare as the "sweet swan of Avon."

3. navibus aut equis expresses the conventional land-sea dyad. As Agrippa had won signal victories on both land and sea, the formula is appropriate.

5-15. I don't attempt epic themes, Agrippa: the Muse forbids me to wear out Caesar's good name, or yours, with my faulty talent. Who can

do justice to Mars in armor, a Meriones, or a Diomede?

6. Pelidae stomachum: the wrath of Peleus' son Achilles was the theme of Homer's *Iliad;* for the stomach as the seat of emotion, cf. 1.16.16. **cedere nescii:** with *Pelidae,* stubborn, unyielding.

7. duplicis ... Ulixeï: double-dealing because of his use of deception; this pejorative view of Ulysses was widespread in later antiquity, as early as Sophocles' *Philoctetes* (409 B.C.).

8. Pelopis domum: Atreus, Thyestes, and Agamemnon were descendants of Pelops. Varius had recently written a tragedy *Thyestes,* to which Horace is alluding here.

9. tenues grandia: contrasting juxtaposition. In calling himself (or his talent) *tenues,* Horace is being disingenuous; 2.20 and 3.30 give a more generous self-appraisal.

10. imbellis ... lyrae characterizes lyric as unsuited to narrative verse about battles, and downplays the more earnest types of lyric, such as 1.2.

12. culpa ... ingeni: a feature of any *recusatio* or refusal to take up a theme was the author's polite self-depreciation; cf. *tenues* (9). **deterere:** wear down, diminish, completing *vetat [me].*

13-14. Quis ... digne scripserit? is a rhetorical question, implying not the inability of Varius but the sheer difficulty of the epic mode. **adamantina:** poetic for any hard substance such as steel or diamond.

15. Merionen: not a major figure in Homer, Meriones was the henchman of the Cretan leader Idomeneus. Horace could be alluding to a now-unknown poem featuring Meriones. **ope Palladis:** in *Iliad* 5 Pallas Athene inspires Diomedes to go on a glorious rampage in which he wounds both Aphrodite and Ares.

16. Tydiden: son of Tydeus, the Homeric patronymic of Diomedes. Cf. *Pelidae* (6).

17-20. My specialty is parties and lovers' quarrels.

17. convivia: symposiums, around which grew a

literary tradition of light poetry.

18. sectis ... unguibus: abl. with *acrium,* once taken to mean that the girls' fingernails have been pared smooth so as not to hurt; but NH *ad loc.* argue that they were sharpened to a point so as to inflict damage. **in iuvenes,** with *virginum ... acrium,* = girls swift to take severe measures against young men, i.e., standing by to repel boarders.

19. vacui, sive quid urimur: with ellipsis of the first *sive,* whether I am free of passion or on fire with some love. For *vacuus* as sexually uninvolved, "available," cf. 1.5.10 *semper vacuam.* Horace is contrasting poems such as 1.5 where he is the amused observer, and others such as 1.13 where he adopts the point of view of the lover. **quid** is acc. of respect or cognate acc. with *urimur.*

20. non praeter solitum: litotic, = as usual. **leves** is emphatic by position, continuing the poetic plural begun on line 5, *nos.*

7

This ode begins as an encomium of Tibur, the pleasant suburb east of Rome where those who could afford to do so went to escape the heat and noise of the city (see maps 5 and 6). Horace advises Plancus, a native of the town, to drown his troubles in wine, offering the legendary precedent of Teucer giving similar advice to his followers. The poem's rambling structure is in the tradition of Pindar, whose victory odes move freely from one topic to another. The meter is Alcmanic strophe.

1-14. Earth has many lovely places, but my favorite is Tibur. For the priamel structure, compare 1.1.2ff. and see appendix C.

1. Laudabunt alii: the opening words signal that the poem is encomiastic and begins with a priamel or funneling device that will lead to the subject of praise. For the concessive sense of *laudabunt,* some may praise, cf. 1.20.10 *bibes.* **claram:** famous. Rhodes enjoys an ideal climate year-round; it was a center of sea trade, art, and schools of rhetoric.

The adjective applies also to Mytilene and Ephesus. **Mytilenen:** capital of Lesbos, home of the poets Alcaeus and Sappho.

2. Epheson: in Horace's day, the metropolis of the Roman province of Asia, noted for its temple of Artemis (Diana), which ranked as one of the seven wonders of the world. **bimarisve:** Corinth had two harbors, one on each side of the Isthmus: on the Corinthian gulf on the west, and on the Saronic gulf to the east. The city was destroyed by Memmius in 146 B.C., but restored in some degree by Julius Caesar.

3. moenia: in Horace's time, these were probably the last surviving reminder of Corinth's past glory. **Baccho:** abl. of cause with *insignis*; Dionysus (Bacchus) was born in Thebes to Cadmus' daughter Semele. **Apolline:** for the shrine of Pythian Apollo.

4. Tempe: n. pl. acc.; the wild and beautiful valley of the Peneus in northern Thessaly.

5. Sunt quibus continues the priamel announced in line 1; *quibus* is abl. with **opus est:** there are some who need only celebrate **intactae Palladis urbem:** Athens, named after the virgin goddess Pallas Athene.

6. carmine perpetuo: a continuous long poem (of the sort Horace did not write). Cf. Callimachus *Aetia* 3, ἄεισμα διηνεκές, Ovid *Met.* 1.4 *perpetuum carmen.*

7. undique decerptam ... olivam: i.e., honorific lore about Athens drawn from many sources; *undique* suggests that such "plucking" has not been very discriminating. **fronti praeponere:** fringe their brow (with a hint of ostentation). The olive was sacred to Athene.

8. plurimus: collective, many a one. **Iunonis:** Argos was a favorite city of Juno: Virgil *Aen.* 1.23f., *ad Troiam pro caris gesserat Argis.*

9. aptum ... equis Argos paraphrases Homer's formula Ἄργεος ἱπποβότοιο, horse-pasturing Argos (*Il.* 2.287). Its flat alluvial plain made it fit for horses. **dites Mycenas:** another quasi-Homeric epithet; Homer called it πολύχρυσος (all golden) because of its fabled wealth in the bronze age. In

the center of the Argolid, it was the site of Agamemnon's palace, as Lacedaemon was the site of Menelaus'.

10. me: contrasted with *alii* in line 1. Cf. *me* in 1.1.29. **nec tam,** repeated on the next line, is completed by *quam* (12): not as much as. **patiens:** hardy, because of the harsh Spartan regimen. These three favorite cities of Juno had lost their importance by Horace's time; Mycenae was long abandoned, already an ancient ruin.

11. Larisae: a city in the heart of Thessaly, on the river Peneus. Achilles was its local hero. **percussit:** has smitten me, made an impression. **opimae:** cf. Homer's Λάρισσα ἐριβώλαξ (*Il.* 2.841). As with *albus* in line 15, Horace characteristically uses a simple Latin epithet to translate a Greek compound. Like *dites Maecenas* (9), Larisa was famous for the wealth of its fertile plains; it was (and still is) the breadbasket of Greece by virtue of its grain crops.

12. domus Albuneae resonantis refers to the grotto where the Sibyl Albunea lived (cf. Virgil *Aen.* 7.83ff.) The epithet is transferred; it is the grotto that echoes, not the Sibyl.

13. praeceps Anio: the steep or tumbling river Anio goes over a series of falls and rapids at Tibur. **Tiburni:** Tiburnus or Tiburtus was one of the three mythical founders of Tibur (mod. Tivoli). **lucus:** a sacred grove, as distinguished in Horace from the ordinary *nemus.* Cf. 1.4.11, *lucis.*

14. mobilibus ... rivis: moving channels, instrumental with *uda.* The reference is to irrigation, by which water would be channeled into the rows of trees as needed. **pomaria:** orchards.

15-21. As the south wind clears a cloudy sky, so you should forget your troubles with mellow wine, at war or at home in Tibur.

15. Albus ... Notus recalls the Gk. λευκόνοτος; the epithet "clear" indicates the south wind's clearing effect on the sky; cf. 1.5.7 *nigris ventis,* 3.27.19 *albus Iapyx.*

17. sapiens: adverbial and predicative: be wise

and remember to, etc., or remember to put a wise end to your *tristitia*.

18. labores: in the bad sense, troubles.

19. molli ... mero: mellow wine; *merum [vinum]*, straight wine undiluted with water, is often used loosely of wine as actually consumed. Unmixed, it would be anything but *mollis*. **Plance:** for more about this person, see appendix A. **signis:** with military standards.

20. tenent ... tenebit: if Plancus was now in the field, the ode may be as early as 30 B.C. or earlier; the future anticipates his return home.

21. Tiburis ... tui: these words form the connecting link to the opening section of the ode. Porphyrio says Plancus was born at Tibur; he must at any rate have owned a villa there.

21-32. Teucer had the sense to drown his cares, when driven by Telamon from his native Salamis.

21. Teucer: son of Telamon and half-brother to Ajax, used as an example of courage under difficulties, hence in an emphatic position. **Salamina:** Gk. acc. of *Salamis*.

22. fugeret: i.e., when he went into exile. When Ajax and Teucer set out for the Trojan War, their father Telamon asked that neither should return alone. Ajax, driven mad by Athena after he failed to win the arms of the dead Achilles, tortured and killed cattle in the camp, thinking he was killing his enemies, then in disgrace took his own life. Telamon stubbornly refused to accept the return of Teucer without his brother, and banished him from Salamis. Plancus, like Teucer, was blamed for the death of his brother (in the proscriptions of 43 B.C.); the suggestion here is that both were blamed unfairly. **uda Lyaeo:** poetic periphrasis, soaked with wine. By metonymy Bacchus Lyaeus, the Releaser from cares, stands for wine itself.

23. populea: the poplar was sacred to the wandering Hercules and hence appropriate to Teucer's present situation.

24. affatus: sc. *est*, from the deponent *affor*.

25. Quo ... cumque: tmesis, as in 1.6.3. **melior ... parente:** i.e., kinder than my father Telamon.

26. ibimus: future with hortatory force.

27. Nil desperandum: sc. *est*. Never despair: the impersonal idiom, as in *de gustibus non disputandum*. **duce et auspice:** a variant of the technical phrase *ductu et auspiciis*, referring to the authority of a consul conducting military operations in a province.

28. certus translates the Gk. epithet of Apollo, called νημερτής because his prophecies were never wrong.

29. ambiguam ... Salamina: i.e., a second Salamis, big enough to dispute the original Salamis' claim to the name. **tellure nova:** on Cyprus. Cyprian Salamis is on the east coast, facing Syria. The "feminine" caesura after *tellure* is unusual in Horace.

30. O fortes peioraque passi: cf. the words of Homer's Odysseus, *Od.* 12.208 and 20.18. Horace's treatment of the theme may be compared to Virgil's in *Aen.* 1.198-9:

O socii *(neque ignari sumus ante malorum),*
o passi graviora, dabit deus his quoque finem.

31. nunc vino pellite curas: cf. Cheiron's advice to Achilles in *Epod.* 13.17, *illic omne malum vino cantuque levato.*

32. iterabimus aequor: i.e., resume our voyage; having just sailed home from Troy, we will "repeat the deep" by sailing on to our new home.

8

The incompatibility of love and athletics, the subject of this ode, was a commonplace of Hellenistic comedy and romance. Formally, the poem is simply a catalog of symptoms, built around the repetition *cur ... cur ... cur ... cur ... cur ... quid?* This ode is Horace's only experiment with the second, or greater, Sapphic strophe.

1-3. Lydia, why are you trying to ruin Sybaris by love?

1. Lydia: a sensuously oriental name, common in love poetry, appropriate to hetaeras. Cf. Lydia in 1.13, 1.25, 3.9, Lyde in 2.11, 3.11, 3.28.

2. Sybarin: another suggestive name, evoking the proverbially luxurious town of Sybaris on the Gulf of Tarentum; to this day a *sybarite* is a voluptuary. **properes** is the first of a series of subjunctives (*oderit, equitet, temperet*) in indirect question after *dic ... cur*. **amando:** abl. of the gerund: by loving him.

3-12. Why has he abandoned his masculine sports—riding, swimming, and the discus? Neobule is impressed by the similar activities of Hebrus in 3.12.7-9.

3-4. apricum ... campum: in Horace's time the Campus Martius was still a large, sunny, open area used for athletics and equestrian exercises.

4. patiens: that is, before he fell in love.

5-6. militaris ... aequalis: his fellow soldiers. Sybaris is imagined as an equestrian officer, not a common foot-soldier.

6. equitet: an exercise encouraged by Augustus, who revived the *lusus Troiae* or Game of Troy; Virgil *Aen*. 5.545ff, Suetonius, *Aug*. 43.2. See note on 3.7.25. **Gallica ... ora:** i.e., the mouth of his Gallic steed. The best horses were imported from Gaul. **lupatis ... frenis:** horses' bits were made jagged ("wolfed") with spikes to hurt the tongue and palate. The plurals refer to repeated occasions.

7. temperet: rein, control.

8. timet ... Tiberim tangere: the Tiber was much used for swimming. The infinitive object of *timere* was a poetic construction of Horace's day. The chattering of Sybaris' teeth is suggested by the alliteration of *t*'s here, as the pounding of horses' hooves was suggested by the *p*'s at the end of the first stanza. **flavum:** a standing epithet for the Tiber because of its alluvial mud; cf. 1.2.13. **olivum:** the oil used for rubdowns after exercise, hence (by metonymy) all exercise.

9. sanguine viperino: abl. of comparison with *cautius*; mentioned in *Epod*. 3.6 as a deadly poison.

10. cautius: more warily. **livida:** black and blue from combat training (abl. *armis*); **gestat:** carry on display, like battle ribbons.

11-12. saepe disco ... nobilis expedito: often (in the past) famed for clearing discus or javelin across the *finis*, which marked the standing record.

13-16. Why is he hiding, like Achilles avoiding the Trojan War?

13. Quid = *cur*, continuing the chain of questions begun in line 2. **latet:** for the theme of the lover in hiding, cf. Callimachus A.P. 12.73 (GP 4), Catullus 55, 58b.

14. dicunt: sc. *latuisse*. **Thetidis:** Gk. gen. of Thetis, mother of Achilles. She had heard the prophecy that he would die in the Trojan War and tried to keep him out of it by disguising him as a girl and leaving him in the care of King Lycomedes of Scyros, where he fell in love with the king's daughter Deidamia. Like Sybaris in this poem, Achilles thus became a willing prisoner of love. Thetis is called *marina* because she was a sea nymph. **sub:** temporal, just before. This was ten years prior to the actual fall of Troy, but the fatal war itself was at hand.

15. funera: the metaphorical "death" of the city, plural because so many died. **virilis cultus:** male costume that would make him easy to recognize. He was so young at the time that he had not yet passed puberty and was not conspicuously masculine.

16. Lycias catervas: the troops are called Lycian because these were the main Trojan allies. **proriperet:** hustle him forth.

9

The Soracte Ode, whose first two strophes are based on an ode of Alcaeus (338 LP), of which six lines are preserved. Horace changes the setting to Italy. This poem is antithetical to the ode to Sestius (1.4), where spring brings thoughts of death. It develops the *carpe diem* theme of 1.11 in a way that has made this one of the best-loved odes of Horace. The meter is Alcaic strophe.

1-4. You see the snow and ice on Mount Soracte.

1. ut: how, introducing indirect questions, *stet ... sustineant ... constiterint.* **stet:** i.e., stands out distinctly against the sky; picturesque for *sit.*

2. Soracte: a mountain about 28 miles north of Rome (see map 5) that "from out the plain / heaves like a long-swept wave about to break," Byron *Childe Harold* 4.75. **nec iam:** and no longer. **onus:** the load of snow.

3. laborantes: straining. **gelu ... acuto:** a hard freeze, which has congealed the streams.

4. constiterint: pf. subj. of *consto,* have stood still, have frozen.

5-8. Pile wood on the fire and bring out some old wine.

5. dissolve suggests melting, as in 1.4.1, *solvitur acris hiems.* **super:** with *large* in the next line, high upon; cf. the use of *sub* in 1.5.3, with the note.

6. reponens: piling; *re-* here indicates both restoration and repeated action. **benignius:** more generously than usual.

7. depromе: draw off from the jar. **quadrimum Sabina ... merum diota:** interlocking word order as in 1.5.6f. **quadrimum:** lit. four-winter, of wine that has been aged four years; *quadrimus,* from *quadri-him-us,* contains the root seen in *hiem-s;* other compounds are *bimus* and *trimus.* **Sabina:** poetic transference of the epithet from the wine to the jar; strictly, it is the wine that is *Sabinum.*

8. Thaliarche: a fictitious name, but suggestive; it means master of the revels. **merum** = *vinum,* as in 1.7.19. **diota:** a "two-eared" jar or amphora, so called because of its two handles.

9-12. Leave all else to the gods, who are all-powerful.

9. cetera: i.e., all things other than the pleasures of the moment. **qui ... stravere:** the clause gives

the reason for *permitte divis cetera.* **simul:** for *simul ac,* as in 1.4.17 and regularly in the *Odes.*

10. aequore fervido: locative abl.: on the stormy sea, with *deproeliantis.*

11. deproeliantis: fighting it out with each other; *de-* is intensive, as in 1.3.13 *decertantem Aquilonibus,* a passage that is similar to this one; *deproelior* is a *hapax legomenon,* found only here in Latin. **cupressi:** tall, slender trees, in shape something like the Lombardy poplar, and hence particularly exposed to the action of the wind.

12. orni: ash trees.

13-24. Do not think of tomorrow, but enjoy what fortune bestows—love, dancing, and the other pleasures of youth.

13. fuge quaerere: a poetic alternative for *noli quaerere;* cf. 2.4.22, *fuge suspicari.*

14. quem ... cumque: tmesis, as in 1.6.3 and 1.7.25. **Fors,** like *Fortuna,* is chance personified. **dierum** depends on *quemcumque:* whatever day, lit. whatever of days. **lucro appone:** a metaphor from bookkeeping, lit. assign to profit, set down as gain. Cf. *debes* and *reddas* in 1.3.6-7.

15-16. nec ... sperne: *nec* occurs repeatedly in Horatian lyric where we should normally expect *neve* (*neu*): i.e., in prohibitions and in jussive and optative subjunctives, e.g., 3.7.29f. *neque in vias despice,* Epod. 10.9 *nec sidus amicum appareat.*

16. puer: perhaps almost adverbial, while you are young. Horace does not specify who the *puer* is. Often, in sympotic settings such as this, it is the slave "boy," but considering the advice given, it is probably the master of revels addressed in 8 *o Thaliarche.* **neque tu:** sc. *sperne;* in disjunctive sentences, *tu* is often reserved for the second member, as here, partly for rhythmic effect and partly to emphasize the injunction; cf. *Epist.* 1.2.63 *hunc frenis, hunc tu compesce catena,* "check it with reins; check it, I tell you, with a chain." **choreas:** dances; cf. *chori* (1.1.31).

17. donec: while, a meaning for this word that occurs first in the Augustan period. **virenti:** understand *tibi*: while you are in the bloom of youth, and ... ; it is contrasted with *canities*, hoariness, the white hairs of old age.

18. morosa: irritable, to be taken with *canities*. **Nunc:** i.e., in youth, repeated for urgency in 21. **campus:** the Campus Martius, the field where sports and military exercises took place; cf. 1.8.4. **areae:** the plazas around temples and public buildings. At this point in the poem, the imagination is momentarily taken from the cold winter to a hot summer scene.

19. lenes ... susurri: the gentle whispers of lovers. **sub noctem:** at nightfall; the use of *sub* is the same as that in 1.8.14, *sub funera*.

20. composita ... hora: at the arranged or settled hour. **repetantur:** by zeugma, be remembered, sought, or claimed; the meaning differs somewhat with the different subjects: *campus et areae, susurri, risus, pignus*. For the force of *re-*, see note on line 6, *reponens*.

21. et is intensive: also, too. We return now to an indoor winter scene, but equally hot. **latentis proditor intimo ... puellae risus ab angulo:** the arrangement is carefully studied; the three modifiers are placed together, succeeding each other in the same order as the three nouns they qualify, which are likewise placed together: a, b, c, A, B, C. This is in English "the tell-tale laugh of the girl hiding in the farthest corner," but in Latin we also get "the laugh from the corner." Cf. the complex word order in 1.5.13ff.

23. pignus is a pledge or token of love, a bracelet or ring as shown by the following *lacertis* and *digito*, which are best taken as datives of separation. **lacertis** are arms, lit. the upper arms.

24. male pertinaci: resisting ineffectually or half-heartedly, *male* being a weak form of *non* as in Virgil *Aen.* 2.23, *statio male fida carinis*; for another picture of a love-tussle, cf. 1.6.17-18, *virginum sectis unguibus acrium*.

10

One traditional role of the ancient poet was to enrich the meaning of myths. This ode to the Roman god of commerce (*comMERCium, MERCator*), already connected in the Roman mind with Greek Hermes, celebrates the complexity of a Hellenized Mercury. Recasting a hymn of Alcaeus of which only the beginning survives (frag. 308 LP), Horace uses the catalog form of the hymn to list the virtues of the god. Meter: Sapphic strophe.

1-8. I will sing of you, Mercury, who formed human culture in speech and exercise; messenger, inventor of the lyre, clever thief.

1. facunde: eloquent, appropriately the first of several *aretaí* mentioned (see appendix C, hymn). Horace calls himself a *Mercurialis vir* in 2.17.29; in his other hymn to Mercury (3.11), Horace concentrates first on the god's patronage of song. In 2.7.13, it is Mercury who rescues Horace from Philippi. **nepos Atlantis:** his mother Maia was Atlas' daughter.

2. feros cultus: savage customs; in *Sat.* 1.3.100 Horace calls primitive man a *mutum et turpe pecus*. **recentum** = recently created, hence early.

3. voce implies song, speech, and language. **catus:** adverbial, shrewdly. His Greek counterpart Hermes was seen as an inventive trickster.

4. more: the custom and institution. **palaestrae:** wrestling place.

6. lyrae parentem: though he was only an infant at the time. The Homeric Hymn to Hermes tells how he fashioned the first lyre from the shell of a tortoise. Cf. *Epod.* 14.11 *cava testudine*, 1.32.14 *grata testudo*. For his gift of the lyre to his half-brother Apollo, see 1.21.12 and note.

7-8. callidum ... condere: clever (enough) to hide. Complementary inf. with adjective, a common poetic construction. **iocoso ... furto:** his sense of humor has been linked to his thievery since the Homeric Hymn.

9-12. Apollo laughed when he threatened you

over the theft of his cattle: you also stole his quiver.

9. Te: cf. line 5 *te*, 17 *tu*. Traditional hymnic anaphora. 1.35.5, 9, 17, 21 and many other examples in Horace follow the same pattern. **boves ... amotas:** the theft of Apollo's cattle was a frequent theme of poetry and vase painting.

10. per dolum: he drove the cattle backward, so Apollo would track them in the wrong direction. **puerum:** baby. Mercury stole Apollo's cattle on the same day he was born. When Apollo caught up with him the next day and taxed him with his theft, Mercury answered from his cradle "Do I look like a cattle rustler? ... I was born yesterday!" (*H. Merc.* 265-73).

11. terret: hist. present, tried to frighten. **pharetra:** abl. of separation with *viduus*. According to a scholium on *Iliad* 15.256, while Apollo was raging on about his cattle Mercury filched his quiver, literally disarming his accuser and making him laugh. Porphyrio attributes this part of the story to the hymn of Alcaeus.

13-16. You also took Priam from Troy into the enemy camp of the Greeks.

13. Quin et: not only that, but also. Having told a comic story about Mercury, the poem continues with a serious one, drawn from *Iliad* 24, where Hermes conducts a grieving King Priam unseen to the tent of Achilles to supplicate the return of his son Hector's body. **Atridas ... superbos:** object of *fefellit*. Atreus' sons Agamemnon and Menelaus were often represented as arrogant leaders in the Trojan War.

14. dives Priamus: as an eastern monarch, Priam is represented in Greek legend as fabulously rich.

15. Thessalos ... ignis: the campfires of Achilles' Thessalian followers, by metonymy the Thessalians themselves. **Troiae:** dat. with *iniqua*, unfriendly to Troy.

16. fefellit: escaped their notice. Takes *Atridas*, *ignis*, and *castra* as object. Emphatic word order links this deception with the one in the previous

stanza.

17-20. You conduct pious souls to the underworld and hold back the shades with your wand, a friend to the upper and the lower gods.

17. reponis: with the *re-* prefix, this is variously intrepreted as signifying "duly conduct," "put away," or "restore" to their original place (for which cf. Virgil's metempsychosis passage in *Aen.* 6.713-51). **laetis ... sedibus:** cf. Virgil *Aen.* 6.638f.: *locos laetos et amoena virecta fortunatorum nemorum sedesque beatas*, viz. Elysium. These lines invoke Mercury in his role as *psychopompos*, conductor of souls.

18-19. virga ... aurea: Hermes' staff, a type of caduceus, is used here to keep the *levem turbam* of bodyless spirits from escaping into the upper world. As a herald's staff, it represents his ambassadorial role between the lower and the upper gods, *superis deorum et imis*.

11

A much-admired sympotic poem expressing an Epicurean distrust of divination or other speculation about the future. Horace admits elsewhere (*Sat.* 1.6.114, *adsisto divinis*) to some interest in soothsayers, and it was an idle curiosity that he shared to some degree with all Romans of his time. Here, though, the point of view is practical and rational. The ode is closely connected in theme with the Soracte Ode (1.9). The meter is the fifth or greater Asclepiadean.

1-6. Don't try to find out, Leuconoë, how long a life the gods have granted us. Better just to take what comes.

1. ne quaesieris: perf. subjunctive in prohibition, a poetic and colloquial usage. **scire nefas:** sc. *est*. The metrical pauses strengthen the parenthetical sense of this phrase.

2. finem: sc. *vitae*. **Leuconoë:** it is unusual for a sympotic poem to be addressed to a woman.

Nothing about her can be guessed from the name, which is probably fictitious and nicely fits the choriambic meter. **Babylonios numeros:** Babylonian tables of numerology. "Babylonians," actually Chaldeans, are typical representatives of the art of astrology, using numerical charts in their calculations. Beginning before Horace's day, their influence continued for centuries at Rome. Although officially expelled from the city in 139 B.C., they continued to do a brisk business. It appears from 2.17 that Maecenas had more than a casual interest in their work.

3. temptaris: try out, experiment with. **Ut** is exclamatory: how much better, etc. **quicquid erit:** obj. of *pati.*

4. pluris hiemes: i.e., more years than you have already lived; "winters" is both poetic metonymy for years and a transition to the winter scene against which this ode is set, like the Soracte Ode (1.9). **Iuppiter:** traditionally represented as a disposer of events, like the Fates.

5. oppositis debilitat, etc.: the winter is represented as wearing out the sea on the cliffs that face it (*oppositis pumicibus*).

6-8. Do your work, enjoy the hour, and put no trust in the future.

6. Sapias: jussive, be wise. **vina liques:** strain the wine (through a cloth or a colander to remove the sediment). Leuconoë is imagined as an attendant at a symposium. **spatio brevi:** with *reseces,* within the short time span allotted us.

7. spem longam reseces: cut back hope for a long life; the phrase is compressed. *reseces* suggests the pruning of vines. For a similar thought, cf. 1.4.15, *vitae summa brevis spem nos vetat incohare longam.* **fugerit:** will be gone; the future perfect here, as frequently, denotes the immediate consummation of the future act. **invida aetas:** envious time, which begrudges us enjoyment of life's pleasures.

8. carpe diem: the original and *locus classicus* of this famous phrase, which picks up the vine-tend-

ing metaphor of *reseces.* The present day is to be "plucked" as if it were a grape. Addressed to Leuconoë, *carpe diem* may carry a note of erotic suggestion. **quam minimum:** as little as possible, i.e., not at all. **credula** implies foolish trust, like our "credulous." **postero:** to the future, sc. *tempori.*

12

A Pindaric encomium of Augustus, opening with a tag from Pindar's victory ode in honor of Theron, *Ol.* 2.2, and proceeding by a similarly lengthy path to the object of praise. Having begged off praising either Augustus or his crony Agrippa in 1.6.9-12 because his *lyrae Musa potens* will have none of it, Horace finds a more willing Muse this time in Clio. His formal framework is the priamel, working his way to Augustus through a series of catalogs. Meter: Sapphic strophe.

1-12. What man, hero, or god are you about to celebrate, o Muse? Whose name will echo in the Muses' haunts?

1. Quem virum aut heroa, etc.: a climactic series of three questions, culminating in *cuius ... nomen?* The three classes (man, hero, god) are later taken up in reverse order, beginning with line 13. **heroa** is Gk. acc., and trisyllabic. **lyra ... tibia:** the lyre implies the Greek tradition, the reed-pipe the Roman; according to Cicero (*Tusc.* 4.3), the Romans accompanied their early songs with the *tibia,* a shrill (*acri*) reed-pipe.

2. sumis celebrare: undertake to celebrate; for the poetic infinitive of purpose, cf. *Epist.* 1.3.7, *quis sibi res gestas Augusti scribere sumit?* **Clio:** the Muse of history, appropriate for the purpose here, although Horace does not as a rule clearly distinguish the attributes of the Muses; see 1.1.33, and note.

3. recinet: will sing back, repeat. **iocosa:** playful, a common epithet of the echo.

4. imago: echo; originally *imago vocis,* but abbreviated by usage.

5. Heliconis: Mt. Helicon in Boeotia, like Mts. Pindus and Haemus a celebrated haunt of the Muses (see map 3). **oris:** borders, slopes.

6. super Pindo: on Pindus' top; cf. the usage in 1.9.5, *super foco*. Mt. Pindus is between Thessaly and Epirus. **gelido ... Haemo:** Mt. Haemus, cool because of its elevation, is in Thrace, and associated with Orpheus.

7. unde: the antecedent is *Haemo*. **temere:** pell-mell, under the spell of his music. The word is the locative of an obsolete nom. *temes* meaning darkness; hence (originally) in the dark, blindly, in confusion. **insecutae** sc. *sunt*. **vocalem:** sweet-voiced, with *Orphea*.

8. Orphea: Gk. acc. of *Orpheus*. **silvae:** even the trees are said to have yielded to the spell of Orpheus's lyre; cf. Shakespeare *Merchant of Venice*, 5.1.79ff.:

> Therefore the poet
> Did feign that Orpheus drew trees, stones, and floods,
> Since naught so stockish, hard, and full of rage
> But music for the time doth change his nature.

9. arte materna: i.e., the skill imparted by his mother, the muse Calliope.

10. lapsus: downward courses.

11-12. blandum ... ducere: persuasive enough to lead. Same construction and metrical position as *callidum ... condere*, 1.10.7-8. **et:** intensive, even. **auritas:** provided with ears, hence attentive; really proleptic: to make them hear and follow. **fidibus canoris:** poetic pl., his resonant lyre. It is a regular feature of Horace's high style to give as many nouns as possible some kind of attributive; eight of the nineteen nouns in the first three stanzas have been so ornamented.

13-24. Praise of the gods—Jupiter first of all, then Pallas, Bacchus, Diana, Apollo.

13-14. solitis ... laudibus: abl. of comparison with *prius*. **parentis:** i.e., Jupiter, father of gods and men. Cf. Virgil *Ecl.* 3.60, *ab Iove principium musae; Iovis omnia plena.*

14. res hominum, etc.: cf. Virgil *Aen.* 1.229f., *O qui res hominumque deumque aeternis regis imperiis.*

15. mundum: the heavens; usually = the universe, but here contrasted with *mare et terras.*

16. temperat: rules. **horis:** seasons, a poetic sense of the word.

17. Unde = *ex quo*, from whom. The antecedent is *parentis*.

18-19. secundum, proximos: the distinction is between a close second (Jupiter has none) and the nearest in honor, viz. Pallas (Minerva, Athene).

21. proeliis audax: modifying Pallas Athena or Minerva, the warrior goddess.

22. Liber: Bacchus. **inimica virgo beluis:** Diana, the huntress and destroyer of monsters (*beluis*).

24. Phoebe: Apollo, preeminent for his skill in archery (*certa ... sagitta*). Augustus was thought by some to be a son of Apollo (Suetonius *Aug.* 94.4), and did much to promote his worship; cf. 1.2.32, and note.

25-32. Praise of heroes: Hercules, Castor, and Pollux.

25. Alciden: Hercules, grandson of Alceus. **pueros ... Ledae:** Castor and Pollux; *puer* is for *filius* as often in poetry, e.g., 1.32.10.

26. hunc: Castor. **equis:** instrumental with *superare*. **illum:** Pollux. **superare:** used intransitively, completing the sense of the adjective (*nobilem*), as in line 12. **pugnis:** with the fists, i.e., in boxing.

27. simul: for *simul ac*, as often. **alba:** bright, clear; cf. 1.3.2, *lucida sidera.*

28. stella: loosely of the constellation Gemini. Castor and Pollux were the patrons of mariners. See 1.3.2 and note. **refulsit:** has shone out.

29. defluit: down flows the *umor*; note the emphatic position of this and the following verbs. **saxis:** the coastal cliffs. **umor:** water.

30. concidunt: subside; cf. Virgil *Aen.* 1.154, *sic cunctus pelagi cecidit fragor.*

32. recumbit: lies down, settles.

33-44. Praise of Roman kings and patriots: Romulus, Pompilius, Tarquin, Cato, Regulus, Scaurus, Paulus, Fabricius, Curius, Camillus. This catalog is like the gallery containing statues of Rome's *summi viri* set up to the right of the temple of Mars Ultor in the Forum Augusti (see Zanker, pp. 210ff.). Cf. the catalog of Romans in Virgil *Aen.* 6.756ff. All reflect Augustus' interest in early history.

34. Pompili: Numa Pompilius, whose reign, according to tradition, was marked by the cessation of war and the founding of elaborate religious ceremonials. **superbos:** implicitly refers to the rule of the last Tarquin, called Tarquinius Superbus. The epithet refers (a) to his arrogance, which led to his overthrow and the establishment of the Republic, and (b) to the magnificence that Rome attained under his regime.

35. fasces: the bundles of rods containing axes, carried by the lictors as symbols originally of the authority of the kings, later of the consuls. **Catonis:** Cato Uticensis, who ended his life by suicide at Utica in 46 B.C. after Caesar's victory at Thapsus, was the champion par excellence of the Republican cause. Hence the present allusion, in an ode whose climax is the praise of Augustus, has not only caused surprise, but has even led some critics to suggest change in the text. But Cato had not been a personal opponent of Octavian, and the interval of some twenty years since his death had doubtless led to forgetfulness of the old party strife. Cato's character and motives, moreover, had been recognized by all as of singular purity and sincerity. A similar allusion to Cato occurs in 2.1.23, *et cuncta terrarum subacta praeter atrocem animum Catonis*; cf. also Virgil's tribute in *Aen.* 7.670, *secretosque pios, his dantem iura Catonem.* Similar encomiums occur in other contemporary writers.

36. nobile = *clarum*, as often.

37. Regulum: said to have been put to death with cruel tortures after his return to Carthage from Rome, where he had dissuaded the Senate from making an exchange of prisoners with the Carthaginians. The story is told in full in 3.5.13ff. **Scauros:** i.e., men like Scaurus; M. Aemilius Scaurus (163-89 B.C.) served with distinction in the Cimbrian war, and was twice consul. Valerius Maximus calls him *lumen ac decus patriae* (5.8.4), but the reputation of some members of the family was dubious. **animae:** gen. with *prodigum*, generous of his great life (because he died for his country).

38. Paulum: L. Aemilius Paulus, who fell at Cannae in 216 B.C. **Poeno:** i.e., Hannibal; the abl. absolute denotes time.

39. gratus: with adverbial force, gratefully. **insigni ... camena:** in verse that makes famous; *camena* by metonymy = *carmine*, song. In praising the national heroes Horace uses the native word *camena* instead of *musa*, with *insignis* in the causative sense. **referam:** I will tell of, celebrate.

40. Fabricium: a hero in the war with Pyrrhus (281-275 B.C.), famed for the integrity and simplicity of his character. Cicero calls him "the Roman Aristides": *Fabricio, qui talis in hac urbe qualis Aristides Athenis fuit* (*De Off.* 3.22.87).

41. incomptis Curium capillis: Manius Curius Dentatus was a contemporary of Fabricius, and like him served in the war against Pyrrhus. His simplicity of life is emphasized in the words *incomptis capillis*, with untrimmed hair. Like the early Greeks, the first Romans wore longer hair and beards.

42. utilem bello: i.e., fit for war, in predicate relation to *Curium*. **tulit:** bred, bore. **Camillum:** M. Furius Camillus, the hero of the Gallic invasion of 390 B.C.

43. saeva paupertas: stern poverty, personified as the mother of Curius and Camillus. The father, in this conceit, is the *avitus fundus*. **apto lare:** a home appropriate to his *avitus fundus*, a small ancestral farm; *lar*, originally the god of the hearth or household, is here used by metonymy for the dwelling.

45-60. Praise of the Marcelli and the Julian

house, particularly Augustus.

45. Crescit occulto aevo: grows with the silent passage of time.

46. Marcelli: the younger Marcellus, nephew and son-in-law of Augustus, whose untimely death, in September of 23 B.C., the year this ode was published, is commemorated by Virgil in *Aen*. 6.863ff. The name would also call to mind M. Claudius Marcellus, the conqueror of Syracuse, who won the *spolia opima* in 222 B.C., and was five times consul between that date and 208 B.C., when he was killed in action. **micat**: shines. **omnis**: i.e., all the other Roman worthies previously mentioned.

47. Iulium sidus: the star of the Julian line; *sidus* = fortune, as often, and though the allusion is to Augustus the word would naturally suggest the comet that appeared in broad daylight after the murder of Julius Caesar (Suetonius *Jul*. 88). **ignis ... minores**: the lesser stars; cf. *Epod*. 15.2, *minora sidera*. The metaphor of the moon outshining the stars is a commonplace, going back to Sappho and Pindar; the pictorial enclosure of *luna* by *ignis minores* is a Horatian touch.

49. pater atque custos: i.e., Jupiter. This brings us back to the beginning of Horace's catalog (line 13). The point of what follows is that Augustus is Jupiter's vicegerent on earth (as later the Christian church in Rome was to assert that the Pope is the *vicarius* or deputy of Christ, and kings were to declare their "divine right" to rule).

50. orte Saturno: vocative, son of Saturn. Horace is now addressing Jupiter. Saturn, the ancient Latin god of agriculture, was identified with Cronos as the father of Jupiter, Neptune, and Pluto.

51. data: sc. *est*. **tu secundo Caesare regnes**: may you reign with Caesar next to you in authority. The distinction between *proximus* and *secundus* observed in line 18 is conveniently forgotten here.

53. Ille: Augustus Caesar. **Parthos**: Horace's favorite foreign bogey, exaggerated as usual (*Latio imminentis*), though they were formidable enough

on their own ground and an acute embarrassment to the myth of Roman invincibility. See note on 1.2.22, *Persae*.

54. iusto triumpho: in a well-earned triumph, to be understood with *egerit*. *iusto* implies fulfillment of the conditions required for the celebration of a triumph.

55. subiectos: bordering on (with dat.). **orae**: used, much as above in line 5, in the general sense of region or district, but with the added notion of distance.

56. Seras: Gk. acc., from nom. *Seres*, lit. "Chinese," loosely applied to peoples living east of the Roman frontier in the vicinity of modern Bukhara, now in Soviet Central Asia. **Indos**: famed for their riches and treasures. The Romans had not yet come in contact with either *Seres* or *Indi*, but it was a natural ambition to include these peoples in the Roman empire.

57-59. te ... tu ... tu: the anaphora, coupled with the emphatic position of the pronouns at the beginning of these lines, closes the ode with due recognition of the supremacy of the god. **te minor** = subordinate to you (Jupiter). **aequus** is adverbial, justly or with justice.

58. gravi curru: Jove's "heavy chariot" was heard as thunder. **Olympum** = *caelum*.

59. parum castis = *incestis*, "polluted" by the vile orgies of the time. **inimica fulmina**: cf. *iracunda fulmina*, 1.3.40 note.

60. lucis: (sacred) groves. Dat. instead of the more regular *in* with the acc., as in 1.2.1 *terris*.

13

Horace's insane jealousy at Lydia's love of Telephus and his anger at Telephus' violent passion yield to words of advice about a better kind of love. The situation is not necessarily autobiographical; Lydia is a common erotic name in Horace (see note on 1.8.1), and Telephus is borrowed from Greek legend. The passionate persona in the first three stanzas is more Catullan or elegiac than

Horatian, while the role of observer that emerges in the last two is more typically Horatian. Meter: second Asclepiadean.

1-8. When you praise Telephus, Lydia, I go mad with jealousy.

2. roseam, cerea: his complexion is that of a very young man; he is a *puer* (line 11), like the lover in 1.5. *cerea* does not imply the unhealthy pallor of our "waxen," but a clear, smooth complexion. Suntans were not in vogue. Cf. Chloris' shoulder in 2.5.18.

4. difficili bile: with intractable anger. The **iecur** or liver, considered the seat of anger, secretes *bilis*, which was thought to affect the mind with anger, madness, or folly. By metonymy, therefore, *bile* = anger.

5. mens ... color, etc.: the list of physical symptoms is probably meant to recall Sappho 31 LP 5-16 and Catullus 51.

6. umor: i.e., a tear

7. furtim indicates he is trying to conceal his emotion.

8. quam ... penitus: how deeply. **macerer ignibus:** a near oxymoron, as the verb means to soak (as in Eng. *macerate*; its derived meaning is to exhaust, torment). But by convention, the inner fire of love is also liquid: see Catullus 51.10 *flamma demanat.*

9-12. I am fired with resentment at his fits of passion.

9. Uror combines the passivity of *macerer* and the fire metaphor of *ignibus;* the language reveals the speaker as the victim of his passions.

10. turpa(ve)runt: have disfigured (with bruises). **immodicae mero rixae:** drunken quarrels; we are meant to infer that Telephus has a nasty streak that comes out when he drinks. Cf. Cyrus in 1.17.23f., *cum Marte confundet Thyoneus proelia.*

12. memorem ... notam: a mark that reminds (i.e., that he bites when he makes love). Lucretius 4.1079ff. describes love-bites with disapproval,

remarking dryly that all this *non est pura voluptas.* **labris:** on your lips.

13-20. Don't expect such love to last; thrice happy are they whose love is free of quarrels and lasts for life.

13. audias, followed by a comma, gives us the only end-stopped line in the poem (except for the full stops at the end of each stanza). It suggests the slower pace of reflection.

14. speres: jussive or hortatory subj. **perpetuum** (esse): the subject is *(Telephum) laedentem.* **dulcia barbare:** contrasting juxtaposition—sweet lips, barbaric damage.

15. oscula = *labra,* lips.

16. quinta parte: a 1:5 dilution, suitable for mortal use, not "quintessence," which (though originally Aristotelian) comes in with medieval alchemy. **imbuit:** steeps, drenches. The idea of love as a divine nectar enters poetic vocabulary with Meleager A.P. 12.133 (GP 84); cf. Ben Jonson "To Celia":

The thirst, that from the soul doth rise,
   Doth aske a drink divine:
But might I of Jove's nectar sup
   I would not change for thine.

17. ter et amplius: a variation of the usual *terque quaterque,* as in Virgil Aen. 1.94.

18. irrupta, unbroken, is a *hapax legomenon* (see appendix C). **nec** governs both *divulsus* and *solvet.*

19. querimoniis: complaints, grievances. Gravestones of married couples sometimes bore the abbreviation *S. U. Q.* for *sine ulla querella.*

20. suprema ... die: euphemistic for *morte,* abl. with *citius.* **solvet** takes an understood *copulam* or *quos* (18) as object. An unbroken bond holds them, and a love not sundered by evil complaints will not break that bond (or will not separate them) before the final day.

14

An allegorical poem, generally said to be about the

ship of state. Fragments of Alcaeus (6 and 326 LP) use the same allegory. The metaphor of the state as a ship is deeply embedded in Greek, Latin, and English (*government* < Gk. κυβερνήτης, helmsman). Commentators as early as the rhetorician Quintilian (ca. A.D. 90) identified the allegory as political: *navem pro re publica, fluctus et tempestates pro bellis civilibus, portum pro pace atque concordia dicit* (8.6.44). The poem has also been seen as reflecting an actual storm that twice hit Octavian's ship and fleet after the battle of Actium (Suetonius *Aug.* 17.3), but many scholars believe that Horace wrote these lines before 32 B.C. W. S. Anderson (1966) has persuasively argued that the ship is not the state at all but a woman, already somewhat the worse for wear, about to embark once again on the stormy sea of love. There is an Alcaean model for this interpretation, too (frag. 306.14.ii LP), and Hellenistic epigrams kept alive the sexual metaphor of a woman as a ship: Dioscorides *A.P.* 5.54 (GP 7) 3-4, Asclepiades *A.P.* 5.161 (GP 40), Meleager *A.P.* 5.204 (GP 60). For the sea of love, cf. Horace 1.5.6-7, 13-16. Others interpret the ship as an allegory of love poetry or the poet's *ingenium*. For more on allegory, see appendix C. Meter: fourth Asclepiadean.

1-9. O ship, avoid the storm and make for port! Don't you see the damage already suffered? The ship cannot endure the storm.
1. referent in mare: will sweep you back out to sea. Early mariners kept close to shore. **novi fluctus:** new swells from another storm, i.e., fresh civil disturbances (or new love affairs).
2. quid agis: a common form of reproof; cf. Cicero *In Cat.* 1.11.27: M. *Tulli, quid agis!* **Fortiter occupa portum:** make every effort to reach port. *occupare* usually implies anticipation; so here, reach port before the storm gets worse.
3. ut: adverbial, how.
4. remigio: oarage, abl. of separation with *nudum*. **latus:** subject of *nudum [sit]*.
5. mālus: the mast. Note the interlocked order,

and the quantity of *malus*. The quantity of some words of this type (not including the word for mast) is illustrated by the hexameter line *mala mali malo meruit mala maxima mundo*, "the jaw of a bad man with an apple brought great evils upon the world." **saucius,** wounded, helps build the ship's personification.
6. antemnae: yardarms. **funibus:** ropes carried lengthwise along the hull from stem to stern, to strengthen the vessel; cf. Acts 27:17: "they used helps (i.e., reinforcements) to undergird the ship."
7. durare: endure, withstand; first used in this sense by the Augustan poets; later, it appears in post-Augustan prose writers. **carinae:** hull, a somewhat bold poetic plural; cf. *puppibus* below, line 14.
8. imperiosius: with *aequor*, more forceful or too powerful.

9-15. Your sails are torn, your shipboard gods are gone; your pedigree is useless, your crew demoralized.
9. lintea: linen or canvas, i.e., the sails (an adjective used as a substantive).
10. di: small images of the gods were often set up in the sterns of vessels; here, these have been swept away, and with them (by implication) the protection of the gods. **quos ... voces:** relative clause of purpose, to call upon. **iterum pressa malo:** when again beset by trouble.
11. Pontica pinus: Pontus (like Cyprus in 1.1.13) was famous for the ship timbers from its pine forests; cf. Catullus. 4. 10ff. *pinus* and *filia* (line 12) are both appositives of the subject of *iactes*. You (who are) Pontic pine, daughter of a famous forest. More personification, as in Catullus 64.1.
12. nobilis: with *silvae*.
13. iactes: boast, flaunt. Concessive subj. taking *genus* and *nomen* as objects. **inutile:** with both *genus* and *nomen*.
14-15. nil ... fidit: puts no trust; *nil* is acc. of result produced. **pictis puppibus:** like today's

wooden vessels in the Mediterranean, ancient ships were often painted in bright colors; in this context, *pictis* has almost the force of "gaudy," and may by *double entendre* refer to female cosmetics.

15-20. Beware! My annoyance has changed to concern; avoid the waters of the Cyclades.

15. nisi ... debes ludibrium: i.e., unless you are doomed to be the sport of the winds; cf. Virgil *Aen.* 6.75, *rapidis ludibria ventis*.

16. cave: beware! used absolutely.

17. Nuper: from *novomper*, newly, lately. **sollicitum ... taedium:** anxious weariness, hence repugnance, loathing, annoyance; *sollicitum* is causal, being transferred from the person to the thing. **quae:** sc. *fuisti* with *taedium* and *es* with *desiderium* and *curaque*; the verb is rarely omitted in subordinate clauses.

18. desiderium curaque non levis: my longing and my anxious care. *Desiderium*, longing for something absent, makes the attribution to the ship of state problematical. If the erotic interpretation of the allegory is correct, Horace is addressing a woman with whom he recently (*nuper*) had a less-than-idyllic affair (*sollicitum taedium*), but now he misses her and would not like to see her embarking on some new, tempestuous romance. *non levis* is litotes for *gravissima* or the like.

19-20. interfusa ... aequora: in Horace's word order, the seas are literally "poured between" the shining Cyclades. **nitentis ... Cycladas:** sometimes explained as a reference to the marble quarried at Paros, Naxos, and other islands in the group. Cf. Virgil *Aen.* 3.146, *niveam Parum.* Alternatively, the epithet may be transferred from the sea to the islands in it. The Cyclades are mentioned by name once elsewhere in Horace, as the haunt of Venus (3.28.14).

20. vites: jussive subjunctive.

15

After a poem about an unwise metaphoric sea

journey, this is about Paris' unwise legendary sea journey, back to Troy with Helen. Horace says in 2.12 that such lyric treatments of epic themes are unwise, but he repeats the effort in 3.11 and 27. Porphyrio states that the inspiration for this ode comes from a Greek poem of Bacchylides representing Cassandra's prophecy of Troy's fall. Here, the prophet of doom is the sea god Nereus. Most of the references are to heroes and events in Homer's *Iliad.* But as Horace's treatments of legend usually have some relevance to his contemporary world, it is reasonable to see in this ode a suggestion of the ill-fated affair of Antony and Cleopatra. Meter: third Asclepiadean.

1-5. While Paris was taking Helen over the sea to Troy, Nereus stilled the winds to utter his prophecy:

1. Pastor: in the position of emphasis, this downgrades Paris to a mere shepherd, so characterized because he was herding sheep on Mt. Ida when he made his famous judgment of Juno, Pallas, and Venus. **traheret:** a forceful word, as in the "rape" of Helen. Although neither raped nor dragged away against her will, she was stolen from her spouse Menelaus. In ancient law, any seduction was legally rape, a crime not against the woman but her proprietor.

2. Idaeis: i.e., Trojan, so called because of the mountains south of Troy. **perfidus hospitam:** contrasting justaposition. Paris' "rape" of Helen was especially perfidious because she was his hostess at Sparta.

3. obruit: overcame, overpowered (*OLD* 4c).

5. Nereus: disyllabic. Myth attributed prophetic powers to the sea gods; cf. "the ever truthful old man of the sea" Proteus in *Odyssey* 4.384ff.

5-12. "All of Greece is sworn to wreck your marriage to Helen, and Priam's city. What trials await your people! Already Pallas is preparing war.

5. Mala ... avi: with evil omen; cf. *Epod.* 10.1,

mala alite. Observation of the flight of birds was a standard mode of prophecy. The root of *avis* appears in *augur, auspex,* and *auspicium.*

6. quam: the understood antecedent is Helen. **repetet:** will seek to recover (also the technical term for a legal claim, e.g., *res repetundae*).

7. coniurata: legend had it that when Menelaus won the hand of Helen, the other Greeks swore to defend their marriage against interlopers. Cf. also the oath to sack Troy, *Il.* 2.286ff., *Aen.* 4.425f.

9-10. quantus ... sudor! Another echo from Epode 10, *O quantus instat navitis sudor tuis* (15). **moves:** you are causing (OLD 16). **funera:** deaths.

12. currus ... et rabiem parat: a slight zeugma, making wrath itself a weapon of war.

13-20. "In vain you preen your hair and play pretty songs; in vain you avoid battle; the time will come when dust will foul your locks.

13. Veneris praesidio ferox: arrogant because of the protection of Venus; in *Il.* 3.380ff. she rescues him from Menelaus. His sexuality and the golden apple he awarded her create a special bond between them.

14. pectes caesariem: will comb your flowing hair, part of Paris' good looks; cf. his *comptos crines* in 4.9.13. For voluptuous male locks, see note on 4.10.3.

15. carmina divides: a unique expression = will sing, suggesting an excessive refinement that has been variously explained. Whatever it is, the women like it (14, *grata ... feminis*).

16. thalamo, in your bedchamber, abl. with *vitabis;* Horace is alluding to the scene in *Il.* 3 where Venus takes Paris to his bedchamber after rescuing him from Menelaus.

17. calami spicula Cnosii: lit. points of the Cretan arrow (collective sing.) Cnossus stands by metonymy for all of Crete, famous for its archers.

18-19. celerem sequi Aiacem: this is the second of two Ajaxes in the *Iliad,* the son of Oileus, famous for his speed (*Il.* 14.520f.).

19. serus: because so many others will have died

before him.

20. collines: you will soil or defile, an ironic reminder of line 14, *pectes caesariem.*

21-32. "Think of the adversaries you will face: Ulysses, Nestor, Teucer, Sthenelus, Meriones, and Diomedes; you will flee like a hunted animal.

21. Laërtiaden: Gk. acc., son of Laertes: Ulysses' patronymic.

22. Nestora: king of Pylos; no physical threat, but the oldest and wisest of the Achaeans. See *Il.* 2.371ff. **respicis:** look back at (as they pursue), have regard for.

23. Urgent: they are hot on your trail.

24. Teucer of Salamis, great Ajax' half brother. See on 1.7.21. **Sthenelus:** Diomedes' charioteer, not a major figure in the *Iliad.*

25. sive, etc.: compressed diction, omitting the first *sive* before *pugnae.* He is knowledgeable, whether of battle or whether it is necessary to exercise command over horses.

26. Merionen: squire of Cretan leader Idomeneus (see 1.6.15), but also mentioned in Homer as a companion of Diomedes, hence linked here with Sthenelus.

27. nosces: sinister understatement, you will get to know.

28. Tydides melior patre: alludes to Sthenelus' claim about himself and Tydeus' son Diomedes in *Il.* 4.405.

29-31. Relieved of hyperbaton, this could be paraphrased *quem tu mollis fugies sublimi anhelitu uti cervus, graminis immemor, fugit lupum visum in altera parte vallis.* *vallis* is gen. with *parte;* *sublimi anhelitu:* with shallow, panting breath; the phrase seems to have been suggested by Gk. πνεῦμα μετέωρον. See *sublimis,* OLD 3d. The epic simile is in the manner of Homer.

32. non hoc pollicitus tuae: adversative: though this isn't what you promised your (Helen). For the semi-colloquial ellipsis, using the feminine pronominal adj. as a substantive, cf. 1.25.7 *me tuo* and

Ovid *Rem. Am.* 573 *ut posses odisse tuam, Pari.*

33-36. "The wrath of Achilles will postpone the end, but after a set time Greek fire will burn Trojan homes."
33-34. Iracunda ... classis Achillei: i.e., the wrath of Achilles in his quarrel with Agamemnon, during which he withholds his Myrmidons from the fighting. This is the main theme of the *Iliad*. For the rhetorical figure, see appendix C, hypallage. **Phrygum:** gen. pl., the Trojans. The Troad is in western Phrygia (see map 4).
35. Note the asyndeton, which omits an adversative conjunction (e.g., *sed, tamen*). **certas hiemes:** the ten years determined by fate until the fall of Troy.
36. ignis: the short second syllable in a glyconic is abnormal in Horace; some editors have tried to repair the line by substituting for *Iliacas* a word such as *Pergameas* that starts with a consonant. But as Homer often treated ˇΙλιος as if it began with the consonantal digamma, it is likely Horace has in mind Ϝιλιακᾶς, making the second syllable of his line long by position. Such antiquarian flourishes were common in Alexandrian poetry.

16

A peacemaking overture to an unnamed woman, said by the scholiasts to be an imitation of the *Palinode to Helen* by the Greek poet Stesichorus. The main body of the poem (5-21) is "a hyperbolical and mock heroic development on the power and danger of anger" (NH *ad loc.*). Seeking some autobiographical relevance, Porphyrio connected the woman addressed with Tyndaris of the following ode, and others have referred it to the attacks on Canidia (*Gratidia*) in Epodes 5 and 17. But the personal remarks more likely reflect Horace's evolution from the mainly satiric author of the *Epodes* to the erotic and encomiastic poet of the *Odes*. For this oblique self-revelation, it may be compared to Epode 14. Meter: Alcaic strophe.

1-4. Destroy my abusive iambs however you like.
1. matre pulchra: abl. of comparison. Horace's riddling form of address could describe Leda's daughter Helen, who came up in Ode 15 and was the subject of Stesichorus' recantation as described in *Epod.* 17.42-44. It could even be Horace's Muse (daughter of Memory), who though not the object of any iambic attack may have been offended by his writing of abusive verses. For flattery of a woman's mother in conciliatory verses, cf. Archilochus S478 Page (P. Colon. 7511) 10-12.
2. quem ... cumque: tmesis, as in 1.6.3, and frequently. **criminosis:** full of accusations (*crimina*), hence abusive. **modum** = *finem*, as in 2.6.7.
3. pones: future indicative with the force of an imperative (or possibly permissive), you may put; cf. 1.7.1, laudabunt. **iambis:** iambic poetry, by traditional account first cultivated among the Greeks by Archilochus, is the conventional vehicle of invective and personal abuse. Hence in Latin *iambi* often = invective verses. This meaning occurs frequently in Horace, who calls his epodes *Iambi* (e.g., in *Epod.* 14.7) from their frequent polemic character. **flamma, mari:** alternative modes of disposal.
4. libet: with *sive*, whether it is pleasing. **Hadriano:** for the use of a particularizing epithet to avoid a general term, see appendix C, synecdoche.

5-12. No divinity shakes up the mind as much as anger; no fear can deter it. Discourses *de ira* were a commonplace in antiquity, and warnings against its destructive power were so universal that Homer's *Iliad* was reduced in the schools to a cautionary tale: *mihi contigit ... doceri iratus Grais quantum nocuisset* (*Epist.* 2.2.41f.).
5-7. The repetition of **non** four times in this stanza gives Horace's language a humorously portentous flavor. **Dindymene** is Cybele, the goddess of Dindymon, a mountain in Phrygia. For the mental frenzy of her worshippers, see Catullus 63 and note on *Corybantes* below. **adytis,** from

adytum (Gk. ἄδυτον = not to be entered), refers to the innermost part of the temple, where the priestess had her seat. **quatit:** shake up, perturb; the verb is to be understood with each of three subjects: *Dindymene, incola Pythius,* and *Liber.*

6. sacerdotum: generalizing plural; there was only one priestess at a time. **incola Pythius:** Apollo, the god that dwells in Pytho's shrine. Pytho was the ancient name of Delphi. The frenzy of the Pythia, priestess of Apollo, is described in Virgil *Aen.* 7.77ff.

7. Liber: Bacchus. **aeque:** i.e., as much as anger. **acuta:** with *aera,* sharp sounding (of the clash of cymbals).

8. geminant: clash together, of the pairs of cymbals. There is a change of construction here: Dindymene, Apollo, and Liber do not shake the minds of their priests as much as anger; the Corybants do not clash their cymbals with the same mind-shaking effect as anger. The *non ... sic ... ut* construction governs all four items in this stanza. **Corybantes:** priests of Cybele, whose religious ceremonial consisted in wild music and frenzied dancing, in which they would beat their breasts and gash their bodies with knives. Since the introduction of the worship of Cybele in about 200 B.C., it had been possible to witness these orgies at Rome itself. **aera:** neut. pl., bronze cymbals. *aes* is used of various objects made of copper, brass, or bronze such as statues, coins, vases, etc.

9. irae: plural, because separate instances are thought of. **Noricus:** Noric steel (from Noreia in Styria) was famous for its hardness. Cf. *Epod.* 17.71, *ense Norico.*

12. ruens: rushing down, as in Virgil *Georg.* 1.324 (of rain) *ruit arduus aether.* **tumultu:** not of any single phenomenon (thunder, lightning, hail, snow, rain, etc.), but of all together.

13-21. Prometheus gave us the lion's wrath when he made us. Wrath brought Thyestes down, and has laid low entire cities.
13. Fertur: is said. This version is found only

here, but the myth of the creation of man from clay by Prometheus goes back to Plato (*Protagoras* 11). **principi limo:** the primeval clay from which man was first created.

14. coactus (with *addere*): when forced to add. Apparently the animals were formed first and there was not enough clay left for the creation of man. **undique:** i.e., from every creature.

15. desectam: cut away. **et,** also, intensifies what follows.

16. vim: violence, fury. **stomacho:** as the seat of the emotions; cf. 1.6.6, *gravem Pelidae stomachum.*

17. Irae: emphatic by position and context, wrath it was that laid Thyesten low; the plural as in line 9. **Thyesten:** the feud between Atreus and Thyestes led the former to kill Thyestes' sons and serve their flesh at a banquet to their father. Horace's friend Varius (1.6.1) had recently published his tragedy *Thyestes.*

18. stravere: *straverunt,* laid low. **urbibus:** e.g., Thebes, destroyed when it defied Philip II in 338 B.C. Horace may be thinking also of Corinth and Carthage, both of which were vengefully razed to the ground by Roman armies but subsequently rebuilt. For the walls of Corinth, sacked by Memmius in 146 B.C., see on 1.7.3. *urbibus* is dat. with *stetere* (for tall cities). **ultimae causae:** the original cause, pl. in agreement with *irae*; *causae* is predicate nom. with *stetere.*

19. stetere, stronger than *fuere,* implies fixity and inevitability.

20. funditus: utterly, from their foundation. **imprimeret ... aratrum:** to drive a plow over the ruins of a city symbolized its permanent destruction; cf. Jeremiah 26:18, "Zion shall be plowed like a field." **muris:** i.e., fragments of the ruined walls.

21. insolens: arrogant in its victory.

22-28. I too gave in to rage in my youth and wrote iambic poems; but now I repent and beg forgiveness.
22. Compesce: curb, restrain. **pectoris:** gen. with *fervor.*

23. temptavit: tempted, led astray.

24. celeres: swift because of the meter; also impetuous.

25. misit furentem: drove me in madness; in *Epist.* 1.2.62 Horace says *ira furor brevis est*, anger is short-lived madness. **mitibus:** abl. of price, here governing the thing taken in exchange, with *mutare*; I want to supplant harsh things with gentle ones. For the alternative construction, see 1.17.2 below.

26. mutare: *quaero* with the infinitive is found only in the Augustan poets and later prose writers. **tristia:** i.e., my truculent words. **dum:** with the subjunctive *fias*, if only, provided only.

28. opprobriis: causal abl. absolute with *recantatis* above; this may refer to the harsh words of Horace's *iambi*, but Horace leaves it ambiguous whether he or the woman is recanting. **animum:** sc. *tuum*, your good will. If the *filia* of line 1 is the Muse, these final words make the poem a playfully conceived invocation; cf. the oblique invocation of Euterpe and Polyhymnia near the end of 1.1.33f.

17

The Tyndaris Ode. Horace invites a lady friend to visit him and enjoy the pastoral delights of his Sabine farm. The poetry contrasts safety with violence, protection with predation. The poem may be read as a seduction ode, but it has traditionally been understood as emphasizing the poet's unique access to the *pax deorum* bestowed by Faunus. For other picnic invitations, see 2.3.9-16, 2.11.13-17. Meter: Alcaic strophe.

1-12. Faunus often comes to the mountain near my farm and spreads his benign influence.

1. Lucretilem: a Sabine hill, like Ustica (line 11), near Horace's country retreat.

2. mutat: this verb may mean to give or take in exchange; here it has the second meaning. Faunus (identifiable here with Pan) takes the acc. *Lucretilem* in exchange for the abl. *Lycaeo*, a mountain

in southwestern Arcadia associated with the cult of Pan.

3. aestatem: the midsummer heat; see note on 17f., *Caniculae ... aestus.* **capellis ... meis:** dat. of separation with **defendit**, wards off from my goats.

4. usque: always, when he is here. The sense of permanence and timelessness is strengthened also by *saepe* (1) and *utcumque* (10). **pluvios ... ventos:** rainy winds.

5. Impune: harmlessly, emphasized by juxtaposition with **tutum**. The benign security of Horace's pastoral retreat is a central idea of this ode. **arbutos:** prized for their shade; cf. 1.1.21.

6. latentis: with both *arbutos* and *thyma*, hiding or hidden among the other greenery. **thyma:** neuter, appropriately plural like the *arbutos* because the goats wander from plant to plant. **deviae:** wandering.

7. olentis uxores mariti: a playful periphrasis for *capellae*, wives of a rank husband; for the personification of the billy goat, cf. Virgil *Ecl.* 7.7, *vir gregis ipse caper.*

9. Martialis ... lupos: warlike predators, identified with Mars because a she-wolf suckled his sons Romulus and Remus; Virgil *Aen.* 9.566, *Martius lupus.* **haediliae:** kids, a diminutive of *haedus.* Subject of *metuunt*, understood from the previous line.

10. utcumque: whenever. **Tyndari:** a fictitious name, suggesting a second Helen (daughter of Tyndareus). **fistula:** the syrinx or panpipe, made of seven reeds of unequal length bound together with cord and wax. The idea is that Faunus comes and protects the flocks whenever he hears the sound of the panpipe.

11. Usticae: probably the hill near Horace's Sabine villa on which the village of Licenza now stands. **cubantis:** sloping.

12. personuere: have echoed, making the animals feel secure. The subjects are *valles* and *saxa.*

13-16. The gods watch over me; here you will have plenty of the countryside's best.

13. Di me tuentur: because of his *pietas* and his *Musa*. A strong personal statement, placed for emphasis at the center of the ode.

14. cordi: idiomatic dat. of purpose with adjectival force (*OLD* 5b), dear to the gods, *dis*; a double dat. construction. **est:** with *pietas* and *Musa*, properly a plural. **hinc ... Hic** (17) **... hic** (21): repetition to emphasize the almost mystical sense of place with which Horace invests his Sabine retreat, a *locus amoenus* in which life can be enjoyed at its best. **copia,** as subject of *manabit*, is abstract, but there is a suggestion of the allegorical goddess Copia.

15. ad plenum: adverbial, to the full; note the cumulative tone of *ad plenum, benigno,* and *opulenta.* **benigno ... cornu:** the abundant horn, the so-called horn of plenty or cornucopia. Originally belonging to the goat that suckled Zeus, it was an attribute of Earth and Fortuna and became a symbol of the Augustan regime, e.g., on the cuirass of the Prima Porta statue of Augustus.

16. ruris honorum can be taken as depending on *opulenta, cornu,* or *copia*; the honors of the field are its crops; cf. *Epod.* 11.6, *silvis honorem decutit,* where the "honor" is foliage. **cornu:** abl. of source with *manabit.*

17-28. Here you will sing and drink in safety, with no fear of your boyfriend's jealous violence.

17. reducta: set back. **Caniculae:** the dog star and the oppressive summer heat that it brings; though a diminutive, *Canicula* refers to Sirius, "the greater dog," rather than Procyon, "the lesser dog" (3.29.18). Its rising on July 26 heralded the "dog days." Cf. Spenser, *Faerie Queene* 1.3.31, "scorching flames of fierce Orion's hound."

18. aestus: heat. **fide Teïa:** on a Tean string, viz. on a lyre from the town of Teos on the Ionian coast of Anatolia (see map 4) where the poet Anacreon lived in the sixth century B.C. Tyndaris will sing a love song in the style of Anacreon.

19. laborantis: acc. plural, referring to Penelope and Circe, who are afflicted with love for Ulysses.

Laborare is often used of diseases and other troubles, but it also means "take pains over," as both characters in the Odyssey aided the hero. **in uno:** for a single man, Ulysses, who spent a year with Circe before returning to his wife on Ithaca.

20. vitream: probably glassy, an enigmatic epithet applied to the enigmatic goddess who turned men into animals but took a shine to Odysseus and gave him useful advice for his return journey. In 4.2.3 *vitreo ponto,* the sea is glassy by virtue of its glitter.

21. innocentis ... Lesbii: his Lesbian wine is harmless because it does not lead to drunken quarrels, as the *nec-* clause explains.

22. duces: drink slowly. **Semeleïus ... Thyoneus:** two matronymics for Bacchus, son of Semele or Thyone. The second name is derived from Gk. θύ-ειν, to rage like a Bacchant. The heavy diction is slightly mocking.

23-24. confundet ... proelia: denotes confused brawling; cf. American slang "mix it up."

24. protervum: headstrong, impetuous.

25. suspecta indicates the suspicion of Cyrus that Tyndaris is being unfaithful to him. **male dispari:** sc. *tibi.* She would be no match for him in a fight. The phrase is asseverative: only too unmatched; cf. *Sat.* 1.3.31, *male laxus calceus, ib.* 45, *male parvus.*

26. incontinentis: unrestrained, violent.

27. crinibus: dat. with *haerentem.* **immeritam,** her dress, nearly personified, is as undeserving of abuse as she is. The nasty scene at the end contrasts with the sheltered calm Horace offers on his Sabine farm.

18

In praise of wine when used in moderation. The opening line is based on a line of Alcaeus (342 LP) in the same meter, but as usual Horace gives his Hellenistic poem an Italian setting. Meter: fifth Asclepiadean.

1-6. Plant grapevines first, Varus. Life is hard without wine; it relieves troubles.

1. Vare: either Virgil's literary friend Quintilius Varus or the jurist P. Alfenus Varus, for whom see appendix A. **severis:** from *sero*, plant. The perfect subjunctive in prohibitions is practically confined to poetry and colloquial prose. Cf. 1.11.1, *tu ne quaesieris*. **arborem:** so called also in the original line of Alcaeus (the diminutive *dendrion*). The elder Pliny (*Nat. Hist.* 14.9) says that vines, because of their size, were rightly called trees by the early Romans, and gives some instances to illustrate the statement.

2. circa mite solum Tiburis: loosely put for *in miti solo circa Tibur*. A soft, mellow soil is suited to the vine. **Tiburis:** praised in 1.7.11ff. Varus evidently had a villa in the neighborhood. **moenia Catili:** tradition had it that the Arcadian brothers Catilus, Tiburtis, and Coras founded Tibur; the town was named from Tiburtis, and the mountain overhanging it, still called Monte Catillo, from Catilus; cf. 1.7.13.

3. siccis: like today's "drys," nondrinkers are often designated *sicci*, just as *madidus, uvidus*, etc. are used of those who indulge; cf. 4.5.39, *siccus* and *uvidus*. **nam:** postponed, like *enim*. **dura:** in predicate relation to *omnia*, has ordained that all shall be hard (lit. has set forth all things hard). **deus:** not Bacchus, but the supreme power generally conceived.

4. mordaces: biting, consuming; cf. Virgil *Aen.* 1.261, *quando haec te cura remordet*. **aliter:** in any other way than by the gift of Bacchus.

5. crepat: harps on, rattles on about.

6. Quis non, etc.: sc. *crepat*, now in a more cheerful sense, prattles about. **Bacche pater:** the Greeks conceived of Bacchus as always young. The epithet *pater* implies reverence, but not necessarily age. **decens:** comely, as in 1.4.6 *Gratiae decentes*.

7-11. Yet past examples prove the dangers of excess.

7. Ac: with adversative force, and yet. **ne quis**

depends on *monet*, line 8. **modici ... Liberi:** of a moderate Bacchus; cf. *verecundum Bacchum*, 1.27.3. To vary his language Horace uses four different names for Bacchus; cf. *Euhius* (9), *Bassareu* (11). **transiliat:** overleap, carelessly abuse; cf. 1.3.24, *non tangenda rates transiliunt vada*.

8. Centaurea ... rixa: the battle of the Centaurs and Lapiths at the marriage-feast of Pirithous. The Centaurs, invited to the wedding by Pirithous, drank too much and tried to carry off the bride, Hippodamia. This was a favorite subject of art, e.g., on the western pediment of the temple of Zeus at Olympia and on the metopes of the Parthenon. **monet ... monet** (9): repetition emphasizes the importance of the warning. **Lapithis:** described in the myths as a Thessalian people; Pirithous was their king.

9. debellata: fought out to the bitter end; cf. 1.3.13, *decertantem*. The Centaurs were all slain. **Sithoniis:** a Thracian tribe, put here for the Thracians in general; cf. 1.27.1f., *Natis in usum laetitiae scyphis pugnare Thracum est.* **non levis:** litotes for *iratus* or the like. **Euhius:** Bacchus; the name came from the cries of his worshippers, *euoi! euoi!*

10. exiguo fine libidinum: by the small limit set by their passions, the point being that passions are a poor guide to good and evil. Cf. Shakespeare *Timon* 5.4.5, "making your wills the scope of justice."

11. discernunt: distinguish. **avidi** may be taken substantively, people who are greedy.

11-16. I don't want to stir you up, Bacchus: hold off your noisy music, and the follies that go in your train.

11. Non ego: emphatically placed: I won't be the one to .... **candide:** as being young and fair-skinned (notwithstanding the *Bacche pater* of line 6), also happy, good-natured. **Bassareu:** another designation for Bacchus; the word (in Gk. βασσαρεύς from βασσάρα, fox-skin mantle) was applied to Bacchus as the god whose votaries wore the fox-skin in their worship.

12. quatiam: shake up, apparently in the sense of rouse (cf. 1.16.5, *quatit mentem*); i.e., I will not provoke you by excessive indulgence. **variis obsita frondibus:** sc. *sacra*, mystic emblems covered with leaves of various kinds (such as the vine and ivy, which were sacred to Bacchus), and carried by the worshippers in wicker boxes, as described by Catullus in 64.259f. Any uninitiated person who looked at the mystic emblems was said to become mad.

13. sub divum: to the light of day; cf. 2.3.23 *sub divo*, beneath the heaven. **Saeva:** the drums are wild or savage because their beating drives the worshipper to frenzy. **tene:** hold back or check, as in American slang "hold the mustard." **Berecyntio:** from Berecyntus, a mountain in Phrygia noted for the celebration of the wild rites of Cybele (see note on 1.16.8, *Corybantes*). The Berecyntian horn belonged to the worship of Cybele, but similar horns were used in the Bacchic orgies. In fact, the two cults were often conflated, e.g., in Catullus 63.23 and 69.

14. caecus Amor sui: blind self-love, the first of three personified follies who follow in the train of an excessive Bacchus.

15. plus nimio: with *tollens*, too high. This use of *nimium* (more by very much) is colloquial and poetic. **Gloria:** here Vainglory personified. **verticem:** crown, i.e., head, appropriately empty (*vacuam*).

16. arcani ... Fides prodiga: the third personified follower. A faith lavish of secrets is one that betrays its trust. Such *perfidia* would be a natural result of the intemperate use of Bacchus' gift. For *prodigus* with the gen., cf. 1.12.37, *animaeque magnae prodigum Paulum*. **perlucidior vitro:** more transparent than glass because it hides nothing. The second metrical pause is here neglected, as often where Horace uses a compounded preposition: cf. 2.12.25 *de* || *torquet* and Ars P. 263 *im* || *modulata*.

19

Horace plays here with some love motifs, reviving the in-love-again theme of Epode 11 and the *recusatio* first essayed in Epode 14, where the poet begs off writing about Roman warfare because he is hampered by love. Glycera, the mercenary hetaera who invokes Venus in 1.30, is the human agent of his affliction, but the agony may be more literary than autobiographical. Meter: second Asclepiadean.

1-8. Venus, Bacchus, and Misrule call me back to love. Glycera's looks and boldness have me on fire.

1. Mater ... Cupidinum: this conception of Venus is as old as Pindar, frag. 122.4 μᾶτερ Ἐρώτων. The entire line is repeated in 4.1.5.

2. Thebanae ... Semelae puer: Bacchus; see appendix C, periphrasis.

3. lasciva Licentia: outrage or hybris personified as sexually unrestrained, wanton. Horace is cheerfully unromantic about his driving forces even while clothing them in mythological garb.

4. finitis ... reddere amoribus leaves it unclear whether this affair with Glycera is old business renewed, or a new discovery that has brought him out of retirement. For the literary pedigree of the in-love-again theme, see the intro. to Epode 11.

5. Glycerae: a common name of hetaeras in real life and New Comedy. A Glycera is the title character of Menander's *Perikeiromene*. See also 1.30, 1.33, 3.19. **nitor:** radiant beauty. Cf. 1.5.13, *miseri, quibus intemptata nites*, 2.8.6 *enitescis*.

6. splendentis: gen. with *Glycerae* above. **Pario marmore:** marble from Paros was the whitest. For comparison of fair skin with marble, cf. Asclepiades A.P. 5.194 (GP 34), 3 and Virgil Geor. 4.523 (of Orpheus) *marmorea cervice*.

7. protervitas: forwardness, a virtue among Horace's women. Cf. Lalage *proterva fronte*, 2.5.15f., Lycymnia's *flagrantia oscula* and *facili saevitia*, 2.12.25f.

8. nimium lubricus aspici: quite hazardous to

look at because of its effect on the beholder's equanimity.

9-16. Venus has descended on me, and I cannot write of war. Prepare a sacrifice! She will be gentler if appeased.
9. tota ruens: rushing in full force. The language is Euripidean, *Hipp.* 443; a common theme of Euripidean tragedy was the destructive force of erotic passion. By Horace's time it was a cliché, no longer necessarily tragic.
10. Cyprum: an ancient center of the cult of Aphrodite; Venus is often called *Cypris*, the Cyprian. **Scythas:** used vaguely of any primitive enemies in the general area of the Black Sea. See NH 1.xxxiv.
11. versis animosum equis: collective singular, bold when their horses are turned in flight. A favorite tactic of the Parthians was to feign retreat, and then to turn suddenly and fire a volley of arrows at their pursuers, whence the proverbial "Parthian shot," used of a cutting remark made in parting.
12. quae nihil attinent: things of no importance. This point of view is diametrically opposed to what Horace says in his patriotic poems.
13. vivum caespitem: fresh turf, normally used to top off sacrificial altars.
14. verbenas: generic for the aromatic greenery used to trim out an altar; cf. Eng. *vervain.* **tura:** incense.
15. bimi ... meri: two-year-old wine, i.e., wine aged more than one year. See on *quadrimum,* 1.9.7. Wine for sacrifice had to be straight *merum,* i.e., undiluted with water. A *patera* was a shallow bowl used for pouring libations.
16. mactata ... hostia: abl. abs., if a sacrificial animal has been slain. **lenior:** more kindly.

20

Invitation poems such as Philodemus A.P. 11.44 and Catullus 13 supply the framework for this ode.

Addressed to a person of greater wealth or higher standing, they contrast the poet's modest standard of living with the magnificence of the guest. The combination of themes is useful to Horace, who frequently in the *Odes* dwells on the simplicity of his personal arrangements, and just as often finds ways to flatter his patron Maecenas. The meter is Sapphic strophe.

1-3. You will drink cheap wine that I bottled myself.
1. vile: cheap, not vile or distasteful. For more on Horace's preferences in wine, see *Epist.* 1.15.17ff. **potabis:** Horace skips the actual invitation. **modicis:** plain or common, referring to the material of which they were made. **Sabinum:** sc. *vinum;* it was local wine, one of the poorer grades.
2. cantharis, Graeca ... testa: Latin wine in Greek containers. The cups (Gk. κάνθαροι) are plain, deep, two-handled drinking pots. The Greek jar, *testa,* was treated with salt to preserve the wine. NH 1.247, Cato *De Agr.* 24, Plautus *Rudens* 588. The wine from such jars, like modern Gk. retsina, was anything but a delicacy.
3. conditum: put up, stored. **levi:** (from *lino*) sealed with wax or gypsum. Participle-verb combinations like this are usually treated in English as coordinate verbs, *put up and sealed.*

3-8. I bottled it when you came into the theater to thunderous applause.
3-4. datus ... plausus: after his recovery from a dangerous illness in 30 B.C., Maecenas was greeted with tumultuous applause upon his appearance in the theater; the event is again alluded to in 2.17.25f. With *datus* understand *est.* **in theatro:** the Theater of Pompey, situated in Rome's Campus Martius. The theater was far too distant from the Vatican hill and the west bank of the Tiber to produce the echo mentioned in the second stanza. That is purely the poet's fanciful exaggeration.
5. care Maecenas eques: Horace adds *eques,* in apposition with *Maecenas,* as a complimentary title

(cf. 3.16.20, *Maecenas, equitum decus*) and because he too was an *eques*. Maecenas held aloof from political ambition and the promotion to senatorial rank that it entailed, remaining by preference a member of the equestrian order. **paterni fluminis:** the Tiber, called Maecenas' native river because he was born in Etruria and descended from Etruscan kings (cf. 1.1.1, *Maecenas atavis edite regibus*), and because the Tiber was *par excellence* the Etruscan river; cf. *Sat.* 2.2.32, *amnis Tusci*; Virgil *Aen.* 2.781, *Lydius* (= Etruscan) *Thybris.*

6-8. iocosa ... imago: the playful echo, as in 1.12.3-4, *cuius recinet iocosa nomen imago*. The delay of *imago* imitates the delay of the echo.

7. redderet: returned, brought back to your ears. **Vaticani:** the name was originally applied to the northern spur of the range of hills on the west side of the Tiber, of which the Janiculum is the highest. Later poets, e.g., Martial and Juvenal, treat the antepenult as long.

9-12. You have better vintages at home than any that fill my cups.

9. Caecubum: sc. *vinum*; the Caecuban, like the three other wines mentioned in this stanza, was one of the choicer Italian vintages. It was grown in Caecubum, a marshy district of southern Latium. **prelo ... Caleno:** in a Calenian wine-press, i.e., at Cales (mod. Calvi) in northern Campania. **domitam:** crushed, poetic for *pressam.*

10. bibes: you may drink, i.e., at your own home; for the concessive future, cf. *laudabunt*, 1.7.1. This verb brings us back to the theme of *potabis* with which the poem began. **uvam:** grape, wine by metonymy. **mea:** in strong contrast with *tu*, and so placed at the beginning of its clause. For a similar contrast, cf. 2.16.33-37, *te greges centum ... mihi parva rura*. **Falernae ... vites:** metonymy for *Falerna vina*, a superior family of wines produced in the *ager Falernus*, in Campania at the foot of Mount Massicus; this is the sweet variety of Falernian; for the dry, strong variety, see note on 1.27.9-10.

11-12. temperant: flavor; strictly, *vinum temperare* means to dilute wine with water. The implication is that Maecenas' expensive wines are smoother. **Formiani ... colles:** metonymy for *Formiana vina*, which grew near Formiae in southern Latium, close to the borders of Campania.

21

Here Horace uses one of his favorite poetic forms, the hymn, to praise Augustus. The formal package is a hymn to Latona and her children Diana and Apollo. The second half of the ode concentrates on Apollo, whose agent turns out to be Augustus. The strategic reservation of this political tribute to two words near the end is tactful but effective. This ode has many similarities to Catullus 34, *Dianae sumus in fide*. Meter: fourth Asclepiadean.

1-8. Girls and boys, sing of Diana, Apollo, and Latona; girls, praise Diana goddess of the grove.

1. Dīanam: the quantity of the *i* in *Diana*, here long, varies. **dicite** = sing of, as in 1.6.5 *dicere*, and often.

2. intonsum ... Cynthium: Apollo is regularly imagined as young and long-haired. The hill on Delos, birthplace of Apollo and Diana, is named Cynthus; cf. Diana's epithet *Cynthia.*

3. Latonam: Latona or Leto is mentioned by Hesiod *Theog.* 918 as Jove's wife before he married Hera. Her rank in his affections is acknowledged in the adverb *penitus* (4).

4. dilectam ... Iovi: dat. of agent with the pf. participle, a common construction.

5. Vos (sc. *dicite*) is addressed to the girls. **laetam:** used substantively, (the goddess who is) happy in the rivers and foliage, i.e., Diana of the groves, *Diana nemorensis*. **coma**, abl. with *laetam*, is the standing metaphor for foliage. Cf. Catullus 4.10, *comata silva.*

6-8. Algido, Erymanthi, Cragi: Algidus, the ridge running between Tusculum and the Alban hills a few miles southeast of Rome, is characteristically linked with Erymanthus in northwest Arcadia and Cragus in western Lycia (Asia Minor, east of Rhodes; see map 4). Part of Horace's literary agenda is to link places in Italy with the Greek world; cf. 1.17.1-2.

7. nigris: dark green with heavy foliage.

9-16. Boys, sing of Apollo, who wards off war, famine, and pestilence, and will (with Caesar's help) inflict them on our enemies.

9. Tempe: neut. acc. pl. (as in 1.7.4), object of an understood *dicite*. This scenic valley between Mt. Olympus and Mt. Ossa had long been associated with the cult of Apollo. Note the repetition of *t-* sounds in this line.

11. insignem may be taken as substantive for Apollo (balancing *laetam* for Diana in line 5) with acc. of respect *umerum*, or simply as modifying *umerum*.

12. fraterna ... lyra: for the lyre as the invention of Apollo's half-brother Mercury, see 1.10.6 and note. It was Mercury's gift to Apollo.

13. Hic ... hic: Apollo, characterized in this stanza as the one who wards off evils, Gk. ἀλεξίκακος. He is represented in Horace and in official propaganda as Augustus' particular Olympian patron.

14. principe Caesare: abl. abs., under Augustus' principate. In 1.12.49ff. Augustus is represented as Jove's vicegerent; here, Horace implies that he is likewise Apollo's agent.

15. Persas atque Britannos: representative barbarian bogeymen. When Augustus went campaigning in Gaul in 27 B.C., it was thought he would also invade Britain (1.35.29f.). But even before that, Horace entertained fantasies of captive Britons in chains (*Epod.* 7.7-8).

22

Horace's eye for glib ideas that lend themselves to mockery comes to rest here on sentimental romanticism, fixing on the charming notion that a lover

pure of heart cannot be harmed by anything in nature. Where in Epode 2 he gave pretty expression to the trite joys-of-country-life theme, now he is so felicitous in his statement of the nothing-can-hurt-the-pure-of-heart idea that the first stanza of this poem was set to music and sung as a hymn in German schools. This opening, in fact, sounds like a respectable Stoic precept, but Horace gradually leads us on until we realize the nature of the joke. Echoes from Catullus point to the source of the romantic ideal being parodied, but the baldest declarations of the lover's invulnerability come from Horace's contemporaries Virgil (*Ecl.* 10.64-69), Propertius (3.16.11-18), and Tibullus (1.2.25-30). Meter: Sapphic strophe.

1-8. The man whose life is pure needs no weapons of defense, wherever he goes.

1. Integer vitae: gen. of specification or reference, a poetic construction. **sceleris** with **purus** is a similar construction, with a sense of separation more common in the Greek genitive.

2. non eget: a Stoic note, the insistence that we do not really need all sorts of things. **Mauris:** the specifying epithet lending color to a generic noun is a commonplace of Horace's poetic language. The reference to the Moors here and in line 15, *Iubae tellus*, however, is topical (see note below).

4. Fusce: Aristius Fuscus, a literary critic, close personal friend, and sometime wag (see appendix A). Addressing him in this context may be an early hint that Horace has something up his sleeve.

5-6. sive ... sive: with the catalog of distant places, this is like Catullus 11.2-9, also written in Sapphics.

5-8. Syrtis ... aestuosas, inhospitalem Caucasum, fabulosus ... Hydaspes: descriptive epithets are vaguely Homeric in tone; they swell the rhetoric as Horace heats up his language. The Syrtis are the hot coastal flats between Carthage and Cyrene; *inhospitalem Caucasum* echoes *Epod.* 1.12. The Hydaspes is a tributary of the Indus river about which there were many exaggerated stories featuring monstrous wild animals.

8. lambit: licks, washes.

9-16. For while I was wandering unarmed in the forest singing of my Lalage, a monstrous wolf ran away from me.

9. Namque, implying that what follows is a proof of what has been said, introduces a note of bogus logic. The position of **me** is emphatic.

10. Lalagen: Gk. acc.; the name suggests a babbler (Gk. λαλαγή = prattle).

11. terminum: supposedly the border of his own Sabine farm; the area, still forested, is a possible habitat for wolves, but it is more likely if Horace saw anything at all it was a neighbor's dog. Wolves regularly avoid contact with humans, rarely if ever attacking—contrary to folklore (e.g., 1.17.9, *martialis lupos*).

12. inermem: adversative, though I was unarmed.

13. portentum: both the supposedly miraculous retreat of the wolf and the wolf itself—particularly the latter, as the context shows.

14. Daunias = Apulia, Horace's homeland; its mythical king was Daunus. The valor of its warriors wins it the epithet *militaris*. **aesculetis:** oak forests (*aesculus* is a variety of oak).

15. Iubae tellus: Mauretania, mod. Morocco. After the battle of Thapsus in 46 B.C., Juba II, still an infant, was taken back to Rome as a hostage and raised as a Roman. He accompanied Octavian on his campaigns, fought on his side at Actium, and was restored to his father's throne in 25. His great learning and patronage of the arts made him anything but a savage: hence the strong irony of using his name to suggest a place of fearsome wild animals.

16. arida nutrix, an oxymoron, is also a touch of high rhetoric: Homer calls Mt. Ida μητέρα θηρῶν, "mother of beasts." By Juvenal's time, north Africa had become a "mother of lawyers," *nutricula causidicorum*, because of its schools of rhetoric

(Juvenal 7.148).

17-24. Put me in any frozen waste or sweltering desert—I will love sweet Lalage anywhere.

17. pigris ... campis: torpid plains or steppes; cf. Lucretius 5.746 (of ice) *pigrum rigorem*, Horace 2.9.5 *glacies iners*, 4.7.12 *bruma recurrit iners*.

19-20. malus ... Iuppiter: by metonymy, bad weather. A typical Indo-European sky god, Jupiter was always associated with weather phenomena such as rain, clouds, lightning, and thunder.

21-22. nimium propinqui solis: Aristotle, Pliny, and the poets agreed that climate is affected by the proximity of the sun rather than the angle of its rays.

23. dulce ridentem: a tag from Catullus 51.5, the second of his two poems in Sapphics (see note on lines 5-6 above).

24. dulce loquentem: from the source of Catullus 51, Sappho 31.3-4.

23

The comparison of a young girl to a fawn appears in a poem of Anacreon (408 Page). The name Chloe (Gk. χλόη, a young shoot) was doubtless chosen for its appropriateness, like Lydia and Sybaris in 1.8. The meter is fourth Asclepiadean.

1-8. You avoid me like a fawn, Chloe, who looks for its mother and trembles at every passing sound.

1. inuleo: a fawn, dat. with *similis*.

2. pavidam: a standing epithet of the deer, appropriate here because even the mother is timorous; cf. 1.2.11, *pavidae dammae*. **aviis:** trackless, lonely.

3. non sine: the litotes lends emphasis. **vano:** empty, needless.

4. siluae: trisyllabic, as in *Epod.* 13.2.

5. mobilibus ... foliis: among the quivering leaves. **veris ... adventus:** i.e., the arrival of a spring breeze. **inhorruit:** has made a rustling sound.

6. rubum: bramble.

7. dimovere: have pushed aside (in their sudden movements). **lacertae:** lizards.

8. tremit: sc. *inuleus*, the fawn.

9-12. I won't hurt you. Stop clinging to your mother; you are ready for a man.

9. Atqui: and yet.

10. Gaetulus: Gaetulia was a frontier region of northern Africa, south of the settled coastal area. **frangere:** infinitive of purpose: to crush with the jaws, as the lion does in *Il*. 11.113f.

12. tempestiva ... viro: causal, since you are ready for a man. The adjective is used of various states of readiness, ripeness, or timeliness; cf. Lavinia in Virgil *Aen*. 7.53 *iam matura viro, iam plenis nubilis annis*.

24

A poem of consolation, addressed to Virgil on the death of their mutual friend Quintilius Varus, on whom see appendix A. This type of dirge or threnody, combining lamentation with eulogy, later came to be known as an *epicedium*. Meter: third Asclepiadean.

1-4. What decent limit can there be to our grief? Teach us a sad song, Melpomene.

1. desiderio: dat. with *modus*, longing for someone absent. **sit:** deliberative subjunctive. **pudor:** decent restraint.

2. capitis: strongly emotional for *hominis*, as we might say "soul." Cf. Virgil *Aen*. 4.354, *capitisque iniuria cari*. **Praecipe:** teach, suggest. **lugubris cantus:** plural for singular, a song of mourning.

3. Melpomene: invoked not as the muse of tragedy (i.e., drama), but as a representative muse; so also in 3.30.16, 4.3.1. **liquidam:** clear-toned, melodious. **pater:** the nine muses were daughters of Jupiter and Mnemosyne (Memory).

5-8. Is he really dead? When will the virtues find his peer?

5. ergo: is it then true that (*OLD* 4). An exclamation of surprise and grief. **Quintilium:** see appendix A.

6. urget: weighs down, lies heavy on. **cui:** relative, dat. with *parem*. **Pudor:** personified Gk. αἰδώς: decency, honor.

7. nuda Veritas: i.e., the simple honesty of Quintilius' literary judgments. The metaphor "naked truth" is still current. In accordance with the conventions of Hellenistic statuary, Horace's allegorical goddesses are sometimes nude; cf. Gratia in 4.7.5f. In *Ars P*. 438ff.

8. inveniet: the singular verb with compound subject, as in 1.22.20, *urget*, and regularly in Horace. **parem:** with *cui*, his equal. Cf. Antony in Shakespeare *JC* 3.2.245: "Here was a Caesar. When comes such another?"

9-12. He was dear to many, but dearest to you, Virgil. You pray for his return in vain.

9-10. flebilis ... flebilior: mourned, deserving of grief. The point of the repetition, brought out in the next lines, is that neither his worthiness nor their grief will bring him back.

11. frustra: with both *pius* (devoted) and *poscis*. Cf. 4.7.23f., *non te restituet pietas*. **non ita creditum:** (a) not entrusted to the gods on the condition of his return to life (b) not entrusted to you, his friend, as a permanent possession.

12. Quintilium deos: double acc., of the thing asked for and the person asked.

13-20. Even if you played the lyre more sweetly than Orpheus himself, you could not restore the dead. Endure with patience what you cannot change.

13. Quid: sc. some such verb as *valeat*: what use is it? **Si ... moderere:** i.e., if you played the lyre (*fidem*) more sweetly than Orpheus himself; perhaps a subtle compliment to Virgil for his skilful treatment of the Orpheus myth in his fourth

Georgic, published not long before.

14. auditam: (once) heard, i.e., heard and heeded. Orpheus attracted not merely the beasts but even the trees by the charm of his music; cf. 1.12.7 *vocalem temere insecutae Orphea silvae*, 1.12.11 *blandum et auritas ducere quercus*. **moder-ere:** *modereris*, manage, modulate. **arboribus:** dat. of agent, frequent in Horace with the perfect passive participle. Cf. 1.1.24 *bella matribus detestata*.

15. num ... redeat, etc.: this question simply repeats in more specific form the query begun by *quid*; the same protasis (*si ... moderere*) is to be understood. **vanae imagini:** dat. with *redeat*, to the empty shade.

16. virga ... horrida: abl. with *compulerit* (18). Mercury's caduceus is so characterized because it is the symbol of passage to the dismal underworld. See 1.10.17-19 and note. **semel:** once and for all, as in 1.28.16 *calcanda semel via leti*, 4.7.21, *cum semel occideris*.

17. fata = *portas fatorum*. **recludere:** open, unlock, completing the sense of *lenis*.

18. nigro compulerit ... gregi: has gathered to his dark herd, dat. of direction instead of *ad* with the acc. For the meaning of the verb, cf. *omnes eodem cogimur*, 2.3.25. *nigro gregi* has a more sinister flavor than the *levis turba* of 1.10.

19. Durum: sc. *est*. **patientia:** instrumental abl. with *corrigere*. It is easier to set right with patience what it is *nefas* to set right (in any other way).

20. corrigere est nefas: it is forbidden by divine law to set right (because the dead cannot be restored to life); the oxymoron emphasizes the discrepancy between *fas* and *rectum*. The infin. *corrigere* is used ἀπὸ κοινοῦ as subject of *fit* and *est*. For the use of *nefas*, cf. 1.11.1, *scire nefas*.

25

The neglected state of an aging hetaera, taken from a traditional motif of Hellenistic poetry in which a lover locked out of his girlfriend's house reminds her in his *paraclausithyron* or serenade that she will one day be less attractive to men. Compare, for example, the epigram of Asclepiades *A.P.* 5.164 (GP 13). Catullus 8.14ff. uses the same themes against Lesbia; Horace applies the technique later to Ligurinus in 4.10, and to Lyce in 4.13. For a fuller account of the theme, see NH 1.289-292. The chilling vividness of Horace's account is especially striking, recalling Goethe's phrase about Horace's "dreadful reality" (*furchtbar Realität*). Meter: Sapphic strophe.

1-8. Admirers come less often, and you hear fewer appeals for pity than before. The present tense of *quatiunt, adimunt, amat*, and *audis* show that Lydia is already in the declining phase of her career.

1. Parcius: placed in the emphatic position: more sparingly, less often. **iunctas fenestras** are double shutters fastened by a wooden bar.

2. iactibus: lit. throwings, i.e., the blows of sticks or stones thrown by lovers to attract her attention; the windows are in the second story. **protervi:** bold, disorderly, impetuous.

3. tibi: dat. of separation; the final *i* is long, as in line 13 and often in poetry, a retention of the original quantity. **somnos:** poetic plural, as in English "slumbers." **adimunt:** steal, by the noise they make.

3-4. amatque ... limen: the only loving in a once-amorous house: the door that stays closed hugs the threshold. For the personification of a sexually active woman's door, cf. Catullus 67.

5. multum: adverbial acc. with *facilis*. This use of *multum* is frequent in Horace. **facilis:** with *quae*, more of the personification suggested by *amat* in the previous stanza; the door was once "quite easy" or complaisant.

6. cardines: hinges.

7. Me tuo ... pereunte, etc.: While I your lover pine away, etc. Words of a type of serenade known as a *paraclausithyron*, sung "outside a closed door" (hence the Greek name) by locked-out lovers. Vignettes of the aging hetaera were often a part of such songs. For the substantive use of *tuo*, cf. 1.15.32, *non hoc pollicitus tuae*. **longas ... noctes:** acc. of duration of time. **pereunte:** the usual exaggeration of the "dying" lover and the common poetic term; cf. 1.27.11, *quo vulnere pereat*.

8. Lydia: for this common hetaera's name, see note on 1.8.1.

9-20. Your turn will come to be out in the cold, a frantic hag complaining that young men prefer fresh greenery to withered leaves. The future tense of *flebis* (10) and *saeviet* (15) indicates a further stage of Lydia's decay.

9. Invicem = *vice versa*, *vicissim*. The scornful becomes the scorned. Emphatically placed, like *parcius* in line 1. **moechos ... arrogantis flebis:** you shall lament the disdain of your lovers; *arrogantis* is predicative. The phrase contrasts with *iuvenes protervi*; **moechos** (lit. adulterers) implies that the customers she will miss after becoming an *anus levis* are dirty old men rather than exuberant youths.

10. solo ... angiportu: a deserted alley, any of the narrow side streets where prostitutes plied their trade; her admirers no longer frequent her *angiportus*, having moved on to others. The phrasing recalls Catullus' abusive description of Lesbia whoring *in quadriviis et angiportis* (58.4). Now Lydia is out in the street, instead of her lovers. **levis:** with *anus*, negligible, weak, skinny, a mere hag.

11. Thracio, etc.: the allusion to the howling wind and the moonless night heightens the picture of Lydia's loneliness. It is the first of several verbal parallels with a fragment of Ibycus (5 Page) describing the pain of unrequited love. For wintry winds as a correlative of aging, see also Archilochus S478b Page. *Thracio vento* is the north wind, whose home was represented as being in the wilds of Thrace; cf. *Epod.* 13.3, *Threicio Aquilone*. **bacchante:** with *Thracio vento*, wildly reveling. **magis:** i.e., more than usual. The poet juxtaposes the woman's frantic grief to the wild revels of a cold wind. **sub interlunia:** on moonless nights;

interlunium was the period between the old and the new moons, commonly believed to have an effect on weather. For the breaking of a word at the end of a Sapphic verse, cf. 1.2.19, *ux-orius amnis* and note.

13. tibi: dat. of reference with *saeviet*. **flagrans amor et libido:** now she is the one who is sexually needy. The collection in this stanza of *flagrans*, *furiare*, and *saeviet* emphasize Lydia's turbulent state.

14. quae: such as. **matres equorum:** poetic periphrasis for mares; see 1.17.7 for a similar paraphrase. **furiare:** madden; for the *furor* of mares in heat, see Virgil *Georg.* 3.266 *scilicet ante omnes furor est insignis equarum*. Lydia is reduced to a state that is less than human.

15. iecur ulcerosum: inflamed liver; for the liver as the seat of anger and similar passions, cf. 1.13.4.

16. non sine: emphatic litotes, as in 1.23.3.

17. laeta: with *pubes*, contrasting with her own angry state. **pubes:** frequent in the poets for *iuventus*.

17-19. hedera ... myrto, aridas frondes: Horace's metaphoric language has been variously interpreted. One reading of the youth-as-foliage conceit finds here three stages of a hetaera's life and desirability:

I. *hedera virens* (e.g., her fresh and youthful past);

II. *pulla myrtus* (e.g., her drab, middle-aged present);

III. *aridae frondes* (e.g., her dried-up future).

This reading fits the *OLD* definition of *pulla* as "drab, dingy, somber." For the metaphor, cf. Archilochus 188 West, οὐκέθ' ὁμῶς θάλλεις ἁπαλὸν χρόα. **atque,** with *magis*, is "more than" (*OLD* 15).

18-20. gaudeat ... dedicet: subjunctive in informal indirect discourse, depending on *quod* (17).

19. hiemis sodali ... Euro: i.e. to the winter wind. Eurus, properly the east or southeast wind, is used generically. *Euro* is an emendation preferred by many editors to the ms. *Hebro* (a river in Thrace) because Horace's scenes are as a rule set in Italy.

20. dedicet: adversative asyndeton, but consecrates, used ironically because it was customary for lovers to dedicate festoons of flowers at their girlfriends' doors. The religious connotation of *dedico* makes the sarcasm more powerful, but the culminating image of a woman cast off like trash is more pathetic than malicious. **Euro** is in a position of emphasis as the last word. The idea of dismissing something by throwing it to the winds is picked up in the beginning of the next ode.

26

This poem, by some accounts Horace's first in the Alcaic meter, is less about Lamia than about Horace's poetry and its powers. It is not even clear which member of the Lamia family is being honored. Meter: Alcaic strophe.

1-6. My friendship with the muses lets me set aside worries about what is happening in the world.

1. Musis amicus: emphatic by position and in an implicitly causal relation to the verb *tradam*: since I am the muses' friend. **metus:** acc. pl.

2. mare Creticum: individualized as usual; the Cretan sea was proverbially stormy, and appropriately far from Horace in Rome.

3. portare: exegetic inf., explaining the purpose of *tradam*. **sub Arcto:** beneath the constellation of the Bear, standing for the north generally.

3-6. quis ... quid ... securus: two indirect questions (with subjunctives *metuatur* and *terreat*), comprising the subjects Horace is unconcerned about. Cf. 2.11.1ff., *Quid bellicosus Cantaber et Scythes ... cogitet ... remittas quaerere*. For the dependent question after *securus*, see *Sat.* 2.4.50, *quali perfundat piscis securus olivo*; *Epist.* 2.1.176, *securus cadat an recto stet fabula talo*.

5. Tiridaten: an exiled Parthian king who appealed to Augustus for help in 30 B.C.; see also on 2.2.17. **unice:** intensive rather than exclusive, with

securus = supremely unconcerned. For the thought, cf. 1.17.13, *di me tuentur, dis pietas mea et Musa cordi est*.

6-12. O muse, weave a garland of sunny blossoms for Lamia; he is the one for you and your sisters to consecrate with a new lyre from Lesbos.

6. fontibus integris: abl. with *gaudes*, pure springs of inspiration. This recalls the Callimachean motif of the uncontaminated spring symbolizing unhackneyed poetry, and Lucretius 1.927, *iuvat integros accedere fontis*. The ideal is not so much total originality as the avoidance of styles and subjects that have been written to death.

7. apricos ... flores: these sunny blossoms contrast with the *tristitiam et metus* that Horace throws to the winds in stanza 1.

8. necte ... coronam: it is left unclear what garland the muses are asked to weave with Horace. The reference may be to this poem iteslf or to a collection of odes. Meleager of Gadara called his anthology of Greek epigrams his *Stephanos* or Garland, but in *Epist.* 2.2.96 Horace uses *corona* of a single poem. The frequent anaphora in this half of the ode (*necte ... necte, hunc ... hunc, teque tuasque*) is in the high style that Horace adopts whenever he talks about his poetry; cf. 1.17.13, 2.20, 3.30. **Lamiae:** see appendix A.

9. Pipleï: Gk. vocative singular of *Pipleïs*, dweller at Pipleia, a fountain in Pieria north of Mt. Olympus dear to the muses. Cf. Catullus 105.1, *Pipleium montem* for Olympus.

9-10. mei ... honores: in a double sense, honors bestowed by me and on me. **fidibus novis:** poetic plural, repeating the idea of *fontibus integris* in line 6. The novelty suggested here would be the use of Greek lyric meters (like the present Alcaic) in Latin verse. Pioneered by Catullus in some half dozen surviving poems, these meters became Horace's standard medium in the *Odes*.

11. Lesbio ... plectro points directly to the Alcaic meter of this ode, but also includes Sapph ics and Asclepiadeans. The plectrum was a "strik-er" (Gk. πλῆκτρον) that plucked the strings of the lyre. The word end after *Lesbio*, i.e., following the fourth syllable of the third line, is rare in Alcaeus and occurs only here in Horace.

27

A symposiac scene, this dramatic monologue was according to Porphyrio inspired by a poem of Anacreon (sixth to fifth cent. B.C.). Frag. 356b Page seems to have suggested at least the opening motto, which condemns drunken brawling. The poet enters a party where a brawl has broken out and rebukes his friends for violating the spirit of the symposium. He then steers the conversation in a more appropriate direction, asking a member of the party about his current love. The dramatic techniques are comparable to those used by Catullus in poem 42, *Adeste hendecasyllabi*. Meter: Alcaic strophe.

1-12. Drunken brawling is barbaric; back to your couches, friends! Do you want me to drink? Then let Megilla's brother tell with whom he is in love.
1. Natis: made or intended for. **scyphis:** large, two-handled goblets, instrumental abl. with *pugnare*. The symposiasts have started throwing their cups at each other.
2. Thracum: gen. pl. of characteristic, limiting *pugnare*: it is typical of Thracians to fight; cf. *Miserarum*, 3.12.1. The Thracians were even heavier drinkers than their Macedonian neighbors, and were considered only half-civilized. For their butchery of women and children at Mycalessus in 413 B.C., see Thucydides 7.27: "the Thracian race, like all the most bloodthirsty barbarians, are always particularly bloodthirsty when everything is going their own way" (tr. Warner). **tollite:** away with, as in *Epod.* 16.39, *muliebrem tollite luctum*.
3. verecundum: restrained, modest; cf. 1.18.7, *modici Liberi*.

4. prohibete: defend from.
5. Vino et lucernis: abl. of separation with *discrepat*. **Medus acinaces:** the Persian dagger, another alien intrusion.
6. immane quantum discrepat: is monstrously at odds; a Greek construction, used only here in poetry. In prose, cf. Sallust *Historiae* 2.44, *immane quantum animi exarsere*.
8. cubito ... presso: i.e., with your weight on your elbows instead of your feet, referring to the custom of resting the weight on the left elbow while reclining at parties.
9. Vultis, etc.: we are to understand that between the stanzas Horace's friends have invited him to have a drink of their wine.
9-10. severi ... Falerni: the only Latin note in an otherwise Hellenic scene; this Falernian is of the strong or dry variety, normally called *austerum*; the milder, sweet Falernian is implied in 1.20.10f., *Falernae temperant vites*; for the distinction, see Pliny *Nat. Hist.* 14.63, Athenaeus 26c. Another way of taking *severi* is as nom. pl. with *vultis*: are you getting strict about the rules of the *magister bibendi* and demanding that I drink my share (*partem*)? **Opuntiae:** adj., of Opus, a Locrian town on the Euboic Gulf. We are back in a Greek context.
11. frater Megillae: the periphrasis implies that instead of a patriarchal Roman setting, we are in a more liberated Hellenistic group where a young man might be identified by his kinship with a prominent woman rather than his father.
11-12. beatus vulnere: a romantic oxymoron. **sagitta** is Cupid's arrow.

13-24. I will drink only if you tell. Surely your love does you credit, and we can be trusted. What a Charybdis you used to love! But now, you are tied up with a Chimaera. The first half of the ode was addressed to his *sodales*; this half is to Megilla's brother, the suffering lover.
13. Cessat voluntas? This implies a pause between the stanzas, during which the lover has

hesitated to explain the cause of his love. For the convention of the tongue-tied lover at a symposium, see Asclepiades *A.P.* 12.135 (GP 18), Callimachus *A.P.* 12.134 (GP 13).

14. domat: tames, masters. **Venus:** by metonymy, either the lover's heartthrob (the object of his passion) or love itself.

15-17. non erubescendis ... ignibus: with no fires that you need blush for, and **ingenuo ... amore:** with a love worthy of a free-born man (*ingenuus*). The former is instrumental with *adurit* [*te*], the latter with *peccas*. Megilla's brother is assured that there is no question of his falling in love with some vulgar flute girl or πόρνη instead of a classy hetaera. In symposiac poetry men do not fall in love with women of their own social rank. Cf. 2.4, where Xanthias is in love with a slave girl. **peccas:** stumble, slip. The word implies no moral wrong, but an forgivable lapse of prudent self-control.

17. Quicquid habes, etc.: cf. Catullus 6.15f., *Quare, quidquid habes boni malique, dic nobis.* But Catullus assumes in that poem that Flavius' affair is utterly tawdry, and he cheerfully threatens after he finds out to tell the world. Horace is knowingly playing against that background.

18-19. A miser, etc.: in mock horror, Horace recalls the young man's last heartthrob. **Charybdi:** a well-known symbol of rapacity, esp. a hetaera's.

20. puer may remind us of the hapless *puer* who falls for Pyrrha in 1.5.

21-22. saga ... magus: witches and sorcerers were supposed capable of inducing or curing love by means of **Thessalis ... venenis,** though Canidia's efforts to involve Varus in *Epod.* 5 are unsuccessful. Thessaly was witch country, the source of magical herbs and potions.

23. illigatum: entangled, as with the Chimaera's snaky tail. **triformi:** the Chimaera had the head of a lion, the body of a she-goat (Gk. χίμαιρα), the tail of a serpent. Lucretius 5.905 *prima leo, postrema draco, media ipsa, Chimaera.*

24. Pegasus: the winged horse mounted by

Bellerophon when he slew the original Chimaera. This Chimaera, Horace implies, will not be so easy. **Chimaera:** abl., *apo koinou* with *illigatum* and *expediet.* The name was already, like Charybdis, associated with hetaeras. In graduating from a Charybdis to a Chimaera Megilla's brother has fallen from the frying pan into the fire.

28

A somewhat enigmatic dramatic monologue, this ode consists of two parts: an address to Archytas, the celebrated general, statesman, and philosopher of Tarentum, followed by reflections on death as the fate of all men (stanzas 1-5). The second part (stanzas 6-9) is the appeal of a shipwrecked sailor for burial. The connection between the two is not obvious, and the transition (lines 21-22) is rather abrupt, "a sudden, wrenching twist" (Armstrong), after which it turns out that the poem as a whole is the monologue of a sailor shipwrecked near the tomb of Archytas—a highly wrought adaptation of the Hellenistic shipwreck epigram. The meter is Alcmanic strophe.

1-6. A small mound of earth now confines you, Archytas, and your past explorations are of no use to you.

1-2. Te ... Archyta: the bracketing word order ironically encloses the parts of the earth that now confine the geographer's remains.

1. maris ... terrae ... harenae: gen. with *mensorem,* referring to Archytas' achievements as a geographer. **numero ... carentis harenae:** the commonplace expression of "countless sand" is applied with irony to the famous mathematician, but there may be a reference to a lost work.

2. mensorem: makes a slight oxymoron with the previous phrase; *terrae mensorem* is equivalent to Gk. γεωμέτρης, "geometer." **cohibent:** confine; emphasizes the paradox of a little earth enclosing a man whose mind spanned the globe. The subject is *munera.* Note the spondaic third foot here and in line 24. **Archyta:** Gk. vocative. This friend and contemporary of Plato was a famous Pythagorean philosopher who flourished around 400 B.C. in Tarentum. Among other achievements, he used mathematical methods to measure the globe.

3. pulveris exigui ... parva ... munera: appositional gen. with a poetic plural. For the paradox of a great spirit in a small grave, cf. Shakespeare *1 Henry IV* 5.4.89ff:

> When that this body did contain a spirit,
> A kingdom for it was too small a bound;
> But now two paces of the vilest earth
> Is room enough.

litus ... Matinum: either on the Adriatic coast, on the "spur" of the Italian boot (Mt. Gargano), or a shore near Tarentum (see map 6). In 4.2.27 Horace compares himself to a Matine bee; either possible location puts this site within Horace's personal ambit in southeastern Italy, not far from his native Venusia (cf. line 26).

4. quicquam: acc. of result produced.

5. temptasse: to have explored; the word implies audacity. **aërias ... domos:** poetic for the spaces occupied by the heavenly bodies (regarded by the Pythagoreans as divinities), which Archytas studied as an astronomer.

6. polum: the vault of heaven; *polus* (properly the pole of the axis of the heavens) is often used figuratively for the heaven itself. **morituro:** causal, and in a position of emphasis: since you were to die. Agrees with *tibi*, line 4.

7-20. So all great men have died: Pelops and Tithonus, Minos and Pythagoras. No one escapes death.

7. Occidit et: reversed for juxtaposition of *occidit* with *moriture*. **Pelopis genitor:** Tantalus. **conviva deorum:** with adversative force, though a table companion of the gods.

8. Tithonus: son of Laomedon, made immortal by his lover Aurora, the dawn goddess. But because she failed to ask the gods to give him perpetual youth, he shriveled away until he became a

mere voice, like a cicada. Cf. 2.16.30, *longa Tithonum minuit senectus*. **remotus in auras:** translated to the heavens as a divinity.

9. Iovis arcanis ... admissus: Minos, King of Crete, is described as admitted to Jove's secrets because his laws were said to have been suggested by Jove, like the commandments given to Moses on Mt. Sinai (Exodus 19-20).

10. Tartara: neut. pl. nom., a variant of *Tartarus*; here it is not where the wicked are punished, but the lower world in general. **Panthoïden:** the son of Panthoüs is properly Euphorbus, a Trojan who helped kill Patroclus in the *Iliad* and was in turn killed by Menelaus. But the patronymic is here applied ironically to the philosopher Pythagoras (flourished 540 B.C.), apostle of the doctrine of metempsychosis or transmigration of souls, who said that he had been Euphorbus in a previous life. To prove it, he entered the Argive temple where Menelaus had dedicated the shield of Euphorbus, and reclaimed it. **iterum Orco demissum:** first, when Euphorbus was killed, and a second time when his supposed reincarnation Pythagoras died. He is said to have been killed in a political uprising in Croton. *Orco* here = *ad Orcum*.

11-13. quamvis ... concesserat: *quamvis* with the indicative first appears (with certainty) in the Augustan poets Horace and Virgil; later it became common in prose. **clipeo refixo:** by taking down the shield; instrumental abl. absolute. **Troiana ... tempora testatus:** he bore witness to Trojan times, and yielded only his sinews and skin (*nervos atque cutem*) to death, not his soul.

12. ultra = *praeter*.

14. iudice te: in your judgment; Archytas reveres Pythagoras as the founder of his philosophical school. **non sordidus:** litotic for eminent. **auctor:** a judge or authority.

15. una ... nox: a common euphemism for *mors*. Cf. 1.24.5, *perpetuus sopor* and Catullus 5.6, *nox perpetua dormienda*. Note juxtaposition of *omnis una* and the emphatic monosyllabic verse ending as in

Catullus 5.5, *brevis lux*.

16. calcanda semel: must be trodden once and for all; cf. 1.24.16, 4.7.21. **via leti:** death's path.

17. alios: some; the correlative *aliis* is supplanted by *nautis*; cf. 1.7.1f., *laudabunt alii ... ; sunt quibus unum opus est.* **torvo:** grim, savage. **spectacula:** in apposition with *alios*, as spectacles to entertain the war god; cf. 1.2.37, *longo satiate ludo*.

18. exitio: end or ruin, in a double dat. construction with *nautis*.

19. mixta: emphatically placed; the lack of distinctions in the underworld was one of its most depressing features. The impression is strengthened by **densentur**; the funerals of young and old are packed together. *denseo, -ēre* is a poetic variant of the commoner *denso, -are*. **funera:** funeral processions.

20. caput: alluding to the lock of hair taken by Proserpina from the head of each victim of death; cf. Virgil *Aen.* 4.698, of Dido, *nondum illi flavum Proserpina vertice crinem abstulerat Stygioque caput damnaverat Orco.* **fugit:** shuns, hence spares.

21-25. I too am a victim of the Adriatic waves. But do you, mariner, cast a grain of sand on my unburied head.

21. Me quoque: i.e., *me* as well as *te* (Archytas), line 1. At this point we begin to realize that the speaker is not Horace but a dead man. **devexi:** sloping downward, hence setting. According to the Elder Pliny, Orion set early in November, at the beginning of the stormy season. **rapidus:** violent, rapacious; cf. *rapio.* **comes Orionis:** in apposition with *Notus*. Note the spondaic ending of the verse, as in line 2.

22. Illyricis: of the Illyrian Sea, that part of the Adriatic that borders on southern Italy (see map 2). **obruit:** overcame, overpowered, as in 1.15.3.

23. nauta: vocative, to some passing mariner. **vagae ... harenae:** shifting sand, with indication of its worthlessness. **malignus:** with adverbial force, grudgingly; the opposite of *benignus*, 1.9.6; i.e., do not be so stingy as to refuse. **ne parce ... dare:** do

not neglect to give; *parco* with the infinitive occurs first in Livy and the Augustan poets. **harenae** is partitive gen. with *particulam* (25).

24. capiti inhumato: notice the striking hiatus. No similar instance occurs in the *Odes*, but in *Epod.* 5.100 we find *Esquilinae alites* and in 13.3 *Threicio Aquilone. inhumato* (unburied) qualifies *ossibus* as well as *capiti.*

25. particulam dare: three handfuls (see line 36) were regarded as sufficient to meet the requirements of formal interment and to secure rest for the waiting spirit. Cf. Antigone's burial of her brother Polyneices in Sophocles' *Antigone* 429ff.

25-36. So may Jove and Neptune grant you safety and wealth; but do not neglect this duty! Three handfuls of sand are enough.

25. sic: then (i.e., if you grant my prayer). This is a customary formula of supplication: see note on 1.3.1. The use of *sic* to resume the substance of a previous imperative or jussive subjunctive is common in poetry. **quodcumque ... fluctibus:** respectively, the direct and indirect object of *minabitur.*

26. Hesperiis: the Hesperian waves could be anywhere off Italy; the context (*Illyricis undis*, line 27) suggests the Adriatic. **Venusinae ... silvae:** near Horace's birthplace, Venusia. Though about forty miles from the sea, these forests were high enough to feel the force of the east wind.

27. plectantur ... te sospite: the emphasis is on the abl. construction: may Eurus buffet the forests and leave you safe. **multa ... merces:** many a wage, reminding us that the person addressed is an ordinary *nauta* (line 23).

28. unde potest: sc. *defluere. unde* is explained in the next stanza by *ab Iove Neptunoque.* **aequo**, kindly or propitious, is to be understood with both *Iove* and *Neptuno.*

29. Neptuno ... custode: because Tarentum's legendary founder was Neptune's son Taras, the god is its guardian. **sacri ... Tarenti:** a common honorific epithet for a famous city; cf. 3.19.4 *sacro sub Ilio* and Homer's Ἴλιος ἱρή.

30-31. neglegis ... committere, etc.: do you take it lightly (*neglegis*) that you are committing a wrong (*fraudem*) destined to be harmful (*nocituram*), etc.? *te* is the subject of *committere*; *postmodo* modifies *nocituram*. The phrasing suggests that the sailor is about to disregard the appeal.

31. Fors et = *fortasse*.

32. debita iura: rights (of burial) still unpaid. **vices ... superbae:** disdainful retribution; a similar lack of burial would be fitting *vices* for the passing sailor's present negligence.

33. te ... ipsum: i.e., as well as your children (*natis*, line 31). **maneant:** potential subjunctive, usually confined to verbs of saying, thinking, or the like. **precibus inultis:** with my prayers unavenged, i.e., my curses on you for leaving me unburied. Note how the good wishes (lines 25-29) predicated on compliance are balanced by bad wishes (30-34) if the sailor does not help.

34. teque ... resolvent: no expiatory offerings will absolve you.

35. non est mora longa: the action requested will not detain you long. **licebit ... curras:** you may move on.

29

Horace's friend Iccius has put aside his study of philosophy to join Aelius Gallus' expedition against Arabia Felix in 26 B.C., hoping to make himself rich on the spoils of war. Struck by the irony that a student of ethical philosophy would become a plunderer and enslaver of others, Horace twits him lightly. With its reflection on the corrupting influence of Roman power, this is an interesting and unusual poem for Horace, who is typically uncritical in his enthusism for foreign warfare and empire. Meter: Alcaic strophe.

1-5. Do you now cast greedy eyes on the wealth of Araby, prepare war against the kings of Sheba and chains for the dreadful Mede?

1. Icci: a note of surprise in this initial vocative.

For more on the person, see appendix A. **Arabum:** the people of Arabia Felix, the fertile portion of mod. Saudi Arabia and Yemen near the Red Sea. **invides:** with dat. *beatis ... gazis*, look askance or with jealousy at.

2. gazis: an exotic eastern word for wealth.

3. non ante devictis: unconquered even by Alexander and his successors. Aelius Gallus' campaign was also to end in disaster (Dio 53.29.4 says most of the army was killed), and Trajan left them unconquered. In Gibbon's time they remained "dangerous to provoke and fruitless to attack." **Sabaeae:** biblical Sheba, approximately the area of mod. Yemen.

4. horribili ... Medo: comic hyperbole. Horace uses "Mede" loosely for the unconquered Parthians or Iranians.

5-10. What barbarian girl will be your slave? What eastern boy will serve your wine, once taught to shoot his father's bow? For the tricolon crescendo of questions (*Quae ... quis ... Quis*), see appendix C.

5. virginum: grandiose partitive gen., implying that Iccius will have plenty to choose from. Cf. 1.38.3, *quo locorum*.

6. sponso necato: abl. abs.; her promised husband has been killed, like Briseis' in *Iliad* 19.291f. Cf. the situation in 3.2.6-12.

7. Puer ... ex aula: i.e., *ex aula regia*; a royal page, belonging to a noble family. Contemporary documents mention a *glaber ab cyatho* among the emperor's household servants in the time of Augustus and Tiberius (Griffin p. 30); this boy, with his *unctis capillis*, may have sexual duties as well; see Seneca *Epist.* 47.7-8.

8. cyathum: wine ladle.

9. sagittas ... Sericas: Chinese arrows, a rarity for a king's personal armory; it was imagined at this time that the *Oceanus Sericus* was a mere 480 miles from the Caspian Sea. See NH on 1.12.56. The detail of the boy trained in archery being perfumed and stationed at a wine-ladle is an ironic reminder that the Roman conquerors are up to no good.

10-16. Who would deny that rivers can run uphill when you are bent on trading your philosophic books for Spanish armor?
10. neget: deliberative subjunctive in a question implying doubt, indignation, or impossibility.
11. pronos: sloping downward, emphatically juxtaposed with *arduis*. **relabi:** flow backward. For this rhetorical way of expressing impossibility, cf. the catalog in *Epod.* 16.25-34 and see appendix C, *adynata*.
13. tu: emphatic, you of all people.
13-14. coëmptos undique ... libros: books bought up from all over; libraries were difficult and expensive to build before printing. Now all that trouble and expense is about to be thrown away. **nobilis ... Panaeti:** Panaetius of Rhodes (185-109 B.C.) did much to adapt Stoicism to the active Roman virtues. His treatise *On Duties* was the basis of Cicero's *De Officiis*.
14. Socraticum ... domum: the philosophic schools were small, closely knit communities. Cicero *De Div.* 2.1 refers to the *Peripateticorum familia*; cf. Horace *Epist.* 1.1.13, *quo lare tuter*. Here the phrase is metaphoric, as though Iccius were still living among the Socratics in Athens.
15. mutare: with abl. of price **loricis Hiberis**, to trade away the books and the Socratic home for Spanish corselets. Cf. the same construction in 1.16.26. Spanish steel was already famous for its hardness.
16. tendis, indicating intention, is strong in meaning and placement: you are hell-bent upon. Stoicism emphasized a serenity that stretched out only for virtue in the spirit of Xenophanes' τόνος ἀμφ' ἀρετῆς (1.20).

30

An epigram in the spirit of the Hellenistic miniatures depicting the lives of ordinary people. Glyc-

era, who makes this invocation, is a hetaera with a little shrine (4 *aedem*) to her patron Venus. Following one of the standard hymnic formulas, she mentions the goddess's haunts in the first stanza and her companions in the second. Similar invocations can be found among the early Greek authors (e.g., Alcman 55 Page, Sappho 2 LP); a closer Hellenistic model may be Posidippus *A.P.* 12.131 (GP 8). Meter: Sapphic strophe.

1-4. Venus, leave your usual haunts and come to Glycera's shrine.
1. Cnidi: home of Praxiteles' famous statue of Aphrodite, for which the hetaera Phryne is said to have modeled. See note on *Epod.* 14.16. About forty miles northwest of Rhodes, this was a celebrated tourist attraction in Horace's time. **Paphi:** on the southwest coast of Cyprus, Aphrodite's home in the earliest Greek sources (Homer *Od.* 8.362f., Hymn to Aphrodite 59); the eastern Greek cult was closely related to that of the Phoenician Astarte.
3. ture ... multo: instrumental with *vocantis*; in traditional religion, the goodwill of the god invoked is purchased with an offering. **te:** obj. of *transfer*. **Glycerae:** a common name for a hetaera, like Lydia. Cf. 1.19.5 note, 1.33.2, 3.19.29. There is no reason to suppose they are all the same person.
4. aedem: shrine or house, a play on meanings. A hetaera's house would naturally be a shrine of Venus. Many prostitutes were in fact at an earlier time temple prostitutes, e.g., in classical Corinth.

4-8. Bring your attendants with you: Cupid, Graces and nymphs, Youth, and—last but not least—Mercury.
5-6. solutis Gratiae zonis: for the nude or semi-nude Graces, see 1.4.6 note and 3.19.16f., *Gratia nudis iuncta sororibus*. **properent** governs all five nom. nouns in this stanza.
7. parum comis ... Iuventas: i.e., not gracious or elegant if sexually inactive. Augustus revived the

old veneration of *Iuventas* by assigning it a place in the religious calendar, October 18.

8. Mercurius: the god of persuasive eloquence (cf. Lat. *Suadela, Suada,* Gk. Πειθώ), but also the god of commerce (see note on 1.10). This gives the poem an ironic twist at the end; cf. the ending of *Epod. 2, Beatus ille,* and the ironic strategy of 1.22, *Integer vitae.* Along with all the other benefits of Venus' presence, Glycera wants to profit from what she does best.

31

A poem on the occasion of Augustus' dedication of a spectacular new Temple of Apollo on the Palatine, October 9, 28 B.C., and the vintage festival of the Meditrinalia two days later. Instead of a grand state poem, Horace presents a few lines on the question "What does the wise man pray for?" After rejecting a series of material ambitions (lines 3-15), Horace offers his prayer for good health and a sound mind. The same theme was memorably stated years later by Juvenal: *orandum est ut sit mens sana in corpore sano* (10.356). Meter: Alcaic strophe.

1-8. What does the poet ask of Apollo after his dedication? Not crops, herds, treasure or land.

1. dedicatum: just consecrated, i.e., following the dedication of his temple. This building would have been of special interest to Horace because it included a large library. Like Propertius and Ovid, he also seems to have liked the statues of the Danaïds placed between the columns of the portico outside; see notes on 2.14.18, 3.11.25. **poscit** takes the acc. of the thing asked for (*Quid?*) and the acc. of the god beseeched; cf. 1.24.12, *poscis Quintilium deos.*

2. vates: the poet-prophet, as in 1.1.35, where see note. **patera:** the flat bowl used for libations.

2-3. novum fundens liquorem: at the October 11 Meditrinalia, marking the end of the grape harvest, libations of the old wine and new grape juice were poured in a prayer for health (Varro *De Ling.*

Lat. 6.21). Hence the prayer in the last stanza.

3-7. Non ... non ... non ... non: the catalog of things not prayed for, following the questions *Quid poscit, ... Quid orat?* makes the poem as a whole a priamel, focusing on the blessings prayed for in the last stanza.

4. Sardiniae segetes feracis: Sardinia's fertile grainfields. Sardinia, Sicily, and north Africa were the three breadbaskets of ancient Rome: Cicero *Pro Manilio* 34.

5. aestuosae ... Calabriae: in ancient times the heel of the Italian boot, dry as well as sultry (*aestuosae*). **grata:** pleasing to look at (especially to the owner).

7. Liris: rising in the Appenines east of Rome, the river Liris flows through Latium and enters the sea near Minturnae. See NH 1.352f. on the river and its territory.

7-8. quieta ... aqua (instrumental abl. with **mordet,** erodes) combines with **taciturnus amnis** to make an idyllic picture, less easily resisted than the other forms of wealth so far mentioned.

9-15. Let others prune the vine, and let the wealthy trader visit the Atlantic three or four times a year with impunity.

9. Premant: concessive subj., check, prune (OLD 19b). **Calena falce:** lit. with a pruning knife from Cales, the sense being that such people have a vineyard at Cales. Cf. 1.20.9, *prelo Caleno* and note.

10. et: some mss. have *ut* here, making the lines describing the merchant a digression.

11. mercator: for this disapproving vignette of the merchant and his audacity, Cf. 3.24.40. **culillis:** a rare word for cups; Porphyrio says they were usually of clay, and used for sacred purposes. The use of golden ones here implies excess. Cf. *Ars P.* 434.

12. Syra: the standing epithet for any luxury import, as in Catullus 6.8 and Horace 2.7.8.

13. dis carus ipsis: ironic, with a touch of contempt, as is **quippe,** introducing the supposed reason why we can tell the gods love him.

15. impune: emphatic enjambment, continuing the ironic tone: we know he leads a charmed life because the gods let him get away with repeated incursions into outlandish waters.

15-20. My diet is country fare. Grant that I enjoy what I have, Apollo, in good health with a sound mind; a graceful old age, and my poetry.

16. cichorea: chicory or endive, used for salads. **malvae:** mallows. The plant's soft, downy leaves were eaten as a demulcent (hence *leves*), to promote regularity. Cf. *Epod.* 2.57, *gravi malvae salubres corpori.*

17. Frui: object of *dones*, takes abl. **paratis,** things I already have handy. **et valido mihi:** and (grant them) to me in good health.

18. Latoë: vocative of *Latoüs*, son of Leto (Apollo); this brings us back to the subject of line 1.

20. degere: object of *dones*; pass, live out. **cithara:** abl. with *carentem*, by metonymy his poetic powers.

32

This ode has the appearance of a prelude, perhaps to an earlier collection of poems. It anticipates the production of a *Latinum carmen*, viz. poetry in a more native idiom than mere adaptations of Greek models. Some speculate that this refers to patriotic poetry, such as the Roman Odes (3.1-6), but the emphasis in the third stanza is on love poetry. The meter is Sapphic strophe.

1-4. I pray you, lyre, if I have ever written a poem that will live, give me a Latin poem.

1. Poscimus, si, etc.: the prayer formula reminds the god prayed to (here the lyre) of past benefits conferred. Some mss. give *poscimur*, as if the poet were being asked to write something. But the form of the poem is a prayer by the poet, not a response to another person's request as in 1.6, *Scriberis Vario.* **quid:** obj. of *lusimus*, if I have written anything

for fun. **vacui:** with the subject of *lusimus*, at leisure, free from care, not "on stage"; cf. 1.6.19, *cantamus vacui.* **sub umbra:** cf. the *gelidum nemus* in 1.1.30, and the link often made by Horace between his natural environment and his poetry.

2. lusimus: poetic plural, like *poscimus* above. The word is chosen to characterize the playful quality of the poet's lyrics. For *ludo* to signify the composition of verses, cf. Catullus 50.2 and 5, 61.225, 68.17. **quod:** referring to *quid* above, introducing a relative clause of characteristic.

3. vivat: subjunctive of characteristic. Horace frequently expresses a proud confidence in the immortality of his poetry. **pluris:** sc. *in annos.* **age:** as in 1.27.17. **dic:** sing. **Latinum ... carmen:** the key phrase of the ode, long taken to refer to patriotic verse but more likely to mean poetry with a native flavor. This was also a goal of the *poetae novi* of Catullus' generation.

4. barbite: a Greek type of lyre, contrasting pointedly with *Latinum carmen.* In this prayer, the *barbiton* is addressed as if it were a divinity beseeched for a favor.

5-12. You who were first played by Alcaeus, who even between wars and seafaring sang of wine and love.

5. Lesbio ... civi: Alcaeus (born about 620 B.C.); *Lesbio* is emphatically placed at the beginning of the stanza, contrasting with *Latinum carmen.* The word *civis* is chosen in view of Alcaeus' participation in the politics of his native city; *civi* is dat. of agent after the participle; cf. 1.1.24, *bella matribus detestata.* **modulate:** played. For the passive use of the deponent participle, cf. 1.1.25, *detestata.*

6. ferox bello: Alcaeus fought against the Athenians and the tyrants of his native city, Mitylene, on the island of Lesbos. **tamen:** i.e., in spite of his warlike spirit (*ferox bello*). **inter arma:** it is clear from the context that this means between wars, i.e., during intervals of peace. For *arma* = wars (OLD 6), cf. Virgil *Aen.* 1.1, *Arma virumque cano.*

7. sive: as correlative with this we must under-

stand a *sive* with *inter arma* above; the two con-
trasted members are poetic equivalents of *sive terra
sive mari*; for the omission of the first *sive*, cf.
1.3.16, *tollere seu ponere vult freta*. **religa**(ve)**rat:**
had moored.

9. Liberum et Musas Veneremque: roughly =
Wein, Weib, und Gesang, i.e., sympotic and amatory
poetry. **illi ... haerentem puerum:** Cupid, imagined
as a child clinging to his mother, Venus.

11. Lycum: a boy loved by Alcaeus. **nigris oculis
nigroque crine:** dark hair and eyes are repeatedly
mentioned as characteristics of special beauty,
though Horace seems personally to have preferred
blondes. Note that the initial syllable is long in *nig-
ris*, but short in *ni-groque*, possibly because of the
muta cum liquida combination -*gr*-. See appendix B.

**13-16. O lyre beloved of Apollo and Jove,
sweet solace of labors, hear my greeting as I call
on you.**

13. decus Phoebi: *decus* is in apposition with
testudo. For Mercury's invention of the lyre from a
tortoise shell, see note on 1.10.6.

15. lenimen: solace; cf. *lenite*, 1.27.7. **mihi:**
ethical dat. with *salve*; cf. Virgil Aen. 9.97, *salve
aeternum mihi, maxime Palla*. The phrase is adopted
from the Gk. hymnic formula, χαῖρέ μοι. **cumque**
perhaps = *quandocumque*, whenever; a unique use
of the word, but intelligible to Porphyrio. It is
adverbial with *vocanti*, whenever I call on you.
salve: imperative, accept my greeting, i.e., be
propitious to me.

16. rite vocanti: when I invoke you duly; *vocanti*
agrees with *mihi*.

33

On the natural tendencies and vicissitudes of love.
The theme of the poem is paradox: love makes
strange bedfellows, joining *imparis formas atque
animos* (10-11). This ode is closely related in sub-
ject to 2.9, *Non semper imbres*. The Albius ad-
dressed here is probably the elegiac poet Tibullus

(see appendix A), although the name Glycera does
not appear in his poems. Meter: third Asclep-
iadean.

**1-4. Do not grieve too much, Albius, if a
younger rival has displaced you in Glycera's
affections.**

1. plus nimio: colloquial and poetic, lit. more by
too much; adverbial with both *doleas* and *memor*.

2. immitis Glycerae: an oxymoron, playing on
the bittersweet love theme; *immitis* is ungentle or
unripe, hence bitter: Glycera, a common name of
hetaeras in comedy, means "sweet" (Gk. γλυκύς).
It is the name of Polemon's concubine in Men-
ander's *Perikeiromene*, and, according to Athenaeus
594d, of Menander's own mistress. In Book 2 of
his elegies, Tibullus calls his love Nemesis, which
is metrically equivalent to Glycera. **miserabilis:**
plaintive, a conventional feature of Latin love
elegies. Cf. the elegist Valgius' *flebilibus modis* in
2.9.9. A second implication is that they are pretty
sorry stuff. Horace was no admirer of the Latin
love elegy.

3. decantes: keep singing; for *de*- as an intensive
prefix, cf. 1.3.13, *decertantem*. **elegos:** generally,
poems in the elegiac meter; specifically, love
elegies, an important Augustan type. **cur ... prae-
niteat:** indirect question, depending on the plain-
tive question implied in *decantes elegos*. **tibi** is dat.
with *praeniteat*.

4. laesa fide: ablatives absolute are often best
treated in English as coordinate constructions: he
outshines you, *and* your faith is wronged. In such
contexts, *fides* applies equally to the trust of the
lover and the good faith of the beloved; cf. 1.5.5
and note.

**5-12. It is always so: Lycoris is on fire for
Cyrus, and Cyrus prefers Pholoë, who finds him
disgusting. Venus delights in mismatched love.**

5. tenui fronte: i.e., with the hairline low over
the forehead, a favored hair style for either sex; cf.
the young Horace as described in *Epist*. 1.7.26,

nigros angusta fronte capillos. **Lycorida:** Gk. acc.; the name Gallus used for his love, the actress Cytheris, in his love elegies.

6. Cyri: objective gen. with *amor*.

7. declinat: inclines toward; a novel word choice, perhaps suggested by Lucretius' use of the word for the swerve of atoms from their regular course. It suggests something irregular in Cyrus' attraction to Pholoë. **Pholoën:** for Pholoë as the type of the balky lover, cf. 2.5.17 *Pholoë fugax* and Tibullus 1.8.69. The name recurs also in 3.15.7.

8. iungentur: with reflexive or middle force, will mate with. **capreae:** roes, small European and Asian deer. Note the juxtaposition with **lupis** (abl. of association). Such impossibilities (*adynata*) were a standard topos of poetry (see appendix C).

9. turpi ... adultero: Cyrus as perceived by Pholoë. Cf. the *moechos arrogantis* in 1.25.9. **peccet:** stray from the straight and narrow, with special reference to offenses against the sexual code. Cf. 1.27.17, *amore peccas*.

10. visum: sc. *est*, has seemed best; cf. Virgil *Aen.* 2.428, *dis aliter visum.*

11. sub iuga aënea: combines the image of sexual pairing or "yoking" with that of submission: defeated soldiers were made to walk under a "yoke" made of spears.

12. saevo ... ioco: another oxymoron, like *immitis Glycerae* (2) and *grata ... compede* (14). Venus is as cruel as *immitis Glycera* (2), *aspera Pholoë* (6-7), and *Myrtale ... acrior Hadriae* (14-15).

13-16. I too have known this fate. Though I could have had a better love, shrewish Myrtale has held me in pleasant bondage.

13. melior ... Venus: a worthier passion. For the figure, cf. 1.1.25, *sub Iove frigido* and see appendix C, metonymy.

14. grata compede: oxymoron. *Compes* is a slave's fetter; rare in the singular, it appears first in Horace. **Myrtale:** a common name of freedwomen.

15. libertina: see note on Phryne in *Epod.* 14.15f., *me libertina neque uno contenta Phryne*

macerat. **Hadriae:** proverbially stormy, as often in Horace. Cf. Shakespeare *Taming of the Shrew* 1.2.71, "Were she as rough as are the swelling Adriatic seas." **fretis:** waters; abl. of comparison with *acrior*. For the comparison of tempestuous temptresses to stormy seas, see the Pyrrha Ode, 1.5.13ff.

16. curvantis: hollowing out the **Calabros sinus,** i.e., the Gulf of Tarentum. The force of the storm erodes the sandy shore of Calabria (the heel of the Italian boot). Like his native Apulia, Calabria exerted a strong pull on Horace's imagination.

34

A mock-solemn renunciation of his Epicurean ways brought on by a miraculous roll of thunder in a clear sky. Though not enough of a believer to hold impassioned views one way or another on this abnormal phenomenon, Horace concludes his ode on a less ironic note than he started. The change of tone makes this a suitable prelude to the Hymn to Fortune, 1.35, which follows. The beginning may be adapted from some lines of Archilochus (122 West) commenting on an eclipse. Meter: Alcaic strophe.

1-5. Once a skeptic about the gods, I am now forced to change my views.

1. Parcus ... cultor is deliberately vague, reflecting the indifferent religiosity of educated Romans in Horace's time, for whom traditional religion was mostly ceremonial.

2. insanientis ... sapientiae: oxymoron. In the context, we are to infer that this was Epicureanism. Epicureans challenged the pious claim that Jupiter sometimes hurls lightning from a cloudless sky. They also taught that the gods are indifferent to human affairs: *Sat.* 1.5.101, *deos didici securum agere aevum.*

3. consultus: an expert in (with gen. *sapientiae*), as in the phrase *iuris consultus.* As in the previous line, Horace is being disingenuous. Though he cheerfully admits in *Epist.* 1.4.16 to being an *Epicuri de grege porcum*, he is also no true believer, *nullius addictus iurare in verba magistri* (*Epist.* 1.1.14). **erro** (present after *dum*): while I was straying.

4-5. iterare cursus ... relictos: i.e., retrace abandoned courses of thought, renew his old-time religion. But *Epist.* 1.18.96-103, published three years after *Odes* 1-3, shows that Horace's views did not really change: he remained more or less Epicurean. Horace's declaration in this ode is rhetorical rather than autobiographical.

5-12. Jupiter thundered in a clear sky, shaking earth and the underworld.
5. Namque: introduces not a demonstration (as in 1.22.9) but an explanation of what precedes. **Diespiter** is archaic and grandiose for Jupiter.
6. nubila is predicative; clouds are what Jupiter usually (*plerumque*) splits with his *igni corusco*, but this time he thundered *per purum*.
8. equos ... currum: the idea was that the hoofs and wheels made the thunder.
9. bruta: heavy, inert, as opp. to the *vaga flumina*.
10. Taenari: the southernmost point of the Peloponnese, traditionally an entrance to the underworld; Virgil *Georg.* 4.467, *Taenarian fauces, alta ostia Ditis*. By metonymy, the underworld itself.
11. Atlanteus ... finis: the end of the world, viz. the western end of the Atlas range in Mauretania where Atlas holds the sky on his shoulders. The presumptuous merchant sails beyond this point into the Atlantic regularly in 1.31.14.

12-16. The god can raise the lowest and reduce the lofty; Fortune makes and unmakes kings.
The theme is a commonplace of classical and Hebraic wisdom literature: Homer *Od.* 16.211f., Hesiod *W&D* 6, Archilochus 130 West, I Samuel 2:7, Psalms 147:6, Sirach 10:14, etc.
12-13. ima summis mutare: take in the lowest in exchange for the highest, i.e., exalt the humble

at the expense of the exalted; the same construction as 1.17.1f., *Lucretilem mutat Lycaeo*. This power is attributed to Fortuna at the beginning of the next ode.
14. apicem: crown; cf. 3.21.20, *regum apices*.
15. cum stridore acuto: the swishing sound (emphasized by the *s-* repetitions in the closing line) is made by her wings; being *rapax*, she is like a harpy. Some interpret the *stridor* as a screech.
16. sustulit: perfect of instantaneous action, like the Gk. aorist. **gaudet:** like Venus in the previous ode, she enjoys human discomfiture.

35
The hymnic form of this ode gives way in the eighth stanza to a prayer for Augustus as he sets forth on his campaign into Gaul in 27 B.C. For an earlier dating, see NH 1.387. Fortuna, who is never actually named in the poem, is identifiable by her attributes. Less fickle than her Greek counterpart Tyche, she is the stern but kindly patron of the Roman people. Meter: Alcaic strophe.

1-16. O goddess of Antium, ready to help or hurt, everyone seeks your help and fears your power to overthrow states.
1. Antium: mod. Anzio, a town on the coast of Latium (see map 6) containing two temples dedicated to Fortuna. It was the old capital of the Volscians.
2. praesens: ready, prompt, powerful. It governs the infinitives *tollere* and *vertere*. **imo ... de gradu:** from the lowest rank. Servius Tullius, a slave's son who became the sixth king of Rome, was credited with founding several Fortuna cults.
3. mortale corpus: of the human condition; cf. "our mortal clay" and similar expressions.
4. vertere funeribus triumphos: i.e., to turn victory to tragedy. Possibly an allusion to the tragic fate of the two sons of Aemilius Paullus, who died a few days on either side of their father's triumph

for the victory at Pydna in 168 B.C. (Livy 45.41.9).

5-9. te ... te, etc.: the catalog of suppliants (lines 5-16, in place of the usual catalog of powers) is introduced with this hymnic anaphora. **ambit:** courts, entreats; a figurative meaning of *ambire,* primarily used of "going about" canvassing for votes. The verb, though singular, has multiple subjects: *pauper* (5), *colonus* (6), and *quicumque ... lacessit* (7).

6. ruris colonus: tiller of the field, a tenant farmer. Some readers take *ruris* with *dominam,* a strong hyperbaton. **dominam:** in apposition with *te.* The conception of Fortune as presiding goddess of agriculture and the sea, both subject to her vicissitudes, appears on ancient coins, which represent the goddess with a cornucopia in one hand and a rudder in the other.

7. Bithyna ... carina: the forests of Bithynia and Pontus, on the south shore of the Black Sea, provided prime timber for ships; another famous source was Cyprus (1.1.13). The adjectives are, however, merely poetic specification, a common practice of Horace. **lacessit:** provokes. For the idea of sailing as a risky defiance of nature, see 1.3.9ff.

8. Carpathium pelagus: another poetic specification, as in the previous line. It is a stormy section of sea between Crete and Rhodes; cf. 4.5.10.

9. Dacus: with *Scythae* and the nouns that follow, subject of *metuunt.* The Dacians lived in what is now Romania. **profugi:** fleeing, an allusion to their treacherous fighting retreat, like that of the Parthians (see on 1.19.11). NH 1.391f. speak of "the well-known Russian stratagem of retreating before an invader." The epithet is repeated in 4.14.32, *profugus Scythes.*

11. regum matres barbarorum: the influence of the queen mother among the polygamous Eastern peoples was often great; cf. 3.2.7, *matrona bellantis tyranni.*

13. iniurioso: wrongful (from the standpoint of those whose *iura* she does not respect), harmful.

14. columnam: i.e., the pillar of the state, public

order. **populus frequens:** a thronging crowd. In this passage Horace again shows his distaste for popular politics.

15. ad arma ... ad arma: the repetition suggests the cries of an excited mob. **cessantis:** those who are holding back, the moderates; object of *concitet.*

17-28. Your attendants are Necessity, Hope, and Faith, who remains steadfast when you abandon the powerful and those once friendly fall away.

17. saeva Necessitas: because Fortuna's decrees are inevitable, Necessity is conceived of as one of her attendants, *saeva* (according to one interpretation) because she is represented with implements of torture and execution. The alternate reading *serva* supports the interpretation of her implements in the next three lines as construction equipment. **anteit:** disyllabic by synizesis (see appendix C).

18. clavos trabalis: her implements of power include large spikes (for fastening criminals to the cross?) and **cuneos,** tapered dowels or wedges. Nails were traditional symbols of fixity (cf. 3.24.5ff.); the temple of the Etruscan goddess Nortia, identified by Juvenal with Fortuna, used *clavos* to mark the passage of years (Livy 7.4.7, NH 1.394f.).

19. aëna = *aënea,* symbolic of her hardness.

20. uncus ... plumbum: the iron clamp used to fasten large blocks of stone together, and the lead poured into the cavities in which the ends of the clamp were inserted. Here their uses are more sinister, as instruments of torture.

21. Te: here the conception of Fortune changes from the universal power to that of a family or an individual. **Spes ... Fides:** the last supports of those whose luck has changed. **albo ... velata panno:** refers to the veiling of her hand. In Livy 1.21.4 the priests of Fides offer sacrifice to Fortuna with their hands bound with a cloth to show that the seat of faith was in the right hand and deserved to be protected. **colit:** for *colunt,* attend upon, worship.

22. nec comitem abnegat: understand *se* as

object of *abnegat*; she does not deny her companionship.

23-24. mutata ... veste: abl. abs. with *linquis*; she is imagined changing to dark raiment as a sign of her disfavor (24 *inimica*).

25. meretrix ... periura: mentioned matter-of-factly as a normal part of the rich man's retinue. **retro ... cedit:** fall back, i.e., give him a wide berth where before they would have crowded around. Singular for plural verb, like *ambit* (5) and *colit* (21).

26. cadis ... siccatis: (abl. abs.) i.e., after the wine is gone.

27. cum faece: dregs and all; stronger than merely "to the dregs" (*faece tenus*).

28. ferre dolosi: (too) treacherous to bear. *dolosi* completes the triad that includes *infidum* (25) and *periura* (26). **iugum:** the yoke of adversity. **pariter:** in common with the victim of adversity.

29-40. Preserve Caesar as he sets out for Britain, and our recruits as they set out for the east. Forgive our past iniquity and guide our weapons against the foe.

29. Serves: jussive subj. Here Horace returns to the conception of Fortune with which he began, the *Fortuna populi Romani*. **iturum Caesarem:** Dio reports three projected campaigns against Britain, in 34, 27, and 26 B.C., none of which were carried out.

30-31. recens examen: probably the new levy made in 26 B.C. for the expedition of Aelius Gallus into Arabia Felix, as alluded to in 1.29.

31-32. Eois ... partibus: the eastern regions, locative or dat. of agent with *timendum*. **Oceano rubro:** in Roman parlance, not only the Red Sea but all of the Indian Ocean near Arabia as well as the Persian Gulf.

33. cicatricum: scars. With *sceleris ...fratrumque* (hendiadys for fraternal crime), gen. depending on *pudet*, we are ashamed of. The reference is to the civil wars that preceded Octavian's *coup d'etat*.

34. Quid nos ... refugimus: from what have we

shrunk? **dura ... aetas:** we, a hardened generation.

36. Unde: from what (crime)? **manum ... continuit:** withheld their hand, i.e., restrained themselves.

38. pepercit aris: *parco* + dat. Implies that suppliants have been denied the protection of the sanctuaries to which they fled. **O utinam:** hiatus after the monosyllabic interjection. **nova incude:** on a new anvil (*incus*).

39. diffingas: forge anew. The word occurs only twice in classical Latin, here and in 3.29.48. With *in* + the acc., the word has the pregnant sense of reforge and turn against. **retusum:** blunted (in the civil wars).

40. Massagetas: a branch of the Scythians east of the Caspian Sea, somehow associated in Horace's mind with the Parthians. **Arabas:** for this unconquerable people, see note on 1.29.3, *non ante devictis*. **ferrum:** the emphatic final word. What began as a pious hymn ends as a "blood and iron" poem.

36

Personal friendship is a major theme in both Catullus and Horace. This celebration of Numida's return from the west, probably from the Spanish campaign of Augustus in 27-25 B.C., may be compared with Catullus 9, welcoming Veranius back from Spain. Numida is a crony of Horace's friend L. Lamia (see appendix A). The last half of the poem calls for a wild party to celebrate, the main attraction being the great drinker and femme fatale Damalis. Meter: second Asclepiadean.

1-9. It is a pleasure to thank the gods for Numida's return from Spain; he will be overjoyed to see his boyhood friend Lamia.

2. debito: the calf's blood is owed *ex voto*, i.e., as previously promised in a prayer for his safe return. Having kept their part of the bargain, Numida's tutelary deities must now be appeased (see *placare*) with incense, music, and sacrifice.

4. Hesperia: in poetry, any western land; in 1.28.26 and the *Aeneid*, it means Italy; from a more Italian perspective, Spain.

5. multa: with *oscula* (6).

6. dividit: shares out (*OLD* 6c), with dat. *caris ... sodalibus, nulli,* and *dulci Lamiae.* For kissing among long-absent friends, cf. Catullus 9.8-9, *applicansque collum iucundum os oculosque suaviabor.*

8. non alio rege perhaps refers to children's games where the leader is the *rex:* see *Epist.* 1.1.59-60 *pueri ludentes "rex eris" aiunt, "si recte facies."* Lamia was the *rex* in Numida's crowd. **puertiae** is a syncopated form of *pueritiae.*

9. mutatae ... togae: exchanged for the *toga virilis* between fifteen and seventeen years of age.

10-20. Let there be nothing lacking in our party, including Damalis.

10-16. ne ... neu ... neu, etc.: this litotic catalog of requests, with the jussive subjunctives *careat, sit, vincat,* and *desint,* belongs to the preparations-for-a-party topos. Cf. Asclepiades *A.P.* 5.181 and 185 (GP 25-26), Catullus 13.3ff., Horace 3.14.17-24, 4.11.1-12. Such catalogs usually include a female companion; here it is Damalis, whose name is repeated thrice.

10. Cressa ... nota: a Cretan or white mark, so-called because of the confusion of *Creta* and its adj. *Cressa* with *creta,* clay or chalk, which Romans thought came from Crete. Any especially *pulchra dies* would be marked with a *Cressa nota.*

11. modus: limit or stint.

12. morem in Salium: the Salii, priests of Mars, had a lively ritual dance; hence no *requies pedum* would be in their style.

13. multi ... meri: gen. of description: not just another pretty face, Damalis can drink with the best of them, including the otherwise unknown Bassus.

14. Threïcia ... amystide: in the Thracian chug-a-lug, from Gk. ἄμυστις. For Thracian drinking habits, see note on 1.27.2.

16. apium: celery provided the greenery for

flower arrangements and garlands. It is called *vivax,* hardy, because it did not wilt easily—unlike the *breve lilium.*

17-18. putris ... oculos: a humorous coinage for bedroom eyes, swimming glances, or the like. Like the Soracte Ode (1.9), this ends in a comic love vignette. All the boys are looking piteously at Damalis, but she already has her *adulter* (Numida, no doubt) well in hand.

20. lascivis hederis ambitiosior: more clinging than wanton ivy (which twines around whatever is available). Damalis' clinging ivy act is surely for the benefit of her all-male audience.

37

This celebrated ode marks the death of the last of the Ptolemies, Cleopatra VII of Egypt. With her lover Antony, she had been the last obstacle between Octavian and the monopoly of power that made him the first Roman emperor. Defeated in the Battle of Actium off the west coast of Greece (September of 31 B.C.), she and Antony retreated to Alexandria, at the mouth of the Nile. When their land forces were finally defeated and Octavian entered Alexandria in August of 30 B.C., Antony and Cleopatra both committed suicide, and the *pax Augusta* was assured. In the first five stanzas, Horace voices Roman satisfaction in the defeat of what is made out to be a monstrous and perverse enemy; then he suddenly turns the poem into a moving tribute to Cleopatra's courageous spirit (for more on Cleopatra, see appendix D). Because official propaganda was representing Actium as a foreign rather than a civil war, no mention, even indirect, is made here of Antony or his Roman forces. The poem takes its motto or opening phrase from Alcaeus frag. 332 LP, celebrating the overthrow of a tyrant: "Now we should get drunk and drink with all our strength, since Myrsilus is dead." The meter is Alcaic strophe.

1-12. Now it is right to drink, dance, and feast

in thanksgiving; before this it was a crime to celebrate, while a mad queen and her diseased eunuchs were plotting Rome's destruction.

1-2. Nunc ... nunc ... nunc: emphatic repetition expresses a note of final relief and strengthens the contrast with *antehac* (5). **pede libero:** suggests wild dancing and freedom from fear; with a play on the wine god Liber, it strengthens the metaphor of intoxication that runs through lines 1-14.

2. pulsanda tellus: i.e., in the dance. Cf. 1.4.7 *terram quatiunt*, 3.18.15 *pepulisse terram*. **Saliaribus ... dapibus:** The banquets of the Salii were proverbial for their sumptuousness. Suetonius (*Claud.* 33.1) reports that the emperor Claudius, when holding court, was so attracted by the aroma of a meal being prepared for the Salii that he left the tribunal and took his place at their table. For their energetic dance, see note on 1.36.12.

3. pulvinar: neut. acc., collective singular; *pulvinaria* were couches on which images of the gods were set while the feast was placed before them. The ceremony was called a *lectisternium*, "couch-spreading."

4. erat: strengthens the sense of *nunc*, implying that the time for this celebration came in the past and it is high time to get started.

5. Antehac: i.e., before the complete annihilation of Antony and Cleopatra; synizesis makes this a disyllable, *ant'hac*. **nefas:** sc. *erat*. The metrical pause after *nefas* is unusual for the Alcaic meter; cf. line 14, where the usual pause is also neglected. **depromere:** cf. *deprome* (1.9.7) and *promptae* (1.36.11, note). **Caecubum:** used substantively, as usual (sc. *vinum*). For more about this wine, see note on 1.20.9.

6. cellis avitis: ancestral wine cellars; presumably the wine too is well aged. **dum ... parabat:** *dum* with the imperfect indicative, only here in Horace. **Capitolio regina:** a good example of Horace's strategic juxtaposing of contrasting words. Although powerful queens were not unknown in the Hellenistic world, the patriarchal Romans perceived the idea of a woman in power as perverted;

moreover, the very name *rex* had been odious since the days of the Tarquins. On this point, cf. Propertius 3.11.47-49: *quid nunc Tarquinii fractas iuvat esse securis ... si mulier patienda fuit?* The choice of *Capitolio* raises the specter of Cleopatra supplanting official worship of the Capitoline deities (Jupiter, Juno, Minerva) with some hideous Egyptian rites. She was, at all events, reputed to have made frequent boasts that she would issue her foreign decrees from the Capitol.

7. dementis ruinas: Horace transfers the epithet from *regina* to *ruinas*.

8. funus et: and destruction. For *et* in second place, cf. 1.2.9, *piscium et summa*.

9. contaminato ... grege: polluted herd. Horace's lurid presentation of the averted calamity reaches its height with this description of Cleopatra's eunuchs, on which see *Epod.* 9.13 note. *grege* is contemptuous.

10. morbo: with *turpium*, foul with sickness or vice. Horace leaves to our imagination the life in which these un-sexed court attendants must wallow. **virorum** is ironic and contemptuous. **quidlibet impotens sperare:** mad enough to hope for anything at all. *Impotens [sui]* means lacking the self-control that the Stoic Romans admired.

11. fortuna ... dulci: i.e., her previous run of luck. She had an affair with Julius Caesar in 48 B.C., and a son by him the following summer; she lived two years in Rome by his invitation, 46-44 B.C. This would now be a somewhat delicate subject under the regime of Caesar's nephew and heir Octavian, whom she tried but failed to seduce.

12-21. But her crushing defeat at Actium sobered her wild dreams of conquest, as Caesar drove her in terror over the sea.

13. vix una sospes navis ab ignibus: subject of *minuit:* the survival of scarcely a single ship, etc. This is something of an exaggeration: during the sea battle at Actium, fire broke out among the ships of Antony and destroyed them; Cleopatra escaped with sixty vessels.

14. lymphatam Mareotico: crazed by Mareotic wine (*lympha* is a collateral form of *nympha*, at the sight of which it was said the unfortunate beholder lost his wits). This wine, Shakespeare's "juice of Egypt's grape" (*A&C* 5.2.277), came from the region of Lake Mareotis, near Alexandria. It was a sweet wine with a high bouquet.

16. ab Italia: really from Actium; but the poet wishes to emphasize that instead of proceeding *in Italiam* as she wished, she was forced to flee in the opposite direction. The normally short *I* of *Italia* is lengthened, as often in poetry. **volantem:** understand *reginam*; Cleopatra is never mentioned by name in Augustan poetry.

17. remis adurgens: pursuing her with oared galleys. Another poetic liberty: Octavian did not follow up his victory with immediate pursuit. He returned to Italy to suppress sedition (Dio 51.4.3), then wintered at Samos and pushed on to Egypt the following spring (30 B.C.). **accipiter velut:** an Iliadic simile (*Il.* 22.139ff., where Achilles sweeps down on Hector like a hawk on a dove).

20. Haemoniae: the old name for Thessaly, whose fields are called snowy (19 *nivalis*) because the hare (18 *leporem*) was hunted in the winter. **daret ut catenis:** conjunction delayed for emphasis on the verb, to throw into chains. The subject is Caesar (line 16).

21. fatale monstrum: no mere dove or hare. Emphasized by enjambment into the next stanza, this epithet concludes Horace's treatment of the unnamed Cleopatra as a lethal bogey-woman. He now dramatically shifts his perspective.

21-32. Yet she showed no fear, and boldly took in hand the fatal serpents, too proud to be shipped away for a Roman triumph.

21. Quae: but she; adversative, the gender of the pronoun contrasting with the neuter *monstrum*. **generosius:** more nobly than Octavian intended her to die, first displayed in his triumphal procession and afterward executed in the Tullianum. See

2.13.18 note.

23. expavit: intensive *ex-*, hence fear greatly or excessively. According to Plutarch, Cleopatra first attempted suicide with a dagger, but was prevented by Proculeius. **latentis ... reparavit oras:** took hidden shores in exchange (for her palace at Alexandria); Cleopatra thought of hauling her fleet over the isthmus of Suez to the Red Sea until Arabs from Petra burned her ships.

25. iacentem ... regiam: sc. *urbem*; her fallen city, the royal quarter of Alexandria. *iacentem* is figurative for its loss of the power to rule Egypt, which now became a Roman province.

26. vultu sereno: i.e., with the philosophic equanimity that the Stoic Romans admired. The sources report that she concealed her despair, and even exhibited a cheerful demeanor in the presence of her guards. **asperas:** rough to the touch; easily provoked to attack with their deadly bite. The repetition of *s-* and *t-* sounds in this clause adds drama.

27. tractare: completes the sense of *fortis* above. **serpentes:** according to the traditional account, she met her death from the bite of an asp, which she had hidden in her bosom. **atrum:** metaphoric, as bringing death.

28. combiberet: intensive *com-*, drink up; a final reference to the drinking theme with which the ode began.

29. deliberata morte: abl. of cause, fiercer because of her resolution to die.

30. saevis Liburnis: dat., indirect object of *invidens*; the direct object is the infinitive *deduci*. She begrudged them the honor of bringing her to Rome. The "Liburnians" were swift galleys patterned after those of the Liburnian pirates, who lived in a part of what is now Albania. Because these galleys had rendered special service in the victory at Actium, they are *saevae* to Cleopatra. **scilicet:** evidently, obviously.

31. privata: as a private person, stripped of her rank as queen of Egypt. **superbo ... triumpho:** abl. with *deduci*. Cf. Shakespeare *A&C* 5.2.55:

Shall they hoist me up
And show me to the shouting varletry
Of censuring Rome?

Livy (quoted by Porphyrio) reports that she vowed not to be led in triumph: οὐ θριαμβεύσομαι. But her effigy was carried in the triumph.

38

This little epigram, significantly placed at the end of Book 1, makes a statement for simplicity. The language is symposiac, but the underlying content is a statement about poetic values. In the Hellenistic tradition, Horace tells the slave attending him not to gild the lily: the greatest elegance is simplicity. Suiting form to content, Horace writes in short, simple phrases unconnected by conjunctions (see appendix C, asyndeton). This coda to Book 1 contrasts with the grandiose predictions of Horace's immortality that come at the end of Books 2 and 3. Meter: Sapphic strophe.

1-8. I dislike elaborate decorations of woven garlands and scarce flowers; simple myrtle is good enough for you, my servant, and for me as I drink beneath my compact vine.

1. Persicos: emphatically placed, this adjective connotes luxurious decadence and everything alien, far-fetched, even barbaric; cf. Callimachus *Aetia* 1.18. **puer:** slave. In the vocative at this point, it signals a sympotic context; cf. Catullus 27.1, *Minister vetuli puer Falerni*. Horace specifies his role as waiter in line 6, *te ministrum*. **apparatus:** acc. pl., paraphernalia, trappings. On their avoidance in plain rhetoric, see Cicero *Orator* 24.83.

2. philyra: instrumental abl., the bast or fibrous bark of the linden or lime tree, used to bind flowers together into garlands. For *corona* as a poem, see note on 1.26.8.

3. mitte: do not. Cf. *Epod.* 13.7, *cetera mitte loqui*. Completed by the iterative **sectari**, don't keep looking for. The three dismissive verbs *odi, displicent,* and *mitte* give the stanza a Callimachean flavor. Callimachus, the great arbiter of Hellenistic taste and distaste, was known for such phrases as μέγα βιβλίον μέγα κακόν: "a big book is a great evil." **quo locorum:** where of (all) places. For the partitive gen., cf. 1.29.5, *quae virginum* and note.

4. sera: i.e., the last of the season.

5. nihil: emphatic negation, governing **allabores** = *adlabores*, do extra work on. *Simplici* here contrasts with *Persicos* in stanza 1; *allabores* likewise echoes the sense of *apparatus*.

6. sedulus curo: emphatic redundancy, I am earnestly concerned. Governs the optative subjunctive *nihil allabores*. Some take *sedulus* with the preceding *allabores*, translating "you needn't exert yourself to add anything" (NH *ad loc.*)

7. arta: compact, dense, thrifty, narrow. Horace pictures himself outdoors under a trellis or *pergola* of vines that have been pruned to stimulate the growth of leaves for denser shade. On a metaphorical level the trellis, like the simple myrtle, represents the plain, economical style of which lyric poetry is capable. Fraenkel calls all of this "an enormous understatement," meaning that Horace's style is far from the last word in simplicity. Commager likewise notes "the exaggerated language of [Horace's] repudiation" and the "playful tension of attitudes."

1

A tribute to the *Historiae* of Gaius Asinius Pollio, a work in progress as this poem was written. Covering the civil turmoil that began with the First Triumvirate and concluding with the Battle of Philippi in 42 B.C., Pollio's (no longer extant) account of domestic bloodletting was a theme of concern also for Horace. Poems in praise of literary achievement were a Hellenistic type adopted by the Romans: Callimachus A.P. 9.507 (GP 56, on Aratus' *Phaenomena*), Catullus 1 (Nepos' *Chronica*) and 95 (Cinna's *Zmyrna*), Virgil *Ecl.* 6 and 10 (Gallus' Elegies). Horace's tribute allows him to reiterate his political theme while (in the closing stanza) detaching himself from it in favor of lighter love poetry. Meter: Alcaic strophe.

1-8. You are chronicling the civil upheaval that began in Metellus' consulship, a task full of danger and hazard.

1. Motum ... civicum: euphemistic for civil wars; object of *tractas*, which is delayed until line 7. *civicus* is archaic for *civilis*, like *hosticus* for *hostilis* in 3.2.6. **ex Metello consule:** from the time of Metellus' consulship. Quintus Caecilius Metellus Celer was consul in 60 B.C., the year Caesar, Pompey, and Crassus formed the First Triumvirate. This coalition is regarded as marking the real beginning of the civil commotions that, with few interruptions, continued for the next thirty years. Actual hostilities, however, did not commence until 49 B.C., when Caesar returned from Gaul and crossed the Rubicon.

2. bellique causas et vitia et, etc.: the triple repetition of *-que* and *et* highlight the complexity of Pollio's undertaking. For more about this polysyndeton, see appendix C. **vitia:** the evils of the civil war, or blunders in its conduct. **modos:** tactics and strategies.

3. ludum ... Fortunae: *tychē* (Gk. τύχη), chance, was an irrational component featured in Greek historiography; personified in Horace, she mocks the plans of humankind. Cf. 1.35.38-40 and

3.29.49ff., *Fortuna saevo laeta negotio et ludum insolentem ludere pertinax.*

3-4. gravis ... amicitias: momentous alliances such at that of Pompey and Caesar; *gravis* also implies that they were troublesome and costly to Rome.

5. nondum expiatis ... cruoribus: i.e., not yet expiated by the slaughter of foreign enemies such as the Persians; the same sentiment as in 1.2.29, *cui dabit partis scelus expiandi?* **uncta:** soaked. **cruoribus:** grandiloquent plural, suggesting the many battles in which Roman blood has been shed.

6. periculosae: because there was danger of giving offense to the surviving partisans. **opus:** a task; the word is in apposition with the preceding sentence. **aleae:** hazard by a common metaphor from dicing, as we say "dicey."

7. incedis per ignes, etc.: it is reasonable to speculate that this and other statements in lines 1-8 about Pollio's history paraphrase the author's own exordium. Cf. Macaulay, *History of England*: "When the historian of this troubled reign (James II) turns to Ireland, his task becomes peculiarly difficult and delicate. His steps—to borrow the fine image used on a similar occasion by a Roman poet—are on the thin crust of ashes beneath which the lava is still glowing" (chap. 6). For *per* in the sense of over, cf. 1.6.7, *per mare.*

9-16. Briefly set aside your tragic muse; soon you will resume, Pollio, famous lawyer, statesman, and soldier.

9. severae: austere, grave, serious. **Musa tragoediae:** Pollio's reputation as a tragic poet is well attested; cf. Virgil *Ecl.* 8.10, *sola Sophocleo tua carmina digna cothurno.* In *Sat.* 1.10.42 Horace cites him as the representative tragic poet of Rome. None of his plays have survived, however.

10. desit: jussive subj. **publicas res ordinaris:** *ordina(ve)ris* = set down, arrange the events of state in a formal chronicle.

11. grande munus: your lofty calling (as a tragic

poet).

12. Cecropio ... cothurno: instrumental abl., with Attic buskin, i.e., in your role as playwright. The buskin or *cothurnus* was the elevated shoe worn by tragic actors to add to their stature and stage presence. Tragedy is called Cecropian (from Cecrops, a mythical king of Attica) because tragedy originated and developed in Athens. **repetes:** resume. The future has the force of a polite imperative, implying confidence that Pollio *will* return to his plays.

13. insigne ... praesidium: famed support. Pollio was a prominent lawyer, especially in the defense of criminal cases; eight of the nine known titles of his speeches are for the defense. **reis** are defendants, described as **maestis** because of the custom of displaying their (allegedly) undeserved misery during trials.

14. consulenti ... curiae: to the Senate in its deliberations. The *curia* was the meeting hall of the Senate, by metonymy the Senate itself. **Pollio:** the final *o*, regularly long, is here shortened. This practice is relatively rare in the Augustan period, but later became quite general. For more about Pollio, see appendix A.

16. Delmatico ... triumpho: he was awarded a triumph for his defeat of the Illyrian Parthini in 39 B.C. **peperit:** has procured; from *pario*.

17-24. Your vivid descriptions already dazzle my mind: trumpets, gleaming armor, horses, generals dusty from battle, and all the world save Cato at Caesar's feet.

17. Iam nunc: even now; the poet conceives himself as already listening to the recital of Pollio's history. **cornuum:** trumpets curved nearly in the shape of a **C**, and strengthened by a crossbar.

18. perstringis: deafen. **litui:** a long, straight horn, curved slightly at the end. Cf. 1.1.23.

20. equitum ... vultus: a pictorial detail, possibly alluding to Caesar's order at Pharsalia, *faciem feri:* "strike them in the face."

21. Audire ... videor: I seem to hear them

(shouting to their troops). With *cuncta ... subacta*, the same verb means "hear of." Some editors amend to *Videre*, but the paradox is deliberate to highlight Pollio's vivid style.

22. sordidos: grimy. Horace's (and by extension Pollio's) imagination is visual and auditory at the same time.

23. cuncta terrarum subacta: all the lands subdued (sc. *a Caesare*); a combination of neuter plural substantive followed by a gen. of the whole is found only in the poets and later prose writers. Cf. 4.12.19 *amara curarum*.

24. atrocem: used here in a good sense, stern. M. Porcius Cato Uticensis, great-grandson of Cato the Censor, received his surname from the north African city that he governed, and where he committed suicide in 46 B.C. rather than live under a dictator. Cf. 1.12.35, *Catonis nobile letum.*

25-36. Our civil strife may well be regarded as a sacrifice to our enemy Jugurtha's shade. What field, river, or sea has not been stained with Roman blood?

25. Iuno: the Carthaginian goddess Tanit, identified by the Romans with Juno. The mention of Cato recalls the battle of Thapsus and the wars in Africa. After the sack of Carthage in 146 B.C. and the execution of Jugurtha in 104 B.C., the Africans would have felt abandoned by their gods. These lines suggest that the shedding of Roman blood on both sides of the battle of Thapsus in Africa would please the dead Jugurtha. **deorum quisquis:** whoever (else) of the gods.

26. cesserat: had withdrawn, abandoning Africa when they found themselves no longer able to protect it. Cf. the gods abandoning Troy in Virgil *Aen.* 2.351: *excessere omnes, adytis arisque relictis, di quibus imperium hoc steterat.* There may be a reference here to the Roman ritual of *evocatio,* conjuring away the city's tutelary deity. **impotens:** helpless; the meaning is glossed by the abl. absolute *inulta ... tellure;* they are helpless because the land is unavenged for its defeats by Rome in the Punic and Jugurthine wars.

27. victorum nepotes: the present victims of civil war are seen as descended from the Romans who conquered north Africa. Q. Metellus Scipio, commander of Pompey's losing faction at Thapsus, was in fact the grandson of Metellus Numidicus, who fought Numidian King Jugurtha in 109-107 B.C. and paved the way for Marius' victory in 106. The 10,000 Romans who fell fighting each other at Thapsus in 46 B.C. may well have been descendants of the earlier victors.

28. rettulit: has offered them in return as **inferias,** a funeral sacrifice; the noun is used predicatively. **Iugurthae:** Sallust's account of the Numidian king's war against Rome was published about 41 B.C.; see on *Epod.* 9.23.

29-32. Quis ... campus, etc.: three rhetorical questions are compressed into a single construction, which might be restated *Quis campus non est pinguior ... ? Quis campus non testatur ... ? Quis (homo) non audivit sonitum ... ?*

29. Latino: instead of *Romano;* throughout his patriotic poetry, Horace emphasizes the regional Italian components of Roman power. Cf. *Dauniae* (34). **pinguior:** fatter because of the blood spilled on it.

30. sepulcris: by its tombs, instrumental with *testatur.*

31. testatur: bear witness to, limited by *non* (29). **Medis:** dat. of agent with *auditum.* On *Medis* for *Parthis,* see 1.2.51. Like the shade of Jugurtha, these enemies of Rome will naturally rejoice at her disasters. There may be a reference here to the opportunistic Parthian invasion of Syria and the southern coast of Asia Minor after Philippi.

32. Hesperiae: the land of the West, from the viewpoint of easterners, would be Italy. Cf. 1.36.4 note. **sonitum** is acc. obj. of *testatur.*

33. gurges: another of many poetic words for sea. **lugubris:** dismal or gloomy, gen. with *belli.*

34. ignara belli: sc. *est;* i.e., do not bear traces of the conflict. **Dauniae:** properly Apulian, as in 1.22.14, but here in the general sense of Italian,

Roman. Daunus was a legendary king of Apulia, famous for its soldiers.

35. decoloravere: stained, with the added metaphoric sense of disgraced. **caedes:** for the plural, see on *cruoribus,* line 5.

37-40. But enough of such dismal themes. O Muse, help me find a lighter verse.
37-38. ne ... retractes: lest you take up again; dependent on *quaere.* Horace suddenly checks himself, as he sometimes does when using a grand or serious style. Cf. 3.3.70, *quo, Musa, tendis?* This is in the manner of Pindar, e.g., *Ol.* 9.40. **relictis ... iocis:** abandoning more familiar humorous themes. **procax:** slightly outrageous, audacious, assertive, playfully licentious; an apparent admission (as also in 1.6.17-20) that the poet feels his natural métier to be light poetry.

38. Ceae ... munera neniae: the functions of the Cean dirge, so called because of the solemn style of Simonides of Ceos (556-467 B.C.), who was noted for his pathos. He wrote elegies honoring the Greeks who fell at Marathon and Thermopylae.

39. Dionaeo sub antro: i.e., in love's preserve; *Dionaeo,* belonging to Dione (the mother of Venus), is the equivalent of *Veneris.* On *sub antro,* see 1.5.3.

40. modos leviore plectro: measures of a lighter plectrum, i.e., verses of a lighter type of poetry. Horace means not so much the actual *modus* or meter (he uses the meter of this poem in many of his lighter odes) as poetry itself. For the literal meaning of *plectro,* see note on 1.26.11.

2

The first of a pair of odes setting forth an ethical precept, this poem contrasts the possession of good character with the ownership of material riches. Though criticized as "somewhat mechanical" (Commager), it is an excellent example of the use of recent history (Proculeius, Phraätes) and nature (the *dirus hydrops* in stanza 4) instead of myth for examples of virtue and vice. Meter: Sapphic strophe.

1-8. Silver hidden in the earth has no luster, Sallust: only our use of it makes it shine. Proculeius won lasting fame by sharing his inheritance with his brothers.

1. color: luster; introduces the metaphor repeated in *splendeat*. **avaris:** either dat. of agent with *abdito*, hidden by misers, or locative abl. with *terris*, in the miserly earth. It became a commonplace of moralists that silver in its natural state is not shiny.

2. abdito: hidden away. **inimice:** vocative, despiser of wealth or **lamnae** (syncopated from *laminae*), a strip of precious metal equivalent to our gold bars. Used contemptuously of wealth not even coined into money, and hence of little immediate use.

3. Crispe Sallusti: where the *praenomen* (Gaius) is omitted, it became common even in prose from the time of Cicero to reverse the *nomen* (Sallustius) and *cognomen* (Crispus). C. Sallustius Crispus had inherited a large fortune from his great uncle and adoptive father, the historian Sallust (see appendix A).

3-4. nisi temperato ... usu: i.e., avoiding the extremes of prodigality and meanness. The clause is best understood as qualifying *inimice* rather than the opening motto. Sallustius is complimented as a despiser of unused or misused wealth. For the utilitarian standard in ethics, cf. *Sat.* 1.3.98 *utilitas, iusti prope mater et aequi.*

5. extento ... aevo: with life prolonged beyond the grave by his reputation for generosity. **Proculeius:** C. Proculeius Varro, son of Aulus Terentius Varro and brother-in-law of Maecenas. When his two brothers lost their property in the civil war, Proculeius gave each a third of his fortune.

6. notus ... animi paterni: known for his paternal attitude (gen. of specification).

7. penna metuente solvi: poetic singular, on wings that refuse to tire; *timeo* and *metuo* are sometimes used by poets in the sense of *nolo*; cf. 1.8.8, *cur timet ... Tiberim tangere.* But there is also a latent allusion to Icarus, whose wings melted: 2.20.13, 4.2.2-4.

8. fama superstes: Horace's poetic figure represents Proculeius' surviving fame as like an eagle carrying him along.

9-16. Control of one's own desire for more is the highest form of power; greed grows by indulgence, like the thirst of a man with dropsy.

9. regnes: generalizing potential subjunctive. This alludes to the Stoic paradox that self-government is greater than political power. The corresponding Epicurean teaching was that you increase your riches by decreasing your desire for them. Cf. Proverbs 16:32, "He that ruleth his spirit is mightier than he that taketh a city."

10-11. Libyam ... Gadibus: i.e., Africa to Europe. Gades (mod. Cadiz) is in Southern Spain, outside the straits of Gibraltar (see map 1).

11. iungas: as owner or ruler. Potential subjunctive, like *regnes*. **uterque Poenus:** both the north African and the Spanish Punic colonist. Long after Rome's final defeat of Carthage, Punic settlements survived in Spain, e.g., *Nova Carthago* (mod. Cartagena), and elsewhere in the western Mediterranean. Modern Maltese is a Punic dialect.

12. uni: sc. *tibi*, a single master.

13. Crescit, etc.: greed is like dropsy or edema (*hydrops*), made worse by trying to satisfy its symptom, thirst. *Crescit* is emphatic by position, and *hydrops* is personified.

15. fugerit venis: fut. perf., emphasizing the importance of the prior condition; the disease occurs when water from the blood accumulates in the tissues. **aquosus ... languor:** the watery weakness that results from the accumulation of water. **albo corpore:** another symptom; note the inclusive word order. The literary description of disease had become a poetic *topos*, as for example Lucretius' description of the Athenian plague in *De Rerum*

Natura, 6.1138ff.

17-24. No potentate is truly happy: rather the one who can look at vast treasure without envy.

17. Redditum ... Phraäten: *redditum* is put first for emphasis on the antithesis. Though he is restored to power, *Virtus* will not admit him to the ranks of the *beati.* Phraätes (or Prahates) won the Parthian throne by murdering his father and brothers. In 30 B.C., Tiridates appealed for Roman help against the usurper. See 1.26.5 note. He contrasts effectively with the fraternal Proculeius (line 5). **Cyri solio:** Arsaces, the founder of the Parthian dynasty of the Arsacidae, claimed descent from Cyrus, founder of the Persian empire. In 3.9.4, *Persarum rege beatior* is used to express the height of happiness, but see note on line 19 below.

18-19. dissidens plebi ... Virtus: a personified Virtue (lit. *vir-tus,* manliness), representing the Stoic ideal of rectitude, excludes the tyrant Phraätes from the *numero beatorum* contrary to the opinion of the *plebs.* Horace's distrust of the general citizenry is a frequent note: Cf. *Epod.* 16.37, 1.35.14-16, 3.1.1, 3.2.20, 3.3.2. **beatorum:** the Stoics believed that only the just are happy (*beatus* also = wealthy). Line 18 is hypermetric, with the final *-um* eliding with the initial vowel in the next line (see appendix C, synapheia). The effect here is to dramatize the title of "happy" being snatched away by *Virtus.*

20. dedocet, teaches ... not, is like our idiom "warn off."

21. vocibus: words: the particular *vox* in question is *beatus.* Enjambment into the next stanza stresses this word. **diadema, laurum:** i.e., the outward marks of royalty. The Stoics taught that royalty lay in character rather than rank: cf. *Epist.* 1.1.59, *rex eris si recte facies.* **tutum:** secure against political misfortune.

22. deferens uni: conferring on him alone. **propriam:** inalienably his own, just as his diadem is *tutum.*

23. irretorto: a new word, coined here by Hor-

ace. The just man's eye is undistracted by mere wealth. He sees it (*spectat*) but does not look back.

24. acervos: piles (of money); cf. *Epist.* 1.2.47, *aeris acervus at auri.*

3

The Stoic flavor of the previous ode yields to an Epicurean cast of thought here, but without the glib tidiness of traditional Epicurean doctrine. As the poem moves past its midpoint, we sense a tension between the rational Epicurean consent to extinction after death and an emotional protest against being herded off like animals to Charon's boat. Meter: Alcaic strophe.

1-8. Be steady in adversity, moderate in prosperity.

1. Aequam ... arduis: the virtue of equanimity, with a playful metaphor about a level head in steep situations. The theme is as old as Archilochus, eighth to seventh cent. B.C. (see frag. 128 West).

2. non secus: and likewise. Asyndeton and litotes.

3. insolenti: orig. = unusual, this word had come to mean also excessive, arrogant, hybristic. **temperatam:** sc. *mentem.* These lines explain what was adopted as the Christian virtue of *temperantia.*

4. laetitia, euphoria, was the Stoic Gk. ἡδονή. **moriture:** vocative of the future participle with causal force: because you are mortal, keep a level head. **Delli:** see appendix A.

5. omni tempore: abl. instead of acc. for duration of time.

6. te: with *bea(ve)ris,* make yourself happy, reflecting the Horatian view that happiness is self-engendered. **in remoto gramine** reminds us of the pastoral *locus amoenus:* cf. 1.1.21-22.

7. reclinatum: with middle force, reclining.

8. interiore nota Falerni: lit. with an interior label of Falernian. Vintners marked wine jars with a *nota* or *titulus* giving the date of the vintage. The jars in the inner (*interiore*) part of the storeroom naturally contained the oldest and best wine. On Falernian wine, see note on 1.20.10. Plutarch *Ant.* 59.4 mentions Dellius' love of this wine.

9-16. Why does nature work as it does? Let us seek its pleasures while we may.

9. quo: the interrogative adverb, in a rhetorical question: why do trees make shade, if not for our enjoyment? **pinus ingens:** the word order (noun-adjective : adjective-noun) suggests that the pine is dark as well as tall, and the poplar less massive than the pine. Horace's attribution of idealized gender features makes them seem like a human couple. **alba** refers to the silvery leaves of the white poplar.

10-11. umbram ... ramis: as *consociare* is intransitive, *umbram* is an acc. of result produced; with **amant,** the effect is close to personification: the trees love to get together and produce shade (for our benefit). Nature's sympathy with man is a pastoral fiction, the "pathetic fallacy" explored first in Greek by Theocritus (ca. 300-260 B.C.) and more recently in Latin by Virgil's *Eclogues.*

11. Quid: used in the same sense as *quo* above. **obliquo:** probably winding rather than sloping.

11-12. laborat ... trepidare: suggests purposeful, bustling labor as the brook hurries along, contrasted with the relaxed sociability of the trees.

12. lympha: connected in popular etymology with the *nympha* of a spring, *lympha* becomes the poetic word for fresh water.

13-14. Huc ... ferre iube: have someone bring, "someone" being a slave. The language is sympotic. **et ... et:** the repetition conveys urgency, as in line 15. **unguenta:** a typical part of any well-planned party; cf. 2.11.15, *canos odorati capillos.* **nimium brevis:** modifies *flores;* the short life of the flower is an example of our own frailty; cf. *breve lilium,* 1.36.16.

15. res et aetas: circumstances and youth. **sororum ... trium:** the three Fates: Clotho spins the thread of life; Lachesis twists it, and Atropos

determines how long we will live by cutting it.

17-28. Rich or poor, high or low, we will all be herded off to the same place.

17. Cedes: you will depart from your **coëmptis saltibus,** upland pastures that have been bought up (*co-emptis*) from various smallholders and united in one vast tract. Such consolidations into large *latifundia* worked by slaves were checked by confiscations under the Second Triumvirate and by Augustus' policy of giving free loans to family farmers. **et ... -que:** emphatic polysyndeton as in lines 13 and 15, here with a note of doom. **domo villaque:** the city *domus* and the country *villa,* which included grounds.

18. flavus: the Tiber was proverbially yellow with alluvial mud; cf. 1.2.13. **lavit:** indicative; in the *Epodes* and *Odes* Horace treats *lavo, -are* as a third-conjugation verb.

19. cedes: portentous or pathetic anaphora (line 17). **in altum:** on high, or into the deep. Romans of the time were building seaside villas that extended via landfill into the deep water.

20. heres: The unworthy heir who fritters away a carefully hoarded fortune is a commonplace in Horace, who got it from the Stoic diatribes. Cf. 2.14.25ff., 3.24.61, *indigno heredi.* The feeling is that of Ecclesiastes 2:18, "Yea, I hated all the labor which I had taken under the sun: because I should leave it to the man that shall be after me."

21-22. Dives ... pauper: in apposition to the subject of *moreris;* it makes no difference whether you linger *sub divo* as a *dives* or a *pauper.* **Inacho:** the first king of Argos, and so suggesting ancient lineage.

23. moreris: tarry or linger, a more colorful variant of *vivis.* With *divum* as a word for the open sky, cf. *sub Iove,* 1.1.25.

24. victima: sc. *cum es,* victim as you are. The word usually implies an animal for sacrifice. The harsh ellipsis and the speeding-up dictated by the meter are effective in dramatizing our ultimate helplessness.

25. eodem: i.e., to the realm of Orcus, where there are no distinctions between rich and poor. **cogimur:** the herdsman's term for gathering a scattered flock, as in Virgil *Ecl.* 3.20, *Tityre, coge pecus.* Cf. 1.24.18. We are being rounded up like sheep. The philosophic tone yields at the end to a mood of protest.

26. versatur urna: everyone's lot is shaken in an urn until someone's bounces out; lotteries were traditionally conducted by this method. **serius ocius:** disjunctive asyndeton (sooner *or* later), modifying *exitura.*

27-28. exitura ... impositura: future participles implying doom, as in line 4 *moriture* and the gladiators' *nos morituri salutamus.* **aeternum:** hypermetric, eliding with the next line and increasing the effect of terminal acceleration: *et nos in aetern' exsili' impositura cumbae.*

28. cumbae: Charon's skiff, the ferryboat to Hades. Emphatic as the last word of the ode. The dat. depends on the prefix *im-* (will place on the boat).

4

A bantering consolation to a lover who has fallen for an *ancilla.* Horace's sympotic poems are usually given a touch of Roman color such as a local place name (the mountain Soracte in 1.9), an Italian wine (*Caecubum* in 1.20), or a Roman personal name (Corvinus in 3.21). Here, as in 1.27, where the theme is similar, everything is Greek. But there is a humorous personal note at the end where the speaker claims to be too old for sex because he is over forty. The meter is Sapphic strophe.

1-12. Do not be ashamed of your love for a slave, Xanthias; there are good precedents.

1. Ne sit: with the pres. subj., less a prohibition than a purpose clause depending on the arguments advanced in the first half of the poem. The construction is elliptical: lest you be ashamed of loving a slave, consider the following. Negative prohibi-

tions with *ne* regularly take the perf. subj., *tu ne quaesieris* (1.11.1). **ancillae:** objective gen. with *amor.* **tibi ... pudori:** double dat., combining dat. of reference (*tibi*) with dat. of purpose or effect (*pudori*).

2. Xanthia Phoceu: Gk. vocative of *Xanthias Phoceus.* Phocis is the district of central Greece around Delphi. **Prius:** before this, referring to the three following examples. It may, though, be taken with **insolentem,** haughty, and hence (before falling in love) unlikely to consort with a mere *serva.* In *Epist.* 2.3.122, Achilles *iura neget sibi nata, nihil non arroget armis.*

3. Briseis: the theme of Homer's *Iliad* is the wrath of Achilles, brought on when Agamemnon takes back the former's concubine Briseis. See *Il.* 1.184ff. Each of the precedents (Achilles, Ajax, Agamemnon) took one of his captive women as concubine. **niveo colore:** an untanned, snowy complexion was essential to the blonde look; cf. 2.5.18, *Chloris albo ... umero nitens* and in this ode *Phyllidis flavae* (14); Xanthias' name implies he too is fair-haired.

5. Aiacem Telamone natum: Ajax the son of Telamon (brother of Teucer in 1.7.21), as opposed to Ajax the son of Oileus; both served with the Greeks in the Trojan War.

6. forma: beauty. **captivae dominum:** the juxtaposition of words emphasizes the contrast, and the paradox of a master enslaved by love for a slave. Tecmessa was the daughter of a Phrygian king whom Ajax killed in single combat. **Tecmessae:** the initial syllable is short by an extension of the *muta cum liquida* rule to Greek words containing *cm* and *cn.*

7. arsit: with love; from *ardeo.* **Atrides:** Agamemnon, son of Atreus. **medio in triumpho:** i.e., at the fall of Troy.

8. virgine rapta: abl. of cause with *arsit.* The girl is Cassandra, first seized at the sack of Troy by Ajax son of Oileus, and then taken by Agamemnon.

9. barbarae: to the Greeks, any non-Greek. Roman poets used it as equivalent to "Phrygian," i.e., Trojan. **turmae:** properly, troops of cavalry; used here of troops in general.

10. Thessalo victore: instrumental abl.; the troops fell to the Thessalian victor Achilles, whose victory over Hector was the decisive event of the war. **ademptus Hector:** the loss of Hector, lit. Hector removed, subject of *tradidit*.

11-12. fessis ... Grais: exhausted by the ten-year siege. **leviora tolli:** easier to be taken. **Pergama:** the Trojan citadel, not to be confused with the city of Pergamum to the south in Mysia (see map 4).

13-20. You never know: she could be of noble birth; her qualities all point that way.

13. Nescias an: potential subjunctive, you wouldn't know but that, i.e., for all you know. **generum:** son-in-law, in apposition with *te*. **beati:** rich; with *parentes*. Horace is joking about the plots of comedies such as *The Carthaginian* of Plautus where the romantic young man is in love with a slave-girl who turns out to be the kidnapped daughter of wealthy parents.

14. flavae: her blonde hair makes her special: see note on 1.5.4. **decorent:** do credit to, with *te* as object. Horace is leading Xanthias on with the notion that she could really be a fine match for him.

15-16. regium ... genus, penatis ... iniquos: both objects of *maeret*. Her tutelary household gods are cruel because they have allowed her to fall into slavery. **maeret:** note the shift to indicative as Horace warms to his idea.

17. tibi: dat. of agent with *dilectam [esse]*. **de scelesta plebe:** humorously exaggerated snobbery. For Horace's own scorn of the "wicked mob," see note on 2.2.19.

18. sic goes with *dilectam, fidelem*, and *aversam*. She is like the excellent young courtesan Philematium in Plautus' *Mostellaria*.

19. lucro aversum: aloof from gain; she is not like the mercenary hetaeras of the comic stage.

20. pudenda: lit. to be ashamed of, i.e., of low birth or character. Phyllis could never have the virtues she does if her mother were a mere commoner or otherwise a potential embarrassment to Xanthias. There is more mockery here of the fictions of comedy.

21-24. My own motives in praising her are pure; I'm too old to want her for myself.

21. teretis ... suras: smooth, well-rounded calves; shapely lower legs were a quality of beautiful goddesses and women as early as Homer (*Il.* 9.557, 560, etc.).

22. integer: disinterested, pure of motive. **fuge suspicari** = *noli suspicari*. Cf. 1.9.13, *fuge quaerere*.

23. cuius: one whose; its antecedent is the understood object of *suspicari*. **octavum ... lustrum:** i.e., fortieth year. Horace is playing on young Xanthias' naivete by suggesting that a man of forty is tottering on the edge of the grave, far beyond the reach of sexual desire. **trepidavit** = *properavit* (cf. 2.3.12), with an additional note of the aging man's anxiety. The subject is *aetas*.

24. lustrum: the sacrifice of purification, performed by the censors every fifth year after completing their work; hence, any period of five years. The technical expression was *condere lustrum*, which Horace as usual avoids.

5

The second of a pair of odes about love, this one advises an impatient lover to bide his time. As no one is addressed by name, the ode may be a soliloquy. It is built around a series of vignettes, beginning with a girl who is not yet a woman and ending with a boy who is not yet a man. The meter is Alcaic.

1-9. The girl you want is like a heifer who is not ready for a mate.

1-2. subacta ... cervice: suggesting submission to sex, as to a yoke. **valet** = *potest*, governing *ferre*, *aequare*, and *tolerare*.

2-3. munia comparis aequare: to match the duties of a partner, as in drawing a plow or the like. Animals working in a yoke had to be matched in size and strength.

3-4. tauri ... pondus: the bull's weight is metaphoric for the lover's vehemence. The metaphor is somewhat coarse, in the tradition that compared human to animal sexuality (cf. 1.23, 3.11.9ff.).

4. in venerem: into the physical act of sex.

5. Circa ... est animus: her mind is dwelling on the *virentis campos*.

5-6. tuae ... iuvencae: i.e., Lalage, who is not named until line 16. The reference to her here follows the metaphor of the two opening strophes. A *iuvenca*, heifer, is a young cow that has not begun its reproductive cycle.

6-7. gravem solantis aestum: relieving the oppressive heat; for a similar picture, cf. 3.13.10-12. *Solantis* modifies *iuvencae*.

7-8. udo ... salicto: a moist willow grove, of the sort that would grow around the river where she went to cool off.

8. vitulis: calves of either gender.

9. praegestientis: modifies *iuvencae*; intensive *prae-* added to *gestio* means to desire eagerly. She is like the Thracian filly in Anacreon 417 Page.

9-16. Soon it will be otherwise, and she will be the pursuer.

9. Tolle: get rid of, as in 1.27.2, *tollite barbarum morem*.

10. immitis uvae: unripe grape; an abrupt transition to a new metaphor for this strophe only. **iam:** soon now, repeated three times (lines 10, 12, 15). Most of what Horace does in this ode comes in threes. **tibi:** dat. of advantage or reference.

10-11. lividos distinguet ... racemos: will mark off the blue clusters; *lividus* is the leaden blue of the half-ripe grape. The metaphor therefore denotes progressing adolescence rather than full maturity.

12. purpureo ... colore: denoting full ripeness.

Purpureus varies from violet to scarlet depending on the amount of dye used. **varius:** many-colored; the fall colors are attributed to a personified *Autumnus* himself.

14-15. illi ... annos: the idea is that as he passes beyond maturity, *ferox aetas* will have taken years away (*dempserit*) from him, while as she improves with time, it will give them (*apponet*) to her. Horace inverts the theme of 1.25 where the woman grows more decrepit and the men younger.

15-16. proterva fronte: figurative of audacity, like our "cheek." The heifer metaphor is now forgotten.

17-24. She'll be more loved than flighty Pholoë, pale Chloris, or girlish Gyges.

17. dilecta quantum non: more loved than. Some readers hear an echo of Catullus 8.5, *amata nobis quantum amabitur nulla*. **fugax:** coy, reluctant, or evasive, not *proterva* like the future Lalage. She is like the Pholoë of 1.33.7-9.

18. Chloris: the name suggests the Greek word for pale, χλωρός. **albo ... umero:** For the ancient taste for untanned skin, cf. note on 2.4.3, *niveo colore*.

19-20. pura ... luna: i.e., a clear moon. **renidet:** gleams.

20. Cnidiusve Gyges: this Gyges is a young *puer delicatus*; his name is Near Eastern, and the epithet tells us he is from Cnidos, home of Praxiteles' famous Aphrodite statue.

21. puellarum ... choro: probably an allusion to the story of the young Achilles, whose mother Thetis tried to save him from the Trojan War by disguising him as a girl and entrusting him to Lycomedes, king of Skyros. When the clever Odysseus came in search of him, he picked him out from the other girls in the court of Lycomedes by including a shield and spear among a pile of gifts. Achilles naturally seized the weapons, and Odysseus collared young Achilles. Cf. 1.8.13-16.

22. mire: with *falleret*; he would amazingly fool even *sagaces hospites*, such as Odysseus in the story about Achilles.

23. discrimen obscurum: the difference between him and a girl; subject of *falleret*. **solutis crinibus**: abl. absolute; the touseled look, much admired in boys, as opposed to the fashionably chaste neatness of women's hair (1.5.4f. and note), and the look of Lyciscus in *Epod.* 11.28, *longam renodantis comam*. Cf. Juvenal 15.137, *ora puellares faciunt incerta capilli*.

24. ambiguo ... vultu: ancient Greeks and Romans were culturally bisexual, and men sometimes found themselves attracted to girlish boys in their early teens. Cnidian Gyges, described in this stanza as like a young Achilles, represents the type. None of this was perceived as being at all perverse, though the effect here is humorous. What Gyges and Lalage have in common is that they are both in early adolescence, and both appeal to the man addressed in this ode. Cf. Anacreon's poem to the boy with a girlish look (frag. 360 Page).

6

Having praised Tibur in 1.7, Horace mentions it here only in passing (lines 5-6) to concentrate his praise on Tarentum in southern Italy. References to his old age (6) and death (22-24) are puzzling: are these an autobiographical intrusion during a period of bad health and depression, or a rhetorical posture to set off his praise of restful places? The latter is a plausible answer if we can imagine Horace owning property in Tarentum as he did in Tibur and the Sabine country, and inviting Septimius to do likewise. The first strophe is strongly reminiscent of the beginning of Catullus 11, also written in Sapphics.

1-8. Septimius, my loyal friend, let Tibur be the place of my retirement.

1. Septimi: see appendix A. **Gadis**: to Gades (mod. Cadiz), a Punic town in southern Spain just beyond the Straits of Gibraltar. Acc. plural, object of *aditure*, like *Cantabrum*. **aditure**: ready to go to.

The three places dependent on this verb = "the ends of the earth," so to speak, making the stanza as a whole a rhetorical tribute to Septimius' friendship.

2. Cantabrum: collective singular; the Cantabrians of northwestern Spain were defeated by the Romans in 29 B.C. but were in constant revolt, hence "untaught to bear our yoke." Augustus himself led two campaigns against them (26-25); Agrippa finally subdued them in 19 B.C. **iuga**: poetic plural.

3. Syrtis: the shoals off north Africa between Carthage and Cyrene, in fact considerably east of Mauretania "where the *Maura unda* seethes" (see map 1). Like most of his contemporaries, Horace has a sketchy sense of geography.

5. Tibur: now Tivoli, about eighteen miles east of Rome, on the top and sides of a steep hill (see map 5). It was a favored refuge from the noise and summer heat of Rome, and much loved by Horace. Tradition had it that it was founded (**positum**) by an **Argeo colono** named Tiburnus or Tiburtus. *Argeo* is a poetic variant of *Argivo*; *colono* is dat. of agent.

7. modus: here equivalent to *finis*. **lasso** sc. *mihi*. **maris, viarum, militiae**: genitives completing the meaning of *lasso*. Cf. Virgil *Aen.* 1.178, *fessi rerum*. Horace is posturing a bit here in the manner of Alcaeus, as if his life has been one of endless roaming and warfare.

9-20. If the Fates keep me from Tibur, I'll seek Tarentum's mild weather and fine honey, oil, and wine.

9. Unde: from Tibur. For the sentiment, cf. *Epist.* 1.7.44, *mihi iam non regia Roma, sed vacuum Tibur placet aut imbelle Tarentum*. **Parcae**: the three Fates. **prohibent**: present tense, as in English; Latin regularly uses the future in such conditional statements. **iniquae**: adverbial with *prohibent*; not the standing epithet of the Fates.

10. dulce pellitis ovibus: Tarentum is dear to skin-covered sheep, whose fine wool is protected by hide jackets even before shearing. Never mentioned by name in this poem, Tarentum is identified indirectly by its river Galaesus and its founder Phalanthus. **Galaesi:** appositional gen. with *flumen*.

11-12. regnata ... Phalantho: the fields (once) ruled by Spartan Phalanthus, who founded Tarentum as a Spartan colony after the second Messenian war, ca. 708 B.C. *Regno* is transitive in poetry and post-Augustan prose. *Phalantho* is dat. of agent, a regular construction with the passive participle.

14. angulus: Tarentum (mod. Taranto) is at the inside corner where the heel meets the boot of Italy. The noun also implies remoteness and seclusion. **ridet:** with *mihi*, smiles upon; the *ē* retains the original quantity of this ending. **Hymetto:** i.e., to the honey of Hymettus, a mountain near Athens famous for this product. Greek honey is still labeled "Hymettus type."

15. decedunt: yield in comparison to. **viridi ... Venafro:** Venafrum was a Samnite town in Campania near the border with Latium, identified by Pliny (*Nat. Hist.* 15.8) as the source of the best olive oil. For the dat. with *certare*, cf. 1.3.13, *decertantem aquilonibus*.

16. baca: the olive "berry."

17-18. ver ... longum tepidasque ... brumas: chiasmus. **ubi:** for the delay of the introductory relative, cf. 1.2.7, *omne cum*. Note the *ī* in *ubi*, a reminiscence of the original quantity. **brumas:** winters; *bruma* (<*brevi-ma*, superl. of *brevis*) is literally the winter solstice, *brevissima (dies)*.

18-19. amicus Aulon ... Baccho: Aulon, a locale near Tarentum, is dear to fertile Bacchus because of its wine grapes.

19-20. minimum ... invidet: a personified Aulon produces such a fine grape that it has little envy for **Falernis ... uvis**, on whose product see 1.20.10 note. *minimum* is adverbial; *uvis* is dat. with *invidet*.

21-24. Tarentum invites us both, Septimius; there you will weep over my ashes.

22. postulant: summon. **arces:** the heights of the

city, or perhaps "the prosperous hilltop villages of the region around Tarentum" (Quinn). **calentem ... favillam:** his ashes, still warm from the funeral pyre. The inclusive word order imitates the tears absorbed in the ashes.

23. debita ... lacrima: the tears due to his memory. The ending is characterized by Santirocco as "almost Propertian" because of the elegist's tendency to fantasize about his own death. Further projections of this kind in Book 2 occur in Odes 13 and 17.

24. vatis amici: a closing *sphragis* or personal signature, echoed years later in the end of 4.6, *vatis Horati*. The words combine the private claim of friendship with the public claim of Horace's prophetic role.

7

A welcome home poem, like 1.36 (to Numida). The Pompeius greeted here is otherwise unknown. The good-humored recollections of Horace's misadventures as a supporter of Brutus in 42 B.C. supplement what he tells us in *Epist.* 2.2.46-50 without adding much detail. Meter: Alcaic strophe.

1-8. Who has returned you home, Pompey, comrade in pleasure and in arms?

1. saepe: Brutus and his forces were in the field for two years before the end came at Philippi, and several minor engagements occurred during this period. **tempus in ultimum:** into extreme peril. The rhetorical tone of this line is elevated and Horace may also be exaggerating slightly, as he does in line 7 of the previous ode.

2. deducte ... duce: word play, like *fregi* and *fracta* in lines 7-11. The abl. absolute has temporal force. **militiae:** the campaign of Brutus and Cassius against Octavian and Antony in 43-42 B.C. Depends on *Bruto duce*.

3. quis: a rhetorical question. After the battle of Actium, Octavian granted amnesty to all who had been in arms against him. **redonavit:** restored; a

Horatian coinage, used only twice in Horace. **Quiritem:** predicate acc., as a citizen, in apposition with *te*. This term is normally used in the plural, of citizens in the fullest and highest sense of the term as opposed to soldiers under military law. Horace's friend has been restored to full civic rights and privileges.

4. dis patriis: the tutelary gods of family and fatherland. **Italoque:** the initial vowel, often long in poetry, is properly short, as here.

5. Pompei: See appendix A; not to be confused with Sextus Pompey "the Great," who was killed in 36 B.C. (see line 16 note). The word is here disyllabic by synizesis.

6. cum quo: Horace always avoids *quocum* and *quibuscum*. **morantem ... diem:** generalizing singular; as usual in the military, time passed slowly.

7. fregi: an appropriate metaphor for killing time with wine breaks. **coronatus:** passive with middle force, taking *capillos* as object.

8. malobathro Syrio: to be taken with *nitentis*. Malobathrum is the Greco-Latin corruption of Sanskrit *tamālapattram*, leaf of tamala tree, from which a fragrant oil was made. It is called Syrian because the Romans bought it there, like most of their eastern products. Horace was actually in Asia Minor during most of his time with Brutus (see *Sat.* 1.7), and it is likely that such luxuries as malobathrum were locally available.

9-16. I fled the defeat at Philippi with you: Mercury whisked me away in a misty cloud, but you were carried into other battles.

9. Philippos: the town in eastern Macedonia where Antony defeated Cassius and Brutus in two battles, 42 B.C. It controlled east-west traffic on the Via Egnatia.

10. sensi: experienced, often used of unpleasant events. **relicta non bene parmula:** abl. abs.; the detail is literary rather than autobiographical. Though we must assume that Horace fled this rout with the rest of his comrades-in-arms, he wraps himself in the poetic mantle of Archilochus,

Alcaeus, and Anacreon, all of whom admitted in verse to throwing away their shields ingloriously (*non bene*) on the field of battle (Archilochus 5 West, Alcaeus 428 LP, Anacreon 381b Page). As a *tribunus militum*, Horace would not actually have carried a shield. Moreover, the small round *parmula* was at this time obsolete.

11. fracta: sc. *est*. **minaces:** (once) menacing hosts, a grandiloquent reference to the republican army overrun by Antony at Philippi.

12. turpe solum, etc.: the ground is *turpe* because they prostrate themselves upon it in humiliating defeat—though Horace seems less humiliated than diverted by this historic occasion. The words suggest an epic phrase for death on the battlefield, such as Homer's ὀδὰξ λαζοίατο γαῖαν (*Il.* 2.418), "bite the dust." There is also a subtle compliment to Augustus, whose allies won the day.

13. me: in antithesis with *te* (15). **Mercurius:** patron of poets, who are *Mercuriales viri* (2.17.29), and inventor of the lyre (*curvae lyrae parens*, 1.10.6). Some see this Mercury as a projection of Augustus, under whose auspices Horace was politically rehabilitated; cf. 1.2.43, *filius Maiae patiens vocari*.

14. denso ... aere: in epic, defeated heroes are wrapped in mist and spirited off to safety by their tutelary god: so Aphrodite rescues Paris in *Iliad* 3.380ff. Though Horace admits to having a bad fright at the time (*paventem*), he jokingly paints his escape home to Italy in epic colors.

15. in bellum: with both *resorbens* and *tulit*. **resorbens:** the receding wave of war draws Pompey back into stormy water after throwing Horace up on the beach.

16. fretis tulit aestuosis: these troubled waters would be the eleven years of continued civil strife between Philippi (Oct. 23, 42 B.C.) and Actium (Sept. 2, 31 B.C.). He probably joined those who took service under Sextus Pompey, and may have joined Antony after Sextus' defeat in 36.

17-28. So now you owe Jove a feast of thanks-

giving. Let us get on with some frenzied drink-ing.

17. obligatam: strictly applicable only to the one who makes a pledge, here applied to the thank-offering for his safe return. **redde:** render; *re-* indicates this is in return for Jove's favor in return-ing him safely to Italy (line 3, *quis te redonavit?*) **dapem:** properly of a sacrificial feast, as here and at 1.37.4.

18. latus = *membra* or the person as a whole. Martial calls the imperial bodyguard *sacri lateris custos* (6.76.1).

19. sub lauru mea: an essential part of any com-fortable home was a shady garden. The laurel or bay tree was cultivated for its thick shade, like the plane tree in 2.11.13. It is also emblematic of the lyric poet's calling, which is contrasted in this poem with *militia*.

20. cadis: wine jars with Pompey's name on them, so to speak (*tibi destinatis*).

21. Oblivioso: because it brings forgetfulness of troubles.

21-22. levia ... ciboria: polished metal cups, shaped like the blossom of the Egyptian bean. **Massico:** for this famous Campanian wine, see 1.1.19 note and the encomium to its powers in 3.21.

22. exple: fill up; the prefix *ex-* denotes full mea-sure. The chiastic asyndeton indicates the poet's impatience to get on with the business at hand.

23. conchis: shells used as table ware, here for ointment, in 1.3.14 for salt. **quis:** sc. *puer*, i.e., a slave. The language is sympotic; for the prepara-tion topos, see note on 1.36.10-16. **udo:** moist, pliant, soft.

24. deproperare: with intensive *de-*, hurry up with. One of the regular preparations for a party was the weaving of garlands from parsley (instru-mental abl. **apio**).

25. curatve myrto: the disordered flurry of lan-guage implies impatience: lines 23-5 might be in prose *quis udo apio myrtove coronas deproperare curat?* (Who's in charge of the garlands around

here?) For the position of the enclitic, cf. 2.19.28 *pacis eras mediusque belli*, 2.19.32 *ore pedes tetigitque crura*. **Quem:** which one of us at the party. **Ve-nus:** the "Venus," like our "boxcars," was the highest throw of the dice (*tali*), but for the Venus each *talus* had to come up different. **arbitrum bibendi:** predicate acc. with *quem*; master of the revels, toastmaster, *magister bibendi*. Cf. 1.4.18, *regna vini*.

26. dicet: appoint or declare; cf. the technical term for appointing a dictator, *dictatorem dicere*. **Non ... sanius** = *insanius*, more wildly than.

27. Edonis: a Thracian tribe famed for the wild-ness of their Bacchic orgies. **recepto:** like *recuper-ato*, recovered.

28. furere: part of Horace's sanity was his love of letting go of it from time to time; cf. 4.12.28, *dulce est desipere in loco* and Erasmus' *Encomium Moriae*, "In Praise of Folly."

8

With comic exaggeration, Horace builds up the perjuries of Barine until she looks like Public Menace Number One. Nature is indifferent to her lies, and the gods just laugh. Pyrrha (1.5) exerted her fatal attraction on one victim at a time; Barine seems to mow them all down at once. Meter: Sapphic strophe.

1-8. If lies were punished with physical blem-ishes, Barine, I would believe what you say. But when you tell a lie, you look even better.

1. iuris ... peierati: coined by analogy with *ius iurandum*, an oath; hence a broken oath, gen. of charge with *poena* (Allen and Greenough §352).

2. Barine: the name suggests Barium on the southeast coast of Italy, and perhaps the easy virtue of a port city where all things are negotiable.

3-4. dente ... nigro, uno ... ungui: abl. of degree of difference with *turpior*. The blemish on the fingernail would be a white mark. For the "Pinoc-chio's nose" effect, where a lie is punished with a physical blemish, cf. Theocritus 9.30 and 12.24. Ovid *Am.* 3.3.1ff. represents a woman like Barine who is immune to such penalties.

7. prodis: come forward, make your appearance.

8. publica cura: everybody's darling (limited by *iuvenum* above).

9-16. Dread oaths are a convenience for you; Venus, the nymphs, and Cupid laugh at all this.

9. Expedit plays off *obligasti* (5); her oath, which should bind her, instead is an expedient (*OLD* 8), extricating her from tight spots (*OLD* 2) and clearing up problems (*OLD* 3). The subject here is *fallere.* **opertos:** covered, euphemistic for buried.

10. fallere: to escape the notice of powers invoked as witnesses to her oaths (mother's ashes, stars, sky, gods), hence to deceive them.

11. signa: stars. **gelida**, to be taken with *morte* below, is appropriately juxtaposed with the sky. The frequent hyperbaton in this stanza (*toto ... cum caelo, taciturna ... signa, gelida ... morte*) emphasizes her elusiveness.

13. Ridet ... rident: these words repeated at the center of the poem emphasize that the tone is comic, not bitter or sardonic. **Venus ipsa:** since Homer, she was laughter-loving Aphrodite; cf. 1.2.33, *Erycina ridens*. For her sense of humor, see 1.33.10-12.

14. simplices: the nymphs are straightforward and ingenuous themselves, but it seems they enjoy deception in others.

16. cote cruenta: Cupid's whetstone (*cos*) is wet with the blood of lovers struck by his arrows.

17-24. New victims keep coming, and old ones won't leave. Mothers, fathers and brides are all afraid of you.

17. Adde quod: a formula of Lucretius, giving a finger-wagging, mock didactic note. **pubes ... omnis** is hyperbolic: the entire (male) population **tibi crescit,** ripens for your use (dat. of advantage).

18. servitus: a collection of slaves, like the submissive lovers in Roman elegy. **priores** are the old lovers, already addicted to her favors.

19. dominae: another reminder of the love elegies being written by Tibullus and Propertius, where the woman is dominant.

20. saepe minati: though they often threaten to do so. The serenade outside the mistress' house (see appendix C, paraclausithyron) sometimes included a warning that the shut-out lover would not stay around forever.

21-23. te ... te ... tua: the repetition parodies the formulaic recital of powers in hymns, strengthening the sense of Barine as something more than human. Cf. the repetitions in the hymn to a wine jug, 3.21.13-21.

21. suis ... iuvencis: metaphoric for their adolescent sons—with a hint of their naive clumsiness, like that of the boy in 1.5.

22. senes parci: the tight-fisted old men are a fixture in comedy, where the more or less standard plot features a romantic youth spending his father's fortune on a greedy hetaera.

23. virgines nuptae: oxymoron. The brides are so recently married as to be still almost virginal—or entirely so, if their new husbands find themselves called out on important business (with Barine) on their wedding night. **ne retardet:** subj. clause of volition with a verb of fearing (21 *metuunt*; see Allen and Greenough §564).

23-24. tua ... aura: the nautical love metaphor is so common in Horace's tradition that it is brought up with a word. Barine's wind is the power of her way with lovers, who like ships can be blown off course and never make it to port (their wives). Cf. Pyrrha's treacherous wind in 1.5.11, where her young man is *nescius aurae fallacis.*

9

Having dealt in 2.8 with a too faithless Barine, Horace turns here to a too devoted Valgius. C. Valgius Rufus, a friend and fellow poet of Horace, has been writing weepy elegies about the loss of a boyfriend, and Horace teases him out of it with a mock consolation suggesting they turn out some bracing verses on the military triumphs of Augustus. Horace was not entirely sympathetic to Latin love elegy's melancholy sentimentalism. Cf. the advice to Tibullus in 1.33, *Albi, ne doleas.* Meter: Alcaic strophe.

1-8. Bad things do not go on forever in nature, Valgius, and good things also end.

1. Non semper: emphatically placed here, the *non semper* theme is frequent in Horace: 2.11.9, 3.10.19, 3.29.6. The appeal to nature as an argument against sorrow is also typically Horatian: 1.7.15-18, 2.3.9-16. **nubibus:** from the clouds, abl. of separation with *manant.* **hispidos,** shaggy or unkempt, suggests the roughness of a winter landscape unsoftened by foliage.

3. inaequales: rough because of their effect on the *mare Caspium*, or irregular, as in sudden squalls.

4. usque repeats the sense of *semper* (line 1). **Armeniis in oris:** in Armenian territory, as Armenia was at the time virtually landlocked.

5. amice Valgi: see appendix A.

7. querqueta Gargani: oak groves of Garganus, the wooded mountain that protrudes into the Adriatic like a spur on the Italian boot, exposed to the northeast winds (*Aquilonibus*).

8. viduantur: the elms are bereft of their leaves as Valgius is of Mystes. The verb provides a transition to Valgius, but other words in this section (*imbres ... manant, vexant, laborant*) also suggest tears, stress, and grief.

9-17. But you never stop mourning for Mystes. Think of old Nestor, who recovered from mourning Antilochus, and the family of Troilus.

9. tu semper answers to *Non semper* (line 1). For the adversative asyndeton, see appendix C. **urges:** dwell upon, with an implication that he is overly solicitous, like the eager lover in 1.5.2, *urget.* **flebilibus modis:** the weepy verses of Valgius' love elegies.

10. ademptum: dead, according to Porphyrio, but the usual meaning of *adimo*, take away or steal, better fits the context. Mystes is a *puer delicatus* who has been lured away by a rival. His name in Greek means "initiate," as one initiated into the mysteries of love.

11. surgente decedunt: a typically witty juxtaposition of contrasting words: when the evening star rises your loves do not fall (or abate).

12. rapidum fugiente solem: i.e., at dawn. Depending on the season, the planet Venus is visible around sunset (and is called Vesperus) or near dawn (when it is called Lucifer, and fades before the rising sun).

13. ter aevo functus: lit. having thrice gone through a lifetime. The deponent *fungor* governs the abl. *aevo.* The prodigious age of Nestor is a tradition from Homer, *Il.* 1.250.

14. Antilochum: after the death of Patroclus, Nestor's young son Antilochus became Achilles' companion. Shortly after the action of the Iliad, he was killed in battle by Memnon.

15-16. impubem ... Troïlon: Priam's young son Troilus, a Trojan counterpart of Antilochus, killed in battle by Achilles.

17-24. Cease your laments, and let us rather sing of Augustus' victories in the east.

17-18. mollium ... querellarum are soft laments in a way that is specific to love elegy: *mollis*, "the stock epithet of the elegiac poet" (Quinn), is linked with a noun associated in Propertius (1.17.9, 1.18.29, etc.) with love elegy. See also Horace's Sappho, *querentem ... puellis de popularibus* in 2.13.24f.

20. Niphaten: a branch of the Taurus range in central Armenia, called **rigidum** (with ice) because its name suggests Gk. νιφάδες, snows. Some later poets thought it was a river.

21. Medum ... flumen: the Euphrates, subj. of *volvere.* Horace shifts to indirect statement, still dependent on *cantemus* (line 19).

22. minores volvere vertices: the river, nearly

personified, rolls smaller wavetops because it has been humbled by Roman might and assigned to the *gentibus victis*. Cf. Virgil *Aen.* 8.726, *Euphrates ibat iam mollior undis*.

23. intra ... praescriptum: within (our) rule, i.e., within a range dictated by Roman prescript. **Gelonos:** a Scythian tribe, here vaguely lumped with conquests nearer the opposite end of the Black Sea. They were a bogey also for Virgil: *pictos Gelonos, acer Gelonus, saggitiferos Gelonos* (*Georg.* 2.115, 3.461, *Aen.* 8.725).

24. exiguis equitare campis: the Romans regarded nomadic movements as mere barbaric unruliness and arbitrarily curtailed their range. Horace approved, though there is no record of Roman conflict with this Scythian tribe. As far as is known, this victory, like the one over the *Medum flumen* above, is a Horatian fantasy. See note on 3.8.23.

10

Aphorisms on moderation, addressed to a Licinius who may have been Maecenas' brother-in-law L. Licinius Murena (see appendix A). The form of these *sententiae* is typical of Aristotle's Peripatetic school, which defined each virtue as a midpoint between extremes. This middle ground is Horace's *aurea mediocritas* (line 5). While Horace's advice may have had particular relevance to Augustan politics, its meaning is universal. The theme is close to that of 2.3, *Aequam memento*. Meter: Sapphic strophe.

1-8. You will live better, Licinius, by avoiding extremes; whoever cherishes the golden mean avoids squalid poverty and the excessive wealth that brings trouble.

1. Rectius: Horace's ethical argument is pragmatic rather than moral. **altum:** the deep, open sea. The poem begins and ends with a sailing metaphor.

2-3. urgendo ... premendo: nearly synonymous

gerunds, by neither pressing out to sea (where the winds are more violent) nor by hugging the shore (where there is less room to maneuver).

3. cautus: adverbial, like *tutus* (6) and *sobrius* (8).

4. iniquum: harsh, treacherous, unfriendly.

5. auream ... mediocritatem: the source of our "golden mean," with no negative undertones of mediocrity.

6-7. caret ... caret: Horace stresses an ethic of avoidance; cf. *cautus* (3), *tutus* (6). **obsoleti sordibus tecti:** the squalor of a run-down house.

7-8. invidenda ... aula: abl. of separation with *caret*. Properly, *aula* = a royal hall or palace. With *invidenda* it is any mansion whose conspicuous magnificence attracts envy. People will plot against you to get your wealth. Many of the proscriptions under Sulla (and later Octavian and Antony) were motivated by the need for money to pay various personal armies.

9-17. High things are the first to suffer harm. The wise man is hopeful in adversity, cautious in success. The same Jupiter who brings the winter also takes it away.

9-12. Examples from nature of the dangers of prominence were a commonplace since Artabanus' advice to Xerxes in Herodotus 7.10ε.

11-12. summos ... montis: acc. pl., mountain tops.

13. infestis ... secundis: sc. *rebus.* In this context, *infestus* = exposed to danger, troubled, adverse. *Secundus*, by a latent sailing metaphor, is favorable.

14-15. bene praeparatum pectus: the Stoics taught that personal preparedness, especially for misfortune, is the best posture in life. For a thumbnail portrait of the *sapiens* and his immunity, see *Sat.* 2.8.83-88.

15. informis: ugly, unsightly.

16. idem: he likewise (*OLD* 7). The enjambment between stanzas is especially noticeable because every other stanza is strongly end-stopped.

17-24. Things will not always be as they are: Apollo changes to god of song from destroyer. Be cheerful when things are tight, but prudent in success.

17-19. nunc ... olim ... quondam ... semper: the emphasis is on change in the course of time. **olim** = sometime in the future (*OLD* 4).

20. Apollo: Apollo's bow was from an early date a metaphor of his association with death by disease, e.g., in *Il.* 1.45-52.

21. Rebus angustis: as in English idiom, when things are tight, viz. in hardship.

22. idem: you likewise (see note on 16).

23. contrahes, etc.: will reef, or shorten, your sails (24 *vela*) in an overly favorable wind, i.e., one that blows too strongly. To this day it remains a truism of sailing that the prudent skipper will not put up too much canvas in a strong following wind.

11

Though elsewhere he is as ready as any Augustan propagandist to celebrate foreign victories or call for new wars abroad, Horace can also speak as a peace-loving Epicurean. In this role, he invokes the pleasures of the symposium and finds arguments in nature that urge us to set larger cares aside and enjoy life as we find it. Such poems come as early in Horace's *Odes* as 1.9 and 11, and as late as 4.12. This ode fits the type; it is appropriately placed midway in Book 2 of the *Odes*, with its themes of moderation and human limits. Meter: Alcaic strophe.

1-12. Don't ask what is going on abroad, Hirpinus. Youth and beauty are fleeting; nothing endures.

1. Cantaber et Scythes: collective sing.; these are tribes on the far northwestern and northeastern frontiers of the empire. On the fierce Cantabrians of northern Spain, see 2.6.2 note. Though only the Cantabrian is referred to as *bellicosus* and

only the Scythian as remote (*Hadria divisus obiecto*), the context naturally suggests that both tribes are warlike and both are separated from Rome by separating seas; cf. the abbreviated construction of *ingens albaque*, 2.3.9. Horace's preference for what is nearby over what is far away is a frequent theme.

2. Hirpine Quincti: for the transposition of *nomen* and *cognomen*, cf. 2.2.3, *Crispe Sallusti*. This Quinctius is apparently addressed also in *Epist.* 1.16, but is otherwise unknown. **cogitet:** is plotting; the use of a singular verb with compound singular subjects (*Cantaber et Scythes*) is normal in Horace.

3. remittas quaerere: for similar periphrastic constructions, cf. 1.9.13, *fuge quaerere*; 1.38.3, *mitte sectari*.

4. trepides in usum: be nervous about the means of using or enjoying, i.e., the needs.

5. poscentis aevi pauca: a life that demands little. The natural simplicity of the good life is a Stoic and Epicurean theme found often in Horace. *Aevum* is used as a synonym of *vita*. **Fugit retro:** another Horatian theme is the speed of passing time: youth is soon behind us. Cf. 1.11.8, *dum loquimur, fugerit invida aetas*.

6. lēvis: sleek, contrasted with the *arida ... canitie* of age; cf. Shakespeare's "dry antiquity" in *AYL* 4.3.104. **decor:** good looks.

7. lascivos: not as pejorative as English "lascivious," more playful and sexy than lewd.

8. canitie: grayness is a frequent poetic synonym for age; cf. 1.9.17, *canities morosa*.

9. Non semper: for the theme, cf. 2.9.1 and note. **honor:** nearly synonymous with *decor* (6), glory or beauty; cf. *Epod.* 11.5f., *December silvis honorem decutit*, where the glory shaken from the forests is their foliage.

10. uno: with *vultu*, the same or a single face. The constantly waxing and waning moon is a classic metaphor of change: cf. Shakespeare *R&J* 2.2.109:

> th' inconstant moon,

That monthly changes in her circled orb.
rubens: a standing epithet of the moon, perceived as blushing: cf. *Sat.* 1.8.35, *lunam rubentem.*

11-12. aeternis ... consiliis: the plans are eternal because they look too far into the uncertain future. Cf. 1.11.7, *spem longam.* The abl. *consiliis* is governed by both *fatigas* (instrumental abl.) and *minorem* (abl. of comparison); for such *apo koinou* constructions, see appendix C. The mind is **minorem,** unequal to, the *consiliis.*

13-24. Why don't we relax here in the shade and enjoy ourselves instead?
13. platano: the plane tree or oriental sycamore was extensively cultivated by the Romans as a shade tree. Here it provides shade for Horace's imagined suburban *locus amoenus,* a pleasant nature spot. Cf. 1.1.21, where the tree is an arbutus. **hac** should be taken with both *platano* and *pinu.* It emphasizes that the good life is right here, not far away like the *Cantaber et Scythes,* and it sets the scene midway through the ode.
14. temere: carelessly, at random; for the etymology see 1.12.7 note.
15. canos recalls *canitie* (8). In *Epist.* 1.20.24 Horace describes himself as *praecanus,* prematurely gray. **odorati:** used as a middle passive with the acc. *capillos* and the instrumental *rosa*; cf. 1.1.21, *membra sub arbuto stratus.*
16. Assyriaque nardo: an aromatic plant imported from Arabia or India via Syria (here "Assyria"). *nardo,* here feminine, is neuter elsewhere in Horace.
17. potamus: hortatory question with *cur non* (13). **uncti:** same const. as line 15, *odorati.* Living as they did in a less deodorized world than ours, ancient men and women used scents freely to cover other smells. **Euhius:** Bacchus; see note on 1.18.9.
18. curas edacis: cf. 1.18.4, *mordaces sollicitudines.* **Quis puer,** calling for a slave to see to some party arrangement, signals a sympotic context; cf. *Epod.* 9.33, 2.7.23, 3.14.17. Like American slave-holders, Romans called their male slaves "boy"; cf. 1.38.1. **ocius:** comparative with asseverative force, very quickly.

19. restinguet: carries out the metaphor of "hot" (*ardentis*) unmixed wine that must be "quenched" with water; cf. Shakespeare *Cor.* 2.1.42, "a cup of hot wine with not a drop of allaying Tiber in't." On Falernian wine, see note on 1.20.10; as in 2.3.8, this is a picnic wine.
20. praetereunte lympha: i.e., water from a passing stream.
21. devium scortum: according to Porphyrio, a call girl available by appointment only as opposed to a street-walking public prostitute. *devium* has the force of "private," and *scortum* (orig. "skin") is as blunt as "hooker." This is something of a humorous oxymoron, as there is not much private about a *scortum.*
22. Lyden: acc. of *Lyde*; the name is Greek, and is a more or less generic professional name, meant to suggest an exotic Lydian origin. The best Greek-style hetaeras, much sought after in Horace's Rome, were sophisticates trained in the Near Eastern traditions of Lydia. **eburna:** i.e., inlaid with ivory. **dic, age:** to the *puer* (18): go tell.
23. maturet: sc. *venire,* hurry on over. The subjunctive, dependent on *dic,* is jussive.
23-24. in comptum ... nodum: the neat knot or bun in the chaste style of a Spartan girl (*Lacaenae more*) is a provocatively modest get-up, a kind of erotic oxymoron. For the simple but sexy tied-up hairdo, cf. 1.5.4f. (*Cui flavam religas comam, simplex munditiis?*), 3.14.21, and Ovid *Met.* 8.319 (of Atalanta; *crinis erat simplex, nodum collectus in unum*).
24. comas religata: another middle participle-cum-acc., like *odorati capillos* in line 15. The closure of this ode with a little detail in what Quinn calls a "characteristic decrescendo ending" contrasts significantly with the opening, *Quid bellicosus Cantaber.*

12

A *recusatio* in the same tradition as 1.6, slipping away from an invitation to write of Rome's triumphs in war and proposing instead to write an erotic encomium in honor of Licymnia. Meter: third Asclepiadean; this is the first poem in *Odes* 2 not in Sapphic or Alcaic.

1-9. You wouldn't want Roman wars or epic battles fitted to the soft measures of the lyre.

1. Nolis: a courteous potential subjunctive. **Numantiae:** a Celtiberian town in northwest Spain that led the resistance to Roman rule, 195-133 B.C.

2. Hannibalem: the Carthaginian leader who invaded Italy in the Second Punic War, 218-201 B.C. The **Siculum mare** was made red with Punic blood in two naval battles of the First Punic War, Mylae (260 B.C.) and the Aegatian Islands (242 B.C.). Horace's list of Roman wars goes backward in time.

3. sanguine mollibus: contrasting juxtaposition emphasizes the unfitness of lyric verse to bloody subjects. *Mollibus* also plays off *durum* (2).

5-6. Lapithas, Hylaeum: Centaurs invited to the wedding of Pirithous and Hippodamia became drunk and attempted to make off with the bride. The ensuing battle was immortalized on the metopes of the Parthenon and the western pediment of the temple of Zeus at Olympia. Cf. the *Centaurea rixa* in 1.18.8. Hylaeus was one of the Centaurs.

7. Telluris iuvenes: the Giants born from the earth attacked the gods; their defeat, a familiar metaphor of political poetry, was also a traditionally unsuitable theme for light poetry. **unde:** from whom, referring to the Giants. **periculum:** obj. of *contremuit*.

9. Saturni veteris: though Saturn (Gk. Cronus) was not involved in the Gigantomachy, his house (now inhabited by Jupiter) was threatened by the attack.

9-20. You are the one to tell of Caesar's battles

in prose; as for me, the Muse wants me to celebrate the charms of Licymnia.

9. tu: emphatic, you are the one. **pedestribus:** prose.

10-11. dices ... melius = you will do a better job, and it is better that you do it. **ductaque per vias:** captive kings, their necks in chains (*regum colla*), were led in triumphs through the city to the Sacra Via, the Forum, and the temple of Capitoline Jupiter.

13. me: contrasting with *tu* (9). This use of *me* is typically Horatian: 1.1.29, 1.5.13, 1.16.22, 1.31.15, 2.17.13, 4.3.29. **dominae:** playfully suggestive of love elegy, where the poet's mistress is a dominating figure. Cf. 2.8.19. **Licymniae:** a perhaps fictitious hetaera; it is the name of a *serva* in Virgil *Aen.* 9.546. Some ancient commentators (recorded by Pseudo-Acro) took this to be a pseudonymn of Maecenas' wife Terentia, but the marriage was too much the target of scandalous gossip for such compliments as we find in the closing stanza to have been a safe subject, even under cover of a pseudonymn.

14. lucidum: adverbial with *fulgentis*.

15-16. bene ... fidum: right faithful (as in colloquial English), governing the dat. **mutuis ... amoribus,** for mutually shared love.

17. ferre pedem: to dance.

18. certare ioco: to bandy jokes; certain Greek festivals (and apparently similar rites of Diana in Italy) featured ritual mockery. **dare bracchia:** to join arms in group dancing.

19. ludentem: taking part in the public entertainment (*OLD* 6).

20. Dianae celebris: lit. of festive Diana, i.e., of her temple on the Aventine thronged by crowds. Her *sacer dies* was August 13.

21-28. Would you accept the biggest fortunes of the east for so much as a lock of Licymnia's hair when she is in the mood for love?

21. num anticipates that the answer to Horace's rhetorical question is no. **Achaemenes,** mythical founder of the Persian Achaemenid dynasty, is an Iranian equivalent of Solomon or Croesus.

22. Mygdonias opes: i.e., the wealth of Mygdon, a legendary Phrygian king.

23. permutare: to receive the acc. (wealth) in exchange for the abl. (a lock of hair); cf. the same construction with *mutat* in 1.17.2. **crine:** abl. of price.

25. The absence of the usual metrical pause suggests a torrid scene; for compound prepositions at caesuras, see note on 1.18.16, *per‖lucidior.*

26. facili saevitia: oxymoron, suggesting that her indignant resistance is easily overcome. Cf. 1.9.24, *digito male pertinaci.*

27. poscente magis: more than a woman who asks for them; *oscula* is the understood object. **eripi:** that they (viz. kisses) be taken by force.

28. rapere occupet takes us back to the military images with which the poem began: Licymnia seizes the initiative (OLD 12) to plunder kisses. Licymnia enjoys sexual tussles in which the aggressive role can suddenly shift.

13

The first of four odes in which Horace mentions being nearly hit by a falling tree (see also 2.17.27ff., 3.4.25-28, and 3.8.6-8), this one develops into a reflection on the power of poetry even in the underworld. The ode begins with a humorously exaggerated apostrophe abusing the tree and whoever planted it, but ends with a captivating picture of Hades' inhabitants delighting in the spell of Alcaeus' poetry. Meter: Alcaic strophe.

1-12. Cursed the day you were planted, dismal tree, and evil the man who planted you.

1. Ille ... illum (5) ... **ille** (8): emphatic anaphora in mock wrath. **et:** correlative with *et* in line 2. **nefasto ... die:** technically, a day on which it was not lawful for the magistrates to give judgment; in general, an ill-omened day.

2. quicumque: sc. *te posuit.*

3. produxit: tended, reared. **in ... perniciem:** for the destruction.

4. pagi: of the district, presumably the one called Mandela in which Horace's Sabine farm lay.

5. et: emphatic: even, actually. **crediderim:** potential subjunctive.

6. penetralia: properly an adjective, used substantively for hearthstone, where the images of the Penates were set up.

7. nocturno: transferred from the verb *sparsisse* to the blood that is spattered. The horror of the act is progressively emphasized by *penetralia, nocturno,* and *hospitis.*

8. hospitis: crimes against a host or guest (either = *hospes*) were the worst imaginable. **venena Colcha:** Medea's Colchis, at the eastern end of the Black Sea, was famous for sorcery and poisons.

10. tractavit: has dealt with, had a hand in.

11. triste lignum: comic invective, wretched log; *lignum* is contemptuous for *arbos.* **caducum:** doomed to fall, as in Virgil *Aen.* 10.622, *caduco iuveni.*

12. immerentis: undeserving, as in 1.17.28, *immeritam vestem.*

13-20. You can't be too careful: death lurks everywhere, unexpected.

13. Quid ... vitet: subjunctive in indirect dubitative question. **homini ... cautum est:** impersonal with dat. of agent and gnomic perfect passive of *caveo.* One is never careful enough. Though the mood has changed from mock invective to reflective, a touch of humorous irony lingers in this section, which resembles any of the less profound tragic choruses.

14. in horas: from one hour to the next. **navita:** archaic and poetic variation of *nauta*; the Punic sailor is the first of three exemplary proofs (with *miles,* 17, and *Parthus,* 18) of the truism that you can't be too careful. **Bosphorum:** the straits near Byzantium (mod. Istanbul), proverbially stormy. Cf. *insanientem Bosphorum,* 3.4.30.

15. perhorrescit: transitive. **ultra ... caeca ...**

aliunde: emphatic redundancy. In our folly we have no thought of the risks we cannot see immediately.

16. caeca: in a passive sense, unseen. **timet:** the *ē* retains its original quantity as in 2.6.14, *ridēt*.

17. miles: i.e., a Roman infantryman. **sagittas et celerem fugam:** objects of *perhorrescit*. Hendiadys, with reference to the proverbial "Parthian flight," the tactic of wheeling in retreat and firing arrows at the pursuing enemy; cf. 1.19.11 and note.

18. catenas: the chains of captivity. **Parthus:** On Rome's Iranian adversaries in Asia Minor, see notes on 1.2.22, 1.12.53. **Italum robur:** Italian oaken ruggedness, with additional reference to the traditional name of the Tullianum, the *Robur*, a dungeon on the Capitoline where foreign chieftains were executed by strangulation after being led in a triumph.

19. improvisa: predicative, emphasized by its placement in the construction.

20. vis rapuit rapietque: the triple emphasis on the violence of death at the center of the poem, aided by the rapidity of the line, signals a change of mood.

21-40. How narrowly I escaped seeing the realms of Proserpina, where Sappho and Alcaeus charm the shades with the music of their lyres.

21-22. quam paene ... vidimus: how close I came to seeing. **furvae:** dusky, because of the darkness of the underworld; transferred epithet. **Proserpinae:** the *o* is short; it is normally long, as in 1.28.20.

22. iudicantem Aeacum: Aeacus (grandfather of Achilles), Minos, and Rhadamanthus are frequently mentioned as judges in the underworld.

23. discriptas: marked out, assigned, allocated.

24. Aeoliis: Sappho's lyre is Aeolian because the dialect of Lesbos where she and Alcaeus lived was Aeolic. **querentem:** in love poetry; the verb is appropriate to what we know of Sappho's poems of love. The love elegies of the Augustan age also adopted a plaintive note.

25. Sappho: acc. **puellis de popularibus:** the girls of her *populus* or community, about whom she wrote love poetry.

26. te: the apostrophe marks Horace's emphasis in this ode on the latter of the two poets. Unlike Catullus, Horace never tried to imitate Sappho, but he often took Alcaeus as a model. **sonantem plenius:** sounding more fully or resonantly; the verb is used transitively; its object is *dura*.

27. Alcaee: the most famous of the Greek lyric poets; hence his golden plectrum. **dura ... dura ... dura:** Like Sappho (line 24 *querentem*), Alcaeus has troubles to sing of. **dura navis** are his hardships at sea.

28. fugae: exile, caused by his opposition to local strong men. It is the only one of his troubles that warrants the epithet *mala*, as exile was considered tantamount to capital punishment.

29. utrumque: each; emphatic by position. **sacro digna silentio:** things worthy of a reverent silence; object of *dicere*.

30. magis pugnas, etc.: popular taste runs to poetry of war and revolution, even in the underworld.

31. exactos tyrannos: viz. the exile of tyrants, a construction like *ademptus Hector* in 2.4.10. Alcaeus' brothers overthrew the tyrant Melanchros, and frag. 332 LP celebrating the death of Myrsilos inspired the opening line of Horace's Cleopatra Ode (1.37).

32. densum umeris: packed shoulder to shoulder, to get near the singer. **bibit aure:** cf. Virgil *Aen.* 4.359, *vocemque his auribus haesi*: Shakespeare *R&J* 2.2.58:

My ears have yet not drunk a hundred words
Of that tongue's utterance.

34. demittit: droops. The treatment of scary or grandiose mythical subjects with disarming realism was a favorite Hellenistic technique. Here, the drooping of Cerberus' ears, like any house dog's, is a sign of his pleasure. **belua centiceps:** Cerberus is elsewhere represented with three heads.

36. recreantur: rest (from their usual ceaseless

writing).

37. quin et: a stronger *quin*, yes, even (as in 1.10.13). **Prometheus:** this is the only passage in Latin that alludes to Prometheus as undergoing punishment not in the Caucasus but in Hades; but see also 2.18.35 and note. **Pelopis parens:** Tantalus.

38. laborem decipitur: collective singular, lit. beguiled with respect to their suffering.

39. Orion: a giant who was famed as a hunter and continued to enjoy his sport in the underworld (*Od.* 11.572f.)—but now he forgets it. After his death he became a constellation.

40. timidos: elsewhere *lynx* is usually feminine; **agitare:** pursue. The peaceful ending is a good example of Horace's closing diminuendos.

14

The Postumus Ode, a melancholy reflection on the inevitable coming of death. The Epicurean tone of the ode as a whole is particularly marked in the last stanza, with its suggestion that enjoyment of the present, and not wealth, is the true purpose of life. The meter is Alcaic strophe.

1-12. The years glide by, Postumus, and no virtue or sacrifice can put off age or the death that comes to us all.

1. fugaces: position indicates that the predication of the sentence lies in this word. **Postume, Postume:** the name, emphasized by repetition, is appropriate to the theme of mortality: it was given to a boy born after his father's death. The Postumus addressed here may be the person addressed by Propertius in *Elegies* 3.12.

2. pietas: as in Virgil's *Aeneid*, this includes a sense of personal responsibility to family and society as well as religious piety. Cf. 4.7.24, *non te restituet pietas*.

3-4. rugis ... senectae ... morti: a climactic arrangement of ideas (and syllables). **instanti:** looming, insistent.

5. non, si: not even if. **trecenis ... tauris:** the distributive numeral, three hundred bulls at a time. The Homeric hecatomb was a sacrifice of epic proportion, one hundred cattle. Three hundred is often used for a large number, especially in Catullus (9.2, 11.8, 12.10, 48.3); here the exaggeration is colossal.

6. places: appease (or try to appease) **illacrimabilem:** with active force: tearless, pitiless.

7. ter amplum: lit. triply large; Geryon was a Spanish giant with three bodies. Hercules killed him and carried off his cattle.

8. Tityon: a son of Terra, Tityos tried to rape Latona and was killed by the arrows of her children Apollo and Diana. He is represented in Tartarus as covering nearly six acres with his vast frame: *per tota novem cui iugera corpus porrigitur* (*Aen.* 6.596). **tristi ... unda:** the gloomy water of the Styx.

9. scilicet: <*scire licet*; surely. **omnibus** is dat. of agent with the gerundive *enaviganda*. The stream must be sailed by all.

10. quicumque ... vescimur: explains *omnibus*; the deponent *vescor* (enjoy, eat) takes the abl. *munere* (bounty) instead of an acc. object.

11. enaviganda: i.e., in Charon's skiff; in the transitive sense, *enavigare* is found first in Horace. The three gerundives, *enaviganda, visendus* (17), and *linquenda* (21), give Horace's statements about death a striking emphasis. **reges:** i.e., men of rank. For this usage in a universalizing rich-poor couplet, cf. 1.4.14, *pauperum tabernas regumque turres*.

12. coloni: farmers (<*colo* = cultivate).

13-24. It is useless to try to avoid death: we must make our trip to the underworld, and we must leave behind the pleasures of life.

13-15. Frustra ... frustra emphasizes the futility of the three ways of cheating death cataloged in this stanza: avoiding war, seafaring, and unhealthy weather.

14. fractis ... fluctibus: breakers, dramatized by interlocking word order. The reference is to the risk of shipwreck.

15. per autumnos: the unhealthy season in Rome; in *Sat.* 2.6.19, *Autumnusque gravis, Libitinae quaestus acerbae*, it is "sickly Autumn, profitable for hateful Libitina," the goddess associated with funerals. **nocentem:** describing *Austrum*, takes the dat. *corporibus:* harmful to our bodies.

16. Austrum: the hot wind that blows up from the Sahara, today called the Sirocco. It is the prevailing wind in August and September.

17. Visendus: emphatically placed, like *frustra* at the beginning of lines 13 and 15 and *linquenda* at the beginning of the sixth stanza.

18. Cocytos: another river in the underworld, derived from Gk. κωκύω, lament; hence, the river of lamentation. **Danai genus infame:** the fifty daughters of Danaus, the Danaïds, had (with the exception of Hypermnestra) slain their husbands on their wedding night. Their penalty in the underworld consisted in endlessly bearing water in leaky vessels, or trying to fill a leaky jar. The subject was familiar from Polygnotus' painting at Delphi, but what made it popular for the Augustan poets was the statues of the Danaïds placed between the pillars of a colonnade at Augustus' recently opened temple and library of Apollo on the Palatine (see note on 3.11.25).

19-20. longi ... laboris: gen. of the penalty, depending on *damnatus*. Condemned to long labor.

20. Sisyphus Aeolides: legendary founder and king of Corinth, the evil trickster; his punishment was forever to roll a huge stone uphill, only to have it roll down just as he reached the top.

21. linquenda tellus, etc.: a condensation of Lucretius' famous lines (3.894-6):

Iam iam non domus accipiet te laeta, neque
    uxor
optima nec dulces occurrent oscula nati
praeripere et tacita pectus dulcedine tangent.

22. harum: deictic, placing Horace's address to Postumus in a garden of carefully tended shady trees (*quas colis*). Cf. *hac* in 2.11.13.

23. invisas cupressos: cypress trees are hateful

because of their association with death and mourning. An evergreen shaped like a Lombardy poplar, its branches were used at funerals as ornamentation, and the trees were planted near graves.

24. ulla: governs the gen. *harum arborum* (22). **brevem:** short-lived; cf. 2.3.13, *nimium brevis flores.*

25-28. An heir will squander your carefully hoarded wine and spill it on your mosaic floor.

25. absumet heres: for the wastrel heir, cf. 2.3.19f. and note. **dignior:** ironic: wastrel though he is, he deserves the wine more than Postumus, who only saves it up.

27. tinguet pavimentum: a vivid picture of the heir's careless extravagance; Horace invites us to picture a mansion's bright mosaic floor stained with wasted vintage wine. The juxtaposition of *pavimentum* with *superbo* (here in a good sense, close to our "superb") heightens the effect.

28. pontificum potiore cenis: a compendious expression for banquets even better than those of the priests (which were proverbial for their magnificence). See note on 1.37.2, *Saliaribus dapibus.*

15

A protest against the growing luxury and extravagance of the day. The theme was a Stoic topos in prose as well as poetry (cf. Sallust *Cat.* 12, 13, 20), and remained so into the Imperial period, when it was vulgarized into a rhetorical cliché (e.g., the diatribe of Eumolpos in Petronius' *Satyricon*, 88). Octavian assumed the censorship in 28 B.C. and undertook a program to regulate conspicuous consumption, but there is no reason to tie this ode to any particular date. Meter: Alcaic strophe.

1-10. Soon princely estates and pools will leave no room for farms; shade trees and flowers will supplant the vine and olive.

1. iugera: a *iugerum* was about two-thirds of an acre. **regiae moles:** princely piles; *moles* means any large building, *rex* was used with a certain contempt of any big shot or VIP. An era of magnificent building began in the peaceful times following the civil wars. The rich competed with each other to lay out ever more ostentatious country estates. A late and extreme example that can still be seen is Hadrian's villa near Tibur (mod. Tivoli).

2-4. latius ... Lucrina ... lacu: a slight exaggeration. The Lucrine Lake was a shallow lagoon near Baiae, separated from the gulf of Pozzuoli by a natural dike about a mile long. Famous for its shellfish and oysters, it had recently been linked with Lake Avernus by Agrippa to form the Portus Iulus, a first-class naval harbor (cf. *Epist.* 2.3.23) in 37 B.C. See NH 2 *ad loc.*

4. stagna: artificial lagoons in which fish were bred. **platanus caelebs:** because the plane tree cast a heavy shade, it was not suitable to be "wed" to vines to make a natural trellis, as was the elm (*ulmos* below).

5. evincet: defeat, drive out. Cf. line 10, *excludet;* one theme of the ode is that excessive private wealth is an assault on nature. **violaria** are beds of violets.

6. myrtus: here fourth declension, nom. plural. **omnis copia narium:** all the wealth of the nostrils, a contemptuously colorful expression for all the aromatic flowers and plants cultivated on the great estates.

7. olivetis: i.e., former olive groves. For the formation, cf. *aesculetis* (1.22.14 note) and *querceta* (2.9.7).

8. fertilibus: with predicative and retrospective force, that once bore fruit. This strengthens the suggestion of *caelebs* (4) that the great villas are sterile and useless.

9. spissa ramis laurea: the purely ornamental laurel (*laurus*, here *laurea* [*arbor*]) is pruned to make it thick with branches, like the dense *platanus* (4). For the abl. construction, cf. 2.13.32 *densum umeris.*

10. ictus: acc. pl., the strokes or impact of the sun.

10-20. This was not the way with Romulus or Cato, when men were poor and the state rich; houses were humble, and public buildings were grand.

11. praescriptum: sc. *est.* **intonsi Catonis:** Cato the Censor (234-149 B.C.), often cited as typical of the old-fashioned sturdy simplicity. Untrimmed hair was symbolic of that simple style. Cf. *incomptis Curium capillis,* 1.12.41 and note.

12. auspiciis: as today, "under the auspices of" means under the regime of, originally because only those in high authority took the auspices (<*avis* + *spex,* interpreted the behavior of birds as omens of the future). **norma:** by the standard.

13. census: wealth, orig. as determined every five years by the state appraiser or *censor.*

14. commune: public property (spec. the national treasury, τὸ κοινόν) as opposed to *privatus census.*

14-15. decempedis metata: measured in ten-foot units. Horace implies that such measures are appropriate only for large public works, not for the colonnades of private villas.

15. privatis: dat., for private citizens, or abl. with *decempedis,* transferred epithet to be understood with *porticus.*

16. porticus: nom. fem. sing., a covered walk whose roof is supported by columns; symbolic of indecent private wealth. **excipiebat Arcton:** the heavy stonework would catch and retain the coolness of the "shady North."

17. fortuitum ... caespitem: chance turf, dug up casually in the good old days to build an altar or thatch a roof. Contrasted with *novo saxo* (20). **spernere,** like *decorare* (20), has no stated subject: laws did not allow people to disdain a chance piece of turf that could be used for a pious sacrifice.

18. leges: Horace projects Augustan reform laws back into the misty past, when the law was simply an unwritten code of behavior. **publico sumptu:** at public expense.

20. novo saxo: newly quarried stone, as appropriate for public buildings as *fortuitus caespes* was for private. This has an obvious bearing on Augustus' public building program. Suetonius records his boast that he found Rome a city of sun-dried brick and left it a city of marble (*Aug.* 28.3). On the theme of public wealth vs. private simplicity, cf. Sallust's description of the early Romans: *in suppliciis deorum magnifici, domi parci erant* (*Cat.* 9); he quotes the younger Cato as complaining in the closing days of the Republic *habemus luxuriam et avaritiam, publice egestatem, privatim opulentiam* (*Cat.* 52.22). For an early variant of this theme, see Aristophanes *Ecclesiazusae.* 206-208.

16

This lyric essay is addressed to a rich Sicilian rancher named Pompeius Grosphus. Its subject is *otium* (Gk. ἀταραξία), the leisure and peacefulness of spirit necessary to businessperson, diplomat, philosopher, and poet alike. The point of view is Epicurean, and its expression ends on a strongly personal note. Meter: Sapphic strophe.

1-8. The frightened sailor asks for peace when the sky grows stormy; so do savage tribesmen, Grosphus, but it cannot be bought for any price.

1. Otium, repeated at the beginning of lines 5 and 6, was likely to remind Horace's readers of the last stanza of Catullus 51—also in Sapphics—where the word was used in the bad sense of "idleness":

Otium, Catulle, tibi molestum est:
otio exultas nimiumque gestis:
otium et reges prius et beatas
     perdidit urbes.

The identity of meters makes the parallel even more striking; Horace was writing for a generation that is likely to have felt the need for peace and quiet more keenly than ever before; the political tumult that led to the Battle of Actium had exacted a heavy emotional cost, as reflected in several Horatian epodes and odes. Horace's mellow perso-

na was a conscious response to the pressures of his time, which did not disappear entirely after Actium.

2. prensus: sc. *nauta.* The anxious sailor is a commonplace in Horace (e.g., 1.1.14, *pavidus nauta*). The picture here evokes the famous proem to the second Book of Lucretius' *De Rerum Natura,* where the tumult of the sailor in a storm is contrasted to the philosopher's calm.

4. sidera: constellations. The Greeks and Romans looked for the Ursa Major when locating the North Star for navigation.

5. furiosa Thrace: the region east of Macedonia was proverbially wild (cf. 1.27.2, *scyphis pugnare Thracum est*), but even these savages pray for peace.

6. pharetra decori: suggests both the ornamented quivers prized by the "Medes" or Parthians, and their distinction as archers. For the latter meaning, cf. 3.2.13, *dulce et decorum est pro patria mori.*

7. Grosphe: for the presentation of philosophic maxims to a particular person, Cf. 2.10.1, *rectius vives, Licini, ...* For more on Grosphus, see appendix A.

7-8. ve-nale: one of three places where Horace's treatment of the third Sapphic line and the adonic as a single unit (see appendix C, synapheia) results in hyphenation.

9-16. No wealth or bodyguard will move aside the troubles of the rich; the good life is a simple one, without anxiety.

9-10. consularis ... lictor: lictors were bodyguards or attendants assigned to magistrates to clear their way through crowds and protect them from angry mobs; one assigned to a consul would be the best available, but useless against an angry mob of cares. **summovet:** clear away, disperse. This verb is the technical *vox propria* for the task of the lictor, as **tumultus** (acc. pl.) means riots. Horace applies a significantly political metaphor to a turbulent state of mind.

11-12. laqueata ... tecta: paneled ceilings,

symbolic of vast wealth; Horace seems again to have the beginning of Lucretius Book 2 in mind, line 28: *laqueata aurataque templa*.

13. vivitur parvo bene: suitably epigrammatic, with the impersonal passive. Both Stoics and Epicureans advocated a minimalist formula for the achievement of happiness (Gk. εὐδαιμονία) through simplicity of life. The emphasis on smallness recurs in the next line (*in mensa tenui*) and in the final stanza: *parva* (37), *tenuem* (38).

13-14. paternum ... salinum: a single heirloom, the salt cellar. Pliny the Elder (first century A.D.) tells of an imperial decree forbidding the possession of more silver than a dish and a *salinum*.

15. levis somnos: easy sleep, rather than light or fitful. **timor aut cupido** are the extremes of repulsion and attraction that people in the state of *otium* (*ataraxia*) make it their business to avoid. *Cupido* is always masculine in Horace, usually feminine in other authors except when personified.

17-24. Why are we so ambitious, always on the move? Worry climbs aboard our ships and harries our cavalry, faster than stags or the southeast wind.

17. brevi fortes: the juxtaposition of contrasting adjectives, suggesting paradox, was a feature of Augustan style; cf. *parvo bene* (13). The qualifiers are causal: since we are *fortes* for only a *brevi aevo*, why do we aim at so many things (*iaculamur multa*)? *iaculamur*, aim at, plays on the name of Grosphus: Gk. γρόσφος is a kind of javelin.

19. mutamus: take in exchange [for our usual haunts], i.e., travel to. This critique is echoed in Emerson's dictum "Travel is a fool's paradise." **alio ... sole** is instrumental with **calentis**, sweltering with an alien sun. Horace's philosophy disapproves of the Roman infatuation with anything exotic.

20. fugit: gnomic perfect or present perfect, "is in the position of having escaped" (NH *ad loc.*) The thought is, What exile but has fled himself as well? Cf. Lucretius' description of the restless man in *De Rerum Natura* 3, ending with *hoc se quisque*

modo fugit (1068).

21-22. Scandit ... Cura: rephrased in 3.1.38, *Timor et Minae scandunt eodem quo dominus*. Here Cura is like an enemy warrior, attacking both at sea and on land. **aeratas ... navis** are armored with bronze for ramming.

25-32. The happy spirit should avoid bitterness, because nothing is wholly blissful. Achilles died, Tithonus withered, and occasion may give me what it has denied you.

25. praesens: used as a neut. acc. substantive with *in*, for the present (*OLD* 16a).

26. oderit: jussive subjunctive, like *temperet* (line 27). **lento**: leisurely, untroubled.

29. Achillem: the classic example of the hero whose life is glorious but short.

30. Tithonum: the opposite of Achilles; his divine lover Aurora made him immortal but neglected to ask that he also be granted eternal youth, so he shriveled away until at last he turned into a cicada.

33-40. You have cattle, racehorses, clothing; to me, Fate has given a little farm, a slender Muse, and the means to scorn the spiteful crowd.

33. Te is governed by **circum**; its repetition in 34-35 *tibi, te* heightens the contrast with *mihi* in the final stanza.

34. mugiunt applies properly only to cows, but is extended to the sheep in *greges centum* above. **hinnitum** is hypermetric, eliding with *apta* in the following line. See appendix C, synapheia.

35. equa: collective sing.; mares were considered better racehorses.

35-36. Afro murice: the shellfish used for purple dye was harvested at Djerba, on the North African coast. Double-dyed (*bis ... tinctae*) fabrics had the richest color (cf. *Epod.* 12.21, *muricibus Tyriis iteratae vellera lanae*), but Horace has already told us (line 7 above) that they cannot buy *otium*.

37. parva rura, referring to Horace's Sabine farm, recalls line 13, *Vivitur parvo bene*.

38. spiritum ... tenuem: the muse's breath of inspiration is *tenuis* for Horace with reference to his light verse as opposed to epic poetry or Pindaric encomium; there is also an echo of the smallness theme: *in mensa tenui* (14) and *parva* in the preceding line. It is in the tradition of Callimachus, who cherished a Μοῦσαν λεπταλέην, and Catullus, who called his poems *nugae* (1.4). **Graeae ... Camenae**, using the old Latin name for the Muse, refers to Greek meters and poetic techniques in Latin poetry.

39. Parca non mendax: Cf. Catullus 64.306, *veridicos Parcae ... cantus.* "His fairy godmother is not just the Muse but Fate herself" (NH *ad loc.*) whose name implies economy and restraint (*parcus, -a, -um*). Horace's preferred style of living merges with his chosen style of poetry.

40. spernere: object of *dedit.*

17

Maecenas' poor health was made worse for him by hypochondria, depression, and a morbid fear of death. Sometime after his patron's recovery from illness in the autumn of 30 B.C., Horace wrote this to cheer him up. The tone changes from real seriousness in the opening stanzas to light irony in the middle and final stanzas as Horace moves tactfully between his own indifference to supernatural influences and Maecenas' belief in astrology. Meter: Alcaic strophe.

1-4. Why do you fret? Neither the gods nor I want you to die before me, Maecenas.

1. querelis exanimas: kill me with your complaints. Cf. *Epod.* 14.5 (also to Maecenas), *occidis saepe rogando.* The initial note of exasperation is soon balanced by the expression of esteem in line 4.

4. decus columenque rerum: comparable in magniloquence to 1.1.2, *praesidium et dulce decus meum.* The *columen* is the ridgepole of the roof, not to be confused with *columna.*

5-12. If an early death took you away, why would the rest of me linger? Whenever you go, we will go together.

5. meae ... partem animae: Horace calls Virgil *animae dimidium meae* in 1.3.8 (see note), the idea being that a close friend is like another self (Aristotle *Nicomachean Ethics* 1166a31, Cicero *Amic.* 80, *verus amicus ... est tamquam alter idem*).

6. maturior vis: euphemistic for an earlier death (than mine). **altera:** sc. *pars*, in apposition with the subject of *moror.*

7. nec carus aeque: sc. *cuiquam*, not as beloved to anyone as I am to you.

7-8. nec superstes integer: nor whole if I did survive. Horace did in fact die fifty-nine days after Maecenas.

8. utramque = *utriusque*; (the ruin) of both of us.

10. dixi sacramentum: the technical jargon for the soldier's oath to his commander was *sacramentum dicere.*

11. utcumque: whenever, as always in Horace.

13-22. No power imaginable will tear me from you, no sign of the zodiac: our signs are in conjunction.

13. Chimaerae spiritus igneae: proverbially fantastic, this monster had the body of the goat, the head of a lion, the tail of a serpent, and a breath of fire. Horace waxes cheerfully fanciful as he approaches the delicate subject of Maecenas' horoscope.

14. Gyas: one of the hundred-handed (*centimanus*) giants who tried to overthrow the Olympians and were buried under Mt. Aetna.

16. placitum (*est*) governs both datives, *Iustitiae* and *Parcis.*

17. Libra ... Scorpios: with *Capricornus*, three signs of the zodiac; whichever constellation was in the ascendant (i.e., rising above the eastern horizon) at the time of one's birth was thought to influence one's character and destiny. Romans were superstitious about things that came in threes; Horace could be referring to three events or crises shared by Maecenas and Horace, symbolized by these constellations. **me ... adspicit:** looks on me; the present is used because the influence was supposed to be lifelong.

18. pars violentior: as the more violent (because of its influence on the time of death); predicative, in apposition with the subject of *adspicit*.

19-20. tyrannus Hesperiae Capricornus undae: because of his fishy tail, Capricorn influences the sea. He was also believed to control the western part of the world: Manilius 4.791, *tu Capricorne, regis quidquid sub sole cadente / expositum*. Some readers find here a reference to Horace's escape from shipwreck near Palinurus Point mentioned in 3.4.28, and speculate that Maecenas was with him at the time.

21. incredibili: for the missing caesura in a moment of excitement, cf. 2.12.25.

22-32. Jove saved you from Saturn's bane; Faunus saved me from a falling tree. Remember to build a shrine in thanksgiving; I will sacrifice a lamb.

22-23. Iovis impio tutela Saturno: interlocking word order emphasizes the contrast between Jove's protection and the malign influence of Saturn (Gk. Cronus, who castrated his father and ate his children). Horace's meaning is that a benign influence (Jove's par excellence) overcame the unhealthy influence of Saturn (god of fevers and diseases) when Maecenas recovered from his illness.

25. cum: on the occasion when. Because this happened after his illness, some interpret *cum* as continuative, "whereat." When Maecenas was well enough to appear in public at the theater of Pompey, he was welcomed with applause: 1.20.3-4, *datus in theatro cum tibi plausus*. NH 1.248 comment dryly "this demonstration must have been one of the red-letter days in his neurotic life."

26. laetum ... sonum: object of *crepuit*.

27. truncus illapsus: the tree on Horace's farm

that is so roundly cursed in 2.13 for falling on its master; see also 3.4.27, 3.8.6-8.

28. sustulerat, nisi, etc.: In this past contrary-to-fact condition, the apodosis *sustulerat* is indicative to emphasize that it was all but a sure thing.

29. levasset: lit. lightened. As in 2.13.11-12, Horace implies that the tree did actually hit him, though he never claims that it injured him. Faunus' intervention is comparable to that of Athena in *Il.* 4.130ff., deflecting the arrow of Pandarus so that it slightly wounds Menelaus instead of killing him.

29-30. Mercurialium virorum: men under the protection of Mercury (Gk. Hermes, inventor of the lyre). On an astrological level, this would refer to people born under the influence of the planet Mercury. Such "mercurial" people were credited with a bent for poetry, eloquence, and wit. Horace is less than dead serious in these lines.

30-31. victimas aedemque votivam: Maecenas' thank-offering will cost him plenty; though not necessarily a full-sized temple, the *aedes* will be no simple affair, especially when compared to Horace's *humilem agnam*. For the contrast of sacrifices, cf. 4.2.53f., *te decem tauri totidemque vaccae, me tener solvet vitulus.*

18

Horace contrasts his own contentment in modest circumstances to the restless arrogance of a plutocrat whom he addresses as the latter builds mansions and drives poor clients from their lands. The death that awaits rich and poor alike is inexorable. These themes recur frequently in Horace's odes. Meter: Hipponactean, also called trochaic strophe. It is not clear whether it was meant to be divided into four-line stanzas.

1-14. No precious panels, rare marbles, or flashy luxuries adorn my house, but trust and talent, and the rich man seeks me out. I ask for nothing more, happy with my Sabine farm.

1. Non ebur, etc.: the series of negatives (1-7 *Non* ... *non* ... *neque* ... *nec*) and the theme of simplicity suggest Horace used Bacchylides frag. 21 (Athenaeus 11.500b) as a motto or model for his opening.

2. lacunar: an ornamental ceiling panel.

3. trabes Hymettiae: beams of gray-blue marble quarried from Mt. Hymettus, just east of Athens.

4-5. columnas ultima recisas Africa: columns of Numidian marble quarried at Simitthus (mod. Chemtou, northwest Tunisia). The yellowish *giallo antico* had recently become fashionable. **ultima** is rhetorical exaggeration: Chemtou is about as close to Italy as any point in Africa.

5-6. Attali ... regiam: the palace of Attalus II of Pergamum, bequeathed to the Romans along with his entire kingdom in 133 B.C. This is more rhetorical exaggeration: Horace means he has not taken possession of a palatial mansion as if he were some long-lost heir (*ignotus heres*) in a comedy.

7-8. Laconicas ... purpuras: purple garments from Gythium in S. Laconia (or the Spartan colony of Tarentum). The plutocrat that Horace claims not to be is so rich that even his clients' wives (*honestae clientae*) wear purple.

10. benigna vena recalls the veined marble of lines 3-4; Horace has a generous vein of *ingenium*, his poetic talent. **pauperem:** with *me*, poor man though I am. Though Horace is exaggerating, the word does not necessarily imply complete destitution; decent poverty is an important part of Horace's self-image throughout his writings. Note his compassionate portrayal of the *pauperem* (39) at the end of this ode.

12. lacesso: importune (OLD 4d), taking the accusatives *nihil* and *deos*. **potentem amicum:** Maecenas. Horace's patron may indeed be an intended likeness of the wealthy man to whom Horace contrasts himself in this ode. Maecenas was notorious for his extravagant habits and Etruscan luxuries such as carved ivory (*ebur*, line 1) and brightly garbed women (7-8, *Laconicas ... purpuras*). See NH 2.289f. ·

13. flagito: same meaning and construction as *lacesso* above, but with *amicum* and *largiora*.

14. unicis Sabinis: the pl. suggests not just the Sabine farm provided by Maecenas, but the incomparable (*unicus*) region where it lay. We know from Catullus 44.1-4 that it was not fashionable, so it contrasts well with the gleaming mansions of the very rich described in lines 1-6.

15-28. Time hurries on, while you build sprawling mansions out into the water without a thought of your mortality. You evict your clients, with their household gods and ragged children.

15-16. Truditur, pergunt: the emphasis is on the destructive haste of time: each day is driven on, and new moons hurry to their own demise. The theme appears with many variations in Horace: 1.11.8, 2.3.15, 4.7.7-12, etc.

17. Tu (the anonymous *avarus*) focuses the poem on personal morality as opposed to the public morality addressed in 2.15. The Hellenistic diatribe to which this poem is related tended to personalize its attacks to make them more dramatic.

17-18. secanda marmora locas: you let out a contract to have marble cut (into thin sheets to face a house wall).

18. sub ipsum funus: i.e., to your very last day, as if building were more important than life iteslf.

20. Baïs: at Baiae, the stylish resort on the Bay of Naples.

20-21. urges summovere litora: the fashion of building homes out over (and into) the water is made to seem an offense against nature; the theme is repeated in 3.1.33-37.

22. parum locuples: ironic, as if you were not rich in *continente ripa* (the mainland fronting the beach). Horace is playing on the root meaning of *locuples*, rich in lands, and *continens*, confining or restricting. *Continentia* is self-restraint: Pseudo-Acro titled this ode *De Continentia*.

24. revellis agri terminos: a second violation of nature, as the boundary markers were under religious protection; the verb, balancing *summovere*

(21), denotes violent removal: tear up, wrench loose.

25. clientium: your rural tenants; such clients were protected by the most ancient laws: *patronus si clienti fraudem fecerit, sacer esto* (XII *Tables*). But the newly rich of the late first century B.C. bought and developed real estate with no concern for decent obligations.

26. avarus: adverbial, you greedily leap. **Pellitur,** emphasized by position and alliteration, echoes the roughness of *truditur* (15).

27. in sinu: in the crook of his arm. Horace picks out details that make the cruel eviction more vivid, beginning with the oldest (*paternos deos*) and ending with the youngest (*sordidos natos*, the tattered children).

29-40. But no hall awaits its master more certainly than death. It is the same for rich and poor, for clever Prometheus, for proud Tantalus and his tribe: Charon, called or not to ease the poor man at his labor's end, hears.

29-32. Hyperbaton suits the disruptiveness of death awaiting the wealthy: no hall awaits its wealthy master more certain than the destined end of greedy death. **rapacis Orci** is gen. of specification with *fine*. The *avarus* (26) meets his match in *rapax Orcus* (Dis, Hades), god of the underworld.

32. Quid ultra tendis? Why do you press on further? The verb suggests unseemly straining after what cannot or should not be attained, like *urges* (20). This is a frequent motif in Horace. **Aequa tellus** denotes impartiality (as in 1.4.13 *aequo pede*) and an equal amount of space in the grave. Nature plays no favorites.

34. pueris: the fourth syllable, regularly long, is resolved into two shorts: *pŭĕr-*. **satelles Orci:** probably Mercury, conductor of souls (ψυχο-πομπός), rather than Charon.

35. callidum Promethea, etc.: suggests an unknown story in which the trickster hero tries to escape the underworld by bribery. For Prometheus in the underworld, see 2.13.37 and note.

36-38. Hic ... hic: Mercury, here represented as strict with the arrogant (*superbum Tantalum ... coërcet*) but kindly to the poor (*levare functum,* etc.). For this picture of Mercury, cf. 1.10.18f., *virgaque levem coërces aurea turbam.*

39. laboribus: abl. *apo koinou* with the deponent *functum* (having performed his labors) and *levare* (relieve him of his labors).

40. vocatus atque non vocatus: i.e., whether or not invoked in prayer. **audit:** regularly used for a god who pays attention to a prayer, it makes an oxymoron here with *non vocatus.*

19

The poet's claim to have seen a god or Muses in an epiphany is an old topic, going back in Greek poetry to Hesiod, Archilochus, Alcman, and Pindar. Departing from his more typically detached and rational style, Horace makes a bold claim for the power of his visionary imagination, and demands our belief—*credite posteri* (line 2). What follows is a dithyrambic poem, a song in honor of Bacchus/Dionysus. The recital of companions, episodes, and powers is in the hymnic tradition. With Dionysus, the emphasis is on miraculous achievements: flowing milk, wine, and honey (stanza 3), the apotheosis of his mortal spouse Ariadne (stanza 4), power over water and serpents (stanza 5), the victory over the Giants (stanzas 6-7), and finally his journey to Hades to recover his mother Semele (stanza 8). Meter: Alcaic strophe.

1-8. I saw Bacchus teaching his songs to nymphs and satyrs, and my mind thrills with fear and joy. Have mercy, Bacchus!

1. in remotis rupibus: Bacchus is a mountain god, associated with wild and isolated places.

2-3. docentem ... discentis: the emphasis on teaching and learning contrasts with the wild aspects brought out in the second stanza.

5-7. Euhoe ... Euhoe: the ritual cry of the Bacchant, from which Bacchus gets his name *Euhius* (as in 2.11.17).

5. recenti: because the fear is still fresh in his mind.

6. pleno ... pectore: circumstantial abl. abs., with my heart full of Bacchus. Cf. 3.25.1, *tui plenum*. This state of mystic ecstasy (Gk. ἐνθυσιασμός) where the god enters into his worshippers is dramatized in Euripides' *Bacchae*. **turbidum** is adverbial.

7. Liber is another name of Bacchus, because his wine and worship free the mind.

8. gravi ... thyrso: causal abl.; the thyrsus carried by Bacchants is a fennel stalk with a bunch of ivy leaves tied to its top. Though light and easy to wave about, it is *gravis* by virtue of its power: it makes Bacchus *metuendus* because its touch can induce madness. See Dodds's commentary on *Bacchae* 113.

9-16. It is meet and right for me to sing of tireless Bacchants, the spring flowing wine, rivers flowing milk, and honey dripping from trees; the starry crown of Ariadne, the ruin of Pentheus' house, and the death of Lycurgus.

9. pervicacis ... Thyiadas: the women worshippers of Bacchus (also called Maenads, Bacchants) are called tireless (*exsomnis* in 3.25.9) because of their long and frenzied rituals.

10. et connects *lactis uberes rivos* to the *vini fontem*. Cf. Euripides' *Bacchae*, 706-10.

12. iterare: repeat the story of; takes the neut. acc. pl. *lapsa ... mella*. In Exodus 3:8 God promises Moses he will deliver the Hebrews out of Egypt to Canaan, "a land flowing with milk and honey." Cf. also the prophecy of a golden age in Virgil *Ecl.* 4.30, *durae quercus sudabunt roscida mella*.

13. beatae coniugis: the Cretan princess Ariadne, married by Dionysus and made immortal after she was abandoned by Theseus.

13-14. Ariadne's **additum stellis honorem** is her bridal crown, set among the stars as the Corona Borealis. For this use of *honor* as honorific gift, cf. 1.17.16 *ruris honorum*.

14-15. tecta ... Penthei disiecta: when Bacchus' cousin Pentheus tried to suppress his worship, Bacchus destroyed his palace; see Euripides' *Bacchae* 576-603.

16. Thracis ... exitium Lycurgi: another king, Lycurgus, tried to harass Bacchus; he was blinded and eventually killed.

17-28. You divert rivers and seas; you control snakes; you defeated the Giants. Though called a god of song and dance, you are great in both peace and war.

17-21. Tu ... tu, etc.: the repetition of the personal pronoun is a typical feature in hymnic catalogs of powers.

17. mare barbarum: the Indian Ocean or the Red Sea. This exploit, comparable to the parting of the Red Sea for Moses, is unknown except for a brief mention in Seneca *Hercules Furens* 903f., *Lycurgi domitor et rubri maris*.

18. uvidus: flushed with wine. **separatis ... iugis** may be a reference to the twin peaks of Parnassus, on whose slopes an annual Bacchic ritual was held. Some understand *separatis* as remote.

20. Bistonidum: women of a Thracian tribe named *Bistones*, whose Bacchic rites were considered especially orgiastic. Snake handling was a widespread feature of the cult, as is sometimes seen in vase paintings. **sine fraude:** without harm (the root meaning of *fraus*).

21-22. regna ... scanderet: climbed or tried to climb to the domain of Jove (*parentis*). The resulting Gigantomachy is the subject of this stanza. The Giants piled Mt. Pelion on Ossa in an attempt to reach Olympus. See also 2.12.6-9, 3.4.49-75.

23. Rhoetum: one of the Giants.

24. mala: the lion's jaw; in this version of the battle, Bacchus takes the form of a lion.

25-27. quamquam ... sed: although ... still. The concessive clause governs the participle *dictus* and the indicative *ferebaris*, both with the same meaning: said to be.

28. medius governs both *pacis* and *belli*, "not

only a mediator of peace but midmost in the fight" (NH *ad loc.*).

29-32. Cerberus saw you when you visited the underworld, and was friendly. Fraenkel comments: "After the grim fight against the Giants, this peaceful picture with its delicate detail comes to the reader as an unqualified delight, and the very sound of the stanza contributes to the effect of a perfect diminuendo." The ending is comparable to that of 2.13.

29. vidit insons: saw you harmlessly, i.e., without hurting you. Cerberus, the *belua centiceps* of 2.13.33-35, guards the exit from the underworld. The purpose of Bacchus' *katabasis* was to bring back his mother Semele.

30. cornu: Bacchus' horn recalls another of his animal forms, the bull; it may also be understood as his drinking horn. **atterens caudam:** sc. *te*, brushing his tail against you.

31-32. trilingui ore: usually three-headed, Cerberus is domesticated here to a one-headed dog with triple tongue. Hellenistic poetry often downgraded the scary monsters of myth and familiarized them by giving them more ordinary features—here the wagging tail and the friendly lick of the foot as Bacchus passes through. Cf. note on 2.13.34. **recedentis:** i.e., of Bacchus going back out of the underworld. Cerberus was a one-way watch dog, driving back anyone who tried to leave Hades.

32. tetigitque: the suffix joins *pedes* and *crura*.

20

Concluding the second book of the *Odes*, with its recurrent themes of mortality and human limits, this ode strikes a contrasting note by asserting the poet's transcendence. Having transcended his allegedly humble birth (*ego pauperum sanguis parentum*) he also transcends the limits of space and death. Like the beginning of the preceding hymn to Bacchus, this ode is extravagant and far removed from Horace's usual posture of detachment. The metaphor of flight to express the poet's celebrity may have been inspired by the Greek elegiac poet Theognis (ca. 550-480 B.C.), lines 237ff. The meter is Alcaic.

1-8. I am borne above the lands and cities on no weak or common wing; I will not perish, Maecenas, or be imprisoned by the river Styx.

1. usitata: common, ordinary; cf. 3.1.2f., *carmina non prius audita*. Horace is probably thinking of his use of Greek lyric meters in Latin poetry. **tenui:** slight, feeble. But cf. 2.16.38, *spiritum Graiae tenuem Camenae*, and note.

2. penna: cf. 2.2.7 (also of fame), *penna metuente solvi*. **liquidum:** clear, as in 1.24.3 *liquidam vocem*.

2-3. biformis ... vates: a bard in the form of a swan, both man and bird; *vates* (orig. = prophet) is an early word for poet; cf. 1.1.35.

4. longius: temporal, like *diutius*. **invidia ... maior:** greater than envy. Since at least the time of Pindar, it was customary for poets to advertise the envy of their rivals. Cf. 2.16.39, *malignum vulgus*; *Sat.* 1.6.46, *quem rodunt omnes libertino patre natum*.

5-6. pauperum sanguis parentum: Horace made a virtue of his supposedly humble origins (cf. *Sat.* 1.6.46, quoted above), but his claim was exaggerated: see Introduction.

6. quem vocas: whom you send for, i.e., invite to share your company. In his *Satires* as well as the *Epodes* and *Odes*, Horace frequently calls attention to his friendship with Maecenas.

7. obibo: a euphemism for *moriar*: I shall not meet [death]. Cf. 3.30.6, *non omnis moriar*.

9-16. Already I feel myself turning into a swan; soon I will see the roaring Bosporus, the African coast, and the regions of the north.

9. residunt: shrink. **cruribus:** locative abl., on my legs. **asperae pelles:** the wrinkled skin of the swan's legs and feet. The details of a metamorphosis were a challenge to Hellenistic poets, who made such poetry a category of literature, emulated in Augustan poetry by Ovid's *Metamorphoses*. But many critics have taken exception to such a description by Horace in the context of this poem.

10. album ... in alitem: i.e., a swan.

11. superne: above, as opposed to *cruribus*; the final *e* is short, as in Lucretius 6.544.

11-12. lēves ... plumae: smooth feathers, as opposed to the *asperae pelles*.

13. notior: more famous. **Daedalio Icaro:** for the patronymic adjective, cf. 1.17.22, *Semeleius Thyoneus*. The comparison with Icarus, who flew too high and crashed, is curious—though he gave his name to a sea. Cf. 4.2.3-4, where *daturus nomina ponto* suggests disaster.

14. gementis ... Bosphori: the strait between Thrace and Bithynia, north of Byzantium, roaring with the noise of surf.

15. Syrtis: the shoals and coast of modern Libya. Gaetulia was a frontier region of north Africa west of the Syrtis; cf. 2.6.3 note. **canorus ales:** tuneful bird, conflating the song of the poet with that attributed to the swan.

16. Hyperboreos campos: the land of the mythical people who lived beyond the north wind (Boreas). They were represented as passing an idyllic existence in a sunny land, but here Horace refers merely to the far north.

17-24. Outlanders everywhere will come to know me. Let there be no unseemly mourning at my death, or needless honors to my tomb.

17. Colchus: collective sing.: the Colchians lived at the eastern end of the Black Sea, where Medea grew up. **qui dissimulat metum ... Dacus:** the fearlessness of Rome's enemies was a patriotic commonplace. Dacians inhabited the area of

modern Romania.

18. Marsae cohortis: an elite Roman infantry corps, rustics from central Italy whose name suggested the war god Mars.

19. Geloni: a Scythian tribe of southern Russia, legendary bowmen and fearless riders: cf. 2.9.23. **peritus ... Hiber:** Spain had an advanced culture, as Horace shows by distinguishing their study (*discet*) from the mere acquaintance (*noscent*) of the eastern European Dacians and Geloni. In the next generation Spain produced the Senecas and Lucan, and later Quintilian and Martial.

20. Rhodani potor: the Gaul, perhaps also to be taken with *peritus*. Though not as cultured as Spain, the Rhone valley was settled and relatively civilized even in the time of Caesar's campaigns of the fifties.

21-24. This closing stanza recalls an epigram of Ennius quoted by Cicero (*Tusc.* 1.34):

Nemo me dacrumis decoret, nec funera fletu
Faxit. Cur? Volito vivos per ora virum.

inani funere: the funeral is empty because Horace has turned into a swan and there is neither a corpse nor an actual death. **neniae:** the lamentations of professional mourners or *praeficae*.

22. luctus ... turpes: unseemly acts of grief, such as tearing the hair, beating the breast, etc.

23. compesce clamorem: restrain the noise of the *conclamatio* (the last call to the dead or dying to determine whether any life remains). Cf. Virgil *Aen.* 4.674, *morientem nomine clamat.* **sepulcri ... honores:** the superfluous tribute of a tomb, appositional gen. (Allen and Greenough §343d).

24. mitte: omit. **supervacuos:** superfluous; a new word, in place of *supervacaneos*, which will not scan.

1

Book 3 begins with a cycle of six poems in the Alcaic meter, the so-called Roman Odes, setting forth the values of Augustan Romanism. The first is a series of sharply drawn vignettes showing that the more we achieve the trappings of success, the more we fall victim to forces beyond our control. Though there is nothing patriotic about this ode, it fits the pattern of the Roman Odes by promoting the personal values without which a better Rome is impossible. The first stanza serves as a proem introducing the series of six. Meter: Alcaic strophe.

1-4. Keep a holy silence: the Muses' priest, I sing songs unheard before to maidens and boys.
1. Odi: Horace begins his ode, as he will end it, on a personal note. As in 1.38.1 *Persicos odi ... apparatus*, the meaning is closer to aversion than outright hatred. **profanum:** lit. outside the shrine. Mystery religions did not admit the uninitiate into their holy place. Horace's use of sacral language to introduce a cycle of state poems shows how close patriotism and religion had been brought together under Augustus. A similar nexus of politics and religion can be seen in Virgil's *Aeneid*.
2. favete linguis: lit. be propitious with your tongues, i.e., avoid words of ill omen by keeping a holy silence.
2-3. Carmina non prius audita are public or national songs in lyric meters (as opposed to Virgilian hexameters).
3. Musarum sacerdos: high rhetoric to convey an appropriately Augustan "sense of the high seriousness that could belong to poetic activity" (Williams).
4. virginibus puerisque: i.e., to the younger generation. **canto** combines the meanings of poetic composition and prophecy (*OLD* 2 and 7c).

5-8. Kings have power over their own people, but Jupiter rules the kings themselves.
5. Regum: gen. with *imperium*. To the Roman

ear, *reges* suggests foreign potentates, but it was also used of any big shot of the sort presented in lines 9-14 (*OLD* 4b, 8).
6. reges in ipsos: adversative asyndeton, emphasized by repetition of the key word.
7. clari Giganteo triumpho: famous for his victory over the Giants, for which see the fourth Roman Ode, 3.4.42-76. Horace's contemporaries may have seen this as a reference to the struggle of Antony against Octavian.
8. cuncta supercilio moventis: for the tradition that Jove accomplishes everything by a nod or a twitch of his eyebrow, cf. *Il.* 1. 528-30, *Aen.* 10.115.

9-16. One man is successful in one way, another in another; but Necessity chooses high and low alike.
9. Est ut ... ordinet: the substantive clause of result continues through line 14, governing *descendat, contendat, sit*. The first VIP in Horace's catalog is a planter with a large *latifundium*. **latius** suggests the generous spacing of his trees as well as the extent of his groves and orchards.
10. arbusta sulcis: the planter arranges his trees in shallow trenches dug for irrigation. **generosior:** i.e., with a better pedigree. Roman politicians made the most of noble ancestors if they had them.
11. Campum: Roman elections—and electioneering—went on in the Campus Martius, which was still open land. **petitor:** as a candidate, in apposition with *hic*.
12. melior governs both *moribus* and *fama*. Politicians like Cicero, who had no illustrious ancestors to brag about, capitalized on their own personal reputation.
13. contendat: for political office. Enjambment with the preceding line helps pair these stanzas; similar enjambment of lines 20-21 and 36-37 indicates the ode as a whole is organized in paired stanzas. The **turba clientium** surrounding Horace's fourth successful type testifies to his success as a

patronus, dispensing and accepting political favors.

14. aequa, etc.: adversative asyndeton, significantly juxtaposed with *maior*. **Necessitas:** the inevitability of doom. Cf. 1.3.32, *tarda necessitas leti*, personified in 1.35.17 as *saeva Necessitas* and in 3.24.6 as *dira Necessitas*. Here too she is a personification, not only of death but of any disaster.

15. sortitur: chooses by lot.

16. The rapidity of the meter dramatizes the action: Necessity shakes the urn in which each person's *nomen* is tumbled. For the image, see 2.3.25ff. *omnium versatur urna serius ocius sors exitura*. For the golden line, of which this is a chiastic variant, see appendix C.

17-24. Whoever lives beneath the sword of Damocles can enjoy neither food nor sleep. But sleep does not scorn the homes of peasants or pleasant outdoor places.

17. Destrictus ensis: the story of the sword of Damocles is well enough known to Horace's audience not to require any reference by name. Our source is Cicero, *Tusculan Disputations* 5.61-2. Dionysius, tyrant of Syracuse (430-670 B.C.), loses patience with one of his flatterers and suspends a sword above his head by a horsehair to teach him the anxiety that plagues a ruler. Damocles is unable to enjoy the splendid feast that is then set out before him. **cui:** dat. of reference with *pendet* and *elaborabunt*.

18. Siculae dapes: Sicily was famous for its luxurious cuisine; the epithet is also appropriate as the scene of the original tale.

21. Somnus: for the adversative asyndeton, cf. lines 6 and 14. With *fastidit* (23), sleep is nearly personified, contrasting it with *Necessitas* in 14.

23. umbrosam ... ripam: the shady stream bank associated with the *locus amoenus* (see appendix C).

24. Tempe: neut. acc. pl., object of *non ... fastidit*. This famous valley in Thessaly between Mts. Olympus and Ossa is another *locus amoenus*,

closely associated with the Muses. Horace often connects the simple rustic life with his own poetic gift.

25-32. The man who desires only what is enough has no cause to fear stormy weather or damaged crops.

25. Desiderantem: used substantively, obj. of *sollicitat*.

26. tumultuosum ... mare: the nemesis of anyone who tries to make a fortune in shipping; cf. the *pavidus nauta* in 1.1.14. In Horace, the sea is generally a scene of danger, storms, and shipwreck; for a possible reason, see note on 3.4.28.

27-28. Arcturi cadentis ... orientis Haedi: constellations that cross the horizon around the end of October, at the beginning of the stormy season.

29. vineae: subj. of *sollicitat* (26). As often in poetry, multiple nouns (here *mare, impetus, vineae*, and *fundus*) govern a singular verb.

30-31. fundusque mendax, arbore ... culpante: humorous personification. Like lazy workers, the farm is making false excuses while the tree is blaming various weather conditions (*aquas, sidera, hiemes*) for its low yield of fruit or olives.

32. sidera: constellations that appear during times of severe heat are seen as themselves scorching the fields. Cf. 1.17.17, where Horace tells Tyndaris that she can avoid the heat of the dog star on his farm.

33-40. The rich man builds his villa out into the water; but Fear, Portents, and Tension never leave him alone.

33. pisces sentiunt: i.e., nature senses the invasion of its domain. Man trifles with natural boundaries of land and sea at his peril.

34. iactis ... molibus: abl. abs., when landfill is dumped into the sea. In search of sea breezes and good views, wealthy Romans of the Augustan age built as far out into the water as possible. **frequens:** busy.

35. caementa: lit. cuttings, i.e., rubble from the dressing of stone used in building the villa. **redemptor:** the building contractor.

37. fastidiosus plays off *fastidit* in line 23. Sleep does not scorn the peasant's cottage, but the fat cat who builds his villa into the water scorns the land.

37-40. Timor, Minae, Cura: personifications of the constant worry that prevents the rich man from enjoying his wealth.

38. scandunt eodem quo dominus: Horace imagines the owner climbing around on his villa during construction.

39. aerata triremi is contemptuously hyperbolic. The rich man's boat is not actually an armored warship with three banks of oars, but a pleasure galley with ornamental bronze plates.

40. post equitem sedet: i.e., she sits behind him when he goes riding.

41-48. If luxury does not relieve unhappiness, why should I build a mansion, or trade my Sabine valley for more troublesome riches?

41. dolentem: a person suffering mental pain, hence unhappiness. **Phrygius lapis:** marble imported from northwestern Asia Minor.

42. sidere clarior has been transferred from the purple fabrics to their *usus*.

43-44. Falerna vitis: i.e., expensive wine. **Achaemenium costum:** Persian perfume, properly the aromatic root imported from India, but called Achaemenid (after the Persian dynasty) because it came via Persia. Horace appeals to a Greek tradition that scorned oriental luxuries—in particular anything "Persian"—as unwholesome.

45. invidendis postibus: with columns likely to incur human or divine envy because they are too much for a mere private residence. Cf. 2.10.7, *invidena aula*.

45-46. novo sublime ritu ... atrium: a high courtyard in the new style, where callers would be received (and impressed). **moliar**, heap up, is contemptuous.

47. permutem, like *moliar* above, is a subjunctive of indignant question. Here the acc. (*divitias operosiores*) is taken in exchange for the abl. (*valle Sabina*). Cf. 1.17.2, *mutat*.

2

The second Roman Ode begins with praise of *pauperies*, which links it to its predecessor. The first half draws a romantic picture of the prowess in foreign wars that the young Roman (line 2, *puer*) will display in the field. *Virtus* in the second half is by contrast domestic and political: its cardinal features are the ability to rise above the popular will as shown in elections, and the ability to keep a secret. At least two tags from Simonides are brought into this ode, highlighting Horace's avowed purpose of putting the Greek lyric tradition at the service of Augustan ideology. Meter: Alcaic strophe.

1-6. Let the youth be trained to endure a rugged life in the open, and harass the savage Parthians.

1. amice: cheerfully. **pauperiem** has none of the connotations of failure or squalor implicit in contemporary Eng. "poverty." For its meaning here, cf. the monastic oath of poverty, chastity, and obedience.

2. puer: since he is already *robustus acri militia*, we should expect *iuvenis* here, but Horace is preparing for the romantic fantasy of lines 6-12. Cf. the erotic *puer* in 1.5.1

3. Parthos ferocis: since the defeat and capture of Crassus' army at Carrhae in 53 B.C., Roman militancy against the Parthians had hardened into a crusade mentality; "Parthian" became synonymous with any eastern barbarian foe.

5. sub divo: under the open sky, a form of metonymy deriving ultimately from the identity of the Indo-European *Dyaus* (Lat. *divus*) as the sky god.

6-12. Let women see him from the enemy walls

and pray their prince will not provoke his wrath. This scene has little to do with actual warfare in Horace's time. It is rather a loose conflation of scenes from Homer, *Il.* 3.146ff., where Helen looks down at the Greek heroes from the walls of Troy, and 22.25ff., where Priam and Hecuba plead with Hector not to meet Achilles in a duel.

7. matrona: the wife of the enemy potentate is also the mother or prospective mother-in-law of the *adulta virgo* in the next line.

9. suspiret: say with a sigh. Though singular, it is to be taken with two subjects: the *matrona*, and the *adulta virgo*. The jussive subjunctive continues the construction of *condiscat* (3), *vexet* (4), and *agat* (5). **agminum:** gen. of specification with *rudis*: unlike the seasoned Roman *puer* (line 2, *robustus acri militia*), the barbarian princeling has never been drawn up in a battle line.

10. sponsus ... regius: the local champion is engaged to the *adulta virgo*.

11. leonem: the warlike Roman youth, as seen through the anxious eyes of the barbarians.

12. ira implicitly compares the Roman youth to Homer's Achilles, whose wrath is the first word and the theme of the *Iliad*.

13-16. It is a fine thing to die bravely for the fatherland, since death pursues even him who runs away.

14. mors et fugacem, etc.: a translation of Simonides frag. 19 Page. Many commentators argue that this tends to undercut the noble sentiment of the previous line. But the paradox goes as far back as the justification of the heroic life given by Sarpedon in *Il.* 12.322-28: because we are mortal and will not live forever, we must win immortality in battle.

16. poplitibus: the backs of the knees, dat. obj. of *parcit*. The only honorable battle wounds are those received while facing the enemy.

17-24. *Virtus* knows nothing of electoral defeat; she does not take office or give it up at public whim. Her immortal path is skyward, spurning the damp earth.

Though *virtus* fits the manly courage of the *puer* in lines 1-16, the personified *Virtus* in these stanzas is strictly political and civilian.

17. repulsae: the regular term for electoral defeat. Augustus' moral reforms were unpopular, and Horace, who makes no secret of his contempt for the *profanum vulgus*, assures his audience that true *virtus* (in the sense of moral excellence) has nothing to do with popularity.

18. intaminatis: a rare archaism for *intactis*, undefiled.

18-19. honoribus, securis: both refer to public office. The axes symbolize the authority of elected Roman magistrates.

20. popularis aurae: the shifting breeze of public opinion. Horace implicitly endorses the dictatorial powers of the Augustan principate.

21. immeritis mori: to those who do not deserve to die. This is a thinly veiled allusion to Augustus, whose deification was a pet project of the Augustan poets. A more overt call for deification is made in 1.2. The theme is repeated in 3.3.10f., 3.5.2f., 3.25.4-6. Though against the traditional Roman grain, deification of rulers was a characteristically Hellenistic institution, reflecting oriental tendencies. As such it was deeply distrusted by conservative Romans, but it exerted an increasing allure on the successors of Julius Caesar and their propagandists.

22. negata temptat iter via: tries a journey along a path denied to others, because no Roman had been deified since the apotheosis of Romulus as Quirinus (3.3.15). Julius Caesar was well on his way to deification when he was assassinated in 44 B.C. With his adoptive father's official recognition as a god on January 1, 42, Octavian became *divi filius*.

23. coetus ... vulgaris: political assemblies. Like the clammy earth (*udam ... humum*) itself, these are beneath the dignity of Horace's authoritarian *Virtus*, who is imagined like a winged Victory.

25-32. Trusty silence has its reward as well. I would have no profaner of Ceres' sacred rites share house or ship with me. Often Jupiter punishes the innocent with the guilty, and the offender never escapes.

25-26. Est et fideli tuta silentio merces: The Greek original of this tag (Simonides frag. 77 Page) was a favorite motto of Augustus, according to Plutarch *Apophthegms of Kings and Emperors* 207c.

26-27. Cereris sacrum arcanae: the Greek cult of Demeter (Lat. Ceres) practiced secret rituals that it was an acknowledged crime to reveal. Here, as in the opening of the first Roman Ode, Horace pushes politics into the realm of religion.

28. trabibus: roof beams.

29. solvat: launch, loose from its moorings. **phaselon:** Gk. acc. of *phaselus*, lit. bean pod, a light, fast ship of the type Catullus brought back from Bithynia (Catullus 4). **Diespiter:** an impressive archaism for Jupiter, the sky god; see note on line 5 above.

30. neglectus: when not duly respected. **incesto addidit integrum:** has involved the innocent with the guilty.

31. raro is adverbial, with *deseruit*.

32. pede ... claudo: abl. of description, with concessive force: Punishment, though of limping foot.

3

The third Roman Ode pays tribute to *iustitia* and *constantia*, with special mention of a deified Augustus (line 11). More than fifty of the poem's seventy-two lines are a mythological digression consisting of Juno's comment on the fall of Troy and her conditions for the subsequent rise of the Roman people. This speech makes stirring reference to the spread of Roman power, but is not especially relevant to the original topic. The poem ends as the poet rejects a topic not well suited to short lyric meters. Meter: Alcaic strophe.

1-8. The just and purposeful man is undeterred by public furor, a tyrant's frown, a stormy wind, or Jove's fulminations. Even if the world collapsed around him, he would be unafraid.

1. propositi: an intention or objective, gen. of specification with *tenacem*. **virum,** obj. of *quatit* (4), recalls the *vir-tus* featured in the preceding ode.

2. prava: crooked, corrupt, or wrong actions; obj. of *iubentium*.

3. instantis tyranni: a threatening tyrant; like *bellantis tyranni* in 3.2.7, this would be some barbarian strong man, not a Roman.

4. mente solida: from his firm resolve, abl. of separation with *quatit*.

6. magna manus: the hand that throws the mighty thunderbolt; fourth subject of *non ... quatit*.

7. si fractus illabatur: if it should break and fall upon him. The future less vivid condition uses a future indicative (*ferient*) in the apodosis to emphasize the sureness of the man's unintimidated state, *impavidum*. Both Stoic and Epicurean cosmology predicted such cataclysmic events; in Stoicism they were periodic.

9-18. This is how Pollux and Hercules attained immortality, and how Augustus will attain it. So it was with Bacchus, and Quirinus, when Juno spoke to the assembled gods.

9. arte is ironic, since the virtues mentioned in line 1 are more a matter of natural character or *ingenium* than acquired skill or craft, *ars*. Horace thus emphasizes that good character is *not* some trick. **Pollux** and his brother Castor were worshipped in a temple in the Roman Forum.

10. enisus ... attigit: struggled upward and attained. Euhemerus wrote a novel ca. 300 B.C. in which the Olympian gods were originally kings whose services to their subjects caused them to be worshipped as gods after their death. Ennius and Posidonius popularized the idea among the Romans, whose propagandists later exploited it to deify the Caesars. **arces ... igneas:** the fiery vault of the Stoic heavens, or more loosely the starry heights of heaven.

11. Augustus: the title conferred on Octavian in January of 27 B.C. He also wanted the title *Romulus*, and coins were struck with the inscription *Romulo Augusto* to suggest he was Rome's second founder. The digression beginning line 18 on the deification of Romulus as Quirinus is a pointed argument for the deification of his alter ego Augustus.

12. bibet: fut. indicative of confident prediction; the nectar certifies Augustus' immortality as it does Romulus' in line 34.

14. tigres indocili: the yoking of tigers or panthers symbolizes Bacchus' power over the forces of nature.

15. Quirinus: god of the Quirinal hill, identified with Romulus in the late Republic. His name is sometimes given as the origin of *Quirites*, Roman citizens (see note on 57).

17. gratum: i.e., a welcome speech, obj. of *elocuta*.

17-18. elocuta ... Iunone: abl. abs., when Juno spoke out. **consiliantibus ... divis:** to the gods in council. This is the epic *concilium deorum*, where the gods decide how things will work out. Virgil's version of this scene comes in *Aen.* 12.791-842.

18-24. "Troy is turned to dust, destroyed by Paris and Helen, and doomed by Laomedon's ancient fraud.

18. Ilion: acc. obj. of *vertit*.

19. iudex refers to the judgment of Paris, in which he awarded the golden apple to Venus; she in turn made him fatally attractive to Helen.

20. The **mulier peregrina** is Helen, brought from Sparta to Troy. Horace's contemporaries might associate her with another *femme fatale*, Cleopatra, who took up residence in Rome from 46 to 44 B.C. (see appendix D).

21. destituit: Priam's father Laomedon hired Apollo and Neptune to build the walls of Troy, but left them without (*destituo*, OLD 7) their agreed pay, abl. *mercede pacta*.

23. castae ... Minervae: dat. of agent with *damnatum*. In the *Iliad*, Juno (Hera) and Minerva (Athene) pair up to do as much harm to the Trojans as possible.

24. duce fraudulento: there is nothing fraudulent about Homer's Priam; he suffers for his father's fraud. Cf. 26-7, *Priami domus periura*.

25-36. "Paris no longer shines, and Priam's house no longer fights with Hector's aid. Now I will give up my wrath and let my grandson Romulus enter the ranks of the gods.

25. Lacaenae ... adulterae: dat. of reference with *splendet*. Juno, goddess of marriage, so hates Spartan Helen that she will not mention her by name; cf. line 20, *mulier peregrina*.

26. famosus hospes: another hostile periphrasis; cf. 19, *fatalis incestusque iudex*.

29. nostris ... ductum seditionibus: the quarrels of the gods, who took sides in the Trojan War, drew it out.

30. resedit: has subsided. Horace plays on *seditionibus* in the preceding line.

31-33. iras et ... nepotem ... redonabo: zeugma: she will give up her wrath and return her grandson Romulus to his father Mars. In this version of the myth Juno is the mother of Mars, who fathered Romulus on Ilia. **invisum:** hated because of his Trojan ancestry; his mother Ilia is here Aeneas' daughter, the **Troïca sacerdos** of line 32. Also known as Rhea Sylvia, she was a Vestal Virgin. The family tree in the version followed by Horace is as follows:

Juno	Aeneas
Mars ——————— + ———	Ilia/Rhea Sylvia
Romulus	

33-34. lucidas ... sedes: heaven; cf. *arces igneas* (10).

35-36. adscribi ... ordinibus ... deorum: borrows Roman administrative jargon for assigning a citizen to a social rank, a colony, or a military unit.

37-48. "As long as a sea separates Troy from Rome and Troy stands abandoned, let the Roman empire extend its power far and wide.

38. exsules: because the founders—Aeneas and his fellow refugees—were originally Trojans.

38-39. qualibet ... in parte regnanto: fut. imperative. This expansive view of the empire is also voiced by Jove in the *Aeneid*: *imperium sine fine dedi* (1.279).

41. insultet: trample on, with connotations of insult.

42. inultae: unpunished, with impunity, because the grave mounds will be left untended.

43-44. triumphatis ... Medis: this is wishful thinking. Augustus had no taste for eastern conquest, and recovered the Roman ensigns lost at Carrhae by negotiation with Parthian king Phraates. Cf. 3.5.3-4 *adiectis ... Persis*, and see notes on 1.2.22 and 3.2.3.

46. medius liquor: periphrastic for the Straits of Gibralter at the western limit of the empire, opposite Egypt near its eastern limit.

47. ab Afro: from the (collective) African, i.e., from Africa.

48. tumidus Nilus: referring to the Nile's annual flood, which makes Egypt fertile. After Octavian's victory in the Battle of Actium, Egypt became a Roman province under a prefect responsible directly to Octavian, who confiscated its large treasures for his personal benefit.

49-56. "As long as she resists the lure of gold, Rome will take her conquests to the ends of the earth, exploring the hottest and the coldest climes.

49. Aurum irreptum: obj. of *spernere*, to scorn gold and leave it undiscovered, lit. to scorn undiscovered gold.

50. spernere fortior: more courageous to scorn it (than to dig it up).

51. cogere humanos in usus implies that man's use of gold is forced and unnatural. Horace probably means to suggest Augustus' moral reforms, in particular his sumptuary laws against the conspicuous display of wealth.

54. tanget: fut. indic. of confident prediction, like *bibet* (12). The subject is *Roma* (44). **visere gestiens:** eager to observe. Horace portrays the Romans as inheriting the Greek zest for scientific investigation.

55. debacchentur ignes: the heat of the sun revels unchecked (intensive *de-*).

56. nebulae pluviique rores: rain and fog typify the extreme north for the Romans because of their contact with northwest European climates affected by the Gulf Stream. Cf. Homer's Cimmerians, "shrouded in fog and cloud," *Od.* 11.14-15, and Horace 1.22.19f., *quod latus mundi nebulae malusque Iuppiter urget.*

57-68. "But all this is on condition the Romans not rebuild Troy. A rebuilt Troy will meet a sorry end; even if it were thrice restored, my Greeks would thrice lay it waste, and thrice the captive wife would mourn."

57. Quiritibus = Roman citizens; the ancients derived it from the Sabine town of Cures.

58. hac lege: under this condition (*OLD* 12c); governs a clause of proviso, *ne ... velint.*

59. rebusque fidentes: being too confident in their circumstances.

60. tecta ... reparare Troiae: the rumor reported in Suetonius' life of Julius Caesar (79.3) of a scheme to move the capital of the empire to Troy or Alexandria is probably not foremost in the poet's mind here. The point is more symbolic, that the Romans should leave the dead past buried.

61-62. renascens ... iterabitur: if, under an *alite lugubri*, Troy's fortune revives, it will be repeated with a *tristi clade.*

65-68. si resurgat ... pereat ... ploret: Juno's prophecy modulates to a less vivid future condition because she does not anticipate it happening.

65. aëneus: i.e., even if it were rebuilt in bronze, a proverbially durable material. Cf. *Epist.* 1.1.60, *hic murus aëneus esto.*

66. auctore Phoebo: i.e., even if Apollo built it; see note on 21.

69-72. But this subject will not suit a lyric line; where are you off to, Muse? Leave off shrinking great subjects into little verses.
69. iocosae: humorous, light. **lyrae** = poetry in a lyric meter. This breakaway form of closure, like the long digression, is modeled after the style of Pindar, the fifth-century author of Greek victory odes. See notes on 4.2, *Pindarum quisquis studet aemulari*, and cf. the breakaway ending of 2.1.
70. pervicax is adverbial: persistently, stubbornly.

4

Horace's longest and most difficult ode, this praise of *consilium* and the power that keeps order has a strongly Pindaric flavor. Like a victory ode of Pindar, it dispenses with the easy transitions and linear movement of thought that we expect in ordinary discourse. The theme of universal order and harmony links the personal topics of the early stanzas to the mythical battles of the later stanzas. The underlying conception that the Muses supply *consilium* to both poet and ruler gives the poem its unity. Meter: Alcaic strophe.

1-8. Come down from heaven, Calliope, and tell us a long poem. I seem to hear her voice, and to walk through sacred, pleasant groves.
1. Descende caelo: the opening words serve a dual purpose, recalling the *Quo Musa tendis?* at the end of the previous ode and announcing the purpose of the present ode. For the language of sacred invocation, cf. 3.21.7. **tibia:** on the pipe (suggesting the accompaniment of choral lyric, which was Pindar's medium).
2. regina ... Calliope: Horace does not sharply define the Muses by type; here Calliope (Gk. Καλλιόπη, "fair-voice") is invoked probably because Hesiod named her as the Muse who attends on kings and poets alike, *Theog.* 79ff.

longum ... melos: acc. obj. of *dic*.
3-4. seu voce ... acuta seu fidibus citharave: as usual in the language of prayer, the Muse is given choices for the form of her epiphany; cf. *Carm. Saec.* 15f., *sive tu Lucina probas vocari seu Genitalis*. **acuta** = clear, high pitched. **fidibus citharave:** hendiadys, on the strings of the lyre (the instrument associated with lyric monody).
5. Auditis: Horace addresses his audience.
6. et links the infinitives *audire* and *errare*.
7. amoenae, to be understood with both *aquae* and *aurae*, suggests the pastoral *locus amoenus* that Horace often mentions as the ideal site of his poetic inspiration.

9-20. When as a child I wandered from my nurse and fell asleep in the woods, doves came and covered me with fresh laurel and myrtle leaves: a miraculous sign to the people thereabout, protecting me from snakes and bears.
9. fabulosae: with *palumbes* (12); in mythic *fabula*, doves pull the chariot of Venus; they also bring ambrosia to Zeus (*Od.* 12.62-3). **Vulture in Apulo:** Mt. Vultur, a peak in Apulia a few miles from Horace's birthplace, Venusia (see map 6).
10. Pulliae, if correct, is the name of Horace's *nutrix*; some good manuscripts read *Apuliae*, a difficult reading because it repeats the final word of the preceding line for no apparent reason, and because the meter would require the natural quantities of the first two syllables to be reversed.
11. ludo fatigatumque somno: zeugma: worn out by play and overcome by sleep. The enclitic *-que* connects the two nouns.
13. mirum quod foret: rel. clause of purpose. A standard feature in the early life of any poet-prophet such as Moses or Hesiod is a miraculous event attesting to divine selection.
14-16. Acherontiae, Bantinos, Forenti: three neighboring villages, ranged in order of altitude. Their modern names are Acerenza, Banzi, and Forenza.
17. tuto ... corpore: for this idea of a poet's

divine protection, cf. 1.17.13f.: *de me tuentur, dis pietas mea et musa cordi est.*

18-19. sacra, collata: to be understood with both *lauro* (symbolizing Apollo and the serious themes of high poetry) and *myrto* (symbolizing Venus and the lighter themes of Horace's love poetry).

20. non sine dis: litotic emphasis, combined with juxtaposition of contrasting words, **animosus infans,** to point up the miracle: infants are fearless or spirited only under divine influence.

21-28. I am yours, Muses, in the Sabine hills, cool Praeneste, sloping Tibur, or cloudless Baiae. Because I am your friend, I was unharmed by the battle of Philippi, a falling tree, and a shipwreck.

22-24. Sabinos, Praeneste, Tibur, Baiae: places of refuge from Rome in the hot summer weather, arranged in order of altitude like the villages in lines 14-16. Sabini [sc. *colles*] was the site of Horace's villa; slightly nearer Rome was the fashionable Tibur, called *supinum* because it lies on a hillside. Praeneste, also a few miles east of Rome, was cooled (*frigidum*) by mountain breezes and much favored as a site for the villas of the rich. Baiae, the resort town on the bay of Naples, had many villas built out into the water, as the epithet *liquidae*—both clear and liquid—suggests. See note on 3.1.34.

26-28. Three moments of physical danger in Horace's mainly sedentary life: the battle of Philippi where Horace and the rest of Brutus' army were defeated (see Introduction and notes on 2.7.9-16), the tree that nearly fell on him at his Sabine farm (see note on 2.13), and an otherwise unknown shipwreck on the Lucanian promontory of Palinurus.

29-36. Whenever you are with me, I will gladly go anywhere.

30. navita: as a sailor. Cf. 2.13.14 *navita Bosphorum*, identically placed in an Alcaic stanza. The entrance to the Black Sea was proverbially stormy.

32. litoris Assyrii: vaguely of any eastern shore; **viator:** as a traveler, appositive to the subject like *navita* (30).

33. Britannos hospitibus feros: probably because their Druid priests were said to make human sacrifices of their captives (Tacitus *Annales* 14.30).

34. Concanum: Virgil (*Georg.* 3.463) says it was the Geloni who drank milk with horses' blood. The Concani were a Cantabrian tribe on the northern coast of Spain.

35. Gelonos: a Scythian tribe of what is now southern Russia, famous for their mounted archers. See also 2.9.23, 2.20.19.

36. Scythicum ... amnem: the Tanaïs (mod. Don R.), flowing through Scythian territory (see map 1). Like Horace the lover in 1.22, Horace the *vates* is above harm, *inviolatus.* But here he is being serious.

37-48. You refresh the spirit of Augustus, and give gentle counsel. We know how the Titans and their mob of giants were removed by Jove who controls all things with his just rule.

37-38. militia ... fessas cohortes: after the Battle of Actium, Octavian faced the task of deactivating his legions by settling them in towns throughout Italy (*abdidit oppidis*). His reduction of the military from sixty to twenty-eight legions in a few months was one of his greatest achievements as peacemaker.

40. Pierio ... antro: lit. a cave of the Muses in the highlands north of Olympus; metaph. anywhere poetry is enjoyed. According to Donatus' life of Virgil, Augustus, after returning from his eastern campaigns in 29 B.C., spent four days vacationing at Virgil's villa in Atella in Campania, during which Virgil and Maecenas read him Virgil's recently completed *Georgics*.

41. lene consilium is the gentle advice of good literature; on another level, it may refer to Octavian's moderate treatment of his one-time adversaries, including Horace himself at the Battle of Philippi (line 26). **consilium** is contracted to three syllables, of which the last is elided; the diaeresis is neglected. See note on *principium*, 3.6.6.

42. almae = nourishers (of the spirit).

43. Titanas immanemque turbam: Horace conflates the Titanomachy with the Gigantomachy; as in 3.1.7, we are also meant to think of the recent civil war between Antony and Octavian.

44. sustulerit: got rid of (*tollo*, OLD 13). The subject is *qui* (45).

45. qui ... qui: Jupiter. Like his Indo-European prototype, this Jove rules his two brothers' realms—sea and underworld—as well.

46. regna ... tristia: the underworld.

47. turmas, squadrons, may have been used here to suggest the units into which Augustus organized the equestrian order (OLD c). Horace hints at an allegory in which Augustus is the Roman Jupiter.

49-64. The hundred-handed monsters and the brothers who tried to pile Pelion onto Olympus were some terror. But what could any giant do against the armor of Pallas? Here stood Vulcan, here Juno, and the great Apollo.

49. magnum ... terrorem is contemptuous; scary as they were, Jove and his Olympian allies made short work of them.

49-50. illa ... iuventus: that young crowd is identifiable as the hundred-handers of Hesiod's *Theog.* 671 because it is *horrida bracchiis*. But in Hesiod they fight on the side of Zeus against the Titans. One of their number, Gyas, is mentioned by name below, line 69. **fidens** may be read alone as "presumptuous," or with *bracchiis*.

51. The **fratres** are Otus and Ephialtes, whose attempt to pile Ossa on Olympus and Pelion on Ossa to reach heaven is mentioned in Homer (*Od.* 11.307ff.) and Virgil (*Aen.* 6.582ff.).

53. Typhoeus, whose name suggests Gk. τυφώς, typhoon, was sent by his mother Gaea to avenge the Titans or Giants. **Mimas**, like Porphyrion, Rhoetus, and Enceladus, is a Giant.

55-56. evolsis truncis ... iaculator: instrumental

abl., thrower of uprooted tree trunks.

57. Palladis aegida: the goatskin shield is a fixed attribute of Pallas (Minerva); cf. 1.15.11.

58. possent: deliberative subj. implying doubt or impossibility.

61. Castaliae: the sacred spring at Delphi.

62. tenet: holds, i.e., rules; the stanza is a loose paraphrase of Pindar *Pyth.* 1.39ff.

63. dumeta, silvam: for symmetry, Horace contrasts the thickets of arid Lycia, where according to legend Apollo spends the winter months, with the trees of his birthplace Delos, where he summers. For the palm tree near Apollo's altar on Delos, see Homer *Od.* 6.162f. and the Homeric Hymn to Delian Apollo, 117.

64. Patareus: of Patara, the site of his Lycian temple and oracle. **Apollo:** the name is withheld until the end for emphasis. For the attention Augustus paid to the cult of Apollo, see note on 1.2.32. The Battle of Actium was fought within sight of the temple of Actian Apollo; the emphatic reference to Apollo in this stanza strengthens the symbolism of Augustus's struggle against Antony as a gigantomachy.

65-72. Force without judgment destroys itself; the gods promote tempered force and hate sheer violence, as the fate of Gyas and Orion testifies.

65-67. vis ... vim ... viris: polyptoton, the employment of the same word in several forms. **consili**, deliberate judgment, recalls *lene consilium* (41). **viris:** acc. pl., obj. of *odere*.

68. omne nefas animo moventis: that prompts in its heart every misdeed; this conception of violence is one form of Gk. *hybris*, ὕβρις.

69. testis: sc. *est.* **centimanus Gyas** = 2.17.14. See note above on 49-50.

70. integrae: virginal, as in Catullus 61.36 *integrae virgines*.

71. temptator: assailant, a hapax legomenon perhaps suggested by Gk. πειραστής; see LSJ s.v. πειράω, A IV.2, "try to rape". The hunter Orion's attempt to rape Diana appears in Cicero *Arati*

Phaenomena 672; Hyginus *Astronomica* 2.35 cites Callimachus for this story.

73-80. Earth mourns for its defeated offspring, whose imprisonment continues.

73. Iniecta ... Terra: Gaia lies over her children, whose burial beneath the earth prevents another rebellion.

73-74. dolet ... maeret: the note of sadness sets an elegiac tone for the closure of this ode: "Among the fallen *monstra* Horace could recognize his fellow Romans, and might remember his own position not fifteen years before, *cum fracta virtus et minaces turpe solum tetigere mento* (2.7.11-12)." Commager, 1968, 201f.

74. partus: acc. pl., her offspring, the rebel Giants and Titans. **luridum:** pale, ghastly.

75-76. Aetnen: The Sicilian volcano imprisons Typhoeus, Enceladus, or Briareus in various versions; the monster's hot breath eats at the volcano, but has not eaten through (*nec peredit*) enough to set him free.

77. incontinentis ... Tityi: intemperate Tityos. For his attempt to rape Latona, a bird was set to eat his liver (*iecur*, regarded as the seat of passion).

78-79. nequitiae additus custos: a guard set over his depravity.

79-80. amatorem ... Pirithoum: a lover rather than a rapist, Pirithous accompanied Theseus to the underworld to carry off Hades' unwilling bride Persephone. They were caught there and chained to a rock. Hercules was able to rescue Theseus, but Pirithous remains imprisoned. Cf. 4.7.27-8, *nec Lethaea valet Theseus abrumpere caro vincula Pirithoo*. For other examples of the low-key ending, Fraenkel's "concluding diminuendo," cf. 2.19.29-32, 3.29.62-4.

5

Called the Regulus Ode because of the figure who dominates eleven of its fourteen stanzas, this poem condemns the disgrace of Crassus' Roman soldiers living in Parthian captivity. It is the mission of Augustus to restore Rome's prestige by renewing its militancy, which is vividly illustrated by the story of Regulus. Though consistently adulatory toward Augustus, Horace is avidly militaristic and opposed to the *pax Augusta* as it was applied to Rome's foreign adversaries. The meter is Alcaic.

1-4. As Jove's thunder proclaims him god of the sky, Augustus will be held a god on earth because of his subjugation of the Britons and the Parthians.

1. Caelo: emphatic by position, this affects both *tonantem* and *regnare*. It is contrasted by *praesens*. Cf. 3.4.1, *Descende caelo.* **tonantem:** a standing epithet of Jupiter, used here with causal undertones: because he thunders, we have [always] believed he rules. **credidimus:** a gnomic perfect, expressing a general truth.

2. praesens divus: a god on earth. Though never actually claiming that Augustus was divine, Virgil and Horace both encouraged the growth of an imperial cult; cf. Virgil *Ecl.* 1.7, *Georg.* 1.34f., Horace *Odes* 3.2.21f. Euhemerism, popularized by the Stoic Posidonius, gave emperor-worship a philosophic veneer by claiming that all gods were once mortals honored by men for their good deeds (see 3.3.10 note). In the years after Actium, the line between Octavian's resemblance to a god and actual divinity approached the vanishing point, with the aid of poems like this. For a parody of such flattering proclamations of divinity, see Seneca's *Apocolocyntosis*, the *Pumpkinification of Claudius*.

3. Augustus: a newly conferred title in 27 B.C.; the Princeps had been demilitarizing the empire, reducing its standing army from sixty legions to twenty-eight between 29 and 28 B.C. **adiectis Britannis,** etc: circumstantial abl. abs., as soon as they have been added to the empire. Cf. 3.3.43-44, *triumphatis ... Medis* and note. Horace anticipates the subjugation of the Britons and Parthians as if it were all but a fait accompli. But the project of invading Britain, often mooted during the principate of Augustus, was not carried out, and formal peace was made with the Parthians in 20 B.C.

4. gravibus Persis: the dread Parthians, a favorite subject of Horatian jingoism. See note on 1.2.22.

5-12. Can it be that Crassus' soldiers, captured and married to barbarian wives, have forgotten their birthright while Roman temples are still intact?

5. milesne Crassi, etc.: collective singular. Plutarch reports that after the defeat of Crassus at Carrhae in 53 B.C. some 10,000 Romans surrendered, settled among the Parthians, and married Parthian women (*Crassus* 31). Some took service in the Parthian armies, and even fought against the Romans. **coniuge barbara:** abl. of association with *maritus*.

6. turpis maritus: in predicate relation to *miles*, emphasizing his fallen state. **hostium:** in apposition with *socerorum* (fathers-in-law), an oxymoron because one cannot be a kinsman and a *hostis* at the same time.

7. pro: the interjection, with nom. *curia* and *mores*. **curia:** the Senate house, symbol of Roman dignity. **inversi:** with *mores*, changed, perverted. For the phrase, cf. Cicero, O *tempora, o mores!* (*In Cat.* 1.1).

8. consenuit: the veteran of Carrhae would by now have aged more than twenty-five years, and the youngest would be middle-aged.

9. rege Medo, Marsus et Apulus: the juxtaposition of names, the Parthian king (a "Mede" as often in Horace) with the Marsian and Apulian flower of Roman soldiery, emphasizes the disgrace; the effect is further heightened by the use of *rege*, always a hated name to the Romans.

10. anciliorum: the twelve small waisted shields kept in the custody of the Salii. One of them is said to have fallen from heaven in the reign of Numa, who to protect it from theft ordered eleven others made identical to it. *ancile* is elsewhere a

third-declension noun. **nominis:** i.e., his Roman name, evidence of his national birthright. **togae:** the distinctive badge of Roman citizenship; cf. Virgil *Aen.* 1.282 *rerum dominos, gentemque togatam.*

12. incolumi Iove: referring to the temple of Jove on the Capitoline, and perhaps meant to recall the ceremonial formula *salva urbe atque arce.*

13-28. Regulus was vigilant against such disgrace when he warned the Romans not to ransom back its captured troops: "I have seen the insolence of Carthage, and our men in bonds. But as dyed wool will never lose its stain, no ransomed captive will come home a better soldier.

13. hoc: emphatic: *this* is what Regulus guarded against. **Reguli:** M. Atilius Regulus, Consul in 256 B.C. during the First Punic War, was taken prisoner the following year while commanding the Roman forces in north Africa. Tradition had it that the Carthaginians sent him to Rome to negotiate an exchange of prisoners, under oath to return to captivity if negotiations should fail. The dilemma faced by Regulus, knowing that if he returned after opposing an exchange of prisoners he would be killed by torture, had become a debate topic in the Roman schools of rhetoric where expediency (*utilitas*) was opposed to moral rectitude (*honestas*).

14-15. condicionibus foedis: from the disgraceful terms of peace; dat. with *dissentientis*.

15. exemplo trahentis, etc.: taking this *perniciem* as an example for the coming age. *Traho* with the dat. is a legal term for assigning something to a category. Some editors (Williams, Quinn, Smith) change the manuscript reading to *trahenti*: Regulus then warns against "a precedent (*exemplo*) that promised (*trahenti*) destruction for future ages" (Williams).

17. periret: the original quantity of the final vowel is here retained. It was regularly short in Horace's day. The subjunctive represents the future indicative of Regulus' own words. **immisera-**

bilis: to be taken closely with *periret*, die without pity. Having surrendered, they deserved none.

18. Signa: the captured Roman military standards.

19. affixa delubris: hung as trophies on the temples and shrines of Carthage (even as Crassus' standards were at this writing on display in Parthian temples).

20. militibus: abl. of separation with *derepta*. Such trophies should be taken only over the dead bodies of our soldiers.

21. vidi; vidi ego: chiastic repetition (with *ego*, line 18). **civium:** the word evokes the intolerable humiliation of a *civis Romanus* with his arms pinioned behind his back by a foreign enemy.

22. retorta: twisted back, with **tergo libero** as abl. of place. One does these things to slaves, but never to a free Roman citizen.

23. portas: sc. *Carthaginis.* **non clausas:** litotes; the Carthaginians feel so safe they leave their city gates open. On another level, Horace may be hinting with disapproval at Rome's closing of the doors on the temple of Janus in 29 B.C., symbolizing that the empire was at peace.

24. Marte ... nostro: metonymy, by our soldiery; abl. with both **populata**, ravaged, and **coli**, the inf. obj. of *vidi* (line 21; *bracchia* and *portas* are noun objects). Its acc. subject is *arva*. Regulus' point is that fields once ravaged by our soldiers are now being tilled by them.

25. auro: emphatic by position, and contemptuous of the idea that a citizen would be purchased for gold, like a slave; **repensus** (from *rependo*) is used in an uncommon sense, ransomed. **scilicet** is sarcastic, the point being that a ransomed soldier is anything but *acrior* for his experience.

26. flagitio additis damnum: you add the expense of ransom to the dishonor of capture. But as the next lines show, *damnum* also refers to the personal damage caused by the experience of capture, from which (Regulus argues) the morale of the captured men cannot recover; they are damaged goods and should be written off.

27. amissos colores: its original whiteness.

28. refert: regain; **medicata fuco:** stained with dye, implying false, unnatural colors.

29-40. "True courage, once lost, is gone forever. Once he has tasted the fear of death, a soldier is useless. O shame, that Carthage rises through the infamous ruin of Italy!"

30. curat reponi deterioribus: *virtus* does not care to be replaced in lesser men, i.e., soldiers who are the worse for having been captured. As in 3.2.17, *virtus repulsae nescia sordidae, virtus* is nearly personified.

31. Si pugnat: an *adynaton*; the point is that such a deer will not fight, because the experience of capture will have broken his spirit. **densis ... plagis:** the close-meshed nets.

33. perfidis se credidit hostibus: the enclosure of *se credidit* by *perfidis hostibus* strengthens the irony. *Punica fides* was proverbial with the Romans for treachery.

34. proteret: trample, i.e., crush in battle, **Marte:** a war.

35. restrictis lacertis: like *retorta ... bracchia* in line 22.

36. iners: adverbial, has tamely felt the lash.

37. Hic: the *ille* in 32, i.e., the once-captured soldier. **sumeret:** deliberative subjunctive with **inscius.** He doesn't know that he should secure his life by fighting rather than from an enemy's mercy.

38. pacem duello miscuit: he has confused peace with war, forgetting the stern rule of war (*duello* is an archaic form of *bello*, an appropriate usage for the old-fashioned Regulus).

39. probrosis ... ruinis: abl. of means with **altior.** This is rhetorical exaggeration: Rome had been damaged by the loss of an expeditionary force and its commander, but scarcely wrecked.

41-48. Sternly denying himself the comfort of his wife and children, he held the Senate to his advice and hurried on his way, surrounded by grieving friends.

41. Fertur returns us to the poet's narrative; the subject is Regulus.

42. ut capitis minor: the usual term is *capite diminutus.* Here *minor* takes the gen. *capitis; caput* often denotes a person's civil rights. As a prisoner of war, Regulus is legally the slave of his captors and no longer entitled to his rights, even as a *paterfamilias.*

44. torvus: adverbial, sternly. **humi posuisse vultum:** kept his eyes lowered, in respectful shame toward his onetime fellow citizens.

45. labantis consilio: backsliding from his advice not to ransom the Roman captives. **patres:** the Senators, *patres conscripti.*

46. auctor: appositive to Regulus, the author of the *consilium.* **alias:** the adverb, previously. No one had ever knowingly urged a course of action that would cost his own life.

48. egregius ... exsul: oxymoron, a glorious exile. **properaret:** hurrying on his way to avoid the appeals of his countrymen.

49-56. Though he knew what tortures awaited him in Carthage, he left as calmly as a patron going to his country villa when his clients' lawsuits have been settled.

49. quae ... tortor parabat: pious legend had it that Regulus returned to Carthage as promised and was put to death with shocking tortures (Cicero *De Off.* 3.100, Gellius 7.4), but the story is considered apocryphal. The earliest of the ancient sources, Polybius, does not mention an embassy by Regulus at all.

50. non aliter: with *quam si* (line 53). The quiet simile with which this ode closes is Horace's most admired ending, poignant but unsentimental: "the framework of daily routine provides a context in which the heroic becomes meaningful" (Commager).

52. reditus: plural for euphony, to avoid the repetition of *-um, -um, -em.*

53. clientum: poetic form of gen. pl. *clientium.* **longa negotia:** object of *relinqueret.*

54. diiudicata lite: abl. absolute; a *lis* is any dispute, usually legal. As a *patronus,* Regulus would assist his *clientes* in the settlement of their disputes.

55. tendens: heading toward. **Venafranos ... agros:** Venafrum, like Tarentum, had become in Horace's time a resort area. The details add everyday realism to Horace's picture of the departing Regulus. For the olive orchards of Venafrum, see 2.6.15 and note.

56. Lacedaemonium Tarentum: it was originally a Spartan colony; cf. 2.6.10ff. The epithet links the Spartan self-denial of Regulus with his love of beautiful places.

6

Another jeremiad like the previous ode, beginning with an allusion to Augustus' program of temple restoration. At the heart of Augustus' cultural policy was the revival of old-fashioned religious and moral life to offset the revolutionary political changes that marked the end of the Republic. Recent military defeats and near-defeats are the result of religious neglect and sexual immorality, says Horace, adding a romantic vignette of ancient farm life during the early wars of Roman expansion. This ode, believed to be the earliest of the Roman Odes, recalls the period after Augustus assumed the office of Censor in 28 B.C., began the restoration of some eighty-two temples, and attempted by legislation to raise the standard of morality. Meter: Alcaic strophe.

1-8. You will suffer for past crimes, o Roman, until you restore your shrines and statues of the gods. Piety is the source of power; its lack has brought troubles on us.

1. delicta maiorum, the sins of your ancestors, probably refers to nothing more ancient than the civil wars that ran from 88 to 31 B.C. **immeritus lues:** the adjective has adversative force: though innocent, you will expiate. The folk wisdom here is felt in Aeschylus' drama of the House of Atreus;

cf. the God in Exodus 20:5 who "visits the iniquities of the fathers upon the children."

2. Romane: for the collective singular, cf. Virgil *Aen.* 6.851, *tu regere imperio populos, Romane, memento.*

3. labentis: slipping into decay; with *templa* and *aedis*, which are virtually synonymous.

4. foeda fumo: some were damaged by fire; others were sooty from votive lamps and the like.

5. dis te minorem, etc.: The sacred paradox of *imperium:* you rule because you conduct yourself as one less than the gods.

6. principium: here trisyllabic: elided with *huc*, *prin-cip-yuc.* Syneresis makes the third *i* consonantal; the *i* of the preceding syllable then becomes long by position. Cf. 3.4.41, *consilium.* **exitum:** the final (successful) outcome.

8. Hesperiae ... luctuosae: Italy is the land of the evening star (Hesperus) from the point of view of the eastern tribes (lines 9-14) who have defeated her in battle; personified, she is sorrowful as a result of those defeats.

9-16. Twice have Parthian chieftans crushed our attacks; Dacians and Egyptians have nearly destroyed our city.

9. Monaeses: the Parthian leader who defeated Oppius Statianus in 36 B.C. **Pacori:** another Parthian, Pacorus invaded Syria and defeated L. Decidius Saxa in 40 B.C.

10. inauspicatos: ill-omened through neglect of the gods; this may refer particularly to Crassus, who began his campaign in spite of dire portents: Cicero *De Div.* 1.29 and 2.84, Valerius Maximus 1.6.11. **contudit:** pounded to pieces, from *contundo.*

11. praedam: booty from the Roman army.

12. torquibus exiguis: the torque, an ornamental metal collar worn by the ancient Celts and other Indo-European tribes, is here typical of the paltry wealth of the barbarians (hence *exiguis*). Xenophon reports that among the Persians they could be worn only by those upon whom the king had

conferred them (*Cyropaedia* 8.2.8). **renidet:** beams with pride that; takes *adiecisse* as object.

13-14. paene ... delevit ... Dacus et Aethiops: a rhetorical exaggeration, though during the struggle between Octavian and Antony the Dacians did take sides with Antony. *Aethiops* is used loosely of the Egyptian subjects of Cleopatra. Official propaganda exploited their presence at Actium to portray the battle there as a foreign, not a civil, war. The thought is that civil dissensions at Rome had almost put the city at the mercy of barbarians; *urbem* is dramatically juxtaposed with *Dacus et Aethiops.* **occupatam seditionibus** refers to the struggle between Octavian and Antony.

15. hic classe formidatus: the Egyptian fleet at Actium consisted of 200 ships.

17-24. Marriage is the first victim of our vice; from this our families, homes, and state are ruined; the girl who learns Eastern dancing already plans illicit sex.

17. Fecunda culpae: pregnant with vice instead of babies. **saecula:** the present generation, plural as in "modern times."

18. inquinavere: have befouled, sullied.

21. Motus ... Ionicos: the voluptuous dances of the Greek east, frowned on by Roman moralists. Some disapproved of all dancing.

22. matura virgo: Cf. 3.2.8, *adulta virgo.* Teenage girls are the group most endangered by suggestive dances, according to this age-old complaint. **fingitur:** passive with middle force; she trains herself in the arts of seduction.

23. iam nunc: the present first stage: *mox* (25) is the next stage in her decline and fall. **incestos:** illicit but not necessarily incestuous.

24. de tenero ... ungui: from the tips of her young fingers, combines the sense of youth with intensity of feeling (Plautus *Stichus* 761, Gk. ἐξ ὀνύχων, Automedon *A.P.* 5.129, Plutarch *Mor.* 3C.). Cf. Cicero *Fam.* 1.6.2, *qui mihi a teneris, ut Graeci dicunt, unguiculis es cognitus.* **meditatur** means both to think about and to rehearse.

25-32. Soon she is looking for adulterous affairs with younger men; with her husband's consent, she is for anyone who calls her away from the party.

25. Mox: when she is married she will look for **iuniores adulteros,** lovers younger than her husband. Girls were often married at an early age to much older men.

26. inter mariti vina: at her husband's parties. A wife's presence at her husband's entertainments was itself a novelty. **neque eligit:** she doesn't even choose her partners, but performs on demand (29 *iussa*). This would seem to be at variance with *quaerit* in the previous line.

27. cui donet: deliberative subjunctive. **impermissa:** hapax legomenon, illicit. **raptim:** hastily. Her infidelities are not hasty and furtive, but wide open (29 *coram*) and with her husband's knowledge (29-30 *non sine conscio marito*).

30. institor: the peddler, who often sees the lady of the house.

32. dedecorum: gen. pl., unbecoming pleasures. **pretiosus:** contrasting with the preceding word, high-paying. Horace implies that the husband's consent, like the wife's favors, is well paid for.

33-44. Better parents than these raised the victors of our former wars; our rustic soldiers grew strong on hard farm work.

33. Non his ... parentibus: not from such decadent parents as these.

34. infecit ... sanguine Punico: stained with Carthaginian blood (in the great sea battles of the First Punic War, 264-241 B.C.). The Greek historian and philosopher Posidonius (ca. 135-50 B.C.) stated that the degeneracy of Rome began after the destruction of Carthage in 146 B.C. The idea took hold, and was still current in Horace's time; it appears also in the histories of Sallust and Livy.

35. Pyrrhum: defeated by Manius Curius at Beneventum in 275 B.C. **cecīdit** (<*caedo*): smote, cut down.

36. Antiochum: Antiochus the Great, king of Syria, defeated at Magnesia in 190 B.C. **Hannibalem:** overthrown at Zama in 202 B.C.

37. rusticorum mascula militum proles: interlocking words, carefully chosen for their rugged sound value. The *mascula proles* is meant to be contrasted with the sex-crazed *matura virgo* of line 22.

38. Sabellis: the Oscan-speaking Italians, especially the Sabines, known for their strictness and purity of manners. **ligonibus:** hoes.

39. severae matris ad arbitrium: this rustic matriarch, contrasted with the sluttish wife of lines 25ff., is like the *pudica mulier* in *Epod.* 2.39.

40. recisos fustis: cut sticks of wood for the hearth; faggots.

41-42. ubi ... mutaret: subjunctive of repeated action, new in Augustan poetry and common in Livy and post-Augustan prose.

43. amicum: welcome to the tired oxen. Cf. the sentimental vignette of evening on the farm in *Epod.* 2.63f.: *videre fessos vomerem inversum boves collo trahentis languido.*

45-48. Things grow worse with time; our own descendants will be even worse than we are.

45. damnosa ... dies: ruinous time. **imminuit:** has impaired or spoiled.

46. peior avis: compendious for *aetate avorum peior.*

47. daturos = *edituros*, destined to beget.

48. vitiosiorem: still more wicked than ourselves; Horace compresses four generations of entropy into three lines. For the apocalyptic pessimism, cf. Aratus *Phaenomena* 124, ὑμεῖς δὲ κακώτερα τεξεῖεσθε, Epode 7, *Quo, quo scelesti ruitis*, and Epode 16, *Altera iam teritur.*

7

Horace breaks off the solemn tone of the Roman Odes with this tongue-in-cheek romance making fun of the clichés of love elegy. The plot unfolds (and thickens) as we read. Asterie's lover, a merchant named Gyges, is forced to spend the winter in an Adriatic seaport, his voyage home from Bithynia delayed by stormy weather. While his hostess Chloe tries in vain to seduce him, back in Rome Asterie herself is being tempted by her sexy neighbor Enipeus. Horace advises her to ignore his serenades. Meter: fourth Asclepiadean.

1-8. Why do you weep, Asterie, for Gyges who will return loaded with Asian wares in the spring? He has been driven by winter winds to Oricum, where *he* weeps away the chilly nights.

1. Asterie: as in *comoedia palliata*, the names throughout are Greek; but the characters are Roman. Asterie's starry name suggests her radiant good looks (cf. 3.9.21, *sidere pulchrior*).

2. Favonii: the westerly winds of spring, called *candidi* because of the bright weather they bring in.

3. Thyna merce beatum: rich with merchandise from Bithynia, on the Black Sea (where Catullus spent the year 57-56 B.C. on the staff of Memmius). Originally separate Thracian tribes, Thyni and Bithyni came to be lumped together: Horace uses the metrically more convenient name.

4. constantis ... fide: gen. of description; the archaic gen. *fidē* implies old-fashioned virtue.

5. Gygen: a namesake of the seventh-century king of Lydia; by Horace's time the name was generally used in the Greek east, and connotes wealth. There is a younger Gyges in 2.5.20. **Oricum** is a seaport on the Adriatic coast east of the heel of the Italian boot.

6. post insana Caprae sidera: after the late September rising (or the mid-December setting) of the constellation Capra or Capella, named after the goat that suckled Jupiter. Ovid *Fasti* 5.113, *signum pluviale Capellae*. This stormy season made sailing treacherous.

8. insomnis: nom. with *Ille* (5).

9-16. But a go-between from his lovesick hostess Chloe is tempting him in a thousand artful ways, telling how a wicked woman made

Proetus condemn an overly chaste Bellerophon.

9. nuntius: a message or messenger. The role of go-between was traditionally taken by a maidservant of the woman in love.

10-11. suspirare, uri: indirect statement with *dicens*. **tuis ... ignibus:** causal abl. with *uri*: she burns with the same amatory fires (i.e., for Gyges) as you, Asterie.

12. vafer: with *nuntius* (9), artful, cunning.

13. Proetum: ancient king of Argive Ephyra, whose wife Anteia tried to seduce Bellerophon and accused him of trying to rape her when he rejected her. The story is told in the *Iliad* (6.156-170), but it is part of a much older east Mediterranean repertoire; cf. the thirteenth-century B.C. Egyptian "Tale of Two Brothers." It is told in Genesis 39 of Joseph and Potiphar's wife, and Euripides dramatized it with Hippolytus and Phaedra in the starring roles.

15. Bellerophontae: dat. of reference with *maturare necem*. According to Homer, Proetus sent him with a letter to Antea's Lycian father asking that he be killed. This leads to Bellerophon's glorious mission against the monster Chimaera, but the story is used here to drive home the moral "never refuse a lady in love."

17-24. The go-between tells of Peleus' near-fatal rejection of Hippolyte, in vain: Gyges is still faithful to you. But be careful not to fall for your own neighbor Enipeus.

17. Pelea: Achilles' father Peleus was propositioned by king Acastus' wife Hippolyte, with the same unsatisfactory results. The story is told by Pindar, *Nem.* 4.57ff. and 5.26ff.

19. peccare docentis: with *historias*, stories teaching us to sin, *peccare* having a special reference to sexual misconduct (*OLD* 3b). But Chloe's *nuntius* is comically incompetent, having chosen stories in which the hero emerges unscathed, the more glorious for his rejection of the woman's advances.

20. fallax: i.e., the *nuntius* sent by Chloe. **histor-**

ias monet: tells warning stories. Some mss. read *movet*, brings to bear.

21. scopulis surdior Icari: deafer than the cliffs of Icarus, the Aegean island east of Samos.

22. voces: the words of the *nuntius*. **integer:** morally unblemished, as in 1.22.1, *integer vitae*. The moral tone here contrasts with the earnestness of the Roman Odes. **tibi,** placed here for emphasis, is dat. with *placeat*.

23. Enipeus, named after the river in Thessaly, is Asterie's all-too-available neighbor in Rome. The name suggests his horsemanship (Gk. ἐνιππεύω), his river swimming (28), and perhaps also his reproach (Gk. ἐνίπτω; he calls her *duram* in line 32).

25-32. Though he is a great equestrian and a fast swimmer, lock your door at night and don't look out when he serenades you: remain obdurate.

25. flectere equum: obj. of *sciens*. He would do this on the Campus Martius, also the classic trysting-place of lovers (as for example in 1.9.18-20). Augustus approved of equestrian displays and pageantry; he revived the equestrian *lusus Troiae*, which Virgil obligingly wrote into *Aen.* 5.545ff. with Iülus in the leading role. Horace has his ideal young warrior terrorize Parthians as a dashing cavalryman (*Parthos ferocis vexet eques metuendus hasta*, 3.2.3-4) while the barbarian *adulta virgo* looks on in awe, and the sexy athlete over whom Neobule moons in 3.12 is an *eques ipso melior Bellerophonte*.

28. Tusco ... alveo: the Tiber is the Tuscan channel because it marks the eastern and southern border of Etruria. For swimming in the Tiber as a glamorous and manly activity, cf. 3.12.7 and note.

30. sub cantu: while he is playing, adverbial with *despice*.

31. vocanti: dat. with *difficilis*, with adversative force. Remain difficult to him even though he often calls you hardhearted. The juxtaposition of *duram* with *difficilis* emphasizes that she should be

as obdurate as Enipeus accuses her of being. For *durus* as an erotic *vox propria*, cf. 4.1.40.

8

This invitation to Maecenas to relax over a jug of wine takes a dramatic form as Horace explains why he, a bachelor, is getting ready for a party on the March 1 Matronalia, a festival for married women. He is celebrating the anniversary of his escape from the falling tree as described in 2.13, and he asks Maecenas to forget his public cares and enjoy himself like a private person. This type of sympotic poem has many variations in Horace: 1.9 and 11, 2.11, 3.29, 4.12. Meter: Sapphic strophe.

1-12. Do you wonder why I am preparing sacrifice on a woman's holiday? I vowed this when I was almost killed by a tree: I am observing the anniversary by opening a jar of old wine.

1. Martiis Kalendis: March 1 is the date of the annual *Matronalia*, when married women sacrifice to Juno Lucina on the Esquiline. **caelebs:** not celibate but unmarried. Like Eng. bachelor, the word is rarely used of women.

1-2. quid agam ... quid velint: ind. question depending on *miraris*.

2-3. acerra turis plena: a small incense box full of *tus*, an aromatic tree gum burned in religious ceremonies.

3-4. carbo in caespite vivo: a lump of hot charcoal to burn the incense was placed on an altar of fresh turf, as in 1.19.13 *vivum caespitem*.

5. sermones: learned discourses in Latin and Greek (*utriusque linguae*); acc. of specification with *docte*. For all his learning Maecenas, who is not named until the middle of the ode, cannot figure out what Horace is up to.

7. Libero: to Bacchus, a favorite god of Horace, here honored as virtually a tutelary deity. **funeratus:** a Horatian coinage, "funeraled," described by Williams as "humorously macabre."

9. anno redeunte: i.e., on the first anniversary.

10. **corticem adstrictum pice:** wine jugs were corked and sealed with pitch to keep the air from spoiling the wine.

11. **fumum bibere:** wine jugs were put up in a smoky attic *apotheca* over the kitchen fires; the idea was that the smoke percolated through the earthenware jug and mellowed the wine. **institutae** is mock-pompous.

12. **consule Tullo:** in the consulship of L. Volcacius Tullus (66 B.C.), a year before Horace's own birth. Another Tullus was consul in 33, the year Horace received his Sabine farm from Maecenas.

13-16. Drink, Maecenas, a hundred ladles to your friend's safety and party peacefully till morning.

13. **Maecenas:** the delay of the name until the middle stanza following an earlier honorific invocation (line 5, *docte sermones*, etc.) is a hymnic device.

13-14. **amici sospitis:** gen. for toasts where we use the dat., to your safe friend (the safety of your friend).

16. **clamor et ira:** Horace does not expect a rowdy party, as only Maecenas and he will attend; this anticipates the dismissal from their minds of wars (17-24). For the dismissal of rowdiness from parties, cf. 1.27.1, *Natis in usum laetitiae scyphis pugnare Thracum est.*

17-28. Lay aside your cares of state: our foreign enemies are in defeat and you can enjoy the present as a private person.

17. **civilis ... curas:** concerns of state. As the following lines show, these are purely external, and overlaid with a pastiche of happy news, wishful thinking, and official propaganda.

18. **Daci Cotisonis:** Dacian king Cotiso, who had taken sides with Antony at Actium, was defeated by M. Crassus in 29 B.C.

19-20. **Medus ... dissidet:** Parthian king Phraates was fighting off the rival claims of a pretender named Tiridates, rendering "the Mede" (viz. the Parthians) harmful chiefly to himself (*infestus sibi*).

21. **servit:** is a slave, an exaggerated way of saying that the Cantabrians had been utterly defeated. This was far from the truth: though defeated by Statilius Taurus in 29 B.C., they remained actively hostile to Roman dominion until defeated by Agrippa in 19 B.C. **Hispanae ... orae:** of the Spanish coast. If they had been merely coastal instead of natives of the mountains that still bear their name, the Cantabrians might actually have been as harmless as Horace claims.

22. **sera:** adj. with *catena*, with adverbial force: at last.

23. **Scythae:** pastoral nomads living north of the Black Sea, apparently thrown in here to round out the picture because they lived at the opposite end of the empire from the Cantabrians. There is no record of conflict with them, though Suetonius says they sent goodwill ambassadors (*Aug.* 21.3), and both Virgil and Horace exploited their propaganda value as if they were defeated enemies. Cf. 1.35.9, 2.9.23, 4.5.25, etc., Virgil *Aen.* 8.725 *sagittiferos Gelonos.* **laxo ... arcu:** with their bow unstrung because they no longer wish to fight.

24. **campis:** the steppes of southern Russia. Cf. 3.24.9, *campestres Scythae.*

25. **Neglegens ne qua**, etc.: be careless of whether the people are in some difficulty.

27. **dona praesentis cape**, etc.: the symposiac *carpe diem* theme, as in 1.11.8.

9

The only lyric of Horace in dialogue form, this little mime dramatizes the quarrel and reconciliation of Lydia and her boyfriend. The theme of love renewed by lovers' quarrels is expressed in Terence's *amantium irae amoris integratio est* (*Andria* 555). Horace adds life to his scene by giving each character a distinctive style of self-expression; see appendix C on ethos. Lydia outbids her lover in her successive responses, and has the last word.

Compare the love duet of Septimius and Acme in Catullus 45. Meter: Second Asclepiadean.

1-8. He: "When I was in your good graces, I was happier than the king of the Persians." She: "When I wasn't playing second fiddle to that Chloe, I was getting on famously."

1. Donec: as long as.

2. quisquam: adjectival with *iuvenis*, here = *ullus.* **potior:** with a stronger claim (to your love), more valued. The theme of power is noticeable in this lover's conception of happy love: *vigui, rege* (4), *regit* (9), *cogit* (18).

3. dabat = *circumdabat*, with the dat. *candidae cervici.*

4. Persarum ... rege: proverbial for wealth, power, and happiness, as also in 2.12.21. **vigui:** flourished.

5. alia: abl. of cause with *arsiti*; cf. 2.4.7, *arsit Atrides virgine rapta*, and *quo* with *calet* and *tepebunt* in 1.4.19f. Lydia's *arsiti*, stronger than her boyfriend's *gratus eram*, fits her strategy of one-upmanship. Where his language suggested love as power, hers suggests love as ardency; cf. 13, *torret face.*

7. multi ... nominis: gen. of quality, of great renown. She is name-conscious (cf. *clarior*), repeating her own name twice in these two lines; we never learn his, though she names his rival.

8. Ilia: Rhea Silvia, who made love with Mars and bore Romulus and Remus. See note on 3.3.31-33.

9-16. He: "Chloe is my mistress now, and I'd die for her." She: "Calaïs is *my* new lover: I'd die twice for him."

9. me: emphatic by position, as often in Horace. **Thressa:** feminine of the adjective *Thrax*, Thracian. **regit:** as in Augustan love elegy, she is his *domina.*

10. modos: measures, i.e., songs; internal object of **docta,** trained. Cf. 4.13.7, *doctae psallere Chiae.* The *docta puella* was a perfect girlfriend for the

man of taste in the Augustan age; Propertius makes much of this virtue in his Cynthia. As her name implies, Lydia is not so much the marrying type as a professional courtesan from the Greek east (her rival Chloe is from Greece). When they could afford to do so, such women might agree to a long-term commitment, as this love-idyll implies. **citharae sciens:** for the gen., cf. 1.15.24, *sciens pugnae.*

12. animae: sweetheart. **superstiti:** proleptic: and let her live.

13. me: tit for tat with line 9. In amoebean verse, the answering stanza echoes words in the preceding speech; cf. *Donec* (1 and 5), *vigui* (4 and 8). **torret** contrasts with *regit* (9). **face mutua:** metaphoric for requited love, where the feelings are mutual. Lovers still carry the torch for each other and sing torch songs.

14. Thurini, etc.: more names; Lydia's point is that while Chloe is just another pretty face, Calaïs is somebody. Thurii (*Thurinus* is adjectival) is a wealthy city in southern Italy (see map 2), and we are to understand that Calaïs' father Ornytus is a VIP down there.

17-24. He: "What if old love returned—if Chloe got the gate, and Lydia the open door?" She: "Even though Calaïs is handsome and you are a heel, I'd rather spend my life with you!"

17. redit: like *cogit* in the next line, present indicative instead of future, for greater vividness. **prisca Venus:** their former love personified, with an old-fashioned Roman flavor.

18. iugo cogit aëneo: cf. 1.33.11, *sub iuga aënea.* Horace combines two meanings: the durable yoke of bonding in love (see note on *aëneus*, 3.3.65), and the yoke of subjection under which conquered soldiers were made to pass (*OLD* 5). For love as *militia*, see 3.26.2, *militavi non sine gloria.*

19. flava: blonde, with a hint of adversative force: even if she is blonde. On the Roman preference for blondes, cf. 1.5.4 note. **excutitur:** as a concession to Lydia, Chloe is pictured as driven out with blows.

21. sidere pulchrior: revenge for *flava* (19). The metaphor goes back to Homer *Il.* 6.401. Cf. 3.19.26, *puro similem Vespero.*

22. levior: lighter, i.e., more fickle. **cortice:** cork, made from the cortex of the Spanish oak.

23. Hadria: for the notoriously stormy Adriatic, cf. 1.3.15 and 1.33.15, note.

10

The *paraclausithyron*, a serenade outside a locked door, is a well-known theme of Hellenistic poetry. Appeals to pity, accusations of cruelty, and references to bad weather were all part of the usual pitch, along with warnings that these serenades will some day be sung to another, younger woman. See appendix C and cf. 1.25, to Lydia. Like Damalis, the femme fatale of 1.36, the Lyce addressed here is actually married, but her *vir* (line 15) has other interests of his own. Meter: third Asclepiadean.

1-8. Even if you were a straight-laced Scythian, Lyce, you would feel pity for me as I lie at your door. Don't you hear the wind howling and see the frost?

1. Tanaïn: the Don, which flows through the Russian steppes into the Sea of Azov north of the Black Sea. **si biberes:** i.e., if you were a Scythian; cf. 2.20.20, *Rhodani potor,* 4.15.21 *qui Danuvium bibunt.* For the severe virtue of the Scythians and Getae, see 3.24.9-20. **Lyce:** Gk. "she-wolf"; the name suggests cruelty, with a pun on Lat. *lupa,* prostitute.

3-4. incolis ... Aquilonibus: the north winds that inhabit the Russian steppes.

5. ianua: always the focus of attention in a *paraclausithyron*, this door is being rattled by the wind (though a subject of *remugiat*, it would be rattling rather than moaning).

5-6. nemus inter pulchra satum tecta: the finest city houses had trees planted in the courtyard like

a row of columns: *Epist.* 1.10.22, *inter varias nutritur silva columnas,* Tibullus 3.3.15, *nemora in domibus sacros imitantia lucos.* Cf. the *vestibulum* of Peleus' palace in Catullus 64.293. The detail shows that Lyce and her husband are very well off.

7. glaciet: an emphatic redundancy, since the *positas nives* are already frozen. For the Horatian coinage of a verb from a noun, cf. 3.8.7, *funeratus.*

8. puro numine Iuppiter: the clear sky; cf. 1.1.25 *sub Iove frigido.*

9-12. Put away your pride, or your beauty will be wasted; your Etruscan father didn't raise you to be a faithful Penelope.

10. currente ... rota: abl. abs. In a rope hoist, if the drum or *rota* on which the rope is wound runs backward, the line runs out (*retro funis eat*) and the load drops. So if in her *superbia* Lyce does not attend to her admirer, she will get nowhere with her love life. Emphatically inserted at the middle of the ode, this workman's proverb hints that the suitor is not of Lyce's affluent class (see appendix C, ethos).

11. difficilem: aloof, standoffish, resistant; with *Penelopen*, predicate acc. of *genuit*. The adjective reminds us of Asterie in 3.7, who is also being courted by an eager suitor while her man is away. Horace advises her to hold out: *difficilis mane* (32).

12. Tyrrhenus ... parens: far from an austere Scythian, she was born a luxury-loving Etruscan.

13-20. Though neither gifts, prayers, your lovers' pallor, nor even your husband's infidelity moves you, spare your suppliants: I for one will not endure these vigils forever.

14. tinctus viola: i.e., pale yellow. Sappho compares her lover's pallor to yellowish green grass (LP 31.14).

15. Pieria paelice: abl. of cause with *saucius*, lovesick over a Macedonian mistress; for alliteration and glamorous poetic color, she comes from the valley north of Mt. Olympus associated with the Muses. Lyce's *vir* is probably there on business, like Gyges in 3.7, who has been trading in Bithynia.

16. curvat = *flectit*: softens you, makes you relent. Anticipates *rigida* in the next line.

18. Mauris ... anguibus: hardhearted flexibility after the oaken rigidity of the previous line. As in 2.6.3, "Moorish" is used loosely for north African. The snakes of Libya were notorious: see Pliny *Nat. Hist.* 5.26 on the desert road between Tripoli and Carthage and Lucan's nightmarish account in *Bellum Civile* 9.607ff.

19. Non hoc: emphatic after references to plural suitors, *amantium* (14) and *supplicibus* (16).

19-20. aquae caelestis: rain. **latus:** the lover has been lying on his side in Lyce's doorway. For the sequel, see 4.13.

11

A seduction ode to Lyde, a skittish young hetaera. Horace invokes Mercury, patron of poets (as in 1.10) and erotic commerce (as in 1.30.8), and summons the lyre whose persuasive powers charm even the dead. He prays that Lyde hear the story of the Danaïds, who when forced to marry the sons of Egypt plotted with their father Danaus to murder them in their wedding beds. All were punished in the underworld for their crime with the sole exception of Hypermestra, who warned her new husband to escape. Hypermestra's care for her allotted man is to inspire Lyde. But the dramatic story of Hypermestra's compassion is so captivating that by the end we have all but forgotten Lyde. This is because the ode as a whole is a characteristically oblique tribute to Augustus' spectacular new temple of Apollo, whose portico was lined with statues of the Danaïds (see note on line 25). Meter: Sapphic strophe.

1-12. Mercury, teacher of song, and you, lyre made from a tortoise shell, sing verses for the stubborn ears of Lyde, who is as frisky as a three-year-old mare unready for a mate.

1. te ... magistro: under your tutelage.

2. Amphion: Mercury's apt (*docilis*) student whose playing charmed the rocks to leap up and form the walls of Thebes.

3. tu ... testudo: the Homeric Hymn to Hermes tells how the young god found the tortoise and hollowed out its shell to form the first lyre.

4. callida: with *resonare*, expert at echoing with seven strings (*nervis*).

5. et: to avoid monosyllabic line endings, Horace usually elides a final *et* with the preceding word.

6. amica governs both *mensis* and *templis*.

7. Lyde: a common hetaera's name; see note on 1.8.1. Though ostensibly this ode is aimed at her, she is mentioned only in the third person, here and at line 25.

9-12. velut ... equa, etc.: Lyde's comparison to a young mare is like Lalage's to a heifer in 2.5.1-9. **trima:** three years old; see note on *quadrimum* (1.9.7) and cf. *bimi meri* (1.19.15).

10. exsultim, friskily, is a *hapax legomenon*.

12. cruda: (too) wild for a *protervo marito*.

13-24. You can lead tigers and forests and halt rivers; Cerberus in Hades gave in to your allure; Ixion and Tityos laughed in spite of themselves, and the Danaïds' urn stood dry while you charmed them.

13. comites: predicative with *ducere*: lead them as companions, i.e., in your train. The miracles in these lines are associated with the myth of Orpheus.

15. immanis is best taken as gen. with *aulae*, the vast hall being Hades.

17-20. Cerberus, etc.: most nineteenth-century editors bracketed this stanza as an interpolation, citing stylistic irregularities such as the use of *eius* (18), which is rare in poetry. See Kiessling and Heinze for the arguments against, G. Williams for a defense of its authenticity.

17-19. quamvis ... muniant ... manet: concessive subjunctives, suggesting Horace's noncommittal view of such stories.

17. furiale: Cerberus' head is Fury-like because both have snakes in their hair.

20. ore trilingui: as at the end of 2.19 (*trilingui ore*), Cerberus has one head instead of three, and a triple tongue.

21. Quin et recalls the scene at 2.13.37 (*Quin et Prometheus*), where Sappho and Alcaeus are enchanting the denizens of Hades with their song. Ixion is the Lapith king bound to a wheel in the underworld because he tried to rape Juno. **Tityos,** another would-be rapist, assaulted Latona and was slain by her children Diana and Apollo.

22-23. stetit urna paulum sicca, etc.: the Danaïds are also sexual offenders, having murdered their newlywed husbands.

25-32. Let Lyde hear of the Danaïds' crime and punishment: the empty jar and leaking water, the final fate of a wickedness that could slay husbands.

25-26. et: hendiadys, because their punishment *is* the jar empty of water, *inane lymphae dolium.* **pereuntis** modifies the *lymphae* that runs out the bottom, *fundo imo.* The fifty Danaïds could be seen in the portico of the temple and library of Apollo on the Palatine, where Danaüs and his daughters were set up as statues between columns of *giallo antico.* Horace commemorated the opening of this splendid new building in 1.31; Propertius 2.31 also pays tribute to it, with special reference to the statues, as does Ovid, *Tristia* 3.1.59ff. The turning point to the chief subject is characteristically placed in the poem's central stanza.

28. sera: late, but normally so: "after the proper, normal, or expected time" (*OLD* 1).

29. manent culpas: are in store for sins (*OLD* 4).

30-31. Impiae ... impiae: with this anaphora Horace's rhetorical tone begins to intensify.

33-44. Only one was gloriously false to her oath: "Arise," she said to her young husband, "and escape my evil sisters! I am gentler than
they and will not harm you.**

33. una de multis: Hypermestra, one of fifty sisters. In the Callimachean tradition, Horace recasts the myth as a drama centered on a single heroine. **face nuptuali** = marriage, abl. with *digna.* See appendix C, metonymy.

34. periurum ... in parentem: with *mendax,* untrue to her perjured father, who had agreed to the marriage of his daughters to the fifty sons of Aegyptus but now conspired to murder the grooms.

35. splendide mendax: see appendix C, oxymoron.

37. iuveni marito: tradition gave him the name Lynceus, but like Hypermestra herself he remains unnamed in this poem.

38. longus ... somnus: euphemistic for death, as in 4.9.27 *longa nocte* and Raymond Chandler's thriller *The Big Sleep.*

38-39. unde non times: from a source you do not fear, an urgent brachylogy to avoid the awkwardness of *inde, unde non times.*

40. falle: elude. The word also adds to the layers of deception in the story: *periurum parentem* (34), *mendax virgo* (35).

42. singulos eheu lacerant: are carving them up one by one, each sister mauling her own husband. The interjection *eheu* adds an emotional and dramatic note in the manner of Greek tragedy. **Ego:** adversative asyndeton: But I, ...

44. claustra: poetic pl., the confining space of the marriage chambers where the other killings were going on.

45-52. "I know I will be punished for my clemency, but go while you can with happy omen, and engrave a lament on my sepulcher."

45. Me pater, etc.: like Regulus in 3.5.49f., Hypermestra does her noble act with full knowledge of its cost to herself.

46. peperci: reduplicated perf. of *parco,* governing the dat. *viro misero.*

47. extremos Numidarum in agros: into the

wilds of north Africa, southwest of Carthage. The detail is anachronistic, more Roman than Mycenaean Greek.

48. releget: will banish. *Relegatio* was a specifically Roman form of exile, like being sent to Siberia. Augustus relegated his daughter Julia to Pandateria in 2 B.C. for her scandalous adulteries; Ovid was relegated to Tomis in A.D. 8 for an unknown indiscretion and his scandalous poetry.

49. pedes ... et aurae: the classic land-sea doublet, meaning wherever you can.

51-52. nostri may be taken with both *memorem* and *sepulcro*. Fraenkel writes of this ending, "In the speech of the heroine a dignity of thought and expression, worthy of tragedy, is maintained throughout, and its grandeur is not impaired by the gentle diminuendo with which this ode, like many others, concludes" (p. 197).

12

A poem in the same meter by Alcaeus (frag. 10 LP) seems to have provided the inspiration for this lament by a girl in love, with additional help from a couplet of Sappho (frag. 102 LP). Though it is not as easy for Horace as it was for Catullus to assume a female persona, this vignette slips rapidly and convincingly from the thoughts of a girl who seems able to do nothing to her images of a youth who seems able to do anything. The meter, Ionic *a minore*, appears only here in Horace.

1-6. Girls in love can do nothing, or they will face an uncle's wrath. Love for Hebrus has taken away your will to work, Neobule.

1. Miserarum, in the position of emphasis, means girls in love; for this special meaning of *miser*, cf. Catullus 8.1 *Miser Catulle*, 45.21 *Septimius misellus*; Horace *Epod.* 14.13 *ureris ipse miser*, 1.27.18, 3.7.10. The gen. of characteristic goes with *dare*: it is the lot of poor girls not to give play to their love. For the construction, cf. 1.27.2, *pugnare Thracum est*, it is typical of Thracians to

brawl, and see Allen and Greenough §343c.

2. lavere: wash away, as a young man would do when drowning his sorrows at a party. **aut:** or else (if they do these things).

2-3. exanimari metuentis ... verbera, etc.: to be frightened to death of the lashings of an uncle's tongue. For the proverbially harsh paternal uncle, see *Sat.* 2.3.88, *ne sis patruus mihi*, and Catullus 74. *metuentis* is acc. pl. subj. of *exanimari* and takes *verbera* as obj.

4. qualum: the wool basket; **telas:** the web or upright threads in a loom.

5. operosae Minervae: hardworking Minerva (Gk. Athena), asexual goddess of household crafts. **Neobule** is vocative; she is talking to herself. Neobule is the name of the girl Archilochus courted.

6. Liparaeï: of Lipara, a volcanic island north of Sicily. **nitor** is glossy beauty, glamor, elegance. Cf. 1.19.5, *urit me Glycerae nitor*. Hebrus is named after the river in Thrace.

7-12. He bathes in the Tiber, a horseman, boxer, runner, expert hunter of stags and boars.

7. simul: as soon as. The second half of the poem is a catalog of things Neobule imagines Hebrus is good at when she sees him swimming in the Tiber. **unctos:** anointed with oil after exercise; Ovid *Tristia* 3.12.21; Horace *Sat.* 2.1.7-8, *ter uncti transnanto Tiberim* (as a formula for health).

8. Bellerophontē: abl. of Gk. Βελλεροφόντης, the mythical rider of the winged horse Pegasus.

10. catus: clever, with *iaculari*. **idem:** pronoun, used adverbially: likewise, at the same time (OLD 8).

11. celer: with *excipere*. This vigorous and unattainable Hebrus can be contrasted with the drooping Sybaris in 1.8, who has lost his interest in manly sport since falling in love with Lydia.

11-12. arto latitantem fruticeto: hiding in the dense thicket. The crisp *t*- sounds suggest the crackling of underbrush. Cf. Homer's description of the boar's hiding place in the *Odyssey*, 19.439-43.

13

Long admired as one of Horace's masterpieces, this hymn to a spring on the poet's Sabine farm is full of sensation and feeling. The glassy coolness of the spring's water contrasts with the passionate redness of the kid's blood spilled into it as a sacrifice. As a further tribute to its powers, Horace offers the spring immortality through his verses. Here as elsewhere, the poet expresses his love of nature as it relates to his creative powers. Meter: fourth Asclepiadean.

1-8. Tomorrow, glassy spring, you will receive the living sacrifice of a young kid.

1. O opens the poem on a note of impassioned utterance. **Bandusiae:** the name may be transplanted to the Sabine farm from a *Fons Bandusinus* near Venusia where Horace grew up. The spring itself is mentioned in *Sat.* 2.6.2, *tecto vicinus iugis aquae fons*, and *Epist.* 1.16, *fons rivo dare nomen idoneus*. **splendidior vitro:** more brilliant than glass; in *Met.* 13.791 Ovid borrows playfully from these lines in Polyphemus' praise of the nymph Galatea: *splendidior vitro, tenero lascivior haedo*.

2. mero: undiluted wine, poured into the spring as a libation to its divinity. **non sine:** litotic for *cum*, as in 1.23.3.

3. cras donaberis: the occasion might be the Oct. 13 Fontinalia, when farmers threw garlands into springs and decorated wellheads (Varro, *De Ling. Lat.* 5).

4. cui frons: whose brow; dat. of reference equivalent to a possessive gen.

5. et venerem et proelia: love and battles, i.e., butting contests with his rivals. Horniness is an ancient metaphor for sexual drive. **destinat:** designates or destines, with dat. *cui* and acc. *venerem et proelia*. The more sexually vigorous the animal, the better the sacrifice; cf. *lascivi suboles gregis* below and *Epod.* 10.23, *libidinosus immolabitur caper*.

6. Frustra, in vain, strikes an appropriate note of pathos. The killing of a young animal is felt for what it is. **gelidos:** cool (and clear), contrasted

with *rubro*, red (and warm). The sensory contrasts, heightened by inclusive word order, are a kind of literary synesthesia, essential to the effect of this stanza. Commager sees in Horace's phrase "a suggestion of the transformation of life into art." **tibi:** constructed like *cui*, line 4: your cool streams.

8. suboles gregis: offspring of the herd, i.e., the *haedus* of line 3.

9-16. You offer friendly coolness to the herd; you will become one of the world's famous springs through the tribute of my verse.

9-10. te ... tu: emphatic repetition, as in 1.10.5ff. Here as in the Hymn to Mercury the poet is enumerating the powers or *aretai* of the object of praise. **Caniculae:** for the dog star and the oppressive heat at the time of its rising on July 26, see 1.17.17, note. **hora:** both the season and the time of day when the heat was worst.

10. nescit = *non potest*, as in *Epist.* 1.12.10 *naturam mutare pecunia nescit* and *Ars P.* 390 *nescit vox missa reverti*. **frigus:** from its water as well as the shade trees around it.

11. vomere: lit. plowshare, by metonymy the plow. For the language, cf. *Epod.* 2.63-4, *fessos vomerem inversum boves collo trahentis languido*.

12. pecori vago: the wandering herd, as opposed to the yoked bullocks.

13. nobilium ... fontium: the celebrated springs of legend, such as Castalia (3.4.61), Dirce (4.2.25), and others associated with poetic inspiration. Predicate gen. of the whole, ellipsis for *fies unus nobilium fontium*.

14. me dicente: causal abl. absolute. *dico* here, as often, means to sing, celebrate. **ilicem:** Horace uses *quercus*, *ilex*, and *aesculus* interchangeably for oak.

14-15. cavis ... saxis: the rocks are not themselves hollow, but together they form a natural grotto, a favorite Hellenistic spot for poetic reverie. Horace's descriptive lines immediately fulfill his promise to immortalize the spring.

15. loquaces lymphae: the liquids and sharp

consonants in the final three lines help the waters speak: "a perfect evocation of the sound made by water" (Williams). We are probably also meant to consider the relation of *loquaces lymphae* to *me dicente* in the preceding line. **desiliunt:** the waters, animated like the kid sacrificed over them, leap down; Cf. *Epod.* 16.48, *levis crepante lympha desilit pede*, 2.3.12, *lympha fugax trepidare rivo*.

14

Written for Augustus' return from Spain in 24 B.C., this ode combines Horace's public, heraldic voice (lines 1-12) with his private, sympotic one (lines 17-28), with a central transitional stanza. Meter: Sapphic strophe.

1-12. Like Hercules, Caesar returns from Spain a victor; let his wife and sister welcome him, along with Rome's mothers and young people.
1. Herculis ritu: like Hercules, who as one of his appointed Labors slew the monster Geryon in Spain and came back via Rome. Hercules figures prominently as an official image of Augustus; worshipped under the title *Hercules victor* or *Hercules invictus*, his arrival in Rome from Spain was commemorated in the *Ara Maxima*, and by Virgil in *Aen.* 8.202ff. For Hercules as a model for the deification of Augustus, see note on 3.3.10. **o plebs**, an unparalleled way of addressing the people, is emphasized by the monosyllabic line ending.
2. morte venale petiisse laurum: to have sought a victory whose price is death. Augustus had fallen dangerously ill at Tarraco, and rumors of his death had reached Rome.
3. repetit penatis, returns home, plays off *petiisse laurum* above.
5. mulier: Augustus' wife Livia; though honorifically characterized as *unico gaudens marito*, i.e., as belonging to a class of *univirae* who had been married only once, she had divorced T. Claudius Nero in 38 B.C. to marry Octavian.

6. operata divis: making offerings to the gods.
7. soror: Octavia. **ducis** refers to Augustus' military role in Spain; cf. 4.5.5, *dux bone* (where he is in Gaul).
9-10. iuvenumque nuper sospitum: young soldiers safely back from the Spanish war.
10-11. puellae iam virum expertae: if the text is correct, these would be girls now able to find a husband from among the returning soldiers. For *puella* of young wives, cf. 3.22.2, *laborantis utero puellas.* **male ominatis**, etc.: cf. 3.1.2, *favete linguis.* The hiatus is unusual in Horace, and many attempts have been made to amend the line as a whole.

13-16. This festive day will relieve my cares; I will fear no violence while Caesar rules the lands.
14. tumultum: technical for civil insurrection in Italy. While Horace may seem here to exaggerate his *atras curas*, at the time of this ode the *pax Augusti* was by no means an inevitability. Lines 18, 19, and 28 of the final section carry significant reminders of past *tumultus*.
15-16. tenente Caesare terras is echoed in 4.15.17, *custode rerum Caesare*.

17-28. Go, slave, and prepare for a party. Ask Neaera to come over, but if her doorman puts you off, forget it. I'm not as quarrelsome as I was when Plancus was consul.
18. Marsi memorem duelli: i.e., one that was around at the time of the Social War, ca. 90 B.C., so-called because it was a rebellion of Rome's Italian *socii*, chief among them the Marsi, demanding political equality with Rome. The archaic *duelli* for *belli* lends an old-fashioned flavor.
19. Spartacum ... vagantem: Spartacus' slave revolt of 73 B.C. ranged north from Capua to Cisalpine Gaul, then south again to the toe of Italy, defeating five Roman armies before its annihilation by Crassus in 71.
19-20. si qua potuit ... fallere testa: if any jug

was able to escape.

21. argutae ... Neaerae: clear-voiced, talkative, clever Neaera; dat. obj. of *dic*. The adjective combines the singing and conversational talents of Neaera, who is named after a famous Greek hetaera of the fourth century B.C.

22. murreum: reddish-brown. For the exotic coloring and the stylishly tied-back hair, see note on 1.5.4, *flavam religas comam*.

23. per invisum ... ianitorem: a competing lover may have bribed Neaera's doorman to harass other callers.

25. albescens ... capillus: metonymy for advancing age. Having embarked on his lyric career at an age when Catullus was five years dead, Horace made himself the poet laureate of middle age. Though only forty-one at this writing, he was prematurely gray, *praecanus* (*Epist.* 1.20.24).

26. litium et rixae cupidos: though no doubt mellowed from his hot youth, Horace will admit in *Epist.* 1.20.25 that he is still *irasci celer*.

27. non ... ferrem: potential subj., I would not have put up with this.

28. consule Planco: 42 B.C., when he was a student revolutionary at the Battle of Philippi. In this good-humored way, Horace renounces his own tempestuous past.

15

Chloris, a woman of mature years married to a man of no wealth, is carrying on like her sex-crazed teenage daughter Pholoe. This poem advises her to act her age. The names are Greek, the advice Roman, the humor of the situation altogether Horatian. Meter: second Asclepiadean.

1-6. Put an end to your shenanigans, lady; you are closer to your funeral than you are to the games girls play.

1. pauperis Ibyci: the first of several comic nonsequiturs, Ibycus has little money but is named after a famous sixth-century poet and bon vivant.

2. nequitiae: worthless naughtiness. **fige modum:** lit. nail a limit, drives home the poet's message vigorously.

3. famosis ... laboribus: her well-known Herculean efforts to play the nubile girl; cf. 1.3.36, *perrupit Acheronta Herculeus labor*.

4. maturo propior ... funeri: closer to a timely death.

6. stellis nebulam spargere: another nonsequitur: she is trying to scatter her middle-aged cloud among the nubile stars. For stellar metaphors of good looks, see note on Asterie, 3.7.1. **candidis** denotes beauty as well as brightness: *Epod.* 11.27, *ardor aut puellae candidae aut teretis pueri*.

7-16. What suits your daughter Pholoe doesn't suit you, Chloris. She can set upon Nothus like a maenad or a she-goat in heat; you should stick to your wool—not the lyre, roses, and the dregs of the wine.

8. et te: you also, obj. of *decet*.

9. expugnat iuvenem domos: storm his house and overcome his resistance. Horace's readers would see this too as a comic nonsequitur, as such aggression was a normally masculine role.

11. amor Nothi: objective gen.; Gk. νόθος = son of an irregular union of a citizen with a noncitizen. The implication is that except in a purely physical way he would be no great prize.

13. te: adversative asyndeton, in a position of emphasis: but as for *you*, ...

13-14. nobilem ... Luceriam: a town in Apulia famous for its wool. Strabo 6.284 compares it with that of Tarentum (on whose *dulce pellitis ovibus* see 1.6.10 note).

16. poti ... cadi: wine jars drained **faece tenus**, to the dregs. **vetulam**, aging, in apposition with *te* (13), may be read as a substantive, hag. Horace may be suggesting a well-known Hellenistic statuette of a drunken old woman clinging to a wine jar, a Roman copy of which survives in Munich. See also 4.15.5

16

Another ode on the subject of simple living, like
1.31, 2.2.16 and 18, 3.1. The paradox that less is
more fits both Stoic and Epicurean schools of
thought, and is a favorite with Horace. The legend
of Danaë is cited as proof of the power of wealth,
but its cost is *cura* and greed for more. Horace
then offers his own case as proof of the power of
simple living. The poem is addressed to Maecenas,
whose patronage is represented as a kind of safety
net to Horace's poverty (line 38). Meter: third
Asclepiadean.

**1-8. A well-guarded tower would have kept
Danaë chaste, but the gods laughed: for a god
turned into gold would make a sure entry.**
   1. Danaën: daughter of Argive king Acrisius,
who tried to prevent her from bearing children
because of an oracle that death would come to
him from his daughter's son.
   3. tristes excubiae: a savage vigil, with gen.
vigilum canum. **munierant:** pluperfect indic. instead
of perf. subjunctive makes the action more vivid;
not until the next stanza do we learn that this is
the apodosis of a contrary-to-fact condition: they
had defended her—or would have, had not ...
   4. adulteris: illicit lovers.
   6. pavidum: nervous. **Iuppiter et Venus:** he
because he will make love to Danaë and will father
Perseus, she as the patroness of sex.
   7. risissent: emphatically placed for humorous
effect, this is the climactic word of the eight-line
sentence. What follows explains why they laughed.
fore: ind. statement depending on the thought
implied by *risissent.*
   8. converso in pretium deo: causal abl. abs.:
because the god was transformed into a bribe.
Jupiter, who takes on various forms in myth to
gain access to his many "wives," came to Danaë as
a shower of gold. Horace rationalizes the myth.

**9-16. Gold overcomes all obstacles: it ruined
the house of Amphiaraus and overcame Philip of**

Macedon's rivals; gifts ensnare sea commanders
too.
   9. satellites: bodyguards, henchmen.
   10. amat: likes, has a tendency (*OLD* 11-12).
   11-12. auguris Argivi: Amphiaraus. Polyneices
bribed his wife Eriphyle to make him join in the
seige of Thebes. Forseeing his own death, Amphi-
araus charged his son Alcmaeon to avenge him by
killing Eriphyle.
   13. diffidit: pf. of *diffindo*, split open, with a pun
on the pres. of *diffido*, lack confidence in.
   14. vir Macedo: Alexander's father Philip of
Macedon, who said any city could be taken to
whose gates an ass laden with gold could be
driven.
   15-16. navium ... duces: added perhaps as a
reference to the Roman admiral Menodorus, who
kept changing sides in the struggle between Octa-
vian and Pompey. **illaqueant:** pres. indic., snare or
enmesh.

**17-20. Anxiety and greed grow with money. I
have wisely avoided notoriety, great Maecenas.**
   18. maiorum ... fames: the hunger for greater
things, i.e., material wealth. Cf. *Aen.* 3.57, *auri
sacra fames*, Greek πλεονεξία.
   19. conspicuum: proleptic, so that it is in full
view.
   20. equitum decus: Maecenas' refusal to accept
a rank higher than the equestrian gave him a
special distinction, and suited Augustus' political
courtship of the wealthy equestrian order. The
epithet makes Maecenas an example of ambition
under control.

**21-32. The more each person denies himself,
the more he will get from the gods. I avoid the
rich, being richer in my lesser wealth. My little
farm is a better lot than the governorship of
Africa.**
   22. nil cupientium ... castra: the camp of those
who are content with what they have. **nudus:**
unencumbered; in the military context, unarmed.

In this metaphor Horace is a **transfuga**, a deserter from the "party of the rich," *divitum partis*.

25. contemptae ... rei: despised property, possessive gen. with *dominus*.

26-27. quam si ... occultare ... dicerer: than if I should be said to hide in my barns whatever the busy Apulian grows.

28. opes inops: the juxtaposition emphasizes the paradox, a form of expression favored by the Stoics and made popular in works like Cicero's *Paradoxa Stoicorum*.

30. segetis certa fides meae: i.e., the dependable yield of my field. For a less dependable farm, cf. the *fundus mendax* in 3.1.29-32.

31-32. fulgentem ... fallit: goes unappreciated by one who gleams with the command of fertile Africa. Horace refers to the coveted proconsulships of north Africa, whose agricultural wealth made graft highly profitable. **sorte beatior** collectively modifies *rivus, silva*, and *fides*, all of which are to be understood as subjects of sing. *fallit*.

33-44. Though my farm is not in the choicest region, I am not destitute; if I were, you, Maecenas, would help me. Better to reduce my needs than expand my fields. Happy the man who has little, but enough.

33. Calabrae mella ferunt apes: for the fine honey of Calabria (the heel of the Italian boot; see map 6), see 2.6.14f.: *[Tarentum] ubi non Hymetto mella decedunt*.

34. Laestrygonia ... in amphora: a reference to Formiae, said to have been the capital of Homer's Laestrygonians.

35-36. Gallicis ... pascuis: pastures in Cisalpine Gaul, which produced a celebrated wool (Pliny *Nat. Hist.* 8.190).

39. contracto ... cupidine: abl. abs., if my desire for wealth is reduced.

40. porrigam: stretch, make them last.

41-42. quam si ... continuem: than if I made the *regnum* of Alyattes (king of Lydia) continuous with the *Mygdoniis campis*, the plains of Phrygia

(once ruled by King Mygdon, *Il.* 3.186). Horace imagines a ranch covering the entire northwest quarter of Asia Minor.

43. cui: short for *ei cui*, dat. with *bene* and *obtulit*.

44. quod satis est: a favored expression of Horace (cf. 3.1.25, *Epist.* 1.2.46), conveying his Epicurean distaste for excess. This included his literary aesthetic as well: *Sat.* 1.1.20, *iam satis est. ... verbum non amplius addam*.

17

A birthday ode for Lucius Lamia, who belonged to a distinguished family from Formiae (see appendix A). Horace writes him some lines on the fanciful genealogy of which such families were fond. The second half of the poem anticipates the rural celebration of his birthday, for which the crow predicts rain. Meter: Alcaic strophe.

1-9. Aelius, descended from Lamus the Lestrygonian, king of Formiae and the river Liris, ...

1. vetusto nobilis ab Lamo: a tongue-in-cheek compliment, making fun of the fashion of tracing family roots to sound-alike ancient heroes; thus Virgil in the *Aeneid* traces Julius Caesar's lineage back to Aeneas' son Iülus, and in 5.117 derives the Memii from Mnestheus, the Sergii from Sergestus. The hard-headed old emperor Vespasian laughed at flatterers who tried to run his pedigree back to a companion of Hercules (Suetonius *Vesp.* 12). Lamus is mentioned in Homer *Od.* 10.81 as king of the Lestrygonians.

2. quando: the relative adverb, since. **ferunt:** they say that; governs an indirect statement that would be in prose *priores Lamos hinc (ab Lamo) denominatos esse*.

3. et: coordinate with the previous *et* (2); people also say that the whole line of descendants will be so named in the recording *fasti*.

4. fastus: acc. pl., with *memores*, chronological lists of consuls. Horace gallantly predicts (rightly, it happens) that the family will be named on these lists: they were even more prominent during the early empire.

5. auctore ab illo: i.e., Lamus, whose gigantic people attacked Odysseus and his men in hopes of eating them. Ordinary cannibals in the family tree would be nothing to boast about, but these are *Homeric* cannibals. Lines 2-4 are to be read as a parenthetical digression.

6. Formiarum: Formiae, a coastal town in southern Latium near the Campanian border.

7. princeps: adverbial, = *primus.*

7-8. innantem Maricae litoribus ... Lirim: the Liris, which floods Marica's shores. This refers to the mouth of the river Liris, which spreads out into marshes near Minturnae. Marica was a nymph, mother of Latinus (Virgil *Aen.* 7.47). She had a sacred grove near the mouth of the Liris.

9. late: far and wide, as in Virgil *Aen.* 1.21, *populum late regem.*

9-16. Tomorrow there will be a storm, according to the old crow: gather firewood while you can, and prepare to celebrate with your household slaves.

9. cras, repeated in line 14, contrasts with *vetusto* (1) and the fanciful genealogy that occupies the first half of the poem. **nemus:** object of *sternet* (12).

10. alga ... inutili: before its use as a fertilizer was discovered, seaweed was proverbially useless; cf. *Sat.* 2.5.8, *vilior alga.*

11. Euro: the rainy wind, *aquosus Eurus* (*Epod.* 16.54).

12. aquae augur: from the Gk. ὑετόμαντις, augur of rain; folk wisdom attributed to the crow or raven the ability to predict rain. Virgil *Geor.* 1.388-9 describes how it calls rain:

tum cornix plena pluviam vocat improba voce
et sola in sicca secum spatiatur harena.

The superstition about the crow plays off the legend in the first half, which places the Homeric king Lamus in Formiae.

13. annosa cornix: its proverbial longevity was stretched by Hesiod to nine generations of men (Plutarch *Mor.* 415c).

14. Genium: the presiding divinity of each person, conceived of as born and dying with him and often perceived as a kind of alter ego; in Greek, the δαίμων: "thy demon, that's the spirit that keeps thee." Shakespeare *A&C* 2.3.19. In Horace, cf. *Epist.* 2.2.187-9: *Genius, natale comes.* Anyone who denies himself reasonable pleasures is cheating his genius, *suom defraudans genium* (Terence *Phormio* 44). Similarly here, *Genium mero curabis et porco.*

15. porco bimestri: when ready for weaning at two months, the suckling pig was fit sacrifice for a feast in honor of the Lares.

16. famulis: household slaves; the word is cognate with *familia* via Oscan *famelo*. **operum:** gen. of separation with **solutis.**

18

A lover of rustic life, Horace was also a lover of rustic religion, though not necessarily a believer. This prayer on the occasion of the country *Faunalia* recalls the description of Faunus' theophany in 1.17. This idyll of an entire landscape peacefully celebrating its own deity is "a little masterpiece of refined simplicity" (Fraenkel). Meter: Sapphic strophe.

1-8. Come gently to my fields and flocks, o Faunus, if I make sacrifice in your honor.

1. Nympharum ... amator: among the attributes of the Greek Pan that Faunus collected was his tireless sexuality. By the nymph Marica (3.17.7) he was the father of Latinus. **fugientum** = *fugientium.*

2. meos finis et ... rura: i.e., his Sabine farm, as in 1.17.

3-4. lenis incedas abeasque ... aequus: the predication is in the adjectives, chiastically arranged in positions of emphasis. Paganism recognized its deities as potentially hostile; thus the god's mood was as important as his presence. **alumnis:** the nursing young of the flock. *Alumnus* is from *alo*, nourish. Here dat. with *aequus*.

5. pleno ... anno: temporal, lit. at the full year, the Nones of December (line 10), December 5 by our calendar. **cadit:** i.e., as a sacrifice. In accordance with the *do ut des* principle of Roman religion, Faunus is *lenis* and *aequus* in return for what Horace does in this stanza.

6-7. larga ... vina: plentiful wines. **Veneris sodali ... craterae:** because wine and love go together, the mixing bowl is personified as Venus' companion.

7. vetus ara, etc.: asyndeton; *vetus* adds an appropriately old-fashioned note.

9-16. Man and beast alike are happy when you are here.

9-15. Ludit ... vacat ... spargit ... gaudet: asyndeton unifies the details into a connected whole including animals, trees, and peasants.

9. herboso campo: in central Italy the grass would still be green in December.

10. Nonae ... Decembres: complementing *pleno anno* (5), the detail is important to distinguish this rural holiday from the city festival, the February 15 Lupercalia.

11-12. otioso cum bove: the bullock, not the horse, was the Italian draught animal: he too would be idle on a holiday.

12. pagus: i.e., everybody in the district. This is the source of Eng. "pagan," though in the early empire *paganus* came to mean civilian as opp. to military.

13. audaces: predicative in this clause, the point being not that the wolf is strolling around but that the lambs feel no fear. For Faunus' protection of the livestock, cf. 1.17.2ff.

14. spargit agrestis frondes: imputes intention to the *silva*, as if it were scattering the ground with leaves in Faunus' honor.

15. invisam ... terram: the *fossor* hates it as the cause of all his drudgery. **pepulisse:** a humorous

note; he beats the earth in his dance. The infinitive (perfect with present force) completes *gaudet*. **fossor:** lit. "ditcher" or farm worker, with connotations of uncouthness (cf. Catullus 22.10). The final vignette reminds readers today of a painting by Bruegel, who specialized in Flemish peasant scenes.

16. ter: in a three-step dance, *tripudium*; cf. 4.1.28, *ter quatient humum*.

19

In 1.27 Horace restored order at a symposium where a brawl had broken out. Here, a nameless antiquarian has run amok with pedantic prattle, and Horace takes over as *magister bibendi* to propose toasts in honor of Murena, recently elected to the college of augurs. The goal of tonight's activity will be lots of noise (23 *dementem strepitum*) and hot sex (28 *torret amor*). The meter is second Asclepiadean.

1-8. You carry on about ancient chronology, but you are silent on the subject of how to get this party started.

1. Quantum distet: ind. question, how far in time Inachus (the first king of Argos) is from Codrus (the last king of Athens). Antiquity was marred by such discussions: Suetonius reports that the Emperor Tiberius used to ask the grammarians such questions as "Who was Hecuba's mother?" and "What did the Sirens sing?" (*Tib.* 70.3).

2. non timidus mori: An oracle had declared that the Dorians would overrun Attica unless the king were killed. Codrus (like the Roman Decii), determined to sacrifice his life for his city, entered the Dorian camp disguised as a slave, picked a fight with some soldiers, and was killed.

3. narras here (as often) implies that the speaker is saying more than anyone wants to hear. **genus Aeaci:** Aeacus, father of Peleus and Telamon, was the grandfather of Achilles, Ajax, and Teucer, and great-grandfather of Neoptolemos: all Greek heroes of the Trojan War.

4. bella sub Ilio: poetic plural: there were many battles, but one Trojan War "beneath sacred Ilium," i.e., beneath its walls.

5. Chium ... cadum: a jug of wine from Chios.

6-8. mercemur, temperet, caream: indirect questions and deliberative subjunctives dependent on *taces*. These vital questions are not being answered. **aquam temperet:** water for mixing with wine was first warmed to temper its chill.

7. quota: sc. *hora*, at what hour.

8. Paelignis ... frigoribus: proverbial for a deep chill; the district of Paeligni in the Apennine highlands east of Rome was particularly chilly. **taces:** governs the indirect questions in this stanza, *quo ... quis ... quo ... quota*; you are silent about these matters.

9-20. Drink to the day, the hour, and Murena; mix the drinks strong for poets, mild for others to prevent brawls. What a pleasure to rave: where's the music?

9. Da lunae, etc.: addressed to the attendant slave (10 *puer*); the understood object is *cyathos*, measures of wine, which govern the gens. *lunae, mediae,* and *auguris Murenae.* For the idiom, cf. 3.8.13, *sume, Maecenas, cyathos amici sospitis centum.* Greek symposia customarily began with three libations. **propere:** quickly.

10. auguris Murenae: implies that the gathering is to celebrate Murena's recent election to the augurate.

11-12. tribus aut novem ... cyathis: let the cups be mixed with three or nine *cyathi* of wine. The Romans measured by twelfths, the *cyathus* being one-twelfth of a *sextarius*, which was about a pint. The drinks might therefore be one-quarter to three-quarters wine, the rest water. **commodis:** adverbial, suitably to each drinker's preference.

13. Musas ... imparis: the nine Muses make up an odd number.

14. ternos ter: the devotee of the nine Muses will take the strong mixture, nine measures of wine to three of water. **attonitus vates:** the inspiration

of the poet or seer (*vates*) was traditionally associated with the power of wine; for the poet's divine madness, see Plato *Phaedrus* 245a. Horace is indulging in good-humored arrogance in claiming the strongest drink as the poet's privilege.

15. tris ... supra: more than three: the Graces prescribe the weaker mixture.

16. rixarum metuens: fearful of brawls.

17. nudis ... sororibus: as in 4.7.5, and cf. Veritas in 1.24.7. Beginning in the third century B.C., when female nudity in art became accepted, the Graces were regularly represented in the nude. **iuncta:** they are always represented with hands joined.

18-19. cur ... cessant: i.e., why aren't they playing? For the note of impatience, cf. *propere* (9). **Berecyntiae ... tibiae:** flutes of the type used in the orgiastic worship of Cybele, as celebrated on Mt. Berecyntus in Phrygia. One of the pair had a curved end, which gave it a deeper tone.

19. flamina: notes (as produced by a wind instrument).

20. pendet: vase paintings illustrate the custom of hanging musical instruments on the wall of the party room when they were not in use. **tacita:** grammatically with *lyra*, but applicable to *fistula* as well.

21-28. Let's get on with festivities the whole neighborhood will hear. Rhode is after you Telephus, and I am hot for my Glycera.

21. parcentis dexteras: hands that hold back from the work of the party.

22-23. invidus ... Lycus: the grumpy neighbor; the adjective denotes ill will, but not necessarily envy.

24. vicina: a lady in the neighborhood, possibly connected with old Lycus but too hot for him to handle (*seni non habilis Lyco*). She may be comparable to the *devium scortum* Lyde in 2.11.21f.

25. Spissa ... coma: instrumental or causal abl. The dense head of hair suggests Telephus' youth, as opp. to Horace's balding middle age. **nitidum:**

for *nitor* as a mark of beauty, cf. Pyrrha in 1.5.13, Chloris in 2.5.18, Hebrus in 3.12.6, etc.

26. puro vespero: the clear evening star, i.e., in a clear sky. For stars as metaphorical of beauty, see note on Asterie, 3.7.1. **Telephe:** one of the guests, an ideal young erotic type here as in 1.13, 4.11.

27. tempestiva ... Rhode: perhaps the *vicina* of line 24, she is ready for Telephus, even if *non habilis* to old Lycus. Her name is from Gk. *ῥόδον*, rose, perfect in the context of line 22, *sparge rosas*. The adjective is used of ripe fruit and nubile women. Cf. Chloe in 1.23.12.

28. lentus ... amor: slow, like a smoldering fire. Glycerae: a hetaera's name, from Gk. *γλυκερά*, sweet.

20

A friendly warning to Pyrrhus, who has seduced Nearchus away from an unnamed lady whose wrath will be terrible. The looming battle over the handsome boy will be Homeric, and Horace borrows an epic simile from the *Iliad* of a lioness in search of her missing cubs. The poem ends with a vignette of Nearchus coolly taking his ease as he watches the carnage waged for his sake. Meter: Sapphic strophe.

1-8. Don't you see how dangerous it is to disturb the lioness's cubs, Pyrrhus? You will soon run when she comes to reclaim Nearchus, and there will be a mighty duel.

1. moveas: disturb, with abl. of manner *quanto periclo*.

2. Pyrrhe: named after Achilles' brash son, also known as Neoptolemus—the first of many Homeric tags in this little mock epic. **Gaetulae ... leaenae:** except for the local detail (Gaetulia was in the wilds of northwest Africa, outside the Roman *limes*), the metaphor comes from an epic simile in *Il.* 18.318ff.

3-4. inaudax ... raptor: oxymoron; the adjective appears to be a Horatian coinage.

6. Nearchum: the object of the sexual rivalry. Horace reveals the situation slowly, piece by piece.

7. grande certamen: in apposition with *repetens*, which means taking steps to recover. **tibi ... cedat:** whether the *praeda* be given to you, ind. question depending on the sense of *certamen*.

8. maior an illa: or if she prove the stronger. *illa*, accepted by most editors, is Peerlkamp's emendation for ms. *illi*.

9-16. While you and she prepare for battle, the one who will decide the contest indifferently cools himself in the breeze.

11. posuisse: depends on *fertur*; the ind. statement has the effect of putting Nearchus at some distance from the coming fray, though he is both judge and prize.

12. palmam: the palm of victory, trodden underfoot as a sign of his indifference: the winner may go unrewarded.

14. sparsum ... umerum capillis: another picturesque detail, like *nudo sub pede* (11-12). For thick, long hair as a sexual attribute of males, cf. Telephus in the previous ode, *spissa nitidum coma* (25), and contrast the tied-up hairstyle of vamps like Pyrrha (see note on 1.5.4).

15. Nireus: the most beautiful Greek in the Trojan War after Achilles, according to *Il.* 2.673. Cf. *Epod.* 15.22, *formaque vincas Nirea*.

15-16. aquosa raptus ab Ida: Ganymede, the young Trojan prince carried off by Jupiter to be his sexual companion and cupbearer. The epithet *aquosa* echoes Homer's *πολυπίδακος* Ἴδης (*Il.* 14.157), Mt. Ida of the many springs.

21

Whimsically addressed to a jar of old wine bottled in the year of Horace's birth, this follows the formal conventions of a hymn of invocation to a deity, but in substance it is a drinking invitation to Corvinus (see appendix A). The mixture of hymnic and sympotic themes and the frequent wordplay connecting them are especially appropriate for Corvinus, whose interests in poetry, rhetoric, and philology were well known. Meter: Alcaic strophe.

1-12. O pious jar, whatever your powers or title, descend at the bidding of Corvinus; philosopher though he is, he will not neglect your virtues.

1. nata: the jar was "born" when it was filled and stored away in the year of Horace's birth. **Manlio:** L. Manlius Torquatus, cos. 65 B.C. Cf. *Epod.* 13.6, *Tu vina Torquato move consule pressa meo.* Roman years were marked from the traditional date of the city's founding (753 B.C.) or by the name of the consul of the year.

2-4. seu ... seu ... seu: hymnic form includes an initial recital of the powers, virtues, or titles of the god invoked. The items listed in the first stanza fill this requirement. **querelas:** contrasted with **iocos,** and alluding to the different effects or powers of wine.

4. pia testa: Horace stops short of calling the jar a divinity but credits it with pious duty. Wine was stored and shipped in disposable earthenware crocks. There is a hill in Rome between the Tiber and the Porta Ostiensis called the Mons Testaceus (now Monte Testaccio) made up entirely of fragments of such jars.

5. quocumque nomine: under whatever pretext (*nomen, OLD* 15b) a play on the bookkeeper's term for a ledger entry (*OLD* 22) and the catchall phrase in a prayer which ensures that none of the god's titles have been omitted. **lectum:** select. A vintage is prepared in varying degrees of quality. For Massic wine, see 1.1.19 note.

6. moveri = *dimoveri,* i.e., brought down from the attic *apotheca* where it was stored, as in *Epod.* 13.6. There is a ritual meaning here also, as cult objects were "moved" or manipulated during ceremonies. **bono die:** an auspicious day or other special occasion.

7. descende: a play on the invoked god's descent from heaven (cf. 3.4.1, *Descende caelo*) and the

descent of the jar from the attic.

8. languidiora: poetic acc. plural; mellower, after about forty years of aging.

9. ille: Corvinus. **Socraticis ... sermonibus:** philosophical talk, with special reference to the Socratic dialogues of Plato. Philosophy was another of Corvinus' many interests. **madet:** more word play: though soaked in philosophy, Corvinus is not unwilling *vino madere.*

10. negleget carries religious overtones of failure to revere the gods and their rituals (*OLD* 3a, 5b); cf. 3.2.30 *Diespiter neglectus,* 3.6.7 *di multa neglecti.* **horridus:** prickly, austere; used adverbially. He will not be so austere as to neglect you.

11. prisci Catonis: ancient Cato, i.e., Cato the elder (234-149 B.C.), the stern moralist whom Cicero revived as his spokesman in *Cato Maior de Senectute.* The adjective connotes old-fashioned austerity.

13-20. Your powers are many: you make stubborn hearts yield, you unlock the secrets of the wise, you give hope and courage to the troubled and weak.

13-19. Tu ... tu ... tu ... te: a catalog of *aretai* or benign attributes is a standard feature of hymns and invocations.

13. lene tormentum: oxymoron; a gentle twist of the arm (<*torqueo*). **admoves:** apply. **ingenio ... plerumque duro:** a usually harsh nature.

14-15. sapientium curas: the problems of philosophers.

15-16. iocoso ... Lyaeo: instrumental; *Lyaeus* "the Releaser" was one of the titles of Bacchus.

16. retegis: uncover, reveal. While under the influence, men reveal their philosophic problems and secret doctrines.

18. cornua: another way of saying *spem ... viresque,* hope and determination. The horn in Roman literature as in Hebrew symbolizes the assertive virtues. Cf. Psalms 148:14, "He exalteth the horn of his people." Ovid *Ars Amat.* 1.239, *tum pauper cornua sumit* (imitating this passage).

19-20. iratos ... regum apices: transferred epithet, the crowns of angry kings. **trementi** modifies *pauperi* above and takes *apices* as its object: the pauper who fears the great man's wrath. For the generalized meaning of *regum*, see 1.4.14 note.

21-24. Your attendants Bacchus, Venus, the Graces, and bright lights will make you extend your stay till morning.

21. Te Liber, etc.: invocations were also expected to list the companions of the god invoked, as in the second stanza of 1.30. **si laeta aderit:** i.e., in a happy spirit, not as a cause of jealous brawls.

22. segnes nodum solvere: slow to break their clasp; the Graces are usually painted arm in arm; cf. 3.19.17, *Gratia nudis iuncta sororibus*. Called *Charites* in Greek, they personify grace and delight.

23. vivae: alight; as long as they stay burning, the party can go on. Thus the *lucernae* are treated as if they were divine companions of the *pia testa*. **producent:** will prolong you, i.e., your presence among us.

22

Horace dedicates a pine that overhangs his Sabine villa to the goddess of nature. In her character as Diana Nemorensis, she has a special relationship with trees, but the poet also invokes her as the goddess of childbirth. This combination of powers is probably inspired by Catullus 34.9-16. In its economy, Horace's poem emulates Hellenistic dedicatory epigrams, literary compositions in the style of actual inscriptions. Its third affinity is to the formula of prayer. Meter: Sapphic strophe.

1-8. Keeper of mountains and groves and helper of women in childbirth, triple goddess, let the pine overhanging my villa be yours with the yearly offering of a boar practicing his sidelong thrust.

1. Montium custos begins the recital of powers that normally begins any prayer.

2. puellas is a surprise for women in childbirth, but their patron is a *Virgo*, and the word suggests this is their first (and most dangerous) childbirth. Italian girls, regularly married in their early teens, would become pregnant early in life.

3. ter vocata: because she is *triformis* (4), and because prayers and rituals often called for triple repetitions. Cf. the formula of burial in 1.28.36, *iniecto ter pulvere*. **adimis:** rescue.

4. triformis: in her triple aspect, she was the celestial Luna, terrene Diana, and Hecate of the underworld. Her statue placed at three-way crossroads gave her the name *Trivia*.

5. tua is predicative, the point of the entire prayer. For Horace's thoughts about falling trees, see 2.13.1-12, 2.17.27-29, 3.4.27, 3.8.6-8.

6. quam: symmetrical with *quae* in line 2. Object of subjunctive *donem* at the end, it introduces a relative clause of purpose: so that I may present it with the blood of a boar. The antecedent is *pinus*. **per exactos ... annos:** through the completed years, i.e., at the end of each one.

7. verris: gen. of *verres*, an uncastrated male pig, boar. Cf. the kid sacrificed to the *fons Bandusiae* in 3.13. **obliquum meditantis ictum:** practicing his sidelong thrust. The position of the boar's tusk requires an oblique, slashing blow; Ovid *Her.* 4.104, *obliquo dente timendus aper*.

8. donem: *donare* takes the acc. of the recipient, instrumental abl. of the thing offered (here *sanguine*).

23

Horace tells a thrifty country housewife that no showy sacrifice is needed to win the favor of the gods. The ode contrasts simple rural worship with the theatrical grandeur of state religion, and there may be a literary metaphor between the lines: in poetry, as in piety, more is not necessarily better. Meter: Alcaic strophe.

1-8. A simple offering, Phidyle, is all you need to insure your crops from blight and your young animals from sickness.

1. Caelo: to heaven; dat. of direction of motion. **supinas:** palms upward, the customary attitude of prayer; cf. Virgil *Aen.* 1.93, *duplicis tendens ad sidera palmas.* **tuleris** = *sustuleris.*

2. nascente luna: at the beginning of the lunar month, when the household gods received their monthly sacrifice. Cf. 3.19.9, *da lunae novae.* **Phidyle:** from Gk. φειδωλή, sparing, thrifty.

3. placaris: for the long *i*, cf. 4.7.20-1, *dederis, occideris*; the *-i* in the fut. perf. indic. is lengthened by analogy with the original quantity in the perf. subjunctive. **horna fruge:** with this year's crop: probably a sheaf or wreath of the new grain.

4. avida ... porca: cf. the *porco bimestri* of 3.17.15. The pig is lustful, ardent, greedy because its vitality makes it a better sacrifice: cf. the *lascivi suboles gregis* in 3.13.8 and the *libidinosus caper* in *Epod.* 10.23.

5. pestilentem ... Africum: the hot, unhealthy Scirocco withered vegetation. Cf. 2.14.16 and note.

6. fecunda: because it is teeming with grapes. **sterilem:** here active: producing barrenness, crop-killing.

7. robiginem: rust, a blight so prevalent that *Robigo* was propitiated as a goddess at the Robigalia on April 25. Ovid *Fasti* 4.907ff. **alumni:** the young livestock, born the preceding spring.

8. pomifero grave tempus anno: bracketing word order highlights the oxymoron; the oppressive season (cf. *Sat.* 2.6.19, *autumnus gravis*) comes at the fruitful [time of the] year. *Pomifero* has the partitive force that is not uncommon with adjectives; cf. *Epod.* 2.29, *annus hibernus*, Sallust *Jugurtha* 107.1, *nudum et caecum corpus*, the unprotected and blind [part of the] body.

9-16. The sheep now grazing on Mt. Algidus is for priests to sacrifice; enough for you to wreath the household gods with flowers.

9. Nam introduces the justification of the previously stated general idea. **quae:** the *victima* (12). **nivali Algido:** some twenty miles southeast of Rome, on the eastern edge of the Alban Hills. Though proverbially cold (1.21.6 *gelido Algido*), it would not be literally snowy at this time of year.

10. quercus inter et ilices: two kinds of oak, not clearly differentiated; see note on 3.13.14. Livestock fed on the mast from oak trees.

11. Albanis in herbis: pastures in the Alban Hills southeast of Rome. The college of pontiffs owned pasture land in the area, where livestock was raised for the large public sacrifices.

12. victima: used of the larger sacrificial animals, such as oxen and full-grown sheep (*bidens*, line 14). **pontificum securis:** emphasis is on the former word; this is a sacrifice for high priests, not housewives.

13. cervice: ellipsis for *sanguine a cervice.* **te nihil attinet:** it does not concern you.

14. temptare: attempt to influence (*OLD* 6); cf. similar words for beseeching the gods: *fatigent* (1.2.26), *laccesso* (2.18.12). As object understand *deos* from *parvos deos*. **bidentium:** full-grown sheep. According to Hyginus, sheep were ready for sacrifice when two prominent incisors displaced the two front milk teeth on the lower jaw. This happened at about two years.

15. coronantem: with conditional force: if you crown your little gods, you need no big sacrifice. **parvos ... deos:** the Lares, honored with garlands on the Kalends, Nones, and Ides of each month, and on other special occasions. The words are contrasted with *multa caede.* **marino rore:** "sea dew" or rosemary, an aromatic shrub used by those who could not afford incense.

17-20. If your hand is clean, no costly victim but salted meal will propitiate your gods.

17. immunis: free of the obligation incurred by pollution or wrongdoing, and perhaps giftless. The word in all its senses is emphatically placed and contains the climax of the ode.

18. non sumptuosa, etc.: adversative: though not made more persuasive by a costly victim; *blandior* agrees with *manus*.

19. mollivit: gnomic perfect: softens, appeases. **aversos Penates:** indisposed to heed prayer. The assumption in sacrifice is that even if everything seems well the gods *might* be nursing a grudge and should be regularly appeased; hence the epithet. By Horace's time Lares and Penates were interchangeable names of household gods.

20. farre ... et ... mica: hendiadys for salted meal, coarsely ground *far* with a grain (*mica*) of salt. This *mola salsa* regularly accompanied sacrifice. **saliente:** jumping in the heat of the fire as it crackles. The greater the crackling when the salted meal was thrown on the fire, the better the omen.

24

A lengthy sermon on Roman materialism, contrasting the noble simplicity of savage tribes with the corruption engendered in Roman life by the unrestrained pursuit of wealth. Horace ties the civil disorders of the recent past (i.e., before 28 B.C.) to the race for indecent wealth. The subject brings this ode close in spirit to the Roman Odes, 3.1-6. Meter: second Asclepiadean.

1-8. You may be very rich and live in a seaside villa, but if Doom has driven her nails into your roof you will not escape fear and death.

1-2. Intactis ... thesauris: abl. of comparison. **divitis Indiae:** India seemed rich because only her expensive exports (ivory, gemstones, perfumes, silks) reached the Romans.

3-4. caementis ... tuis: instrumental abl., with your landfill; see note on *caementa*, 3.1.35. It was fashionable for the very rich of Horace's time to build houses out into the water on landfill.

4. terrenum omne ... et mare publicum: all the dry land as well as the sea that belongs to everybody; *publicum* stresses the arrogant seizure of public space for private building.

5-7. adamantinos ... clavos: her nails of adamantine, a material harder even than iron. Hyperbaton gives them extra rhetorical impact.

6. summis verticibus: in your rooftops. The nails mean you may go this high and no higher. **dira Necessitas:** fate, personified as a builder. Cf. 1.35.18-20, where *saeva Necessitas* is represented with an array of building materials.

9-16. Better the life of the Scythians and Getae, who live in primitive simplicity and stern morality.

9. Campestres ... Scythae: steppe-dwelling Scythians; for more on these distant nomads, see note on 3.8.24. Their strict marital virtue is touched on in 3.10.1, but this may have more to do with the vaporings of popular philosophy than with the historical Scythians, who according to Strabo (7.300) practiced communal marriage. Like his contemporary Strabo, Horace invests them with the virtues of noble savages.

10. rite: in accordance with tradition, duly.

11. rigidi Getae: the rugged, stern Getae lived north of the lower Danube, in mod. Romania.

12. immetata ... iugera: their acres are unmeasured because they hold land communally. **liberas:** free for all, free from private ownership.

13. Cererem: grain, by metonymy.

14. longior annua: for more than one year at a time (to avoid exhausting the soil, or because it was poor in the first place). Caesar notes this practice among the Suebi (*BGall.* 4.1); Horace treats it less as a practical measure than as a sign of their virtuous indifference to property.

16. aequali ... sorte vicarius: a substitute of equal rank. **recreat:** revives. Horace's point is that instead of a condition common in late Republican Italy where family farms were bought up and turned into large *latifundia* owned by absentee landlords and worked by slaves, land among the Getae stayed in the hands of working proprietors who helped each other. For a picture of the early Italian peasantry as the backbone of Roman strength, see 3.6.33ff.

17-24. There, a mother is kind to her or-phaned stepchildren and a wife is faithful; her dowry is virtue, and the price of sin is death.
17. Illic: among the Sythians and Getae. **matre:** abl. of separation with *carentibus*.
18. temperat: with dat. *carentibus privignis*, exercises restraint toward her motherless stepchil-dren. Stepmothers are proverbially harsh toward their husbands' earlier children because they favor their own children as heirs.
19-20. dotata ... coniunx: another folk type, a wife with a big dowry who browbeats her less wealthy husband. **nitido:** radiant, slick, good-looking. Cf. the handsome Telephus in 3.19.25, *spissa nitidum coma*.
22. metuens alterius viri: apprehensive of any man other than her husband.
23. certo foedere: descriptive abl., *castitas* with an inviolable bond of marriage.
24. est is to be understood both with *peccare* (the regular verb for sexual misbehavior) and with *mori*.

25-32. Let whoever wishes to put an end to civil war restrain license and win the veneration of posterity. We have come (alas!) to hate virtue and want it out of sight.
25. O quisquis: a thinly veiled allusion to Oc-tavian. This ode is relatively early, generally dated ca. 28-27 B.C. Like the Roman Odes, it is ad-dressed to no particular person.
27. Pater urbium: vaguely honorific, meant to suggest *pater patriae*, an official title of supreme honor not officially awarded to Augustus until 2 B.C.
28. subscribi statuis: to be inscribed on bases of statues of himself. Like coins and buildings, statues were an important instrument of Augustan politics. By the time of this ode, the Mausoleum of Augus-tus was already well under way, with a colossal bronze statue of the emperor planned for its peak.

30. postgenitis: grandiloquent for *posteris*. **quate-nus:** inasmuch as, since.
31. incolumem: while it lives, i.e., in a living person. The national savior will be revered only in the distant future, because we hate such men during their own lifetimes.
32. sublatam (*esse*): we want *virtus* removed. **invidi:** envious as we are of it. This and the previous line refer obliquely to Julius Caesar, whose avenger Octavian had declared himself to be.

33-44. What good are laments without laws, laws without morals—if the distant parts of the world do not expel the merchant, and if seamen conquer the seas; if poverty overcomes scruples and deserts the path of virtue?
34. reciditur: is cut back, pruned.
37. pars inclusa caloribus: the torrid zone around the equator, which some geographers believed to be hot only at its northern and south-ern edges (Strabo 2.97).
38. Boreae: dat., to the north.
39. duratae ... solo: hard-frozen to the ground.
40. mercatorem: like other writers of diatribe, Horace often expresses disapproval of merchants and the risks they take in the pursuit of lucre: 1.1.18, 1.31.11, 3.1.26, 3.29.60.
40-41. callidi ... navitae: clever sailors, whose conquest of the sea is perceived as a sin against nature; cf. 1.3.23f., *impiae non tangenda rates transiliunt vada*. Their transgression is implicitly linked with that of merchants who employ them.
42. magnum ... opprobrium: in apposition with *pauperies*, poverty wrongly seen as a disgrace. Horace often maintains the view that decent *pauperies* is an honorable state; in 1.1.18 he mocks the *mercator* who is *indocilis pauperiem pati*. **iubet:** bids people to do or endure anything (*quidvis et facere et pati*), without scruple.
44. arduae: steep, grammatically linked with *virtutis*, logically with *viam*. See appendix C, hypal-lage, and cf. Ophelia's "steep and thorny way to heav'n" in *Ham.* 1.3.48.

45-54. Let us discard our useless gems and gold. We must remove the sources of greed and train weak minds with sterner stuff.

45-47. nos ... nos: subj. of *mittamus* (50).

45. in Capitolium: Suetonius reports that Augustus deposited 16,000 pounds of gold and 50 million sesterces' worth of gems and pearls in the shrine of Capitoline Jupiter (*Aug.* 30).

46. turba faventium: a crowd of approving citizens.

50. scelerum: gen. with *paenitet*, if it repents us of our crimes.

52. elementa: the ingredients or first beginnings of our *cupidinis pravi*.

52-53. tenerae nimis mentes: i.e., the minds of the young.

53-54. asperioribus ... studiis: presumably warfare, as in 3.2.1-6. Augustus revived the organization of upper-class boys into *collegia iuvenum* where they were trained in physical culture and horsemanship before graduating into the *Juventus* at seventeen, where they received military training. For the *lusus Troiae*, an equestrian display put on by the *Juventus*, see note on 3.7.25.

54-64. Boys ingorant of riding and hunting play with hoops and dice, while their fathers cheat their partners. Riches grow, but something is missing.

55. ingenuus: freeborn. Augustus promoted social stratification by creating new forms of social distinction such as assigning theater seats by rank, discriminating between slave-born *libertini* such as Horace's father and *ingenui* such as Horace himself.

57. Graeco ... trocho: a hoop, less manly because it is Greek.

58. seu malis: or, if you prefer. **vetita ... alea:** though dicing had been officially banned for generations, Suetonius *Aug.* 71 reports even Augustus had a weakness for it.

59. periura ... fides: perjured trust, broken promise; subj. of *fallat*.

60. consortem socium: his business partner. *sors*

in this context is shared capital.

61-62. indigno ... heredi: for the unworthy heir as the best argument against accumulating wealth, see 2.3.20, 2.14.25, 4.7.19.

64. curtae: proleptic adj.: something is missing, and it is incomplete. **rei** is dat. of reference, material wealth.

25

Horace reenters the ecstatic dithyrambic world he essayed in his Hymn to Bacchus (2.19). Now he does so with a specific worldly purpose, the praise of *egregii Caesaris*. Nowhere does Horace venture farther from the rational and ironic style of his light poetry than in this ode, whose formal pretext is to introduce some grand poem in honor of Augustus. The single, almost offhand mention of his actual theme (line 4) is characteristic, however; so is the grandiloquent way of describing his own poetry (17f.). Meter: second Asclepiadean.

1-6. Where are you taking me Bacchus? In what grotto will I compose Caesar's praise?

1-3. Quo ... quae ... quibus: three rhetorical questions, arranged in a tricolon crescendo with each question longer than the one before. The structure is appropriate to the tone of magnificence. **tui plenum:** full of your inspiration; cf. 2.19.6, *plenoque Bacchi*. **nemora, specus:** groves and grottos are appropriate to a god whose rituals are celebrated outdoors in the country; they are also suited to a poet who feels the affinity Horace often declares for nature; cf. 13f., *ripas et vacuum nemus mirari libet*. **mente nova:** a new mood. Swift changes of impulse are characteristic of orgiastic states.

5-6. meditans ... inserere: getting ready to place Caesar's glory among the stars; *meditor* is used of practicing lines, e.g., Catullus 62.13; here we are to imagine the poet composing and testing them out loud in the echoing *antris*. **consilio Iovis:** in Jove's council; implies that Jove is already considering the deification of Augustus.

7-14. I shall sing a new song, like a Bacchant in the Thracian wilderness.
7-8. insigne, recens, ... indictum: substantive, something distinctive, original, unsung. Athenaeus 14.622c-d quotes a Greek song to Bacchus containing a similar, perhaps ritual, claim to originality.
8-12. Non secus ... ut: just as ... so, lit. no differently [than] ... so. Horace compares the Bacchant's choice of natural surroundings to his own.
9. exsomnis stupet: lack of sleep promotes the hallucinatory state indicated by *stupet*. **Euhias:** the Bacchant, a name suggested by the ritual cry *euhoi!*
10. Hebrum: river in Thrace, where Bacchus' rituals were especially orgiastic.
12. lustratam: trodden; in the original sense, also purified. **Rhodopen:** a mountain range in Thrace.

14-20. O lord of Naiads and Bacchants, I begin a mighty and perilous but pleasant task.
14. Naïadum potens: lord of the Naiads or river nymphs; cf. 1.3.1, *diva potens Cypri*.
15-16. valentium ... vertere: strong [enough] to uproot tall ash trees; poetic usage substitutes the simple verb for the compound *evertere*. Bacchants in their religious frenzy had miraculous physical strength.
17-18. nil parvum ... nil mortale: asyndeton in the grand style; *nil mortale loquar* indicates both the divine inspiration and the permanence in time of the verses he will utter. **humili modo:** in the low or simple poetic style. **Dulce periculum:** oxymoron, referring to the risk of joining a god in his primal form. But Horace seems also to make the admission here that poetry in the ecstatic high style of encomiastic verse is risky business. Further reflections on such an enterprise can be found in 4.2, where Horace declines the pleasure—and the risk.
19. Lenaeë: Gk. title of Bacchus, god of the wine vat (λην óς).

20. cingentem refers ambiguously to Horace and/or Bacchus. Bacchus is represented in art with his brows in a vine shoot (*pampino*); his followers are likewise adorned.

26

A half-serious farewell to the world of love, written in the style of a Hellenistic epigram. The imaginary inscription in which a retiring tradesperson dedicates the tools of his or her trade to the appropriate deity was a long-established literary type by Horace's time. A similar dedication is suggested in the Pyrrha Ode, 1.5.13ff. The meter is Alcaic strophe.

1-8. Not long ago I served with glory as a soldier of love; now the temple wall of sea-born Venus will hold my weapons.
2. militavi: a common figure, to which Horace returns in 4.1.1f. Cf. Ovid *Am.* 1.9.1: *Militat omnis amans, et habet sua castra Cupido*.
3. arma: the weapons of lovers, as enumerated in line 7. **defunctum bello:** like the empty bottle that is a "dead soldier," the lover's lyre (*barbiton*) is worn out from playing serenades.
4. hic paries: the wall of the shrine where votive offerings are hung, here to the left of the goddess's image.
5. marinae ... Veneris: Hesiod represents her as born from the sea. The epithet is appropriate here because the sea in Horace is typically stormy and disastrous.
6. ponite: to his attendants, as in 1.19.13f., *hic verbenas, pueri, ponite turaque*. The verb, like *hic paries* in line 4 and *hic, hic* here, invites us to imagine an actual scene of dedication rather than the inscribed dedication suggested by Hellenistic epigrams.
7. funalia, vectus, arces: the lover's "weapons." The *funalia* are torches made of rope dipped in wax or resin that light his way as he goes serenading; the crowbars (*vectes*) are used to pry open

the door of an uncooperative hetaera; *arcus*, bows, has puzzled commentators. They may be some tool for opening the proverbially stubborn door of the mistress, or Cupid's bows.

9-12. A final prayer, o goddess: give Chloe a lash for her arrogance.

9. beatam ... Cyprum: blessed as her favorite haunt.

10. Memphin: Herodotus 2.112 mentions a temple in Egyptian Memphis to ξείνη 'Αφροδίτη; the epithet is used of those giving or receiving hospitality, as would be appropriate to the goddess of hetaeras. Bacchylides frag. 30 Maehler also mentions a "snowless Memphis." **Sithonia:** an ornamental epithet for snow; the Sithonii were a tribe of Thrace, which poets had decided was snowy. Also, the Chloe who is giving Horace a chilly treatment in this ode may herself be a Thracian: 3.9.9, *Thressa Chloe*.

11. sublimi flagello: with your uplifted lash. This detail is a novel extension of the conventional image of Venus driving her victims under her brazen yoke (1.33.11, 3.9.18) as if they were defeated soldiers in the ritual of surrender.

12. tange: either to make Chloe fall in love, or to chastise her. In the latter case, *tange* would be understatement: Horace wants her soundly thrashed. English schoolboys refer to corporal punishment as being "touched up." **Chloen:** a reluctant young girl in 1.23, she is Lydia's blonde Thracian rival in 3.9. We are to infer that she is a hetaera who feels she has better things to do than trifle with the likes of Horace. **semel:** with *tange*, implying that once will be enough. **arrogantem** has causal overtones: because she is scornful.

27

A propempticon to a lady named Galatea, who is on her way out of town for a fling with some new lover. Horace good-naturedly suggests she may be headed into stormy waters, and reminds her of the story of Europa, who had bitter regrets after going for a joyride on the back of a bull (Jove in disguise) who took her to Crete. The long mythic digression follows the pattern of the Hypermestra Ode, 3.11. It recalls a Hellenistic epyllion by Moschus, as well as the monologue of Ariadne on the beach in Catullus 64.132-201—though here Horace concentrates more on Europa's feelings of guilt than her anger at a betrayer. The story has a happy ending when Venus appears to inform Europa that she is Jove's "wife" and will give her name to Europe. Meter: Sapphic strophe.

1-12. May bad omens attend the wicked as they start their journey; but for the person I care about, I shall call up a good sign.

1. parrae recinentis: a hooting owl. The *re-* prefix implies revocation (of a journey started) as well as repeated hooting. Horace's satirical love of magical hocus-pocus goes back to his mockery of the witches in *Sat.* 1.8 and in Epodes 5 and 17.

2. ducat: lead or draw, probably more jargon of witchcraft. Its subjects are *omen*, *canis*, *lupa*, and *vulpes*.

2-3. ab agro Lanuvino: from the country around Lanuvinum, a town on the Appian Way leading to Brundisium, Galatea's port of departure (see maps 5 and 6).

3. rava lupa: a yellowish gray she-wolf.

4. feta ... vulpes: a fox who has just given birth.

6. per obliquum: i.e., crossing their path at an angle.

7. mannos: the ponies pulling their cart, fashionable Gallic animals like the ones pulling the cart in *Epod.* 4.14. **cui timebo:** the one for whom I feel anxiety (as opp. to the *impios* in line 1).

8. providus auspex: redundant, a prophetic prophet, augur, diviner.

10. imbrium divina: prophetic of rains.

11. oscinem: acc. of *oscen*, a bird whose cry (rather than its flight) is prophetic. The epithet is comically irrelevant, as in this case it is the flight and not the cry of the raven that will be prophetic. In apposition with **corvum**, the raven. **suscitabo**: with *ego* (7), I will rouse with prayer the prophet raven before the bird that predicts rain (the raven) returns to the standing pools (9, *stantis repetat paludes*).

12. solis ab ortu: from the east, a lucky quarter of the sky. Horace's language, a parody of impressive-sounding magical jargon, indicates that he will prevent rain from spoiling Galatea's trip by calling forth a raven from a lucky direction before it can be seen flying to the swamps, which would mean rain.

13-24. Good luck to you, Galatea, wherever you go, but I worry about stormy weather. May such tempests fall upon the wives and children of my enemies!

13-14. sis ... vivas: concessive subj. with *licet*, granted you should be happy and remember me.

15. laevus ... picus: more superstitious double-talk; in Roman augural practice, a woodpecker on the left would be lucky; but Horace follows the Greek practice here (facing north instead of south while taking the auspices), making it unlucky.

16. vaga cornix: the roving crow, augur of rain (3.17.12, *aquae augur annosa cornix*).

18. pronus Orion: setting Orion (in early November); the tumult is transferred from the weather at this season to Orion itself. **ater**: with *Hadriae sinus*, black with storms.

19-20. quid ... peccet: lit. how it sins, i.e. how it deceives. **albus**: clear, cloudless, free of storms. **Iapyx**, the west-northwest wind, favors anyone sailing from Italy to Greece.

21-22. caecos ... motus: blind or unforeseen outbreaks.

22. orientis Austri: of the south wind as it starts to blow; for the more common formula, cf. Virgil *Aen.* 3.481 *surgentis Austros*.

24. verbere: with the pounding of the surf.

25-32. Europa was similarly trusting of the tricky bull, but then grew frightened when at sea. A moment before, she was picking flowers unawares. The remainder of Horace's poem would have reminded his readers of an epyllion by Moschus (fl. ca. 150 B.C.; Gk. text and comm. in Hopkinson, *A Hellenistic Anthology*), but here we get different details. Moschus concentrated on what happened before Europa reached Crete.

25-26. niveum doloso credidit tauro latus: elegantly chiastic, a golden line were it not spread over two lines. The artful bull is Jupiter in disguise, who lured Europa from the Phoenician shore and carried her to Crete, where she bore him Minos and Rhadamanthus. The story, which now takes over the ode, is brought in as a paraenetic exemplum or paradigm showing how excursions that seem a good idea at the time can go wrong.

26-27. scatentem beluïs: teeming with sea monsters.

27. medias ... fraudes: dangers on every side.

28. palluit audax: oxymoron: brash though she was, she now turned pale with fear at the *pontum* and the *medias fraudes* (for *palluit* + acc., cf. *Epist.* 1.3.10). Horace's treatment of the story concentrates on Europa's state of mind.

29. studiosa: eagerly intent on, with gens. *florum* and *debitae coronae*. These nouns may also be understood as objective gens. with *opifex*.

31. nocte sublustri: in the dim night following her departure.

33-44. As soon as she reached Crete, she was sorry: "What have I done? Is this some dream? Was this trip really better than picking flowers?

33. centum tetigit potentem: the rattling *t*-sounds briefly recall Catullus 63, which is also about a traveler's regrets: *citato cupide pede tetigit* (63.2).

33-34. centum ... oppidis: causal abl. with *potentem*; the tradition of Crete's hundred cities goes back to Homer's Κρήτην ἑκατόμπολιν, *Il.* 2.649.

34. Pater: The first word out of Europa's mouth is significant; the end of her speech consists of his stinging rebuke as she imagines it (57-66). See appendix C, ethos, and cf. the first words of Attis' lament in Catullus 63.50: *Patria o mei creatrix, patria o mea genetrix.*

37. Unde quo, from what place and to where, has less to do with her change of place than her altered state, from a *filia* to an outcast.

38. virginum culpae: for the offence of a girl (generalizing pl.). **Vigilans:** awake, as opp. to dreaming.

39. vitiis carentem: i.e., still innocent, the victim of a nightmarish *imago vana*.

41. porta ... eburna: abl. of way by which. False dreams come out through the ivory gate, true dreams through the gate of horn (Homer *Od.* 19.562ff., Virgil *Aen.* 6.893 ff.).

45-56. "If only I could hurt that monster now! O gods, let me be killed by lions or tigers before I waste away.

45. infamem: infamous. *Infamia* was the legal term for an official state of disgrace under which a citizen convicted of such crimes as seduction or rape of a citizen lost certain rights. **iuvencum,** bull-calf or bullock, is abusive for *taurum.*

47-48. frangere enitar ... cornua: as if she could. The effect is to emphasize her impotence: even if the bull were still there, she could scarcely hurt him by attacking his horns (symbolic perhaps of his sexuality). **modo multum amati ... monstri:** of the just now much loved ... monster; emphasizes her swing of feeling, even as she remembers.

49-50. Impudens ... impudens: adverbial, shamelessly. Europa returns to the feelings of guilt with which she began her lament. **Orcum moror:** put off my death.

52. nuda: she is not so frantic with guilty grief that she does not consider the picturesque aspect of her imagined death: she dwells upon her fine figure, her lovely cheeks (53-4 *decentes malas*), her tender, juicy body (54-5 *tenerae sucus ... praedae*), and her overall good looks (55 *speciosa*). This vanity makes her a less serious and tragic figure

than Catullus' Ariadne, whose semi-nudity in 64.63-67 represents her total self-neglect: *toto ex te pectore, Theseu, toto animo, tota pendebat perdita mente* (69-70).

53. turpis macies: the unlovely shrinkage caused by starvation. C.L. Smith notes here "the outcropping of a deep-seated feeling of the ancients ... that one entered the underworld in the form in which he left life." Cf. for example the mangled shade of Deiphobus in *Aen.* 6.495f. But Europa does not reflect that she too might arrive mangled.

54. sucus: bodily fluid; cf. the girl in Terence's *Eunuchus* 318, *corpus solidum et suci plenum.*

56. pascere tigris: be food for tigers.

57-66. " 'You cheap thing, Europa' my father is saying, 'why don't you hang yourself, or throw yourself from the cliffs? Or would you rather card wool as the slave of some barbarian mistress?' "

57. Vilis perfectly reflects Europa's loss of self-esteem, transferred in her mind to the loss of her father's esteem.

58. cessas: delay. **hac ab orno:** from this ashtree (as if he were not *absens*).

59-61. pendulum ... laedere collum: lit. hurt your hanging neck. **zona bene te secuta:** sarcastic: with the belt that fortunately came with you.

61-62. sive te ... delectant: more sarcasm: or, if you prefer.

63-64. erile ... carpere pensum: to card a master's wool, i.e., as a household slave assigned to menial tasks.

65. regius sanguis: though you are of royal blood; in apposition with Europa, subj. of *mavis.*

65-66. dominaeque tradi ... paelex: to be handed over to your master's wife as his concubine. Early Greek law allowed a man to keep a live-in mistress in the same household as his wife. When Agamemnon comes back from the Trojan War in Aeschylus' *Agamemnon*, he hands over his concubine Cassandra to his wife Clytemnestra, with the request that she be well treated.

66-76. Venus heard her lament, and after having her fun said, "Do not be angry with the bull: you are Jove's wife, and half the world will take your name." Venus' speech is a variation of the happy ending in Moschus' epyllion, where Zeus himself announces the good news.

66. Aderat querenti: appeared to her as she complained. This theophany, a *dea ex machina* ending to Europa's misadventure, tends to undercut its usefulness as a warning to Galatea—but the story has long since taken on a life of its own.

67. perfidum ridens: laughing deceitfully because of the trick that brought her to Crete.

67-68. remisso ... arcu: with his bow unstrung (after having done its work of making Jupiter fall in love with Europa). Cf. 3.8.23, *laxo arcu*.

69. Abstineto: fut. imperative, with gens. *irarum calidaeque rixae*.

71. cum ... reddet, etc.: when the hated bull gives you his horns to be mangled; said with a laugh, because Venus knows that Europa's angry attack (45-48) will be harmless. Jupiter will make love to Europa and make her the mother of Minos and Rhadamanthus.

74. mitte singultus: stop your sobbing; cf. 2.20.24, *mitte supervacuos honores*.

75. sectus orbis: from *seco*, half the world according to the ancient Mediterranean cosmology. The east-west dividing line began with the Nile, ran up the coast of Asia Minor, and continued through the Hellespont and the Bosporus. Europa's migration from Phoenicia to Crete represents a historic path of development and colonization during the Bronze Age.

76. nomina: poetic plural as in 4.2.4, *daturus nomina ponto*. Horace's closing words play off lines 1-2, *omen ducat*.

28

A poem for the July *Neptunalia*, when it was the custom for Romans to improvise pergolas of branches to keep off the sun and enjoy the beach or river bank. Asking himself, What better thing could I do? Horace calls on a musically talented hetaera named Lyde to bring down a jug of vintage wine from storage and enjoy the waning day with him. With wine, woman, and song, the holiday is complete. After exchanging songs on the theme of the day, she will then go on to sing of the goddess of love. Meter: second Asclepiadean.

1-8. What should I do on Neptune's holiday? Break out some wine, Lyde; noon has passed, and you are sparing a wine that idles in storage.

1. quid potius: what rather than the following. The *festus dies* was July 23.

2. reconditum: laid away.

3. Lyde: an amatory rather than servile or domestic name, like the Lyde in 3.11 or the Lydia in 1.8, 1.13, 1.25, 3.9. The choice of name indicates how Horace proposes to spend the holiday. **strenua:** adverbial, energetically. There is a playful contrast between the forceful vocabulary that follows (*munitae, adhibe vim, deripere*) and the way the two of them will spend the day—and night. **Caecubum,** a favorite wine of Horace, came from southern Latium.

4. munitae ... adhibe vim sapientiae: military parlance, lay siege to wisdom's stronghold, it being a sympotic commonplace that drinking lightens up the conversation.

5. Inclinare meridiem: a variant of the usual *inclinare diem*. It is past noon.

7. horreo: from the storeroom.

8. cessantem ... amphoram: the idling jug. **Bibuli:** M. Calpurnius Bibulus, consul with Julius Caesar in 59 B.C.; the name is appropriate not only as suggesting drink (*bibulus* = fond of drink), but because Bibulus' chief activity was to delay Caesar's proposals. This is lazy wine that needs to be dealt with briskly.

9-16. We will sing of Neptune, you of Latona and the moon, and then of Venus, with a final song to Night.

9. invicem: in turns. Amoebean singing was an old and popular type of self-entertainment. The form is reflected in 3.9, Catullus 45 and 62.

11. recines: with abl. *curva lyra*, sing in accompaniment with your lyre.

12. celeris spicula Cynthiae: the arrows of Diana the huntress, daughter of Latona.

13. quae Cnidon: sc. *eam*; you will sing (11 *recines*) of her who holds Cnidos, etc. This way of mentioning Lyde's *summum carmen*, her supreme performance, indicates it will be a hymn to the love goddess. Cnidos was famous for Praxiteles' statue of nude Aphrodite.

14. Cycladas: a deity identifiable with Aphrodite was worshipped throughout the Aegean islands from at least 3000 B.C., as evidenced by numerous Cycladic figurines of a nude goddess. **Paphum:** an early city on the west coast of Cyprus, with an ancient cult of Astarte/Aphrodite.

15. iunctis ... oloribus: Aphrodite and her forebears were often represented with birds, here the joined swans who draw her chariot through the air.

16. merita ... nenia: elsewhere a dirge, here perhaps a slow melancholy song, almost a lullaby, well-deserved by this hour of the evening. The poem has taken us from early afternoon well into the night.

29

Horace invites his patron to leave the responsibilities and heat of midsummer Rome behind and enjoy himself in the country. Most of the poem is a development of the *carpe diem* theme, setting forth the popular arguments for philosophic detachment. The tone is mildly serious, using a skillfully blended variety of images and ideas to avoid the tedium of a mere sermon on the good life. Meter: Alcaic strophe.

1-8. There is an unopened jug of wine for you, Maecenas, with flowers and balsam at my place.

Don't just put it off and think about it!

1. Tyrrhena regum progenies: offspring of Etruscan kings; the opening affects formality, but is less solemn in this context than *Maecenas atavis edite regibus* in the formal dedication of 1.1.1. The epithet is shifted by hypallage from *regum* to *progenies*. **tibi** is dat. of reference with *est* (5).

2. non ante verso ... cado: in a previously unturned (undisturbed) jar. **lene merum:** mellow wine.

4. pressa ... balanus: crushed balsam, used as an aromatic.

5-6. iamdudum ... morae ... nec semper: references to passing time help establish the *carpe diem* theme. *morae* is dat. of separation.

6. udum Tibur: mod. Tivoli. This genteel suburb, a favored site for villas about fifteen miles north-northeast of Rome, was damp (as in 1.7.13) because of its irrigated orchards, which helped keep the area cool in hot weather.

6-7. Aefulae declive ... arvum: an old Latin town, Aefula (mod. Monte Sant'Angelo) lay in the hills between Praeneste and Tibur. **nec ... contempleris:** don't just think about or gaze at. At that time, it was possible to see the distant countryside from vantage points in Rome.

8. Telegoni iuga parricidae: the hills of Tusculum, another of the semicircle of villa towns east and south of Rome. See note on *Epod.* 1.29. Its legendary founder Telegonus unknowingly killed his father Ulysses in combat.

9-16. Leave the splendor and pollution of Rome; often simple meals in a plain house are a pleasant change and smooth a troubled brow.

9. Fastidiosam ... copiam: affluence that produces *fastidium*, a feeling of satiety.

10. molem, etc.: the city's towering mass. The language is inspired by Hellenistic encomia of buildings and cities. Horace may also be thinking of the tower in Maecenas' mansion on the Esquiline, from which Nero is said to have watched the great fire of A.D. 64 (Suetonius *Nero* 38).

11. omitte mirari: don't be overly impressed with. With objects *fumum* and *strepitum* interwoven with *beatae ... et opes ... Romae*, the tone is lightly mocking. For all its splendor, Rome was dirty and noisy. For the philosophic indifference to material things, see *Epist.* 1.6.1 *nil admirari* and Cicero *De Off.* 1.20.66.

13. divitibus: for the wealthy.

15. sine aulaeis et ostro: hendiadys, without purple dining room canopies, such as the one that collapses in *Sat.* 2.8.54ff.

16. explicuere: have taken the wrinkles out.

17-24. Now the midsummer constellations are in view; the shepherd takes it easy in the shade, and there is not a breath of wind.

17. clarus ... Andromedae pater: the constellation Cepheus, named after the Ethiopean king whose daughter was rescued from a sea monster by Perseus. It rose in mid-July.

18. Procyon: from Gk. Προκύων, lit. the pre-dog star, which rises July 15, eleven days before Sirius or *Canis maior*, presaging the "dog days" of midsummer.

19. Leonis: the sun enters the constellation Leo about July 21. Its principal *stella* is Regulus, rising July 30 (Pliny *Nat. Hist.* 18.271).

22-23. horridi dumeta Silvani: thickets of shaggy Silvanus, old Italic god of the forests; the *tutor finium* of *Epod* 2.22.

24. taciturna: part of the predicate. The stream bank is silent because there are no random breezes.

25-32. You worry about the state of Rome and distant enemies; but a provident god keeps the future hidden and laughs at human anxiety.

25. quis deceat status: ind. question depending on *curas*, suggesting questions of constitutional reform too abstract for the moment.

26. urbi: dat. with *times*.

27-28. Seres: lit. Chinese, loosely used (as in 1.12.56) of everybody east of the Roman frontier. **regnata Cyro Bactra:** the capital of Parthia, once

ruled by the elder Cyrus. **Tanaïs:** the river Don, represented as *discors* because the Scythians living nearby are warring with each other.

29-30. Prudens .. deus: like the *deus prudens* in 1.3.21 who separates land from sea, this one conceals the future, according to the Stoic doctrine of a divine *providentia* that does what is best for us: Cicero's *quaedam vis quae generi consuleret humano* (*Tusc.* 1.118).

31-32. si mortalis ... trepidat: if any mortal worries unduly; cf. 1.11.1, *scire nefas*, etc.

32-41. Take care of what is at hand; other things are swept along as by a river, sometimes peacefully, sometimes in a monstrous flood.

33. aequus: with equanimity. Cf. 2.3.1, *aequam memento rebus in arduis servare mentem*.

33-34. fluminis ritu: in the manner of a river; cf. 3.14.1, *Herculis ritu*.

35. cum pace: peacefully.

35-36. Etruscum in mare: hypermetric elision of *Etruscum* in 35 and enjambment of 36 into the next stanza help this section flow like a river. Horace exploits the metrical slowness of 35 for the peaceful river, and the rapidity of 36 for the flood. *Etruscum* shows this is the Tiber, "king of Etruria's rivers" (Fraenkel). **adesos:** lit. eaten, polished by the torrent.

37. stirpesque raptas: uprooted tree trunks. **et pecus et domos:** polysyndeton for the effect of confusion and devastation.

38. una: the adv., all together.

40. fera diluvies: the wild flood; from *diluo*, dissolve, wash away. For the flooding of the Tiber in 27 B.C., see 1.2.13ff. and NH 1.24.

41. irritat: excites, stirs up.

41-48. Whoever can say "I have lived; let tomorrow bring what it may, it cannot undo the past" will be happy and self-reliant.

41. potens sui: in control of himself, self-reliant: a Stoic and Epicurean ideal, Gk. ἐγκράτης ἑαυτοῦ, αὐτάρκης.

42. deget: will pass his time (with predicate *potens sui laetusque*). **in diem:** one day at a time.

44. polum pater occupato: let father Jupiter fill the sky.

45-47. For rhetorical effect, Horace expresses the same idea three ways: **irritum ... efficiet** (make useless, cancel), **diffinget** (unmake), **infectumque reddet** (render undone).

49-56. Mischievous Fortune bestows her favors uncertainly; if she takes flight, I renounce what she has given, relying on my character and honest poverty.

49. saevo laeta negotio: taking pleasure in cruelty, like Venus in 1.33.12, *saevo ... cum ioco*.

50. ludum ... ludere: an emphatic *figura etymologica*, as in Hamlet's "Speak the speech, I pray you, as I pronounc'd it to you" (*Ham.* 3.2.1). For the *ludum Fortunae*, see 2.1.3. **pertinax:** persistent (in playing strange jokes). She is reliable only in her unreliability.

53. manentem: predicative, when she stays put.

54. pinnas: her wing feathers. Like other Hellenistic abstractions, e.g., Victory, she is winged, suiting her flighty nature. **resigno:** relinquish; as a term in accounting, enter as a debt to be repaid.

55. virtute me involvo: I wrap myself in my *virtus* as a protection against the vagaries of fortune. Stoic *virtus* included a state of mind that was immune to material losses, pain, and grief.

55-56. probam ... pauperiem sine dote: virtuous, undowered poverty. Horace personifies *pauperies* as a poor but honest bride, contrasted with the winged but unfaithful *Fortuna*, represented in Shakespeare (e.g., *Ham.* 2.2.236, 493) as a strumpet.

57-64. It is not my way to pray for my cargo when a tempest strikes; I will take to my lifeboat and sail away.

57. meum: predicate adj. with *decurrere* and *pacisci*. For the construction, cf. 1.27.2, *pugnare Thracum est* and note on 3.12.1. **mugiat:** howls in

the *Africis procellis*.

58. malus: the mast of my ship. Horace shifts to the conceit of himself as a *mercator* caught in a storm with a precious cargo.

59. decurrere: have recourse. **pacisci:** middle deponent, make a deal for myself by means of *votis*, vows to make an appropriate offering to the god if one avoided shipwreck.

60. Cypriae Tyriaeque merces: i.e., luxury goods from the East.

61. avaro ... mari: greedy because it devours ships; 1.28.18, *avidum mare*.

62. me: obj. of *feret* (64).

62-63. biremis ... tutum: safe in the protection of a two-oared skiff (the ship's lifeboat); a small craft will ride out a storm better than a heavy ship in the voyage of life.

64. geminus ... Pollux: patron of mariners with his twin Castor, the *fratres Helenae* asked to help Virgil's ship in 1.3.2.

30

In this epilogue to the three books of odes published together in 23 B.C., Horace expresses pride in his accomplishment and predicts lasting fame for his work. The poem's sonorous phrases give it the monumental character that he claims for his entire publication. Meter: first Asclepiadean, used previously only in the first ode of the collection, 1.1.

1-8. I have completed a monument more enduring than bronze and taller than the pyramids, indestructible by age or weather. I shall not altogether die, but will grow with my fame.

1. exegi: I have finished. **aere perennius:** more lasting than bronze, the material of statues and public records. Cf. the indestructable wall in 3.3.65, *murus aëneus*.

2. regali ... situ pyramidum: periphrasis for royal pyramids, unless we understand *situs* as decay or perhaps decaying mass.

3. imber edax: the devouring erosion of rain. **impotens:** as often, *impotens sui*, hence furious. The northeasterly Aquilo is proverbially violent in Horace: *Epod.* 10.7, 13.3, *Odes* 1.3.13, 2.9.6, 3.10.4.

5. fuga temporum: the flight of ages. Cf. the *fugiens hora* in 3.29.48.

6. omnis: adverbial, wholly. The poet's prediction of his own immortality had been a literary topos since Ennius (see note to 2.20.21-24).

7. Libitinam: the death goddess, so called because at the temple of Venus Libitina supplies for funerals were stored and rented, and a registry of deaths was kept. **usque:** on and on, continuously, modifying *crescam*.

7-8. postera ... laude refers to the praise of later generations; abl. of cause with **recens**, fresh.

8-16. While Rome endures, I will be spoken of in Apulia as the first to bring Aeolic lyrics into Latin verses. Accept your well-earned tribute, Muse, and crown me with Apollo's laurel.

8-9. Dum ... pontifex: the chief priest and the Vestal virgins represent Rome's religious institutions and hence Rome herself (though as it turns out the city and Horace's poetry both outlasted official paganism). There is probably no allusion to any particular ceremony. **Capitolium:** the Capitoline hill and the temple had the same name; both symbolize Rome's eternity.

9. tacita: keeping a reverent silence. This contrasts with the roaring river in the next line, *violens obstrepit*.

10. dicar: I shall be spoken of, i.e., famous. **qua ... obstrepit,** etc.: the *qua-* clauses modify *dicar*; Horace means that his fame shall flourish in his native Apulia. Similar statements of local pride are found in other Roman poets. Horace has already spoken of his fame abroad in 2.20.14-20. **Aufidus:** a river in Apulia, a mountain torrent in its upper course near Horace's home.

11. pauper aquae Daunus: Daunus, an early

king, is poor in water because of the proverbial dryness of *siticulosa Apulia* (*Epod.* 3.16). **agrestium populorum:** rural people. The gen. with *regnavit* is a Greek construction.

12. ex humili potens: powerful from humble origin; according to legend, Daunus was a refugee from Illyricum. The phrase is also to be taken with reference to Horace, a freedman's son.

13-14. princeps ... deduxisse: as the first to adapt; the infinitive is governed directly by *dicar*; *princeps* is nearly equivalent to *primus* in the sense of "the first," with the added notion of leadership, which *primus* lacks. Though Catullus wrote two poems in the Sapphic meter (poems 11 and 51), Horace is justified in his claim that he was the first to adopt **Aeolium carmen**, the Aeolic meter of Sappho and Alcaeus. Fifty-five of the eighty-eight poems in *Odes* 1-3 are in Sapphic or Alcaic meters. All but six of the rest are Asclepiadeans, which belong to the same tradition. **Italos:** the *I* here, normally short, is long. Cf. 2.7.4 note.

14. deduxisse: to have converted, developed, adapted (*OLD* 12d). **modos** are meters. Horace might more accurately have said that he adapted Aeolic *modos* to Italian *carmina*, i.e., poems set in Italy and addressed to a Roman audience. **Sume superbiam:** accept the proud honor, since you inspired me. Horace repeats the tribute to Melpomene in 4.3.24: *quod spiro et placeo, si placeo, tuum est.*

15. quaesitam meritis: won by your merits. **mihi:** dat. of reference instead of a possessive adjective with *comam*. **Delphica lauro:** the Delphic bay or laurel sacred to Apollo, the god of poets.

16. volens: gladly, with good will. **Melpomene:** strictly speaking, the Muse of tragedy, but such distinctions were not always observed; in accordance with Horace's usage, she is the Muse in general. Her name means "she who sings," from Gk. μέλπομαι, sing (to the lyre or harp). Cf. note on 3.4.2, *Calliope*. **comam:** my locks.

This Centennial Hymn was written for the celebration in 17 B.C. of an ancient ceremony founded by the Valerian *gens* and converted into a national observance, the *ludi Tarentini*, in 249 B.C. Repeated in 149 but forgotten in the civil confusion a century later, it was revived by Augustus, whose religious officials declared that the fifth *ludi Saeculares* were due in 17 B.C., counting from the foundation of the republic. Following the death of Virgil in 19, Horace was *de facto* poet laureate and wrote a hymn to be sung by a chorus of boys and girls on the third and final day of the festival. There is little doubt that for Horace, this was the high point of his career as *vates* of the Roman world remade by Augustus. A hymn to Apollo and Diana, it is less remarkable as a lyric achievement than as a verbal monument, a ceremonial landmark of the *pax Augusti*.

1-12. Phoebus and Diana, grant our prayers on this holy occasion ordered for a song to Rome's gods. God of the sun, may you see nothing greater than Rome!
1. silvarum ... potens: ruler of the forests; for the gen. construction, cf. 1.3.1, *diva potens Cypri*.
2. lucidum caeli decus, bright glory of the heaven, is in apposition with both Phoebus the solar god and Diana the lunar.
5. Sibyllini ... versus: the original prophetic verses in Greek hexameters, supposedly purchased from the Sibyl by one of the Tarquin kings, were destroyed when the Capitol burned on 83 B.C.; another set was rounded up and suitably edited by the XV *viri sacris faciundis*, then deposited in the temple of Palatine Apollo. These verses prescribed religious observances.
6. virgines lectas, etc.: the inscription made for the occasion (CIL 6.32323) says there were twenty-seven of each; *lectas* and *castos* are to be taken with both boys and girls; they were chosen from families in which both parents were still living and were wed by *confarreatio*, the most sacred form of marriage. Their social rank is indicated by 4.6.31f.,

virginum primae puerique claris patribus orti.
7. dis quibus, etc.: to the gods who love the seven hills of Rome.
9. Alme Sol: Apollo in his character of life-giving solar deity.
10. alius ... et idem: i.e., you are different every day but also the same.

13-24. Goddess of childbirth, protect mothers and bring forth their young; further the decrees of marriage so that this festival may be repeated.
13-14. Rite: duly, in accordance with your role. **aperire:** with *lenis*, gentle in bringing about timely parturition (*maturos partus*).
14. Ilithyia: Gk. Εἰλείθυια, goddess of childbirth identifiable with Diana, Lucina, Genitalis. Naming many titles of the deity invoked increases the likelihood that she will listen. **tuere:** imperative, watch over.
17-18. producas, prosperes: hortatory subjunctives. **super:** with abl., decrees on (a) *iugandis feminis* and (b) the *lege marita*. The former refers to the recently enacted Lex Iulia de maritandis ordinibus, the latter probably to its companion Lex Iulia de adulteriis coercendis. They were not actually *patrum decreta*, but were passed by the Comitia with the grudging assent of the senate, and they were the least successful part of Augustus' legislative program. The marriage law penalized bachelors, widowers who did not remarry, and childless couples; the adultery law (euphemistically labeled here *lege marita*) made infidelity a public offense.
19. prolis ... novae feraci: with abl. *lege marita*, productive of new offspring, in the hope that the roll of Roman citizens could be maintained without giving citizenship to foreigners.
21-22. certus ... orbis: the fixed cycle of the *ludi Saeculares*, set at intervals of 110 years (*undenos deciens per annos*), the theoretical limit of a human life. According to other ancient sources (Val. Antias, Livy, Varro) the interval was 100 years; when the emperor Claudius celebrated these *ludi* in A.D. 47, he too used the 100-year interval.

23. ter die, etc.: for three days and as many nights.

24. frequentis: acc. with *ludos*, festivals thronged with crowds.

25-36. You, truthful Fates, join a good future to what has passed. Let nature be fruitful; do you, Apollo, give kindly ear to the suppliant boys; moon goddess, hear the girls.

25. veraces cecinisse: truthful in having foretold what was once ordained (*quod semel dictum est*). The Parcae or Moerai (Gk. Μοῖραι) were given offerings on the first night of the festival.

26-27. stabilisque rerum terminus servet: parenthetical (and may the steadfast boundary of time preserve it). **peractis**: to fates that have already been completed.

30. donet: jussive subj., let the land present Ceres with a crown made of ears of grain (a *spica* is an ear of grain). The imagery is similar to the personifications of nature on the Ara Pacis.

31. aquae salubres: healthy rains as opp. to the torrents that damage the trees in 3.1.30. The attributives *salubres* and *Iovis* can reasonably be understood with both *aquae* and *aurae*; cf. note on *lectas* and *castos*, line 6.

33. condito ... telo: in a gentle mood, with his bow sheathed: 2.10.19, *neque semper arcum tendit Apollo*.

35. siderum regina bicornis: Diana as Luna, the two-horned moon, rules the nighttime sky.

37-48. If Rome is your work and if Trojan companies led by Aeneas landed on our coast, gods, give our youth good morals and our elders peace; give wealth, offspring, and every glory to the race of Romulus.

37-38. Iliae ... turmae: Trojan companies, subj. of *tenuere*. These references recall Virgil's *Aeneid*, published after the poet's death two years earlier.

39. mutare Lares et urbem: to move their homes and city.

41. cui: refers to the remnant (*pars*, line 39) of

Trojans who made the trip to Italy; dat. of reference with *munivit iter*, for whom he paved the way. **sine fraude**: without harm, the root meaning of *fraus*.

42. castus Aeneas: a characteristically Horatian variant of the Virgilian formula *pius Aeneas*.

43. munivit: the technical word for paving a road (*OLD* 6), with the same metaphorical sense as in English: he paved the way.

43-44. daturus plura relictis: destined to give them more than they left behind.

45. docili: attentive, willing to learn.

47-48. remque prolemque et decus: climactic polysyndeton emphasized by elision of the second *que* into the next line. See appendix C, synapheia and hypermetry.

49-60. May Augustus' prayers be answered: now may Parthian, Scythian, and Indian seek peace; now may the ancient virtues dare return, and abundance appear in the horn of plenty.

49. Quae ... veneratur: the things for which he entreats you; *veneror* takes accusatives of the thing requested and the person entreated. The acc. *quae* is also object of *impetret*, may he obtain.

50. clarus ... sanguis: Augustus, whose Julian *gens* traced its ancestry to Aeneas' son Iülus, grandson of Venus and Anchises.

51-52. bellante prior: sc. *hoste*, superior to a warring enemy. **iacentem lenis in hostem**: lenient toward an enemy prostrate in defeat. The policy, immortalized in Virgil's *parcere subiectis et debellare superbos* (*Aen.* 6. 853), was in fact an old one.

54. Medus: the Parthians, as often in Horace. **Albanas ... securis**: Roman arms, so called after the pre-Roman capital at Alba Longa.

55. responsa petunt: they seek our answers to their peace overtures (as if from a god or oracle). The Scythians had in fact sent a goodwill embassy (see note on 3.8.23).

56. Indi: though the Romans had little direct contact with the Indians, Suetonius (*Aug.* 21.3) says they too sent ambassadors. It is not clear to whom *superbi nuper* refers, as there is no record of conflict with either Scythians or Indians.

59. audet: sing. verb for all the personified virtues; Hesiod (*W&D* 197ff.) had predicted that in the Age of Iron, Shame and Nemesis would abandon humanity and return to their place among the immortals. The implication of their return is that a golden age has come back.

60. Copia: for the horn of plenty, see note on 1.17.15. The spontaneous production of food is another feature of the golden age.

61-72. If Apollo with all his powers looks with favor on his Palatine temple, he is prolonging the Roman state; his sister Diana heeds the priests' prayers and gives friendly ear to the children.

61. Augur: as the god of prophecy, e.g., at Delphi.

62. acceptus ... Camenis: loved by the nine Muses.

63. salutari levat arte: relieves with his healing art.

65. Palatinas ... aras: the spectacular temple of Apollo on the Palatine, dedicated by Augustus in 28 B.C.; Horace wrote 1.31 in honor of the event. **aequus:** kindly, with adverbial force.

66. rem ... Romanam: the Roman state, as in *res publica.*

67-68. alterum in lustrum, etc.: into another period and an always better age. An *ingens lustrum* was a period of 100 or 110 years, the interval of the *ludi saeculares.* Cf. Virgil *Aen.* 1.283, *veniet lustris labentibus aetas.* **prorogat:** prolongs, pres. indic. to express assurance.

69. Aventinum: Diana's temple on the Aventine hill was built originally by Servius Tullius. **Algidum:** in the hills about nineteen miles southeast of Rome, where she was worshipped as Diana Nemorensis, Diana of the groves. Cf. 1.21.6, *gelido prominet Algido.*

70. quindecim ... virorum: *quindecimviri sacris faciundis,* the priestly college instituted by Tarquin as *duumviri* and charged with the keeping and interpretation of the Sibylline books. At this time there were actually twenty-one priests, including Augustus himself and Agrippa.

71. curat: attends to, heeds.

73-76. We report the certain hope that Jove and the gods are listening.

73. Haec Iovem sentire, etc.: in apposition with the *spem* that the chorus report.

74-75. reporto, doctus ... chorus: the collective choral "I," trained by Horace.

1

A tribute to Paullus Fabius Maximus, set in the framework of a prayer to Venus. Rather than an invocation, the address to Venus is a prayer for mercy, suggesting that the young, successful Paullus would be a more fitting recipient of her presence. As is often his way, Horace then undercuts his denial of love by stating his love for Ligurinus. Meter: second Asclepiadean.

1-8. Spare me from further battles, Venus; I am not the man I was. Leave me, now about fifty and resistant to your commands, and go where the prayers of the young summon you.

1. Intermissa … diu: Venus's wars (like Horace's love lyrics) have long been suspended, supposedly because of the poet's age. The words make a suitable opening, as about a decade has passed between *Odes* 1-3 and the publication of *Odes* 4, ca. 13 B.C.

2. bella, with *idoneum* (line 12) and *militiae* (16), recall the valediction to love in 3.26, *Vixi puellis nuper idoneus / et militavi non sine gloria*.

4. sub regno Cinarae: Augustan love elegists saw themselves as ruled by the women they loved; cf. Cynthia's ghost to Propertius (*Elegies* 4.7.50), *longa mea in libris regna fuere tuis*. Cinara or Cinyra may represent a real person, as she is mentioned three other times in Horace, all of them after her death: *Epist.* 1.7.28, 1.14.33, *Odes* 4.13.21-22. The name, from Gk. κινάρα "artichoke," is associated with symposia and wine (Alcaeus 347 LP, Columella *Rust.* 10.235-41).

5. mater saeva Cupidinum = the opening line of 1.19, which has a similar in-love-again theme.

6. circa lustra decem: adjectival phrase modifying *durum*: one about fifty, hardened to your soft commands. **flectere:** obj. of *Desine* (4); the sense is conative: stop trying to bend.

9-20. You will be a more timely guest in the house of Paullus Maximus, a noble, handsome, and eloquent lawyer who will serve you well and build you a handsome shrine at his lakeside villa.

9. Tempestivius: more timely, adv. with *comissabere* (11).

10. purpureis ales oloribus: borne on the wings of radiant swans, lit. winged by means of. For *purpureus* in this sense, see *OLD* 3.

11. comissabere: with *in domum* (9), you will make your carousing way into. Derived from Gk. κωμάζω, burst in upon in the manner of a reveller (LSJ III). A formal prayer asking a divinity to go elsewhere (Gk. ἀποπομπή) suggests an alternative destination; here it is the house of Paullus. For more about Paullus Fabius Maximus, see appendix A.

12. iecur: for the liver as the seat of passion, cf. 1.13.4, *fervens difficili bile tumet iecur*.

14. pro sollicitis non tacitus reis: not exactly an erotic virtue, but suitable for a man about to marry into the family of Augustus. The central five stanzas of this ode are broadly encomiastic—as are most of the odes in this book. **reis:** defendants. This line is paraphrased in Ovid, *ex Ponto* 1.2.115: *vox tua auxilio trepidis quae solet esse reis*.

15. puer: erotic term for any male; cf. *puella* and Eng. boyfriend, girlfriend. The word here also distinguishes Paullus from Horace, who is about twenty years older.

17. quandoque: at whatever time.

18. largi … aemuli: the big-spending rival is a classic source of trouble for lovers, for example in 4.11.23. Paullus, being rich himself, can just laugh at such a rival. **muneribus:** instrumental abl. with *largi* or abl. of comparison with *potentior*.

19. Albanos prope … lacus: prime villa territory in the hills a few miles southeast of Rome, where we are to presume Paullus or his family has a summer home. The *Lacus Albanus* and the nearby *Lacus Nemorensis* are close to the Via Appia and convenient to Rome.

19-20. te … marmoream: a marble statue of you. **sub trabe citrea:** under a roof of citron wood, a finely veined cedar from North Africa. Pliny *Nat. Hist.* 13.101 cites Theophrastus as writing ca. 314

B.C. that it was used in ancient temples. A fragrant wood rich in resins, it was highly resistant to decay.

21-28. There you will enjoy incense and music; boys and young girls will dance in your honor twice a day.
22. duces: with *naribus*, you will inhale. **Berecyntiae ... tibiae:** Phrygian reed pipes. Mt. Berecyntus was associated with the worship of Cybele. Cf. 1.18.13, 3.19.18. The musical instruments probably came to Rome along with the cult at the end of the third cent. B.C.
24. fistula: another kind of reed pipe, higher pitched than the *tibia*.
27. pede candido: i.e., young and well-washed.
28. in morem Salium, etc. refers to the lively three-step dance of the *Salii*, of the ancient priesthood of Mars; cf. 1.36.12, *neu morem in Salium sit requies pedum.*

29-40. I no longer enjoy love or parties—but why do I weep, Ligurinus, and have trouble speaking? Sometimes in my dreams I hold you, sometimes I follow you through the grass or the rolling waves.
29-32. nec ... nec ... nec ... nec ... nec: Horace contrasts his own state (via the emphatic placement of *me*) with the positive virtues of Paullus.
30. spes ... credula: a hope that believes my love could be returned (*animi ... mutui,* gen. with *credula*).
31-32. certare, vincire: subjects of *iuvat*, like *femina, puer,* and *spes*.
33. Ligurine: probably fictitious, Ligurinus recurs in 4.10.5. His name identifies him as an Italian from Liguria, and perhaps also suggests a clear tenor voice, Gk. λιγυρός (in the *Odyssey* of the song of the Sirens, 12.44).
35. facunda: eloquent, persuasive, with *lingua*. **parum decoro:** with *silentio*, unbecoming silence. The line is hypermetric, as the final *-o* elides with *inter* in the next line. When he can speak at all,

his words tumble out.
36. inter verba cadit: between one word and another my tongue falls into an unbecoming silence. Horace conflates the expressions of Sappho 31.9-10 and 13 with Catullus 51.9 *lingua sed torpet* and 10 *flamma demanat*.
37. Nocturnis ... somniis: perhaps suggested by a Greek epigram of Meleager, A.P. 12.125 (GP 117) 1-2: "I constantly have a dream that hunts after the winged apparition" (of the boy he loves). Cf. Medea's dream of Jason in Apollonius *Argonautica* 3.616ff. and Dido's dream of Aeneas, *Aen.* 4.465ff.
38. volucrem: as you run quickly; like Hebrus in 3.12, Ligurinus is athletic; he works out on the Campus Martius, then goes swimming in the Tiber.
40. dure: plays ironically off *durum* (7): now it is Ligurinus, not Horace, who is resistant. **volubilis:** rolling.

2

A polite *recusatio* to the young Iullus Antonius, a close associate of Augustus and an adoptive member of his family, refusing to compose a Pindaric ode to celebrate the return of Augustus from his campaigns in Gaul in 13 B.C. Though at an earlier age Horace had written in the Pindaric manner (e.g., 1.12), he compares himself here to a Callimachean bee and offers the task of eulogizing the princeps to Iullus, an amateur writer of epic. Horace's tribute will be the ordinary cheers of a spectator. Instead of sacrificing twenty cattle, he will offer a single calf. Meter: Sapphic strophe.

1-4. Whoever tries to rival Pindar will suffer the fate of Icarus and give his name to a glassy sea.
1. Pindarum: 518-438 B.C., one of the great authors of choral lyric and the master of a complex and difficult poetic idiom. Except for some fragments, only the victory odes survive.
2. Iulle: here dissyllabic; the *nomen gentile* is

given on line 26. For more about this person, see appendix A. **ceratis ope Daedalea:** waxed with the art of a Daedalus, referring to the wings crafted from feathers bound with wax that Daedalus made for himself and his son Icarus to escape from Crete. Icarus ambitiously flew too near the sun, which melted his wings.

3. nititur: supports himself, with the additional sense of "strains" beyond the limit of his power. **daturus nomina:** doomed to give his name; *nomina* is a poetic plural.

5-24. Like a mountain torrent, Pindar rushes fervently along in bold dithyrambs, hymns and paeans, victory odes, and dirges. These five stanzas in a single sentence mimic the stylistic extravagance of the poet whose achievements they describe.

5. monte decurrens velut amnis: like a stream running down a mountain; for the delayed adverb, cf. 1.37.17, *accipiter velut*.

6. notas ripas: its usual banks.

7. fervet ... ruit: the impression of reckless force is germane to Horace's subtle criticism of Pindar, as is **immensus,** boundless. Horace's Hellenistic taste preferred a concise, economical style. Note that the caesura in this line falls between the paired short syllables; this feminine caesura occurs also in lines 9, 13, 17, 23, 33, 34, 38, 41, 47, 49, and 50. The freer verse style of Book 4 is also evident in the hypermetric lines of this ode, lines 22 and 23.

7-8. profundo ... ore: as the vowel sounds imply, the Pindaric voice is orotund and sonorous, if not bombastic.

9. donandus: worthy to be rewarded; takes the abl. of the gift given.

10. audacis ... dithyrambos: impassioned songs in honor of Dionysus, bold because of the ecstatic freedom associated with Bacchic revels. Mild versions of the form can be seen in 2.19 and 3.25. **nova ... verba:** new coinages, especially the compounds characteristic of Pindar and Aeschylus,

were distrusted by poets in the tradition of Catullus' *novi poetae* except when they attempted to imitate the grand old style.

11. devolvit returns to the metaphor of the mountain freshet. Pindar rolls down big words the way a torrent rolls down boulders.

11-12. numeris ... lege solutis: critics of Horace's time (Cicero *De Or.* 3.285, Dionysius Halicarnassensis *Comp. Verb.* 19) emphasized the metrical license of dithyrambic poetry. Horace did not necessarily mean that all Pindaric verse was so freely structured; for example, scholars half a century later were teaching *qua lege recurrat Pindaricae vox flexa lyrae* (Statius *Silvae* 5.3.151f.). Cf. Horace's criticism of Plautus' meters in *Ars P.* 270.

13. deos regesque canit: in his hymns and paeans. The linkage is euhemeristic because it blurs the distinction between gods and mortals, exactly as Horace and other partisans of Augustus proposed to worship the *princeps* as a god. See note on 3.3.10. **deorum sanguinem:** progeny of gods; shows that the *reges* in question were kings of the heroic age such as Theseus, Peleus, and Pirithous.

14-15. iusta morte: because one of the Centaurs tried to make off with Hippodameia, the bride of Pirithous; cf. 1.18.8 and 2.12.5.

15-16. tremendae flamma Chimaerae: the fire-breathing monster of Lycia killed by Bellerophon; it combined the head of a lion, the body of a goat, and the tail of a serpent. Cf. 1.27.23. As *deos regesque* (13) are comparable to Augustus, monsters defeated by them are comparable to the vanquished Sygambri mentioned in line 36.

17. quos Eleā, etc.: object of *dicit*; refers to victors at the Olympic games held in Elis. These are the victors celebrated in Pindar's *epinicia* or victory odes. The Greek games here seem to anticipate the *publicum ludum* honoring Augustus' return in line 42.

18. caelestis: in apposition with *quos*; for the sentiment, cf. 1.1.5, *palmaque nobilis terrarum dominos evehit ad deos.* **pugilem, equum:** boxing and chariot racing, main events at the panhellenic

games, here representative of all the contests, such
as the track and field events. *Equum* includes
owner, driver, and horses.

19. dicit: celebrates in song (as often); cf. *canit*
(13), *plorat* (22). **centum potiore signis:** better
than a hundred merely physical monuments. In
this sense, a *signum* is a statue, engraved relief, or
painted figure. The poems are *aere perennius*, like
Horace's in 3.30.1.

20. munere: i.e., the ode composed in honor of
the victor. For the abl. with *donat*, cf. *laurea
donandus* (8).

21. flebili sponsae iuvenemve: the *-ve* here
(introducing *plorat*) is transferred from the begin-
ning of the verse. *Flebilis* is used in an active sense:
tearful, as in 2.9.9. *Sponsae* (dat. of separation), lit.
fiancée, is a bride or wife.

22. plorat: i.e., in his lost dirges or threnodies
(θρῆνοι). **moresque** elides with the following word,
making the verse hypermetric.

23. nigroque also elides, giving us two successive
hypermetric lines, perhaps mimicking Pindar's
impetuous style.

24. invidet Orco: by preserving the virtues of
the dead person in his verses. Cf. 3.30.6, *non omnis
moriar*. Orcus or Dis is the god of the underworld,
and by metonymy the underworld itself.

25. Multa ... aura: the mighty breeze of Pindar's
eloquence. **Dircaeum ... cycnum:** Pindar is the
swan of Dirce because of the legendary spring near
Thebes, his birthplace (see map 3). For the swan
as poet, see 2.20, where Horace imagines himself
metamorphosed into a swan.

26. tendit ... quotiens: postponed conjunction,
as often as.

**27-32. I am less a Greek swan than an Italian
bee.**

27. Ego: contrasting himself with Pindar and (by
anticipation) Antonius (33ff.). **apis Matinae:** *mons
Matinus* was a spur of Mt. Garganus on the eastern
coast of Apulia, not far from where Horace was
born (see map 6). **Matinae more modoque:** an

alliterative formula, in the method and manner of
the Matine bee, suggests the appropriate humming
sound.

29-30. per laborem plurimum: the Hellenistic
poetic ideal called for highly polished verses rather
than great volume. This makes the bee image
appropriate. Though Pindar compares his own song
to a bee in *Pyth.* 10.54, the metaphor is more
likely from Callimachus' Hymn to Apollo, 112-116:

> The river Euphrates has a powerful current
> but the water is muddy and full of refuse.
> The Cult of the Bees brings water to Deo
> but their slender libations are unsullied and
>   pure,
> the trickling dew from a holy spring's height.
>   (tr. Lombardo and Rayor)

30-31. uvidi ... Tiburis: because of the water-
falls; see 1.7.13, 3.29.6. *-que* connects *nemus* and
ripas.

31. ripas: of the Anio, which flows through
Tibur. The local details fit the Italian character of
Horace's poetry. **operosa ... carmina:** the product
of the *laborem plurimum* of lines 29-30. Like Edi-
son, Horace credits perspiration more than inspira-
tion. **parvus:** an uncharacteristic but appropriate
posture for the author of this ode, contrasting
sharply with his grandiose image in 1.1.35-6, 2.20,
3.30. Note the effective juxtaposition of *operosa*
with *parvus*.

32. fingo: shape, fashion; the verb is appropriate
to the claim of painstaking workmanship.

**33-44. You, Antonius, will do a better job of
praising our god-given Caesar, and commemorat-
ing the celebration of his return.**

33. Concines: usually = sing together with
accompaniment; here perhaps compose and per-
form, but the sense of being in harmony with the
maiore plectro is intended as a secondary meaning.
maiore poeta plectro: *poeta* is in apposition with
the omitted subject of *concines*, i.e., *tu*, Antonius.
plectro, abl. of quality with *poeta*, is the pick used
to strum the lyre; Antonius is a poet of a grander

style of poetry than Horace's. Cf. 1.26.11, *Lesbio plectro*, 2.1.40 *leviore plectro*.

34. quandoque: in the sense of *quando*, as in 4.1.17. **trahet:** captive chieftains were led in chains in a triumph, then executed.

34-36. ferocis ... Sygambros: characterized in 4.14.51 as *caede gaudentes*; their defeat of Lollius occasioned Augustus' expedition to Gaul in 16 B.C., but they withdrew before his arrival. The fantasy here of their chieftains being led to execution in a triumph is a typically Horatian touch. The defeat of Lollius was one of the two severe and ignominious defeats suffered during Augustus' principate (Suetonius *Aug.* 23.1).

35. per sacrum clivum: the *Sacer Clivus* was that part of the Sacred Way which extended from the *summa Velia* at the Arch of Titus down toward the Forum. The name is found only here and twice in Martial. **decorus:** in the sense of *decoratus*, as in 3.14.7.

36. fronde: i.e., of laurel, the badge of victory.

39. in aurum ... priscum: i.e., to the golden age of old.

41. -que ... et: poetic for *et ... et*.

42. publicum ludum: singular for plural, probably for euphony. Imposing spectacles, such as gladiatorial and other *ludi*, were regular accompaniments of triumphal celebrations. The games took place in 14 B.C., but Augustus declined the triumph and entered the city unannounced and by night. **super:** with the abl., in celebration of. **impetrato:** gained in answer to our prayer.

44. litibus orbum: because of the legal holiday, the Forum would be "orphaned" of litigants.

45-60. My part will be to cheer from the sidelines, and to offer the small sacrifice of a kid.

45-46. meae ... vocis accedet bona pars: the loyal function of my voice will be to chime in. **audiendum:** worth hearing.

46-47. O sol pulcher! Identification of the ruler with the sun was a commonplace of Hellenistic panegyric. Horace implies he will not be composing

a unique poem, but cheering like everybody else. This joining in with the crowd is most uncharacteristic of Horace (cf. 3.1.1 *Odi profanum vulgus*). Cf. note on *canemus*, 4.15.32.

47-48. recepto Caesare: causal abl. absolute with *felix*.

49. Teque: if the mss. are correct, *te* is the triumphal procession personified, object of *dicemus*; we will call out to you as you go along, "Io Triumph!" Some editors prefer *terque*, thrice, or *tuque*, Augustus.

51. civitas omnis: subject of *dicemus*.

53. Te: Horace now turns to Antonius, who will make a grand sacrifice of twenty cattle (to go with the great ode Horace is suggesting he compose for the occasion).

54. me tener ... vitulus: for the small sacrifice appropriate to humble means, see 2.17.30-32, 3.23; Horace's sacrifice is symbolic of his less grandiloquent poetic style. For the metaphor, cf. Virgil *Ecl.* 3.85. **solvet:** with *me*, will fulfull my obligation, assumed when I prayed for Augustus' safe return; also governs *te* in the previous line. **relicta matre:** i.e., newly weaned. The rest of the poem pointedly wanders off into a digression on the sacrificial calf, which interests Horace more than all the pageantry. For the description, cf. 3.13.3-8 and 3.22.6-8.

55. iuvenescit: is growing up, becoming a young ram.

56. in mea vota: to fulfil my vows; *in* + acc., expressing purpose.

57. fronte: with its brow, on which horns are beginning to sprout. **imitatus:** for the perfect participle denoting contemporary action, cf. 1.7.24, *affatus*. But since a *tener vitulus* would be too young to have sprouted horns, the participle is proleptic: he is ready to imitate the horned moon. **curvatos ... ignis:** the crescent light, explained in the next line.

59. qua duxit, etc.: where it has taken on a mark (not there at birth); the clause limits *niveus*.

60. cetera: Gk. acc. of specification: elsewhere. On this closing description, C. L. Smith observes that "it serves to heighten the contrast between the rich Antonius, who can send victims by the score to the altar, and the owner of a modest farm, who knows well every creature in his small herd, and to whom the sacrifice is therefore more of a personal matter; and it furnishes the ode, at the same time, with a pleasing close, drawing the reader's mind away from the stirring picture just described, to rest, in parting, on a quiet rural scene."

3

In this Ode to Melpomene, Horace simultaneously calls attention to his status as a leading poet and gives the Muse all the credit. At the same time, he acknowledges the creative influence of the streams and trees at Tibur. The motto is from Hesiod *Theogony* 81ff. via Callimachus (*Aetia* 1.37-38): "Those whom the Muses have looked on as children with favoring eye, they do not avoid as friends when they are old." Meter: second Asclepiadean.

1-12. The child you favored at birth, Melpomene, will not become famous as boxer, chariot racer, or general, but as lyric poet.

1. Melpomene: invoked here, as in 3.30.16, because her name is derived from Gk. μέλπω, sing. **semel:** once (implying finality).

2. placido lumine: with kindly eye; for this common meaning of *lumen*, cf. *Epod.* 17.44, *adempta vati reddidere lumina*.

3-10. non ... non ... neque ... sed: a priamel like the one in 1.7 leading up to Tibur as the subject to be praised. The three rejected subjects, *labor Isthmius*, *equus impiger*, and *res bellica*, are arranged in a tricolon crescendo. For more on these technical features, see appendix C.

3. labor Isthmius: refers to the panhellenic Isthmian games held every five years near Corinth; by metonymy, the Greek games generally (Olympic, Nemean, Pythian, and Isthmian).

4. clarabit pugilem: make famous as a pugilist (predicate acc., in apposition with *illum*). As in the previous poem (4.2.18 *pugilemve equumve*), boxing and chariot racing are representative of all the sports in the Greek national games.

5-6. ducet ... victorem: i.e., will pull him to victory. The construction in each element of the priamel is similar. **Achaïco:** after the Roman sack of Corinth in 146 B.C., all of southern Greece became the province of Achaea.

6. res bellica: the business of war; subject of *ostendet*. **Deliis ... foliis:** the leaves of bay or laurel were sacred to Apollo, the god born at Delos.

8. quod ... contuderit: because he has crushed the swollen threats of kings; subjunctive in a relative clause of characteristic, expressing cause. As usual in Horace, **regum** suggests foreign, un-Roman potentates.

9. ostendet Capitolio: the Roman triumphal procession culminated in a spectacular ceremony on the Capitoline hill.

10. Tibur ... fertile: a favorite retreat of Horace, about eighteen miles east of Rome. See 1.7.13, 2.6.5, with notes. Suetonius, writing in the early second century A.D., says that Horace's house was pointed out by locals near the little grove of Tiburnus.

10-11. aquae ... comae: the climactic nouns of the priamel; nature serves Horace as the Muse's instrument, making him what he is. **praefluunt:** flow through; the river is the *praeceps Anio* (1.7.13).

12. fingent = *reddent*, will make, implying that a writer is actually fashioned into a poet by his natural setting. Cf. 4.2.32, *carmina fingo*. **Aeolio carmine nobilem:** famous for my lyric poetry. As in 3.30.13, "Aeolic" refers to the part of Greece where Sappho and Alcaeus lived (Lesbos and the nearby coast of Asia Minor), and to the short, highly polished lyrics that made them models of the kind of poetry that Horace particularly emulated. Cf. 2.13.24, *Aeoliis fidibus*.

13-24. Romans have put me beyond the reach of envy and point me out as they go by; it is all your doing, o mighty Muse.

13. principis urbium: queen of cities, as we would say. The gen. depends on *suboles*.

14. dignatur: deems it fitting; takes *ponere* as object. **suboles:** offspring, posterity.

16. minus mordeor: since the time of Pindar, an oblique way of claiming success as a poet was to claim that one was being attacked by envious rivals. An even bigger boast would be that one was becoming too big for the *dente invido*.

17. testudinis: because the sounding board of the lyre was originally made from a tortoise shell, this is by metonymy the lyre.

18. strepitum: not literally din or racket, but (as modified by *dulce*) sound. **Pieri:** Gk. vocative of *Pieris*, Pierian because she comes from Pieria, a valley just north of Mt. Olympus associated with the Muses. **temperas:** shape, not restrain. But the word implies that control is the essence of poetry.

19. quoque: even. A swan's voice in a fish is a novel *adynaton*—though Pausanias 8.21.2 mentions lore of an Arcadian fish that was supposed to sing like a thrush.

20. donatura: the future participle here implies potential, not destiny: you who would give, if you wanted (*si libeat*). **cycni ... sonum:** Horace imagined himself transmogrified into a swan in 2.20, where it is called a *canorus ales*; in 4.2.25 he calls Pindar "the Swan of Dirce." *Cycni* here scans as an iamb.

21. muneris ... tui: predicate gen., a gift of yours.

22-23. quod monstror ... fidicen: the clause explains *hoc*; that I am pointed out as the minstrel. *fidicen* comes from *fides* (lyre) + *cano*. Since the death of Virgil in 19 B.C. and Horace's authorship of the *Carmen Saeculare* for the Ludi Tarentini in 17, Horace was de facto the poet laureate of Rome. These lines testify to the pleasure he took in his celebrity status, unlike Virgil who hated publicity.

24. tuum: predicate adjective with *quod spiro et placeo*. Having placed himself above his critics in line 16, Horace closes on a note of modesty.

4

A victory ode in the Pindaric manner for Augustus' stepson Drusus, who at the age of twenty-three (in 15 B.C.) had brought the eastern Alps under Roman control with the aid of his brother Tiberius, the future emperor. We have it on the authority of Suetonius that this praise of his stepsons was the reason why Augustus wanted Horace to publish a fourth book of odes. Drusus, the emperor's favorite, is the center of attention here; Tiberius is praised in 4.14. Meter: Alcaic strophe.

1-12. Just like the eagle on its first flight swooping upon the sheepfolds and attacking snakes in its love of food and battles, ...

1. Qualem introduces the first part of a long Homeric simile that covers the first sixteen lines of a period seven stanzas long. Acc. obj. of *propulit* (6), *docuere* (8), *demisit* (10), and *egit* (12).

2. regnum, etc.: dominion over the wandering birds.

3. expertus fidelem: having found him trustworthy in the case of fair-haired Ganymede (the Trojan prince abducted to be Jupiter's cupbearer in heaven). In the usual version of the story, Jove turns himself into an eagle.

5-11. olim ... iam ... mox ... nunc: the progressive stages of the fledgling eagle's adventures.

5. patrius vigor: his natural strength.

6. laborum ... inscium: i.e., inexperienced in the tasks of hunting.

7-9. verni ... venti: the spring winds, subject of *docuere*.

8. insolitos ... nisus: unaccustomed efforts.

10. hostem: predicative; his spirited attack has sent him as an enemy upon the sheepfolds. Cf. the lion in Catullus 63.77, *pecoris hostem*.

11. reluctantis dracones: struggling, resisting snakes, like the one described in *Il.* 12.201ff.

13-28. ... **and just like the newly weaned lion that will kill the young roe, so was Drusus to the Vindelici; their once-victorious hordes felt the power of young Neros raised in the household of Augustus.**
13. qualemve: part two of the simile is a single stanza. **caprea:** the roe, a small European deer.
14. intenta: with *vidit* (16), intently.
15. depulsum: with *ab ubere*, and with *lacte*. The lion is newly weaned, as the eagle in the first simile was newly fledged. Readers have been puzzled by the apparent redundancy; one solution has been to understand *matris ab ubere* as referring to the roe and its mother (which like the lioness would also be tawny, *fulva*). The ambiguity is creative, however, as both the Vindelici and Drusus were not-yet-mature antagonists and their conflict a small thing compared to that of Drusus' ancestor C. Claudius Nero with Hasdrubal (lines 37-44).
16. dente novo peritura: doomed to die by the lion's young tooth.
17. videre: sc. *talem*. The subject is the Vindelici, who lived along the southern bank of the Danube. **Raetis ... sub Alpibus:** along the headwaters of the Danube, near L. Constance in what is now the southern edge of Germany (see map 1). The purpose of the campaign was to secure Italy's northern approaches in central Europe.
18. Drusum: see appendix A.
18-22. quibus mos ... omnia: dat. of reference, whose custom. This parenthetical digression, of a type common to Pindar and poetic eulogies of Horace's own time, may be paraphrased "Whence their custom, descended through all time, arms their right hands with an Amazonian axe, I have put off asking, and it isn't right to know everything." Apparently someone had traced their ancestry to the Amazons, citing their double-edged battle axe as evidence; but this may all be invent-

ed to make fun of an overworked panegyric topos by applying it to such little-known small fry as the Vindelici.
23. catervae: bands or squadrons (as opp. to the regular Roman formations).
24. consiliis iuvenis revictae: overcome in turn (*re-*) by the young man's strategies. The rapid meter implies that they were quickly brushed aside, as was in fact the case.
25. rite: properly, with *nutrita*. **indoles:** innate character. The point of Augustan propaganda was to show that the Neros were fit for the succession even though Augustus was not their natural father.
26. faustis sub penetralibus: i.e., in the imperial household, but expressed with religious overtones.
27-28. Augusti paternus ... animus: the paternal enthusiasm of their stepfather Augustus; subject of understood *posset*. **Nerones:** both Tiberius and Drusus, whose cognomen is from their father Ti. Claudius Nero.

29-36. Breeding tells in men as in animals: but training strengthens an inborn character that can bring disgrace if it fails.
29. fortibus et bonis: by strong, upright parents. This may be a play on the name Nero, which according to Suetonius *Tib.* 1.2 means *fortis ac strenuus* in the Sabine language.
30. patrum: of their parents. The comparison of human and animal breeding was a favorite Socratic theme, and the inbred virtue of athletic victors was a favorite Pindaric topos as well.
33. Doctrina ... promovet, etc.: training advances their inborn strength. Horace is giving Augustus his share of the credit.
35. utcumque defecere mores: whenever decency or character has fallen short.
36. bene nata: natural as opp. to acquired virtues. **culpae:** misdeeds.

37-44. Your debt to the Neronian family, Rome, is witnessed in the defeat of Hasdrubal when he was rampaging through Italy.

38. Metaurum flumen: the river in Umbria flowing into the Adriatic (see map 2) where in 207 B.C. C. Claudius Nero, having intercepted a dispatch and secretly raced up the length of Italy with 7,000 picked men, prevented Hasdrubal from joining forces with his brother Hannibal. This was the turning point in the Second Punic War. Hannibal left Italy to defend Carthage and was defeated at Zama in 202.

38-39. Hasdrubal devictus: i.e., the defeat of Hasdrubal, subject of *testis [est]*.
39-40. fugatis ... Latio tenebris: when the shadows were lifted from Latium.
41. primus ... risit: was the first to laugh. **alma ... adorea:** with life-giving glory; Horace uses an archaic noun to make his phrase memorable.
42-44. ut ... equitavit: when he galloped like a flame through **taedas**, pine trees, or the east wind through the sea off Sicily. By a slight zeugma, the wind seems also to gallop.

45-52. From this point on Roman youth increased, and shrines were repaired until Hannibal complained, "We are like stags attacking wolves, and will be lucky to escape.
45. usque: steadily, by dint of *secundis laboribus*. In a veiled allusion to Augustus' program for the improvement of Italy, Horace makes it seem as if Rome sealed its victory by breeding more soldiers (only five years passed between Metaurum and Zama) and repairing temples.
47. tumultu: specific term for war within or on the borders of Italy.
48. deos habuere rectos: had the statues of their gods set up again (*habeo, OLD* 27).
50. Cervi ... praeda: appositional, like stags that are the prey of wolves. Hannibal's situation is a logical *adynaton*. Cf. Virgil *Ecl.* 8.52, *nunc et ovis ultro fugiat lupus*.
51-52. ultro: we (the attackers) are actually hunting down enemies whom it would be a signal triumph (**opimus triumphus**) to escape. *Ultro*

conveys the sense of going beyond what is reasonable or natural. C. Claudius Nero had Hasdrubal's severed head thrown into Hannibal's camp (Livy 27.51.11).

53-60. "The mighty race that came from Troy draws strength and life from the blade that cuts it, like an oak.
55. natosque maturosque patres: such as Aeneas' son Ascanius and his father Anchises. The whole stanza is a pastiche of words and images from the *Aeneid*, which everybody was reading at the time this ode was published.
57. ilex tonsa: as the oak's limbs are cut, new ones grow in to take their place. **bipennibus:** by double-bladed axes. Horace's *durus ilex* simile recalls Virgil's *validam quercum* in *Aen.* 4.441 ff.
58. nigrae feraci frondis: describing *Algido*, fruitful of dark foliage. The reference is to the cool, forested hills about nineteen miles southeast of Rome; cf. *Carm. Saec.* 69.
59-60. ab ipso ... ferro: Hannibal's complaint focuses on a series of paradoxes.

61-72. "No hydra was ever stronger, no soldiers sprung from dragon's teeth. Whatever you do, it will throw down its victor. No more good news for Carthage: all is lost!"
61. hydra: the many-headed water snake from Lerna; for each head Hercules cut off, two grew in its place.
62. vinci dolentem: loth to be defeated.
63. monstrumve, etc.: No greater prodigy did Colchis (lit. the Colchians) grow. As a condition of winning the golden fleece, Jason was required to kill a dragon and plant its teeth, from which armed warriors sprang up.
64. Echioniaeve Thebae: or Echion's Thebes. Europa's brother Cadmus killed a dragon that had attacked his men, and sowed its teeth as commanded by Athena. From the warriors that sprang up, all but five killed each other. One of them, Echion, married Cadmus' daughter Agave and

founded the ruling dynasty of Thebes.

65-66. Merses ... luctere, etc.: concessive hortatory subjunctives: sink it in the deep, it comes out handsomer; grapple with it, it will overthrow its unscathed victor *multa cum laude*.

68. coniugibus: dat. of agent with *loquenda*, for wives to tell of.

69-70. nuntios ... suberbos: after his victory at Cannae, Hannibal sent his brother Mago back to Carthage with three and a half pecks of gold rings taken from Roman knights killed or captured (Livy 23.12).

72. Hasdrubale interempto: since Hasdrubal has been killed (by Claudius Nero's army at the Metaurus river).

73-76. Nothing is impossible for a Claudian, with the help of Jupiter and wise counsel in the trials of war. Readers have been unable to agree whether the last stanza is spoken by Hannibal or Horace.

73. Claudiae ... manus: Claudian powers or deeds. As sons of Tiberius Claudius Nero, Drusus and Tiberius both carried the *nomen gentile* of the Claudii. The line of emperors beginning with Augustus and ending with the death of Nero Claudius Caesar in 68 A.D. was the Julio-Claudian dynasty.

75. curae sagaces: wise care. Horace leaves it to the reader to decide whether this is provided by Jupiter, their stepfather Augustus, or themselves.

76. acuta: dangers, crises.

5

Augustus was absent from Rome for three years from 16 to 13 B.C., securing the northern Rhine frontier against German raiders and reorganizing the finances of Gaul. Having in 4.2 declined to write a Pindaric ode in anticipation of his return, Horace here pleads for that return, arguing that Italy is now an idyll of virtue, safety, and contentment—or would be if only Augustus would come

home. Meter: third Asclepiadean.

1-8. Guardian of the race, you are too long absent; when your spring-like face has shone on us, the days are brighter.

1. Divis orte bonis: as a member of the *gens Iulia*, he is descended from Venus' son Aeneas. The phrase also means he was born under heaven's favor. **Romulae** is for *Romuleae*, as in *Carm. Saec.* 47. For Augustus' wish to be seen as a second Romulus, see note on 3.3.11. These lines echo a passage in Ennius' *Annales* pleading for the return of Rome's first king:

> *Pectora diu tenet desiderium ... simul inter*
> *sese sic memorant: "O Romule Romule die,*
> *qualem te patriae custodem di genuerunt!*
> *O pater o genitor, o sanguen dis oriundum!*
> *Tu produxisti nos intra luminis oras."*

3. patrum: the "conscript fathers" or senators.

4. sancto concilio: ind. obj. of *pollicitus. sanctus* was a regular epithet of the senate.

5. lucem: i.e., the light of your presence. While tactfully skirting the hackneyed "sun king" theme of Hellenistic panegyric, Horace keeps light and solar themes within easy reach: *orte* (1), *adfulsit* (7), *soles* (8), *sol* (40). **dux bone:** repeated in line 37, this refers to Augustus' present function as leader of Roman armies in the field.

6. instar veris: like spring, referring to the emperor's *vultus*.

7. gratior it: passes more pleasantly.

9-16. As a mother longs for her absent son, so the fatherland longs for Caesar.

9. iuvenem: i.e., her youthful son. **invido:** because it takes him away from home.

10. Carpathii maris: the waters southeast of Carpathos, the island between Rhodes and Crete. Like the wind, the sea is made specific for vividness. **aequora:** governing *maris*, the flat expanse of sea.

13. votis ominibusque: i.e., making vows and consulting the omens. Cf. the close of Livy's preface to Book 1 of his history, *cum bonis potius ominibus votisque et precationibus deorum dearumque libentius inciperemus*.

15. desideriis icta: smitten with longings.

16. quaerit: asks for. **Caesarem:** an emphatic substitute for *te*, significantly juxtaposed with *patria*.

17-24. Our farms are safe, the seas are at peace, morality has triumphed over sin.

17. etenim: for (explaining why the *patria* wants him back). What follows is a catalog of blessings that Augustus has achieved and will be glad to see when he returns. **tutus:** adverbial. **rura ... rura:** the rustic scene is emphasized in part because of Augustus' program of aid to farmers, particularly the family farm after the desolation of the civil wars.

18. Faustitas: hapax legomenon; this allegorical figure representing fertility is usually titled *Fausta Felicitas*, to whom offerings were made annually on the Capitol. Horace's coinage carries the solemn ceremonial connotations of *faustus*. As a goddess, she recalls the allegorical figure of Pax on the Ara Pacis, erected about the same time as this poem's publication to celebrate Augustus' safe arrival home from his campaigns.

19. pacatum: like *tutus* above, this carries the predication of the sentence. The reference is to the extermination of the pirates that had formerly infested the Mediterranean, and the defeat of Sextus Pompey at Naulochus in 36 B.C. Suetonius (*Aug.* 98.2) tells us that as the emperor was once sailing past Puteoli the passengers and crew of an Alexandrian ship hailed him as the source of their freedom and prosperity. Augustus boasted in his own *Monumentum Ancyranum: mare pacavi a praedonibus*. **navitae** = *nautae*.

20. culpari metuit fides: the thought is that merchants are concerned about their reputation for fair dealing, which is personified as *fides*. Cf. his previous complaint about its decay in 3.24.59, *cum periura fides consortem socium fallat*.

21. casta domus, etc.: One of Augustus' fondest hopes was that he could improve private morality (whose decline in sexual matters is explicitly described in 3.6.21-32). Yet the reforms indicated in this stanza represent wishful thinking rather than actual achievements. **stupris:** sexual abominations.

22. mos et lex: conventional morality and law; the latter would include the *lex Iulia de adulteriis coercendis* (18 B.C.), which allowed anyone to bring criminal charges against an adulterer and prescribed harsh penalties. Cf. 3.24.35, *quid leges sine moribus vanae proficiunt?* **maculosum ... nefas:** polluted crime. **edomuit:** has thoroughly subdued; *e-* has emphatic force. The statement is an exaggeration.

23. simili: i.e., resembling the husband of the mother; cf. Catullus 61.214-18:

> *Sit suo similis patri*
> *Manlio et facile insciis*
> *noscitetur ab omnibus*
> *et pudicitiam suae*
> *matris indicet ore.*

puerperae: bearers of children.

24. comes: emphatically placed; vengeance follows close on (*premit*) guilt, and no longer limps as in 3.2.32.

25-32. Who's afraid of foreign enemies while Caesar is safe? We tend to our farms, and invoke you as a god in our toasts.

25. Parthum: Horace's number one foreign bogey. The Roman standards captured by the Parthians from Crassus at Carrhae (53 B.C.) had been recovered by treaty in 20 B.C., seven years before the time of this ode. **gelidum Scythen:** a lesser eastern bogey, living north of the Black Sea. Though there is no record of conflict with these pastoral nomads, both Virgil and Horace speak of them as a conquered enemy. See note on 3.8.23.

26. Germania horrida: rough because of its endless tracts of virgin forest: cf. Tacitus *Germania* 5, *terra silvis horrida*. **parturit:** breeds.

27. fetus: acc. pl., offspring. **ferae ... Hiberiae:**

the Greek name for Spain; the epithet refers to the fiercely independent mountain tribes of northern Spain such as the Cantabri (see notes on 2.6.2, 2.11.1) and the Concani, who according to 3.4.34 drank horses' blood. Agrippa had finally subdued them in 19 B.C.

28. curet: would mind, care about.

29. condit ... diem: sees the day out (OLD 8). **suis:** emphatic; the farmers own the land they work, they have not been displaced by civil war or land redistribution, and they are not away on campaign.

30. viduas ad arbores: elms and poplars "wedded" to grapevines were used as trellises; here we see farmers attaching vines to unwed trees. Cf. 2.15.4 *platanusque caelebs* and *Epod.* 2.9, *adulta vitium propagine altas maritat populos.* **ducit:** leads in marriage, the usual term.

31-32. alteris ... mensis: i.e., at the end of the meal; the *mensae secundae* was the second and final course of a farmer's meal, when it was customary to make offerings to the *Lares.* Horace as usual varies the technical term.

32. te ... adhibet deum: invokes (lit. invites) you as a god. After the return of Octavian from Egypt in 29 B.C., the Senate ordained that offerings should be made to him not only at public banquets but also at private meals.

33-40. We invoke you along with our household gods, and pray you will give us happy times.

33. te prosequitur: honors you (OLD 3), i.e., follows up the prayer and libation with the invocation of your name. **mero defuso pateris:** with unmixed wine poured from bowls in a libation.

34. Laribus: compendious for *numine Larium.* The worship of Augustus began with the inclusion of his *genius* (see 3.17.14, note) among the *Lares.*

36. memor: mindful of, i.e., calling them to mind by sacrifices in their honor. The mention of Castor and Hercules is subtly Euhemeristic, reminding the reader of the theory that all gods were originally mortals; see notes on *Pollux et vagus Hercules,*

3.3.9-10, and *praesens divus,* 3.5.2.

37. o utinam: hiatus is normal after the expletive. **ferias:** holidays. Augustus' reign of peace and prosperity is to be one long holiday, if their prayers are answered.

38-39. integro ... die: when the day is whole, i.e., *mane.*

39. sicci ... uvidi: i.e., sober and soaked with wine.

40. cum sol Oceano subest leaves it to the reader's imagination to compare Augustus' absence to that of the sun at night: he will return just as surely.

6

A hymn to the god who will be celebrated with his sister Diana in the *Carmen Saeculare,* with an address to the boys and girls who will be performing the hymn. The dramatic date, if not the date of composition, is just before the opening of the *Ludi Saeculares* in May of 17 B.C. Meter: Sapphic strophe.

1-12. O god, whose punishing force the Niobids and Tityos felt, and even the mighty Achilles—he fell like a cut pine tree, and lay in the dust of Troy.

1-2. magnae vindicem linguae: punisher of a boastful tongue. Niobe had boasted that her seven sons and seven daughters made her superior to Leto, mother of Apollo and Diana. **Tityos** tried to rape Leto.

3. sensit: though singular, it has three subjects: *proles Niobaea, Tityos,* and *Achilles.* **Troiae prope victor:** almost the conqueror of Troy; as he dies in *Il.* 22.359, Hector predicts that Achilles will die at the hands of Paris and Apollo.

4. Phthius: of Phthia, the region of southern Thessaly that was Achilles' home.

6-7. filius quamvis Thetidis ... quateret: even though he was the son of the sea nymph Thetis (and therefore half-divine) and made Troy's towers tremble. The sense of the adversative *quamvis* covers both his ancestry and his power, dramatized by alliteration of *d*'s and *t*'s.

11. procidit late: fell sprawling; this and the dust (*pulvere Teucro*) recall Agamemnon's description of Achilles' death in *Od.* 24.39f., σὺ δ' ἐν στροφά- λιγγι κονίης κεῖσο μέγας μεγαλωστί.

13-24. Achilles would not have stooped to the deception of the Trojan Horse, but he would have burned his captives, had not Jove inter- vened for Aeneas' sake.

13. non inclusus: the negative governs both the participle and the subjunctive *falleret* (16). He would not have shut himself up in the Horse and deceived, etc.

13-14. equo ... mentito: the horse that pretend- ed to be an offering to Minerva.

14-15. male feriatos Troas: obj. of *falleret*, the Trojans keeping an ill-chosen festival (in honor of the Trojan horse). **choreis:** round dances.

16. aulam: Priam's palace, second obj. of *falleret*.

17. palam captis gravis: cruel to those captured openly, in battle. Horace generalizes from Achilles' sacrifice of twelve young Trojans on the pyre of Patroclus in *Il.* 23.175.

18. nescios fari pueros: a clever paraphrase of *infantes*, infant children.

19-20. etiam latentem matris in alvo: even one hiding in its mother's womb. In *Il.* 6.58, during an intense period of fighting, Agamemnon urges the total destruction of the Trojans, including those still in the womb.

21-22. ni tuis flexus ... vocibus: unless bent by your prayers. **Venerisque gratae** may be a remind- er of the scene in *Aen.* 1.223-96 where Venus appeals to Jupiter and is assured of Rome's imperial destiny. **adnuisset:** promised or approved by a nod of his head.

23-24. potiore ductos alite: built under stronger auspices.

25-30. Phoebus, defend the glory of the Latin Muse. Phoebus has given me the inspiration, art, and name of poet.

25. Doctor ... fidicen: two roles of Apollo, teacher of the Muses and player of the lyre.

26. Xantho ... amne: the Lycian river on the south coast of Asia Minor, on whose banks at Patara was a major center of Apollo's cult.

27. Dauniae ... Camenae: i.e., of Italian poetry. Daunus was a legendary king of Apulia, Horace's birthplace.

28. levis Agyieu: smooth-faced lord of the streets. Apollo, traditionally unbearded, was repre- sented by a conical pillar set up at the street-door of houses. From Gk. ἄγυια, street. The title sug- gests the "ways" or themes of song, as in Gk. οἶμος ἀοιδῆς.

31-40. Boys and girls of the chorus, keep well the rhythm of my poem as you sing of Apollo and Diana.

31. Virginum primae, etc.: cf. *Carm. Saec.* 7, *virgines lectas puerosque castos.*

33. Deliae tutela deae: wards of the goddess of Delos, Diana.

34. cohibentis: with *deae*, who stops. The god- dess of the animals is also the one who hunts them.

36. pollicis ictum: the stroke of my thumb on the strings of the lyre. This is to be taken figura- tively, as if Horace were actually playing accom- paniment.

38. crescentem ... Noctilucam: the waxing moon goddess who brightens the night with her torch.

39. prosperam frugum: lit. prosperer of crops. **celerem:** with *volvere*, swift to roll the running months.

41-44. When you are older, you will remember you sang the hymn composed by Horace.

41. Nupta iam: soon, when you are a married woman. **Ego** indicates the pride with which she will speak.

42. saeculo ... referente: when the century brought back the festal days, *festas luces*. For the period of the *saeculum*, see note on *Carm. Saec.* 21.

43. reddidi: I performed. The verb suggests not only repeating, but also uttering in reply, as in a rehearsal where the author-director would recite lines in the manner he wishes them to be performed. **docilis** is nom. with *Ego*: I, trained in verses, performed the poem of *vatis Horati*.

44. Horati: a "signature" in the emphatic final position, this is the only place in the *Odes* where Horace mentions himself by name. Cf. the ending of 2.6, *vatis amici*, where Horace imagines his ashes sprinkled with a friend's tears. Here, he imagines himself a living memory passed down by members of his chorus.

7

T. S. Eliot called April "the cruelest month" because nature's renewal of itself mocks our own unrenewable mortality. Here Horace returns to reflections on the meaning of spring set down earlier in 1.4, *Solvitur acris hiems*, but with more somber results. A. E. Housman considered this the most beautiful poem in Latin. Like 1.4, it is in an epodic meter, in this case the first Archilochian, which "reinforces the contrast between nature's continuity and man's abrupt end" (Reckford).

1-8. The snows have fled, the land resumes its foliage, and nymphs and Graces lead again the dancing bands. But time warns us not to hope for immortality.

1-2. gramina campis arboribusque comae: chiastic arrangement gives a sense of order to the natural cycle.

2. comae: foliage, as in 1.21.5 and 4.3.11.

3. mutat terra vices: earth is going through her (seasonal) changes; for the meaning of *vices*, cf. 1.4.1; it is acc. of the inner object with *mutat*. **decrescentia:** subsiding after the winter floods; cf. *fluvii ... hiberna nive turgidi*, 4.12.3f.

4. praetereunt: flow past their banks, i.e., within them instead of overflowing them in the floods of early spring.

5. Gratia cum ... geminis ... sororibus: see on 3.19.17 and cf. 1.4.5f., where Venus leads the dances (*ducit*).

7. Immortalia ne speres: the clause is object of *monet. immortalia* = *immortalitatem*. **annus ... diem:** i.e., the revolving year with its changes and the flight of time.

8. rapit: snatches away the day that nourishes us (*almum ... diem*) and so robs us of life itself.

9-20. Seasons return and time makes up its losses, but we are dust and shadow, not knowing if we will live another day. Your heirs will lose what you have lavished on yourself.

9-10. mitescunt ... proterit ... interitura, etc.: Horace achieves color in his rapid summary of the seasons through the variety of the verbs describing their changes. **zephyris:** i.e., under their influence. **proterit:** summer tramples spring like a defeated foe, as in 3.5.34 and Virgil *Aen.* 12.330. A gentler interpretation is echoed in Shakespeare *R&J* (1.2.25):

> When well-apparelled April on the heel
> of limping winter treads.

10. interitura: destined to perish.

12. bruma: winter; for the etymology, see note on 2.6.17. **iners:** lifeless; cf. 2.9.5 and the similar force of *piger* in 1.22.17, *pigris campis*.

13. Damna ... caelestia: their losses in the sky, i.e., the losses of the waning moon, which are made up when it waxes. **celeres lunae:** the swiftly changing moons.

14. nos: adversative asyndeton, emphatically placed in the line and at the center of the ode: we mortals as opposed to the *lunae*. **decidimus:** we have descended. The s- endings in this and the next two lines add a sonic effect.

15. pius Aeneas: an echo from the *Aeneid*. **Tullus dives:** cf. Livy 1.31.1, *cum in magna gloria magnisque opibus regnum Tulli ac tota res Romana* *esset.* **Ancus:** Ancus Martius, the fourth king of Rome.

16. umbra: shadow. In this line, *u-* sounds dramatize the hollowness of death.

17. an: whether; for this use of *an,* cf. 2.4.13, *nescias an.* **hodiernae ... summae:** to today's total, i.e., to the number of days that you have already lived. **crastina ... tempora:** tomorrow's time.

19. heredis: for the motif of the worthless heir, cf. 2.3.20 note, 2.14.25, 3.24.61f. **amico ... animo:** usually interpreted dat. "to your own dear soul" (Gk. φίλη ψυχῇ) rather than abl. "with friendly intention" (to the heir).

20-21. dederis ... occideris: the quantity of *-is* is unusual. In the perfect subjunctive the *i* of the second singular was originally long; the fut. perf. indicatives here are lengthened by analogy, as in 3.23.3, *placaris.*

21-28. Nothing can bring you back after you are dead. Even Diana cannot save Hippolytus, nor can Theseus restore his beloved Pirithous.

21. splendida ... arbitria: his glorious verdict; *arbitria = iudicia* (so-called poetic plural); *splendida* is transferred from Minos, who while alive was king at Cnossus, in Crete, and honored by Zeus; cf. 1.28.9. After his death he was a judge of the shades in the lower world, with Aeacus (2.13.22) and Rhadamanthus.

23. Torquate: see appendix A. **genus:** Torquatus belonged to the Manlian *gens,* one of the oldest and most distinguished Roman families. The cognomen of the Torquati was derived from the *torques* or ornamental gold collar taken by T. Manlius Torquatus from a Gaul killed in single combat in the fourth century B.C.

24. pietas, uprightness, recalls *pius Aeneas* in line 15.

25. Diana: the virgin goddess loved the chaste Hippolytus, as in the play of Euripides. **pudicum ... Hippolytum:** his rejection of the advances of his stepmother Phaedra, wife of Theseus, cost him his life. Horace follows the Greek version of the myth,

whereas the *Aeneid* (7.761ff.) represents him as saved by Diana and under the name of Virbius worshiped in her grove at Aricia. Note the parallel position and emphasis of *pudicum* and *caro.* Hippolytus' chastity did not save him from death, nor did the friendship of Theseus save Pirithous. The grim point of the final stanza is that death conquers love.

26. liberat: release. The historical present here and at *valet* suggests they are still trying.

27. Lethaea ... vincula = *vincula mortis,* as Lethe was the river of forgetfulness in the lower world. **caro ... Pirithoö:** dat. about equivalent to a gen. limiting *vincula*; the friendship of Theseus and Pirithous was proverbial. For Pirithous' crime, see on 3.4.79.

8

Horace sends this poem as a gift to Censorinus, with the observation that it is more valuable even than a precious work of art because it confers immortality. Its theme makes this a counter to the previous poem, on the finality of death. It is the only ode of Horace that does not conform to "Meineke's canon" that all Horace's odes are of a length divisible by four, but none of the attempts to bring it down to 32 lines has been persuasive. Meter: first Asclepiadean, used elsewhere only in 1.1 and 3.30.

1-12. I would give my friends bowls, bronzes, and tripods, Censorinus, if I had artworks to give, but *you* like poems, and poems are what I have to give.

1. commodus: with adverbial force, obligingly.

2. Censorine: see appendix A. **aera:** bronze cauldrons such as were given to athletic victors. Pindar's *Isthmian* 1.18 mentions bowls, bronze cauldrons, and tripods as traditional prizes.

5. divite me scilicet artium: conditional abl. abs., if I were rich, of course, in works of art. In this section of the poem Horace's tone is lightly ironic.

6. Parrhasius: painter of the late fifth to early fourth century B.C. **Scopas:** the fourth-century B.C. sculptor.

7. hic ... ille: the latter (Scopas) and the former (Parrhasius), respectively, as usual in Latin.

8. sollers ... ponere: skilled at depicting.

9. haec ... vis: this capacity (to represent men or gods visually, like a Parrhasius or a Scopas). Horace has moved from the question of material possessions (bowls, bronzes, and tripods) to that of artistic capacity.

10. res ... aut animus: the wealth or the inclination.

12. muneri: dat. of reference, place or declare a value on the gift.

13-22. No monumental inscriptions, no military victories win clearer praises than poetry: nor, if its pages were silent about your good deeds, would you reap your reward.

13. notis: mere marks such as a name and a title, as opp. to the connected discourse of poetry.

15. celeres fugae: Hannibal's hasty retreats from Italy after his brother's defeat at Metaurus (see note on 4.4.38) in 207 B.C., and after the battle of Zama, 202 B.C.

16. reiectae ... minae: the threats of Hannibal to sack Rome were thrown back by his defeats in the Second Punic War.

17. incendia Carthaginis: when the Romans destroyed Carthage in 146 B.C. This line's omission of the caesura and the use of *eius* at the beginning of the next line (see below and on 3.11.18) are among irregularities noted by critics who believe that the irregular length of this ode involves a corruption at the midpoint.

18-19. eius, qui ... rediit: two Scipios are conflated here: (a) the elder Scipio, Africanus Maior, who in reply to accusations of profiteering said that he returned from his victory in Africa enriched with nothing but a name (*nomen ... lucratus*, viz. the title *Africanus* conferred in honor of his

defeat of Hannibal at Zama in 202 B.C.), and (b) his adoptive grandson P. Cornelius Scipio Aemilianus, who captured and sacked Carthage in 146 B.C. **eius,** gen. with *incendia* or *laudes*, is rare in poetry. Virgil never uses it, and Horace in lyrics only here and in 3.11.18.

20. Calabrae Pierides: the Muses of Ennius, the native of Calabria whose *Annales*, a national epic, included the Second Punic War.

21. sileant: passed over in silence, with obj. *quod bene feceris.*

22-34. Romulus and Aeacus owe their immortality to poets; Hercules, the Dioscuri, and Bacchus owe their powers likewise to the Muse.

23. Mavortis ... puer: Romulus, son of Mars and Ilia.

25. Aeacum: Achilles' grandfather, after death one of the judges in the underworld (2.13.22, *iudicantem vidimus Aeacum*).

27. divitibus ... insulis: the islands of the blest in the underworld; *Epod.* 16.42, *beata arva divites et insulas.*

29. caelo Musa beat: for the Euhemeristic theory of divinity, see on 3.3.10. Horace nearly reverses the notion that the gods make poets (via inspiration) by saying that poets create the gods by conferring immortality on distinguished mortals. Even the Muse appears in this context an extension of the *virtus et favor et lingua potentium vatum.*

29-30. interest optatis epulis: Hercules, always a hearty eater in comedy, is pictured banqueting at the longed-for meals of Jove.

31. Tyndaridae the sons of Tyndareus, Castor and Pollux, patrons of seamen in the form of a constellation, *clarum sidus.*

33. ornatus: a middle passive, taking the obj. *tempora* and the instrumental abl. *viridi pampino*, green vine of ivy or grape: his brows decked with the green vine.

34. Liber: Bacchus.

9

The third of the central triad of poems in Book 4, this ode continues the theme of poetry and immortality. Ostensibly an encomium of Lollius, a trusted ally of Augustus, this poem is more noticeable for the tribute Horace pays in the first half of his poem to the Greek poets and their achievement. Meter: Alcaic strophe.

1-12. Lest perhaps you think my poetry will perish, consider the fame of Pindar and other lyrists; age has not destroyed Anacreon's verses, and Sappho's love still breathes.

1. Ne forte credas: negative clause of purpose, depending on the indicatives *latent* (6), *delevit* and *spirat* (10), *vivunt* (11). The construction is like a negative command (don't think the words I speak will perish), with the indicatives stating the reason why. **interitura** (esse): ind. statement, obj. of *credas.* **quae:** with *verba* (4), the words I speak.

2. natus ad Aufidum: I, born near the Aufidus, the river in Venusia. For its roar (*longe sonantem*), cf. 3.30.10, *qua violens obstrepit Aufidus.*

3. non ante, etc.: through not previously popularized arts, Latin lyrics in Greek meters.

4. socianda chordis: to be combined with strings, i.e., accompanied by the lyre. The meaning is figurative rather than literal.

5-6. priores ... sedes: the first position in any list of poets. **Maeonius:** of Maeonia, on the Aegean coast of Lydia. Because Chios and Smyrna were often claimed as the birthplace of Homer, the ornamental epithet "Maeonian" was commonly used; cf. 1.6.2, *Maeonii carminis,* of poetry in the Homeric style.

6-7. Pindaricae ... Ceae: adjectives with *Camenae,* the Muses or poems of Pindar and of Ceos, the island home of Simonides and Bacchylides east of the tip of Attica. **minaces:** the Muses of Alcaeus are threatening because of his invectives against the tyrants of Lesbos.

8. graves: serious, dignified. Stesichorus rendered myths into choral lyric, preserving their epic grandeur and weight (see Quintilian 10.1.62).

9. si quid ... lusit: whatever playful love poetry Anacreon once wrote. For *ludere* of amatory verses, see Catullus 50.2-6.

11-12. commissi calores ... fidibus: passions entrusted to lyres or lyrics. **Aeoliae ... puellae:** Sappho of Lesbos. Natives of the Aegean coast around Lesbos spoke the Aeolic Greek dialect. *Puella,* like *puer,* is conventional erotic language having nothing to do with age.

13-28. Helen is not the only woman who burned for an adulterer, nor Teucer the first to shoot an arrow. Not once was Troy besieged, or heroes fought and died; many brave men lived before Agamemnon, but are forgotten for lack of a poet.

13-14. comptos ... crinis: object of *arsit* and *mirata,* the well-combed hair of Paris, as in 1.15.14 (to Paris), *pectes caesariem,* and *Il.* 3.55, ἥ τε κόμη τό τε εἶδος. **illitum:** hyperbolic of gold "smeared" on his clothes.

15-16. regalis ... cultus et comites: Spartan Helen is dazzled by Paris' oriental finery and retinue.

17. Teucer: the best of the Greeks in archery, *Il.* 13.313. **Cydonio:** Cretan, from a city in Crete. The Cretans were famous for bows and archery.

18. non semel: not a single time; legend had it that Hercules sacked it a generation before the Trojan War. Horace's words recall the other sack of Troy that was *not* celebrated in epic verse, but he also suggests a generic sense in which there have been many unsung Troys, as in Gray's country churchyard: "some mute inglorious Milton here may rest." The Stoics revived a cyclical cosmology punctuated with conflagrations. Virgil hinted at this in his description in *Aen.* 2 of Troy's burning. Cf. *Ecl.* 4.35, *erunt etiam altera bella / atque iterum ad Troiam magnus mittetur Achilles.*

20. Idomeneus Sthenelusve: two Greek heroes in the *Iliad.*

22. acer Deïphobus: Hector's brother, a leading

Trojan warrior who succeeds Paris as Helen's husband. His mangled shade appears to Aeneas in *Aen.* 6.494.

27. urgentur: are weighed down by the long night of deathlike obscurity. Horace is paraphrasing Pindar *Nem.* 7.12-13 ταὶ μεγάλαι γὰρ ἀλκαί | σκότον πολὺν ὕμνων ἔχοντι δεόμεναι.

29-44. Virtue hidden differs little from laziness buried. But I will not leave you unhonored, Lollius; you have a prudent and honorable character.

29. sepultae ... inertiae: dat. with *distat.*

31. chartis: my pages, i.e., my poems.

33. impune: without my doing something to fight them off. **Lolli:** see appendix A. **carpere:** reduce or wear away the fruits of your labors, *tuos labores;* the subject is *lividas obliviones,* dark forgetfulness.

35. rerum ... prudens: practical.

36. dubiisque rectus: like *aequus,* even-headed in crises. After suffering the loss of his legion's standards in Gaul, Lollius' reputation needed considerable rehabilitation. Horace concentrates on the qualities of character that would most likely be questioned. To call him courageous under the circumstances would have invited ridicule, but prudence and level-headedness might charitably be conceded to Lollius.

37. vindex ... et abstinens: a punisher of greedy deception and not covetous. Another charge against Lollius was corrupt greed, a charge countered with dogged persistence over the next two stanzas. A *novus homo* without wealthy family connections, Lollius accumulated a vast fortune before his death. Compare Horace's words of praise with Velleius Paterculus 2.97.1, M. *Lollio, homine in omnia pecuniae quam recte faciendi cupidiore et inter summam vitiorum dissimulationem vitiosissimo.* But as a partisan of Tiberius (whom Lollius hated), Velleius had his own axe to grind. There was no middle ground in the political infighting of imperial Rome.

39. consul ... non unius anni: Lollius was in fact consul only once (in 21 B.C.), but the rank of *consularis* continued for life. We are also to understand this tribute in the Stoic, philosophic sense: only the wise man is a true king—or consul. The referent has changed from Lollius' *animus* (34) to the man himself.

41. honestum praetulit utili: preferred the honorable to the expedient, like Regulus; see note on 3.5.13, and Cicero *De Off.* 3.99-101. *Honestum* is the regular philosophic term for Gk. τὸ καλόν. Its opposite in Stoic philosophy is *utile,* Gk. τὸ συμφέρον.

42-43. alto ... vultu: with his head held high in lofty disdain. **dona nocentium:** the bribes of guilty parties.

43-44. per obstantis catervas, etc.: having tactfully skirted the subject of Lollius' behavior in the battlefield, Horace concludes with a metaphoric picture of Lollius as warrior. **explicuit sua ... arma:** gnomic perfect, has brought his arms (of virtue) safely out through the *obstantis catervas,* opposing hordes (of vice). The metaphor is bold, as this is exactly what Lollius had failed to do with his legionary standards against the Sygambri in 16 B.C. Horace's point is that Lollius' ethical victories outweigh his military defeat.

45-52. The truly happy man is not the rich one, but one who makes the most of his talents, lives simply, and fears wickedness more than death.

46-47. beatum, beati: the regular Stoic word for the felicity of the virtuous: *Zeno in una virtute positam beatam vitam putat* (Cicero, *Luc.* 134). The idea goes back to Democritus' conception of εὐδαιμονία. **occupat:** makes claim to, assumes.

49. callet: is knowing enough to, with *uti* and *pati.* **pauperiem pati:** cf. 1.1.18, on the *mercator* who is *indocilis pauperiem pati.*

10

In this sequel to the last two stanzas of 4.1 where Horace has fallen in love with Ligurinus, the poet warns the conceited boy that he will not be pretty forever. Like 1.5, the Pyrrha Ode, this may be read as a song of experience, sung by a man who has been through a humbling experience and is contemplating a boy who has not. The theme is a common one in Hellenistic love epigrams. Meter: fifth Asclepiadean.

1-8. O cruel and desirable boy, when your bloom has given way to shaggy whiskers you will say, "Alas, why did I not feel the same when I was young, or why can I not reclaim my youthful face?"

1. adhuc: still; gives prominence to the poem's theme of change.

2. insperata ... pluma: the unexpected plumage will be rough whiskers. Some editors have found this metaphor a strained one; Bentley emended *pluma* to *bruma*: when the winter of maturity comes unexpected to your haughtiness.

3. umeris involitant comae: like Nearchus' voluptuous locks in 3.20.14, *sparsum odoratis umerum capillis*; cf. also Telephus in 3.19.25, *spissa te nitidum coma*, and the daydream in *Epod.* 11.28 of the sleek boy *longam renodantis comam*. **deciderint comae:** when his long hair is shorn on assumption of the *toga virilis*. Ligurinus is a citizen, not a slave-boy.

4. color: antecedent of *qui*, subject of *verterit*. **puniceae ... rosae:** better than the flower of a crimson rose. Cf. Telephus' *cervicem roseam*, 1.13.2.

5. mutatus ... verterit: has changed and turned *in faciem hispidam*, to a bristly, shaggy look.

6. speculo: in the mirror. **alterum:** changed, a different person.

7. mens: disposition as well as knowledge. Now he wants the attentions that he rejected when he was a boy with many male suitors. **puero:** dat. of possession: why did I not have it as a boy.

8. his animis: my present repentant mood.

incolumes ... genae: cheeks unmarred with whiskers.

11

A springtime invitation to Phyllis encloses a birthday invitation to Maecenas, who is mentioned only here in Book 4. The opening stanzas are bright and full of life, but the ode moves to a conclusion that is "all gentleness and mellow resignation" (Fraenkel). Meter: Sapphic strophe.

1-12. I have a cask of aged wine, Phyllis, and green plants in the garden for garlands; the household is bustling, and the fires are smoking.

1-4. Est ... est ... est: anaphora with asyndeton for an insistent feeling of readiness in the present that is basic in sympotic poetry. The first three stanzas are asyndetic, with only one subordinate clause (line 5) slowing the pace.

1. nonum superantis annum: past its ninth year. The detail introduces the theme of improvement with years that recurs in the middle of the ode.

2. Albani: sc. *vini*, wine from the Alban hills southeast of Rome.

3. Phylli: vocative, from Gk. φυλλάς (= green foliage) suggesting the greenery with which she will crown her head, and fresh youth. **apium:** a green plant related to celery and parsley used for weaving garlands (*nectendis coronis*).

4. hederae vis: a large supply of ivy; *vis* fits the energetic tone of the opening stanzas.

5. religata: passive with middle force, lit. bound up with respect to your hair (acc. *crinis*). Cf. 4.8.33, *ornatus viridi tempora pampino*.

6. ridet: gleams cheerfully.

6-7. castis ... verbenis: vervain, an aromatic shrub, pure because of its use to bind an altar.

7-8. avet .., spargier: as if it were also a conscious participant, the altar is eager to be sprinkled with the blood of a sacrificed lamb, *immolato agno*. The archaic pass. inf. (*spargier* for *spargi*) occurs only here in the *Odes*.

9. **cuncta ... manus:** the entire staff of the house. For the preparations-for-a-symposium topos, see also 3.14.17-24.

10. **mixtae pueris puellae:** i.e., male and female slaves. *Puer* and *puella*, in the servile sense as in the amatory, have nothing to do with age.

11-12. **sordidum ... fumum:** sooty smoke from torches or cooking fires. **trepidant rotantes vertice:** dance about as they twist the smoke from their peak. Horace uses *trepidare* to describe the quick movement of running water in 2.3.12, *lympha fugax trepidare rivo*.

13-24. **We are celebrating the Ides of April, which is my Maecenas' birthday. Don't think about your boyfriend Telephus, who has been taken over by a rich and lusty rival.**

13. **tamen** signals a change of pace and subject. **noris:** syncopated from perf. subj. *noveris*.

14. **Idus:** nom. fem. plural, the thirteenth day in April.

15. **mensem Veneris:** because of increased sexual activity in the spring, and perhaps by a popular etymology connecting *Aprilis* with Gk. ἀφρός, sea-foam, and Aphrodite.

16. **findit:** divides, because it comes in the middle. Another popular etymology derived *Idus* from Etruscan *iduare*, divide (Macrobius *Sat.* 1.15.17).

17-18. **sanctior ... natali proprio:** almost more sacred than my own birthday (*dies natalis*) because of our close friendship.

19. **luce:** day. **Maecenas meus:** particularly emphatic, placed as it is at the midpoint in the ode. This, the only reference to Maecenas in *Odes* 4, may be intended to quell speculation that the friendship between Horace and his original patron had cooled. Maecenas had fallen from official favor and retired from public life, and Augustus insisted on taking over the role of patron.

19-20. **adfluentis ... annos:** plays off the wine in the first stanza *nonum superantis annum* (1), implying that Maecenas too is aged to perfection. The

prefix *ad-* implies improvement rather than loss; contrast the aging effects in 2.5.14-15, *illi quos tibi dempserit apponet annos*, where *illi* is a girl not yet in her prime accumulating years as an asset, and *tibi* is a man past his prime, losing time.

20. **ordinat:** counts, with the implication that he is setting them in orderly rows, like one in control of his aging.

21. **Telephum:** the fast cut to a new character emphasizes a contrasting situation. Phyllis is not in control of her life, having lost her boyfriend Telephus (the young Adonis of 1.13.1 and 3.19.26). **occupavit:** has seized.

22. **non tuae sortis:** not of your rank. **puella:** Phyllis' unnamed rival. No *psaltria*, this woman is a well-connected and affluent (*dives*) denizen of the Roman *dolce vita* that Maecenas so enjoyed and Augustus so regretted. The rich rival is a theme from comedy: see 4.1.18 *largi aemuli*, and *Epod.* 11.11, 15.17ff. The suprise is that here she is a woman, not the usual male interloper.

23-24. **grata compede:** oxymoron, pleasing bondage. The strong *puella* who has seized and bound Telephus is like the *domina* of Augustan love elegy.

25-36. **Phaëton and Bellerophon teach us to check our ambitions. Come now, last of my loves, and sing some lines; by song we will abate black cares.**

25. **Terret:** deters, teaches us to avoid. **ambustus Phaëton:** the burning of Phaëton, who lost control while trying to drive his father's sun chariot.

27. **gravatus:** OLD 4b: when he refused (found too heavy) the earthly horseman Bellerophon. Pindar *Isth.* 7.44 is the source of this story, that Bellerophon became overly ambitious and tried to ride his winged steed to heaven. The participle puns on *exemplum grave* in the previous line; Horace is having fun with his grandiose examples.

29. **digna:** worthy or appropriate goals. **sequare** = *sequaris*, subjunctive in an *ut*-clause of purpose depending on the sense of *exemplum grave* (26).

The frequency of feminine caesuras (after the sixth syllable) is noticeable in this part of the ode: see also lines 23, 30, 34.

29-31. et ultra ... vites: and that you should avoid hoping for more than is proper by deeming (*putando*) an unequal partner to be a crime (*nefas*, sc. *esse*). The poker-faced, intricately arranged statement of the κηδεῦσαι καθ᾽ ἑαυτόν theme (Aeschylus *Prom.* 890, Callimachus A.P. 7.89.12, GP 54.12) is lightly ironical in tone.

31. Age iam: like *tamen* in 13, this signals a change of tone and topic.

32. finis amorum: Phyllis is the last woman Horace will address in an amatory way in a poem.

33. alia calebo: fall in love with another. For heat as synecdoche for love, cf. 1.4.19, *quo calet iuventus nunc omnis et mox virgines tepebunt.*

34. condisce modos: learn with me some lines of poetry, i.e., let me teach you. As Horace taught the singers of the *Carmen Saeculare*, now in a less serious mood he proposes to teach Phyllis some lines to sing. Horace leaves us to guess who wrote the lines and which lines they are.

35. quos reddas: relative clause of purpose, so you can sing them back to me in your lovely voice—like the girl performing the *Carmen Saeculare* in 4.6.43: *reddidi carmen docilis modorum vatis Horati* (see note).

35-36. atrae ... curae: the usual phrase in Horace for depression: 3.1.40, 3.14.13f. The adj. was perhaps suggested by Gr. μελαγχολία, a condition brought on by an excess of black bile. On the supposed characters of atrabilious men, see Aristotle *Problems* XXX: "Problems Connected with Thought, Intelligence, and Wisdom"(953a10-957a36).

12

Another springtime invitation like the preceding ode, this time concentrating on the seasonal theme as in 1.4, *Solvitur acris hiems,* and 4.7, *Diffugere nives.* In a kind of priamel that takes us in succes-sive stanzas through natural, mythological, and pastoral evocations of the season, Horace arrives at his sympotic theme in the central stanza. The dominant mood is cheerful, with a counterpoint of darker notes (5-8, 19-20, 26). The stanzas are end-stopped with unique regularity in a poem of this length. Meter: third Asclepiadean.

1-12. Now spring winds press the sails, fields thaw, and rivers quiet; the mourning swallow builds her nest, and shepherds pipe to please the god of Arcady.

1. Iam veris: the opening evokes Catullus' spring poem, *Iam ver egelidos refert tepores* (46.1). The theme is a common topos in Hellenistic epigram: *Iam* echoes the ἤδη in A.P. 9.363.9-11, 10.1.2, 2.3, 4.5, 5.1, 6.1, 15.1, 16.1.

2. animae ... Thraciae: the Thracian winds. *Anima* for *ventus*, found only here in Horace, is cognate with Gk. ἄνεμος. The conception of the zephyr or spring breeze as Thracian is Homeric: *Il.* 9.5, Βορέης καὶ Ζέφυρος, τώ τε Θρῄκηθεν ἄητον.

3. nec fluvii strepunt: the spring flooding of colder climates is a winter phenomenon in Italy. Horace's spring is the post-flood season. Cf. 4.7. 4, *decrescentia ripas flumina praetereunt.*

5. Nidum ponit: builds her nest. **Ityn:** son of Thracian king Tereus and Athenian princess Procne. When Tereus raped and mutilated her sister Philomela, Procne took revenge by killing her son Itys and feeding him to his father Tereus. All were metamorphosed into birds, Tereus into a hoopoe, Procne into a swallow, Philomela a nightingale. Several playwrights dramatized the myth, including Sophocles, Livius Andronicus, and Accius. Cf. Horace *Ars P.* 187 on the metamorphosis of Procne; the story is part of Silenus' song in Virgil *Ecl.* 6.78-81. The best surviving account is in Ovid *Met.* 6.424ff.

6. infelix avis: Procne, because she killed her own child, making herself an *aeternum opprobrium* of the Athenian house of her ancestor Cecrops.

8. est ulta: with *male*, wickedly avenged the barbaric lusts of kings, viz. king Tereus. The moral of the story as Horace gives it is that one wrong (the rape of Philomela) does not justify another (the murder of young Itys). Horace likewise simplifies the *Iliad* in *Epist.* 2.2.42: *iratus Grais quantum nocuisset Achilles.*

9-10. Dicunt ... carmina: play tunes, with instrumental abl. *fistula*, shepherd's pipe. **custodes** = *pastores.*

11. deum: Pan. **nigri:** with *colles*, dark with foliage and shade.

12. Arcadiae: the locale of Virgilian pastoral. Arcadia was an isolated, mountainous area in the central Peloponnese, whose pastoral inhabitants, according to Polybius 4.20, were primitive in everything except music. See R. Coleman on Virgil *Ecl.* 7.4.

13-24. These are thirsty times, Vergilius. If you want to share my wine, bring some aromatic nard and forget your troubles; it is a pleasure to indulge in silliness sometimes.

13. Vergili: not necessarily Virgil the poet, who was now about six years dead. *Cum tua ... merce* (21f.) and *studium lucri* (25) suggest he is a merchant. But the identification is much disputed, because there are many echoes of Virgilian poetry in this ode.

14. Calibus: at Cales, in northern Campania; its wine, *prelo domitam Caleno*, was offered Maecenas in 1.20.9f. **ducere:** drink. **Liberum:** Bacchus, wine by metonymy.

15. iuvenum nobilium: his young patrons are unknown. One theory is that this refers to the young Octavian, the *iuvenem* of *Ecl.* 1.42, who is said to have saved the poet Virgil's farm from confiscation in 41 B.C.

16. nardo: a popular aromatic imported from the east; cf. 2.11.16 *Assyriaque nardo*, and note. **merebere:** you will earn it, i.e., pay for it. The idea of inviting a guest and then demanding that he supply the treat is from Catullus 13, *Cenabis bene.*

17. parvus onyx: a small stone perfume jar. **eliciet:** will entice a jug. Both little perfume jar and big wine jug are personified.

18. Sulpiciis horreis: warehouses by the Tiber at the foot of the Aventine, used for wine, oil, and similar commodities.

19. donare ... largus: generous enough to give new hopes. For this virtue of wine, see 3.21.17, *tu spem reducis mentibus anxiis.*

19-20. amara ... curarum: bitter anxieties; cf. *Ars P.* 49, *abdita rerum* for obscure things.

20. eluere efficax: capable of washing away the bitter taste of cares.

21-22. tua ... merce may indicate Vergilius' profession of merchant, but it may as well simply continue the joke of line 16, *merebere.*

23. immunem: without having to pay; the adjective denoted exemption from taxation or duties. Cf. Gk. ἀσύμβολος, not making a contribution to a feast. **tinguere poculis:** to soak you in my cups as if you were a rich man in a *plena domo.*

25. pone moras: i.e., hurry up.

26. nigrorum ... ignium: oxymoron, of the fires that cremate. Cf. *Aen.* 4.384 and 11.186 *ignibus atris*, of funeral pyres. **dum licet:** the familiar sympotic carpe diem theme.

27-28. stultitiam, desipere: of drunken silliness. For the last line see Menander 354 Körte (421 Kock), οὐ πανταχοῦ τὸ φρόνιμον ἁρμόττει παρόν, καὶ συμμανῆναι δ' ἔνια δεῖ. **in** loco denotes time and place, like Gk. ἐν καιρῷ.

13

Perhaps a sequel to 3.10, where Lyce had the poet locked out. The topos of the aging courtesan appears first in Hellenistic epigram. Horace put it to rough use in Epodes 8 and 12; it recurs in 1.25 *Parcius iunctas quatiunt fenestras*, and 3.15, *Uxor pauperis Ibyci*. It is thematically related to seduction themes warning a boy or woman that "Youth's a stuff will not endure" (Shakespeare *Twelfth Night* 2.3.51). The malicious tone turns briefly elegiac in the sixth stanza with the memory of an old love, Cinara. Meter: fourth Asclepiadean.

1-12. Lyce, my prayers have been answered: you are a hag. You try to be seductive, but Cupid hates the way you look.

1. Audivere ... di ... di audivere: repetition with chiasmus, giving the words a jeering tone. **mea vota:** perhaps those attendant on his lockout in 3.10, when he warned her that he would not put up with this treatment forever.

2-3. fis anus ... vis, etc.: the *f-* and *s-* sibilants give his malicious glee a hissing sound.

4. ludis: i.e., as if she were still a girl.

5. cantu tremulo: abl. with *sollicitas*; her singing voice has gotten unsteady. Compare hers with Phyllis' *amanda voce* in 4.11.34. **pota:** the drunken old woman is a traditional type: see note on 3.15.16. **Cupidinem lentum:** personification, a reluctant Cupid.

6. sollicitas: conative, you try to arouse. **virentis:** gen. with *Chiae*: blooming, as in 1.9.17. Contrasted with *aridas* in line 9.

7. Chiae: the name of a younger hetaera, derived from the island of Chios. Cf. Lesbia, Delia, etc. **doctae psallere:** trained to play the lyre. On the *docta puella*, see 3.9.10 and note.

8. excubat: keeps watch. The *locus classicus* of this conceit is Sophocles' ode to Eros in *Antigone*: "you spend the night on a girl's soft cheeks," ἐν μαλακαῖς παρειαῖς νεάνιδος ἐννυχεύεις (784).

9. Importunus: both unsuitable to aging Lyce and relentless in his pursuit of youth. **aridas quercus:** figurative for desiccated former beauties; cf. Lydia's comparison to *aridae frondes* in 1.25.19.

10. luridi: a sickly yellow color.

12. turpant: disfigure. **capitis nives,** the snows of your head, are gray hair as in Catullus 64.309 *niveo vertice*.

13-22. But Coan silks and jewels cannot bring back the dazzling looks that swept me off my feet in the old days.

13. Coae ... purpurae: the professional dress of hetaeras was made from gauzy dyed silks made on the island of Cos—but not usually dyed purple.

14. cari lapides: precious stones, like the jewels in 3.24.48. **semel:** once and for all, as in 4.7.21 and often in Horace, for whom the finality of time is nearly an obsession.

15. notis ... fastis: in the public record; a *fasti* (pl. for sing.) was a list of regular festivals or consuls. Here it means approximately what we mean by "the record book." The book on her salad days has been closed and put away. **condita ... inclusit:** has locked up and put away.

16. volucris dies: as in 3.28.6. Horace has several variants of the expression, e.g., *invida aetas* (1.11.7), *fugiens hora* (3.29.48).

17. venus = *venustas*, sexy good looks and elegance.

18. illius, illius: i.e., of that Lyce of old; note the short penult.

20. me surpuerat mihi: one of the philosophic arguments against falling in love was that it deprived the lover of self-mastery, Gk. ἐγκράτεια. The verb is a colloquial syncopated form of *surripuerat*.

21. felix: modifies understood *tu*, Lyce. **post Cinaram:** either after her death, or second only to Cinara, who is so often mentioned by Horace as an old flame that she may be a real person: 4.1.3ff., *Epist.* 1.7.28, 1.14.33.

22. facies: to be taken both with *nota*, a well-known beauty, and with descriptive gen. *artium gratarum*. In her prime Lyce had both the looks and the musical talents of a first-class hetaera.

22-28. Now you are old as a crow, and young men laugh because your fire is out.

24. servatura: of the Fates, destined to preserve. **parem:** with *Lycen* below.

25. cornicis vetulae: for the proverbial longevity of the crow, cf. 3.17.13, *annosa cornix*. **temporibus:** years or age, dat. with *parem*.

28. facem: Lyce is compared to a burned-out

torch, no match for the *iuvenes fervidi* (26).

14

Ostensibly a victory ode for Tiberius to commemorate his conquest of the Vindelici in 15 B.C., this complements the ode to Drusus, 4.4. Horace duly mentions the emperor's stepson in lines 14 and 29, but his chief emphasis is on Augustus, to whom the ode is addressed. Meter: Alcaic strophe.

1-9. How can the senate and people immortalize your virtues, Augustus, since your victory over the Vindelici?

1. Quae cura: what solicitous action; subject of *aeternet* (5). **patrum ... Quiritium:** of the senate and citizens, as in the SPQR formula.

2. plenis honorum muneribus: instrumental abl., with tributes full of honors.

3. virtutes: obj. of *aeternet*. **in aevum,** forever, reinforces *aeternet*.

4. per titulos, etc.: specifies *muneribus* above. *Tituli* are commemorative inscriptions as well as honorific titles such as *Augustus, divi filius, princeps*. **fastus:** acc. pl. of *fasti*, consular lists and other commemorative (*memores*) records. This line echoes 3.17.4, *per memores genus omne fastus*.

5. aeternet: a rare word for immortalize; deliberative subjunctive. **qua:** the rel. adverb, where.

5-6. habitabilis ... oras: the inhabited world or *oikoumene*.

7. quem: Augustus, obj. of *didicere*. **legis expertes Latinae:** lacking Roman law, therefore (in our Roman eyes) lawless and barbaric.

8. didicere: have come to know, through the military operations of his stepsons Tiberius and Drusus in 15 B.C.

9. quid Marte posses: a Greek "I know thee who thou art" construction, glossing *didicere*. Although Augustus was not the field commander, he was under imperial law the supreme military commander and the officer to whom the *auspicia* formally belonged.

9-24. Under your command Drusus and Tiberius have defeated the Genauni, Breuni, and Raeti: like a wind driving the waves before it, Tiberius rode his bellowing steed through the flame of battle.

10-11. Genaunos ... Breunos: tribes of the Tyrolean Alps on the river Inn. The Breuni survive in the name of the Brenner Pass. Both are obj. of *deiecit*. **implacidum** appears first here in extant Latin.

11-12. arces ... tremendis implies they had great fortresses high in the Alps.

13. deiecit acer: climactically placed at the beginning of an enjambed stanza, eagerly threw down. **plus vice simplici:** in a more than simple requital; the punishment he dealt them was greater than they bargained for.

14. maior Neronum: Tiberius Claudius Nero was older than his brother Drusus by four years. The nom. *Tiberius* will not fit in an Alcaic meter. **mox:** Tiberius' attack on the Raeti came a little after his brother's on the Genauni and the Breuni. The campaign is described in Velleius 2.95 and Dio 54.22.

15. immanis: savage; according to Strabo (4.6.8), when they captured a town they murdered their male captives, including infants and women who according to their seers were pregnant with male children.

16. auspiciis ... secundis: under favorable omens. This, like *milite tuo* (9), reminds the reader that the auspices were Augustus', with the young Neros acting as his agents only.

17. certamine Martio: warfare. The caesura is not observed, as also in 1.37.14.

18. devota morti ... liberae: sworn to death as free men.

19. fatigaret: subjunctive (ind. question) depending on the idea in *spectandus*: remarkable with what ruins he exhausted hearts set on death, etc.

20-22. indomitas ... nubes: epic simile: almost as the Auster drives the unmastered waves, when the band of Pleiades splits the clouds.

23-24. vexare, mittere: with *impiger*: energetic in harassing and at driving. The **ignes** through which Tiberius drives his horse are the metaphorical blaze of combat or the burning villages of the Raeti.

25-40. Like the river Aufidus in flood, Tiberius wrecked the lines of barbarians with your aid. Since the fall of Alexandria, Fortune has brought your missions to a glorious end.
25-29. sic ... ut: a rare inversion of the usual form of comparison. **tauriformis** is also rare in Latin poetry since Catullus and the *neoterici*, who avoided compounds made up in the Greek style. **Aufidus**, the river in Apulia near Horace's birthplace, is torrential also in 3.30.10, *violens obstrepit Aufidus*.
26. Dauni Apuli: the legendary king of Apulia; cf. 1.22.14, 3.30.11.
28. diluviem meditatur: plans or threatens a flood.
29. Claudius: another synonym for the metrically intractable *Tiberius*. For more on Tiberius Claudius Nero, see appendix A.
31. metendo: by mowing down, instrumental abl. with *stravit*. Cf. the simile in Catullus 64.353-55.
32. sine clade: i.e., without casualties in his own army.
33-34. te ... te ... tibi: Horace returns to his main topic, Augustus, with the reminder that he is ultimately to be credited with this victory.
35. portus: acc. pl. obj. of *patefecit*. The city had two harbors, one on each side of the mole linking Pharos to the mainland. **Alexandrea:** Cleopatra's capital, taken by Augustus fifteen years earlier on August 1, 30 B.C.
36. vacuam ... aulam: Cleopatra's palace, emptied by her suicide.
37. lustro ... tertio: in the third five-year period; cf. Horace on his own age in 4.1.6, *circa lustra decem*.
39-40. peractis ... imperiis: through the execution of your commands. **arrogavit:** has claimed for Augustus (*OLD* 4), with the additional notion that

Fortuna has added *laudem et decus* to *belli secundos exitus* (*OLD* 2b).

41-52. Barbarians marvel at you; the rivers and lands heed you and venerate you.
41. Te: repeated seven times in three stanzas as counterpart to the parade of tribes, rivers, and lands, *victae longo ordine gentes* (Virgil Aen. 8.722). **Cantaber:** collective sing., the most resistant of the Spanish tribes; see note on 3.8.21.
42. profugus Scythes: a more ornamental than actual enemy, as far as is known. For the epithet, see note on 1.35.9 *profugi Scythes*. Further notes at 3.8.23, 4.5.25. Like the Indians, they were known only by hearsay (*auditu modo cognitos*), Suetonius Aug. 21.3.
43. tutela praesens: an effective defense.
44. dominae ... Romae: personified, as she would later appear on coins; cf. 4.3.13, *Romae principis urbium*.
45. fontium qui celat origines: the Nile's headwaters remained unexplored until the nineteenth century.
46. Nilus: representing the Egyptians and the Ethiopians. **Hister:** the lower Danube, by metonymy the Dacians. **Tigris:** representing the Parthians.
47. beluosus: full of *belua*, sea monsters. A *hapax legomenon*, another of several coinages apparently made for this poem. The Romans were ready to believe the ocean was full of strange and monstrous marine life. The troops of Drusus' son Germanicus, driven into the North Sea by a storm in A.D. 16, saw *monstra maris, ambiguas hominum et beluarum formas, visa sive ex metu credita* (Tacitus Annales 2.24.6).
48. Britannis: dat. with *obstrepit*, roars about the Britons. The only British sea the Romans would have encountered was the sometimes stormy English Channel. Strabo 4.5.3 reports an embassy of British chieftans to Augustus, but the conquest of Britain talked about earlier in the principate was never carried out; see note on 1.35.29.

49. non paventis funera Galliae: gen. with *tellus.* For the Druid belief in the immortality of the soul and their consequent fearlessness in battle, see Caesar *BGall.* 6.14.5 *imprimis hoc volunt persuadere, non interire animas, ... atque hoc maxime ad virtutem excitari putant, metu mortis neglecto.*

50. audit: heeds. The subjects are the rivers and ocean in the previous stanza as well as *tellus* here.

51. Sygambri: the Germans whose incursion into northern Gaul and defeat of Lollius in 16 B.C. occasioned a personal campaign by Augustus and Tiberius; see note on 4.2.34-36, *ferocis Sygambros.*

15

Turning from the military subject of the previous ode, Horace devotes his final ode to a eulogy of Augustus' peaceful achievements. Written soon after the princeps' return to Italy on July 4, 13 B.C. (see intro. to 4.5, to which it is closely related), this concentrates on the benefits of the *pax Augusta:* restoration of past virtues and suppression of foreign and domestic violence. Meter: Alcaic strophe, the meter of choice for Horatian patriotism.

1-4. Apollo forbids me to sing of warlike themes.

1. volentem: adversative, though I was willing. **proelia:** i.e., Augustus' victories in war. **loqui =** *canere,* as in 4.2.45.

2. increpuit: chided me. The rebuke from Apollo is probably inspired by Callimachus' *Aetia* 21-24: "when first I set the tablet on my knees, Apollo said to me 'singer, raise a fat animal for sacrifice, but keep a slender Muse.' " **lyra:** instrumental abl. with *loqui.*

3-4. ne ... darem: the substantive clause depends on the idea of ordering contained in *increpuit.* He chided me that I should not spread my little sails, etc. **parva Tyrrhenum:** the juxtaposition emphasizes the disparity between Horace's lyric style and the large themes of Italian warfare. The opening lines are thus a *recusatio,* rejecting an epic warlike theme.

4-16. Your regime, Caesar, has restored our farms, rescued our standards from the Parthians, made peace, restrained vice, and called back the virtues that made Rome master of the world.

4. Tua, Caesar, aetas, etc.: The abrupt transition to a catalog of blessings gives it special emphasis. Forbidden to sing of war, the poet enumerates Augustus' peaceful achievements.

5. fruges ... uberes: refers to Augustus' agrarian reforms, which broke up many large *latifundia* and redistributed land to his veterans. Augustus' program of free loans to smallholders further strengthened the family farm. **et ... et ... et:** the polysyndeton (*et* is repeated seven times in stanzas 2-4) underscores the great number of the princeps' achievements.

6-7. signa ... derepta: though true in a limited sense (they *were* taken down), this is a bald misstatement of the well-known facts. In 20 B.C. Rome established Tigranes as a client king in Armenia (Parthia's northern neighbor). By a simple show of force, Augustus' stepson Tiberius could now persuade Parthian king Phraates to enter into a compact of friendship under whose terms the soldiers and standards of Crassus, captured at Carrhae in 53 B.C., were peaceably returned. **nostro ... Iovi:** note the emphatic position of *nostro;* "our Jove" is the temple on the Capitoline. The standards were later transferred to the temple of Mars Ultor, dedicated in 2 B.C.

7-8. superbis postibus: dat. of separation with *derepta;* this is a contemptuous reference to the Parthian temple where the trophies had hung for over thirty years.

8. vacuum duellis: free from wars; *duellis* is archaic.

9. Ianum Quirini clausit: the temple or arch of Janus near the north end of the Forum was closed when no wars were in progress. Prior to Augustus, this had happened only twice in Roman history; it

happened three times during his principate. Horace
varies the usual phrase, *Ianus Quirinus*.

9-10. ordinem rectum: obj. of *evaganti*. **licentiae,**
indirect obj., agrees with *evaganti*: Augustus has
imposed restraints on license that strays from right
order. The figure is military, of breaking ranks in
the order of battle; used here of anybody straying
"from the straight and narrow," as we might say.
The reference is to his moral legislation.

10-11. frena ... iniecit: put a rein on license; cf.
3.24.29, *refrenare licentiam*.

12. veteres ... artis: the traditional virtues that
had made Rome great, as enumerated in the
Roman Odes, 3.1-6. For *ars* as a virtue, cf. 3.3.9,
hac arte. **revocavit,** with *rettulit* (5) and *restituit* (6),
emphasizes a fundamental tenet of Augustan
ideology, that the principate was a restoration
rather than a revolution.

**13-15. Latinum nomen et Italae ... vires, fama-
que et imperi ... maiestas:** the three stages in the
extension of Roman dominion.

15. porrecta: sc. *est*; as often in lyric, the subject
is plural, *fama et maiestas*. **ortus:** acc. pl. of repeat-
ed occurrence; the reference is to the empire in
the east, which extended as far as the Caspian
Sea. The oriental magniloquence with which this
long sentence (4-16) ends fits the subject.

16. ab Hesperio cubili: from its western bed,
Italy.

**17-24. While Caesar guards the empire, no
domestic madness or foreign wars will disturb
the peace.**

17. Custode rerum Caesare: cf. 3.14.15, *tenente
Caesare terras*, and *Aen*. 1.282, *Romanos, rerum
dominos*. For the image of the princeps as *custos*, cf.
1.12.49, *pater atque custos*, 4.5.2, *Romulae custos
gentis*.

18. exiget otium: drive out peace.

19. ira: like *furor civilis* and *vis*, rage is half-per-
sonified. Both *furor* and *ira* are key words in the
Aeneid as causes of tragedy in both love and war.
procudit: hammers out, forges.

20. inimicat: a Horatian coinage; makes enemies
of.

21. qui ... Danuvium bibunt: Augustus' exten-
sion of the Roman frontier to the Danube was one
of his greatest and most lasting achievements,
cementing Roman influence in central and eastern
Europe. Horace refers here to the recently defeated
Vindelici and other Alpine tribes on the south
bank of the Danube (in mod. Germany; see map
1), referred to in 4.2 and 14. The Rhine and the
Danube remained the northern boundary of the
Roman empire for centuries. For the figure of
speech, cf. 2.20.20, *Rhodani potor*.

22. edicta Iulia: the general name for the poli-
cies and treaties of Augustus that made the *pax
Romana* possible. **Getae:** the people north of the
lower Danube (mod. Romania), praised for their
stern morality in 3.24.11.

23. Seres: lit. Chinese, used vaguely of people
beyond the eastern frontier.

24. Tanaïn prope ... orti: the Scythians; the
Tanais is the Don river, in southern Russia.

**25-32. Therefore let us daily, with wine, music,
and song, celebrate the glorious men of old,
Troy, Anchises, and the progeny of Venus.**

25. Nos: subject of *canemus* (32) in a strong
hyperbaton putting heavy emphasis on the poem's
final word. **profestis lucibus:** on ordinary working
days. *lux = dies* as in 4.6.42 and 4.11.19.

28. rite: in due form. **apprecati:** having prayed
to; another Horatian coinage, not found again
until Apuleius, two centuries later.

29. virtute functos duces: lit. leaders who per-
formed their *virtus*, i.e., did their virtuous duty; but
the phrase also approximates various euphemisms
for "die" such as *officio fungi*: hence "died glori-
ously." *Duces* is object of *canemus* (32) with *Troi-
am, Anchisen*, and *progeniem*. **more patrum:** Cato's
Origines alluded to the early custom of singing
songs of old glories: *in Originibus dixit Cato morem
apud maiores hunc epularum fuisse, ut deinceps qui
accubarent canerent ad tibiam clarorum virorum*

laudes atque virtutes (Cicero *Tusc.* 4.3). For a free reconstruction, see Macaulay's *Lays of Ancient Rome*.

30. Lydis remixto, etc.: abl. absolute, with song mingled with (the sound of) Lydian pipes. Plato mentions the Lydian style as soft banquet music. The prefix of *remixto* suggests repetition or persistence.

31. Troiam, Anchisen, etc.: the source and founders of the Roman race as for example set forth in Virgil's *Aeneid*. The *progeniem Veneris* includes the *gens Iulia*, of which Augustus was an adoptive member. Cf. *Carm. Saec.* 50, *Anchisae Venerisque sanguis*. The fourth book of the *Odes* thus ends with a reference to Venus, as it has begun: *Intermissa, Venus, diu*.

32. canemus plays off *me loqui* at the end of the first line. Horace lays aside his persona as the isolated *vates* who shuns the mob (as in 3.1.1, *odi profanum vulgus*) and speaks in a communal voice, as in 4.2.49-52: "he had to go a long way before he was able to speak like that" (Fraenkel).

APPENDIX A

PEOPLE

A note about Roman names: By the Augustan age, it had long been the custom to name freeborn men with a *praenomen* or personal name, a *nomen gentile* derived from the person's clan or *gens* (usually ending in adjectival *-ius*), and a *cognomen* or family name. Horace's father, having been born a slave, would likely have adopted the old Roman name *Horatius* in the same way American ex-slaves adopted names like Washington, Adams, and Jefferson. Quintus Horatius Flaccus, like Publius Vergilius Maro and Publius Ovidius Naso (*praenomen* + *nomen gentile* + *cognomen*), is generally known by his gentile name, though in referring to himself by name he twice uses *Flaccus* and twice *Horatius*. There was no regular system for the naming of women.

The names in this list are chiefly male, consisting of people known to be (or, like Numida, likely to be) historical personages. Hetaeras, who often used pseudonymns in real life, are assumed for the purposes of this list to be types in Horace rather than actual individuals: no attempt therefore is made to identify people bearing such names as Barine, Chloë, Chloris, Damalis, Glycera, Lalage, Leuconoë, Lyce, Lyde, Lydia, Neaera, Pholoë, Phyllis, Pyrrha, or Tyndaris. The same anonymity applies to male lovers or boyfriends, e.g., Calaïs, Cyrus, Enipeus, Gyges, Lyciscus, Sybaris, Telephus, and Xanthias. Mythological characters are explained in the notes as they appear.

M. Vipsanius **Agrippa** (64-12 B.C.), friend and supporter of **Augustus**, commanded the left wing at the battle of Actium and was chiefly responsible for Antony's defeat. Thrice consul (37, 28, 27) and probably Augustus' most trusted ally, he is mentioned in Horace (1.6) for his achievements as a military commander who deserved to be celebrated in epic verse. His second wife, Augustus' daughter Julia, bore him five children, including Agrippina, through whom he became grandfather of the Emperor Caligula, great-grandfather of the Emperor **Nero**.

Iullus **Antonius**, son of Marcus Antonius the triumvir and his third wife Fulvia, was brought up in Rome by Augustus' sister Octavia, Antony's cast-off fourth wife. In 21 he married Octavia's daughter Marcella. At the time of Horace's ode addressed to him (4.2, 13 B.C.), he was close to **Augustus** and seems to have suggested that Horace write a Pindaric ode in honor of Augustus' return from his Gallic campaigns. An amateur poet, he composed an epic *Diomedeia* in twelve books. He later was condemned for adultery with Augustus' daughter Julia and conspiracy to take over the principate, and committed suicide in 2 B.C. Knowing what we do, it is easy for us to read between Horace's lines a sense of Iullus' fatal excessiveness.

Gaius Octavius **Augustus** (63 B.C.-A.D. 14) is generally called Octavian when speaking of events prior to 27 B.C. Grandnephew and adopted successor of Gaius Julius Caesar, he appointed himself Caesar's avenger when the dictator was assassinated in 44 B.C. While Horace fought on the side of the assassins at the battle of Philippi in 42, the party of Octavian defeated the self-styled tyrannicides, and the triumvirate of Antony, Lepidus, and Octavian became Rome's ruling junta. This alliance unraveled with the deposition of Lepidus in 36, and the struggle between Antony and Octavian was decided at a battle off the western coast of Greece near Actium in September of 31. By this time, Horace had returned to Rome under a general amnesty, and under the patronage of **Maecenas** became a vociferous partisan of the *pax Augusti*, which became the life work of the first *princeps*. Honored by the Senate in 27 with the title Augustus, the first emperor gave his name to an era through a program that was as much cultural as political or military. He enacted laws to promote marriage, penalize adultery, and curb excessive private spending; he undertook the restoration of temples, and promoted a vast program of image-making on behalf of old-fashioned *Romanitas*, which included the efforts of **Virgil** and Horace, the historian Livy, and many lesser writers. Suetonius preserves fragments of letters from Augustus to Horace that indicate a warm personal friendship, though Horace declined Augustus' offer of a post as his personal secretary. Horace's poetry is unabashedly adulatory, and like Virgil he took every opportunity to promote the official deification of Augustus.

Censorinus, to whom Horace offers a gift of poetry in 4.8, is commonly identified as C. Marcius Censorinus, who became consul in 8 B.C.; but a strong case can be made for Lucius Marcius Censorinus, who attempted to defend Caesar on the Ides of March in 44 B.C. Made consul in 39, he served as one of the *quindecemviri* in charge of the *ludi saeculares* of 17 B.C.

Cleopatra VII Philopator, queen of Egypt, was the last of a dynasty created by Alexander's general Ptolemy. Antony's lover and ally in the Battle of Actium, she died by suicide in 30 B.C. Her defeat and death are described in 1.37. For E.M. Forster's brief biography, see appendix D.

Marcus Valerius Messalla **Corvinus** (64 B.C.-A.D.

8), invited to Horace's drinking party in 3.21, was a student at Athens with Horace and Marcus Cicero; when Julius Caesar was assassinated, he fought on the side of Brutus and Cassius at the Battle of Philippi in 42. Later converted to **Octavian**'s side, he served as consul in 31 and joined the battle against Antony's forces at the Battle of Actium. As proconsul in Gaul, he defeated the Aquitani and was given a triumph in Rome (27 B.C.). Retiring thereafter from politics, he became a prominent orator and historian; he was patron of a literary circle that included **Tibullus**, Sulpicia, and Lygdamus. He wrote treatises on grammar and style, an interest reflected in the elaborate wordplay of 3.21. Fragments of his writing are still extant.

Crispus Sallustius: see C. **Sallustius** Crispus.

Quintus **Dellius** changed sides so many times in the Roman civil wars (first Dolabella, then Cassius, after that Antony, finally **Octavian**) that Valerius Messalla **Corvinus** called him "the circus-rider of the civil wars," *desultor bellorum civilium*. Both learned and colorful, he wrote a history of Antony's war against the Parthians as well as *epistulae lascivae* to **Cleopatra** (Seneca *Suasoriae* 1.7)—all now lost. *Odes* 2.3, about the importance of keeping a level head, is appropriately addressed to him, as Horace's odes of advice tend to name individuals who exemplify the virtue recommended (NH 2.52).

Nero Claudius **Drusus** (38-9 B.C.), son of Livia Drusilla and Tiberius Claudius Nero, was raised with his older brother **Tiberius** in the imperial household and adopted by his stepfather **Augustus** after his father's death in 33 B.C. In 15 B.C., at the age of 23, he and his brother commanded successful operations against the Raeti and Vindelici north of the Tyrolean Alps, an exploit for which Horace wrote a Pindaric victory ode, 4.4. His later campaigns in Germany earned him and his descendants the surname Germanicus. He died of illness in 9 B.C. after a fall from a horse. He was father of the Emperor Claudius, grandfather of the Emperor Caligula, and great-grandfather of the Emperor Nero.

Aristius **Fuscus**, a close friend of Horace, is addressed in 1.22 with the declaration that the pure-hearted lover is immune to all dangers. Known to the ancient commentators as a *grammaticus doctissimus*, he was something more than a schoolmaster: **Porphyrio** says he wrote comedies, and in *Sat.* 1.10.83 he is mentioned as one of the critics who has approved the early work of Horace. In *Sat.* 1.9.60ff. Fuscus shows his waggish side by leaving Horace at the mercy of an adhesive social climber despite Horace's desperate signals. *Epist.* 10.1-5 describes Horace and Fuscus as intimates (*paene gemelli fraternis animis*), though he is a city man while Horace is a *ruris amator*.

Pompeius **Grosphus**, the wealthy Sicilian rancher addressed in the Ode to Tranquillity (2.16), may be related to the Grosphus of Agrigentum mentioned in the Second Punic War by Silius Italicus (*Punica* 14.208ff.) and the Eubulidas Grosphus praised by Cicero *In Verrem* 2.3.56. Porphyrio says he was an *eques Romanus*. Horace recommends him to **Iccius** in *Epist.* 1.12.22f.: *utere Pompeio Grospho et, si quid petet, ultro / defer; nil Grosphus nisi verum orabit et aequum.*

Iccius, once a devoted student of moral philosophy, is about to give it all up and embark on a plundering expedition into Arabia Felix in 1.29. That campaign, led by Aelius Gallus in 26-25 B.C., was a disaster, but Iccius survived and in *Epist.* 1.12, written in 20 B.C., he is depicted as managing **Agrippa's** estate in Sicily

Lucius **Lamia** could be any of three members of a distinguished family from Formiae mentioned by Horace. Lucius Aelius Lamia, an ally of Cicero,

was aedile in 45 B.C. and praetor in 42. His son Lucius served in Spain two decades later, and his grandson Lucius was consul in A.D. 3, governor of Africa in 15-16, and *praefectus urbi* in the year of his death, A.D. 32. The Lamia of 1.26 may be the Aelius named in 3.17, who served as legate in Spain. The Lamia in 1.36 is a young man, probably Aelius' grandson, as is the Lamia in *Epist.* 1.14.6.

The **Licinius** addressed in 2.10, *Rectius vives*, is identified in one group of manuscripts as Licinius Murena. The full name may be A. Terentius Varro Licinius Murena, and he may be the Murena mentioned in 3.19 (and the Murena who is host to Horace's party of travelers in *Sat.* 1.5), but all of this is hypothetical. A Licinius Murena was adopted by one Terentius Varro, making him half-brother by adoption of the Proculeius mentioned in 2.2.5 (see note) and of **Maecenas'** wife Terentia. This Licinius shared the consulship with Augustus in 23 B.C., but his candor in opposition to Augustus and his alleged involvement in Caepio's conspiracy against the Princeps led to his execution after trying to escape (Dio 54.3.5). The advice on moderation in 2.10 may, if the identification is correct, have a bearing on the character of Licinius. The identification with Licinius Murena is tempting because this personage was the patron of a leading Peripatetic (Athenaeus of Seleuceia), and because he was involved in dangerous political maneuvering that eventually cost him his life.

Marcus **Lollius**, cos. 21 B.C., the object of Horace's praise in 4.9, was a prominent supporter of **Augustus**. While on the one hand Horace praises his integrity, other ancient sources including Velleius Paterculus and Tacitus portray him as rapacious, corrupt, and incompetent. In 16 B.C. he lost the standards of a legion he was commanding against the Sygambri, a misfortune Tacitus would later label the *clades Lolliana* (*Annales* 1.10.4). Some time after Horace's ode he fell from favor, was accused of taking bribes from the king of

Parthia, and died in 2 B.C., possibly by suicide, leaving behind a spectacular daughter and an enormous fortune.

C. **Maecenas**, Horace's patron, traced his ancestry to Etruscan kings but preferred to remain a member of the equestrian class. A person of great wealth and something of a voluptuary, he was a close friend of **Octavian** during the early years of his principate, serving in sensitive diplomatic and political tasks. Though he never held public office, he played a major role in the regime, most notably as the orchestrator of literary work that would consolidate the Augustan image of piety and high public morals. As **Virgil's** patron he is credited with encouraging progress on the *Aeneid;* Virgil brought Horace into the literary circle, which also included Propertius. Horace is fulsome in his praise of Maecenas, who provided the Sabine farm where Horace spent much of his time and the financial support necessary to free him for a poet's life. Relations between Augustus and Maecenas cooled considerably in 22, when Maecenas leaked a state secret to his wife Terentia (see NH 2.155). Though Horace mentions him only once in *Odes* 4, the reference is affectionate (11.19) and there is no evidence of a falling-out between poet and patron. Maecenas died in 8 B.C., less than two months earlier than Horace himself.

Licinius **Murena**, newly elected to the college of augurs in 3.19, is generally presumed to be the **Licinius** of 2.10, q.v.

Numida, the friend of **Lamia** being welcomed home from Spain in 1.36, is otherwise unknown. **Porphyrio** says his name was Pomponius Numida, and many manuscripts of the *Odes* call him Numida Plotius, but neither identification can be confirmed.

Octavian: see **Augustus.**

Paullus Fabius Maximus, the dashing and successful lawyer to whom Horace sends Venus in 4.1, belonged to an ancient and noble family and was one of **Augustus'** close friends. Sometime after the composition of 4.1, he married Augustus' cousin Marcia, the grandniece of Julius Caesar. He was also a friend of Ovid, who wrote the hymn sung at his wedding and who later asked him to intervene on his behalf when exiled to Tomi (*Pont.* 1.2 and 2.3, *vox, precor, Augustas pro me tua molliat aures,* 1.2.115). Two years after the publication of *Odes* 4 he became consul (11 B.C.).

Lucius Munatius **Plancus**, consul in 42 B.C., was a prominent politician and correspondent of Cicero. That he was considered an opportunist we have from Cicero himself in a letter to Plancus (*epist.* 10.3.3). He and his ally M. Lepidus had their own brothers proscribed, and soon after had themselves honored in a triumph for their earlier victories *ex Gallia* before sharing the consulship of 42—a set of accomplishments their former soldiers mocked with the punning ditty *de germanis, non de Gallis, duo triumphant consules.* A one-time supporter of the republican cause and later of its adversary Antony, he deserted to **Octavian** in 32, and in 27 authored the proposal that Octavian be given the honorific title Augustus. Horace addresses a consolation to him in 1.7, but it is not clear what *tristitia vitaeque labores* occasioned the poem.

Gaius Asinius **Pollio** (76 B.C.-A.D. 4), addressed in the opening poem of *Odes* 2, was a friend of Catullus (poem 12) and saved **Virgil's** property from confiscation in 41 B.C. Statesman, historian, and patron of letters, he earned a triumph for his victory over the Parthini in the Balkans and used the spoils to found a national library, Rome's first public library. His tragedies were praised by Virgil (*Ecl.* 3.86) and Horace (2.1.9); his *Historiae,* covering the period of civil wars from 60 to 43 B.C., are the subject of 2.1. All of his writings, except for three letters in Cicero's *Epistulae ad* *familiares* (10.31-33), are lost.

Pompeius, the comrade-in-arms welcomed back to Italy in 2.7, is identified as Pompeius Varus in Ps.-Acro and some mss., but nothing else is known about him except what Horace says in this poem, viz. that he fought on the losing side at Philippi in 42 B.C. and was involved in later battles of the civil war. He is not to be confused with Pompeius Grosphus. The *nomen gentile* Pompeius was common in Horace's century, and this Pompey may be one of many whose family owed its citizenship to a member of the great Pompey family that included Caesar's rival Gnaeus Pompeius Magnus and Octavian's rival Sextus Pompey.

Pompeius Grosphus: see **Grosphus.**

Pomponius Porphyrion, generally referred to as Porphyrio, wrote a commentary on Horace's poems for school use in the early third century A.D. Using older commentaries that are now lost, he commented on Horace's subject matter, grammar, and style. Though his work is still useful, he reports gossip uncritically and interprets all personal statements in Horace's poems as strictly autobiographical.

Quintilius: see Quintilius **Varus.**

Gaius **Sallustius** Crispus, addressed in 2.2, was the grandnephew and adopted son of the historian Sallust. Like **Maecenas,** whom he succeeded as **Augustus'** chief private counsellor, he remained a member of the equestrian order. But he was enormously rich, and Tacitus remarks that there was nothing old-fashioned about his love of luxury: *diversus a veterum instituto per cultum et munditias copiaque et adfluentia luxu proprior. Suberat tamen vigor animi ingentibus negotiis par, eo acrior quo somnum et inertiam magis ostentabat* (Annales 3.30.2-3). He was also a generous patron of literature, according to an epigram of Crinagoras, *Anth. Plan-*

udea 40 (GP 1975ff.).

Septimius, addressed as a loyal friend in 2.6, is introduced to **Tiberius** in *Epist.* 1.9 as *fortem bonumque.* Suetonius has preserved in his *Vita Horati* part of a letter of **Augustus** to Horace mentioning him as a mutual friend: *tui qualem habeam memoriam poteris ex Septimio quoque nostro audire.* **Porphyrio** says he was an *eques Romanus* and a comrade in arms of Horace, perhaps speculating in the latter case on the basis of 2.6.8, *militiaeque.*

Lucius **Sestius,** addressed as *O beate Sesti* in 1.4.14, first appears in literature as the son of P. Sestius, tribune of 57 B.C. Cicero, in a speech defending the father, brings the tearful young son in for pathetic effect: *video hunc praetextatum eius filium oculis lacrimantibus me intuentem* (Pro Sestio 144). He joined the republican allies of Brutus in 44 and served (like Horace) under Brutus in Macedonia. Proscribed and then pardoned, he won the respect of Augustus for his principled republicanism and was appointed *consul suffectus* in 23 B.C., the date *Odes* 1-3 was published.

Tiberius Claudius Nero (42 B.C.-A.D. 37), brother of Nero Claudius **Drusus,** was adopted by his stepfather **Augustus** after his father's death. His mother was Augustus' powerful wife Livia. In 20 B.C. he accompanied his stepfather to the east and received back the Roman standards lost to the Parthians at Carrhae in 53 B.C. A capable military commander, he was honored in a Horatian victory ode (4.14) for the victory over the Vindelici won in combined operations with his brother Drusus. He became the second of the Julio-Claudian emperors when Augustus died in A.D. 14.

Albius **Tibullus,** the elegiac poet, was a friend and younger contemporary of Horace. Born some time between 55 and 48 B.C. to the equestrian rank, he wrote love elegies in a refined, plain style at about the time Horace was writing his *Odes*. Horace addresses him in 1.33, *Albi, ne doleas*, and *Epist. 1.4, Albi, nostrorum sermonum candide iudex*. He died in 19 B.C.

Torquatus, invited to dinner in *Epist. 1.5* and addressed in *Odes* 4.7, may be a son of the L. Manlius Torquatus who was consul in the year of Horace's birth. Horace's references in the epistle to a case he was pleading and in the ode to his *facundia* suggest he practiced oratory and law in Rome. His ancestor Titus Manlius Torquatus Imperiosus, consul in 347, 344, and 340 B.C., won the cognomen by stripping the torque or gold neckpiece from a Gaul whom he killed in single combat.

C. **Valgius** Rufus, twitted for writing weepy love elegies in 2.9, is mentioned in *Sat.* 1.10.82 as a critic in the circle of **Maecenas** and **Octavian**, who approves of Horace's work. A few surviving fragments confirm that he wrote various kinds of poetry. He also wrote learned monographs on rhetoric, grammar, philology, and even herbal medicine. He was given a suffect consulship in 12 B.C., perhaps more for his cultural than his political achievements.

L. **Varius** Rufus, author of elegiac, epic, and tragic poetry during the age of Augustus, was a friend of **Virgil** and **Maecenas** before Horace joined their circle, and joined Virgil in introducing Horace to Maecenas (*Sat.* 1.6.55). Considered by Horace one of the top poets of his time, he wrote a highly praised tragedy *Thyestes* in 29 B.C. and a Panegyric of Augustus. After Virgil's death in 19 B.C., he

was appointed, with Tucca, the task of preparing the unfinished *Aeneid* for publication. In 1.6 Horace suggests him as the one to write a poem celebrating the military achievements of **Agrippa**. See also *Sat.* 1.5.40, 93; 1.9.23, 1.10.44, 81; 2.8.21, 63; *Epist.* 2.1.247, *Ars P.* 55.

P. Alfenus **Varus** may be the person addressed in 1.18. A distinguished jurist, he became suffect consul in 39 B.C. He has also been tentatively identified as the Alfenus of Catullus 30, the Varus of Catullus 10 and 22, and the Varus of Virgil *Ecl.* 6.6-12 and 9.26-29. See also Quintilius Varus below.

Quintilius **Varus**: the Varus addressed in 1.18 and the Quintilius mourned in 1.24 are traditionally identified as this friend of **Virgil** and Horace. A native of Cremona living in Tibur and a member of the equestrian order, he is remembered in the *Ars Poetica* (438-44) as a helpful critic of poems in progress. See also P. Alfenus Varus above.

Publius **Vergilius** Maro (70-19 B.C.), the poet of the *Aeneid*, was a contemporary and friend of Horace. Like Horace, he lost his farm to Octavian's confiscations during the turbulent years before Actium and the *pax Augusta*, but he regained his lands through the intervention of friends and became a close friend of **Maecenas** and **Augustus**. In *Sat.* 1.6.55 Horace tells how Virgil introduced Horace to Maecenas, who became his patron. The Virgil mentioned in 1.3 as setting out on a voyage to Greece is probably the poet; the one invited to dinner in 4.12 could be a businessman with the same *nomen gentile*.

APPENDIX B

METERS

Meter (Lat. *modus*) is the rhythmic pattern of poetry, without which language cannot be poetry, just as sound without rhythm cannot be music. Meter is as instinctual as the beat of the heart. English meter is based on the natural syllabic emphasis of words: blank verse (unrhymed iambic pentameter) uses the natural rhythms of word accent, as in this line of Marlowe describing Helen of Troy:

Was thís the fáce that laúnched a thoúsand shíps?

Latin and Greek meter also uses the natural rhythms of words, but instead of accent or ictus it uses quantity—the length of a syllable—to establish its rhythms:

Persĭcōs ŏdī, pŭĕr, āppărātŭs.

Here, instead of bearing down harder on the long syllables (marked —), the idea is to hold them a bit longer than the short ones (marked ‿), as in music you would hold a half note twice as long as a quarter note. The Sapphic rhythm of the sample above can be sounded as follows:

Dumm de dumm dumm dumm, de de dumm de dumm dumm.

Words keep their stress accent in poetry, but stress is subordinated to quantitative rhythm. When stress-accent and meter correspond, the resulting harmony is *homodyne*; when they conflict (as is more often the case), the effect is *heterodyne*.

Latin meter is not hard to learn. The first step is to recognize the basic rules of quantity that distinguish long "half-note" syllables from short "quarter-note" syllables. A syllable is short and can be sounded rapidly unless

(a) It contains a vowel that is *long by nature*, like the ablative ending of *puellā* or the accusative ending of *Persicōs*. Other long quantities are built into the stem, like the *ē* in *Homērus* or the *ī* in *ruīna*. Latin-English dictionaries will always mark long vowels, and because Latin is not a silent language it is a good idea to keep track of the sound of words as you learn them. Diphthongs (ae, au, ei, eu, oe, and ui) are also long by nature.

(b) It is followed by two consonants, making it *long by position*. For example, in the sample line above, the first syllable of *apparatus* is long by position because the two *p*'s, always sounded separately in Latin, slow down that first syllable, making it long even though the vowel itself is short. The double-consonant rule applies even if one or both of the consonants are in the following word. Also, *x* counts as a double consonant (=cs), so although the *a* of *vivax* is naturally short, its syllable "makes position" because of the double consonant that follows it. Where there is a combination of a mute (*b, c, d, g, p,* and *t*) followed by a liquid (*l, m, n,* or *r*), as in *acris*, the preceding syllable may be long or short depending on the demands of the meter. For example, in *Epod.* 17.57 the first syllable of *sacrum* scans long, but in *Odes* 3.2.26 the same syllable is short. This option is the "*muta cum liquida*" rule.

Like riding a bicycle, this is more complicated to explain than to do. The best way to learn the meters of Horace is to memorize a few samples. When the basic patterns have become second nature, the rest is easy.

Read out loud, Latin poetry has a musical quality that is reflected in the Latin word for poem, *carmen*, which also means song. Horace called his poems *carmina*; we call them odes from the Greek word for song, *ōdē* (ᾠδή). The *Odes* are of a particularly musical type called *lyric* (as opposed to epic, iambic, or elegiac). Traditionally, such poetry in early Greece was sung to the lyre, and though that instrumental accompaniment had ceased to be customary, the lyre remains the chief symbol by which Horace refers to the poetry of his *Odes*. Horace regarded it as his greatest achievement that he brought Greek lyric meters into Latin poetry (see for example 3.30.13).

The chief building block of meter is the metron or foot, a particular sequence of long and short syllables. The typical foot around which Aeolic or lyric meters are built is the choriamb. Here are the most common feet:

- the choriamb, as in *scīrĕ nĕfās, cōnsĭlĭō,* and *quae nĕmŏra aut.*
- the spondee, as in *audāx, ōdī,* and *nūnc tē.*
- the iamb, as in *dĕōs, vĭdēs,* and *mĕae.*
- the trochee, as in *nāvĭs, pēctŭs,* and *mōrtĭs.*
- the dactyl, as in *sōlvĭtŭr, crēdŭlŭs,* and *fābŭlă.*

Though lyric meters are not as a rule broken down into feet, it is convenient to know these building blocks. They are used not only in lyric meters, but in the originally epic dactylic hexameter and in various iambic meters. As the first of these examples shows, a foot does not necessarily begin or end with a word.

Feet are combined into verses or lines, which in turn may be combined into stanzas or strophes. Particularly in the *Odes*, Horace has a strong tendency to compose in units of four lines: about 78 of Horace's 103 odes are written in meters that fall into four-line stanzas (such as the Alcaic and the Sapphic), and only one ode (4.8) is of a length indivisible by four.

Scansion (< Lat. *scandere*) is the business of marking the long and short syllables in a line or stanza of poetry. Usually written above each line, it uses the *longum* (—) to mark long syllables, the *breve* (˘) for short syllables, and an × figure to mark *syllaba anceps* at any point where the syllable may by long or short. Two vertical lines (‖) mark a pause (diaeresis or caesura) in the middle of some meters; a single vertical line (|) is sometimes used to mark foot divisions. Elision, where the vowel or diphthong at the end of one word is absorbed into the initial vowel of the following word in the same line, is marked by a connecting line beneath the two vowels affected (e.g., *ausa et*). In such cases, the first vowel is said to *suffer elision* because its quantity (and also its sound, at the reader's option) is overridden or slurred with that of the second vowel. Because final *-m* and initial *h-* are weak consonants, both are susceptible to elision (e.g., *illum et, doctarum hederae, Acheronta Herculeus,* pron. *ill'et, doctar'ederae, Acheront'erculeus*). Any exception to the rule of elision is called *hiatus*.

Substitution: to allow flexibility in composition and avoid monotony in the simpler, repetitive meters, long or short syllables may be substituted by the poet within certain limitations. To indicate such options, a metrical scheme indicates acceptable substitutes *above* the usual long or short marks, as in this schema of the dactylic hexameter:

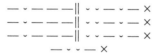

Such double marking occurs only in a metrical scheme, not in actual scansion.

The following metrical schemes are arranged in order of their frequency in the *Epodes* and *Odes*. For explanations of technical terms, see appendix C.

Alcaic Strophe

$$\times - \smile - - \| - \smile \smile - \smile \times$$
$$\times - \smile - - \| - \smile \smile - \smile \times$$
$$\times - \smile - - - \smile \, - \times$$
$$- \smile \smile - \smile \smile - \smile - \times$$

Horace's favorite lyric meter, used in thirty-seven odes, is named after the Greek Archaic poet Alcaeus of Mytilene, a Lesbiot who wrote in the early sixth century B.C. Horace shows a strong preference for a spondaic opening in the first three lines. The diaeresis is occasionally neglected, e.g., in 1.37.14 and 4.14.17. One distinguishing feature is the rapidity of the fourth line, which is sometimes exploited for expressive purposes.

Sapphic Strophe

$$- \smile - - - \| \smile \smile - \smile - \times$$
$$- \smile - - - \| \smile \smile - \smile - \times$$
$$- \smile - - - \| \smile \smile - \smile - \times$$
$$- \smile \smile - \times$$

Named after Sappho of Lesbos, a slightly older contemporary of Alcaeus (b. ca. 630 B.C.), this meter occurs in twenty-five odes. It consists of three Sapphic lines and a shorter Adonic, which gives a feeling of closure since it is also the regular ending of a dactylic hexameter. The pause after the fifth syllable is sometimes delayed until after the sixth, especially in the *Carmen Saeculare* and *Odes* 4. The lines of this meter are felt to flow into each other, a feature called synaphaea. Horace therefore tends to end each Sapphic with a longum (by nature or by position with a consonant in the succeeding line), and to avoid ending a line with a vowel if the next line of the same stanza begins with a vowel. Sometimes when this occurs there is elision from one line to the next (e.g., 2.2.18, 2.16.34, 4.2.22 and 23). Another symptom of synapheia is hyphenation of a word from one line to the next: *ux-orius* (1.2.19-20), *inter-lunia* (1.25.11-12), *ve-nale* (2.16.7-8), always between the third Sapphic and the Adonic. This suggests that originally the Adonic was seen as a lengthening of the third Sapphic rather than a metrically autonomous line. Such elided and hyphenated words are said to be hypermetric.

Asclepiadean Meters

Though named after the Hellenistic poet Asclepiades of Samos (fl. 290 B.C.), these meters go back to Sappho and Alcaeus. They are based on a Glyconic

— — — ˘ ˘ — ˘ ×

augmented with an extra choriamb.

First Asclepiadean

— — — ˘ ˘ —||— ˘ ˘ — ˘ ×

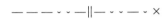

Sometimes called the lesser Asclepiadean, this is the basic form of the meter, used by itself only three times (1.1, 3.30, 4.8). The metrical pause (here a diaeresis because it falls between the two choriambs) is rarely disregarded (2.12.25, 4.8.17).

Second Asclepiadean

— — — ˘ ˘ — ˘ ×
— — — ˘ ˘ —||— ˘ ˘ — ˘ ×

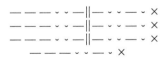

The first line is a Glyconic, the second a first Asclepiadean. The most-used Asclepiadean meter, this occurs in twelve poems. In this edition, poems in this meter are printed in four-line stanzas though the meter itself is not stanzaic.

Third Asclepiadean

— — — ˘ ˘ —||— ˘ ˘ — ˘ ×
— — — ˘ ˘ —||— ˘ ˘ — ˘ ×
— — — ˘ ˘ —||— ˘ ˘ — ˘ ×
— — — ˘ ˘ — ˘ ×

A stanza composed of three first Asclepiadean lines and a Glyconic, used nine times in the *Odes*.

Fourth Asclepiadean

— — — ⏑ ⏑ —||— ⏑ ⏑ — ⏑ ×
— — — ⏑ ⏑ —||— ⏑ ⏑ — ⏑ ×
— — — ⏑ ⏑ — ×
— — — ⏑ ⏑ — ⏑ ×

Horace uses this in seven odes; it combines two first Asclepiadeans with a Pherecratic (line 3) and a Glyconic (line 4).

Fifth Asclepiadean

— — — ⏑ ⏑ —||— ⏑ ⏑ —||— ⏑ ⏑ — ⏑ ×

Sometimes called a greater Asclepiadean because of its extra choriamb, this appears three times in the *Odes*.

Iambic Strophe

⏒ — ⏑ — ⏒ || — ⏑ — ⏒ — ⏑ ×
⏒ — ⏑ — ⏒ — ⏑ ×

Iambic trimeter (three pairs of iambs) followed by iambic dimeter (two pairs of iambs). Used in the first ten epodes because the iambic rhythm carries connotations of mockery, this meter admits substitutions and (rarely) resolutions in the odd-numbered iambs, but keeps its flavor by avoiding them in the even-numbered feet, which always open with a short syllable. Because of its flexibility, it may produce spondees and dactyls, as well as an occasional tribrach (⏑ ⏑ ⏑) or anapest (⏑ ⏑ —).

Archilochian Meters

Named after the iambic and elegiac poet Archilochus (early seventh century B.C.), this family of epodic meters appears in both the *Epodes* and the *Odes*.

First Archilochian

— ⏕ — ⏕ —||⏕ — ⏕ — ⏑ ⏑ — ×
— ⏑ ⏑ — ⏑ ⏑ —

The first line is an ordinary dactylic hexameter; the second is a hemiepes, repeating the first as far as the caesura, but without substitutions. The meter is used only in 4.7, in four-line stanzas.

Second Archilochian

$$— \breve{\breve{}} — \breve{\breve{}} — \| \breve{\breve{}} — \breve{\breve{}} — \smile\smile — \times$$
$$\bar{\smile} — \smile — \bar{\smile} — \smile \underset{}{\smile} \| — \smile\smile — \smile\smile \times$$

A dactylic hexameter is followed by an iambic dimeter (two pairs of iambs) combined with a dactylic trimeter catalectic. It is the meter of Epode 13.

Third Archilochian

$$\bar{\smile} — \smile — \bar{\smile} \| — \smile — \bar{\smile} — \smile \times$$
$$— \smile\smile — \smile\smile \underset{}{\smile} \| \bar{\smile} — \smile — \bar{\smile} — \smile \times$$

The first line is an iambic trimeter; the second combines a dactylic trimeter catalectic with an iambic dimeter (thus reversing the halves of the second line of the second Archilochian). It is used in Epode 11.

Fourth Archilochian

$$— \breve{\breve{}} — \breve{\breve{}} — \| \breve{\breve{}} — \breve{\breve{}} \| — \smile — \smile — —$$
$$\bar{\smile} — \smile — \bar{\smile} \| — \smile — \smile — —$$

A greater Archilochian, consisting of four dactyls and an ithyphallic ($— \smile — \smile — —$), followed by an iambic trimeter catalectic. Paired in four-line stanzas, this distich is used in 1.4.

Pythiambic Meters

These meters, used in three of the epodes, combine epic with iambic meters.

First Pythiambic

$$— \breve{\breve{}} — \breve{\breve{}} — \| \breve{\breve{}} — \breve{\breve{}} — \smile\smile — \times$$
$$\bar{\smile} — \smile — \bar{\smile} — \smile \times$$

Dactylic hexameter followed by iambic dimeter, used in Epodes 14 and 15.

Second Pythiambic

$$— \breve{\breve{}} — \breve{\breve{}} — \| \breve{\breve{}} — \breve{\breve{}} — \smile\smile — \times$$
$$\smile — \smile — \smile \| — \smile — \smile — \smile \times$$

Dactylic hexameter followed by iambic trimeter, with no substitutions in the iambic line. See Epode 16.

Alcmanic Strophe

— ⏔ — ⏔ —|| ⏔ — ⏔ — ⏑ ⏑ — ×
— ⏔ — ⏔ — ⏑ ⏑ — ×

A dactylic lyric meter named after the early Spartan poet Alcman (later seventh century B.C.), this epodic meter pairs a dactylic hexameter with a dactylic tetrameter (four feet). Printed here without stanzas in Epode 12, and with four-line stanzas in *Odes* 1.7 and 1.28.

Iambic Trimeter

⏒— ⏑ — ⏒||— ⏑ — ⏒— ⏑ ×

Three pairs of iambs, with substitution permitted in the first, third, and fifth breve. Used in Epode 17, this is not strictly speaking an epodic meter because it does not alternate with a longer or shorter line. Its flavor of Roman comedy is appropriate for a humorous poem. Like the iambic strophe, this meter admits substitutions and resolutions in the odd-numbered iambs, but keeps its flavor by avoiding them in the even-numbered feet, which always start with a short syllable. Its flexibility admits spondees, dactyls, and tribrachs (⏑ ⏑ ⏑) in place of iambs.

Second Sapphic Strophe

— ⏑ ⏑ — ⏑ — ×
— ⏑ — — —|| ⏑ ⏑ —||— ⏑ ⏑ — ⏑ — ×

The first line, an Aristophanic, is a Sapphic minus the first four syllables; the second line is a Sapphic with an extra choriamb. See *Odes* 1.8.

Hipponactean

— ⏑ — ⏑ — ⏑ ×
⏒ — ⏑ — ⏒||— ⏑ — ⏑ — —

Also called trochaic strophe (though it is not clear that Horace used it in four-line stanzas) this is a trochaic dimeter catalectic (two pairs of trochees "stopping short" of the last syllable) followed by an iambic trimeter, also catalectic. See *Odes* 2.18. It is said to have been used often by Alcaeus.

Ionic a Minore

⏑ ⏑ — — ⏑ ⏑ — — ⏑ ⏑ — — ⏑ ⏑ — —
⏑ ⏑ — — ⏑ ⏑ — — ⏑ ⏑ — — ⏑ ⏑ — —
⏑ ⏑ — — ⏑ ⏑ — ×

The name of the foot, two short syllables followed by two long syllables, is the same as that of the strophe. Each of the first two lines has four feet; the third has two feet. This is a virtuoso meter, especially in Latin, which has fewer short syllables than Greek; moreover, no substutions are allowed. Found only in Odes 3.12.

For a fuller account of meter in general, see *The Meters of Greek and Latin Poetry* by James Halporn, Martin Ostwald, and Thomas Rosenmeyer (1980).

APPENDIX C

GLOSSARY OF LITERARY TERMS

adynata, Gk. ἀδύνατα, "impossibilities," sing. *adynaton*, are a rhetorical **topos** used to color a declaration that nothing will ever happen, or that the inconceivable is happening. For the former, see *Epod.* 16.25-34, *Odes* 1.33.7-9; for the latter, 1.29.10ff.

allegory: a compound of Gk. ἄλλος "other" and ἀγορεύειν "to speak." Defined by Quintilian 9.2.92: *Totum ... allegoriae simile est aliud dicere aliud intellegi velle*. In 8.6.44 he quotes Horace *Odes* 1.14.1-3 as the *locus classicus* of the figure that says one thing but means another. Allegorical interpretations of Homer were common as early as the fifth century B.C., but already by the early sixth century B.C. Alcaeus was writing about the ship of state (frags. 6 and 326 LP) and the ship as a woman (frag. 306.14.ii), providing Horace with inspiration for his ode. See Angus Fletcher, *Allegory, the Theory of a Symbolic Mode* (1964) and Jon Whitman, *Allegory: The Dynamics of an Ancient and Medieval Technique* (1987).

anacoluthon, a syntactic nonsequitur in which a new construction is started in mid-sentence before the old one is completed, imitating the natural compression of impassioned speech. In *Epod.* 15.7-8, *dum pecori lupus et nautis infestus Orion / turbaret hibernum mare*, there is a slight anacoluthon because *infestus* must be retrospectively applied to *lupus* with an *esset* to be supplied by the reader. A more complex but grammatically consistent anacoluthon occurs in the eighth stanza of *Odes* 2.1 (see note on lines 29-32), where three rhetorical questions are compressed into one.

anaphora, repetition for emphasis, is a standard device for raising the rhetorical level. In hymns, some types of anaphora are traditional (e.g. the repetitions of *te* in *Odes* 1.10 and 1.35); elsewhere,

it may indicate strong feeling. Fraenkel asserts that it is "almost always a sign of serious emphasis." Sometimes it simply connects related clauses or sentences (as in 4.12.16f. *nardo ... nardi*), but even in such cases there is often an effect of special dignity.

anastrophe, reversal of the normal order of two words, is a form of **hyperbaton** common in Horatian lyric: in *Odes* 1.2, *grave ne* (5), *omne cum* (7), *piscium et* (9), *prece qua* (26), *quam ... circum* (34). As in each of these examples, it delays the adverb, preposition, conjunction, or other word which is seen as less important, resulting in a more emphatic diction. Though this is a poetic usage, it conforms to the general tendency of Latin to put more important words first.

anceps, or more properly *syllaba anceps*, is an "uncertain" or "equivocal" metrical quantity, conventionally marked (especially at the end of a line) by the symbol ×. The first and last syllables of the first three verses in the Alcaic strophe are anceps (see appendix B).

antithesis: an important determinant of word order in Horace, not only in **oxymoron** but wherever he can juxtapose words of contrasting meaning: *obducta solvatur* (*Epod.* 13.5), *tenues grandia* (*Odes* 1.6.9), *perfida credulum* (3.7.13), *dulci mala* (3.12.1-2), *opes inops* (3.16.28), *palluit audax* (3.27.28). Its effect is to emphasize paradox and to heighten the color of language by calling attention to contrasts.

apo koinou: from a Greek expression for two constructions depending "on a common [word]," this term describes a compressed phrase in which a single word has a double syntactic function. In *Epod.* 3.11, *ignota tauris illigaturum* is a kind of Siamese-twin construction in which the dative *tauris* goes with *ignota* (unknown to the bulls) and with *illigaturum* (about to fasten onto the bulls. See also *Chimaera* (1.27.24), and note on *consiliis*, 2.11.12. Cf. **zeugma**.

apostrophe: Gk. "a turning away" to address an audience that is absent, dead, or inanimate. Most of Epode 7 is an apostrophe to Romans bent on civil war; cf. Cicero's *O tempora! o mores!*

asyndeton (Gk. "non-linkage") is the lack of a conjunction such as *et*, *aut*, or *sed* between two words or clauses. Especially effective in an inflected language such as Latin and a favorite device of Horace, it gives his style a distinctive speed and economy, as in the phrase *serius ocius* (disjunctive asyndeton: sooner *or* later, 2.3.26). Originally, it was a feature of paratactic poetry such as Homer's, whose eloquent bluntness left logical connectives up to the audience. **Adversative asyndeton** is the omission of a word such as *sed* or *tamen* that would indicate that the second clause is contrary to the first. In such cases (e.g., 2.9.9, 3.1.14), an English translation would interpolate *but* or *however* to clarify the relation of ideas. The effect of asyndeton can be drily ironic; see notes on *Epod.* 2.70, *Odes* 1.25.20. Asyndeton is a feature of classic English style, as when the ghost of Hamlet's father describes himself

Cut off even in the blossoms of my sin,

Unhouseled, disappointed, unaneled (1.5.76-7). For its opposite, see **polysyndeton**.

caesura is the "cutting" of a metrical foot in the middle of a poetic line by the regular placement of word ending. The resultant pause, less marked than the pause at the end of a line, may be emphasized by phrasing and punctuation. Word ending in dactylic hexameter after the first syllable of the third foot is traditionally known as a "masculine" caesura; if the pause falls between the two short syllables of a dactylic third foot, it is called a "feminine" caesura. Because feet count for little in

lyric meters, the distinction between caesura and **diaeresis** is unimportant and *pause* is a good synonym.

catalectic (Gk. "leaving off"): an adjective describing metrical lines in which the last syllable of a foot is omitted at the end. Catalectic lines occur in the Archilochian meters and the trochaic strophe (see appendix B).

catalog: any list in poetry, such as the list of occupations in 1.1.3-28 with which Horace prefaces his statement about his own poetic vocation. A basic poetic form that can be as long as Homer's catalog of Greek ships that went to Troy (nearly 400 lines of *Iliad* 2) or as short as a four-line Horatian strophe, the catalog is ubiquitous in Horace. See also **priamel** and **tricolon crescendo**.

chiasmus is the arrangement of words into a symmetrical structure resembling the Greek letter *chi* (X): A, B, B, A. For example, in 1.1.22 *aquae lene caput sacrae*, the two genitives *aquae sacrae* are crossed by the two accusatives *lene caput*. This use of **hyperbaton** to make an inclusive word order is one of the features that distinguishes Latin poetry from prose and makes it especially difficult to translate effectively.

conceit (It. *concetto*, "notion") is an imaginary conception, usually metaphoric, put in to make a description fresh and striking, as when Horace describes water splashing down from the mountains "with clattering foot": *montibus altis / levis crepante lympha desilit pede* (*Epod.* 16.47-8). The conceit remains a field for virtuosity in writing: in *This Side of Paradise*, F. Scott Fitzgerald describes the protagonist's thoughts in a moment of reflection: "His poor, mistreated will that he had been holding up to the scorn of himself and his friends, stood before him innocent, and his judgment walked off to prison with the unconfinable imp, imagination, dancing in mocking glee beside him."

diaeresis: the "pulling apart" of a metrical line between two feet by the regular placement of word ending at that point. It is one type of regular pause in a line of poetry (see also **caesura**). Because feet as such are unimportant in most lyric meters, the distinction between diaeresis and caesura is somewhat academic, and *pause* is often used instead. Such pauses are often accentuated by punctuation.

ellipsis is the omission of a word that can be supplied from the context. Though sometimes a source of confusion at first, ellipsis contributes to the economy of language that keeps Horatian poetry lively and sometimes discreetly funny, as in *Epod.* 12.15, where a woman with sex on her mind says, "*Inachiam ter nocte potes.*"

encomium: a laudatory ode, generally any eulogy or panegyric in prose or verse. One of the basic forms of ancient poetry, encomiastic verse may praise a god (see **hymn**), a person, or even something inanimate like a moral virtue (e.g., in the Roman Odes, 3.1-6) or a wine jar (3.21). Pindar's victory odes, which had a great influence on Horace, are the best example of this type in Greek. Most of Horace's encomia praise Augustus, Maecenas, and other leaders of the Augustan establishment (see especially *Odes* 4), but he also uses the conventions of the form playfully (3.21) and in numerous hymns. The form survived antiquity in both prose (e.g., Erasmus' essay *Encomium Moriae*, "In Praise of Folly") and poetry (e.g., Keats' "Ode to Autumn").

end-stopping follows the natural tendency in poetry for the end of a line to correspond with the end of a unit of meaning such as a phrase, clause, or sentence. We normally expect to pause at the end of a line, and we expect the language to pause also. Lines with punctuation at the end are said to be heavily end-stopped. They are easier to follow, and feel neater because the main metrical pause is reinforced by the sentence structure. The opposite of this practice is **enjambment**.

enjambment, the running-on of meaning from one line to the next, is a way of emphasizing the part that runs on. It takes advantage of our expectation that the end of a line is also the end of a unit of meaning (see **end-stopping**), forcing us instead to go on to find the completion of the thought. In this line from Shakespeare, enjambment expresses contempt:
> Yet I know her for
> A spleeny Lutheran (*Henry VIII* 3.2.99f.).

In *Odes* 1.3.32-3, "the formerly slow necessity of distant death" is made more striking by the postponement of the last word:
> *semoti*que *prius tarda necessitas*
> *leti corripuit gradum.*

Enjambed lines also tend to move more rapidly because they override the pause at the end of a line. For other effects, see notes on 1.31.15 and 3.1.13.

epode (*epōdus*, <Gk. ἐπῳδός): originally the shorter verse of a couplet, as in the meters invented by Archilochus, and hence short poems written in such meters (LSJ). In Horace, it is a dactylic or iambic poem combining two lines of unequal length. First written in the Greek archaic period by the Ionian poets Archilochus and Hipponax (seventh to sixth cent. B.C.), epodic poems were revived in Callimachus' third-century *Iambi*. The Iambic Strophe, used in Horace's first ten epodes, is the most popular epodic meter; the Archilochian, Pythiambic, and Alcmanic meters are also epodic. Besides the *Epodes*, these meters are also used in *Odes* 1.4 (fourth Archilochian), 1.7 and 28 (Alcmanic strophe), and 4.7 (first Archilochian).

ethos: ἦθος, the Gk. word for character, means also the representation of character in dramatic speeches. A skill borrowed from Homer and the tragedians (also called *ethopoiïa*), ethos can be found wherever Horace is quoting somebody's words in a longer poem. Perhaps the best example is the speech of Europa in 3.27.34-66. For its use in a shorter lyric, see the contrasting language of Lydia and her lover in *Odes* 3.9.

golden line: any poetic line "of two substantives and two adjectives with a verb betwixt to keep the peace" (Dryden, preface to *Sylvae*). The term usually applies to a five-word line arranged adjective a, adjective b, verb, noun A, noun B. A variant employing **chiasmus** is 3.1.16:

> *omne capax movet urna nomen.*

Such deployments of language in **hyperbaton** were a prized achievement of poetic artistry as early as Catullus (e.g., 64.59, 129, 163, 172, etc.). Sometimes Horace spreads this arrangement of words over two lines, e.g., 3.27.25-26.

Grecism: any usage borrowed from the Greek. Though Horace disapproved of introducing Greek words into Latin poetry, he takes advantage of the more flexible syntax of Greek and some Greek idioms in constructing a poetic dialect. Constructions such as the accusative of specification began as poetic; after Horace's time they worked their way into prose.

hapax legomenon, ἄπαξ λεγόμενον, Gk. "once said," is a word that is unattested elsewhere in Latin, and is possibly therefore a new coinage produced for special effect: *Epod.* 5.34 *inemori*, 16.38 *inominata*.

Hellenistic: belonging to the period of Hellenic culture beginning with the death of Alexander the Great in 323 B.C. and ending with the battle of Actium in 31 B.C. The Hellenistic age is so called because during this time non-Greek societies throughout the Mediterranean and the Near East, such as Rome and Alexandria, adopted Greek culture (or had it imposed on them). Hellenistic art, poetry, philosophy, and religion dominated the Romans even as they were adding Greece to their empire: hence Horace's famous apothegm *Graecia capta ferum victorem cepit* (*Epist.* 2.1.156). Hellenism's most influential literary figure was Ptolemy's court poet Callimachus, whose literary personality Horace virtually adopted as his own. See Peter Green, *Alexander to Actium* (listed in Introduction).

hendiadys: (Gk. "one through two") the expansion of a single idea into two separate ones, as in "nice and warm." Its effect is to add emphasis. In *Epod.* 16.41-2 Horace recommends escape to some distant utopia: *beata / petamus arva, divites et insulas,* meaning "let us head for the happy fields *of* the wealthy isles." Cf. 3.4.4, *seu fidibus citharave Phoebi,* "or on the strings *of* Phoebus' lyre."

hetaera or **hetaira:** ἑταίρα, Gk. "companion," a euphemism for the highest rank of prostitute in the Greco-Roman world. Originally from the great cities of the Asia Minor coast such as Miletus, the profession is rooted in the tradition of temple prostitution, but by Horace's time had long since become purely secular. These women of pleasure, like the Japanese geishas, were as a rule highly trained in music and dance, and sometimes better educated than their male clients. They were the most cultivated and independent women in the ancient world, widely imitated in their makeup and attire by other women. With exotic professional names such as Lydia, Lyde, Pyrrha, and Neaera, they appear regularly in Horace's urbane poetry of love and parties.

hiatus, a phonetic "yawning," is the omission of elision where it would normally occur. Hiatus occurs regularly after the interjections *o* and *a*, for example in *Odes* 1.1.2, *o et praesidium.* See also *Epod.* 5.100 *Esquilinae alites*, *Epod.* 13.3 *Threicio aquilone*, 1.28.24, *capiti inhumato*.

hymn: a poem to a god, closely related to the **encomium** because it includes praise. A hymn will contain more than one of the following: the name or names, epithets, and titles of the divinity addressed; the god's genealogy or parentage; the god's haunts (usually places famous for his or her worship); the virtues (Gk. ἀρεταί), powers, or functions attributed to the god. These naturally fall into one or more **catalogs**, which were considered in archaic ritual to give the performer a greater claim upon the deity's goodwill the more complete they were. The hymn may then culminate in a **prayer**. See *Odes* 1.10, 21, 30, 35, 2.19, 3.13, 21-22, 4.6, *Carmen Saeculare*.

hypallage, Gk. "exchange," is the transference of an epithet from the noun it logically describes to some other word. In *Epod.* 10.14, *impiam Aiacis ratem*, the impiety of Ajax is transferred to his ship in a kind of guilt by association. Cf. 1.15.33-4, *iracunda ... classis Achillei* for the anger of Achilles, who withheld his *classis* from the fighting. It is closely related to **metonymy**.

hyperbaton, a leap-frogging of normal prose word order, is a basic technique of poetry in Latin and Greek, made possible by the use of inflection rather than word order to indicate syntax. Hyperbaton separates noun from adjective, for example, to allow the artful arrangements of words found in inclusive or interlocked word order, **chiasmus**, and the **golden line**. See also **anastrophe**, and notes on 1.3.32, 2.8.11, 3.24.5-7.

hypermetry, a symptom of **synapheia**, is elision from one line to the next, where the last syllable of a line is lost in elision with the initial vowel at the beginning of the next. See for example 2.2.18f., *beator(um)/ eximit*, 2.16.34 *hinnit(um)/ apta*, 3.29.35 *Etrusc(um)/ in mare*. An uncommon feature, this is generally used to heighten a special effect; like **enjambment**, it hurries us along to the next line without the expected pause.

iambic poetry: poetry dominated by iambic rhythms (see appendix B) had traditional associations of mockery. Catullus called his abusive poems "iambs" (see 36.5 40.2, 54.6) in a tradition that goes back at least as far as Archilochus (seventh cent. B.C.), whose lampoons are said to have caused one of his victims to hang himself. The iambic spirit is prominent in the iambic strophes of Epodes 2-6, 8, and 10, and in the iambic trimeter of Epode 17.

litotes: from Gk. "plainness, simplicity," is assertion by means of negation. We are *not unaccustomed* to this device in English, though it is perhaps not exactly plain or simple. A form of emphasis by understatement, as when we say a certain politician is wicked but *no fool*. In *Epod.* 16.26, *ne redire sit nefas* means "let it be lawful to return [when stones float]." The infant Horace sleeping fearlessly on Mount Vultur is *non sine dis animosus* (3.4.20).

locus amoenus: the "pleasant place" outdoors in nature. This had become a celebrated **topos** of Hellenistic poetry, made popular by Theocritus in his pastoral idylls. Its features usually include a stream or spring, cool shade, the song of birds or cicadas, and a grassy bank to lie on. See, for example, *Epod.* 2.23-28 and *Odes* 2.3.6-12. Horace repeatedly refers to such an environment in connection with his role as a poet (e.g., 1.1.30, 1.17, 4.2.30).

locus classicus: the "classic spot" exemplifying a particular usage in an especially memorable way. For example, the traditional *locus classicus* of **oxymoron** is 3.11.35, where Hypermestra is praised as *splendide mendax*, gloriously untruthful for violating an oath to kill her husband.

lyric: originally meaning poetry accompanied by the lyre, this came to be the term distinguishing one type of poetry from epic, iambic, elegiac, expository, and dramatic. It is also called *melic* from Greek μέλος, "song." Though not actually sung, its performance in Roman times had a semimusical quality that distinguished it from ordinary speech (see appendix B). In its broadest definition, lyric includes both the *Epodes* and the *Odes* of Horace, but more narrowly it refers to poems whose meters follow the Aeolic patterns used by Sappho and Alcaeus of Lesbos. "Lyric" is a Hellenistic coinage, and the scholars of Alexandria handed down a canonical list of nine lyric poets to parallel their list of nine Muses. It included the monodists Alcaeus, Sappho, and Anacreon and the choral lyrists Alcman, Stesichorus, Ibycus, Simonides, Pindar, and Bacchylides, all of whom were emulated by Horace. Lyric meters are typically not broken down into feet, and they are frequently stanzaic. The subject of lyric poetry varies from love to politics, its tone from lightly ironic to heavily moralistic. Sometimes personal, it can also be as public and ceremonial as the *Carmen Saeculare*. Like Catullus a generation earlier, Horace was a pioneer in bringing lyric into the mainstream of Roman literature.

metonymy, "change of name," is the rhetorical figure by which a thing is named by referring to a part of it: *trabs*, beam, means ship by metonymy in 1.1.13; in another context, it means shrine (4.1.20). Quintilian equates it with hypallage in prose, and cites *pauperum tabernas* in 1.4.13 as an example where the paupers' huts refer indirectly to the paupers themselves. In another type of metonymy, Neptune = the sea, Bacchus = wine, and Venus = sex or love. See also **synecdoche** and **hypallage**.

motto: the beginning words or lines of a poem are sometimes adapted from a Greek source (usually Alcaeus) in the same or a similar meter. A motto may be significantly different from the Greek original, as is the direction in which Horace then develops his ode. For Alcaean mottoes, see *Odes* 1.9, 10, 14, 18, and 37, and 3.12. For a motto

from Bacchylides, see 2.18. For the history of the term, see Fraenkel (159 n.2).

oxymoron: paradox arrestingly expressed by the juxtaposition or combination of opposite words, as in *splendide mendax* (3.11.35), describing the "gloriously untruthful" Danaïd who broke her oath to kill her husband on their wedding night. In Latin as in English (e.g., "military intelligence"), it is a vehicle of epigrammatic wit. Horace is especially fond of antithesis, arranging words in such a way as to create strange bedfellows; oxymoron is one form that stylistic tendency takes: 1.34.2, *insanientis sapientiae*, 2.12.26, *facili saevitia*.

paraclausithyron: a histrionic scene "outside a closed house-door" put on by a lover seeking admission, featuring the lover's sung complaint to the woman who has locked him out. As the woman is usually a **hetaera**, such serenades are excellent advertising for her, but the chief note struck is one of pathos. Remarks about inclement weather, **apostrophes** to the moon and stars, complaints about the woman's insensitivity and the hardness of her threshold, and warnings that she will not always be so fervently sought after are common themes of this **topos**, for which see *Epod.* 11.21-22, *Odes* 2.8.19-20, 3.10.19-20. The standard work on the subject is Frank Copley's *Exclusus Amator* (1956).

paraenetic (Gk. "hortatory") poetry exhorts the reader to live according to certain values or to adopt a certain course of action. Horace's Roman Odes (3.1-6) are strongly paraenetic along old-fashioned patriotic lines. Many of his philosophic poems offer advice about living well, e.g., *Odes* 1.11 to Leuconoë, *Tu ne quaesieris*, and 2.3 to Dellius, *Aequam memento rebus in arduis / servare mentem*.

periphrasis, Gk. for "roundabout diction," is a common feature of the ornate style enjoyed in

Hellenistic and Roman poetry. In the taste of Horace's time, *Thebanae Semelae puer* (1.19.2) is an elegant way of referring to Bacchus. Learned periphrasis also appealed to connoisseurs. Sometimes its intention is humorous, as when Horace calls she-goats "wandering wives of a rank husband," *deviae olentis uxores mariti* (1.17.6-7).

persona, Lat. for theater mask, is the rhetorical image or role assumed by a speaker or writer. Horace's personae include the impassioned patriot or lover, the detached observer, even the pugnacious mocker. Because classical audiences did not expect poetry to be frank, sincere self-revelation as much as a public artifact, they expected any poet or speaker to adopt a personality that would make his message more effective. The image of himself projected in Horace's *Odes* should therefore not be confused with the historical Horace.

polysyndeton is the multiplication of connectives such as *-que* and *et* for rhetorical effect. In 2.1.2-4, *bellique causas et vitia et modos*, etc., Horace is emphasizing the complexity of Pollio's historical task; in 3.29.37, *stirpesque raptas et pecus et domos*, it "enhances the effect of a devastating rush" (Fraenkel). In 4.15.5-14, it suggests "an almost unlimited sequence of beneficial achievements" (Fraenkel). See also **asyndeton**: "a great chain or series is of its essence impressive, whether connectives are inserted or omitted. Whether asyndeton or polysyndeton is the more impressive in a particular place, depends on the nature of the context" (Denniston, *The Greek Particles*, 1954, xlv).

prayer: closely related to the form of the **hymn**, the prayer is a formal supplication. Two early examples can be found in Chryses' supplication to Agamemnon and his subsequent prayer to Apollo in Homer's *Iliad*, 1.17-21 and 36-42. Following the customary *do ut des* approach of ancient religion, the prayer combines a statement of good will toward the addressee or a reminder of past services

with a request for some favor. See note on the *sic* formula in 1.3.1ff., and Glycera's prayer in 1.30.

predication: the chief point of a clause, sentence, or poem. The predication of *Odes* 2.17, for example, is that Horace will not outlive Maecenas. In Latin, predicative words tend to take precedence in word order, while less important words can be delayed (see **anastrophe**). In Horatian poetry, the predicative word is often pushed to the front of a line to give it emphasis (see note on *Epod.* 8.17).

priamel: "a focusing or selecting device in which one or more terms serve as foil for the point of particular interest" (Bundy, *Studia Pindarica* 1.5). The term, coined in 1921 to describe a feature of Pindar's style, is widely applicable to poetic rhetoric: for example, in 1.7.1-10 Horace runs through a **catalog** of places that others have praised before reaching Tibur, the place he wishes to praise. In 1.1.3-28, he lists a number of other occupations before focusing on his own. 1.31 lists all the things Horace does not pray for as a means of emphasizing what he really wants in the final stanza.

prolepsis or anticipation is the description of an event before it has actually happened. In *Epod.* 16.33, *credula nec ravos timeant armenta leones*, the herds are trusting (*credula*) before they do not fear the tawny lions, and in the following line, *ametque salsa levis hircus aequora*, the (normally shaggy) goat is sleek (*lēvis*) before loving the salt seas. At the cost of a slight inconsistency in logic, proleptic language gives poetic language more concentration and economy.

propempticon: a "send-off" poem wishing someone a good voyage, such as *Odes* 1.3, written on the occasion of a trip to Greece by Virgil. It includes a prayer for good weather and favorable winds, as well as a cautionary or disapproving note suggesting that the writer would rather his friend did not go away at all. See also 3.27, and a reverse propempticon, Epode 10, wishing Mevius a bad voyage.

protreptic: didactic, designed to instruct or persuade. Like earlier poets, Horace sometimes uses myth in this way, e.g., in 3.4.69ff., where the examples of Gyas and Orion are used to show that force without wisdom is self-destructive. In 3.7.13-20, Chloe's emissary uses the legends of Bellerophon and Peleus in an attempt to persuade Gyges that it is best to cooperate when a woman wants to seduce you. Cf. also 1.7.21ff., the example of Teucer. In classical rhetoric, a protreptic *exemplum* normally supports a passage of *paraenesis* or advice.

recusatio: a poetic statement declining to take up a particular theme or type of poetry. A rhetorical device used regularly by Pindar, it forms the basis of Epode 14, *Odes* 1.6 and 19, 2.12, and 4.2. The Horatian *recusatio* typically sets aside war themes in order to deal with love.

resolution: a form of metrical variation where two short syllables are substituted for an initial anceps or a longum. In the iambic trimeter, (see Epodes 1-11, 16-17), the first syllable or either longum of the first iambic metron may be resolved into two brevia or short syllables. See diagram in appendix B.

ring structure is the device of marking off a rhetorical unit by repeating at the end something said at the beginning. In Horatian lyrics, the unit so marked is usually an entire poem. Ring structure gives a sense of wholeness to such a poem; its counterpart in music is the repetition of the opening theme at the end of a movement or other unit of composition. It is closely related to **chiasmus**.

standing epithets are more or less ornamental adjectives attached by custom to certain nouns without any special relevance to the context.

Descended from the formulaic language of Homer (white-armed Hera, laughter-loving Aphrodite, rosy-fingered dawn), they fit the diction of Horace with its strong tendency to attach an adjective to every noun. Examples: *flavum Tiberim* (1.8.8, 1.2.13, 2.3.18), *pavidae dammae* (1.2.11, cf. 1.23.2), *Syria merce* (1.31.12, cf. 2.7.8), *luna rubens* (2.11.10).

strophe: from Gk. "turn," suggesting that it originally accompanied a choral dance movement, this is a stanza of poetry. Nearly two thirds of Horace's odes are written in stanzaic form, almost always in four-line stanzas.

substitution: the generic term for all metrical variation, including **resolution**. In any metrical scheme, permissible substitutions are written in above the normal longa or brevia. Aeolic meters such as the Sapphic, Alcaic, and Asclepiadean generally do not admit substitution. See diagrams in appendix B.

sympotic or **symposiac:** having to do with the symposium or drinking-party (Lat. *convivium*), a traditional Greek gathering of affluent males at which wine, women, and song were the main business. Since the time of Alcaeus (sixth cent. B.C.), the symposium had been a typical setting of lyric poetry. Its themes included politics and philosophy, but in Hellenistic times the love theme predominated. Sympotic motifs include the carpe diem advice of 1.11, requests to a slave (*puer*) or **hetaera** to pour the wine (e.g., *Epod.* 9.33, *Odes* 3.19.10), the preparation **topos** (3.14.17-24, 4.11.1-12), and scenes where a lover is discovered and offered counsel (e.g., *Epod.* 11.8-10, 19-20, *Odes* 1.27.14ff.). Alcaeus, Anacreon, and the Hellenistic love epigrammatists were important sources.

synapheia is the "fastening together" of lines in an Aeolic meter such as the Sapphic strophe as if they were a single line or colon. Though relatively uncommon in Horace, it manifests itself in occasional hypermetric lines (e.g., 2.3.27, 3.29.35) and three cases where a word is hyphenated. See **hypermetry** and appendix B on the Sapphic strophe.

syncope is the abbreviation of a word, usually a verb, for phonetic and metrical economy, e.g., *repostum*, syncopated from *repositum* in *Epod.* 9.1, *puertiae* from *pueritiae* in 1.36.8.

synecdoche, Gk. "a receiving together," is a figure of speech that "has the power to give variety to our language by making us realize many things from one, the whole from a part, the genus from the species, ... or the opposite" (Quintilian 8.6.19). It is closely related to **metonymy**. In the phrase *trabe Cypria*, lit. "in a Cypriote keel" (1.1.13), Horace combines the two figures, *trabe* meaning "ship" by metonymy and *Cypria* particularizing the ship by synecdoche to give it local color. Synecdoche is a favorite device of Horace to make general situations more vivid: wine is Falernian, a hound is Molossian, the sea is Tyrrhenian or Adriatic—not necessarily because that detail is important, but because it sharpens the language. Such adjectives of specification have therefore an otiose quality, as do such standing epithets in Homer as "wine-dark sea" and "laughter-loving Aphrodite."

synizesis: the "collapsing" of two vowels into one for metrical purposes. Each of the following, normally trisyllabic, scans as two syllables: *anteit*

(1.35.17), *antehac* (1.37.5), *Pompei* (2.7.5).

tmesis or "cutting" is the breaking up of a compound (*what god soever it be* for *whatsoever god it be*), as in 1.6.3, *quam rem cumque*, 1.7.25, *quo nos cumque*, 1.9.14, *quem Fors dierum cumque*. It lends a Homeric and thus poetic note, because Homer treated as separate words prefixes that later became inseparable.

topos: lit. a "place" or passage that is familiar as a type, e.g., a **locus amoenus**, preparations for a party, and the formula of prayer. Horace wrote for a public that was familiar with such formulas and enjoyed them with or without the humorous twists that he gives them.

tricolon crescendo: also called a rising tricolon, an arrangement of three clauses or periods in such a way that each is longer than its predecessor, as for example in 1.29.5-15 *Quae ... quis ... Quis*, 3.25.1-6, *Quo ... Quae ... Quibus*, etc, and the vignettes of Pholoë, Chloris, and Gyges in 2.5.17ff. It is one of the artful arrangements of poetic language like **chiasmus** that was appreciated for its own sake.

zeugma: the "yoking" of two different constructions or meanings to a single common word, typically the verb. Thus in 1.1.19-21, *spernit* takes both a noun object (*pocula*) and an infinitive object *demere*. Closely related to the **apo koinou** construction, zeugma involves a shift of grammatical construction, or a change of sense, e.g., from literal to metaphoric.

APPENDIX D

THE DEATH OF CLEOPATRA
by E. M. Forster

After Plutarch's account at the end of his *Life of Antony* and Shakespeare's 1606 dramatization of North's Plutarch in *The Tragedy of Antony and Cleopatra*, the best (and perhaps least-known) supplement to Horace's Cleopatra Ode (1.37) was written during World War I by E. M. Forster while he was living in Alexandria. It appears in the History section of *Alexandria: A History and a Guide*.

The girl who came to the throne as Cleopatra VII Philopator was only seventeen. Her brother and husband Ptolemy XIV was ten; her younger brother eight, her sister fifteen. The Palace at Alexandria became a nursery, where four clever children watched the duel that was proceeding between Pompey and Caesar beyond the seas. Pompey was their guardian, but they had no illusions, either about him or one another. All they cared for was life and power. Cleopatra failed in her first intrigue, which was directed against her husband. He expelled her, and in her absence the duel was concluded. Pompey, defeated by Caesar, drifted to Egypt, threw himself on the mercy of his wards, and was murdered by their agents as he disembarked.

With the arrival of Caesar, Cleopatra's triumphs began. She did not differ in character from the other able and unscrupulous queens of her race, but she had one source of power that they denied themselves—the power of the courtesan—and she exploited it professionally. Though passionate, she was not the slave of passion, still less of sentimentality. Her safety, and the safety of Egypt were her care; the clumsy and amorous Romans, who menaced both, were her natural prey. In old times, a queen might rule from her throne. Now she must descend and play the woman. Having heard that Caesar was quartered at the palace, Cleopatra returned to Alexandria, rolled herself up in a bale of oriental carpets and was smuggled in to him in this piquant wrapper. The other children protested, but her first victory had been won; she could count on the support of Julius Caesar against her husband.

Caesar's own position, was, however, most insecure. He was Lord of the World, but in his haste to catch Pompey he had hurried ahead of his legions. When the glamour of his arrival had worn off the Alexandrians realized this, and in a fierce little war (Aug. 48 - Jan. 47 B.C.) tried to crush him before reinforcements arrived. ... The war was after all decided outside Alexandria. More reinforcements were coming down the Canopic mouth of the Nile and the Alexandrians marched out to intercept them there. The young Ptolemy XIV was their general now. He was defeated and drowned, his army was destroyed, and Caesar returned in triumph to its city and to Cleopatra.

Cleopatra's fortune now seemed assured. Having married her younger brother (as Ptolemy XV), she went for a trip with Caesar up the Nile to show him its antiquities. The Egyptians detested her as their betrayer but she was indifferent. She bore Caesar a son and followed him to Rome, there to display her insolence. She was at the height of her beauty and power when the blow fell. On the Ides of March, 44 B.C., Caesar was murdered. She had chosen the wrong lover after all.

Back in Alexandria again, she watched the second duel—that between Mark Antony and Caesar's murderers. She helped neither party, and when Antony won he summoned her to explain her neutrality.

She came, not in a carpet but in a gilded barge, and her life henceforward belongs less to history than to poetry. It is almost impossible to think of the later Cleopatra as an ordinary person. She has joined the company of Helen and Iseult. Yet her character remained the same. Voluptuous but watchful, she treated her new lover as she had treated her old. She never bored him, and since grossness means monotony she sharpened his mind to those more delicate delights, where sense verges into spirit. Her infinite variety lay in that. She was the last of a secluded but subtle race, she was a flower that Alexandria had taken three hundred years to produce and that eternity cannot wither, and she unfolded herself to a simple but intelligent Roman soldier.

Alexandria, now reconciled to her fate and protected by the legions of Antony, became the capital of the Eastern world. The Western belonged to Octavian, Caesar's nephew, and a third duel was inevitable. It was postponed for some years, during which Antony acquired and deserted a Roman wife, and Cleopatra bore him several children. Her son by Julius Caesar was crowned as Ptolemy XVI, with the additional title of King of Kings. Antony himself became a God, and she built a temple to him, afterwards called the Caesareum, and adorned by two ancient obelisks (Cleopatra's needles). This period of happiness and splendour ended in the naval disaster of Actium in the Adriatic, where Octavian defeated their combined fleets. The defeat was hastened by Cleopatra's cowardice. At the decisive moment she fled with sixty ships, actually breaking her way through Antony's lines from the rear, and throwing it into confusion. He followed her to Alexandria, and there, when the recriminations had ceased, they resumed their life of pleasures that were both shadowed and sharpened by the approach of death. They made no attempt to oppose the pursuing Octavian. Instead, they formed a Suicide Club, and Antony, to imitate the misanthrope Timon, built a hermitage in the Western Harbour which he called Timonium. Nor was religion silent. The god Hercules[1], whom he loved and who loved him, was heard passing away from Alexandria one night in exquisite music and song.

Arrival of Octavian. He is one of the most odious of the world's successful men and to his cold mind the career of Cleopatra could appear as nothing but a vulgar debauch. Vice, in his opinion, should be furtive. At his approach, Antony after resisting outside the Canopic Gate (at "Caesar's Camp") retreated into the city and fell upon his sword. He was carried, dying, to Cleopatra, who had retired into their tomb, and their story now rises to the immortality of art. Shakespeare drew his inspiration from Plutarch, who was himself inspired, and it is difficult through their joint emotion to realise the actual facts. The asp, for example, the asp is not a certainty. It was never known how Cleopatra died. She was captured and taken to Octavian, with whom even in Antony's life-time she had been intriguing, for the courtesan in her persisted. She appeared this time not in a carpet nor yet in a barge, but upon a sofa, in the seductive negligence of grief. The good young man was shocked. Realising that he intended to lead her in his triumph at Rome, realising too that she was now thirty-nine years old, she killed herself. She was buried in the tomb with Antony; and her ladies Charmion and Iras, who died with her, guarded its doors as statues of bronze. Alexandria became the capital of a Roman Province.

---

[1] Not Hercules but Bacchus, according to Plutarch *Ant.* 75.6.

REFERENCES

J. H. Allen and James B. Greenough, *New Latin Grammar*. New York: Ginn & Co., 1888/1903.

William S. Anderson, "Horace *Carm*. 1.14: What Kind of Ship?" *Classical Philology* 61 (1966), 84-98.

David Armstrong, *Horace*. New Haven, Conn.: Yale Univ. Press, 1989.

Elroy Bundy, *Studia Pindarica I: The Eleventh Olympian Ode*. Berkeley and Los Angeles: Univ. of California Press, 1962.

T.V. Buttrey, "Halved Coins, the Augustan Reform, and Horace, *Odes* 1.3." *American Journal of Archaeology* 76 (1972), 31-48.

Corpus Inscriptionum Latinarum. Berlin, 1863-.

Steele Commager, *The Odes of Horace. A Critical Study*. New Haven, Conn.: Yale Univ. Press, 1962.

Frank Copley, *Exclusus Amator*. Baltimore, Md.: Johns Hopkins Univ. Press, 1956.

J. D. Denniston, *The Greek Particles*. 2nd ed. Oxford: Clarendon, 1954.

Angus Fletcher, *Allegory, the Theory of a Symbolic Mode*. Ithaca, N.Y.: Cornell Univ. Press, 1964.

Eduard Fraenkel, *Horace*. Oxford: Clarendon, 1957.

P. G. W. Glare, ed., *Oxford Latin Dictionary*. Oxford: Clarendon, 1968-82.

A. S. F. Gow and D. L. Page, *The Greek Anthology. Hellenistic Epigrams*. Cambridge: Cambridge Univ. Press, 1965.

A. S. F. Gow and D. L. Page, *The Greek Anthology. The Garland of Philip and Some Contemporary Epigrams*. Cambridge: Cambridge Univ. Press, 1968.

James Halporn, Martin Ostwald, and Thomas Rosenmeyer, *The Meters of Greek and Latin Poetry*. Norman: Univ. of Oklahoma Press, 1980.

Neil Hopkinson, *A Hellenistic Anthology*. Cambridge: Cambridge Univ. Press, 1988.

Adolf Kiessling, *Q. Horatius Flaccus: Oden und Epoden*. 11th ed., rev. by Richard Heinze with bibliographical supplement by Erich Burck. Zürich and Berlin: Weidmann, 1964.

H. G. Liddell and R. Scott, *A Greek-English Lexicon*. rev. by H. S. Jones. Oxford: Clarendon, 1940.

Edgar Lobel and Denys Page, *Poetarum Lesbiorum Fragmenta*. Oxford: Clarendon, 1955.

R. G. M. Nisbet and Margaret Hubbard, *A Commentary on Horace: Odes Book I*. Oxford: Clarendon, 1970.

R. G. M. Nisbet and Margaret Hubbard, *A Commentary on Horace: Odes Book II*. Oxford: Clarendon, 1978.

D. L. Page, *Poeti Melici Graeci*. Oxford: Clarendon, 1962.

Pomponius Porphyrio, *Commentum in Horatium Flaccum*. resc. Alfred Holder. Innsbruck: Wagner, 1894.

[Pseudo-Acro], *Acronis et Porphyrionis commentarii in Q. Horatium Flaccum*, ed. F. Havthal. Berlin: Springer, 1864-66.

Michael C. J. Putnam, *Artifices of Eternity. Horace's Fourth Book of Odes*. Ithaca, N.Y.: Cornell Univ. Press, 1986.

Kenneth Quinn, *Horace: The Odes*. New York: St. Martin's Press, 1980.

Kenneth J. Reckford, *Horace*. New York: Twayne, 1969.

Paul Shorey and Gordon J. Laing, *Horace: Odes and Epodes*. New York: Sanborn, 1919.

Clement Lawrence Smith, *The Odes and Epodes of Horace*. New York: Ginn & Co., 1894/1903.

M. L. West, *Iambi et Elegi Graeci*. 2 vols. Oxford: Clarendon, 1971.

Jon Whitman, *Allegory: The Dynamics of an Ancient and Medieval Technique*. Cambridge, Mass.: Harvard Univ. Press, 1987.

Gordon Williams, *The Third Book of Horace's Odes*. Oxford: Clarendon, 1969.